AKBA
154

TIBET   LHASA

KATHMANDU

HIMALAYAS

BRAHMAPUTRA

AWADH
LUCKNOW
GANGA   JAUNPUR
ALLAHABAD   BANARAS   PATNA   GANGA   TANDA
BIHAR
BENGAL

ORISSA
MAHANADI

THE EMPEROR'S WRITINGS

THE EMPEROR'S WRITINGS
Memories of Akbar the Great

A Novel

Dirk Collier

AMARYLLIS

AMARYLLIS

Copyright © Dirk Collier 2011

All rights reserved. No part of this book may be used or reproduced, stored in or introduced into a retrieval system, or transmitted, in any form, or by any means, (electronic, mechanical, photocopying, recording or otherwise) without the prior written permission of the Publisher. Any person who does any unauthorised act in relation to this publication may be liable to criminal prosecution and civil claims for damages.

Dirk Collier
asserts the moral right to be identified
as the author of this work

This edition first published 2011

AMARYLLIS
An imprint of Manjul Publishing House Pvt. Ltd.

Editorial Office:
J-39, Ground Floor, Jor Bagh Lane,
New Delhi 110 003, India
Tel: 011-24642447/24652447 Fax: 011-24622448
Email: amaryllis@amaryllis.co.in
Website: www.amaryllis.co.in

Registered Office:
10, Nishat Colony, Bhopal 462 003, M.P., India

ISBN: 978-81-910673-6-1

This edition is for sale only in the Indian subcontinent, Southeast Asia and UAE.

Typeset by
Mindways Design
1410 Chiranjiv Tower
43 Nehru Place
New Delhi 110 019

Printed and Bound in India by
Thomson Press (India) Limited

*To
Anne, Bart and Ellen*

*Since wars begin in the minds of men,
it is in the minds of men
that the defences of peace
must be constructed*

(UNESCO Constitution, 16 November 1945)

Contents

List of Characters	*xi*
Author's Preface	*xv*
Cover Illustration	*xx*
1. Jahāngīr	1

Part I
2. Kalānor	11
3. Jālandhar	34
4. Pānīpat	46
5. Dillī	69
6. Mānkot	92
7. Lāhor	118
8. Jālandhar, Sirhind	129
9. Dillī, Āgrā	137
10. Bairām Khān (1)	152
11. Bairām Khān (2)	159
12. Makhfī	165
13. Māham Anaga, Adham Khān	183
14. Ājmīr	196
15. Māham Anaga, Adham Khān (2)	204
16. Sulh-i-Kul	211
17. Saltanat	225

Part II
18. Raf-e-Hejāb (1)	233
19. Raf-e-Hejāb (2)	248
20. Fath, Shuresh, Molk	270

21. Rājāstān	284
22. Sīkrī (1)	300
23. Sīkrī (2)	318
24. Makhfī	327
25. Gujarāt (1)	351
26. Gujarāt (2)	367
27. Abū-l Fazl	384
28. Bengāl, Mewār	410
29. Ibādat-Khāna (1)	418
30. Ibādat-Khāna (2)	431
31. Ibādat-Khāna (3)	445
32. Kābul	463
33. Dīn-e-Illāhī	474
34. Zōhr	486
35. Saltanat	491
36. Tanhāyī-e-'Asr	499
37. Murād, Asirgarh	508

Part III

38. Allāhābād (1)	519
39. Allāhābād (2)	522
40. Allāhābād (3)	537
41. Dānyāl	542
42. Saltanat	549
43. Shām	554

Epilogue (1)	559
Epilogue (2)	569
Epilogue (3)	572
Annexure I: *Akbar's first letter to the Jesuits of Goa*	578
Annexure II: *Letter of Pope Gregory XIII to Akbar – Rome, 18 February 1582*	579
Annexure III: *Jahāngīr's account of the murder of Abū-l Fazl*	581
Annexure IV: *Jahāngīr's account of his own drinking habits*	582
Annexure V: *Jahāngīr on his father*	583
Historical Notes and Acknowledgements	585
Bibliography	597

List of Characters[1]

Abū-l Fazl
Shaykh Abū-l Fazl 'Allāmī (1551-1602), minister at Akbar's court; author of the *Akbar Nāmā* (History of Akbar) and the *Ā'īn-i-Akbarī* (Institutes of Akbar).

Adham Khān
Māham Anaga's son; Mughal army officer.

Akbar
Abū-l Muzaffar Jalāl-ud-dīn Muhammad Akbar (1542-1605), third and greatest of India's Mughal Emperors.

Bābur 'The Tiger'
Gītī-Sitānī Firdaws-Makānī Zahīr-ud-dīn Muhammad Bābur, grandfather of Akbar and founder of the Mughal Empire.

Bairām Khān
Akbar's guardian; *Khān Khanān* (Lord of Lords), head of the Mughal army, and regent of the empire.

(Rājā) Bhagwān Dās
Hindū general at Akbar's court; son of Rājā Bihārī Mal.

(Rājā) Bihārī Mal
King of Amber (Jaipūr) in Rājpūtānā; Akbar's faithful ally; father of Akbar's first Hindū wife.

(Rājā) Bīrbal
Hindū minister at Akbar's court.

(Prince) Dānyāl
Akbar's third son.

Gulbadan
Akbar's aunt, half-sister of Emperor Humāyūn.

(Prince) Muhammad Hakīm
Akbar's half-brother; ruler of Kābul.

---

1. Names not appearing in this list will be clear from the context.

Hakīm Alī Gilanī
Akbar's physician.

Hamīda Bānū Bēgam
Akbar's mother.

Hēmū
Hindū general; prime minister of one of
Shēr Khān Sūr's successors, and Akbar's bitter opponent.

Humāyūn
Jahānbānī Jannāt-Ashyānī Nasīr-ud-dīn Muhammad Humāyūn, Akbar's father, second of the Mughal emperors of India.

Jī Jī Anaga
One of Akbar's nurses; spouse of Shams-ud-dīn.

Kāmrān
Humāyūn's brother and bitter rival.

Khān Khanān, Khān-e-Khanān
Khān of the Khāns, Lord of Lords; honorary title.

Māham Anaga
Akbar's favourite nurse and foster mother; mother of Adham Khān.

(Rājā Kūwar) Mān Singh
Hindū general at Akbar's court; nephew, adopted son and heir of Rājā Bhagwān Dās.

Makhdūm-ul Mulk
Leading Muslim cleric.

Mīr Abdul Latīf
Akbar's personal teacher and trusted friend.

(Shaykh) Mubārak (of Nāgaur)
Abū-l Fazl's father.

Mun'im Khān
Prince Muhammad Hakīm's guardian and governor of Kābul; later Akbar's prime minister.

(Prince) Murād
Akbar's second son.

Pīr Muhammad Khān
Mughal army officer; Bairām Khān's assistant and later rival.

Salīmā Sultān Bēgam
Akbar's favourite cousin and wife; widow of Bairām Khān.

(Prince) Salīm
Nūr-ud-dīn Muhammad Jahāngīr, Akbar's eldest son and successor, fourth of the Mughal emperors (1569-1627). Nicknamed Shaykhu Bābā (Dear little Shaykh, Daddy Shaykh) by his father.

Shams-ud-dīn
Husband of Akbar's nurse Jī Jī Anaga; faithful and competent Mughal army commander; later prime minister.

Shaykhu Bābā
Daddy Shaykh, Dear little Shaykh, nickname given by Akbar to his eldest son Salīm.

Shēr Khān Sūr
Afghān king, who forced Emperor Humāyūn into exile after defeating him twice; Humāyūn was able to regain his throne only after Shēr Khān's death.

Sikandar Sūr
Afghān commander and pretender to the throne of Shēr Khān Sūr; Humāyūn's (and later Akbar's) opponent.

Tardī Beg
Mughal army officer and governor of Delhi at the beginning of Akbar's reign.

Tānsēn
Famous singer and courtier at Akbar's court.

(Rājā) Todar Mal
Highly talented Hindū general and administrator, one of the most important ministers at Akbar's court.

Author's Preface

No man's life can be encompassed in one telling. There is no way to give each year its allotted weight, to include each event, each person who helped to shape a lifetime. What can be done is to be faithful in spirit to the records and try to find one's way to the heart of the man . . .
   Richard Attenborough's film Gandhi, *opening scene.*

Si j'ai choisi d'écrire ces Mémoires d'Hadrien à la première personne, c'est pour me passer le plus possible de tout intermédiaire, fût-ce moi-même.[1]
   Marguerite Yourcenar on her Memoirs of Hadrian *(1951).*

One could argue that it is hardly necessary to add an *Author's Preface* to this novel. The historical notes at the end provide ample historical information and references for the interested reader. Besides, to use the words of the renowned Italian semiologist and novelist Umberto Eco, written texts are in fact *machines to generate interpretations*: each reader, from her or his individual cultural background and personal experience, will engage in a different internal dialogue with the text, and in so doing, will discover in it layers of meaning that even the author was not aware of or had not even intended. In fact, as Eco pointed out, only half-jokingly: from that point of view, the best thing for an author to do after his or her book has been published, is to die! However, as I am not in any hurry

---

[1] *'If I have elected to write these* Memories of Hadrian *in the first person singular, it is because I wanted as much as possible to avoid any intermediary, even myself'.*

to prove Eco's point, and since *The Emperor's Writings* is not a 'regular fiction book', the publisher and I have thought it advisable to provide the reader with a bit of context.

My fascination for Emperor Akbar dates back to the autumn of 2002, when I was reading a few books on the history of Goa, with the vague intent of writing – some day, after retirement, as it had always been my dream – a historical novel about the Goan inquisition and the first pre-colonial contacts between India and the nascent imperialist European powers. I discovered, to my surprise, that the then ruling 'Great Mogul' Akbar the Great had invited no less than three Jesuit missions to his court, eager to learn about the Christian faith and very much looking forward to erudite and profound debates between those foreign priests and representatives of Islām and other faiths. At a time when Europe found itself plagued by fanaticism, persecution and bloody religious wars, this seemed to be a remarkably tolerant and open-minded attitude for an absolute monarch.

Intrigued, I began to document myself about the life and times of this remarkable individual, of whom, I am ashamed to admit, I had never heard before. In my defence, I should point out that at least in my time, high schools in continental Western Europe paid little to no attention to Asian history in general, and Indian history in particular . . .

I soon found myself fascinated with Akbar's story: his swift and spectacular rise to absolute power, amidst strife and intrigues, often against overwhelming odds; his exotic, yet remarkably modern vision of a prosperous, diverse and tolerant India; and his eventful, not to say tragic personal life, with the bitter and never fully resolved conflict with Salīm (Jahāngīr), his only surviving son and successor. And while I will readily admit (as I'm sure, he would do as well) that he was by no means a saint[2], I found true greatness in him.

I abandoned my earlier book project, and decided, first, that my debut novel would be about Akbar, and second, that I would not wait until retirement before writing it. Little did I realise that this decision would rob me of every free moment of the next seven years of my life, including every single morning from 6 to 7 am, and the better part of

---

2. See the historical notes at the end of this book.

every single weekend; in my rashness and naiveté, I thought I would have a go at it.

I soon decided to make my book a fictional autobiography. I have always had a profound admiration for Marguerite Yourcenar's majestic *Mémoires d'Hadrien* (Memoirs of Hadrian); and many other, less ambitious but equally entertaining novels like Robert Graves's *I, Claudius*, Margaret George's *Autobiography of Henry VIII*, Amin Maalouf's *Léon l'African* (Leo Africanus), Bernard Simiot's *Moi, Sylla, dictateur* (I, Sulla, Dictator), to name but a few, have always held a great attraction for me. Besides, I had come across a well-known seventeenth-century painting of Emperor Jahāngīr holding his father's portrait[3]: it is as if Akbar is talking to his son from the hereafter! That was exactly what I wanted: 'my' Akbar would be talking to his recalcitrant son, from yonder side of the grave, just like Yourcenar's Hadrian had written to Marcus Aurelius. I could of course have had one of the emperor's confidants – his physician, perhaps? – take dictation from him, but like Yourcenar, I wanted to *eliminate all intermediaries*; and so, I had the old emperor secretly overcome his dyslexia.

Fictional autobiography is arguably the most challenging, certainly the most ambitious, but in my opinion, definitely the most authentic, genre in historical fiction. As Yourcenar points out in the quote above this introduction, the would-be author of any authentic, honest fictional autobiography will need to practice the most rigorous self-effacement: not his or her own feelings and opinions are important, but the subject's. Every thought, every statement in the text needs to be challenged: is this really a thought that could have crossed my subject's mind? Would he or she really have felt this way? What could have been his or her motivation for this or that particular deed? Alas and of course, such a noble endeavour will always be, to a certain extent at least, doomed to failure. Complete self-effacement is impossible; the author's character and personal experience will inevitably influence his or her perception of the facts at hand. Moreover, as it was pointed out so honestly and eloquently in the above quote from the opening scene of Attenborough's *Gandhi*, it is, alas, quite impossible to fully capture a human life in a single narrative. Choices have to be made, digressions and omissions are inevitable . . .

---

3. See, e.g., http://eu.art.com/products/p12266045-sa-i1635678/posters.htm

I certainly have to plead guilty to all of the above. To name but a few examples:

- I have discreetly glossed over (as probably he would have) the failed attempt on Akbar's life at age twenty-one: an attempt which was, most probably, the direct result of his scandalous misconduct with a number of married women, whereby he tried to forcibly marry certain ladies belonging to distinguished Delhi families, and even compelled one Shaykh to divorce his wife in his favour. However, he quickly mended his ways, and in the words of the great historian Vincent Smith, from then on 'we do not hear again of scandals like those which tarnished his good name at Delhi'[4]. I therefore decided that Akbar's youthful lapse was not important enough to interfere with the story I/he wanted to tell.
- While I am by no means a military man myself, I have devoted a considerable amount of attention to Akbar's conquests and his abilities as a strategist and army leader – as I am sure he would have done, when talking to his successor: There is no denying that he was, in today's terms, a shameless imperialist, and that the lust for power and military conquest was his driving ambition.
- Akbar enjoyed female companionship, but he was not a very romantic man and never seemed to have experienced the passionate love that, for instance, Jahāngīr felt for Nur Jahān, or Shāh Jahān for Mumtaz Mahal. Nevertheless, it is well documented that his cousin Salīmā Sultānā, whom he married after Bairām Khān's death, was clearly his favourite, in spite of the fact that she did not bear him any children. She was intelligent, learned and highly influential, much more than any other woman at Akbar's court (including his own mother), and Akbar greatly valued her opinion. I have therefore devoted several chapters to their relationship, even though their personal feelings will of course remain a matter of conjecture.
- Throughout his life, Akbar has always been a deeply religious man, a mystic with a highly unorthodox, but deep and unfeigned

---

4. Smith, pgs 47-8.

reverence for the Creator and an almost obsessive interest in religious truth. The public debates he organised between representatives of various creeds were probably much less systematic and erudite than is suggested in *The Emperor's Writings*, but I have thought it necessary to devote a considerable amount of attention to the profoundly held convictions of Akbar's teacher Mīr Abdul Latīf and his close friend and advisor Abū-l Fazl: that universal friendship and brotherhood across the boundaries of creeds and religions is possible, and that true Islām is a religion of tolerance and peace.

As I have readily admitted in the historical notes at the back of this book, *The Emperor's Writings* is, and remains, a novel. It is a romanced attempt, by a twenty-first century Western European, to read into the mind of a sixteenth century Indian monarch. An incomplete one, admittedly; an imperfect one, undoubtedly; but an honest one, most definitely.

Cover Illustration

The illustration on the front cover is that of Akbar, and has been created by carefully arranging words written in Arabic calligraphy. The word that forms the face under the turban is 'Abū'l Fath', and means 'Father of Victory'. Embodying the chest and back, 'Jalāl-ud-dīn' means 'Splendour of Religion'. The abdomen or lower arm of the figure is shaped by the word 'Muhammad'. 'Akbar' constitutes the back of the head and turban. 'Pādshāh', which means 'Emperor', forms the inside part of the left leg. The hand holding the flower has been shaped by 'Ghāzī', meaning 'Emperor'. Lastly, the crossed legs at the bottom and the lower arm are formed by 'Akbar-e-Āzam', which means 'Akbar the Great'.

First Letter

جهانگیر

Jahangir

In the name of god, the compassionate, the merciful

From the King of Kings,
Shadow of God on this Earth,
Splendour of Faith,
Slayer of the Infidel,
Bower of all Necks and Bender of all Knees,
Jalāl-ud-dīn Muhammad Akbar Pādshāh Ghāzī,
Shāhān Shāh,
By the Will of God, Supreme Ruler of Kābul and Qandahār,
Thatta, Multān, Lāhor and the Panjāb, Kashmīr,
Dillī, Āgrā, Oudh, Awadh, Allāhābād, Ājmīr, Ahmedābād, Mālwa,
Bihār, Bengāl, Urīsā, Khāndesh, Berār and Ahmadnagar,
All the lands of the Hind and the Gangā[1] from ocean to ocean,
To his beloved son,
Shāhzāda Sultān Muhammad Salīm,
King of Allāhābād,
Governor of Bengāl and Urīsā,

---

1. Indus and Ganges

The Emperor's Writings

And God willing, soon to be
Nūr-ud-dīn Muhammad Jahāngīr Pādshāh Ghāzī,
Shāhān Shāh.

In this fiftieth and, most probably, last year of the Ilāhī Era,
This day of Doshanbeh, the eleventh day of Mehr
Yawm al-'Ithnayn, 20 Jumādā-l-Ūlā, 1014[2]
about three hours before dawn.

My dearest son, impatient heir and eager successor, My dearest Shaykhu Bābā,[3]

You will probably be surprised to find out that I can write, after all.

I know everybody believes I'm illiterate – that I cannot read more than a few very simple words here and there, and that I can barely sign my own name. Until a few years ago, they were quite right. To a large extent, they still are, much to my regret, I might add.

Although my mind is much quicker than most, and notwithstanding my lively interest in the limitless, beautiful, fascinating world of learning and books, I have always had this strange ailment – not being able to see written texts as other people apparently can. You know, with time, normal people seem to acquire an effortless ability to instantly recognise the shape of familiar words. But to me, reading has remained as difficult as it is for children who are still in their first months at school. I, who can give you thousands of quotes from thousands of books that have been read to me, find myself laboriously deciphering written texts, word

---

2. The dates refer to the Persian solar calendar as well as the Muslim (Hijri) lunar calendar. 20 Jumādā-l-Ūlā, 1014 AH corresponds to Monday morning, 23 September 1605 of the Julian calendar (which remained applicable in Great Britain until 2 September 1752), or 3 October 1605 of the Gregorian calendar, i.e. the current Common Era.

The *Ilāhī* Era was established in 1584, in Akbar's twenty-ninth year of reign.

3. Shaykhu Bābā: 'Daddy Shaykh; dear little Shaykh': Nickname used by the Mughal emperor Akbar the Great (1542-1605) for his son and successor Salīm, later Emperor Jahāngīr (1569-1627).

for word, letter by letter. Countless hours of practicing secretly, under the patient and respectful guidance of Abū-l Fazl, have been of little avail: It has become painfully apparent that further progress will not be possible.

Abū-l Fazl, my trusted friend! Writing his name still brings tears to my eyes; when I think of how he was murdered and his body desecrated, how his head was cut off and thrown in the latrines and left to rot in stinking excrements, I feel again the anger and rage rising in me – I feel hatred, acid and burning in my throat, like filthy vomit.

Had Abū-l Fazl's murderer been anyone else, I would have persecuted him to the end of the world. I, who have never enjoyed the execution—much less the torturing—of an enemy, would have made him suffer days, nay, weeks of unspeakable, agonising pain, before finally watching him choke to death, his windpipe stuffed with the excrement from his own ripped-out guts.

But, of all the people in this world, the murderer of my dearest friend happens to be you, Salīm – you, my dearest son, my heir, my only hope for the future!

I am the king of kings, and although I should be careful not to pay too much attention to flatterers, I am indeed, most probably, the mightiest ruler on earth.

Yet, for all my might and wealth, there is no one more utterly powerless than I am. For how could revenge appease my tormented mind? It would simply wreck my life! It would destroy all my hopes and dreams of true immortality; my life-long ambition for an everlasting, glorious dynasty of powerful and just rulers who will continue my bloodline and forever honour my name in grateful remembrance.

Therefore, for my own sake, and even for the sake of poor Abū-l Fazl, I must make sure that his life of tireless dedication and hard work for the good of our realm and the welfare of our Gurkaniyya dynasty has not been in vain. I must put aside my anger, and substitute it with calmness, kindness and understanding. . . .

Maybe Abū-l Fazl's death has been a sign from god to me. Maybe He, who is the lord of the Day of Judgment, but also the acceptor of repentance, the pardoner and the all-forgiving, wanted to show me that in order to achieve my worldly ambitions, I must follow the path of the Hindū and Jain and Pārsī saints whom I so fondly listened to for so many nights. At least this time, I must admit that only the path of ahimsa, the path of non-violence, will lead me to real victory.

I believe I do understand you quite well, my dear Bābu Shaykhujī. You are not too different from me, you know.

You definitely have the potential to become an even greater king than I have been, but I regret to say, there is also a very real danger that you might become an utter failure. A child of many prayers, you were raised in a protected, loving environment of unequalled wealth and luxury. Luxury breeds self-indulgence and laziness; it makes one weak – weak, like your unfortunate brothers Murād and Dānyāl, who drank themselves to death; weak, like the many opponents I encountered and defeated, despite their vast territories, their wealth and their armies so much larger than mine. What has become of all their might? Those among them who are not dead, now make haste to kiss my stirrup upon my arrival. So easy is it for power to slip away from the careless. . . .

But you can be a great king, Salīm. In your veins flows the strong blood of our glorious ancestors, the great Chingīz Khān and Amīr Temūr the Iron, the Unconquered Ruler of the Seven Climates.[4] Like me, you combine the bold audacity and strength of Turk and Mongol warriors with the shrewd refinement of Persian kings. Moreover, it is clear from your pleasant appearance that you have also inherited many of your noble mother's Rājpūt traits. All this should amply suffice to make you a strong ruler.

However, you will not become a truly great king, one whose memory will be revered by generations to come, unless you also attain wisdom, my son. Wisdom is a precious gift that god only bestows on those who truly seek to acquire it – on those who have the openness to listen to others with genuine respect and humility.

Never be afraid to listen to others, my son, no matter how different they might be from you and no matter how alien their manners may seem to you. Wisdom, I have learned, can be found in conversations with black-robed Jesuits and white-robed shaykhs; skeleton-like, ash-smeared Hindū renunciants or well-fed mullāhs.

---

4. Genghiz Khān (1162-1206) and Timur [Lang Tamerlane (1336-1405)].

Truth, my son, is like a beautifully shaped diamond. It is one; yet it has thousands upon thousands of facets, colours, aspects and reflections. Every person who honestly seeks the truth will have something important to say to you, but remember that no one will ever possess it entirely. The whole truth is the privilege of god Himself; god, to whom alone belongs the beautiful name *al-Haqq*,[5] as the Holy Qur'ān teaches us.

Therefore, put your trust in those who seek the truth in humility. But keep a safe distance from those who claim to have found it. And remember: A wise man, much more so a wise king, opens his mind to others, but never surrenders it.

As you well know, all my life, the quest for wisdom and truth has haunted me. Fortunately, god has graciously blessed me with ample opportunities to meet wise and learned people from many faiths and many different parts of the earth.

How to convey to you this little wisdom that I have managed to acquire, my son? This question has never left my mind, since I first sensed how your burning ambition to become the king was pushing you towards insurrection against me. Mind you, I think I understand what may have been your motives, and I do not really want to blame you too harshly. I have been forced to succeed my father—may god grant him the eternal bliss of paradise!—at the much too tender age of thirteen. But who knows what I would have done, if I had still been a mere crown prince at the age of thirty? Most probably, like you, I would have wanted a kingdom of my own. Most probably, like you, I would have been courting the idea of insurrection.

What was I to do? I so badly wanted to talk to you for days and nights in a row, exchange views with you, offer you my advice – but I painfully realised that you would never really listen to me, until I would cease to be a rival to you.

So, with the help of poor Abū-l Fazl—may god reward him in abundance for his faithfulness and dedication!—I acquired the skill of writing.

Fortunately, for a person with my ailment, writing is much easier than reading. When you are writing, you do not have to decipher the

---

5. Al-Haqq: The Truth – one of the ninety-nine divine names in Islamic tradition.

meaning of someone else's signs, and guess which vowels go with which consonants; you just have to put on paper the sounds of the words that enter your own mind.

Finding myself capable of writing down my thoughts with relative ease opened up a whole new world for me. Now, I thought, I would be able to speak to you at the only time you would really listen: after my death.

It took me countless hours and every free moment of my days and nights to compile all these writings and documents, which I thought would be of interest to you. For all the pain and effort it took, I thought it was well worth it. It was a good plan: Nobody but my faithful old friend Abū-l Fazl knew about my newfound skill and secret activity. After my death, he would have made haste to show you the hiding place of my writings, under one of the stone floor slabs in the court archive. You would then read these letters, and through them, in a few hours time, acquire what has taken me years of reflection.

But then, Abū-l Fazl was assassinated, and it turned out you were behind the murder! For all my grief and anger, I realised I needed to act quickly and take the matter in my own hands.

First, I had to re-establish full authority and bring you back in the fold. For weakness never breeds respect. The weak only get contempt – maybe sometimes, when they are lucky, they are pitied. But I don't want anybody's pity. I want to be respected. Admired, revered and loved, if possible; hated and feared, if necessary; but always respected.

By the will of the almighty, I succeeded. We are now officially reconciled; you, a respectful crown prince and obedient vassal, and I, the undisputed monarch. What is even more important is that you are back to being in control of yourself, and no longer under way to drink yourself to death like Murād and Dānyāl did.

Now is the time for me to act, and take care of my succession. If I wait any longer, we will grow apart again. Worse still, there may even be a war of succession between you and young Khusrau, between my son and my grandson!

This, I must prevent at all cost.

As you know, yesterday afternoon, I arranged for a fight on the banks of the Jumna between your champion war elephant, Girānbār, and Khusrau's champion, Ābrūp. To me, it was much more than just one of the many hundreds of elephant fights I have ordered for my amusement and distraction. Girānbār's victory was a reassuring sign to me. It made me feel that you and you alone should be my successor. As is taught by the age-old laws and customs of our great Chagatai[6] nation, it would be contrary to nature to bypass the father in favour of the son.

But the elephant fight also made it distressingly clear to me that there is no time to lose. The unseemly squabble between your supporters and Khusrau's clearly warned me to act immediately if I am to prevent a struggle between my blood and the blood of my blood, a struggle that could ruin everything I had worked for. . . .

Be it so. I will not hesitate any longer. Tonight, I will start taking the poison, at irregular intervals and in varying doses. I guess it will take me a couple of weeks to die from the ensuing dysentery. I trust even good Hakīm[7] Alī Gilanī's potions and medicines will be quite powerless against it. Not a very glorious death, I admit, but an effective and not too painful one, and one that will not arouse too much suspicion.

And when I shall feel the end is near, when I approach the unfathomable, black abyss of death, and prepare to prostrate myself before the unspeakable majesty of the giver of life, I will have you called to my bedside. I will have you girded with Jannāt Āshyānī's[8] sword, and as a formal sign of the commencement of your reign, I will adorn your head with the imperial turban. I trust it will not take you long to find this letter inside the turban, and I trust you will thereafter go to the archive, and retrieve the remainder of my writings, underneath the fifth floor slab in the outer right corner of the room, underneath the place where my revered grandfather Bābur's memoirs are kept.

Take some time to read these writings, Shaykhu Bābujī. Through them, you will get to know me better. Keep them to yourself, and use

---

6. Chagatai: Turkish-speaking Turko-Mongol tribe in Transoxania and adjacent territories in Central Asia, named after Chagatai Khān, second son of Genghis (Chingīz) Khān, who had inherited those regions after his father's death. Emperor Akbar's grandfather, Bābur, was a Chagatai Turk who, after being driven from his homeland by Uzbek rivals, established himself in Kābul, and from there, invaded India and established the Mughal dynasty. The word 'Mughal' is Persian for 'Mongol'.
7. Hakīm: Doctor, physician.
8. Jannāt Āshyānī: 'Who is nested in the garden of paradise', posthumous title of Emperor Nasīr-ud-dīn Muhammad Humāyūn (1508-56), father of Akbar the Great.

them to your benefit – I hope they will help you to avoid making some of the mistakes I made.

Do not blame yourself for my death, my son. My time has come. The joys of life, the hunting parties, the nights of laughter and friendly conversations, the cups of wine, the soft-scented musk melons of Kābul and Kashmīr's sweet grapes, the tender breasts and firm thighs of harem girls, even the wisdom of sādhus and sūfis . . . they all seem to have lost their attraction to me.

I must now finish the task that I have been created to accomplish, and in good order, hand over my realm to my successor. I now leave you my world – seize it, Jahāngīr[9] pādshāh, and rule over it with justice and wisdom.

May you lead a good and glorious life, my dear son, and may you receive guidance and blessings in abundance from the ultimate ruler of this world and all worlds to come; the one of thousands upon thousands of most beautiful names; the first and the last; the one, to whom lead thousands upon thousands of paths.

May He, the compassionate, the merciful, the acceptor of repentance, the pardoner, the all-forgiving, graciously nullify my sins – the small and the great, the known and the hidden. May He repair what was wrong in my life, complete what I should have finished, and multiply in infinity what little good I have done or intended to do.

May He engulf me in the unfathomable and limitless ocean of His tender mercy.

---

9. Jahāngīr: Seizer of the world, world conqueror – the official name chosen by Akbar's son and successor Salīm upon his accession to the throne.

Part I

10 سحر

---
10. *Sahar*: Dawn

Second Letter

کلانور

Kalanor

I was thirteen years of age, growing taller and stronger with every passing day, and things were going well. As the young crown prince of the empire, I thoroughly enjoyed my first official assignment, and I felt immensely proud and important.

My blessed father, Emperor Jahānbānī Jannāt-Ashyāni Nasīr-ud-dīn Muhammad Humāyūn[11]—may god's gentle light forever shine upon him—had just appointed me as the governor of the entire Panjāb! I headed a strong force of elite horsemen, under the able guidance and watchful eye of Bairām Khān, my strong and competent new atālīq[12], a battle-hardened Shī'a Turkomān warrior, sipahsalār[13] of the imperial army. He had been my father's iron right arm for years.

---

11. Humāyūn (6 March 1508, Kābul—26 January 1556, Dillī), second of the Mughal emperors of Hindustān. Nasīr-ud-dīn: Helper of Religion. Posthumous titles: Jahānbānī: Guardian of the World, Refuge of the World; and Jannāt Ashyāni: Who is nested in the gardens of paradise.
12. Atālīq: Guardian
13. Sipahsālār: Commander-in-chief of the army, marshal.

Our task was to deal with Sikandar Sūr and his followers, who were still roving the Siwālik hills up north, hoping for an opportunity to come back into the plains and challenge my father's throne.

God was smiling upon us. Sikandar Sūr was really no match for someone as deadly as Bairām Khān. Never wasting any time, hardly ever allowing himself a moment of leisure, he went about his task of eliminating the enemy forces, with the same effortless efficiency as a tiger killing a herd of goats.

His tall, sinewy, broad-shouldered figure seemed to be everywhere in the imperial camp. He talked to regular soldiers as well as army leaders, dealt with supply matters, listened intently to all scouting reports, ordered hit-and-run attacks and all-out assaults. Our men blindly obeyed him – they would have followed him to the very gates of hell! I guess they somehow sensed that he would never order them to do anything he would not be prepared to go through himself.

Although he would always dress quite plainly, not very different from the ordinary soldiers, he looked invincible in his armour and dark blue clothes. The black turban he wore when we were not engaged in battle, gave him an even darker appearance. His face was tanned and lined, with high cheekbones, a long hooknose and a thick, black beard. The piercing eyes under bushy, wild eyebrows, and the thin-lipped, disdainful mouth gave his face a stern, haughty expression. He hardly ever smiled or laughed, but when he did, he showed a row of strong, white, rather sharp, teeth.

While he painstakingly kept me out of danger, he did make sure I saw plenty of action, and would always take the time to explain to me every move of ours and the reasons behind it. I was learning every day, and never felt more excited in my life. Everything was going well, extremely well. . . .

Late in the afternoon on Shanbeh, the fourteenth of Bahman, corresponding to the twelfth of Rabī al-Awwal, 963,[14] after yet another day of successful military operations, we were resting in the imperial army camp on the banks of the river Ravi near Kalānor, admiring the

---

14. Corresponds to Saturday, 27 January 1556 of the Julian calendar.

beauty of god's creation, as the setting sun was painting the water and the rocks with colours of copper and gold.

We had just finished washing and were getting ready to turn towards Mekkah and start our evening prayers, when a messenger from Dillī came galloping into the camp.

One could see it immediately, from the disconcerted look on his face, from the way his horse had been driven to utter exhaustion that this was highly important and very bad news. Faulting, stammering, the messenger informed us that my blessed father had been critically injured in an accident in his library. There was little hope for his recovery.

What had happened? It appeared that my revered father had been studying for a few hours in his cherished library in the Shēr Mandāl building, as he had always been so very fond of doing. At sunset, he had gone to the rooftop observatory with several of his astrologers and other learned men, to observe the first visible movements of the celestial bodies. In the west, Esfand[15] was vaguely discernible on the horizon. From the observer's perspective, the sun was setting three fingers' breadth away from it, towards the south. A half hour later, Venus would be setting close to exactly the same spot. Saturn, high up in the sky, and Mars, in the Bahman[16] constellation, would then form a straight line above it. My blessed father was deeply convinced that it was all of profound significance. . . .

He was about to retire to his quarters for a moment, and stood on top of the steep staircase, when suddenly, the muezzin's *ādhān*[17] to the Salāt al-Maghrib was heard. My unfortunate father hastened down the flight of steps, in order to properly face the *qiblah*[18] and start his prayers, when his foot got caught in his robe, and he fell headlong down the stairs. He received a violent blow on his right temple, blood seeping out of his ear. The court physicians later said that his skull had been fractured.

---

15. Esfand: Pisces
16. Bahman: Aquarius
17. Adhān: The call to prayer. Salāt al-Maghrib: The sunset prayer, one of the five daily obligatory Muslim prayers.
18. Qiblah: The direction of Mecca.

Before losing consciousness, he found the strength to order Shaykh Nazr Culī Turkistānī to send a messenger to the Panjāb, to warn me and Bairām Khān about the accident. His last words, according to those present, were: 'I accept the divine summons.' Three days later, he passed away.

My poor, unfortunate father! May god grant him the peace of the gardens of paradise, for the life he has led on this earth has brought him but little of it. . . . So many grand ambitions, plans and dreams! So many interests and occupations! So few of them fulfilled. . . .

He was born a mighty prince, heir to the throne of the vast dominions conquered by Bābur the Tiger, my blessed and glorious grandfather – may almighty god reunite them in the eternal bliss of His paradise!

Yet, despite this auspicious and noble birth, it was god's sovereign will, that most of the years of his life be fraught with danger, hardship, humiliation and worries: After nine and a half years on the throne of Hindustān, he found himself ousted from his kingdom by Shēr Khān Sūr, his Afghān neighbour and erstwhile vassal.

Shēr Khān Sūr was a conniving, treacherous snake, no doubt about that, but, much as I hate to admit it, he was an abler soldier and ruler than my father was, and he organised and defended his stolen empire well. My poor father spent the following fifteen years of his life in bitter exile, at times little more than a common marauder, with a dwindling group of ragged followers, before god finally chose to restore him to power, after Shēr Khān's death.

Alas, little time did he get to enjoy the sweet taste of victory. A mere six months later, it pleased god to ordain, that he should lose his life in a silly accident on the stairs of a library. . . .

My father and his library . . . I do not think there was a single place in the world he liked any better. Although it had been built by his mortal enemy, he simply adored the building, 'the navel of wisdom' as he would call it, with its perfect octagonal shape, its elegant, canopy-shaped dome on the roof, its cool interior, packed with thousands upon thousands of precious manuscripts, on every subject conceivable or imaginable. . . .

He was really a scholar at heart, my blessed father, a man with a mind more restless than mine. Whenever he found the time—provided he was not wasting it in opium's false paradise!—he would be working on some kind of contraption, feverishly drawing, calculating; or he would sit in his library, reading voraciously, adding yet another insight to his vast knowledge, about the movements of celestial bodies, the properties of metals and precious stones, flowers, herbs and plants, the four elements and their relationship to the letters of the sacred Arabic alphabet, and many other such lofty matters.

Unfortunately, he deluded himself into thinking that all these learned endeavours were vitally important to the art of successful governing. Literally everything and everybody in his court and army was referring in some way or other to the stars and the planets, and to the colours, numbers, substances and attributes associated with them. He would wear different colours each day of the week, each colour referring to a different planet. Similarly, the nobles, officers, artisans and the like were all divided into categories, each referring to the stars and the elements. He designed and built a vast array of complicated inventions and contraptions, of varying, and often doubtful, practical use, ranging from portable bridges to a floating palace, and a huge tent with twelve partitions, corresponding to the twelve signs of the zodiac, with lattice openings at the exact spots where the light of the corresponding stars would fall through. He also had a large, perfectly round carpet woven, with circles representing the orbits of the planets and colours symbolising the elements. He used to play a strange game on it, whereby the courtiers present had to take their places on the carpet near the planet corresponding to them. My father, seated on a throne, would occupy the circle of the sun. A dice with pictures of a person standing, sitting, reclining, crouching, ect., on each of its sides was used. Every participant would throw the dice, and assume the position indicated, inviting, of course, laughs from the others. My father would then comment on the astrological significance of constellations, and link them to events past, present and future. All members of the court pretended to be very fond of the game.

So many learned and intricate pastimes, inventions, rules, arrangements, divisions and subdivisions! Each and every one of them, the result of so much lofty thought! Yet, virtually none of them served any practical purpose whatsoever. Not one of his ingenious inventions managed to halt, or even delay, his enemy Shēr Khān, who drove him out of his own kingdom. Not a single one of his learned observations and calculations warned him that he would fall to his death from the stairs of his own library. . . .

I do not mean any disrespect to my revered father in telling you all this, my son. I loved my father; I honour and cherish his memory; I owe him my life and my throne. He has given me love, protection, and education; and with you, I share his admiration for men of wisdom, learning and science.

However, there is no doubt in my mind: My blessed father's lot in life was a direct warning from god to me, and to you, and to all the Gurkaniyya pādshāhs following us – in this world, god only favours the people who *act*!

It may very well be that the universe is one, that the eternal decisions of god (who owns the past, the present and the future) can be revealed to us through the constellation of the stars, the properties of numbers and the like, but one thing has become very clear to me throughout my life: God only helps those who are willing to help themselves, my dear son. The world of study and knowledge, fascinating and enchanting as it is, may help us to understand Him better, but will in itself not bring us any nearer to Him. God favours people who *do* something! He wants us to take our destiny into our own hands, not to leave it to the stars and numbers!

Intricate rules of protocol, elaborate and arcane ceremonies, conspicuous display of fabulous wealth serve their own useful purpose – they are pleasing to the eye and ear; they instill appropriate awe and respect in the hearts of the king's subjects, and appropriately remind them of his divine mission on this earth.

Nevertheless, the king himself should not be fooled by them. He should never lose sight of the challenges of the real world, which lies *outside* his palace! Those challenges do not require all those calculations, studies and ceremonies, my son. On the contrary, most of the time, the matters of this world are surprisingly uncomplicated; more often than not, they simply require dedication and swift action, rather than indolent reflection. Wars are not won by astrologers, but by warriors who act boldly and swiftly!

When the news of my father's death was brought to us, I fell to the ground, weeping and lamenting, as a loving son at that young age would be expected to do on such a mournful occasion.

But to be honest, I found it very difficult at that time to feel any of the appropriate feelings. I should have felt overwhelming, gut-wrenching grief and sadness, but instead, my head felt numb, as if I had been drinking wine, and all kinds of confused, inappropriate, unworthy and disgraceful thoughts were galloping through my mind.

However much I tried to picture my father as I had known him during his life, I could not stop myself from thinking about what would be happening to his dead body. I had seen festering corpses of Afghān insurgents in the monsoon rains, bloated, black, ghastly, spreading the pestilent, nauseating, unbearable stench of death, hideous worms crawling through their rotting intestines. I had seen mummified corpses of men, fallen years before in the blazing furnace of the desert, dry, dark brown and brittle, as if they had been made out of petrified wood, their faces still recognisable, with parched, tan skin stretched over their skulls, their mouths gaping wide open, as if stiffened in hellish laughter.

What did my father's body look like? Were his eyes and mouth open or shut at the moment of death? Did he pass away like heroes are supposed to, with a noble, serene, impassable expression on his face, like the stone statue of a sleeping god? Or did he die miserably, like a scared animal, his mouth wide open, frozen in the last, agonising attempt to catch a breath of air, his eyes open, staring in horror down the black abyss of death?

I thought of his imposing face, the black eyes under stern eyebrows, the stringy, pointed black beard, which would move up and down when he spoke, and which he always fondled absentmindedly, whenever he was reading something. How many days would have to go by before this face had disappeared, before this noble head had turned into a stinking, fleshless skull, grotesque and dirty, plucks of scalp and beard still sticking to it?

I also found myself questioning all the things I had earlier assumed to be true. How was it possible that my father, who was so well acquainted with celestial sciences and versed in the mysteries of the stars, had been unable to foresee this catastrophic event? Why had god allowed him to be fatally injured, precisely at the moment he was answering the call to prayer? Could this not be used as an argument by the infidels against the truth of our religion? Did god care at all about our hopes and plans? Would He protect me against my enemies, or was He just watching all our strife and wars, the way cruel young boys look at the desperate struggles of a termite in an anthill?

I do not recall feeling afraid, but I very clearly realised that my own future was far from certain. I was only thirteen, yet I knew more than enough about the world, in general, and about Hindustān, in particular, to realise that I would have to fight for my father's inheritance. And the determined, stern look on Bairām Khān's face proved to me that he was thinking exactly the same.

Bairām Khān, who had been the driving force behind my father's restoration to power, once again proved himself the ablest of generals and the most loyal servant of the empire.

Khān Bābā, my strong protector! When I think of him, I have this disturbing, nagging feeling of guilt, this feeling that many people have when they remember their own parents: the painful awareness of having received much more than one deserves or could ever repay, the regretful understanding that one should have shown them much more gratitude, obedience, love and respect, when there was still time to do so. May god reward him in eternity for his faithfulness, and may god forgive me for the misguided, short-sighted ungratefulness with which I later treated him!

As always, he acted swiftly and without hesitation. My father's death was kept a secret for as long as possible. False messages about his recovery were sent to Lāhor, and back in Dillī. A loyal cleric by the name of Mullāh Bekasi, who happened to have my father's build and the same shape of beard, was dressed up in my father's robes, and made the usual daily appearance to the public from the balcony on the riverside of the fort.

Meanwhile, Bairām Khān moved on all fronts. First of all, he secured the loyalty of his personal rival, Tardī Beg, an influential Turkomān officer, raising him to the rank of commander of five-thousand horses, and appointing him governor of Dillī. He made sure the amīrs shared his view on the things that needed to be done.

He also very aptly persuaded me to resist the temptation of riding into Dillī ourselves.

'You see, Your Majesty,' he explained, 'we have to realise that our hold on Hindustān and the other dominions is not as strong as we would like it to be!'

He drew a map in the sand. 'Kābul and Qandahār, up here in the far west behind the Khyber pass, is not our concern right now. As arranged by your blessed father, they are under the government of Prince Muhammad

Hakīm, your younger brother, and his guardian Mun'im Khān. To be honest, I do not like Mun'im Khān very much, and I do think there is a very real danger that he and your brother will sooner or later try to become independent from your throne; but as I said, they are not our immediate concern. At least for now, Kābul is secure and could even become our refuge, if ever—god forbid!—some kind of disaster would befall us.

'The situation back here in Hindustān is far more dangerous, Your Majesty! Yes, our troops do hold Dillī, Lāhor and the other main cities, but the fight is far from over! Sikandar Sūr and the other would-be heirs of Shēr Khān are waiting for an opportunity to strike again and drive us out of these lands, just like they did to your blessed father fifteen years ago. I know, we have defeated them twice, seven months ago, first at Māchhīwāra and then at Sirhind; however, as you know, they are still roving the Siwālik hills. We must continue to smoke them out, chase them and reduce their forces as much as possible before we head back to Dillī. Otherwise, before long, they will be back to challenge us!'

The following weeks were spent in preparation for my formal accession to the throne. A brick platform was built in a garden at Kalānor, while astrologers engaged themselves in learned and complicated calculations and feverish disputes about the most auspicious moment for the enthronement ceremony to take place.

In the meantime, we kept harassing Sikandar Sūr's forces. Compared to my later battles and conquests, it was of course but a small scale war, and I was only an immature boy, but I'm proud to say that with Bairām Khān's wise counsel, I fought it skillfully – not as a hard-hearted, ruthless conqueror who leaves nothing but death and devastation, but as a prudent and wise king who desires the welfare of his subjects. Towards the enemy troops, we showed nothing but merciless, vengeful, stern determination. We killed anyone who dared to oppose us, whenever and wherever we could, pursuing them tirelessly, at all times of the day and night, attacking them when and where they least expected it, gradually wearing out their will to resist. On the other hand, we painstakingly avoided causing any harm to the peaceful inhabitants of the region, whether Muslim or Hindū. The strictest orders were given to pay, promptly and generously, for whatever supplies we obtained from them. We treated their village elders with respect, and left their possessions, temples, homes and women untouched.

Thus it should be, my son. The common people should know their king to be powerful and just. They should realise they have nothing to fear if they stay loyal to him; but nowhere to hide, if they do not.

When children came near our camps, we did not chase them away. On the contrary, we put some effort into teaching them to ride a horse, wield a sword and handle bows and arrows with some accuracy. It is good that the boys of the country aspire to fight for their king when he needs them. Small armies of motivated and skilful volunteers fight so much better than large hosts of mere conscripts.

A few more raids against the weakening followers of Sikandar Sūr, and we would be making our triumphant entry into Dillī. That was our plan.

Little did we realise, it would take us nine more months, and a devastating battle against a formidable new adversary, before we would finally be in a position to enter my father's capital. . . .

≈

The astrologers had finally come to an agreement on a felicitous day and hour for my formal accession to the throne. It was to be scheduled exactly at noon, on Ādīneh, the second of Rabī ath-Thāni of the Hijrī year 963.[19] Three days before, the khutbah[20] had been read in my name for the first time in the mosques of Dillī, Āgrā, Lāhor and the other cities of the empire.

I ascended the coronation platform, wearing a heavy golden robe and a dark blue, almost black, turban, lavishly adorned with precious pearls, accompanied by the sound of blaring trumpets and thundering war drums. The long, golden fringes of the shiny red-and gold imperial canopy were gently swaying in the warm breeze.

The amīrs, khāns, mansabdars and other nobles, all stood around the platform in a hexagon, symbolising the six sides of the universe: north, south, east, west, up, and down. In the entrancing rhythm of the

---

19. Corresponds to Friday, 14 February 1556 of the Julian calendar.
20. Khutbah: Formal prayer for the reigning monarch.

war drums, they chanted, over and over, the same two words: 'Pādshāh salāmat, pādshāh salāmat'![21]

Bairām Khān handed over my father's sword to me. The sword had been brought in from Dillī. I accepted the sword like a reigning monarch would, without bowing my head, yet hoping no one would notice my shaking hands. I unsheathed the sword, and pointed it high towards the sun. All those present followed my example. I slowly turned around, saluting the cheering nobles on all six sides of the platform, and finally sat down on the throne.

My first official deed of government was to appoint Bairām Khān as wakīl of the empire, and bestow on him the lofty titles of Khān Khanān and Sipahsālār I'tizād-i-Daulat Qāhira.[22]

The astrologer had suggested I do this, probably following Bairām Khān's orders, but I would have taken the initiative of my own accord anyway. I sensed it was vitally important to strengthen Bairām Khān's position vis-a-vis the other high officials of the empire.

I made a sign, and two guards handed me a black and gold robe made especially for the occasion. I took it in my hands, briefly touched my shoulders with it, and laid it on the shoulders of Bairām Khān, who knelt down on one knee in front of me, bowing his head. The amīrs, khāns and other nobles cheered to congratulate him, but to my satisfaction, they did so with audibly less enthusiasm than when they had been acclaiming me.

The astrologer proceeded to talk to the assembly about the future of my reign. His sermon was lengthy and learned. He did his very best to convince everybody about the invincibility of my stars by explaining the astrological significance of the moment of my birth. He demonstrated at length how my birth horoscope predicted, without a shadow of doubt, that god Himself had clearly and unequivocally decided that I would become one of the greatest monarchs the world had ever seen, stronger, more victorious, more wise, than Chingīz Khān, Temür, Sargon, or Iskandar.

---

21. Pādshāh salāmat: Hail to the emperor.
22. Wakīl: Administrator of the imperial household. Khān Khanān, Sipahsālār, I'tizād-i-Daulat Qāhira: Lord of lords, commander-in-chief of the army, stay of victorious dominion.

I must confess; his pompous, extravagant flattery pleased me more than I cared to admit. I felt shivers going down my spine when he solemnly, one by one, read out the names of all my ancestors, up to Adam.... Peace be upon all of them, and may their graves be holy and filled with god's light!

Hearing this long list of glorious and important ancestors, I once again stood in awe before the miracle of our existence. Take away just one of them, or any of the ancestors of their mothers and wives, have just one of these thousands upon thousands of people conceive his or her offspring with a different partner or at a different moment, and we would not be here! How wondrous is this life! How magnificent is god's creation! Praise be to Him in eternity!

Yet, what a heavy burden to hear all those glorious and important names, the names of my father Humāyūn; of my grandfather Bābur the Tiger; of Amīr Temür the Iron, founder of our blessed Gurkaniyya Dynasty[23], and his glorious ancestor Chingīz Khān the Great, all of them mighty and glorious kings of kings, all of them dead and buried and no longer there to help me....

Here I was, a thirteen year old boy king, with no safe territory to call my own, surrounded by strong and experienced enemies, and the fate of this entire glorious and mighty dynasty on my shoulders....

When the astrologer had finished his allocution, all the amīrs, khāns, sirān, sidārān, sipahkashān, sipahsālārān[24], all the officers and grandees, all the supporters of our dynasty, one by one, came forward, took a solemn oath on the Holy Qur'ān, and pledged their allegiance to me.

Along with gold and jewels, bags of coins—the first ones minted in my name—were distributed among the participants.

---

23. The Mughal emperors never referred to themselves as *Mughal* (i.e., Mongol) at all. They called themselves *Silsila-i-Gurkaniyya*, the Gurkanid Dynasty, in reference to Tamerlane's (Amīr Temür's) title of *Gurkan*, from the Mongolian *gürägän* or *kürägän*, which means son-in-law, a title accorded to all those who had married a princess of Genghīz Khān's blood, as did Amīr Temür, and as did Bābur's father (Akbar's great-grandfather), Umar-Shaykh Mirza.

24. Sirān and sirdārān: Lords and overlords; sipahkashān and sipashālārān: generals and commanders-in-chief.

The rest of the day was spent eating and drinking and exchanging kind and pleasant conversation. Bairām Khān made sure I met and spent an exclusive amount of time with every one of the nobles. The time spent with each noble was proportionate to their rank and merit. During my meetings with the nobles, Bairām Khān would recount their glorious deeds and accomplishments, and the services they had rendered to my father and grandfather.

And in the night, as I lay wide awake and unable to sleep, I thought about my father. I saw before my mind's eye his gentle face, his charming, engaging smile, and that dark, pointed beard of his. It was as if I could feel his strong hands lovingly fondle my hair, as they used to do when I was just a little boy. I remembered how he had tried to explain to me the many things he knew, and I understood that even in anger, he had always wanted to show me how much he loved me.

Suddenly, with unbearably painful clarity, the harsh, bitter truth stood before me.

For the first time, I truly and fully realised, not only with my head, but also deeply in my heart, that my father was dead and gone, that I would never see him smile again, that I would never again have the opportunity to ask for his advice, never again enjoy a meal with him, or hear his soft, endearing and pleasant voice.

And I wept bitterly.

The following khutbah having been read in his name since three days, His Majesty, the king of kings, ascended the glorious throne at Kalānor.

From the Archives of the Imperial Court of Hindustān

On the Glorious Enthronement
of His Majesty
Abū-l Muzaffar Jalāl-ud-dīn Muhammad Akbar Pādshāh

At Kalānor,
on this most felicitous and auspicious day and hour, to wit

At noon, this Friday,
the second of Rabī ath-Thānī of the Hijrī year 963,
the tenth of Isfandarnaz of the Jalālī year 477,

the fifteenth of Tir of the Yazdajirdi year 925,
and the fourteenth of Shabat of the Rumi year 1867,

The universe has been adorned with the accession to the
Most Glorious Throne of Silsila-i-Gurkaniyya,
the World-seizing Dynasty of Temür the Iron,
by His World-Adorning Majesty,

Hazrāt Shāhānshāh[25]
Abū'l Muzaffar Jalāl-ud-dīn Muhammad Akbar,
Shadow of God,
King of Kings,
the Most Glorious and Radiant Sovereign of our age,
Theatre of God's power,
Bezel of God's signet-ring,
Glory of the Gurkaniyya Dynasty,
Lamp of the Tribe of Sāhib Qarān Qutub-ud Dunyā-wa-ud-dīn, Amīr
Temür Gürgān,
Heir to the Glorious Throne of Jannāt-Ashyāni Nasīr-ud-dīn
Muhammad Humāyūn Pādshāh,
Commander of the Armies of World-Government,
Author of Universal Conquest,
Shining Forehead of the Morning of Guidance,
Focus of the Sun of Holiness,
Sublime Concentration of Humanity,
Heir-Apparent of the Sultān of the Skies,
Leader of Triumphant Armies,
Quintessence of Day and Night,
Sublime Progeny of the Pure Elements and Heavenly Bodies,
Sun of Benevolence and Bounty,
Cheek-Mole of Sovereignty and Fortune,
Vice-Regent of God,
Knower of the Gems of the Wise,
Appreciator of the Pearls of Lofty Genius,
Balm of Ulcerated Hearts,
Incarnate Reason,

---

25. Hazrāt: His Majesty (lit. The Presence); Shāhānshāh: King of kings.

Enlightened Seer of the Truth,
Lover of the Way of God,
Wakeful Occupant of the Throne of Morning,
Knower of the Boundaries of the Paths,
Illuminator of the World,
Achiever of Universal Peace,
Site of Wondrous Gifts,
Grand Master of the Grades of Sanctity,
Initiated in the Mysteries of Darkness and Light,
Perceiver of the Links between the Visible and the Invisible,
Knower of Temporal and Eternal Secrets,
Fountain of those who Thirst for the Waters of Knowledge,
Goal for those who Strayed from the Path of Perfection,
Library of Refined Subtleties and Exalted Sciences,
Dwelling of Knowledge and Inspired Mysteries,
Beacon of Benevolent Society,
Pilot of the Ship of the Universe,
Rescuing Ark of the Boundless Ocean,
Keen-Sighted Guardian of Honour,
Subtle Distributor of Dignities,
Monarch of Fortunate Genius and Auspicious Glance,

Strong Bearer of Heavy Burdens,
Brilliant Master of Quick Understanding,
Ornament of Wisdom,
Cherisher of the Wise,
High-Born of Auspicious Horoscope and Happy Stars,

World-Adorning Conqueror,
Supporter of Friends, Scatterer of Foes, Binder of Enemies,
Cutter of the Bonds of the Oppressed,
Opener of Countries and Dominions,
Exalted Occupier of the Throne,
Glistening Sword of Justice,
Lord of the Seven Worlds,
Protector of the Faith and Prosperity,

Breaker of Enemy Ranks,
Beautifier of the Seven Climes,

Hero of Holy War's Battlefield,
Builder of the Unassailable Bulwarks of Sovereignty and Dominion,
Base of the Pillars of Instruction and Discipline,
Holder of the Handle of Perfect Reason,
Riveter of the Chain of Universal Justice,
War Hammer of Triumphant Battle,

Ocean of Generosity,
Equitable Equinox of Justice,
Waving Fan of Pleasantness,
Experienced and Disciplined in the Solution of All Problems,
Key to all Locks,
Socrates of Wisdom,
Plato of Perception,
Source of Smiling Donations,
Forgiver of Transgressions,
Vigilant Controller of Lust and Appetite,

Destroyer of Enemy Courage,
Bringer of Despair to the Wicked,
Fair-Dealing Destroyer of Fraud and Deception,
Source of Powerful Benevolence,

Whose Glorious Dominion humiliates the Rulers
of the Quarters of the World;
Whose Fortune Opens the Ears of the Princes of the Horizons;
Whose Victorious Banners Lift up the Eyes of Monarchs;
Whose Glorious Court has become the Home of the Elect;
Whose Mighty Fame Mingles with the Spheres;
Whose Glory has Passed from Ocean to Ocean,
Whose Glorious Ascension to the Throne is the Ultimate Bounty of
the Felicitous Conjunction of Stars and Planets.[26]

---

26. Most of the titles quoted above are authentic and have been used by Abū-l Fazl Allāmī in the *Akbar Nāmā* (transl. H. Beveridge, as listed in the bibliography), either referring to Emperor Akbar himself, or to his father Humāyūn.

The sound of trumpets and war drums, which turn to water the courage of iron-hearted enemies, making them break their ranks in disgraceful panic and flee in disarray, accompanied his glorious accession. Congratulatory clamours were heard from the six sides of the universe.

The sword of Jannāt-Ashyāni Nasīr-ud-dīn Muhammad Humāyūn pādshāh was handed to the king of kings by Bairām Khān, sipahsalār of the glorious army, and protector, atālīq and foster father of His Glorious Majesty, and was beheld in awe by the multitude standing around the glorious throne.

The preacher, with sweet-tongued, pearl-dropping mouth, enchanted the ears of those present by the awe-inspiring recollection of His Majesty's glorious names and attributes as written above.

He proceeded to evoke, in prayerful remembrance, the names of His Majesty's ancestors, in the following words:

Hail to Hazrāt Shāhānshāh Abū'l Muzaffar Jalāl-ud-dīn Muhammad Akbar,
Heir to the lofty throne of Jannāt-Ashyāni Nasīr-ud-dīn Muhammad Humāyūn Pādshāh,
Son of Gītī-Sitānī Firdus-Makānī Zahīr-ud-dīn Muhammad Bābur Pādshāh Ghāzī,
the world-conquering tiger,
First Gurkaniyya emperor of Hindustān,
Who through his noble father was the fifth descendent of Amīr Temūr Gūrgān, the Iron,
And through his divinely radiant mother, Qutlaq Nigar Khānum Cupola of chastity and veil of purity, grandson of Yunus Khān of Tashkent, grand Khān of the Mongols,
himself the twelfth descendent of the great Chagatai Khān, son of Chingīz Khān!
Bābur Pādshāh being the son of 'Umar Shaykh Mīrzā,
son of Sultān Abū Sa'īd Mīrzā,
son of Sultān Muhammad Mīrzā,
son of Mīrān Shāh,
son of Sāhib Qarān Qutub ud Dunyā wa-ud-dīn, Amīr Temūr Gūrgān,

son of Amīr Tharāghāi,
son of Amīr Barkal,
son of Alankīr Bahādur,
son of Ical Nunyān,
son of Qarācār Nunyān,
son of Sūghuj-cī,
son of Iradam-cī Barlās,
son of Qāculī Bahādur,
son of Tumana Khān,
son of Bāysanghar Khān,
son of Qāydū Khān,
son of Zūtamīn Khān,
son of Buqa Qā'ān,
son of Būzanjar Qā'ān,
son of Ālanqū'ā[27], impregnated by the Divine Light,
daughter of Ju'ina Bahādur,
son of Yaldūz,
son of Mangalī Khwāja,
son of Temūr Tāsh,
descendant of Qīyan,
son of Īl Khān,
son of Tingīz Khān,
son of Mangalī Khān,
son of Yaldūz Khān,
son of Ā-Ī Khān,
son of Kun Khān,
son of Aghuz Khān,
son of Qarā Khān,
son of Mughal Khān,
son of Alinja Khān,

---

27. According to the Mongol chronicles, Princess Ālanqū'ā, wife of King Zubun Biyān, became a childless widow after her husband's premature death. One night, however, a ray of light entered her body, and she miraculously became the mother of triplet brothers, the eldest one of whom was Akbar's forefather. (J.F. Richards in Alam & Subrahmanyam 1998, pgs. 143-4.)

son of Kayūk Khān,
son of Dīb Bāqūi,
son of Alinja Khān,
son of Turk,
son of Yafeth,
son of Noah,
son of Lamech,
son of Methusalah,
son of Enoch,
son of Yared,
son of Mahalalil,
son of Kenau,
son of Enosh,
son of Seth,
son of Adam, whom Allāh made from clay.[28]
Peace and abundant blessings of Allāh be upon them all!
May their graves be holy, and filled with god's light until the Day of Judgment!

Wearing the four-gored cap of knowledge and fourfold sincerity, the preacher then proceeded, with pleasant, awe-inspiring words of great learning and astute intelligence, to expound the felicitous truths about the auspicious horoscope of His Majesty's ascension, and of the hidden meaning and significance of His Majesty's celestial name:

> It is not hidden from the enlightened minds of the wise and the learned, how it has pleased divine providence to arrange the affairs of the universe in such a manner, that the current state and future of one can be derived from the situation of another. The exact occurrence of any event enables the initiated to predict, with precision and certitude, the eternal divine decrees that govern it. Various delightful points arise from the consideration of the auspicious horoscope[29] of His Majesty's ascension to the throne.

---

28. Based on Abū-l Fazl's *Akbar Nāmā*, I, 143 ff.
29. The *Akbar Nāmā* (I, 69-128) provides a much more lengthy analysis of horoscopes, according to both Indian and Western astrology.

In the tenth angle, which is the house of sovereignty, the sun, undisputed sultān of the skies, is shining its golden light. It is well known that the tenth house is of paramount importance for the hour of an ascension to the throne. The presence of the sun in this house is a clear and unequivocal sign of the advent of a world-conquering monarch!

The second house, which is that of property, is Tīr,[30] and the moon, which is the regent of this house, has attained the position of Fauq-al-arz, ascension above the earth, a clear proof that the keys of this earth's treasures will fall into the hands of this most august monarch.

The third house, which is that of kinsmen and connections, is Mordād, and its dominant, the sun, is in the tenth angle. All His Majesty's relatives and connections will be obedient and submissive to him and his just decrees!

The fourth house is Shahrīvar, the terrestrial house, pertaining to the result of actions and to earthly possessions. Mercury, its dominant, is in the ninth house, which is that of travel. This is a clear indication of lasting conquests of unsurpassed importance!

The fifth house is Mehr, that of children, enjoyment and presents. Its regent is Venus, which is in Esfand, which is her house of ultimate exaltation. His Majesty will be blessed with auspicious children, and his cup of joy will run over. Caravans of priceless gifts from the four corners of the world will be unloaded at his threshold.

The sixth house is Ābān, the house of slaves and servants, and of diseases. Its dominant, Mars, is in the tenth house, the house of sovereignty! His Majesty will have numerous faithful and devoted servants and be protected against disease.

The house Āzar is the Nadir of the ascendant. It is devoid of auspicious stars, a clear indication that the enemies of the empire will all be overcome with ease.

The eighth house, Dey, rules heritage. Saturn, its regent, is in

---

30. Tir: Cancer; Mordād: Leo; Shahrivar: Virgo; Mehr: Libra; Esfand: Pisces; Ābān: Scorpio; Āzar: Sagittarius; Dey: Capricorn; Bahman: Aquarius; Khordād: Gemini; Esfand: Pisces; Farvardin: Aries; Ordibehesht: Taurus.

the eleventh house, a clear proof that His Majesty is abundantly blessed with the perfect qualities of his glorious ancestors.

Bahman, the ninth house, has to do with knowledge, faith, and travel. Mercury, who is the lord of the ascendant (as regent of Khordād), is adding a kind aspect to this house, and causing the abundant acquisition of the lights of wisdom.

The tenth house, Esfand, is the house of sovereignty, and of mothers. The sun, Venus, and Mars are there, meaning that the days of sovereignty will always be pleasant. His Majesty's glory and splendour will increase continuously! The mothers of high rank in his household will see their desires attained, and be blessed with the birth of many glorious princes.

Farvardīn, the Eleventh house, is associated with hopes, and with sincere friends. It is the house where the sun is exalted and where the Moon is waxing. Every desire that arises in His Majesty's holy soul will be fulfilled, and trusted friends will surround him.

The twelfth house is Ordibehesht, the house of enemies. It is void of any auspicious stars. Moreover, Mars, Jupiter, the moon and the sun are positioned as clear opponents of these enemies, indicating they will drink blood from His Majesty's sharp sword. His Majesty's victorious troops will be well-disciplined, the affairs of the state will advance and prosper, and the royal splendour and glory will increase continually!

Not only the celestial bodies reveal the divine will to the initiated!

God, who is just and the source of all harmony, has ordained that those who are acquainted with Abjad[31] and Rumūz-i-Jafar ū Taksīr,[32] the art of the mysteries of the letters, in which he has caused holy books to be written, and above all, of the letters of the Holy Qur'ān, will have in-depth knowledge of hidden wisdom of great value. Indeed, the state of the entire universe is in harmony with the hidden aspects of divine essence and sacred

---

31. Abjad: The use of the twenty-eight letters of the Arabic alphabet as numerals.
32. Rumūz-i-Jafar ū Taksīr: The 'cabalistic' analysis of words, letters and their combinations and permutations.

revelations that lie under the Mu'jama and the Muhmala.³³ The isolation and combination of these letters, their intricate, subtle and complex relationships to the numbers, the four elements, the temperaments and bodily fluids, the celestial bodies and spheres, the minerals, metals, fluids, herbs and plants: all are manifestations of one majestic divine truth, which it has pleased god almighty—praise be to Him in all eternity!—to reveal to the most diligent of His creatures.

When we now look into His Majesty's august name and the letters in which it is written, many auspicious truths become self-evident to those who carry the lamp of learning into the darkness of human ignorance.

As we all know, the beautiful name that has been given to His Majesty, to wit, اکبر (Akbar),³⁴ directly refers to the most awe-inspiring of all the divine attributes. Allāh, indeed—praise be to Him in all eternity!—truly is the greatest, greater than anything conceivable or imaginable, much greater than the sun, which is but a feeble spark compared to His radiant eternal light, greater than this entire universe, which is less than a tiny speck of dust compared to His inconceivable majesty.

Observe the letters of this august name, how equably proportioned and distributed, are the four elements of the universe: Alif ا is Fire, Kāf ک is Water, Bā ب is Air, and Rā ر is Earth.

Even if the mightiest enemies would surround His Majesty on various sides, they would be scattered and annihilated by the unbeatable core of His Majesty's glorious name, since Kāf, the first medial letter, is watery, and therefore drives off the jinns and other supernatural influences made of fire; while Bā, the second medial letter, which is aerial, will scatter the human opponents, made of earth.

Notice how baiyināt-I-hurūf analysis of the word آفتاب āftāb (sun) yields the number 223, corresponding exactly to the numerical value of the name Akbar. His Majesty is clearly destined to be

---

33. Mu'jama and Muhmala: Dotted and undotted Arabic letters.
34. Akbar: Greater, greatest. *Akbar* is the Arabic comparative/superlative of the adjective *Kabir*, great.

sultān of the earth, just as the sun is the undisputed sultān of the skies!

Akbar – this glorious name is so made up that no element is wanting in it, and no element is redundant. Its august bearer will possess bodily health, length of life, lasting joy and exaltation of sovereignty. His will be beauty, bounty, majesty, and perfection.

Glory to god!

Glory to His shadow on this earth!

Glory to Hazrāt Shāhān Shāh Jalāl-ud-dīn Muhammad Akbar Pādshāh!

All the world-subduing Sirān, Sidārān, Sipahkashān, Sipahsālārān, and all the other pillars of empire and eyes of sovereignty, took solemn oaths on the Holy Qur'ān, pledging their everlasting allegiance, unlimited submission and total surrender to the king of kings.

Gold, pearls and other priceless jewels were distributed in abundance. Any and all of the nobles, whether they were called upon to serve in the presence of His Majesty, or were stationed in the provinces or on the borders, received the royal favours in accordance with their position and merit.

Third Letter

جالندهر

Jalāndhār

Later in life, I have been back to Kalānor a number of times. I never liked it very much. Those rural, provincial surroundings, the unadorned, plain brick coronation platform, the unimpressive, ill-kept gardens, none of them really help convey the impression that this is the place where one of the greatest kings in history ascended the throne.

I have given orders for the garden to be embellished, and a few decorative constructions to be built around it, to add a bit to its standing and dignity. It may be good and wise for a king to remember the humble circumstances of his own beginnings, but his subjects should not be reminded about them too often.

I really ought to have more fond and grateful memories of the place. After all, this is where my reign started – a relatively humble and hesitant start for what became an unparalleled series of glorious victories and conquests, the foundation of one of the most powerful and prosperous empires the world has ever seen. If anything, the humility of my origins should increase my satisfaction and pride over the results I achieved.

Yet, as I walk in the peaceful silence of the garden, it seems I still sense the tension in the air, the doubts and fears of my army commanders, the almost tangible threat of defeat and disintegration. No matter how proud I was at the coronation ceremony, I knew very well, despite all the solemn oaths of allegiance and the astrologer's pompous grandiloquence, how precarious my hold on my father Humāyūn's heritage was. Kalānor reminds me, all too clearly, how narrowly I escaped defeat and oblivion, and how much I owe my good fortune to sheer luck.

But to be completely honest with myself that is not the main reason why I dislike the place so much. Kalānor reminds me, more than I care to admit, all the sad mistakes of my youth. It painfully reminds me, how much I owe my success to the loyalty and dedication of other people, whom I later misjudged and paid back with arrogant ingratitude. . . .

No matter how good my excuses, no matter the amends I made, the forgiveness I did obtain: My sins will stay with me until the day I die. The wrong we have done can be forgiven, its consequences mitigated, but no one can undo the fact that it has actually occurred, through our fault. No matter how much we would want it otherwise, our errors become part of our lives. We can only hope that when we are admitted in the gardens of paradise, god Himself—praise be upon Him!—will somehow be able to re-write the stories of our lives, and make them perfect. Will this not be the ultimate blessing of paradise: that god will heal every wound, remove every scar, reunite us with those we have harmed, and allow us to see them again, without any trace of sadness, guilt or remorse? How I wish it would be like this! May I be reunited one day with my friend and teacher Bairām Khān, and may there be nothing but joyful laughter between us!

In the days following my ascension to the throne, Bairām Khān had to intervene more than once to restore discipline among the troops. Such is life, my son: In a herd of animals, be they sheep or cattle, horses, dogs or elephants, there is always rank and order. Each and every animal knows its place – the higher in rank will eat and mate before the lower; all is in balance and harmony. But when a newcomer is added to the herd, or if one of the leading animals gets sick or dies, or there is another incident that upsets the balance inside the group, a series of conflicts breaks out, until the old order is confirmed, or a new one is established. The stronger the leading animal, the sooner the period of unrest will end, and the more peaceful will be the period that follows.

As you will no doubt experience when I'm gone, my dear son, people are no different. The death of a king and the advent of a new reign always brings unrest and strife among the royal family members and the nobles.

Rank and hierarchy will be challenged and disputed, until the new king restores rest and order.

The worst incident happened on the third day after the coronation. Bairām Khān had convened an assembly of all the nobles in the coronation garden to discuss the military situation. One of the leading amīrs, Abū-l M'aālī, who had been a close confidant of my blessed father, at first bluntly refused to attend, unless guarantees would be given for a place of honour for him at the meeting. When he finally did join us, under the obvious influence of more than a few cups of wine, he came to sit down just next to me on my right, without having been invited to do so. He sat himself down without even properly paying his respects. He greeted me kindly, but without reverence, as if I was his pupil, instead of his king. . . .

I was young and did not know what to do, but Bairām Khān did not hesitate for one moment – he had the rascal put in chains immediately. At first, he wanted to have him executed, but I advised against such radical action, and had him carted off to prison in Lāhor. He was later released and allowed to undertake the Hajj[35] to Mekkah. How very convenient it is, when the interests of religion coincide with those of the empire. . . .

If I say so myself, this was indeed the most appropriate course of action. Sentencing Amīr Abū-l M'aālī to death would have undermined the loyalty and trust of the others, for he was a brave and respected soldier, and had been one of my father's closest friends and allies for many years. It is never a good idea for a king to apply capital punishment for a relatively small offence, my son. Not only because it is unjust and irreparable, but because it is a mistake! The verse that Abū-l Fazl was so fond of quoting—'The head of the slain cannot be joined again!'—rings true. Capital punishment is a sign of weakness. It provides an easy excuse for those who want to challenge the king's position, and unsettles the loyalty of the king's remaining supporters.

On the other hand, it would have been a much worse mistake to let Abū-l M'aālī get away with his insolent attitude. Mercy and forgiveness can be signs of strength, but just as often, they are signs of weakness.

---

35. Hajj: Pilgrimage to Mecca, which every Muslim is supposed to perform at least once during his lifetime.

A wise king, my son, should know the difference, and above all, never hesitate to act promptly when challenged. What today is only the slightest lack of respect, will become defiance tomorrow, insubordination the day after, and insurrection the next. Remember, my son, it is much easier to kill a tiger when it is still a cub. . . .

The incident with Abū-l M'aālī was a warning signal and reminder to us, that the amīrs' loyalty was conditional at best. Any mistake from our side, any setback in the fight against our enemies, and our host of followers would quickly disappear before our very eyes. The victorious and the powerful may never be short of friends and supporters, but let them not be deceived: loneliness, bitter loneliness is the fate of the defeated. . . .

Abū-l M'aālī's imprisonment did send a clear message to all the amīrs, that the Gurkaniyya throne intended to be obeyed and respected. More disturbingly, it was also a message that Bairām Khān was not going to allow anyone to challenge his own position as the regent of my father's empire. Had he acted against Abū-l M'aālī to protect me? Or did he just want to serve his own interests? Was he nourishing personal ambitions? The first, tiny seeds of doubt, suspicion and jealousy had been sown in my heart. They would later become an overgrowing, tangled mass of poisonous bindweed. . . .

In the course of the following weeks, we continued our military operations in the Siwālik hills, until the torrential rains of the monsoon transformed the entire country into a swamp, making swift cavalry actions nearly impossible. Cavalry unable to move freely is always at risk, and it soon became evident that Sikandar Sūr's forces were even more afraid than we were at the risk of getting pinned down at a single spot. They withdrew further to the north, and we moved south towards Jālandhar, where we remained for some five months.

I spent the time horse riding, hunting, bow and musket shooting, wrestling, and practicing my fighting skills with sword, lance, mace and battle axe. It brought me great joy to feel how I was growing stronger and better every day.

Bairām Khān also saw to it that my education continued. By that time, my teachers had given up all attempts to teach me to read and write, but I very eagerly listened to all kinds of books being read to me by my new teacher, Mīr Abdul Latīf. May god be well pleased with him! Under the old man's guidance, I willingly learned by heart many sūrahs of the Holy Qur'ān, and hundreds of beautiful Persian and Arabic prayers, poems and stories by Jalāl-ud-dīn Rūmi, Sanā'ī, Hāfiz, and many other saintly teachers.

By far the fondest memories I have are of the afternoons and evenings when I was instructed in the history of the great empires of old. Mīr Abdul Latīf of course told me about the conquests of the Prophet Muhammad and the four right-guided Khalīfas. But what I enjoyed even more was the adventures of the great Iskāndar[36]; or Salāh-ud-dīn, the liberator of Jerusalem; or Sultān-i-Rūm Mehmet II, conqueror of Istanbul, and so many other great kings and warriors.

Most of all, of course, I loved to hear about my own glorious ancestors, Chingīz Khān the Great, and Amīr Temür the Iron.

My favourite hero was my own grandfather, the conquering Tiger of Hindustān, the great Gītī-Sitānī Firdaws-Makānī Zahīr-ud-dīn Muhammad Bābur Pādshāh Ghāzī,[37] may his grave be holy. I enjoyed listening to his memoirs, the *Tuzuk-i Bāburi*, or *Bābur Nāmā*, as they call them in Persian these days. How I love these writings! So grand, yet so unassuming; so full of lofty eternal wisdom and practical advice; all those shrewd, astute insights, those honest, candid statements, all of them written in plain, crystal-clear, down-to-earth Turkī.

Many times when my tutor Mīr Abdul Latīf was giving me history lessons, Bairām Khān himself would sit down with us, listening intently to the teacher's reading, sipping fresh sugared water with lime, and eating quite impressive amounts of almonds, figs and dates, ostensibly without being very much aware of it.

After a while, he would stop eating, dismiss the teacher, and start drawing battlefield maps on the ground with the point of his sword, and teach me all there is to know about our strategies and tactics, our weaponry, and those of our opponents. In great depth and detail, he taught me the appropriate deployment and use of cannon, horsemen, and foot soldiers on the battlefield, as well as the rules governing troop movements, encampments and fortifications. He discussed supplies,

---

36. Iskāndar: Alexander the Great.
37. Gītī-Sitānī: Conqueror of the world; Firdaws-Makānī: Abiding in paradise. Zahīr-ud-dīn: Helper of religion.

weaponry, and equipment; the keeping of elephants, horses, camels, mules, and livestock, and many other related subjects, which are highly important for a king to master most thoroughly.

Bairām Khān did so much more than telling me a few fascinating stories. He did not even talk that much about bravery, glory or honour. He explained to me the art of warfare, like a physician demonstrating how to prepare a medicinal potion, like a carpenter or a mason showing how to build homes and furniture, or like a merchant explaining the tricks of the trade to his successor.

≈

Bairām Khān

War is not as messy as it looks, Your Majesty. Victory or defeat is not merely the result of fate or coincidence, not even of bravery. Warfare is an art, a science, just like astrology, or medicine. Like the movements of the sun and the moon and the other celestial bodies, warfare is governed by inescapable, iron laws. The task of an army leader is to thoroughly understand them, and to put them to use, to his own advantage.

The most important law of warfare, Your Majesty, the law that contains all others, is the following: All other things being equal, god favours the larger army!

You see, Your Majesty, any major battle can be thought of as a series of encounters between the two opposing armies, during which every soldier tries to kill as many enemies as possible. Suppose, Your Majesty, there are two such armies, one 30,000 strong, the other 10,000. Suppose one out of ten attempts on either side to kill enemy soldiers is successful. After the first encounter, the smaller army will have killed 1,000 of its opponents, and the larger army will have killed 3,000, leaving 29,000 against 7,000. At the second encounter, the smaller army will only be able to kill 700 enemies, while losing 2,900 of its own troops, leaving 28,300 against 4,100 at the third encounter. At that time, supposing both armies continue to fight as valiantly as before, the large army will lose 410 men, leaving 27,890, but the smaller army will lose 2,830 soldiers! This leaves it with a mere 1,270 men for the last and final encounter, during which it will be completely annihilated, while the victorious army still retains a large fighting force of 27,763 men.

Such is the simple arithmetic of a battle of attrition, Your Majesty – the larger army wins. . . .

There are, however, many ways to influence the working and outcome of this fundamental law of war, and a good army commander knows how to put them to use in his own favour.

Of course, weaponry of superior quality will increase the army's effectiveness: longer-ranging cannons, muskets and bows will allow your soldiers to start killing their enemies before incurring any casualties themselves. Fortifications, entrenchments, bulwarks, and also shields and armour will reduce the effectiveness of enemy attacks.

Even more important than weapons, defences and equipment, is the fighting spirit of your men. You have to remember, Your Majesty, that each army may have its number of heroes, but the vast majority of your soldiers will be ordinary men, afraid to die, and naturally inclined to avoid the heat of the battle and flee from danger. An ordinary soldier, when left to himself, will feel the urge to run away, or in contrast, to attack prematurely, in an instinctive effort to get the battle over with as quickly as possible. He will discharge his bow or musket in the general direction of the enemy, without taking proper aim, thereby wasting and reducing his own army's killing power. When his army suffers a setback, he will flee in panic, and thereby allow himself and his comrades to be slaughtered like the meekest of sheep. When, on the contrary, his army is victorious, he will immediately start plundering and fail to pursue the fleeing enemy, thereby wasting a precious opportunity to annihilate him, allowing him to regroup and come back to fight another day.

This behaviour is of course typical for an army of inexperienced conscripts, but even in an army of battle-hardened professional soldiers, it is always lurking beneath the surface. An able commander, Your Majesty, is aware of these natural weaknesses of men, and knows how to counteract them. He will at all times maintain order and discipline in his army. He will foster his men's courage and eagerness to fight by reminding them of the rewards of war: spoils and booty, security for their families, honour and glory for themselves. When fighting infidels, he will of course remind them of Allāh's eternal blessings awaiting those who die in jihād.

He will keep his army exercising every day, so that the proper behaviour in battle becomes routine to it. He will not only pay attention to the cavalry, but to the foot soldiers as well. He will take time to talk to them, and teach them, for instance that in the face of an enemy cavalry charge, by far the best thing they can do for themselves is to firmly hold their ground, in tightly closed ranks. It may take more than ordinary courage, not to move when thousands upon thousands of thundering hooves are rushing towards you, but it is by far the most effective defence. Horses, no matter how fierce and battle-hardened, no matter how obedient they may be to their master, will never run at full speed into a solid wall. When approaching well-closed ranks of disciplined and determined enemy foot soldiers, they will inevitably slow down, exposing themselves and their riders to arrows and musket fire.

Elephants, on the other hand, should if possible, be fought behind deep trenches, or, if there is no time to dig them, they should be fought with flexible, fast moving infantry battlelines, clouds upon clouds of arrows, volleys of cannon and musket fire, and swift hit-and-run cavalry charges. Elephants are very hard to kill, and will slam through any fixed battle formation trying to oppose them, but when they are wounded and enraged, they are almost impossible to keep under control and can therefore quickly become as dangerous to their own army as to their opponent's. When commanding an elephant force, it is therefore essential to keep them in the rear, out of reach of enemy cannon fire, and to bring them to bear only near the end of the battle, when the enemy formations have been driven together in a compact mass and the time has come to move in for the final kill.

The greatest emphasis, Your Majesty, needs to be put on speed. The commander will have his archers and musketeers train every day, over and over, how to replace each other in quick succession, the front row discharging their weapons, the second, third, fourth and fifth rows ready to replace them, and the following rows reloading, so that the battle formation is able to deliver a constant flow of arrows and musket fire.

When all this is done diligently and put into practice on a regular basis—a king should always seek conquest and war, lest his army become lazy and ineffective!—yours will be a battle-hardened fighting force, able to defeat armies, vastly superior to it in numbers.

Then comes maybe the most difficult part: the proper deployment of your fighting forces. You see, Your Majesty, no matter how good your soldiers and their equipment, that in itself is not enough. Troops need to be deployed and sent into action in accordance with the requirements of the battlefield. This is perhaps the most important, and also the most difficult skill of warfare.

Observe, Your Majesty, how smaller armies fight so much better on narrow, restricted battlefields, where mountains, hills, forests, rivers, lakes and the like are blocking the deployment of their adversary. This kind of terrain enables a smaller army, using its greater mobility and the element of surprise, to transform the war into a series of smaller, hit-and-run battles, in which, when and where it strikes, it can effectively outnumber its opponent.

The whole purpose of troop movements and manoeuvres in open battlefields is to create similar conditions. As demonstrated so ably by your glorious grandfather Bābur pādshāh—may Allāh smile on him and make his grave holy!—an enemy host of overwhelming strength can be turned into an ineffective, helpless mass of cannon fodder, when you succeed in blocking its ability to properly manoeuvre and deploy its fighting force.

Consider, Your Majesty, your grandfather's immortal victory at Pānīpat, on that glorious day of Yawm as-Sabt, the ninth of Rajab, 932[38], the victory that won him the throne of Hindustān.

Bābur pādshāh had less than twenty thousand men, against over one hundred thousand brave and excellent Afghān troops under Ibrāhīm Lodhi, then sultān of Dillī.

Sultān Ibrāhīm's army was thus vastly superior in numbers. He also had about one thousand fighting elephants at his disposal. Our army, as in the days of old, mainly relied on horse archers, but was ably supplemented by 4,000 musketeers, and about 150 cannons of various kinds. These new ways of fighting made the difference that day. Your grandfather had come to realise, long before his opponents in Hindustān, that cannons are not only essential when laying siege to a fortress, but can also be put to great use on the open battlefield.

Bābur pādshāh knew he would not stand a chance unless he could force the enemy army to fight on a narrow front. He therefore positioned his forces to the east of Pānīpat, between the town walls and the Jumna River.

---

38. Saturday, 21 April 1526 (Julian calendar)

The Baranghar[39] wing had the town walls to its right, while the Jawanghar's left flank was protected by ditches, felled trees, and artificial hedges made of thorny shrubbery, all the way to the riverbanks. This made sure that the army could not be bypassed and surrounded by the enemy. Harawal, Gul, and Chandawul[40] forces in the centre were kept behind mobile defences made of series of gun carts, linked together with chains or ropes, behind and in between which were archers and musketeers, protected by movable wooden mantlets. At regular intervals, he left openings in the front, a bit less than a bow shot wide, through which cavalry assaults of up to five thousand horses could be launched.

Bābur pādshāh's preparations were impeccable, but Sultān Ibrāhīm Lodhi refused to give battle, and quite rightfully so; after all, time was very much on his side. He had no difficulties of supply, whereas Bābur pādshāh would sooner or later be forced to withdraw, or leave his entrenched position and attack.

For seven days, in the blazing heat of early summer, the armies faced each other.

With a series of quick cavalry raids, Bābur tried to provoke the enemy into attacking him, but Sultān Ibrāhīm ignored all insults and would not move. As morale in our camp was deteriorating fast, Bābur pādshāh then decided to launch a night attack, on the seventh of Rajab.

Five thousand men of our Jawanghar's main body moved into Lodhi's camp, but they were in for a very unpleasant surprise themselves – the Afghāns were ready and waiting for them! Fortunately, our forces did not confuse bravery with foolishness – they were able to disengage and withdraw without too many losses. Had they continued their attack, they would most certainly have been annihilated.

Ironically, it was this defeat that won the war for us. After another day of waiting, shortly after dawn on the ninth of Rajab, encouraged by their easy victory, the Afghāns moved in for what they thought was the final kill.

It went exactly as Bābur pādshāh had planned. The mighty Afghān cavalry charge, which had started on a broad front, was slowed down

---

39. Baranghar: Right wing; Jawanghar: Left wing.
40. Harawal: Advance guard; Gul: Army centre; Chandawul: Rear guard.

considerably when it had to squeeze itself through the narrow funnel created by our entrenchments, their left flank pushing sideways into their own centre formation.

Bābur pādshāh's forces waited in silence until the Afghān front was well within reach of our artillery. Then, the Dhamaka and Ramjanaki cannon opened up, their projectiles penetrating up to six lines deep into their formation, followed by devastating blasts of the multi-barrelled Arghun fieldguns. As the large guns reloaded, deadly volleys of our infantry muskets and Bān rockets further decimated the enemy vanguard one could see the bullets and missiles piercing enemy shields and armour. The Afghān front-lines tried to turn around and move out of reach of our guns, but the attacking ranks behind slammed into them. Their entire fighting force had turned into a compacted, disorganised mass, those caught in the middle unable to move anywhere, defenceless fodder for our Ghabarah mortar bombs and the clouds upon clouds of arrows that kept raining down on them.

Bābur pādshāh did not waste any time to seize the opportunity.

The best of our cavalry—fearless, battlehardened Turkomān archers on the swiftest Irāqī horses—stormed through the openings in our defences, wheeling round the Afghān flanks and effectively preventing them to manoeuvre.

The Afghāns fought bravely and with honour, repeatedly charging our front lines at the centre, in an effort to break out of the trap, but it was to no avail – very few of them even reached our positions, and those who did were finished off quickly.

As your illustrious grandfather writes in the *Tuzuk-i Bāburi*: 'The sun had mounted a spear high when the onset of battle began, and the combat lasted till mid-day, when the enemy was completely broken and routed, and my friends victorious and exulting. By the grace and mercy of almighty god, this arduous undertaking was rendered easy for me, and this mighty army, in the space of half a day, laid in the dust'.

Sultān Ibrāhīm Lodhi's corpse was found amid sixteen thousand fallen Afghāns. When his head was brought to Bābur pādshāh, he ordered the sultān's remains to be washed and shrouded in the finest cloth, and buried with honour, at the spot where he and his men had fallen.

Your noble grandfather ordered his son, Shāhzāda[41] Sultān Humāyūn, your glorious father, to ride into Āgrā, Lodhi's capital, and sent another contingent of troops to occupy Dillī. The next day, he followed the army into Dillī, where for the first time, the khutbah was read in his name.

Hindustān was his. Praise be to god!

This glorious battle, Your Majesty, contains in itself the entire art of warfare! For generations upon generations, army leaders of all nations will speak in awe and admiration about Bābur pādshāh's magnificent victory at Pānīpat!

≈

Bairām Khān was so right, my son. The study of this battle is indispensable for the education of all generations to come – it contains in itself almost the entire art of warfare! Moreover, it was with this battle that we established ourselves as the rulers of Hindustān! Promise me, my son, on my grave, that you will never allow any of the princes of our dynasty to forget where they came from!

The battle of Pānīpat. . . . How many hours did we spend talking about it, analysing it! Little did we imagine at that time, that only a few weeks later, we too would find ourselves fighting at Pānīpat – fighting desperately for our very own survival. . . .

---

41. Shāhzāda: Prince (literally, offspring of the Shāh).

Fourth Letter

ثانیثت

Panipat

Sikandar Sūr was not the only one coveting the throne of Hindustān. There were, alas, quite a number of other would-be heirs and successors to the throne of Shēr Khān Sūr, eager to revive their predecessor's empire.

Shēr Khān was a devious traitor; he stole my father's dominions. Because of him, my father spent more than fifteen years in miserable exile. As my father's son, I hate him for it. Yet, as my father's successor, much as I hate to admit it, I owe him a debt of gratitude.

For all his conniving treachery, Shēr Khān Sūr was an insightful and wise ruler. He clearly understood that conquest alone is not sufficient to build an empire. In fact, victory in battle is only the beginning of the work. Conquests, my son, are like castles of sand unless they are properly consolidated and strengthened. Consider Bābur pādshāh's victories, even Temür's, or those of the great Chingīz Khān; they were all like grassland fire: awesome, spectacular, impressive to behold, but over very quickly, and not leaving anything of lasting value.

Building a throne is an art, keeping it is another, my son. Never assume that our dynasty rules over Hindustān because it is our god-given right to do so. It will be your duty as pādshāh, to maintain and increase the strength of our empire. Every waking moment of your life should be devoted to the strength of the empire, either expanding it through conquest, or consolidating it through wise government. Dominions and territories need to be administered, populations need to be integrated. Do not take this lightly, my son! It is a never-ending task and a heavy burden, and it should always be on your mind, whether you are waging war, administering justice, securing revenue to the treasury, organising commerce and agriculture, or favouring the arts.

Shēr Khān understood all this and was a much better ruler than I care to admit in public. So much so that I have thought it wise to take over many government institutions and practices that had been installed under his reign. Good ideas are good ideas, no matter where they come from, my son.

Fortunately for my father and for our dynasty, however, Shēr Khān was not allowed to stay in this world very long. God, who is infinite justice, caused him to die in an explosion of one of his own rockets, only five years after he stole my father's throne.

After Shēr Khān's death, the once-powerful Sūr dynasty quickly went into decline.

Shēr Khān's youngest son and successor, Jalāl Khān, who ruled under the name Islām Shāh, died of a painful disease eight years later, before he was able to secure his own succession. He and his father had been competent rulers, but their successors were weak and divided, and quickly squandered their strength in fratricidal civil war.

Jalāl Khān's twelve-year-old son was brutally murdered by his worthless uncle, Mubāriz. That coward son of a bitch cut off the poor boy's head, right before the very eyes of his desperate mother – Mubāriz's own sister! Such can be the lust for power, stronger than the laws of god and men alike, more enchanting than the rapture of opium, sweeter than a woman's embrace.

Mubāriz assumed the title of Adil Shāh. Not only was he a treacherous murderer, he was also an indolent pig who left all the affairs of the state to Hemū, his deceased predecessor's competent minister, a dwarfish, unimpressive Hindū of humble origins and most frail stature, but clever, tenacious, and dangerous like a cobra.

While Hemū's power was on the rise, Mubāriz (Adil Shāh) wasted his days playing music, singing, dancing, drinking, and enjoying the pleasures of the harem. Meanwhile, his empire was crumbling around him.

Let the emptiness of Mubāriz's worthless life be a warning to you, my dear son. The path of self-indulgence may be pleasant and easy to follow, but it does not lead to god. Much less does it lead to success in this world.

As I said, Mubāriz promptly lost control over most of his stolen empire. His cousin Sikandar Sūr seized the Panjāb. Another one of his cousins, Ibrāhīm Sūr, took possession of Dillī and Āgrā, and Muhammad Shāh set up an independent realm in Bengāl, leaving only Bihār to the usurper. One Sūr waged war against the other.

It should be no surprise that all this ruinous infighting quickly brought the proud reign of the Sūrs to an ignominious end. Remember this always, my beloved son, let it be a lesson for us: God does not approve of those who let their blessings go to waste.

Ibrāhīm Sūr was chased out of Dillī by Sikandar Sūr and later, decisively defeated by Hemū. He fled to Orissa, where he died, a forgotten man. As for all the other Sūrs, god almighty, in His benevolent mercy, has chosen our dynasty to be His right arm in chastising them and their followers.

Indeed, the internal squabble between the Sūrs had provided my blessed father Humāyūn with the opportunity to cross the borders of Hindustān again, and take back what was rightfully his. He defeated Sikandar Sūr a first time at Māchhīwāra, and then again at Sirhind, forcing him to flee to the Panjāb, where Bairām Khān and I were chasing him, when my father died in that unfortunate accident on the library roof.

It has thus been god's will, that I would be the one to reunite the lands of Hindustān.

We were still encamped at Jālandhar, preparing ourselves to resume the operations against Sikandar Sūr, when the news was brought to us that Hemū had crossed the border of Adil's dominions and was marching against us from the south.

The history of Hindustān would have been very different indeed, if the plans and ambitions of this conniving devil of a man would have met with god's approval.

Hemū had been fighting Adil's battles against the other Sūrs in the west, proving himself a most able general and leader of men, winning no less than twenty-two battles for his master.

Each time, he grew more powerful. Outwardly, he behaved like Adil's most loyal servant, but very soon he must have come to the conclusion that he could do even better for himself. He accumulated immense wealth, only to spend it with cunning generosity, gradually buying himself the loyalty of the Afghān amīrs. The conquest of Hindustān would be his final step towards absolute power.

Hemū's forces advanced via Gwālīor to Āgrā, which they captured without a fight, as the commander of our garrison in that city, Iskandar Khān Uzbeg, withdrew towards Dillī, to join forces with Tardī Beg, the newly appointed local governor. One would have expected them to hold the city and keep Hemū's army occupied until we joined them with the main body of our army. Instead, Tardī Beg panicked. He allowed his vanguard to be slaughtered before his very eyes without intervening, and fled to the northwest, abandoning 1,000 fine Irāqī horses, 160 war elephants, and other valuable booty to the enemy. So precipitous was his flight that Hemū, suspecting a ruse, did not dare to follow him.

Hemū entered Dillī in triumph. This was the opportunity he had been waiting for all his life. He distributed all the captured treasures and horses among his Afghān nobles, keeping only the elephants for himself. There, he had coins struck in his own name, held his court under the imperial canopy, called himself Rājā Vikramaditya and assumed the dress and style of the great Hindū kings of old. His Afghān commanders started calling him Hemū Shāh, and I suspect his Hindū followers were dreaming of a whole new era. His long years of hard work seemed to be coming to an end. He was ready to claim the throne of Hindustān for himself.

Bairām Khān was livid when the news of Tardī Beg's shameful retreat was brought to us.

'I must have been out of my mind to entrust Dillī to this treacherous, cowardly, stinking heap of dog vomit!' he hissed. 'Measures will have to be taken, Your Majesty,' he mumbled, talking more to himself than to me, 'but we have to be careful! Cowardice is contagious, like the plague. We need to convince the other amīrs first; we desperately need to stay united and bring everybody back in line.'

Preparations were made for a hasty march. Much to our regret, we were forced to leave a sizeable cavalry force behind in the Panjāb, to make sure Sikandar Sūr would not be able to attack us from the rear.

Khīzr Khwāja Khān, a competent and reliable Chagatai leader who had married my father's half sister Gulbadan Begum and was thus related to me, was left in charge of these rearguard forces.

We quickly moved southeast with the rest of the army. A courier was sent to Tardī Beg, carrying a firmān[42] ordering him to meet the imperial army at Sirhind.

Two days later, we met, about two hours before noon. I was pleasantly surprised to see how Bairām Khān warmly embraced Tardī Beg, affectionately calling him his tüqān.[43] He then proceeded to welcome the other commanders of the Dillī and Āgrā garrison, and the two groups of army commanders started greeting each other. As often happens when the situation is grave, the reunion was just a tad too joyful, the embraces over-friendly, the voices exaggeratedly loud, the conversations interspersed with just a bit too many jokes and laughs. Despite the conspicuous display of optimism and joy, the atmosphere felt distinctly awkward and ominous.

Fortunately, this uneasy exchange of courtesies, formalities and civilities did not last very long. Bairām Khān clapped his hands to get everybody's attention and the conversations stopped abruptly.

'We need to talk, my friends,' he said, with a tone of sadness in his voice. Instantly, as if they were performing a ceremony rehearsed many times over, the amīrs went into the main tent in the most orderly fashion, sitting themselves down in a circle, the highest in rank sitting in front, the others in the back.

'My brother Tardī Beg has thus chosen to regroup with the rest of the imperial forces before attacking the enemy,' he said, offering Tardī Beg an elegant way to explain his cowardice as an astute strategic move.

Alas, the dumb fool failed to seize the hand extended to him. How often is arrogance the mother of error, the hallmark of stupidity. . . .

'My brother must have had too much wine, for he confuses his dreams with reality,' he snapped. 'It would be utter folly to try to oppose this accursed infidel with the forces we have! He must have over a thousand war elephants, of a kind nobody has ever seen before! They are terrifying,

---

42. Firmān: Imperial order
43. Tüqān: Elder brother

huge like mountains, their mouths like the jaws of a dragon, daggers and sabers attached to their tusks and trunks. Despite their size, they are of the most amazing swiftness and agility: The fastest Irāqī horse would not able to outrun these rushing mountains of death! Vicious and mean they are, and nothing in this world matches their strength. I saw them uprooting strong trees as if they were mere blades of grass, just for the fun of it! I saw one of them grab a man and his horse, effortlessly fling them into the air and trample both of them to death! Unlike all other elephants, they seem to be impervious to pain when wounded. I saw two of them being hit by at least twenty arrows in their forelegs, trunks and ears – it did not seem to bother them at all! They just kept rushing forward, smashing into our lines, killing everything and everybody on their path. I am telling you, my brothers, this is no normal enemy we are facing! Not only does he outnumber us, ten to one at least; he possesses weapons and animals that he could not possibly have obtained by any normal means! I'm telling you, he is protected by the most powerful magic, supported by ash-Shaytān himself![44] There is only one sensible thing we can do: Go back across the Khyber pass into Kābul, join forces with Prince Muhammad Hakīm and Munim Khān, avail ourselves of the most powerful magic to break this infidel's black witchcraft, and then come back to reclaim what is rightfully ours!'

'If we run away now, without a fight,' Bairām Khān replied, ignoring the insult and trying to control his anger, 'we may never get a chance to take Hindustān again. Don't you see what this infidel is doing? He is trying to rebuild the great Hindū empires of old, and if we do not stop him, he might just be successful! He is an astute general, and an able leader of men. It is obvious that before long, he will have armed and mobilised the Hindū masses! They have been used to foreign Muslim rulers for centuries, but this is their chance to rise again! Ours is a holy task, my brothers: If we don't stop Hemū, it's only a matter of time before he will drive Islām out of these lands. He may allow the Afghāns to stay on as his vassals for a while, but he will wipe them out as soon as he feels strong enough to do so. If we run away now, we will need ten times our current strength to come back. Moreover, if we run away now, we betray

---

44. Ash-Shaytān: (The) Satan, the devil

the cause of Islām, we betray our oath of loyalty to Emperor Humāyūn and his legitimate heir, and worst of all, we forever lose our honour! It will take generations for people to forget our scandalous cowardice! To possess a throne, to possess an army ready for battle, and then to run away without a fight, like a bunch of women! This is not how I wish to be remembered! Do not forget, my brothers, we all have to die some day. When we die, is not so important, and is in the hands of Allāh anyway. Much more important is how we spend our lives! How much better it is to die at the age of forty, sword in hand, fighting like a man, spitting death in the face, than to die a despicable coward twenty years later!'

'All of you Shi'a heretics seem to be obsessed with martyrdom!' Tardī Beg retorted, his face full of contempt. 'Sensible people understand that the cause of Islām is much better served by living men fighting tomorrow than by powerless martyrs dying today!'

Bairām Khān's hand moved towards the hilt of his sword.

At this time, Shams-ud-dīn Muhammad Atga Khān intervened. He was a longstanding and faithful ally of my father, respected throughout the army for his bravery and wisdom. Moreover, as the husband of my dear foster mother Jī Jī Anaga, one of the nurses who had taken care of me as a child, he was related to me as my atga[45], my foster father, and thus one of the most important nobles in the imperial court. He stepped between the two men and thundered:

'Enough of this, my brothers! Is this a time for us to be divided? Tardī Beg Khān, with all due respect, let me warn you, here and now that I will personally kill anybody who tries to incite one Muslim against the other in this time of danger and war! Do we not all worship Allāh? Do we not all recognise the noble Prophet Muhammad as His Messenger, eternal blessings be upon him? We should not fight among ourselves, my brothers – we have to stand united against the threat of this infidel! And I have to agree with my Lord Khān Khanān: We simply cannot afford to run away! Who has forgotten the miserable years of exile before our beloved Emperor Humāyūn was able to recover the throne of Hindustān? I will not be chased out again without a fight! And let Hemū be helped

---

45. Atga: Foster father. As related before, Shams-ud-dīn Muhammad Atga Khān was married to Jī Jī Anaga, one of Emperor Akbar's nurses.

by the devil – we will be the allies of Allāh Himself! Let us prepare for battle, my brothers, let the astrologers help us choose the most auspicious time and place, and let us put our trust in the Almighty! After all, not a single leaf falls from a tree, if He does not want it! How would He then allow this infidel to defeat us, unless it is His divine will?'

The amīrs nodded in consent. One of them started shouting, 'Allāhu Akbar!'[46] and before long, everybody was chanting and proclaiming god's greatness.

Bairām Khān raised his hand and said:

'You have spoken well, my friend! Thus it shall be done! Let the astrologers prepare their horoscopes, by all means. We will head south tomorrow!'

The amīrs retired to their own quarters. As soon as everybody had gone, Bairām Khān started pacing up and down the tent.

After a while, he mumbled:

'No, this time, we need to act – this has gone far enough!'

Then, turning to me as if he had failed to notice me before, he said:

'The coming days will be difficult and demanding – perhaps Your Majesty wishes to go hunting this afternoon? The plains around Sirhind are pleasant and game of all kinds abounds. Your Majesty will not have the opportunity to distract Himself in the coming days. . . .'

I, of course, suspected what Bairām Khān was up to, but chose to say nothing. I realised he was probably right, and to be honest, despite the gravity of the situation, the prospect of being on my own for a couple of hours was extremely tempting.

I rode back into the camp near sunset. My attendants handed the game we had killed to the kitchen servants. I proceeded to the imperial tent, where Maulānā Pīr Muhammad Shirwāni helped me to dismount.

'I need to inform Your Majesty,' he stammered, 'that Tardī Beg is dead.'

---

46. Allāhu Akbar: 'God is greater' or 'God is the Greatest'. Akbar: Comparative/superlative of the Arabic adjective Kabīr, great.

'Tell me how this happened,' I replied, not in the least surprised, yet trying to hide my anger that an important measure like this had been taken without consulting or even informing me.

'Your Majesty, Bairām Khān sent me to Tardī Beg, to invite him for a meeting in his pavilion. At first, he refused to come, but I replied, truthfully, that the Khān Khanān had requested to see him to discuss the strength of Hemū's army and the strategy to be followed. Reluctantly, Tardī Beg then accompanied me to the Khān Khanān, where he received a cool but courteous welcome. The Khān Khanān asked a thousand questions about Hemū's forces, the number and weaponry of his troops, their battle tactics, and so on.

'The conversation went well, as long as they were discussing cannon, cavalry and the like. But when Tardī Beg again started talking about Hemū's elephants, in an effort to explain why he had failed to defend Dillī, Bairām Khān burst into a torrent of abuse:

'"Spare me your imbecile ramblings about elephants raised by the devil!" he yelled. "You are a despicable coward, and an idiot as well! If you had any honour in your miserable carcass, or even a bit of sense in your thick swine's head, you would have *held* Dillī, seizing every opportunity to weaken Hemū's forces and wear him out! A couple of days later, we would have had the opportunity to attack him from behind, cut off his supplies and fight him on two fronts! And now, thanks to your cowardice and stupidity, we will have to face him in the open field!"

'He paused, and resumed, in a much friendlier tone of voice:

"In difficult times like these, Tardī Beg, it is important for us to stay united. The best way to redeem yourself, and to have everybody forget this incident, is to lead your men into battle and fight bravely. If you can promise me that, I will never again mention this incident."

'"I don't need any favours from a Shī'a heretic," Tardī Beg retorted angrily.

'"Besides, I have not decided yet, but I will act as I damn well please," he added defiantly.

'The Khān Khanān did not reply at all. Not a muscle moved in his face. It was as if he had not heard the insult. Addressing himself to me, as if Tardī Beg was no longer present in the tent, he said softly:

"It is almost time for noon prayers. I will go out – I still need to wash and prepare for them."

'As soon as Bairām Khān left the tent, two of his guards stepped in. Before Tardī Beg had a chance to move, they drew their swords and plunged them into his chest. As he sank down, dying, they wiped off the blades on his clothes, courteously bowed to me, and went out again, without a word.

'Tardī Beg still tried to say something, gasping for air, blood gushing out of his mouth, his fingers clasping his own clothes, as if they could save him, but he died a few moments later.

'Soon after, the Khān Khanān stepped back into the tent, his face and hands still wet from washing for prayers.

'"There was no other way, my friend," he said to me, without looking at Tardī Beg's body. "Please join me for the noon prayer."

'We went out and worshipped with the others. After prayers, he ordered his guards to bury the corpse outside the camp, and went out to inspect the troops.'

'Where is Bairām Khān now?' I asked.

'He has requested me to read this letter to Your Majesty,' Pīr Muhammad replied, taking out a folded piece of paper from his clothes. To this day, I still remember how the letter went, almost word for word. . . .

Your most noble and gracious Imperial Majesty, I humbly, respectfully and desperately implore Your Majesty to remain firmly convinced, that the only motives for my decisions and actions have been the strength of Your Majesty's empire, the stability of Your Majesty's throne, and the safety of Your Majesty's life.

Being wise for his age, and gifted with astute insight in worldly matters, Your Majesty will agree with me that the execution of Tardī Beg had become inevitable. He was quickly becoming a source of bitter division in our army. It was only a matter of time before he would have instilled his own treacherous cowardice in the hearts of many of Your Majesty's subjects.

Indeed, it is my honest belief that if this treacherous coward had been allowed to remain alive, Your Majesty would have been at great risk to lose his throne – and maybe even his life. It was therefore my sacred obligation, before Allāh, and before the memory of Your Majesty's blessed father who has entrusted Your

Majesty's safety to my care, to rid Your Majesty's court from the presence of this treacherous element.

I have chosen not to fight and kill him myself, as I would have liked, but to have him summarily executed, as he deserved. Indeed, it should be clear to all, that Tardī Beg's death was not a personal issue between me and him, but a matter pertaining to Your Majesty's throne.

I clearly understand that I have deserved Your Majesty's anger, not having requested Your Majesty's permission before inflicting capital punishment on one of Your Majesty's army leaders. However, knowing the kindness and compassion of Your Majesty's noble heart, and fearing that Your Majesty's youthful inexperience might cause him to underestimate the clear and immediate danger threatening him and his rightful throne, I have thought it advisable to take matters in my own hands. If Your Majesty, in his infinite goodness, had decided to spare Tardī Beg's life, I would have been faced with the most painful of dilemmas: to obey my emperor, and in doing so, betray his best interests, or to serve him through disobedience.

Desiring at all cost to avoid such a difficult choice, I have elected to do what I know was right. I humbly beg Your Majesty to take pity on me, and to continue to admit me in his august and noble presence. However, should my insolence have displeased Your Majesty too much, I shall take my leave, depart from Your Majesty's dominions, and, if Allāh wills it, retire to Mekkah.

I remain at all times Your Majesty's most humble, obedient and dedicated servant,

Bairām Khān Badakhshāni, Wakīl, Khān Khanān, Sipahsalār I'tizād-i-Daulat Qāhira,
Son of Sayf Alī Beg Badakhshāni,
Son of Mahmūd Alī Beg Badakhshāni,
Son of Pīr Alī Beg Kurdistāni,
Son of Mīr Alī Shukr Beg Bahārlü, of the Nation of the Qarāqūilü Turks

Without a word, I went inside the imperial tent, leaving Pīr Muhammad standing outside, still holding the letter in his hands. I had the greatest difficulty not to start screaming and stamping my feet in anger. Such insolence! How did he dare to treat me like a child! How did he dare to take such important decisions on his own, without consulting me!

I forced myself to think as calmly as I could. The tone of his letter was obedient enough, but that did not fool me. Had he not sent Pīr Muhammad as his messenger, rather than talking to me, face to face? Had he not clearly stated that he would leave the empire and go into exile to Mekkah, rather than humbly submitting to my verdict? Did such arrogant, headstrong attitude not clearly show the limits of his obedience and loyalty? Could I still trust him? Whom did he really serve? The seeds of doubt, already sown, grew their poisonous roots in my soul. . . .

But what was I to do? I could not possibly afford to dismiss the most competent and respected leader of my army! Had he not offered me his loyalty? Had he not referred to his forefathers, who had been faithful supporters of my ancestors? Moreover, as far as Tardī Beg was concerned, had his decision not been the right one – as always?

I stepped back outside the imperial tent, where Pīr Muhammad was still standing, nervously crumpling up Bairām Khān's letter.

'Tell the Khān Khanān,' I said, 'that this is no time for us to be divided. Tell him I need him here to help me lead the army against the infidel Hemū and his followers. Tell him, he has done well in punishing Tardī Beg. Tell him . . .'

I wanted to say: 'Tell him I have forgiven him for taking this decision without asking my permission', but I chose not to lie.

'That's all,' I said. 'Go now.'

The coming days were spent in preparation of the impending battle with Hemū.

At least for some time, Tardī Beg's execution had the desired effect. There was no more talk of fleeing to Kābul. Nevertheless, the morale of our troops left much to be desired. Hemū's generalship and the strength of his army was the subject of many whispered conversations. As Abū-l Fazl described it, perturbation found its way into the hearts of imperial servants, through the instrumentality of empty-headed babblers, from whom no army is ever free, or rather, there are armies of such . . .

Bairām Khān and the senior officers did their best to counter the growing defeatism. Through a judicial mixture of encouragement, promises, veiled and open threats, and emotional appeals to the men's sense of honour and religion, they at least managed to keep an outer semblance of order and discipline. The very few deserters got caught, and their severed heads, on spikes near the tents where they had been camping, helped to dissuade others from following their example. The astrologers, after having examined the shoulder blades of a freshly slaughtered sheep, again proclaimed the invincibility of my stars with such vehement authority and persuasion that I started to believe them myself. . . .

Hemū, who must have been informed about our troubles through his spies, eagerly seized the opportunity. He marched north towards us as fast as he could, which was wise: One should never hesitate to seize an opportunity as it presents itself. However, in the process, he got a little overconfident, which was a mistake: One should never underestimate an enemy. . . .

He sent his large fieldguns, rockets, cannon, mortars and the like, ahead towards Pānīpat, escorted by a relatively weak vanguard of ordinary troops. Undoubtedly, his plan was to prepare a defensive artillery position for his army, similar to the one my grandfather Bābur had used thirty years ago. At Pānīpat, he would block our passage, forcing us to turn back and flee, or to risk a suicidal frontal attack. He was out to destroy us, exactly the same way my own ancestor had destroyed his adversary!

Had he succeeded in his plan, we would have had no alternative but to refuse battle and flee further north. Ours was the smaller army – we would most certainly have been annihilated if we had dared to attack a strong defensive position like that.

Bairām Khān immediately sensed the danger when our scouts informed us about the arrival of Hemū's vanguard at Pānīpat.

'We absolutely must seize that artillery before the main body of Hemū's army arrives, Your Majesty,' he explained. 'If the enemy manages to deploy it in the narrow passage at Pānīpat, we have no alternative but to turn back as fast as possible, and build up a defensive position of our own further north. Let us send ahead a strong force of the best of our cavalry. God willing, they still may arrive in time. If they fail, they will still be able to extricate themselves and join us back here.'

Thus it was done. Bairām Khān formed a vanguard of the best and bravest of our cavalry, under the leadership of Ālī Qulī Khān Shaibānī.

He personally handpicked and instructed the commanders: outstanding warriors who had been loyal servants to our dynasty for a long time, like Iskandar Khān Uzbeg, Abdullah Khān Uzbeg, Ālī Qulī Khān Andarābī, Haidar Muhammad Ākhtabegī, Muhammad Khān Jalāir, Muhammad Qulī Cūlī, L'al Khān Badakhshī, Majnūn Khān Qāqshal, and many other brave men. Making sure there would be no doubt or misunderstanding about his personal loyalty to me, he also sent the most devoted of his own personal followers, including Husain Qulī Beg, son of Walī Beg; Shāh Qulī Mahram, Mīr Muhammad Qāsim of Nīshāpūr, Sayyid Mahmūd Bārhā, and Auzān Bahādur.

The vanguard rode towards Pānipat, still about ten kos[47] further south. We followed with the remainder of the imperial army. According to Abū-l Fazl—writing many years later about things he never witnessed and that happened when he was only six years old—I led the troops 'with a tranquil mind, an open brow, a prayerful heart, a just intent, a right principle, a wide capacity, a strong hand, a firm foot, a high spirit, a lofty soul, a right plan, a shining countenance, and a smiling lip. . . .' He was always a shameless flatterer.

The next day, scouts came with reassuring news: Hemū's artillery was ours. Our vanguard had launched an all-out assault upon arrival, and the enemy had fled in disarray without much resistance. There had been no losses from our side.

'This is of course excellent news, Your Majesty,' Bairām Khān said when the scouts had left, 'but the fight is far from over. Hemū can no longer use this artillery against us, but neither can we use it against him, unless we somehow manage to arrive there ahead of his army. This means he would have to stay where he is now, and I don't think he will make that kind of mistake.'

He was right. Hemū, who was closer to Pānipat than we were, drove his army as fast as he could. It was clear what he was up to: get his

---

47. Kos: A unit for measuring distance, roughly equivalent to 2.5 miles or 4 kilometres.

artillery back and bring it into position, or at the very least, prevent us from using those guns against him.

The morning of Panjshanbeh, the twenty-fourth of Ābān of the first year of my reign, the second day of the Hijrī year 964[48], when we were still about three kos removed from the town, scouts came in with the news we feared: Hemū's army had arrived, and was launching a massive attack. Our vanguard troops, knowing their duty, were fighting back as hard as they could. They were, however, vastly outnumbered and in dire need of help.

Leaving the slower-moving artillery carts and the supply train behind us under the protection of a small rearguard, we hurried towards Pānīpat, with as many combat troops as possible: all of our horse archers and heavy cavalry, and a large number of musketeers, crossbow archers and regular bowmen. The foot soldiers were riding, by two or three, on the backs of reserve horses, camels and elephants.

Bairām Khān, in full battledress, with glittering iron scale breast armour over a full body *sirih* suit of mail, was personally leading the march, galloping back and forth alongside the column on a shiny, pitchblack stallion, his dark blue mantle flying behind him. The mail neck and shoulder protection, hanging down from his spiked *dubalgha* Turkish helmet, jumped up and down with each bound of his horse. The men cheered as he passed them by. He looked invincible, and, I hate to admit, I felt jealous of him.

The brave men of our vanguard were on the verge of defeat, by the time we arrived on the battlefield. The left and right wings of Hemū's army war elephants and Afghān cavalry were pushing forward, in an effort to outflank and encircle them. Our men were fighting desperately to prevent this, but it was an uneven battle indeed. Tears came to my eyes when I saw some of the best of our men being picked off by crossbow and musket marksmen before they even had the chance to fight back. Indeed, god does favour the larger army. . . .

Bairām Khān left me in the rear, with a group of close to three thousand of our best men on the fastest horses – they would be able to bring me into safety if things turned out badly for us. He galloped to

---

48. Thursday, 5 November 1556 (Julian calendar)

the front of the ranks, slid down the nose bar of his helmet, and made his horse stand on its hind legs, as he drew his curved Turkomān sabre. Keeping the horse balancing on its hind legs, its forehoofs clawing in the air and iron-scale armour glittering in the sun, he held his sword high, and shouted: 'Allāhu Akbar! Yah Mu'īn! Allāhu[49] Akbar!' The battlecry was taken over by all of our army, as the large Naubat battledrums signalled the order to attack.

The army entered into battle as instructed. The main body of our cavalry stormed forward in a two-pronged attack along the left and right flanks, to relieve the men of our vanguard. They were followed by as many musketeers and archers on foot as could be transported to the front line. The centre was formed by the remaining foot soldiers, about four thousand horsemen, backed up by our elephants, and the returning vanguard cavalry. We were visibly outnumbered. Hopefully, the rearguard would arrive in time.

For some time, our cavalry onslaught halted Hemū's advance on the flanks. The Afghān enemy horsemen, their mounts already exhausted from the earlier battle, suffered heavy losses, and a considerable number of enemy marksmen were killed by a well-directed volley of musket fire. Many of our cavalry reached the enemy lines, and I saw untold acts of bravery, with groups of our horsemen picking out an individual enemy elephant, harassing it with arrows and distracting it, while one or two of them quickly dismounted to stab it deep in the belly with long lances.

Yet, despite those initial successes, the battle did not go well. There seemed to be an unlimited supply of fresh enemy troops, and, as Tardī Beg had warned us, most of the enemy elephants were remarkably well disciplined, obedient to their mahāwats[50] and pushing forward despite many wounds. Slowly but surely, our flanks were driven back to the centre, and our losses started exceeding theirs.

Suddenly, the ground started shaking, as we saw a grey wall of elephants rushing straight towards us. Hemū, who must have seen the weakness of our centre formation, and probably wanting to finish the battle before the arrival of our artillery, was moving in for the final

---

49. Yah Mu'īn: O (Divine) Helper.
50. Mahāwat: Mahaut, elephant driver

kill. Judging by the royal canopies, visible towards the rear of their formation, he was personally leading the charge. Thousands of Hindū soldiers were shouting 'Gopāl, Gopāl!'[51] and I remember wondering, despite the excitement of the moment, what their battlecry meant.

It was clear we were in desperate trouble, our centre being vastly outnumbered, and our left and right wings, in dire straights themselves, unable to come to our rescue.

'You have not won yet, you stinking infidel pig,' I heard Bairām Khān hiss, as he rode forward to direct the defence of our centre.

Despite their small numbers and the desperate situation, our central cavalry performed admirably, charging the enemy front in well-timed, successive waves, each delivering a volley of arrows in quick succession, while our infantry archers and musketeers moved their mobile defences forward to support them, killing most of the enemy troops riding the front line of elephants. Thousands upon thousands of arrows were shot slantwise in the air towards the enemy ranks behind the front line, in an attempt to bring disarray to the enemy onslaught.

Alas, it all seemed to be of little avail. Defeat was now becoming inevitable; there were just too many of them. It would not be long before our cavalry would have no more room to manoeuvre, and would be forced to flee or be annihilated. Bairām Khān and the amīrs started to organise our retreat, creating openings in the rear formations for the front line cavalry to fall back through. Maybe, we could still escape with a sizeable combat force and come back to fight another day.

Then, suddenly, for no apparent reason, the enemy onslaught faltered. Groups of two, four, ten elephants broke the ranks and abruptly turned around; only moments later, the entire enemy host was fleeing in utter panic. We had won! How could this be?

Fortunately, Bairām Khān and the two brave commanders of our left and right wings, Abdullāh Khān and Sikandar Khān, kept their level-headedness, and our troops, despite the hardship of the battle and the heavy losses we had sustained, knew their duty. In circumstances like these, many armies have failed to take advantage of the situation. It is only natural for soldiers who have narrowly escaped death and are

---

51. Gopāl: Cowherd, protector of cows; one of Lord Krishna's names.

exhausted, to rejoice in victory and break off the fight. That, however, is a mistake: A fleeing host of enemies might come back to fight another day, and should therefore always be hunted down.

Wave after wave of our cavalry—including most of the three thousand that had been guarding me—went after the enemy and slaughtered them by the hundreds.

'Spare the elephant drivers and the Afghān horsemen who surrender their weapons,' Bairām Khān instructed. Indeed, a wise conqueror thinks of the battles to come, knows how to combine firmness with magnanimity, and turn some of today's mortal enemies into tomorrow's grateful allies.

The pursuit was still ongoing, when it became clear what had caused the sudden collapse of the enemy host. Shāh Qulī Mahram came to us with a number of his followers, and what seemed to be, strapped to a horseback, the meagre corpse of a dwarfish, bony little man: the great Hemū himself. He had been turned over to us by his own mahāwat.

Two men pulled him off the horse, and held him by the arms to prevent him from falling down. He was still alive, but barely so – an arrow was sticking out of the bleeding socket of his left eye. It had hit him from the right, probably glancing off the nose bar of his helmet, piercing his left eye, and entering the bone in the back of the socket towards his left temple, where it got stuck, ostensibly without entering the brain. It must have been a stray arrow, one of the many hundreds shot randomly in the air to harass the enemy troops in the back. It had been a lucky shot, or, as Abū-l Fazl preferred to put it in more flowery language, 'an arrow from the bended bow of divine wrath. . . .'

I know, my son: Were this an adventure book, I would be accused of bad writing, but there is nothing I can do about it – this is how it actually happened! I would have very much preferred our victory to have been more glorious and heroic, but I cannot help it: Our entire empire has been founded on one lucky stray arrow, and god only knows what Hindustān would have looked like today, if Hemū had stayed a few paces more to the rear. . . .

I do not know whether he was fully conscious when they brought him before me. He did not say a word and did not react to anything we said or did. He just hung there between our men, his left hand covering his injured eye, the arrow sticking out between his fingers, blood flowing over his face and hand. He was breathing heavily, obviously in a lot of pain, moaning slightly each time he exhaled.

I kept staring at this little man. He looked so harmless and pitiful, despite the gold thread loincloth and the shining armour and heavy jewellery covering his frail chest. His head, bald with only a few strands of hair on the sides and the back, looked like the skull of some heinous kind of bird. How could this pathetic, puny, lowborn little Hindū have become so powerful?

Bairām Khān drew his sword and handed it to me. It was time for me to earn the title of Ghāzī.[52]

I know that Abū-l Fazl—as I said, he was but a small child at the time of the battle and so never witnessed it—wrote that I magnanimously refused to kill Hemū, saying that 'there was no honour in slaying a defenceless and wounded enemy'. Like many other such stories, he probably heard this one from the mouths of flattering courtiers and repeated it, in a commendable attempt to demonstrate and exemplify the nobility of my character.

Alas and of course, it is not true. What would have been the point of arguing with my guardian who had just saved my throne, if not my life? How could I leave the death of so many of the best of my men unavenged? Why would I risk undermining my own authority and reputation with those who survived? Besides, in the state Hemū was in, killing him quickly seemed to be the most merciful thing I could do for him.

It is true, however, that I did hesitate for a moment, thinking to myself, as I stood there with Bairām Khān offering his sword to me, how regrettable it was, that a man of such outstanding ability could not be put to better use in my own service. . . .

'Go on, Your Majesty,' Bairām Khān insisted, interrupting my thoughts. I took the sword from him, and the men let go of Hemū's arms. He sunk to his knees, and I struck him in the back of the neck before he could fall to the ground. I could feel the spine crack under Bairām Khān's sabre, but the blow was not strong enough to sever the head completely. Before the body hit the ground, Shāh Qulī Mahram,

---

52. Ghāzī: Slayer (of the infidel).

Iskandar Khān Uzbeg, Pīr Muhammad and the other bystanders sunk their swords into the twitching body, all of them anxious to stain their swords with the blood of so powerful an enemy. Bairām Khān took his own sword back, and severed Hemū's head from the trunk, cutting through the throat with an ostensibly effortless, routine movement of the wrist, like an experienced butcher.

'Iskandar Khān Uzbeg,' he instructed, 'take half of the cavalry, on the freshest horses, and hunt down as many survivors you can find. Proceed to Dillī, and occupy the city. We will join you there as soon as possible with the rest of the army. Shāh Qulī Mahram, instruct the rest of the troops to start building a tower of heads, in front of the north gate, next to the road.

'We will assemble there as soon as it is finished. Organise the collection of the spoils, and get the army ready to head further south, as soon as the rearguard and the artillery arrives.'

About two hours later, the army had assembled, standing before Pānīpat's northern wall in battle array, including the rearguard and artillery, and over fifteen hundred elephants and ten thousand horses taken from Hemū's army. Mounds of spoils had been assembled and sorted: jewellery, gold, food supplies, muskets, gun powder, swords, bows, arrows, spears, pikes and other arms and equipment.

Towering above all the piles was a pyramid of over ten thousand severed heads.

In case you are wondering, Salīm, it had the height of a tall man riding on the back of a camel; and at its foot, you needed about twelve camels to surround it. I saw then, why Chingīz Khān and Amīr Temür had so often done this during their conquests: Nothing sends a clearer message than a pile of enemy heads! I remember feeling horrified and fascinated at the same time – I could not bring myself to stop staring at them. It seems my mind's eye can still see every detail: the heads still wearing their helmets or turbans, and the bare ones; the necks which had been cut off clean and straight, and the ones with frayed edges, which looked as if the head had been torn or twisted off, rather than cut; the faces with eyes and mouths closed as if sound asleep, the ones staring in horror as if still alive, and the ones with a careless, drunken look, with sleepy, half-open eyes and drooling mouths. Most of them were covered with blood and dust as could be expected, but a large number had remained surprisingly clean. Many of them, I would say at least one out of six, judging by the ones where one could see the back of the head, had ostensibly been killed while running away: In the back of their heads was either a short, straight, clean cut, about the length of the middle finger, where the flange of a war hammer had entered their skull, or a broad, deep dent, with reddish, jagged edges, where the mace had slammed into the back of their helmet.

Under the thundering sound of the heavy naubats and the somewhat smaller portable naqqarah kettledrums, Bairām Khān and I rode towards the pile, followed by the twenty main army leaders. Our horses, at a restrained trot, proudly raised their forelegs high at each step. Bairām Khān, still in full battle armour, was guiding his horse with his knees, in the fashion of the great steppe warriors who had been his ancestors.

His left hand carried Hemū's head, holding it by the neck hair. The arrow had been pulled out of the eye socket, undoubtedly in order to avoid any misunderstandings as to the cause of death. In his right hand, he held a heavy cavalry lance with a long, straight, sword-like point, without any barbs. Four Qutā Tibetan yak tails were hanging from its shaft: It was clearly one of the lances brought into Hindustān by my grandfather Bābur the Tiger, made over a hundred years before, in the frigid highlands of the faraway kingdom of Fergāna.

We halted, facing the troops, our backs to the pile of heads.

'Behold, the heads of those who wanted to oppose us!' Bairām Khān shouted, looking over his shoulder, his face and voice full of contempt.

'And behold, the head of the mighty infidel king, Hemū!' he added, holding the severed head high.

'Slain by the noble hand of our august young emperor, his imperial majesty, Jalāl-ud-dīn Muhammad Akbar Pādshāh Ghāzī! Hail to His Imperial Majesty!'

Accompanied by the drums, the troops started chanting 'Pādshāh salāmāt, pādshāh salāmāt!' for what seemed an eternity.

'My friends, my brothers!' Bairām Khān shouted, stopping the clamour, 'our enemies call us Mughals or Mongols, because we came from up north, and most of us are Turks, Tājiks and Uzbegs.

'Our enemies say we are but a bunch of savages. Well, let them. Let them! I for one, consider it the greatest honour to be called a Mongol when I think of our glorious and invincible forefathers!

'Today, my brothers, we have entered history and proven ourselves to be the worthy sons of our fathers. We have wiped out an overwhelmingly powerful enemy army, vastly superior to us in number, animals, weapons and equipment. We have captured many spoils, and rest assured, my brothers, all of you will be much richer tomorrow than you were this morning!

'There is no doubt in my mind, that all this has only been possible with the support of Allāh Himself, praise be upon Him! Indeed, Allāh is just and compassionate! He is the helper of those who worship Him and lead their lives the way He has ordained! Behold, my brothers, He has graciously rewarded us for the bravery we have shown today! It is clearly His will that our beloved young pādshāh become the ruler of this land, the just and beneficent shadow of Allāh on this earth!

'My brothers, we have been victorious in today's battle with only a small army at our disposal. Now, however, we have the means to build one of the mightiest armies the world has even seen! Nothing, absolutely nothing or nobody will stop us now! Allāh Himself will guide us to further greatness and glory!'

The crowd cheered enthusiastically.

'Let our enemies make no mistake,' Bairām Khān said, casually tossing Hemū's head in the sand. He paused for a moment, until it had almost stopped rolling. From the hip, he thrust the lance in the severed neck. He sure knew how to handle a lance. The long pike had penetrated the base of Hemu's skull, and its tip was sticking out at the top of the head – like a bloody, malformed kind of horn. The face looked ghastly, with the bleeding, empty left socket, and the right eyeball, upturned and white that seemed to stare at the crowd. The mouth was hanging wide open, gaping like the jaws of a fish of prey. The long, bony teeth were dirty red with the blood that had entered the mouth at the time of death. A few sticky twines of entangled hair were dangling from the side and the back of the head. I do not think a devil in hell could look any worse than this.

'Let our enemies make no mistake,' Bairām Khān repeated. 'The Mughals are here to stay!'

The army cheered as we paraded it, riding at a slow pace from the left wing to the right. When we had passed by the ranks, we rode back to the small hill overlooking the battlefield, where I had been standing during the battle.

Still in the saddle, Bairām Khān shook the head off the lance, and instructed the amīrs.

'Khwājā Ambār Nāzir, kindly prepare for travel. Take three hundred good men and bring this head to Kābul. Inform the members of the imperial court about our glorious victory. Tell them that it will not take long now, before all the lands of Emperor Humāyūn will be fully under our control again. They will be relieved to hear that the days of the glorious Pādshāh Bābur are back! Request the high-born ladies of the court to kindly prepare themselves for the journey, and join us here in Hindustān in due course.

'Abdullah Khān Uzbeg, have Hemū's trunk taken to Dillī, and have it hung from a gibbet, jewels and all, for everyone to see. Let it stay there, until nothing is left but a few rotten bones!

'The rest of you army leaders, instruct your men to bury the dead, and have the camp prepared for the night! You may tell them to help themselves to extra rations of meat, and feast and celebrate, but not too late into the night: Tomorrow at dawn, we will proceed to Dillī!'

Fifth Letter

دلّی

Dilli

Iskandar Khān Uzbeg and his men had performed their task well – there was not a single incident on our way to Dillī.

Along the road, at irregular intervals, there were small mounds of severed heads, alternated with rows of heads on spikes, and here and there, a corpse that had been hanged or impaled. As Abū-l Fazl put it, 'Iskandar Khān Uzbeg delivered some of the malignant and useless from the prison of existence, and put the distracted inhabitants of the country in order'. He always did have a way with words. . . .

I guess matters had been too pressing, and defeat and annihilation had come too close, for our men to be merciful towards any surviving enemy troops. It is not easy to show magnanimity, when one has seen death's sinister grin. . . .

Dillī itself, its inhabitants having remained as neutral as possible throughout the conflict, had remained unharmed, and was well prepared to welcome us back. It appeared that the entire population—Muslims, Rājputs, Panjābis and local Hindustānis alike—had gathered to witness our return and welcome us. But the Uzbeg had taken no chances: His archers could be seen on every rooftop along the way, and small groups of cavalry were standing guard, ready to disperse the crowd at the slightest sign of trouble.

We entered the city in triumph at an hour chosen by the astrologers.

I will not bore you with a detailed description of the army parade, my son. Suffice it to say, it must have been an absolutely overwhelming sight for the people of Dillī. To be honest, I was quite impressed myself. . . .

In between the parading troops, at regular intervals, there was the deafening noise of *naqqarah* kettledrums, smaller *dankahs*, and thundering, overpowering *naubat* wardrums on carts, together with jingling cymbals and blaring trumpets.

There seemed to be an interminable amount of fighting forces. At the head of the column came several bands of fiercelooking Qalawuri scouts, Qazaqi raiders, Qarawal skirmishers, and Taulqamah ambush troops. All of them were half-wild, bloodthirsty hill and desert tribesmen: Turkomāns, Uzbegs, Baluchistānis, Sindhis. They were followed by Iftali vanguard troops and the main body of light and heavy cavalry, headed by Bairām Khān and the most important amīrs, all of them in full battle dress.

Most of the cavalry were our own men, but there were also a few thousand Afghāns, who had survived the battle of Pānipat and had come over to our side. The necessary precautions had of course been taken: They were not as well armed as our own men, divided in smaller groups and surrounded by superior forces of our own men, but still, they were allowed to participate in the parade and take their place in the imperial army. It is often wise to allow former enemies to become your allies, my son. Defeating your enemies, burning and killing everything that belongs to them, is the way of conquest. Making allies out of them, using sound judgement and prudence, and the right mixture of vengefulness and clemency, is the way empires are built!

Behind the cavalry came various kinds of infantry: musketeers, archers, and regular infantry armed with swords and pikes.

They, in turn, were followed by several hundred pieces of artillery, thousands of bān rockets, and carts full of earthenware grenades and wooden gunpowder vessels.

Behind them came the most impressive sight of all the parade: the fighting elephants, Hemū's and ours, over two thousand of them in total, all in full battle gear. They were carrying marksmen, armed with *gajnal* heavy muskets, crossbows and regular bows.

The elephant column itself was protected at both flanks by three thousand handpicked cavalry troops: heavily armoured assault cavalry with lances, swords and maces, and horse archers, steering their horses with their knees, bow and arrow in hand, ready to shoot at the slightest sign of trouble. About one in four of them was sitting sideways or backwards in the saddle, so that every angle remained under cover at all times.

I was riding the tallest elephant of them all, Hemū's preferred fighting champion Hawāi, an absolutely huge, mean, vicious mountain of muscles, now deceptively meek and docile under the hands of Hemū's mahāwat, one of the many Hindustāni elephant drivers who had been spared after the battle. When Hemū had been injured, he had handed him over to our troops and had been spared as a reward.

I would have much preferred to ride Hawāi myself, as I would do so many times later in my life. You know I always loved the feeling of being in control over such a massive animal, tens of times stronger than the strongest man. In fact, as you know very well, I adore all animals: horses, elephants, camels, dogs, hunting leopards, hawks . . . I don't know whether there is any truth in the Hindū belief of reincarnation, but if there is, I must have been an animal attendant in one of my previous lives. . . .

But of course, I could not be riding an elephant myself on that occasion. Protected by a personal guard with drawn sword, I was sitting on Hemū's elevated throne in the turret on Hawāi's back, under the imperial canopy, wearing my coronation robe and turban, and many jewels of gold and pearls and precious stones, all of which had belonged to my father and his father.

For the first time, I really felt like the true emperor, at the centre of everybody's attention, the focal point of the entire parade. It was one of the very few times since my enthronement that Bairām Khān was not riding next to me. The crowd cheered enthusiastically as I passed them by. I could not help being impressed at the thought that all these people were now my subjects.

Following the rest of the elephants, came another strong body of cavalry: a smaller group on horseback, and about two thousand men riding some of the finest and fastest camels to be found in all of Sindh and Rājasthān.

Near the end of the parade, flanked by a rearguard of horse archers, came the supply train, again combining ours and Hemū's, including dozens of carts with spoils taken from Hemū's army: weapons, clothing, pieces of equipment, jewellery, money, gold and other valuables.

Finally, as in battle, the ranks were closed by a strong band of fierce-looking elite Nasaqchi troops on the swiftest horses, who, as you know, are used to prevent the men in battle from retreating without orders. It is good that the men realise that running away from the enemy will shorten their life, rather than prolonging it. The courage to face evil is often found in fear of things much worse. . . .

With the thunder of the war drums pounding in my chest, and looking at the interminable column in front and behind me, I felt the blessing and protection of god Himself, and despite the excitement of the day, a warm, tranquil, almost peaceful feeling came upon my soul. I made a solemn vow, to myself, to god, to my ancestors, and to the thousands who had died for me at Pānīpat that I would make good use of all this military might. Never again would I allow myself to get into a situation where I would need to fight for my own survival. On the contrary, I would make sure it would be my opponents who would be fighting for theirs. Somehow, I knew that my life, from that moment on, would be one of conquest and triumph. This was clearly my destiny, and god's manifest will. He Himself had given me victory against impossible odds. He Himself wanted me to become one of the greatest kings the world had ever seen. I was determined not to disappoint Him.

The parade arrived at the imperial fortress near the Jumna River.[53]

There, in front of its gates, Bairām Khān and I formally supervised the distribution of the spoils of war. As Bairām Khān had promised the men at Pānīpat, all of them became rich that day.

We kept almost nothing for the imperial treasure. There would be ample occasions in the future to replenish it. Right now, it was more important for us to secure the undivided loyalty of the army upon which our power depended.

Honorary titles and positions were given to army leaders who had distinguished themselves in the battle: Abdullāh and Iskandar Khān

---

53. Jumna River: Also called Yamuna or Jawan.

Uzbeg, Alī Qulī Khān Shaibānī, and a number of others. All of them were rewarded with the governorship of a province. The border regions of our territories were thus entrusted to the care of experienced and competent commanders. All of them would leave after a couple of days, each one with a strong contingent of troops, to take charge of their assigned fiefs.

On Bairām Khān's explicit request, Maulānā Pīr Muhammad Shirwānī was also given the title of Khān, as well as the prestigious function of Nasīr-ul Mulk, Helper of the Realm. He was thus to become the supervisor of my personal service and household.

He was to assume his new duties a few days later. For the time being, he was sent with a strong group of cavalry to Alwar, west of Āgrā, to bring that area securely under our control and deal with Hemū's family, which resided down there.

He came back three days later, with a number of carts laden with treasure, and the head of Hemū's elderly father. There had been a brief struggle with the remaining enemy troops. Many had been killed, and some had escaped southwest towards Ājmīr, duly pursued by a force of trusted men.

Hemū's aged father had been captured and brought before Pīr Muhammad. In a gesture of generosity and religious zeal, he had offered the old man his life, if he would convert to Islām. They say, he refused with dignity:

'For eighty years I've worshipped my god according to my religion,' he said. 'Why should I change it at this time, and why should I, merely from fear of my life, and without understanding it, come into your way of worship?' Pīr Muhammad had not wasted any time on religious debate, and answered him 'in the tongue of the sword', as the chroniclers put it.

I could not help feeling a bit sad when I heard the story. What glory is there in killing a grief-stricken, elderly father? I was also very much intrigued at his last courageous words. 'My god', he had said, rather than 'the gods', in plural. Didn't these Hindūs claim there are many gods, rather than one?

I wondered what god's final verdict over him would be. Would this defenceless old man really be thrown into hell for having refused to accept the true religion of Islām? Somehow, I thought not. Clearly, the old man's intention had been to serve god, however misguided his superstitious idolatry might have been. Would this not suffice to appease god's wrath, and obtain the blessings of His forgiving mercy? If I would already be inclined to forgive him, why would god, who is so much better than I am, not do the same?

For the first time in my life, the thought entered my mind, that religion, at least the way we understand it, might be less important to god than we tend to think. Maybe, I thought, He attaches more importance to what lives in people's hearts, than to the way they have learned to worship Him, or the prophets they believe in.

Anyway, the death of Hemū's father did confirm the fast-growing reputation of Pīr Muhammad Shirwāni as a competent and ruthless army leader. The appointment of this humble mullāh to the position of Nasīr-ul Mulk had been an important promotion indeed, but Bairām Khān clearly had made up his mind to reward a useful helper, who had always proved himself to be his unquestioning, loyal servant.

It would, nevertheless, prove to be one of Bairām Khān's rare mistakes: as will be explained later, Pīr Muhammad soon proved to be an insufferably conceited and arrogant character, and it did not take long before he conveniently forget the duty of gratitude he owed towards his noble benefactor.

I have had many similar experiences myself, my son. The promotion of a meritorious, commendable person is not always a good move: it may bring to surface certain weaknesses, which had hitherto remained hidden. This is the case, in particular, for authority-related vices, such as pride, conceitedness, and arrogance.

Make it a habit, my son, to keenly observe the ones you have recently promoted. Is there a change in how they treat their subordinates? How is their behaviour while meeting their former and current peers? How about their attitude towards you? Any trace of overconfident arrogance? Or, what may be more dangerous, any conspicuous, cringing servility, which may be hiding other, more dangerous feelings?

A wise monarch, my son, should make it his task to know and understand the human soul and its hidden depths. He will constantly be on the lookout for those small and minor outer signs that seem to be of no importance, but that may betray inappropriate and dangerous inner thoughts and motives. It is important for a king to know what people think, for thoughts may drive actions. . . .

Our triumphant entry into Dillī culminated in lavish and sumptuous celebrations, which were organised that same night. They were designed to impress, even more than to entertain, with abundant and delicious food of all kinds, and valuable gifts for everyone in the city of Dillī. The highlight of the evening was a display of fireworks ('a rose garden of fire', as my good old friend Abū-l Fazl called it in his book), whereby a large puppet representing Hemū was burnt, amidst the dancing and cheering crowd.

The next day, for the first time in my life, I woke up as the chief resident of the Dillī palace. Finally, my life as emperor had started!

I must say, I truly have the fondest memories of that moment, and of the weeks that followed.

Bairām Khān did see to it that my education continued. That I did not mind at all. I had grown quite fond of my teacher Mīr Abdul Latīf's lessons: readings from some book or other, followed by a discussion, reflection, comparison with other books—a pastime I have continued to appreciate throughout my entire life.

Other than that, there were very few pressing affairs of state that needed attention those first few weeks. The military situation was stable. The new regional governors were getting organised. I thus had ample opportunity to get better acquainted with the daily life at the court and its organisation.

I was quite impressed with the rituals surrounding my appearance in public, the administration of justice, private and public audiences, meals, and all other aspects of life. The rites that were performed in those early days would definitely seem rather coarse and primitive to us now, but at that time, they appeared to me as refined, elaborate and awe-inspiring.

I love the rituals of the imperial court, the bowing, the hands touching foreheads and hearts. That is not only my personal vanity, my son. I think it is good, and even necessary, for a king to be surrounded with splendid solemnity. People should not look upon him as a normal person, for he is not! A true king, worthy of that title, my son, should aspire to be god's shadow on earth. After all, if he occupies the throne, is it not because god Himself has allowed him to do so? Not a single leaf falls from a tree unless god allows it! Therefore, it is only becoming that in the eyes of the common people, god and the king should almost coincide. The king should be the object of their sincere and undivided admiration and devotion, the source and destiny of all their hopes and fears.

Although he is only a human being, the king should constantly aspire to emulate god, to the best of his abilities. Like god, he should be beneficent, kind and just, but also strong, overwhelming, awe-inspiring and daunting. To those who submit to his authority, the king should be accessible and kind, the fountain of justice, the ultimate abode of peace and tranquillity. To those who dare to oppose him, however, he should be the inescapable bringer of death. . . .

To be honest with you, I must confess that at that time, these lofty and important reflections did not occupy my mind as much as they do now. I was still very young, and I thought of little else but enjoying my newfound life. It was all so new and exciting to me, and I really loved everything about it . . .

I enjoyed walking around in the palace and its large rooms, courtyards and corridors, delighted in the thought that it all belonged to me. I loved the reverence shown to me, the constant attention with which I was surrounded. It seemed that literally hundreds of people went out of their way to please and serve me, to fulfil and even anticipate every wish of mine.

I could not believe the variety and quality of food that suddenly became available to me, day and night: the most exquisite meats, fish, fowl, vegetables, fruits, nuts and sweets, imported from the most faraway places! What a world of difference from the rather frugal, hasty meals I had had in the days before the battle of Pānīpat!

I particularly enjoyed the cold drinks they served me, deliciously chilled with real, genuine ice, shipped to the palace on large, flat-bottomed barks travelling the Jumna. Fresh ice, harvested in the mountains far up north, still very much outside our dominions at that time; acquired at great expense, brought into the palace cellars after a journey of several days, just for my comfort and that of a handful of others, who could afford to pay for it and were fortunate enough to be associated with me.

I believe I can more or less guess what you are thinking as you are reading this, my son. I do realise you are accustomed to so much more than a bit of ice, brought to you from the mountains of Kashmīr. What seemed to me then like the blessed luxuries of paradise, would probably look rather frugal to the both of us now, accustomed as we are to all the opulence the world has to offer. The old palace in Dillī is nothing compared to the lofty buildings and entire cities that were put up later during my reign. I guess this is inevitable: it is very difficult indeed to truly appreciate the things that one has learned to take for granted for so many years.

Nevertheless, if you aspire to be wise, my son, you should often reflect on those many luxuries you enjoy, and understand how much they are dependent on our continuing power and wealth. Never forget, my dear Salīm, that all this power and wealth is not just there for us to enjoy because we happen to be the emperors. It is our god-given task, to see to it that it is maintained and increased!

God does not mind His creatures taking pleasure in the beauty and the many delights of His creation, for He is Himself the source of all pleasure and enjoyment. However, He does not approve of the self-indulgent, the lazy, the weaklings who have become so absorbed in their own little pleasures as to forget their duties.

But again, these were all lessons I still had to learn myself. I was a young boy, who enjoyed life, and who had just become emperor of Hindustān. Little else was on my mind, than to explore and enjoy this wonderful, exciting new life that had been given to me.

I must say, Maulānā Pīr Muhammad Shirwāni—now proudly called Pīr Muhammad Khān since his promotion—was doing an excellent job in his new assignment as Nasīr-ul Mulk, the head of my household and personal assistant.

He entrusted most of the daily management of the palace, the food, the decoration and such things to Māham Anaga. She was a great help to him, always busy, never leaving a detail unchecked. But Pīr Muhammad himself was very personally involved as well. He tried his very best to see to it that every desire of mine was fulfilled, before I even expressed it – sometimes even before I consciously thought about it myself. In considering my needs, he proved himself to be knowledgeable and wise, in a practical sort of way. I will always be grateful to him for that.

Knowing how fond I was of outdoor activities, he immediately organised a hunting party for me. It was a gazelle hunt with some of the best hunting leopards that were as fast as lightning. I have always been very fond of all kinds of hunting: dangerous wild boar hunts on horseback with lances; drives with hundreds of beaters; tiger hunts, with muskets and bows on the back of an elephant; fowl hunting with hawks and falcons; but I've always had a particular weakness for chītahs. They move with such majesty, they are such fast and efficient killers, so wild and dangerous, yet, when tamed so surprisingly meek and docile with people.

When I returned from that first hunt, he had arranged entertainment—acrobats, music and dancing—during dinner.

He must have been watching me look at the dancing girls. And look at the girls I did: the golden jewels adorning their hair, face, body, arms and legs; their beautiful silk and muslin dresses; the graceful curve and roundness of their hips; the elegant shape of their legs in the long transparent skirts or trousers; their breasts, delightfully visible through those gauze fabrics, so aptly called 'woven air',[54] the enchanting movements of their bejewelled arms and long-fingered hands; and the elegant, tip-toe steps of their high-arched, shapely feet, delightfully adorned with golden ankle chains and toe rings.

'Would Your Majesty like a companion for tonight?' Pīr Muhammad Khān inquired discreetly.

I was grateful for his tactful attitude: it was respectful, considerate, without even a semblance of that vulgar tone of conspiracy, which people tend to use when they are alluding to the desires of the body. He had asked the question in the same innocent, self-evident way as if he had been inquiring when and what I wanted to eat. I was very much pleased with him.

'Yes, why not,' I replied, trying to sound as casual and uninterested as possible.

'Unless Your Majesty instructs me otherwise, I will send him a different girl every night,' he replied, again sensing perfectly what were my youthful desires.

Ah, my son, what can I tell you about those carefree, blissful first nights? They were complete, total, sheer heaven! What a world of difference from my first clumsy amorous attempts with young serving-girls in the palace of my father as a twelve year old! Then, it had all been hasty and messy and disappointing. Now, it was absolute perfection. . . .

---

54. The muslin worn by Mughal ladies had such romantic names as *daft hawa* (woven air), *ab-i-rawan* (running water), and *shabnam* (night dew) (Eraly, 2007, p.138).

Truly blessed was I – there was the opportunity created by royal birth, wealth and power; the excitement of newly discovered, untrodden paths of pleasure; and the lust and self-evident vigour of youth.

I hope and pray that after my death, god will not send me to hell, despite my many sins and weaknesses. But even if He does, I will always remain grateful to Him for the glimpse of paradise He has graciously shown me in those first nights in Dillī. . . .

Those wonderful, heavenly nights! How often have I enjoyed their memory!

How could I ever forget them: the luxurious baths; the silk and satin sheets; the scented oils and sweet perfumes; the entrancing dances; the glitter of golden jewels on soft naked skin; the twisting of perfectly rounded hips; the delightful, gentle wiggling of proud, naked breasts; the sweet faces, all eyes and smiling teeth in the soft candle light; the taste of mango juice and honey, trickled on firm, dark nipples; the giggling chases in the rooms and corridors of the royal quarters; the soft veils playfully binding the wrists of sweet, smiling captives; the endearing scent of soft, velvet skin; the tender kisses on moist and avid lips; the soft hands and mouths everywhere; the finger nails, clawing deep in the skin of my back at the moment of divine climax. . . .

There were even times when, in the impetuous rashness of youth, I asked Pīr Muhammad Khān to send me two or three girls at once, but I must say, after a few attempts, I gave up on that practice. Despite the delightful promise the situation had seemed to offer in my young, lustful imagination, it came out disappointingly messy – much less pleasurable than I had hoped. More bodies, it appeared, do not necessarily lead to more passion. No, much sweeter are the memories of the times where there was kindness besides lust, friendly conversation besides passion – the nights where I peacefully fell asleep against the back of my companion, my hand on her breast.

Do not worry, my son. I will not go on describing in detail all the things that happened to me on those blissful nights. I know, children find it distinctly awkward to hear about their parents' amorous relations. And even among friends, and after many cups of wine, only the coarse and the vulgar will go into sordid little details about their own adventures in bed.

Yet, it seems important to me that you should know the whole story of my life, and learn from it. I think I do have to tell you something about the weaknesses of my youth, for it is about time you learned to overcome yours.

I do not want to hurt your feelings too much, my beloved Salīm, but until a few months ago, you were little more than a pathetic drunkard, well under way to drink yourself to death. You may be exquisitely learned, intelligent and refined, my son, but you're also lazy and self-indulgent. This is of course understandable, given the opulence you have known throughout your life, but that does not make it any less worrying.

Be aware, my son, that the first, and by far the most important task of a king, is to conquer *himself*.

Look at me: have you not always known me as a strong-willed emperor, very much in control of everything and everybody, in command of himself in the first place?

I'm fond of good food, yet I eat only once a day. Most of the time, under the influence of the wise teachings of Hindū and Jain saints, I even abstain from the various kinds of meat I liked so much when I was young.

You know how much I like wine and spirits. I admit that I do get drunk every once in a while, mostly on gentle evenings when the moon is soft, and when I'm enjoying good company. Yet, I will often go for days without drinking anything but water, for I believe that is necessary if I want to remain in control of myself. For that very same reason, I rarely enter opium's false paradise.

I adore the pleasures of the harem, even at my advanced age, for god has graciously given me health and vigour. However, I will not allow the women who happen to be sharing my bed to interfere with the affairs of state, or run my life – unlike you, I have the impression. It is all right to love a woman, but that should not dominate your life, my son! For instance, what is that silly infatuation of yours with that Persian girl, Mehr-un Nissah, Ghiyas Beg's daughter? Would you ever see me running after a woman like that, ridiculous and pathetic, like a peacock in heat? Never! And neither should you, my son: an emperor must always, above all things, remain emperor!

It is appropriate and important for you to realise, my son, that your father was not born this strong. I have the same desires and weaknesses as you or any other man. The only thing I have learned, much better than you have, my son, is to allow pleasure into my life, without being ruled by it. I may give in to my passions, every once in a while, but I can usually keep them under the control of my will.

Learn to control yourself as well, for it is unwise and unworthy to allow one's desires to run one's life. There is so much more to life, my son, than the pursuit of vulgar pleasure! But I must acknowledge the truth: moments of worriless pleasure can indeed be enchanting; young was I, and wild at heart, and did not—nor wanted to—understand all these things. . . .

Bairām Khān, at first, cheerfully approved of my amorous adventures. When he saw the joyful memories in the dreaming smile on my face, my tiredness from the lack of sleep, he actually encouraged me:

'It's great to be a man, isn't it, Your Majesty? Is there anything more delightful than the companionship of a willing, beautiful, naked woman? Every morning when I wake up, I thank Allāh that I was not born a girl – I would really hate it, if I had to share my bed with something as ugly as a man!'

He laughed heartily at his own joke. It was one of the rare occasions I didn't see him dead serious. . . .

The next day, after a particularly wild night with very little sleep, I was a bit late for my daily public appearance at the balcony. Bairām Khān looked at me intently, but said nothing.

The day after that, I arrived much too late. He still did not say anything, but publicly reprimanded Pīr Muhammad Khān instead.

'Nasīr-ul Mulk,' he barked, knowing very well that I could hear him, loud and clear, 'next time, kindly see to it that His Majesty is able to attend our public ceremonies on time. You know how important it is to avoid it when people start gossiping!' He was of course right, but I felt humiliated and angry all the same.

The following day, in the afternoon, I deliberately did not show up for a private audience with a messenger who had just arrived from the Panjāb.

Immediately after the audience, my guards announced Bairām Khān's arrival at the entrance of the royal quarters. I did not dare to deny him access, and had him shown in.

He looked at the jars of wine and spirits, the half-empty cups, the ruffled sheets and veils. He sat himself down opposite me, uncomfortably close, clearly smelling my breath reeking of drink, and noticing the dilated pupils of my eyes – I had indeed been drinking some of that opium-laced rose water my father enjoyed so often.

'Your Majesty, I need to talk to you before the evening meal,' he said.

'Why don't you speak to me right now? I'm afraid I have other plans in the afternoon,' I replied defiantly.

'I need to talk to you when you are sober,' he answered quietly, with a sad look on his face.

Seeing that I wanted to answer back, he continued, slightly raising his voice:

'With respect, Your Majesty, I am your atālīq, and I have requested an urgent meeting with you about important affairs of state. I will present myself two hours before evening prayers.'

He got up, and left, clearly not intending to take no for an answer.

I slept the better part of the afternoon and woke up with a terrible headache, in the foulest of moods. I wanted to drink some more wine, just to upset Bairām Khān, but I was feeling too sick and lousy.

When Bairām Khān arrived at the indicated hour, I was starting to feel a bit better. Some cool lime sherbet had just been brought in; I did not offer him any, and started eating.

He ignored the insult.

'Your Majesty needs to be more careful about how he spends his time,' he stated, clearly not bothering to waste any time on civilities. 'There is nothing wrong with entertainment and amusement, but Your Majesty should remain mindful of his duties as the emperor. People need to be able to see Your Majesty, they need to realise he is young, bright and strong; they need to take guidance and leadership from him. That can only happen if Your Majesty remains in control of himself.

'Your Majesty should therefore be very careful with wine, and even more so with opium, for they dull and blunt the mind, and weaken the body. They should be taken sparingly, if taken at all. They can be enjoyed with moderation in the evening, when the day is over and it is time to relax, but not during the day, or when the affairs of state need to be managed.'

'I am the emperor, and I will do as I please,' I said defiantly, looking him straight in the eye.

He stared back, not in the least intimidated. To my astonishment, his stern face suddenly became friendly, and he gave me a warm, almost encouraging smile.

'Of course you will do as you please,' he agreed condescendingly, dropping the formal *Your Majesty*. 'The only real question is – which "you" is it going to be?' He paused, as if he wanted to allow some time for these rather strange words to take root in my soul.

'I am going to tell you two true stories, which have greatly influenced the way I look at life. You will then better understand what I mean,' he explained.

'As you know, a few years ago, after he had been driven out of his dominions by Shēr Khān Sūr, your revered father was forced to spend a number of years in Persia. Back there, he tried to obtain the Shāh's support in winning back his throne. Thanks to Allāh, his efforts have been rewarded with success, but it has taken quite some time and a great deal of worries. As you know, I was among your father's followers and travelled with him everywhere. During our stay, we visited many cities and met many people.

'One evening, in the beautiful city of Herāt, I had the good fortune of making the acquaintance of a learned and saintly Sūfī teacher. He was clad in white and white-bearded. Though he was trembling and weak with old age, he still had the brightest mind one can imagine.

'Years before, when he was a young man, he had been a merchant, and had travelled to the most faraway places. He had visited cities all over the Muslim world: Samarqand, Bukhārā, Isfahān, Baghād, Jeddah, Mekkah, Medīnah, Dimashq, Al-Quds, Al-Qāhira,[55] Istanbul, Tunis, and even to faraway ports in the lands of the Firanghīs,[56] like Jenua and Barshalonā, many hundreds of kos west from here.

'On one of his travels in the countries of the Firanghīs, he visited Rumiyah, a beautiful city, pleasantly located in the fourth climate, in a region called Itāliah. It is the residence of a man they call pāpā, who is

---

55. Dimashq: Damascus. Al-Quds: Jerusalem. Al-Qāhira: Cairo.
56. Firanghī: 'Frank', i.e. European Christian.

the spiritual head of the Nazariyya[57] sect. There, in Rumiyah, the Sūfī had many conversations with Nazariyya men of learning, who all tried to convince him to abandon Islām and convert to their strange religion.'

'What do these Nazariyyans believe?' I asked, finding myself interested in spite of myself. 'Which god do they worship?'

'They do worship the one and only true god – Allāh, the god of Ibrāhīm, like us Muslims, and also like the Jews do, although they call Him by many different names, such as Dīo, Diòs, Deus, and also Ghott, or something like that – a word that sounds a bit like the Persian word Khodā that you yourself often use, Your Majesty. So, these Nazariyyans do worship Allāh, but somehow, they have come to think that He consists of *three* persons – an idea as preposterous as it is blasphemous!

'The first of these three gods, they call the Father. The second, according to them, is actually the prophet Īsā ibn Maryam,[58] whom they call Yehsus or something like that in their languages. They also call him God the Son.

'To be honest, I'm not quite sure who the third divine person is, according to their strange, misguided faith. I think it is Maryam, the saintly mother of the prophet Īsā, may Allāh receive her in His mercy. The Nazariyyans indeed call her Mother of God. They apparently also worship a deity called the Holy Spirit, but I'm not quite sure who that is supposed to be.

'So you see, it all seems very complicated, and in reality, while the Nazariyyans do claim they serve the one true god, they are really not much better than the idol-worshipping Hindū pagans. . . .

'Mind you, it is of course true that the prophet Īsā ibn Maryam—may the blessings of Allāh be upon him—was an extraordinarily holy man! He holds a highly exalted rank among the prophets! Allāh Himself saved him from death on a cross. His mother Maryam gave birth to him while she was still a virgin, and together with Āsiyah, the wife of Pharaoh, Khadīja, the Prophet Muhammad's first wife, and Fātimah, his daughter, she is one of the "four perfect women" of Islām. But it is of course utter blasphemy to state that a mere man could in fact be Allāh Himself, or

---

57. Nazariyya: 'Nazarean', i.e. Christian.
58. Īsā ibn Maryam: Jesus, son of Mary.

that Allāh had a son. Allāh is greater, He is the one, there is nothing and no one like Him. He was, is, and will be. He is the eternal, the first, and the last. He definitely has no mother, no father, and no son!

'Anyway, coming back to this learned Sūfī teacher, he told me about a long and inspiring conversation he had one night back in Rumiyah, with a learned and kind man. This man had not been trying as hard as the others to convert him to the Nazariyyan sect, but had seemed to be more genuinely interested to find out what exactly we Muslims believe, and compare it to what the Jews, the Nazariyyans, and the ancient Greek philosophers believe in. They had stayed up practically all night, both of them quoting from books and prayers from each other's traditions.

'"That night, I truly learned," the Sūfī said, "that god is greater than the differences among men."

'They talked about Allāh's magnificent creation, the heavenly spheres and the earth; they also talked about us, human beings, our position in Allāh's universe, and our duties in this life. The Nazariyyan sage quoted a very interesting small book, written seventy years ago, by a very learned Nazariyyan priest who was also a nobleman, something similar to an amīr. His name, if I remember well, was Mirāndollah.[59]

'In that book, Allāh Himself is described as talking to Adam, the first human being.

'And Allāh says:

> I have created this entire world with everything in it, the sun and moon, stars and planets, mountains, plants, oceans, animals . . . Everything in it has its own particular place and obeys its own, strict laws, which I, Allāh, have ordained in My infinite wisdom. Only you, Adam, whom I made from clay, you are an exception. I have created you in such a way, that you yourself will have to choose your own place in the universe, and make your own laws. It will be up to you, to sink deeper than the lowest animal, or to rise above the Angels . . .'

Bairām Khān paused, looking at the ground.

---

59. The Italian Renaissance philosopher Giovanni Pico della Mirandola (1463-94). The text is *Oratio de Dignitate Hominis* (1486), Discourse on the Dignity of Man.

'I know you love books, Your Majesty. For some strange reason, you are unable to read, but you very much like to listen to books and the stories they hold.

'Well, our lives are just like those storybooks, Your Majesty. We have been thrown into life without asking for it, and we will have to leave it some day, when it is Allāh's will that we do. In between, we are writing our own personal story: it consists of the things that happen to us, and how we react to them.

'Within limits, we can do whatever we want, but one thing is absolutely impossible for us: we cannot avoid writing our story.

'When I leave here, there are so many possibilities open to you, so many things you can write in the book of your life. For instance, you can write: *And then, he made up his mind to become a great emperor*; or, *And then, he got drunk again*; or, *And then, he prayed to Allāh to give him strength*; or, *And then, he sat down, not knowing what to think*; or, *And then, he inquired about the situation in the Panjāb*. . . .

'There are thousands upon thousands of ways the story of your life can continue, Your Majesty. They may lead up, or down. They may go in a straight line, or via all kinds of detours. You, and you alone, are the writer – it is up to you to decide.

'However, there is one thing you cannot do, and that is – *not* writing your story. Even if you would decide to step out of this life and kill yourself, you would necessarily still be writing your story, saying: *And then, he killed himself* . . .'

Much as I resented admitting it to myself, I knew Bairām Khān was right.

I offered him some of my lime sherbet. He accepted with polite gratitude, pretending he had not noticed it up to that moment.

'You spoke of two stories, Khān Bābā. What is the second one?'

'This first story was a general one, applicable to every human being. The second one concerns you more directly and I have to warn you: You will not be pleased to hear it, but I have promised your revered father—may his grave be holy—that I would tell it to you when the time would come.

'It was a little over one year ago. You had just been named governor of the Panjāb, and I had been appointed as your atālīq. As you know, both events had been celebrated with impressive ceremonies, full of rituals, symbols and signs. Towards sunset, I was informed that your father wished to see me. I wondered why – the audience had finished only two hours before. Two guards escorted me to your father's private chambers.

'With all due respect, Your Majesty, I was truly shocked by your father's appearance – so completely different from the extravagantly attired demigod I had seen a couple of hours before, during the ceremony.

'It was truly dreadful to see how he looked. The stately majesty, the jewels, the attributes, the shiny clothes – they were all gone. He wore a simple cotton tunic – not even a lower officer in his army would ever have wanted to wear it. He had even taken off his turban. I had never seen him without a turban before in my whole life, not even when we were camping in the deserts of Sindh. The air in the room was comfortable. Yet, he was sweating profusely and shivering at the same time, as if in fever with cold sweat.

'I entered the room and prostrated myself, touching the ground with my forehead. He made an impatient gesture to approach the platform where he was sitting.

'"Sit next to me, Khān Khanān," he ordered, and clapped his hands.

'"Bring me one-fourth of my usual portion for now", he said to the servant who came in. They brought him a golden beaker holding a milky liquid, which I knew to be a preparation of opium and rose water, which, unfortunately, you seem to be familiar with as well. He drank it immediately, as if overcome with an unquenchable thirst.

'"This will just be enough to ease my discomfort without clouding my mind," he explained apologetically. "As you probably know, I should have had my usual portion of opium about two hours ago. I will have some more when we finish talking. We have had so little opportunity to really talk, my dear friend Bairām, and it is important that we do. You have just been appointed as my son's atālīq and protector, and it is essential that you know my hopes and fears for him. I don't expect to die any time soon, but one never knows. . . . The stars do not always reveal everything, they can be misread. . . ."

'He closed his eyes and leaned back, allowing the opium to work. The trembling stopped, the agitation subsided, but his mind was clearly still not at ease.

"'Maybe it is for the best that you have seen me sweating and trembling like this," he said, guessing what I was thinking. "I am the emperor and I do as I please, but if I'm completely honest with myself, it is no longer me taking and enjoying opium: The opium is taking *me*, and it has been for years.

"'Not that I would want to have it any other way. I simply cannot bear the thought of giving up these blissful moments of total relaxation and well-being, the clear, gentle white light that melts away all my troubles and worries. But if I'm honest with myself, as I intend to be tonight, my dear Bairām Khān, I must confess: I am opium's powerless prisoner. I get very sick when I don't get it on time. I always have to plan the dose I will be taking. Too much of it will cloud my mind, but without it, I am unable to think of anything else until I do get it. I will often break off important activities or conversations with people of my court, just to be able to indulge in my pleasure.

"'I do realise that under the influence of opium, I often do not take things as seriously as I should, but it holds such divine pleasure! When I take a large dose before I glide into a blissful sleep, I can see it all so clearly before my eyes! It seems I am filled with divine knowledge and wisdom: without reasoning, without words, I completely understand the universe, how it all hangs together, the elements, the spheres, the colours, the numbers, the letters, all of Allāh's majestic creation and the symbols that stand for it.

"'At the same time, I then see the magnificent, splendid, glorious calling of our Gurkaniyya dynasty. Then, there is absolutely no doubt in my mind, that it is Allāh's manifest will: we are chosen to conquer and rule. I see how we will follow the footsteps of our glorious ancestors, and go way beyond where they have ever trodden. I see how I and my descendants will regain control of Samarqand, Tashkent, Bukhārā and all the lands that rightfully belonged to our revered ancestors. And after that, who knows? If Allāh wills it, absolutely nothing will stop us! If Allāh is pleased with us, He may allow us, maybe ten generations from now, to unite under our victorious banners, all the Turks, Mongols, Arabs, Afghāns, Persians and Hindūs! Just imagine, Bairām! Nothing would be able to resist our might! With Allāh's help, we would defeat and conquer the Firanghīs, the empire of Cathay, and all of the other infidels in the East and West. In obedience to Allāh alone, we would rule the world –

from the ice-covered wastelands of the north, to the grasslands and the dark forests south of the Maghreb desert!

"'But when the opium has worn out, and before my body starts to become ill and grows restless for a new dose, I see the world and my life as they really are. I see how I have been given power and wealth, and how I squandered it. Let's face it: Most of my life, I have been a king only in name. I was an unimpressive, homeless warlord, very often a fugitive, wandering from one place to the other with a dwindling host of followers, often in great danger, and forced to leave my infant son and heir in the care of dubious allies and unfaithful relatives. Fifteen of the twenty-six years of my reign, including the first twelve and a half years of my son's life, I have spent on the edge of disaster, fleeing from my enemies, humiliating myself and even renouncing my personal beliefs in order to find some shelter and help, hoping, in spite of all odds, to recover the throne from which I had been driven by that dark-hearted Afghān traitor, Shēr Khān – may Allāh's wrath duly punish him for his treachery!

"'Fifteen years, Bairām! Fifteen years of fighting and despairing, before it finally pleased Allāh to grant my armies the sweet taste of victory. . . .

"'Make sure Akbar learns from my mistakes, Bairām! Make sure he does not fall into the trap! The throne, you see, is the loneliest place in the realm. My revered father, the great Bābur pādshāh, used to say: 'No bondage equals that of sovereignty'. How very right he was! In the end, there is no one you can trust but yourself. Tell Akbar that the better he is able to remain in control over his own self, the easier it will become for him to remain in control of others. I know that when you are king, you can do as you please – you can eat and drink whatever you like, enjoy the pleasures of the harem, have all kinds of entertainment organised just for you. Yet, the more you allow your cravings for these things to run your life, the less powerful you will become!

"'When the time comes, Bairām, make sure my son knows all this, before it is too late! Tell him about these things! He will be smart enough to understand. After all, his grandfather Bābur was that age when Allāh put him on the throne. . . .'"

Bairām Khān paused and looked at me intently.

'With all due respect, Your Majesty, that time has come. I do not mean any disrespect to you, or to your father, whom I loved and revered, and supported at the peril of my own life. However, the truth must be told, your father did have the tendency to indulge too much in his own pleasures and private interests. There is, of course, nothing wrong with recreation every once in a while, but a great king should be above his own weaknesses. As Bābur pādshāh, your august grandfather, once wrote to your father: 'Retirement matches not with rule!'

'Your noble father, Emperor Humāyūn—may Allāh grant him peace—was aware of his own weaknesses. He took pride in your strength and resilience, your sharp mind and broad knowledge. He believed in you and wanted you to become a strong emperor, stronger than he himself had been. He himself wanted me to talk to you in this way.

'Do not disappoint him, Your Majesty. Become the great emperor you know you can be!'

He paused again, probably waiting for me to react. I didn't. I couldn't. I knew he was right, but I felt extremely hurt by the brutal way he had described my father, and I could not help resenting him for it.

Nevertheless, I must admit: that evening was a turning point in my life. It would still take me a few more years before I would really take my life in my own hands. Even after that, there have been too many instances where I had too much to drink or lost self-control. However, Bairām Khān's wise words have stayed with me and have remained my guiding principle for the rest of my life.

Let them also be a lesson to you, Salīm! Remember the sad fate of your poor brothers! Learn to control yourself better – you owe it to our empire, and you owe it to yourself!

'I need to brief Your Majesty on the military situation,' Bairām Khān said after a brief silence, returning to the affairs of state, as if nothing had been said or happened.

'I have some outstanding, excellent news, but there is also somewhat disconcerting news, Your Majesty. Let me start with the former: Ājmīr and the surrounding country are ours! Our brave men have done an excellent job – the last remnants of Hemū's followers have been hunted down. Ājmīr, Your Majesty, the sacred city of Ājmīr! Your Majesty is now the guardian of the sacred grave of Khwājah Muīn-ud-dīn,[60] the peace of Allāh be upon him! Never have the lands of Hindustān seen a holier or more erudite Muslim saint; thousands upon thousands of pilgrims—Hindūs and Muslims alike—travel to Ājmīr each year, to invoke his powerful intercession, and seek solace and wisdom near his sacred tomb! It is truly a good sign, a sign from heaven that this holy place is now under Your Majesty's protection!'

'And the bad news?' I asked.

'The messenger who came in from the Panjāb this afternoon, told me that Sikandar Sūr's forces have come down from the Siwālik heights. They are plundering the Panjābī countryside – they actually appear to be threatening the Lāhor garrison!'

'Well, it's probably for the best! We would have had to deal with this vermin sooner or later anyway – we may as well get it over with now!'

---

60. Khwājah Muīn-ud-dīn Muhammad Chishti (1142–1236): One of the greatest Muslim saints in India. His tomb in the city of Ajmer, in Rajasthan, still is a very important place of pilgrimage, for Muslims and Hindus alike.

Sixth Letter

مانکت

Mānkōt

There is not much to tell. Of course we won. From then on, we would always win. For the rest of my life, despite the many wars I had to fight and the uprisings I had to repress, the military situation has hardly ever been a cause of real concern to me.

With but a few exceptions, you being one of them, my dear son, I've never again felt under any real threat. Somehow, I just knew that I was born to conquer and rule. God had clearly chosen me, and would not let me down.

Khīzr Khwāja Khān, our local commander in the Panjāb, who as I told you had been left behind when we set out to confront Hemū, had been doing his best, under the circumstances and considering the forces at his disposal.

Having been informed that Sikandar Sūr was on the move again, he had left Lāhor to deal with a pre-emptive strike against a few local Panjābī traitors who had been taking bribes from Sikandar Sūr's spies.

Unfortunately, he had been forced to withdraw back into the city, when his vanguard of two thousand cavalry had been severely defeated by the enemy's main army.

In order not to let things get out of hand, we quickly sent reinforcements to the Lāhor garrison: a strong body of elite cavalry, under the command of Iskandar Khān Uzbeg.

The Uzbeg was one of our very best commanders, competent, tough, and utterly ruthless.

As I told you, he had been one of the heroes to lead our vanguard at Pānīpat, and deservedly received the title of Khān Aālam for his role in that battle.

Meanwhile, we prepared the main body of the imperial army. On Doshanbeh the twenty-sixth of Āzar[61], we set out for the Panjāb, leaving Mahdī Qāsim Khān behind in charge of the forces guarding Dillī.

It became a leisurely march, with stops and hunting parties underway. The reports from the scouts were reassuring: Iskandar Khān Uzbeg and Khīzr Khwāja Khān clearly had the situation under control.

During the march, we also received excellent news of another kind, news from Bairām Khān's household back in Lāhor: Ten days after we had left Dillī, he had become the father of a healthy son, Abdurrahīm, whom of course you know very well, my son. Out of precaution, Bairām Khān had sent his pregnant wife and the rest of his family to Lāhor at the time we were marching against Hemū.

The child's mother came from the family of the influential Khāns of Mewat.

Bairām Khān's marriage to her dates back to the days of my father Humāyūn – when they had just recaptured Dillī, they had taken a very wise measure to ensure political stability in the area. He and Bairām Khān married the two beautiful daughters of Jamāl Khān, the cousin of Hasan Khān of Mewat, one of the most powerful local zāmīndārs.

In accordance with normal rules of hierarchy, my father married the elder sister, and Bairām Khān the younger one. Thus, the rulers of Mewat had become joined with the Gurkaniyya dynasty and its nobility by bonds of matrimony – a great honour for them, and added security for us. As you very well know, my son, the strength of an empire is not only built on bulwarks and fortifications. . . .

Abdurrahīm's birth was of course seen as an excellent omen for our campaign. Bairām Khān organised a sumptuous celebration, with superb food in abundance.

---

61. Corresponds to Monday, 7 December 1556 on the Julian calendar.

The astrologers had calculated the child's horoscope, and sent lengthy reports about the lines on its hands and forehead. The young Abdurrahīm, they predicted, would have a splendid future, and a position of major importance at the imperial court. At least once they have been proven right.

Even before the imperial army had reached the town of Jālandhar, Sikandar Sūr, who knew very well he did not stand a chance against us in open country, again took refuge in the Siwālik hills.

This time, however, there were no monsoon rains to protect him. We followed him deep into the hills and set up camp, first near the small town of Dēsūhah, next at Dahmirī. There, we celebrated the completion of the first year of my reign.

No doubt, Sikandar Sūr's plan was to harass us with a number of hit-and-run attacks and to draw us into battle in that difficult terrain, criss-crossed with ravines, where our superior numbers would actually be a tactical disadvantage.

His hopes, however, were bitterly crushed as he never even got a chance to put his plan to the test. As he and his supporters would soon find out, we were using exactly the same strategy, and we were better at it than them.

The main body of the imperial army stayed encamped safely at Dahmirī, while Pīr Muhammad Khān was sent out to roam the hills with a rather small but strong and mobile group of experienced horse archers, and some of our most war-like, not to say murderous, scouts. Villages that had provided support to Sikandar Sūr were brutally punished, and the wealth of the local leaders methodically destroyed.

It did not take more than a few days for the local zāmīndārs to drop Sikandar Sūr like a stone. They all made haste to come to our camp at Dēsūhah, throw themselves at our feet, and pledge allegiance to us.

Sikandar Sūr, now without any local support, took refuge with his loyal Afghāns in the stronghold of Mānkot.

As you probably know, Mānkot is quite a strong fortress. It consists of four strong separate forts on adjoining hilltops, providing excellent cover to each other, joined and enclosed by bulwarks, which are very difficult to approach, let alone assault. Inside its enclosure, it has an abundant supply of excellent fresh water, and the neighbouring countryside is rich in all kinds of other provisions.

We, of course, decided to lay siege to the fort. Storming it would have cost us many lives, which we could ill afford to lose at that time, after the heavy casualties we had incurred at Pānīpat.

In a few days, we had the fortress entirely surrounded by our entrenchments, and all its supply lines and escape routes were completely sealed off. The only thing we needed now was time and patience. Slowly but surely, Sikandar Sūr's garrison would be strangled to death.

Indeed, it became a leisurely, if somewhat boring, siege.

From the point of view of fighting, very little happened. Slowly but surely, our trenches were moved closer and closer to the walls. Occasionally, marksmen on their ramparts tried to take shots at the men digging the entrenchments, but our superior numbers of archers and musketeers quickly forced them to take cover. Very soon, each time they dared to show themselves, their losses far exceeded ours.

Brave as always, the Afghāns made a few heroic, if futile, attempts to break through the encirclement. Each time they fought with honour, but never stood a chance. We were always on our guard; they never even managed to cross our first line of entrenchments.

Rather than a military threat, the Afghān sallies were a welcome distraction in the dreariness of those long, identical, boring days, offering an ideal occasion for some of our young and warm-blooded officers to show their courage in close combat.

I was particularly impressed with the courageous, not to say rash, behaviour of my hot-headed foster brother, Adham Khān.

He was the youngest and preferred son of my dear head nurse and foster mother, Māham Anaga. In the Chagatai tradition, he and I were therefore *koka* or *kukultash*, foster brothers, *united by a river of milk*. . . . He was six years older than me, strong and bold, and I liked him.

Ambitious, eager to rise to the highest positions in the army, and utterly fearless, he would throw himself in the middle of the fight, with no other protection than a simple coat of mail, a helmet and a shield, just like the ordinary soldiers. He was fast, and fought well. I saw him killing at least five enemies in a single encounter! Grateful and proud I felt of my *koka*, and resolved to promote him to the highest ranks, as soon as an occasion would present itself. Little did I suspect, what a mistake that would prove to be. . . .

After those first few skirmishes during the early days of the siege, the Afghāns made no further attempts to break out. Each time, their losses had been much heavier than ours, and their numbers had been much smaller to begin with. Indeed, god does favour the larger army.

Still, they remained well entrenched in their fortress, and stubbornly refused to submit. Clearly, despite our promises to the contrary, they were convinced they would all be put to the sword as soon as they surrendered. Possibly, they were still hoping for some kind of miracle: maybe some new enemy would attack us from the rear; maybe we would become reckless and make the mistake to try and storm the fortress. . . .

But of course, nothing of the sort happened. There were no new enemies to attack us. On the contrary, the messages we received from our commanders in the border provinces brought us nothing but encouraging news: recalcitrant opponents were being subdued, new territories were being added to our dominions. Patiently and methodically, we continued the siege, undermining their morale, slowly starving them. We made sure they witnessed the daily arrival of abundant new supplies in our camp. We feasted in sight of their ramparts.

One evening towards the end of Bahman of that year,[62] when I returned from a short hunting trip in the area, Bairām Khān came to greet me when I reached the camp.

'Your Majesty, today's messenger from the court back in Lāhor has brought good news: the highborn ladies of the imperial court have arrived safely from Kābul, and are awaiting Your Majesty's instructions!'

'That is excellent news, indeed! Who is with the group?' I asked. 'I trust they have had a safe journey?'

'There is, of course, Your Majesty's revered mother, Her Majesty Maryam-Makānī-Qadasī-Arkānī-Hamīda Bānū Bēgam.[63] Accompanying her are several other highborn ladies, including Hājī Bēgam, who as you know was one of your father's other spouses. There are also his

---

62. Early February of 1557.
63. Maryam-Makānī: Occupying the place of (the Virgin) Mary; who is of equal rank with (the Virgin) Mary. Qadasī-Arkānī: Pillar of purity.

half-sisters, Gulbadan Bēgam and Gulchihra Bēgam;[64] and Your Majesty's charming cousin, Salīmā Sultān Bēgam.'

I smiled.

'She really is a nice girl, isn't she, Khān Bābā? You still want to marry her, I gather? Don't worry, I have not forgotten that my father promised you her hand in marriage as soon as Hindustān would be under our control again.

'After we have dealt with Sikandar Sūr, let the arrangements be made for the wedding! I'm confident that my revered father would not have wanted it any other way!'

Bairām Khān smiled gratefully.

'Your Majesty is most kind! It is truly a great honour for me to marry such a distinguished and honourable lady of the imperial family! I pledge I will honour and worship her, Your Majesty!'

He kept silent for a while, clearly looking for words to say something unpleasant.

'Anything wrong, Khān Bābā?'

'Your Majesty asked me, whether the ladies have had a safe journey... Well, unfortunately, Your Majesty, I have been informed that your two younger sisters, who were accompanying Her Majesty on her voyage, had become ill and passed away during the journey, peace be upon their chaste souls! Alas, it was Allāh's will. . . .'

I looked at the ground, not knowing what to say. It was hard to believe that those two playful, healthy children were dead. . . .

I paused, picturing their pretty faces before my mind's eye.

'What a terrible, terrible loss for my poor mother! How is she doing now?'

'I do not know the circumstances of their passing, Your Majesty. I was told they became ill during the journey. As for your revered mother, Your Majesty, I was told, she has resigned herself to Allāh's will. She is, so they say, much comforted by the prospect of seeing her son again.'

'How about Prince Muhammad Hakīm, and Mun'im Khān?'

---

64. Gulchihra: Rosy-cheeked; Gulbadan: Rose-bodied.

'Your Majesty's half-brother and his atālīq have elected to remain back in Kābul. They have sent a message that they consider it their duty to keep that important city in secure hands.'

That typical, somewhat disdainful look was on Bairām Khān's face again.

'You don't seem pleased with that, Khān Bābā?'

'To be honest, Your Majesty, neither I do not like nor trust Mun'im Khān. I think he is one of those people who much rather wants to be number one in a small kingdom than number two or three in a large one. . . . I suspect him of wanting to set up an independent kingdom back there in Kābul. I think it is only a matter of time before they declare their independence from the throne of Hindustān. Admittedly, I do not have any tangible proof against him. I must confess, he did behave like an obedient vassal when he learned about our victory at Pānīpat. He did treat our emissary Khwāja Ambār Nāzir like a returning hero; he did have Hemū's head, or what was left of it, duly hung from the eastern iron gate of Kābul; he did order sumptuous celebrations to be held. However, I would advise Your Majesty to remain watchful. I am really not sure how far the ambition of Your Majesty's half-brother will go. He is still very young, but his ambitions may grow rapidly. . . .'

Proper arrangements were made for the reunion with my family.

We sent Māham Anaga ahead to Lāhor, to make sure my mother was all right and well attended to, and request her to travel towards Mānkot. I would meet her under way.

So it happened. Bairām Khān stayed behind, in command of the siege, and I went with an armed escort in the direction of Lāhor to meet my mother and her retinue underway.

We met the imperial cortege at one day's march from Mānkot. Quite an impressive group it was, with a strong, heavily armed escort of about one thousand horses, under the command of the Kābul army leaders. They were guarding the small group of female elephants carrying the beautifully adorned pālkīs in which the ladies were travelling.

There was, of course, also an impressive train of camels and mules, carrying enough supplies to enable an extended stay, wherever it might be decided to pitch camp. Accompanying the royal train was also a multitude of soldiers' wives and children, who had come to visit their husbands and fathers.

All the members of the imperial family seemed to be doing quite well.

Out of the first pālkī came, with some effort, my aunts Gulchihra and Gulbadan – the former, quite frail and terribly shy; the latter, in contrast, plump, merry, and talkative. I could not help smiling when I put my arms around her massive waist to embrace her, remembering that her name means 'rose-bodied'. . . .

The second pālkī was occupied by Hājī Bēgam and Salīmā. I, of course, first paid my due respects to my father's widow, knowing she had been very close to him and still revered his memory. While I was talking to her, however, I found it difficult not to let my eyes wander off towards Salīmā.

You see, more than just my cousin, Salīmā has always been a dear friend and companion to me in my youth, and as you know, she is very wise and kind-hearted, and exceptionally well-read for a woman. I have always been attracted to her.

There she was, my sweet cousin, exactly the way I remembered her – only, much prettier still. As you know, she is a few years older than I am; two years ago, in Kābul, she had still been an overgrown, flat-chested, skinny adolescent; but now, she had turned into quite an attractive young woman, in the prime of her youth, neither too plump nor too skinny, precisely of the kind I have always liked the most. . . .

She must have guessed what I was thinking, because she gave me what I thought was a slightly mocking, but friendly smile.

'I am happy to see my emperor and noble cousin in good health,' she said, a bit stiffly, in contrast with her friendly smile. 'May Allāh be your guide and protector, and grant you victory, in this war and all the others you will have to fight!'

'Thank you, my dear cousin. I am very glad to see you are doing so well! It has been too long since we last met,' I said, and very much wanted to continue the conversation, but did not have the opportunity to do so, for about thirty paces behind her, I saw my mother, being helped by her attendants to climb out of the pālkī she had been travelling in.

I reluctantly but hastily took my leave of Salīmā, and went towards my mother's elephant, to make sure she would not have to walk to meet me. A son, my dear Salīm, should always behave like a son, even when he has become emperor. . . .

I thought to myself, it had again been quite a while since I had last seen my mother. In fact, because of the difficult circumstances of my youth, my father constantly wandering around as a destitute fugitive, I had spent most of my youth separated from my parents, in the care of relatives and foster parents.

Despite that, I have always very much revered and respected my mother, and, I guess, feared her as much as I loved her, for as you know, she was a strong-willed lady – pious and well-intentioned, no doubt, but also opinionated, often moody, and hard to please. The story goes, she refused to consider my father's marriage proposal for over forty days, despite her parents' insistence!

Also with me, our relationship has not always been easy. As you know, Salīm, she would most of the time prefer to live on her own, residing in a palace in Dillī or Āgrā, with just a few of her close friends and confidantes to keep her company. She clearly preferred to run her own quiet household, rather than having to share the busy life in the imperial zenāna in Fatehpūr, and witnessing the comings and goings of all these Hindūs and Christians, the presence of whom she utterly disapproved of, not to say abhorred.

In spite of these frictions, there has always been much tenderness and mutual respect between us, and despite our differences of opinion, she has always done her utmost to further the interests of our family.

But let me come back to all of that later.

My mother was visibly pleased seeing her son, the emperor, respectfully bowing down, kissing her hand and humbly touching her feet.

She made me stand up, and hugged and kissed me. Taking me by the shoulders, she looked at me, smiling and crying at the same time.

In an effort to dispel the awkwardness of the moment, she began babbling enthusiastically in that noble, melodious, elegant Persian of hers.

'My dear, dear boy! I'm so happy to see you! You cannot image how much I have missed you! I have been so worried about you since your father passed away! Look how you have grown! How strong have you become! Your father would have been so proud of you!'

'Let's sit together and talk. It has indeed been much too long since we have seen each other!' I replied.

I courteously bowed to the other ladies, exchanged a few civilities with the army leaders escorting them, and accompanied my mother into her quarters.

Although she had not changed a great deal, and there was still no gray in her black hair—after all, she was only fifteen years older than me—she somehow looked much older. The lines on her face had deepened, and her eyes looked dead-tired. I suspected she had spent many sleepless and tearful nights, mourning the loss of her two young daughters.

'Mother, I was very sad to hear that my dear little sisters have unexpectedly passed away. It must have been a devastating blow to you. May god grant you comfort and consolation,' I said softly.

She gave me a grateful smile.

'Praise be to Allāh under all circumstances,' she said bravely, quoting the expression, which, according to the tradition, the Prophet himself used, when confronted with sad occurrences.

There was an awkward silence.

'Seeing you in good health takes away my sorrow, my son,' she lied, clearly trying to convince herself.

'One person can never replace another,' I answered. 'I know I cannot undo the sad loss of my little sisters, but I will promise you the joy of a loving and respectful son.'

She hugged me, her lower lip trembling, her eyes turning red. She buried her face in my shoulder and started weeping, softly at first, then violently, sobbing like a child, her frail body shaking all over.

'My poor darlings! They were the light of my eyes!' she sobbed. 'My dearest sweethearts! Such good and gentle children! Why has Allāh taken them away from me? Why, why did He bless me with theoe wonderful children, only to take them away from me? How will I ever get over their loss?'

She let go of me and sat down on the pillows on the floor, her face all red and wet with tears, her eyes staring at the patterns of the carpets, without really seeing them.

'Little Taminah[65] was only eight! Such a delightful, beautiful child! So full of life, always playing, laughing, singing . . . bringing a smile on everyone's face!

'She was so excited about travelling to that strange and faraway country, Hindustān, and going to see her elder brother, Akbar, who had become a mighty emperor!

'She thoroughly enjoyed the trip – it was a welcome distraction for a lively child like her. "Travelling is so much more fun than sitting in that dull palace in Kābul!" she would say almost every day.

'She seemed to be everywhere: always on the move, chatting with the soldiers, the cooks, the animal attendants. She adored being around the animals, feeding them, caring for them. More than once, I even had to reprimand her and tell her it was about time she started behaving like a princess, rather than like a stable boy.

'And then suddenly, when we were resting for a few days underway in Jalālābād, she got a fever. In a few hours, she became dangerously ill. The physicians gave her herbal tea to drink, the mullāhs and astrologers used special prayers to Allāh, and magic to avert the evil eye, but nothing seemed to help. Two days later, she was literally burning with fever, her frail little body shaking all over, unable to eat or drink anything. Every once in a while, she would speak, but what she said didn't make any sense at all. She was delirious, the physicians said. On the third day, she did not say anything anymore. She did not move at all, her breathing was shallow and painful, her skin dry as sand. Her eyes remained open, almost all the time . . . she hardly ever blinked. With every passing hour, it seemed her gentle, beautiful little face was shrinking.

'I was desperate. At one point of time, I actually threatened the physicians, yelling and screaming that I would have them executed if they did not quickly come up with a cure; the next, I was begging them to save her . . . I am sure they did everything they could; alas, nothing seemed to work. In the evening of that third day, without a word, without a sigh, my little darling stopped breathing. . . .

---

65. The actual names of Akbar's sisters are, as far as the author has been able to research and ascertain, unknown.

'Raushanā and I howled like wild animals when it happened; we cried our lungs out; implored Allāh to help us, to perform a miracle, to bring her back to us; but it was, of course, all in vain.

'When they carried my little Taminah to her grave, in that distant city of Jalālābād, where she has no one to visit her, no one but strangers to light a lamp on her grave, I thought I would die too. Never in my life had I felt such grief and pain. . . .

'May Allāh forgive me, I even thought about killing myself, and go and lie next to her in that same grave, so she wouldn't be alone. . . .'

Her voice faltered and she covered her face. Her shoulders were shaking violently. My poor mother! My poor little sisters! I felt so immensely sad, so deeply sorry for her, but I could not find any words to say. I just held her tight, and pressed my cheek against hers. Standing before such irreparable loss, what can we say? What can we do? The greatest comfort we can give to those we love, is to hold them, and let our tears mix with theirs. . . .

After a while, my mother let go of me. She smiled through her tears, touched my cheeks and patted my face with her shawl.

'I'm very glad to see that you have a kind heart, my boy. It is a blessing for an empire and its people when their emperor is both strong and kind-hearted!'

She paused.

'The empire . . . that was one of the few things that kept me going. After all, was I not the widow of an emperor, and the mother of his successor? Everybody kept telling me: 'Your Majesty, you must be strong, Your Majesty has a task to fulfill!'

'After three days of mourning, we continued our journey towards Hindustān. While leaving that wretched town of Jalālābād, I constantly kept looked behind me, in the direction where I knew Taminah's grave was. Each time, Raushanā would hug and kiss me, and cry with me, without a word.

'My dearest Raushanā! I owe her so much! She was only twelve. Less than one year had passed since she had become a woman, but I can tell you, very few adults ever grow to be so strong and wise! So gentle and sweet. . . . Wherever she was, wherever she went, everything just became good, and beautiful. . . .

'Such a great support she was to me during that difficult time! She would cry with me when I was in despair; she made me smile when I tried to be strong; she comforted me with words of wisdom and compassion when thoughts and memories tortured my head. . . . It seemed she had eyes only for me. Never would she talk about herself or her own grief.

'"Fortunately, I still have my Raushanā!" I often thought to myself. How I wish I had never done that! The worse things seem to happen to us when we think we are safe, don't you have that feeling as well? It seems that Allāh, or rather ash-Shaytān the devil, does not want us to feel at ease. . . .

'Our caravan arrived at Kotal Sitāra near the Indus River, and we camped there for a few days, enjoying the cool breeze and the majestic view of the water.

'There, to my utter despair, my dearest Raushanā became ill as well. It started with some kind of mild indigestion, but very soon, she became violently ill, vomiting, her bowels indisposed, unable to eat or drink anything. Nothing that the physicians tried seemed to help. She was growing weaker by the hour.

'The poor girl never complained, not even once. She only seemed to be concerned about me. She told me not to worry, and that everything would be for the best. . . . Her last words, when she had hardly any strength left to speak, were to the physician who was feeling her pulse: "Please comfort my poor mother".

'For a week, I stayed at her bedside, watching her die before my eyes, powerless and desperate. I kept praying night and day, and felt utterly guilty when I had dosed off for an hour, out of sheer exhaustion. . . .

'On the eighth day, she quietly left this world. Fortunately, she did not suffer more. All her strength had left her, and she was sound asleep, when her breathing became softer and shallower, until it stopped completely.

'For the first few moments after her death, to my own surprise and shame, I did not cry. I did not seem to have any tears left. I was just sitting there next to her, as I had been during those last days.

'Then, when I bent down to kiss her one last time, something in me seemed to break.

'I started crying, covering her face with my tears, shaking her, telling her to wake up. Gently, the people around me tried to separate me from her and lead me out of the tent. I did not want to go, I let myself fall to the ground, I howled and screamed. . . .

'I tore my clothes and yelled: "Where are you now, Allāh? Where is Your compassion? Where is Your love? Why do You torture me like this? How can you be so cruel? What have I done to You, to deserve a horrible punishment like this?"

'In my heart, I even cursed Him—may He forgive me—and in my thoughts, I called Him a bastard, a murderer of defenceless children. If it had been in my power, I would have cast Him in the deepest dungeons of His own hell. . . .

'Salīmā and Hājī, and Gulbadan and the others tried to calm me down. They took hold of my wrists to restrain me, but the physician sent them away: "Leave her alone, please! Her Majesty is ill with grief! Leave her!"

'Then, he turned to me: "Let me help you, Your Majesty!" he said compassionately. He handed me a beaker of milky fluid, of the kind your late father drank so often.

'"Drink this, Your Majesty," he said. "It will help you in these hours of grief!"

'I tried to push it away – I have always hated what that filthy brew did to your father . . . but the physician gently insisted: "Trust me, Your Majesty. You must drink this; it will help you!"

'I finally gave in and drank it slowly. The potion was bitter. It had a faint, stale smell of roses gone bad and withering greenery. I did not feel a thing at first. Soon afterwards, however, I seemed to calm down a bit, and despite my sadness and despair, beautiful thoughts and visions found their way to my mind.

'It was as if my soul was being filled with a kind, gentle light. I closed my eyes; I saw my Taminah and Raushanā, smiling in the gardens of paradise . . . I saw myself reunited with them, and with your father, and with all other people, in happiness.

'I sunk into a deep sleep. When I woke up, while realising it had been nothing more than a dream, there was a glimmer of new hope in my heart. Some day, Allāh would reunite me with my poor sweethearts, in a world where there will be no more tears.

'Then I thought of my own blasphemous thoughts the day before. I had cursed Allāh! I had insulted Him, rejected Him! I prayed for mercy and forgiveness, but my fears became worse and worse. What if He throws me in jahannum?[66] What if He never allows me to see my daughters again?

'After a few hours, I just could not stand it any longer. I desperately needed to talk to someone.

'I asked to see the old mullāh, who had been present at the time of Raushanā's death.

'"I'm so scared, revered master!" I cried. "I'm so afraid Allāh will punish me for my blasphemous thoughts! When Raushanā died, you know, I cursed Allāh, in my thoughts, I even called Him . . ."

'The mullāh raised his hand, and looked at me earnestly.

'"I do not need to know about any sins you may have committed, Your Majesty," he interrupted. "But I do understand that Your Majesty was overwhelmed with grief. This is why Your Majesty refused to submit to Allāh's will, and your mind harboured rebellious thoughts. This was indeed a sin, but then, none of us is without sins! Surely, Your Majesty, Allāh understands and forgives – He is so much greater than any sin we could commit! The important thing is, Your Majesty has returned to Him and asked for His forgiveness – He will most surely give it to you."

'"Are you sure about that, revered master?" I asked.

'"I am, Your Majesty. The holy Qur'ān itself confirms it unequivocally, in many places. Allāh, may He be praised, is at-Tawwāb, the acceptor of repentance; he is al-Ghaffār, the forgiver; al-Ghaffūr, the all-forgiving; al-Halīm, the forbearing; al-'Afuw, the pardoner. . . . From dawn to sunset, Allāh is there to forgive us during the daytime, and from sunset to dawn, He is there to forgive us at night. The holy Prophet Muhammad—eternal peace and blessings be upon him—described Allāh's mercy as follows:

> O son of Adam,
> were your sins to reach the clouds of the sky
> and were you then to ask forgiveness of Me,
> I would forgive you.[67]

---

66. Jahannum: Gehennah, hell
67. From the Hadīth (traditions relating to the deeds and sayings of the Prophet Muhammad); this passage is from the *Hadīth Qudsī* collected by Abū Īsā Muhammad at-Tirmidhī, author of one of the six canonical collections of Hadīth.

"'You see, Your Majesty, Allāh does understand your grief and has gladly forgiven your sins, but He also wants you to be strong! He wants you to go on with your life, as the mother of His Majesty the emperor. He wants you to help your son, to guide him and support him. Lead a pious and righteous life, Your Majesty, and you will see, Allāh will reward you abundantly!"

'The mullāh's kind words have been a source of comfort to me ever since. Now, each time I think about my daughters, I try to think about how I saw them in paradise. I ask Allāh to forgive my sins, and I do my best to imagine how He will give back my two little darlings and reunite me with them, in a world of total bliss, where there are no more tears. . . .

'These thoughts do give me strength, but I must confess they do not take away the pain, my son. I hate to admit it to myself, but I feel best when I do not have to think and remember at all, when my mind is occupied with other matters.'

She looked up to me, wiped away her tears, and put her hands on my shoulders.

'Now that I see you, my son, I know the good mullāh was right: Allāh wants me to go on living in this world. He wants me to be there to help and support you. You are still so young, my dear boy, and the world is vast and fraught with danger. You need all the help you can get, even from a feeble woman like me!'

I kissed her, bowed and again touched her feet.

'I am most grateful for your help and guidance, Mother! May Allāh grant you comfort and consolation! I promise I will be a respectful and loving son to you, and do whatever is in my power to bring you happiness!'

The next morning, we travelled back to Mānkot. The ladies accompanied us, with their escorts and their retinue. They would stay in the army camp for a few days, before returning to the court at Lāhor.

There were touching scenes of joyful family reunions, after so many months of hardship and fighting; cheerful old comrades, happy to see each other in good health; there was good food, and stories and presents to be exchanged. Everybody could now see with their own eyes: Hindustān was secure enough for the ladies of the imperial court to leave the safety of Kābul. It was even safe enough for them to come and feast in sight of the once-so-dreaded and powerful Sūr family. There was magic in the air; this was only the beginning; we were witnessing the dawn of an extraordinary new era.

Celebrations were held every day, well in sight of the enemy fort. We made very sure the defendants could see the ample supplies, the delicacies, the wealth, the luxury. Siege warfare is a war of minds, my son, more than of weapons.

To be sure, it did not miss its effect on Sikandar Sūr and his Afghāns. Soon, we received the visit of humble and submissive emissaries, bringing us proposals of peace. We treated them with courtesy, but sent them back as soon as we heard they were trying to stipulate terms and conditions. We would accept nothing less than complete and unconditional surrender. We would promise nothing more than clemency and justice. Until they accepted these terms, the siege would have to continue.

After the ladies and their cortege had left to go back to Lāhor, the days went by, in dreary boredom.

I was desperate for ways to pass the free time in hand. I went hunting in the hills. I arranged for wrestling matches. I discussed books with my teacher. I received messengers and discussed their reports with Bairām Khān.

My favourite pastime, however, then as well as now, was elephant fights. Hardly a day went by without one. I really don't know how many hundreds of these fights I've organised in my lifetime. Yet, I have never grown bored of them. I just love it all: the shouts of the mahāwats; the smell of the animals; the trumpeting and snorting; the clouds of dust; the ground shaking with every step; the mighty muscles under the thick, leathery skins; the massive, ramming heads; the tusks, lethal as war hammers, even under their protective cover. . . .

Then one afternoon, things almost went terribly wrong.

Bairām Khān had been ill for a couple of days. He had developed some kind of fever, and a number of nasty, painful boils had appeared on his legs and the lower part of his body. The physician gave him herbal infusions to bring down the fever, and regularly applied hot compresses to the boils, before opening them with lancets and washing the wounds with vinegar.

Bairām Khān, of course, had wanted to go about his duties as before, but the physician had ordered him in no uncertain terms to stay in bed in his tent: "You keep these wounds clean and you rest, for at least a week! If you don't, you will surely contract blood poisoning, and then, you will have to rest forever!"

He had grudgingly accepted and stayed in his tent, passing his time sleeping, listening to messenger reports, and reading – mostly Jalāl-ud-dīn Rūmi's writings, and verses from the Qur'ān and the Hadīth.[68] Slowly, his condition was improving, but he was still very weak.

On the afternoon of the third day of Bairām Khān's illness, I had arranged yet another elephant fight, this time between Fatūhā and Lagna, two of our finest, strongest, and most pugnacious *mast* elephant bulls.

It really promised to be a great spectacle. Both animals were massive and angry and vicious, eager to kill their rival when given a chance. Right from the start, however, it all got out of hand. The mahāwats clearly had very little control over the animals – they hardly managed to hold on to their necks! Very soon, the fighting animals had left the arena, chasing each other all over the camp. More than once, spectators had to quickly jump aside in order not to get trampled.

I thought it was great fun. I did see the pleading looks the mahāwats gave me when they passed by me. I understood very well, what they were hoping for. They wanted me to give the sign to drop the andhiyārī canvass over the elephants' eyes to calm them down. But I didn't. I was just too fascinated by the spectacle.

Suddenly, there was a deafening roar. Lagna's left tusk had lost its protective cover and had rapped across Fatūhā's left flank, leaving a lacerated, profusely bleeding wound. The pain and anger seemed to double the victim's forces. He jumped up on his hind legs, kicking Lagna off balance, nearly throwing off its mahāwat in the process. He then rammed Lagna in the flank with such force that the other recoiled at least fifteen paces, hitting Bairām Khān's tent in the process.

The tent collapsed completely. For what seemed an eternity, the fighting animals were trampling all over it. Then, fortunately, the mahāwats managed to drop the blindfolds. The animals, now unable to see each other, quickly calmed down, and were led away, each to a different corral.

---

68. Hadīth: Traditions or sayings of the Holy Prophet Muhammad.

We all stared at the fallen tent. Everybody cheered with relief when we saw a curved dagger cutting through the canvas. Bairām Khān crawled out, dressed in his sleeping robe, his face grimacing a bit from the pain in his legs, his hair sticky with feverish sweat.

'Khān Bābā, are you all right?' I asked.

With visible effort, he restrained his anger. He bowed, or rather, nodded, stiffly.

'Qorbānat,' he replied, in formal Persian, looking intently at my eyes.

There was an awkward silence, for what seemed like an eternity.

'With Your Majesty's permission,' Bairām Khān said slowly, 'I would like to retire and go lay down again. I am still feeling rather ill.'

Shams-ud-dīn, my atga, reacted immediately.

'It would be a pleasure as well as a great honour for me, if you would care to accommodate yourself in my tent. Meanwhile, new quarters can be built for you.'

'You are most kind, my brother,' Bairām Khān replied. 'With Your Majesty's permission . . .'

Without awaiting my reply, he bowed again, and walked, with some difficulty, to the atga's tent.

I retired to my quarters, wondering what to think about Bairām Khān's reaction. 'Qorbānat,' he had said. Why qorbānat? Why not 'I'm fine, Your Majesty, thank you for asking,' in plain Turkish, or 'alHamdu liLlāh', Praise be to god?' Why this much less common Persian expression? He hardly ever used Persian, most certainly not when speaking to me. In fact, as far as I could remember, this was the very first time he directly spoke to me in that language . . . in reply to a question in Turkish, at that! This was clearly no coincidence.

In itself, there was, of course, nothing wrong with qorbānat: Is it not a normal, polite way to thank someone who has just inquired after one's health and well-being? But, as you know very well, the expression literally means 'thy sacrifice'. Why did he choose to call himself my *sacrifice*? Was it a covert reprimand for my reckless and irresponsible behaviour? Or did he actually mean to imply that I had done this on purpose? Could he really believe a terrible thing like that?

My suspicion was indeed correct. About three hours later, Shams-ud-dīn requested to be admitted to my quarters.

With a grave, worried look on his face, he told me how Bairām Khān had interrogated him—at length—about the incident, how he had wanted to know the exact sequence of events in every minute detail. He had only calmed down somewhat, when Shams-ud-dīn had taken a solemn oath, on the Holy Qur'ān, swearing that to the best of his knowledge, the incident had been nothing more than an unfortunate accident.

I was profoundly upset. I felt insulted and angry that he apparently held me in such low esteem. And to be honest, I also felt quite worried. What was I to do if he were to turn against me?

The following days, I would often pay him a visit in his tent, politely inquiring about his health, asking his advice about the incoming reports from other regions of the empire, the military situation, and many other matters of state. He remained quite courteous, respectful and friendly. Neither of us ever mentioned the incident, but it was all too clear, neither one of us had forgotten about it.

Sure enough, it came to my ears that during the following weeks, he repeatedly interrogated a number of other people, much the same way as he had done in Shams-ud-dīn's tent.

Clearly, the poisonous weeds of suspicion had been planted in his soul as well. . . .

Fortunately, the siege offered some welcome distraction. The situation in the enemy fort was now clearly growing desperate. The visits of Sikandar Sūr's peace emissaries became more frequent. As a sign of good will, Sikandar invited ambassadors of the imperial army into the fort and even sent his own son as a hostage as a guarantee for their safety.

Shams-ud-dīn immediately volunteered to go as our ambassador.

'Even if they still refuse to surrender,' he argued, 'we will at least get some first-hand information about the situation inside.'

He returned with a number of exquisite gifts: gold, silk, carpets, and a couple of magnificent horses and elephants, surprisingly well-fed at that. Most of these gifts were of course presented to me, but Sikandar Sūr had also been shrewd enough, not to forget smaller, yet quite substantial individual gifts for Bairām Khān, Pīr Muhammad Khān, and Shams-ud-dīn Atga Khān himself, with personal and elaborately polite and kind accompanying letters for each one of them.

Shams-ud-dīn went back into Mānkot with the same answer as before: The gifts were a hopeful sign that the beleaguered were willing to give up the rebellion and obey their rightful sovereign. Their lives would be spared, but the emperor would not accept any other terms or conditions of any kind. Their surrender was to be complete and unconditional.

For another two days, the fort remained closed and silent. Then, finally, after six months of siege, our patience was rewarded. On Yeksanbeh, the twelfth of Khordād of the second year of my reign – the twenty-fifth of Rajab, 964,[69] Sikandar Sūr himself solemnly surrendered the keys of Mānkot into my hands.

We granted him one request – he would be allowed to surrender with honour. His son would kneel and rub his forehead in the dust in his stead, thus asking forgiveness for the rebellion, but Sikandar Sūr himself would be allowed to do obeisance according to the protocol observed by the senior members of my court.

At the agreed hour, the gates of Mānkot finally opened up.

Riding their swift Afghān battle horses, Sikandar Sūr and three of his officers came out. Crossing the narrow bridges, which had been laid over the trenches, they entered the imperial camp, dismounted, and approached the platform on which I was sitting.

So, this was the great and dangerous Sikandar Sūr. . . .

He looked disappointingly unimpressive – a middle-aged, weak, tired-looking man, visibly scared for his life. Unlike most Afghāns, he did not wear a full beard, but only a long moustache, more customary with our men. Judging from his pale, flaccid, sagging skin, he had until recently been rather healthy but had lost quite a lot of weight during the siege. Likewise, his officers, though much younger and healthier looking than he, made a tired and weakened impression.

They all bowed and slowly approached the platform, until a slight movement of Bairām Khān's right hand indicated they had come close enough. There again, they bowed elaborately and repeatedly, like obedient and respectful vassals at my court were supposed to bow, touching, three times in a row, their foreheads, their chest and the dust of the ground with their right hand.

---

69. Sunday, 24 May 1557 of the Julian calendar.

One of the Afghān officers handed Sikandar Sūr a set of large iron keys on a small pillow made of red silk. He raised it in front of his chest and stretched his arms towards me.

'Your Majesty,' he mumbled slowly as if he was chewing the words in his mouth. He looked like a guest at an important banquet, swallowing with great difficulty a dish he abhors, yet does not dare to refuse.

'Your Majesty,' he repeated, 'I surrender to you the keys of the fortress of Mānkot.'

He paused again.

'I recognise Your Majesty as my lawful sovereign, to whom—and Allāh is my witness!—I pledge my unwavering loyalty, and that of my men.'

I made a sign for Shams-ud-dīn to come forward and receive the keys on my behalf.

'Sikandar Khān,' I replied, 'eternal praise and thanks-giving be to Allāh! In His infinite compassion and mercy, He has granted us the wisdom to avoid further unnecessary bloodshed. These lands of Hindustān need pious and competent men to administer them and ensure their prosperity. Let us leave behind the differences that separated us, and build a new future!'

He bowed, visibly relieved and grateful to see that we were keeping our promise to spare their lives.

I must confess, we had considered—at length, I might add—the option of executing him anyway. After all, there were many good reasons to do so: Had he not caused us an inordinate amount of trouble? Was it not dangerous, if not outright foolish, to allow a member of the Sūr family to stay alive? Hotheads like Pīr Muhammad Khān and Adham Khān had not failed to use those arguments, convincingly and emphatically.

Yet, Shams-ud-dīn, Bairām Khān and I had, in the end, reached a consensus – living up to our promise, while more dangerous in the short term, could actually prove to be of greater benefit in the future.

'Treating him well sends a powerful signal to our other adversaries,' Shams-ud-dīn had argued. 'It will motivate them to surrender as well. Opposing Your Majesty means running and hiding like a hunted animal, constantly risking one's life and possessions. Submitting to Your Majesty's rule and joining the empire, in contrast, is the easy way out, the key to a life of peace, leisure and prosperity.'

'I very much agree with that point of view,' Bairām Khān nodded.

'Besides, when you come to think if it, subduing a Sūr, and turning him into a vassal, is much greater a victory for us than killing him! If we execute him, he will remain a noble hero in the eyes of many Afghāns, a noble warrior, dying honourably after an unequal, brave and gallant fight. If he submits, the whole era of the Sūrs becomes little more than a vulgar rebellion. Conversely, if you pardon him, Your Majesty, you show yourself to the world as a most wise and noble ruler, a king whose court is the refuge of the just and the lovers of peace, where it is good to live, *zire sayeye lotfe shoma*, as they say in Persian, *under the shadow of your kindness* . . .

'Yes, I would follow your atga's advice, Your Majesty – we are taking a small risk, but we have so much more to gain!'

Thus it was done. Sikandar Sūr was not executed, nor maltreated. He was made to suffer the much worse defeat of subtle humiliation.

I invited him to come closer and sit down on the carpet near the platform where I was seated. He and his men were offered various kinds of ice-cooled sherbets, freshly baked bread, fruits, nuts, and skewers of exquisitely roasted mutton, fowl and lamb.

For one brief moment, they did their best to hide how famished they were.

'Go ahead, enjoy,' I said. 'There is more than enough!' They needed no further encouragement.

For a while, we engaged in pleasant conversation, about the various kinds of bread, fruit and meat; about butter, oil, salt, condiments; about horses, hunting and similar subjects of common interest. When it comes to bringing people together, few things are as effective as good food and benevolent conversation.

Then, as we expected, Sikandar Sūr made his final move.

'Your Majesty,' he started, trying to hide how tense he was feeling, 'I speak on behalf of all of us in thanking Your Majesty for his most kind generosity. May Allāh grant him a long, happy and healthy life! As I have told Your Majesty, I solemnly pledge to him my unwavering loyalty. . . .'

He paused, trying to find the appropriate words.

'I am not a young man anymore, Your Majesty. While I am still in good health, thanks to Allāh, I clearly feel how much of my former strength has left me. I have no other desire than to live in peace and contribute to the prosperity of these lands, which now belong to Your Majesty. I would be most grateful if Your Majesty would allow me to remain here in the Panjāb, as Your Majesty's governor. I know these territories well. I solemnly swear, I will administer them diligently and honestly! The khutbah will be read in Your Majesty's name, every Friday, in all the mosques. I personally guarantee that a steady stream of revenue will flow into Your Majesty's coffers. . . .'

Probably guessing from the expression on my face that I was about to say 'no', he rapidly added: 'Allāh is my witness; may I die in agonising pain and burn in hell if I'm not speaking the truth! And I am willing to entrust my son, who is dearer to me than anything on this earth, to Your Majesty's protection, as a sign of my close alliance with Your Majesty's imperial court, and a guarantee of my unwavering loyalty!'

Maybe, under different circumstances, I would have yielded to these pleas and arguments. But Bairām Khān and I had talked this through – there was no way we were going to allow Sikandar Sūr to remain in the Panjāb. Even if he were speaking the truth—what I was inclined to believe—the Panjāb was much too important a province to leave it under the effective rule of someone else. My control over it had to be direct and absolute.

'Sikandar Khān,' I replied, 'there is much joy in my heart at the kindness of your words. Nothing is dearer to me than the prosperity of these lands, and the friendship among all the people dwelling therein, especially between the brave and noble Afghāns and ourselves.

'We will be most grateful, and our mind will be at ease, knowing that the beautiful province of Bihār prospers under your able governorship!

'There is a subtle, yet important distinction to be made,' I continued, raising my voice, as he clearly wanted to say something in protest.

'There are, in fact, two kinds of governors, Sikandar Khān. On the one hand, you have local rulers, who have accepted, often reluctantly, to become the ally and vassal of another, mightier king. After their formal surrender, they continue to rule their dominions very much like before. Of course, they do recognise the sovereignty of the king, which in practice means they allow the khutbah to be read and coins to be struck in his name, and they pay yearly taxes to him.

'On the other hand, there are, what I would call, regular governors. These are trusted members of the king's court, sent out to administer a province, in the name and on behalf of their lord and sovereign.

'Sikandar Khān, I trust that a man like you clearly appreciates the difference. We would, however, like to avoid any confusion or misunderstanding in the minds of our subjects. Your predecessor, Shēr Khān Sūr—may Allāh forgive his sins—has risen to power after a rebellion against my revered father. That rebellion has now come to a final end!'

For a moment, it seemed he still wanted to say something in protest, but the expression on Bairām Khān's face quickly made him change his mind.

'As Your Majesty wishes,' he whispered, bowing his head, a tired man who had lost his final battle.

Bairām Khān smiled as he watched the Afghāns go to their assigned tents.

'Your Majesty did very well,' he nodded, 'this was really outstanding, spoken like a true king! I wish your father could have witnessed this!'

He had never given me a greater compliment. No satisfaction is greater than that of a task well accomplished . . .

The next morning, Sikandar Sūr, with a handful of followers and a strong escort of ours, left the Panjāb forever. He never caused us any trouble again – or, as Abū-l Fazl would have phrased it, he 'never again removed the neck of submission from the collar of obedience'. He administered his province with commendable diligence and loyalty, until his death, barely two years later.

With him died the last of the remaining Sūr kings.

The other Sūr, that bastard Mubāriz, had already met his well-deserved fate further east. Hemū's death had left him utterly helpless – without his iron right arm, his downfall was only a matter of time. Sure enough, around the time Mānkot fell into our hands, the Sultān of Bengāl attacked and crushed his remaining army. Barely three years had passed, since he had put himself on the throne after butchering his defenceless young nephew. That is how quickly thrones can be lost.

The Bengālīs killed him on the spot, like the scabby dog he was. I hear he was stabbed in the gut with a thin dagger, and left to die for hours, in excruciating pain. The filthy swine deserved every moment of it. I just wish I had been there to kill him myself.

Thus ended the glorious Sūr dynasty: with the execution of a fat, indolent, worthless son of a bitch, and the quiet passing of an obedient provincial administrator. It took a lifetime of hard work for one strong man to build a powerful kingdom. Less than a generation later, his successors let it slide back into insignificance. . . .

Let their downfall be a lesson to us, my son!

After the fall of Mānkot, we chose to stay a few more weeks in the Siwālik Hills. After all, it was the hottest time of the year; where could it be better to stay, than in a pleasant mountainous country with plenty of fresh air and shade from the trees? Finally, on Shanbeh, the nineteenth of Mordād,[70] when the monsoon rains were finally bringing some refreshment to the parched lands, the imperial army left the Siwāliks and marched to Lāhor.

One week later, we made our triumphant entry into the city.

---

70. Corresponds to Saturday, 31 July 1557 of the Julian calendar.

Seventh Letter

لاہور

Lāhör

We stayed in Lāhor for a period of four months and fourteen days. It was not a time I like to remember.

Not that there were that many problems – on the contrary, everything was for the best. The reports coming in from the border regions were quite reassuring. Each day, our hold on the recently acquired territories was growing stronger. The stream of revenues was growing steadier every day. Law and order was in place, insurgents and marauders of all kinds having been eliminated or forced to surrender.

The local chiefs and leaders made haste to pledge their allegiance, bringing gifts, offering their daughters in marriage, requesting the favour to kiss the threshold of the sublime court and do homage, as Abū-l Fazl liked to put it. Fortune was smiling on me. My empire was growing more powerful by the day.

Yet, it was not a pleasant time for me. More often than not, I found myself in a bad mood, bored, dissatisfied with everything and everybody, most of all myself. I guess this is not entirely surprising; after all, I was hardly fifteen years old – at an age where most youngsters are at odds with themselves. Unfortunately, I was no exception.

My problem was rather simple, and, in fact, not dissimilar to yours and my father's, Salīm: I was just lazy. As usual, Abū-l Fazl phrased it very politely: 'in repose and pleasure, outwardly he wore the guise of one who did not attend to affairs. . . .'

Truth is, I wanted to enjoy the pleasures of kingship but not shoulder its burdens and that, alas, is not possible, my son. Laziness is the soft pillow on which Satan smilingly sleeps.

Being king is not about following your passions and interests, my son. It is about serving your empire, being available to your subjects, and guiding them.

This may sound great, but in practice, it means listening to hundreds of reports, requests and complaints, oftentimes about trivial things you're not even remotely interested in. It means sitting in dreary ceremonies and boring discussions for hours on end. It means, spending a whole lot of precious time exchanging civilities with people you do not even like very much.

Above all, it implies working very hard to make sure that you remain in control.

Do not be mistaken, Salīm: Staying in power is not as simple as it sounds. Of course, when you are around, everybody will be polite and obedient enough. Everybody will go out of their way to serve and please you, and to tell you the things you like to hear. Unfortunately, it is all too easy to be lulled asleep by all that. Before you know it, you can become the unwitting prisoner of your own courtiers, a misinformed, misguided buffoon in a golden cage.

A wise king will be careful, my son. He will check, re-check, and check again. He will never confide in just one single individual. A wise king, my son, is lonely, and works hard.

Like you, I was of course aware of all this, but somehow did not have the stamina to act upon it. Most of the time, I went hunting, enjoyed myself with music and dancing girls, and left the day-to-day affairs to Bairām Khān.

When you leave a void, you should not be surprised to find that others make haste to fill it. When the elephant leaves, the tiger returns. . . .

And indeed, Bairām Khān, diligent and hard working as always, readily took charge of everything. Whenever I was around, he would be courteous and obedient enough, but in my absence, he acted as the true head of the empire.

Not surprisingly, this did not fail to raise serious concerns with the people who loved me, like my mother and Shams-ud-dīn, and arouse the bitter jealousy of others, above all, Māham Anaga and Adham Khān, her ambitious son. Soon, I found myself surrounded by rumours, gossip, intrigues. . . .

The imperial court was quickly turning into a hornet's nest. It was sufficient that one party argued one way, for the others to take the opposite view.

In fact, the squabbling had already begun back in Mānkot, when proposals were being made for me to marry my first wife, Ruqayyah, the daughter of Abdullāh Khān Moghul. Bairām Khān was strongly opposed to the idea, because Abdullāh Khān Moghul's sister had been married to Kāmrān, my father's brother and bitter opponent. Marrying this woman was not only a risk, he argued, it was also disrespectful towards my father's memory. But Māham Anaga, Pīr Muhammad Khān and Shams-ud-dīn were very much in favour of the union, as it was a sign of unity and reconciliation in the imperial family. In the end, much to Bairām's dismay, I followed the latter advice, and married Ruqayyah, as a sign of reconciliation and unity.

I did not really mind all these arguments – in the end, there was a valid case to be made for both points of view. Much more disturbing was the animosity, if not outright hostility, between the protagonists. Not a day went by without reproaches, insinuations, accusations, and complaints.

All these incidents further complicated my relationship with Bairām Khān. Despite our mutual affection, we seemed to be constantly irritated at the other's attitude and behaviour. Slowly but surely, we were drifting further apart. . . .

A particularly disturbing confrontation occurred about three weeks after we had set up residence at Lāhor. At the end of a long, boring day, where we had been listening to dozens of requests concerning petty local matters, and endless reports about revenues and expenditures, I felt I had had enough of it all. There was still one more meeting scheduled, an audience with some local Panjābī zamīndārs who had come to pay homage. I did realise this was relatively important, but I just couldn't bear the thought of another two, three hours of sitting on a pillow, listening, nodding and exchanging civilities. I was really desperate to go out and do something else. And so I did. I told Bairām Khān to go ahead and receive the zamīndārs on my behalf.

He was visibly displeased, but to my surprise and relief, made no real attempt to talk me out of it.

'Your Majesty realises this is a very important assembly?' he asked. 'Your Majesty allows me to take the necessary decisions by myself?'

'Sure, sure, whatever,' I answered, and made haste to get out in the open.

I made my way to the stables, and spent the rest of the afternoon elephant-riding, enjoying myself immensely. When I came back, I was in no mood to go back to the affairs of state, much less to listen to another one of Bairām Khān's sermons about the duties of kings.

I did not go to see him, did not send for him, and did not even bother to ask anybody else about the outcomes of the meeting. I went straight to my private quarters to have dinner. I enjoyed some cool wine, some music and a delightful dancing performance, and spent the rest of the night with one of the girls. She was very attractive, with long, black curly hair, and truly understood how to please an eager young man. We enjoyed each other's company until deep into the night.

The next morning, much too early to my taste, I was informed that Shams-ud-dīn was urgently requesting an audience. I reluctantly got out of bed, and invited him to join me for my morning meal.

After the customary civilities, he started to talk about the military and political situation in the Panjāb, and expressed his satisfaction that we now seemed to have this important region tightly under our control.

'The measures taken yesterday were harsh, but necessary, I think,' he added, trying to probe the expression on my face.

I did not have the faintest idea what he was talking about.

'Yes, thanks for your help and support, Atga,' I answered vaguely.

He clearly was shocked, though he did his best not to show it. 'Your Majesty was informed about the execution of Takht Mal?' he asked.

'Of whom?' I asked, painfully conscious of how stupid that sounded.

'Takht Mal, the zamīndār of Pathānkot. I suppose Bairām Khān has asked Your Majesty's permission to have him killed?' he replied, visibly dismayed at my ignorance.

'We briefly talked about it, yes,' I lied. 'So, that was done yesterday, after the audience, atga? Tell me how it went. I have not had the chance to talk to the Khān Khanān yet.'

Shams-ud-dīn hesitated, clearly worried by what he just heard.

'Well, Your Majesty, Bairām Khān had all the zamīndārs assembled in the hall of public audience. He was sitting where he would normally sit, on the right-hand side of the royal platform. One by one, the local leaders were called forward. They paid homage, exchanged a few civilities with the Khān Khanān, and received gold and other gifts in recognition of the renewed alliance and as a reward for their loyalty.

'The fifth to be called forward was Takht Mal of Pathānkot. Bairām Khān started the conversation quite amiably, as he had done with all the others.

'"My lord Takht Mal," he said, "His Majesty is very pleased indeed that henceforth, he will be able to count on the unwavering loyalty of the leader of Pathānkot!"

'"And I am of course very pleased to be able to be of service to His Majesty," Takht Mal answered with a bow.

'"Are you indeed?" inquired Bairām Khān. He looked at the zamīndār, and the smile on his face slowly disappeared.

'"My Lord Takht Mal, I seem to recall that Humāyūn pādshāh, may Allāh receive him in paradise, used to pay you quite generously for your loyalty, did he not?"

'Takht Mal was visibly getting worried.

'"Yes, my Lord Khān Khanān, but . . ."

'"I know," Bairām Khān agreed, "the forces of Humāyūn pādshāh were driven out of Hindustān, and Shēr Khān Sūr came to power. There was very little you could do about that, was there? I agree – you needed to think about the welfare of your family and your people. Nobody will deny that you have acted prudently and wisely for yourself and your dominions! I suppose Shēr Khān has paid you handsomely for your support as well, has he not?"

'Takht Mal tried to smile apologetically and nodded, looking at the carpet at his feet. He was sweating profusely.

'"When Humāyūn pādshāh finally got back what was rightfully his, he understood and forgave you, did he not? He rewarded you for your renewed pledges of loyalty, did he not? And when he died, you did accept the gifts that were presented to you on behalf of his lawful successor, His Majesty Abū'l Fath Jalāl-ud-dīn Muhammad Akbar, did you not?"

'Takht Mal nodded again. He tried to say something. His lips moved, but no sound came out.

'"I know, I know, Sikandar Sūr probably made you an offer you could not refuse," Bairām Khān said with a sad, compassionate expression on his face. "From now on, however, we *really* want to make absolutely sure that we can count on Pathānkot's unwavering loyalty! We will therefore pay you for your services, one last time."

'His eyes went towards the back of the hall. He made a slight, almost imperceptible gesture with his right hand. Before anybody realised what was going on, one of the guards, a Qazaqī raider who had been standing motionless at the back of the hall, dashed towards Takht Mal. In an instant, he threw a piece of thin hemp-string over his head, looped it twice around his neck, and pulled it tight.

'It was an impressive demonstration of fighting skills. Just one short, choking noise escaped from his victim's throat, and then, there was absolute silence – his windpipe had been completely tied shut before he could blink an eye.

'Takht Mal's face immediately turned dark red, then purple. He was struggling violently, kicking his arms and legs, throwing his weight from left to right. It did not seem to bother the Qazaqī one bit. He passed the string one more time around Takht's neck, and skillfully knotted it tight. He let go of his victim, and calmly returned to the place where he had been standing, without even looking back.

'Takht Mal desperately reached for the knot, tried to pull the string away, and loosen it . . . all in vain, of course. He fell to the floor, rolled and kicked a few more times, then lay still, on his back, his eyes and mouth wide open, his black tongue sticking out. It was a ghastly sight indeed. . . .

'Bairām Khān looked each of the remaining zamīndārs in the eye, one by one. Then, his eyes singled out one of them.

'"My Lord Bakht Mal, please come forward," he said softly to the dead zamīndār's brother.

'The poor man obeyed, shaking like a leaf. For a while, Bairām Khān just left him standing there, next to his brother's corpse.

'"My Lord Bakht Mal," he repeated, "on behalf of His Majesty the emperor and in my own personal name, I want to express our heartfelt regrets for the harsh measures that had to be taken. I trust you appreciate that there was no other way. At the same time, I would also like to express our sincere hopes that the new zamīndār of Pathānkot will prove himself a loyal ally of the empire of Hindustān. I trust we will be able to rely on you personally, will we not, my Lord Bakht Mal?"

'He looked at him like a cobra at its prey.

'"Yes, Your Majesty, I mean, my Lord Khān Khanān," Bakht Mal stammered.

'Bairām Khān kept looking at him, without blinking an eye.

'"I can assure you, my Lord Khān Khanān, you can count on me. God is my witness, my Lord Khān Khanān . . ."

'For what seemed an eternity, Bairām Khān said absolutely nothing. He just kept staring at him, his face inscrutable and expressionless. Finally, he nodded, smiling faintly.

'"On your way out, my Lord Bakht Mal, you will receive a bag of gold coins and a pair of the finest horses, as a sign of His Majesty's appreciation of your pledge of unwavering loyalty!"

'"You have our permission to retire, if you wish," he added, looking at the stain between Bakht Mal's legs. The poor man had wet himself. . . .'

Shams-ud-dīn paused.

'This is the story, Your Majesty. I'm sure the Panjābī zamīndārs will not easily forget this lesson they got.'

I looked at the carpets, wondering what to say.

'The Panjāb is of vital importance to us,' I agreed after an uncomfortably long silence. 'It must be very clear to everyone that we can and will not tolerate any insubordination! Examples must be set, if necessary!'

What else could I have answered? What else was there to say?

After Shams-ud-dīn had left, I kept pacing up and down, wondering what to do about Bairām Khān. Was I to reprimand him? Congratulate him? Ignore him?

I sent for him later that afternoon.

'Shams-ud-dīn told me what happened yesterday,' I said. 'I think you did the right thing, Khān Bābā. I'm just disappointed that you did not involve me in the decision, as you should have. This was not like Tardī Beg's execution, when our survival was at stake. I was much younger, and less experienced back then. This time, you really should have involved me in this decision, Khān Bābā!'

For a moment, I thought he was going to apologise, but he apparently changed his mind.

'Your Majesty can be involved any time and to any extent he wants,' he said. 'Meanwhile, I'm trying to do my duty, the best I can.'

'I do not doubt that, Khān Bābā, nobody does. But you should have involved me this time,' I insisted.

This time, I saw him hesitating.

'Yes, Your Majesty is right. I do offer Your Majesty my sincere apologies. However, I can assure Your Majesty that my only motive has been the security of the empire,' he answered.

I just nodded, and said nothing. How could I be sure that he really meant it?

A few weeks later, there was yet another one of these incidents. Admittedly, this one was really a rather trivial matter, far less tragic and important than the previous one, but also a matter of principle, and it made me very angry.

We had received the visit of a messenger from Bahādur Khān, the newly appointed governor of Multān.

Many people had warned me against his appointment, because he was one of Bairām Khān's closest confidants, but a better man for the task could not have been picked: a brave and competent soldier, one of the heroes of our vanguard at Pānīpat, and a dedicated, strong-willed man. The unruly area of Multān was clearly in need of a strong governor like him. In only a few months' time, he had succeeded in ridding the province from the various bands of Balūchī robbers who had been prowling the countryside. A sizeable number of them had been killed, the rest driven back into their rugged mountains. Peace and prosperity was returning, and revenues were flowing to our treasury.

All this was, of course, reason enough to be satisfied and grateful. After hearing the messenger's report, I asked Bairām Khān to send Bahādur a congratulatory letter, as well as a suitable reward.

The next day, I was shocked to find out that on top of a large sum of money and jewels, Bahādur had actually been awarded two of the very finest *mast* elephants of the imperial stables! I kept calm, but inside, I was really beyond myself with rage. Who did Bairām think he was, giving away imperial personal property without my permission? And not just any regular army elephant, but two of the very finest animals in the empire, carefully selected for the imperial stables! Such insolence! Such arrogance!

To make things worse, on my way back to my quarters, I bumped into Māham Anaga, who did not fail to take advantage of the situation – she would rarely miss an opportunity to undermine Bairām Khān's position.

With a rather phony smile on her face, she started congratulating me:

'There is really no limit to the kindness of Your Majesty's noble heart! Such generosity! I just hope a rough soldier like Bahādur Khān will duly appreciate this token of Your Majesty's appreciation!'

'Yes, thank you,' I replied evasively.

She looked at me with a hint of scorn on her face. It was obvious she did not believe me. 'I assume these gifts have been sent on Your Majesty's orders?' she asked, clearly eager to make her point. 'Surely, the Khān Khanān would never have taken a decision like this without Your Majesty's permission?'

I did not answer. What could I say? Did I have to admit that I had not been informed?

She still did not let go of her prey.

'Your Majesty is far too good,' she sighed with an intensely sad and worried look on her face. 'Your Majesty should be more careful, and think more of his own interests.'

'What do you mean, Māhamjī?'

'I mean, Your Majesty has been allowing this Bairām Khān to become way too powerful,' she snapped.

In spite of everything, I was surprised at her bluntness.

'We should not forget, Māhamjī,' I argued, 'that he has been appointed by my father! Besides, without him, we might not have even be here! He was my father's strongest and most trusted army leader; he was the one who defeated Hemū and the last of the Sūrs!'

'Nobody denies that he is competent, and works very hard,' she admitted. 'The only question is, Your Majesty, who does he work for? Do you not see how power-hungry this man is? Your Majesty is still very young, but what in two, three years from now, when you will be an adult, and no longer require an atālīq? Are you sure he will gracefully step down? Are you confident that he will obey you, even if he is of a different opinion than you? Do not forget that there are other candidates to occupy the throne! There is still your younger cousin, your uncle Kāmrān's son. And Bairām Khān may even nourish higher ambitions for himself. He has Shēr Khān or Hemū as his shining examples: a competent minister may one day occupy the throne himself. . . .'

'I think you are exaggerating, Māhamjī, but I do appreciate your concern,' I answered bravely.

I must confess, however, her words made a much deeper impression on me than I cared to admit. She was right, I could no longer allow Bairām Khān to run the empire on his own. I had to set things straight.

But that was much easier said than done. How was I to deal with this? Surely, I could not afford to make a fool of myself and ask my presents to be given back, like some kind of spoilt child? And what was I to do about this incident? Try to ignore it altogether? Make a scene?

After a sleepless night, full of dark and angry thoughts, I made up my mind: I would summon him to meet me in my quarters.

I was just about to have him called, when the guards announced that Bairām Khān requested to be admitted for a private audience with me.

To my surprise and relief, he looked nervous. There was a timid, subservient look on his face – very unlike him, I must say.

'You wanted to see me, Khān Bābā?' I asked, trying to sound as casual as possible.

'I wanted to obtain Your Majesty's permission to give orders to the army chiefs to prepare for a march back to Dillī.'

He hesitated. It was blatantly obvious that he had not requested an audience specially to ask me this. 'As Your Majesty knows, the military situation in the Panjāb and the other territories in west Hindustān appears to be sufficiently stable and under control. I believe therefore, that our presence here in Lāhor is no longer required. If Your Majesty agrees, we could head back east and take up residence in Dillī again, at least for the foreseeable future,' he added.

'That's fine with me, Khān Bābā,' I replied. 'I have to admit, I was getting rather bored here in this palace anyway!'

Bairām Khān nodded.

'Very well, Your Majesty. I will make the necessary arrangements for the march.

'I would also like to request . . .' He hesitated.

'Yes?' I asked.

'I would also like to request Your Majesty's permission to make the necessary preparations for my marriage to the honourable Salīmā Sultān Bēgam. As we have discussed before, Your Majesty's father promised me that I could marry her when Hindustān would be ours again, and Your Majesty confirmed that the arrangements could be made as soon as we had dealt with Sikandar Sūr. . . .'

'This has indeed been agreed,' I admitted. 'Well then, please go ahead with the arrangements! And tell me, when will we see the *zifāf*?[71] Still over here in Lāhor?'

He bowed.

'I am most grateful to Your Majesty for this great honour! I promise that I will be a good and caring husband. The ceremony can be organised on the way. We won't lose any time that way.'

'Very well, Khān Bābā, so it shall be done. Congratulations!'

There was a bit of an awkward silence. Surely, this was not the appropriate moment for me to bring up the issue of the elephants. All things considered, a pair of topclass elephants was maybe a small price to pay for peace in Multān.

'Tell me, Khān Baba, have you eaten yet? Come, sit down with me. It's been much too long since we had a chance to talk in private!'

We ordered some food and sat down together. We talked for hours, about all kinds of subjects, trivial as well as important: the affairs of state; the military situation; the future administration of the territory; and horses, hunting, food, women, poetry, religion . . . it was a delightful morning. Why could it not always be like that?

I watched him walk out after he had taken his leave, and for the rest of the day, I thought of little else than my relationship with this man, to whom I owed my life and my throne – this man, whom I loved, admired, envied, and feared; and I wondered how it all would end.

---

71. Zifāf: Bridal procession.

Eighth Letter

جالندهر، سرهند

Jālandhar, Ṣirhind

The imperial army slowly made its way east. With no major trouble to be expected, it was, once again, more of a leisurely excursion, rather than a military campaign. As usual in the winter season in Hindustān—it was the twenty-sixth of Āzar of the second year[72] when we left Lāhor—the weather was truly delightful, with cool nights full of stars, and mild, sunny days with clear, deep blue skies.

I was extremely relieved to get out of the palace, in the open again at last, and I was not the only one. The air seemed to have a beneficial influence on people's moods – at least, there was much less gossiping, complaining, and bickering.

We had planned our first stop at Jālandhar. Almost two years had passed since I had last set foot there. I must say I was pleasantly surprised: Under the monsoon rains, it had been a rather dull and dreary place, but now, under the clear blue skies of winter, it had an almost festive look to it. The return of peace and order to the region had clearly been a blessing to the local people: They seemed to be better off – their clothes were newer and cleaner, their children more lively, and their animals fatter.

---

72. Tuesday, 7 December 1557 of the Julian calendar.

Timid at first, the locals soon trooped together, eager to catch a glimpse of the imperial cortege, with its conspicuous display of power and wealth. They gladly accepted our gifts, and willingly supplied us with a variety of excellent fruits and vegetables, as well as clean drinking water.

In the course of the following weeks, there would be ample opportunity for them to witness impressive parades and sumptuous royal celebrations.

First of all, there was, of course, Bairām Khān's long-awaited marriage to my sweet cousin Salīmā Sultān Bēgam.

Not surprisingly, Māham Anaga, Pīr Muhammad Khān and others had made more than a few attempts, not all of them very subtle, to convince me that this marriage was not in the best interest of the empire.

It would make Bairām Khān much too powerful, they argued. Was he not wakīl and sipahsālār of the empire already? Was that not more than enough for one man? Surely, they pleaded, it would be ill-advised to grant him the honour of also marrying the daughter of Humāyūn's sister Gulrukh, the granddaughter of the great Bābur pādshāh himself. This would all but elevate him to royal rank! It would only serve to make him even more arrogant and ambitious than he already was!

I must confess, the same thoughts had crossed my own mind as well, and truth be told, I would have very much preferred to marry Salīmā myself, but I really did not want to go back on a promise made by my father. Besides, I thought, there were other sides to the argument as well.

I discussed the matter in private with Shams-ud-dīn, whom I appreciated for his level-headedness and honesty. Although he was by no means a personal friend of Bairām Khān's, he fully agreed with me: I simply *had* to honour my father's promise.

No one had done more for the restoration of the empire than Bairām Khān. The soldiers and officers admired and revered him. Even if I wanted to, I simply could not afford to go back on a solemn promise made by my own father to such a deserving and important man. To do so, without a very clear and evident reason, would certainly undermine my reputation, not to mention my authority.

Moreover, Bairām Khān's marrying Salīmā was much more than a recognition and reward for services rendered; it was a renewed alliance between families. It would reconfirm and strengthen the ties of loyalty that united him and his household to the imperial family. Indeed, Salīmā's father Nūr-ud-dīn Muhammad belonged to the respected Naqshbandī family, which had been connected to the imperial dynasty for generations. Bairām Khān's mother being Naqshbandī as well, it was only becoming that he, in his position, should marry a girl from that family.

Had not the Prophet Muhammad himself declared that matrimonial alliances are the best way to increase friendship among families?

And so, it was done. I do not remember the exact date of the marriage – it must have been about five or six weeks after we had left Lāhor, early in the month of Bahman.[73]

Through my mother and other intermediaries, Salīmā had made it clear that she wished to give her consent in person, rather than through the office of a wakīl,[74] as was customary. In view of her high status and noble birth, nobody dared to argue with her. After all, it was permissible for an adult woman to give her consent herself – under both Shī'a law and our own. Even more importantly, thanks to Salīmā's decision, we did not have to solve the issue of who would act as her wakīl, for this would certainly have led to another argument, for instance, about whether or not it was appropriate for me as emperor to assume that role myself.

The *nikāh*, celebration of the marriage contract itself, took place in the courtyard of the small fortress, in the presence of only a few high-ranking witnesses, including myself. As you know, it is customary for the qāzī and the partners to assemble in a convenient place, other than a mosque, which made the suitable locations at Jālandhar rather limited in number.

After the men had all gathered in the courtyard, Salīmā came in, together with my mother and the other ladies from the imperial court and their main servants. I was glad to see she had not followed the admonitions of some of the mullāhs to veil her face with purdah; instead, she was wearing the classical dress of noble Turkish ladies, with muslin trousers under a long robe of beautiful, gold-coloured silk, and a tall, jewel-

---

73. Early February, 1558
74. In this context: legal representative, proxy holder; male attorney acting in the name and on behalf of the bride during the marriage contract proceedings.

studded headdress from which several strings of pearls were hanging. Her bejewelled hands, and her feet, as far as they were visible in the open-heeled silk slippers, were adorned with intricate henna patterns, which, according to the age-old custom, had been applied the night before.

When everybody was seated, the qāzī formally asked both spouses whether they consented to the marriage and the generous dowry.

He proceeded with a lengthy, rather boring sermon on marriage and the respective duties of spouses, after which the ceremony ended with the *fātiha*[75] being recited by all those present.

Like any other Muslim, I had recited the first Sūrah of the Holy Qur'ān countless times before. Yet, for some reason, this time was special. As I stood there, together with my closest friends and family on that solemn occasion, it was as if I heard those words for the first time. I suddenly became aware of god's majestic, humbling presence. Shivers went down my spine, as I slowly pronounced the solemn Arabic verses:

> *Bismi-Llāhi ar-Rahmāni ar-Rahīm*
> *Al-Hamdu li-Llāhi, Rabbi-l-Ālamīn*
> *Ar-Rahmāni ar-Rahīm*
> *Māliki yawmi-d-Dīn*
> *Iyyāka na'budu wa iyyāka nasta'īn*
> *Ihdinā-s-sirāta-l-mustaqīm*
> *Sirāta-lladhīna 'an 'amta 'alayhim*
> *Ghayri-l-maghdūbi 'alayhim*
> *Wa lā-d-dāllīn*
> *Āmīn*

In the name of god, the compassionate, the merciful,

> *Praise be to God, Lord of the Worlds;*
> *The Compassionate, the Merciful;*
> *Lord of the Day of Judgment*
> *You alone we worship, and Your aid we seek*
> *Lead us in the Straight Path*
> *The Path of those upon whom is Your Grace*

---

75. Fātiha: The opening chapter of the Holy Qur'ān.

> *Not of those upon whom is Your Wrath*
> *Nor the astray*
> *Amīn.*

The wedding ceremony having thus been concluded, Salīmā was carried in a closed pālkī to Bairām Khān's quarters, where, in accordance with our age-old customs, she would sit down to a repast with her old and new female friends and relatives, waiting for her husband to arrive after the night prayers.

Meanwhile, the proud bridegroom paraded through the streets on horseback, accompanied by his closest friends and allies, and a large procession with music and torches. That evening, the army fraternised with the people of the town, feasting on fowl, lamb, mutton, fish, vegetables and fruits in abundance.

I watched Bairām Khān, sitting at the banquet, happy, smiling, relaxed, and I must confess, I could not help feeling more than a bit jealous of him. Tonight, I thought, he would be sharing his bed with Salīmā. . . .

It is true that she wasn't what one would call a ravishing beauty, even when she was still young, but as I told you, I have always found her very attractive. It just shows on her face, the kind of person she is. She has that honest, engaging smile – everybody feels at ease with her, and wants to be with her.

Seeing her coming in, in those beautiful clothes, I thought she looked stunning, and once again, I deeply regretted that this sweet, attractive, healthy looking young woman would be marrying someone else.

Tonight, I thought, tonight he is going to undress her . . . I imagined what a blessing it would be, to lay down with her, to become one with her oh, how I envied him for it!

I could have had all the beautiful girls I wanted, but here I was, fantasising about my cousin. . . . For a number of days, in fact, I thought of little else than Salīmā, imagining what her naked body would look and feel like. . . .

Such is the enchantment of women, is it not, my son? No matter how many of them have come to share our beds, there will always be the other ones, to tempt us, to make us lose ourselves over them. . . .

We stayed encamped at Jālandhar for a few more weeks after the wedding.

Four hours, twenty-eight minutes into Yawm al-Khamis, the twentieth of Jumādā 'l Ūlā of 965, the sun left Esfand and entered the sign of Farvardīn, the new solar year;[76] we thus celebrated the beginning of the third year of my reign. And it seemed only weeks since I had ascended the throne. Such is the nature of time, my son – the months and years of our lives may seem long, but they slip through our fingers like desert sand. We must use them well, my son, we must not waste them in idleness, for they will never come back!

For three days and three nights, we feasted. There was a great hunting-party – a drive hunt, with hundreds of beaters. Back in town, there was of course plenty of food and drink for everyone, with music, dancing and fireworks. For the first time, I had myself weighed on a large pair of scales, and to everybody's joy and amazement, my weight in coins of gold was distributed among the soldiers and the local villagers. The common people should see their pādshāh like god, the lord of the universe, who gives without being asked.

After the celebrations, we left Jālandhar, and headed further south towards Dillī.

When we had crossed the Sutlej River near the town of Ludhiana, messengers informed us about a minor uprising near Hissār – one of the so many I have had to deal with in the course of my reign, and which is of no interest here. We ordered Pīr Muhammad to head straight south through the countryside, with the main body of the army to crush the insurgents, whereas Bairām Khān and I continued along the main road towards Dillī with a smaller army contingent. We would halt underway, at Sirhind, to pay our respects to my father's mortal remains.

Two and a half years ago, when Hemū's army was marching towards Dillī, faithful and prudent servants had taken my father's coffin to a safer place further northwest. Not surprisingly, they had chosen the town of Sirhind: It was an auspicious location, for it was there that my father had defeated Sikandar Sūr's army.

---

76. Corresponds to the late evening of Thursday, 10 March 1558 of the Julian calendar (Muslim days are counted from sunset to sunset). Esfand: Pisces; Farvardīn: Aries.

My father's coffin had remained there, laid out in the central hall of the small fortress guarding the town. Arriving at the hall, before entering, Bairām Khān and I knelt down and touched the doorstep with our foreheads. The room was dimly lit, with only a few candles; there were no guards or custodians of any kind inside.

The coffin had been placed on a small platform and covered with a large white shroud touching the floor. I looked at the oblong shape of the coffin under the shroud. It was rounded at the corners; the head being slightly broader than the foot. As is customary, it was oriented north-south; inside the coffin, I knew my father's head was turned to the right, facing west, towards Mekkah.

I was relieved to notice that there was not even a hint of the stench of death in the room. The coffin must have been well-sealed, I thought; or maybe there were two of them, one inside the other; or maybe, time had already completed its hideous work on my father's body, and reduced it to dry bones. . . .

With difficulty, I managed to suppress these inappropriate musings about the corpse inside the coffin, and occupied my mind with prayer and pious reflections.

I prayed to god that He would admit my father into eternal paradise, together with all the rest of us, and that He would help me to protect my dominions, and rule justly over their inhabitants.

I even prayed to the dead body in the coffin, although I knew very well that it is an abomination for a true believer to pray to anybody or anything other than god Himself.

'My dear father,' I implored, 'if you can, please help me and guide me, grant me wisdom and strength, grant that I may be a worthy successor to you and to our glorious ancestors.'

After a few minutes of silence, Bairām Khān took out a small, hand-written prayer book from a small leather purse attached to his belt. Speaking slowly, word for word, he recited:

> Peace be upon you, O dwellers of the grave!
> May Allāh grant you and us protection!
> We pray to Allāh for security, for ourselves and for you.
> You are those who have gone before us, and we are following you.
> We will meet you, if it pleases Allāh.

We stayed for a few more minutes and left the hall, walking backwards and bowing repeatedly, as if we were taking our leave from a living king.

'As soon as feasible, I will have my father's body brought back to Dillī,' I said to Bairām Khān, looking back over my shoulder as we rode out of Sirhind the next morning. 'I will have a splendid mausoleum built for him, Khān Bābā! It will be one of the most magnificent buildings the world has ever seen, more beautiful and imposing than even Temür's tomb at Samarqand! Thousands of years from now, people will say: "Surely, this must be the resting place of the greatest emperor of all time!"'

Bairām Khān nodded approvingly. 'I am sure your revered father will appreciate that very much. However, there is one thing you can do, which will please him even more!'

'And what would that be?' I asked.

He paused, put his hand on my shoulder, and looked at me, like he had done that afternoon, back at the palace in Dillī, when he had told me that living one's life is like writing a storybook.

'Make him proud, Your Majesty.'

Ninth Letter

دلّی، آگرا

Dilli, Agrā

We proceeded southwest via Samāna towards Hissār, to check on the military operations down there. As we had expected, the rebellion had been crushed by the time we arrived. After a few days of rest in the town, we headed east towards Dillī, and reached the capital on the fourth of Ordībehesht.[77]

The people were visibly more at ease and enthusiastic than at the time of our first triumphant entry into the city. Clearly, after a period of understandable scepticism, people had finally started to believe that Emperor Humāyūn's young successor was here to stay. After all, his armies had defeated the mighty Hemū and Sikandar Sūr; who was now left to challenge him?

We stayed in Dillī throughout the summer and the rainy season. After six and a half months, we decided to move the imperial court to Āgrā, fifty-two kos southward, as we believed this would help us strengthen our hold on the southern border regions.

We travelled downstream on the Jumna River, in an impressive fleet of flat-bottomed barks, their planks beautifully adorned with precious

---

77. Thursday, 14 April 1558 of the Julian calendar.

silks; crowds gathered in awe wherever we were passing by. They would all return to their humble dwellings and, as it should be, spread the news about the unseen splendour of their ruler.

We arrived in Āgrā on the eighteenth of Ābān.[78] I was pleased to find that the city was living up to its reputation, despite the heat of the season. I could see why my grandfather Bābur pādshāh had set up residence there. Although the heat was not any less than what it was in Dillī, the breeze on the river did bring some refreshment, and many well-kept gardens added to the attractiveness of the landscape. The arable land produced excellent fruits and vegetables. I would not go as far as the local poets and claim that the river Jumna 'would make Baghdād ashamed of the Tigris and Egypt of the Nile', but I have to admit, it did have something distinctly majestic over it, and its water was indeed limpid, light and digestible.

I took up residence in the Bādalgarha citadel, and witnessed how the matters of government were put into proper order. As the fort was in a rather dilapidated state, we immediately ordered repair and expansion works, which, after a few years would impart to it the majestic, overpowering aspect it currently has – for it is good that the people of the land get to see the greatness of their king reflected in the grandeur of his buildings.

Twice a week, we discussed the affairs of state in the diwān-i-khas,[79] with Bairām Khān and all the 'officers and pillars of the empire', as they were called, in attendance.

Things went well for the empire. Rest assured, I will not bore you with a detailed account of each of our conquests and victories, my son. You can read about them in the archive records, and Abd-ul Qādir Badā'unī's chronicles, and of course, in Abū-l Fazl's writings.

Suffice it to say, our armies did very well on all fronts.

In the west, we managed to capture Fort Jitaran in Rājpūtānā,[80] despite fierce resistance. As Abū-l Fazl put it, 'many of the stiff-necked

---

78. Sunday, 30 October 1558 of the Julian calendar.
79. Diwān-i-khas: Hall of private audience
80. Near Jodhpur

Rājpūts were conducted to the abyss of annihilation, and the country was cleared of the rubbish of stubborn rebels.'

Perhaps more importantly, in the south, we conquered the important city of Gwālīor, which of course greatly contributed to the safety of our borders.

And far up north, last but not least, the heavily fortified citadel of Jammū fell into our hands – an important first step towards the later conquest of our beloved, beautiful Kashmīr. . . .

Our strategy towards our enemies remained unchanged. Those who dared to oppose us were 'levelled with the dust of annihilation', or 'hastened to the hell of extinction', as it is phrased in the chronicles. However, those who were smart or coward enough to surrender the keys of their fortresses, soon found out, to their own surprise and relief, they had in fact 'opened the gates to their own wishes'. . . .

This is the way a wise emperor should operate, my son. Towards the obedient, he should be the strong and reliable guardian of peace, safety and prosperity; to those who oppose him, he should be inescapable destruction.

Never forget, people are moved by mainly two things: their own self-interest, and fear; a wise ruler knows how to make judicious use of both.

I once heard an instructive anecdote about this. I think it was Mīr Abdul Latīf who once told it to me, about a great emperor in Rūm, who lived many centuries ago, before the advent of the Franks, who at that time were still savages, dwelling in dark, cold, damp forests. It was the time when Rūm's wise men no longer believed in their pagan gods of old, and had yet to become followers of Īsā,[81] a time where people had no other god than their own conscience.

This wise emperor compared the bond between a sovereign and his subjects to a precious, beautiful ring: It should be forged out of the gold of love, adorned with the gems of kindness and magnanimity, but also, hardened through an appropriate alloy of rigour and fear, for pure gold is too soft a material to create a durable jewel.

---

81. Īsā: Jesus

I was, however, barely sixteen years of age at the time, and neither wise nor strong enough to put this into practice.

What can I say, my son? What else can I do, but confess that my life was out of my control? It pleases me not at all to think back on this period, but I have to, for your sake. Please understand, my son, the uncertainty that has been tormenting you these last years: I had to bear that as well! When you become pādshāh, you will face problems very similar to mine. You will soon find out that the enemies at the borders of your realm are usually not your greatest concern. Fighting wars is hazardous and difficult, but having your own people do what you want them to, is often much more difficult an art! There is a lot of truth in the supplication Abū-l Fazl used to pray in mock despair, whenever a dispute at court annoyed him: 'My god, deliver me from my friends, and I will gladly deal with my enemies!'

The atmosphere at the imperial court in Lāhor had been bad enough, but now, it was becoming untenable. The animosity between Bairām Khān's followers and the camp of Māham Anaga and Pīr Muhammad Khān had clearly turned into outright hatred. Behind some outer semblance of unity during the audiences in the diwān-i-khas, there was nothing but spite and intrigue, every protagonist doing whatever he could to thwart his rival's ambitions and discredit him in my eyes and those of the others.

It is hard to believe, and even harder to admit that a strong man like me was unable to call to order a bunch of squabbling, self-righteous courtiers, but what was I to do? After all, I was only sixteen at the time, still very inexperienced. And to make matters worse, I was alone: Apart from my mother, far away in Dillī, who was there to turn to for support and impartial advice?

Not a month went by, without some or other crisis or quarrel between Bairām Khān and the rest, where I would find myself idly standing by, powerless, as if I had nothing to say about it.

'His Majesty was testing the men of the age', Abū-l Fazl wrote. . . . The truth is, His Majesty did not know what to do! I just could not afford to take sides, without risking chaos, possibly even civil war.

And so, I did nothing at all.

Just like in the old days back in Lāhor, I seized every possible occasion to get away from the palace. As usual, Abū-l Fazl made brave attempts to describe my behaviour in polite euphemisms:

'His Majesty was continually engaged in hunting deer with the cītā, and in elephant fights, and such other external matters, which the superficial man regards as matters of insouciance, and left political and financial matters to the lovers thereof.'

Indeed, I would spend days, if not weeks, in a row, in the beautiful hunting grounds south and west of Āgrā. There, amidst the fields and the wilderness, in the awe-inspiring silence, far away from everything and everybody, I did not have to think about the palace and its quarrels. Nothing was more pleasing to my eyes than the graceful step of my leopards, and the sight of my hawks soaring majestically above the land. In the excitement of the chase and the killing, I found peace of mind.

Back in the city, I spent as much time as I could with the soldiers, taking great pride in showing off my growing strength and martial skills. Indeed, I had become one of the very best marksmen in the army, with both musket and bow. I was an accomplished expert at loading and firing any type of cannon or rocket. I wrestled all but the very strongest men to the ground, and there was absolutely no one who could handle animals the way I could. A worthy descendant of my Mongol and Turkish ancestors, I would ride the most unruly horses with the greatest of ease. The most vicious, murderous bull elephants, real man-killers like Dilsankār, Hawāi, Faujbidār, Damūdar, Jhalpa, Lakhna: I rode them all, better than any of the mahāwats; meek like lambs, they became under my hand.

In the palace, I deliberately avoided private conversations, with Bairām Khān, Shams-ud-dīn, or anybody else. I was tired of all the quarrels, the accusations, the self-serving advice, and the thinly veiled reproaches. When my presence in the diwān-i-khas was not required, I would retire to my quarters, usually in the presence of one or the other sweet, docile girl who was proud to comfort me with her firm, soft body.

Unfortunately, demons cannot be driven out by running away from them. The softness of women's breasts, or the excitement found in hunting or sports provide but a passing fuddle of joy. He who tries to escape from the world in the joys of leisure, will soon discover that neglect of duty unsettles the mind, and fills it with remorse and sadness.

The months went by. They became seasons, then years. I was now seventeen years of age, strong as a bull, in possession of all the wealth and luxury anybody could ever want, but unhappy. It was a time of insecurity, and darkness of thought. I felt like a prisoner, in my own palace, in my own life. It seemed to me that the animals in my stables were more free than I was. With each passing moon, I became increasingly unsatisfied with my life, and hated myself for it. . . .

It is not hard to understand why all the elaborate rituals, the hands and foreheads touching the ground, the flowery titles and superlatives are of little help when deep down, one knows one does not deserve them. 'Become the great emperor you know you can be,' Bairām Khān had told me, back in Dillī. How? When? Would I ever be able to attain such a lofty goal? Would I ever become as strong as him? In matters of government, he never seemed to get bored or tired; he always asked the right questions, always took the right decisions. . . .

His attitude, nevertheless, was quickly becoming a source of great concern to me. Something about him had changed. The rivalry with Māham Anaga and Pīr Muhammad Khān had made him irritable, suspicious, and even more stubborn than before. At times, he behaved worse than a squabbling old harem hag. He could not stand anybody disagreeing with him, on anything. Even the slightest sign of divergence, the weakest opposition was taken as a personal insult, as an attempt to take away his privileges as regent of the empire.

Despite my advancing adolescence, he kept on running the affairs of state as if I was still a thirteen year old. In fact, rather than seeking my involvement and approval, as he should have done, it seemed he was taking more and more decisions on his own. Was he not supposed to inform me, discuss things with me? How long was he actually planning to hang on to power? Not once did he speak to me about handing over power, about retiring to another function.

I did not fully realise it at the time, but Bairām Khān, for all his hard work and dedication, was much less capable a leader than I would later become, at least in one important respect. He constantly made that fatal mistake that so many people in positions of power tend to make: being too preoccupied with his own thoughts and activities to take notice of the forces around.

This is not how power should be exercised, my son. A wise ruler is a keen observer of men and their motives; he knows how to be obeyed, respected, loved and feared at the same time. He will use gentle persuasion, or brutal violence, as required by the circumstances.

But Bairām Khān, unfortunately for him, was a soldier, not a court diplomat. He seemed to know only one way to get what he wanted: ordering people around, as if they were dogs, and brutal repression at the slightest sign of resistance. He seemed to care very little that it made him unpopular, and his heavy-handedness made the ranks of his enemies grow larger by the day.

Maybe, I thought to myself, he was just getting old: More often than not, people approaching old age tend to confuse stubbornness with wisdom. But whatever the cause of his behaviour, it was really becoming a major problem.

And so, day by day, he and I grew further apart. . . .

I am really too tired to recount each and every one of the incidents that alienated me from him; they do not add much value to the story I want to tell you, my son. Suffice it to say, not a month went by without one. Each time, I would find myself confronted with decisions that had been taken, things that had been done, situations that had been created, that had been forced down my throat, and that I could do nothing about. . . .

Despite the outrage of all the Sunnīs at the court, I did nothing when Bairām Khān unilaterally appointed Shaykh Gadā'ī Kambū, a fellow Shī'a, to the important office of sadr, responsible for all the imperial lands and the administration of pensions and subsidies. After all, there was no reason for me to intervene. Shaykh Gadā'ī was an extremely competent man, and did his work well. Young and inexperienced though I was, I was wise and broad-minded enough to realise that god stands way above the petty differences between Sunnī and Shī'a. Competence, decency, wisdom and the like: they neither begin nor end at any man-made border, and neither do their opposites. . . .

In spite of Māham Anaga's desperate pleadings, I did not intervene when Bairām Khān sent her son Adham Khān to the fortress of Hatkānt near Gwālīor, where the troublesome Bhadauriyah tribe was in revolt.

After all, I thought to myself, Bairām Khān's motives may have been self-serving, but he was probably right – that truculent and quarrelsome fellow would indeed come of much better use fighting the enemies of the empire. And indeed, Adham Khān did quite well. 'With god's help, he subdued the country, and the seditious received fitting punishment', the chronicles report. . . .

But when Bairām Khān had the audacity to unilaterally dismiss Pīr Muhammad Khān, ordering him to turn in his army standard and kettledrums, and to depart on the sacred journey to Mekkah, I realised things really could not go on like this. Bairām Khān may have had ample reason to be displeased with Pīr Muhammad—it was certainly true that he had become annoyingly arrogant—but the dismissal of a senior official is no small matter. Was it not outrageous that this had been decided and executed without my permission?

I was clearly not the only one to be worried about this state of affairs.

Only a few days after Pīr Muhammad's dismissal, I received a visit from my mother, who had travelled down all the way from Dillī to see me. I did not have to guess what she wanted to talk to me about.

We exchanged a few civilities and went to my private quarters.

'My son, we need to talk,' she said, without any further introduction. 'What are you going to do about Bairām Khān?'

'What do you mean, Mother?' I asked.

'I think you know very well what I mean. Your father has been dead for three years now. You are becoming a grown man, my son. It is high time you started taking matters seriously.'

I wanted to answer something, but she impatiently put up her hand.

'I know what you're going to say, and I agree: Bairām Khān *is* a competent man. But my question is, how much longer is this going to last? Power is a dangerous thing, my son! It poisons even the purest of minds. What if this man gets inspired by Shēr Khān's example? What if he decides to claim the throne for himself? What if he shifts loyalty to Kāmrān's son? And even if he does remain loyal to you, what kind of a king will you become, my son, with a man like that next to you? I cannot believe you would be prepared to settle for a life of indolence in the shade of your own prime minister, like Mubāriz Khān Sūr who was eclipsed by his own prime minister, Hemū. Can't you see how he is eliminating his rivals one by one? Can't you see how he has been putting his Shī'a followers in the highest positions? What gave him the right to confiscate Pīr Muhammad's property when he returned from Gujarāt to Rājputānā, instead of continuing towards Mekkah? Do you think your ancestors would have approved of that? A king does not allow others to take important decisions like that in his stead! A king does not beg, my son: he commands! A king does not hope: he makes sure!'

Noticing the growing anger on my face, she smiled, clearly relieved to see that her words were having the effect intended.

'Nothing has been lost yet, my son. You are still very young, and it is normal that you rely on people who are more experienced than you are. But I'm warning you, time is running out! You are in the fourth year of your reign; you are seventeen years of age. It is time for you to assume full power!'

'What do you think, then, I should do about Bairām Khān?' I asked. 'Surely, I cannot just dismiss him, after everything he has done for us?'

'He has done a lot to be grateful for,' she admitted. 'However, I am confident that there are ways to get rid of him without forgetting your debt of gratitude. There are so many territories to be administered, so many new ones to be conquered. . . .'

It took me a few more weeks before I finally decided to act.

Maybe if Bairām Khān would have bothered to come and see me, if we would have had a chance to talk about all this, I might still have changed my mind . . . I might still have found a more graceful way out.

But it was not to be. A few days later, probably without even being aware of it, he made, what I decided, was his final mistake.

In less than two weeks' time, two of my favourite personal mahāwats, both of them low-caste Hindūs, were executed on his direct order. One of them, a gray-haired, almost toothless, thin man of about fifty, had not been able to restrain an imperial mast elephant, when it suddenly attacked and killed one of Bairām Khān's animals. The poor fellow was beheaded on the spot.

The second one, a boy my age or perhaps a bit younger, lost his life when the elephant he was guiding along the banks of the Jumna River suddenly dashed into the water and almost overturned the small boat on which Bairām Khān happened to be resting. I was just on my way out of the city, leaving for a short hunting trip, when I saw soldiers dragging the mahāwat's corpse away. His head was still lying in the sand, staring at the sky with empty eyes, its mouth half-open, as if it was about to ask how all this could have happened.

Only with great effort was I able to hold back my tears. Probably Bairām Khān had not given it a moment's thought when he had this lad killed. After all, it was only a low-caste servant, an infidel at that, who had endangered his life. An example had to be set. However, I had shared so many fine hours with that simple mahāwat. I had known him, liked him; I had made fun of the Hindustānī mistakes he made in that clumsy Persian of his. . . . And now, without my permission, because of this one silly incident, he was dead.

It is of course just and appropriate that rulers have the right to life and death of their subjects. After all, what would the world come to if there were no punishment? There would be no authority! As the ancient Hindū laws of Manu put it, 'the whole world is kept in order by punishment, for a guiltless man is hard to find. . . .'[82]

However, we kings and holders of authority should never forget that god alone is the source of all power, including our own. His will, and His will alone, should be guiding us in all our decisions. Whether we let someone go free, or sentence him to death, our sole aim should be to serve god, and god alone.

We should, therefore, never confuse the appeasement of our own anger with justice, my son. This is why, already in the early years of my reign, I gave strict orders never to carry out any death sentence, unless and until I had repeated it three times during the same day – lest, in my first anger, I did something irreparable. Indeed, to err may be human, my son, but in matters of justice, error is inhuman!

There was one good thing about the poor mahāwat's death – for the very first time in my life, I had been given a good reason to hate Bairām Khān. And perhaps even more importantly: for the very first time in my life, I knew my own judgement to be better than his. Suddenly, it had become much easier for me to remove him from office. Finally, I made up my mind: Bairām Khān had to go.

The die had been cast. I had taken one of the most painful decisions of my life: I was about to dispose of the man to whom I owed everything.

---

82. Quoted by Stanley Wolpert, p. 201.

It gives me neither pride nor joy to think back on this, my son, but what else was I to do? Surely, you, of all people, should be able to understand what I was going through! When you are born a king, there comes a time when you must take things in your own hands, no matter how great the merits of your predecessor – is it not so, my son?

It took me several more weeks to work out my plan of action. If I may say so myself: I handled it well.

I needed to tread carefully: Bairām Khān was not an opponent to be underestimated. Slowly, carefully, biding my time, I developed my plan.

As I expected, Māham Anaga and Adham Khān were more than eager to help, and I knew I could also count on Shams-ud-dīn's loyalty. Secret messages were sent to Pīr Muhammad Khān, who was in Rājputānā after having travelled as far as Gujarāt, to keep himself ready to return as soon as possible.

Usually, I spoke to each one of them separately when the occasion presented itself. When Bairām Khān was not around, we would meet in my private quarters and discuss the appropriate course of action.

'It is easy enough,' Adham Khān had said with his usual impetuousness. 'There are plenty of opportunities to kill the bastard! If Your Majesty so wishes, I can do it myself! Bairām Khān does not like me, but he trusts me enough to allow me in his presence. Yes, I could do it on any one of the next few days . . . at a moment when his personal guards are not around, or when we visit the mosque, or when we are on our way to a meeting with you. I could also invite him to my quarters for dinner, under some pretext or other, saying I need to discuss something with him in private, and have him assassinated, as soon as he comes in, like he did with poor old Tardī Beg!'

Have Bairām Khān assassinated, after so many years of faithful service? No, I wanted nothing to do with it! To this day, I am proud and grateful I did not take the easy way out – it would have haunted me for the rest of my life.

'There must be another way,' I said. 'A man like Bairām Khān does not deserve a fate like that.'

Adham Khān clearly did not share my views.

'Your Majesty is most kind and magnanimous. However, he should keep in mind that this is a necessary measure for the higher good of his throne! Your Majesty's kindness of heart prevents Him from seeing the clear and imminent danger this man represents. I swear, Your Majesty, if I were in your position, I would not be too sure about his loyalty! Just look at what this man has done over the last few years: there is simply no limit to his ambition and arrogance! Sooner or later, Your Majesty will see that this Shi'a bastard will show his true colours! Sooner or later—'

I raised my hand to silence him.

'I am profoundly moved by my *koka*'s[83] loyalty and devotion, and I am deeply grateful for his courageous offer, but my mind is made up: I will not have Bairām Khān assassinated. Not only would it be unjust, it would also be unwise! Bairām Khān has served my blessed father Humāyūn and me for so many years – his support has been invaluable to us! The officers and soldiers in the army love and respect him, and for good reason – he is an excellent general! If I would have this man executed, after everything he has done for me, how can I expect the others to continue to trust and respect me?'

Māham Anaga wanted to say something, but Shams-ud-dīn interrupted: 'Let us not discuss this any longer. His Majesty is right – killing Bairām Khān would be a grave sin in the eyes of Allāh; moreover, it would probably do His Majesty's interests more harm than good!'

Adham Khān said nothing in reply. From the look on his face, it was clear he was not convinced at all. Knowing his violent temper, I sensed there was a real danger of him going ahead with his plan anyway.

'If Bairām Khān gets assassinated, without my direct order,' I added, looking Adham Khān straight in the eye, 'I would have no alternative but to have the murderer executed!'

Adham Khān bowed, visibly angered and insulted.

'As Your Majesty commands. I hope Your Majesty will never regret this kindness. . . .'

There was an uncomfortable silence.

'How should we then proceed?' Māham Anaga asked. 'Surely, it would be dangerous to wait any longer! Your Majesty, in his kindness, may still not believe it, but this Shi'a bastard is quickly taking control over the army! Over the last two years, he has given the rank of "commander

---

83. Koka: Foster brother. Akbar and Adham Khān had both been wet-nursed by Māham Anaga.

of five thousand" to no less than twenty-five men, all of them his own personal supporters! Soon, all the army officers will be his personal vassals! If we wait any longer, it will be too late – there will be no army left to support us!'

'Who says we need to wait?' I said, trying to sound unperturbed. 'I can do exactly what he did to Pīr Muhammad Khān: I can grant him leave to depart to Mekkah. He is a deeply religious man, and has not completed the Hajj yet – he may even welcome the idea! However, you are right – we must also be prepared to deal with the situation if he refuses to go. It is never a good idea to leave matters of high importance to someone else's discretion! I think we had better assemble a strong fighting force, outside Āgrā – up in Dillī, for instance. If Bairām Khān does rise against me, which I still don't believe he will, we will be in a good position to defend ourselves and crush the rebellion before he has had a chance to organise himself properly.'

And so it was done. On Sehsanbeh, the ninth of Farvardīn of the fifth year,[84] we left Āgrā, with only a small escort, in order not to arouse suspicion, on the pretext of another hunting trip. I admit, it was not very glorious, nor courageous, but I do not think there was another way.

As prudence dictated, we took Abū-l Qāsim, son of Kāmrān, with us. If Bairām Khān would choose to rebel, he would at least not be able to use a grandson of Bābur to legitimise his uprising. The amīrs were bound by an oath of loyalty to us, but it would be foolish to provide them with an excuse to join a rebellion. . . .

We headed north and reached Sikandara. As the latest messages from Dillī had indicated that my mother was not feeling well, it did not arouse any suspicion that I ostensibly changed my mind about the hunting trip, and decided to travel to Dillī, to pay her a visit. A message was sent to Shihab-ud-dīn Ahmad Khān, the governor of the city, to strengthen the defences of the fort and prepare to receive us.

After a few days, we reached Dillī, without any noteworthy incident. As soon as we arrived, messages were sent to all the amīrs, informing them that now that I had reached adulthood, I had decided to relieve

---

84. Tuesday, 17 March 1560

Bairām Khān of his command and take the matters of government in my own hands.

They say that Bairām Khān simply refused to believe the first rumours about his impending dismissal. When, after a few days, he finally realised that what he had been hearing true, he reportedly sat still for hours, completely silent, his face wet with tears.

Yet, he flatly refused to take up arms against me, rejecting the advice of Shaykh Gadā'ī, Walī Beg and his other supporters. When they tried to insist, he reportedly shouted:

'Now, leave me alone! I do not aspire to the throne. My aim was the conquest of Hindustān, and now, my work being done, I only want the king's pleasure. . . .'

There was much unrest, not to say, panic, among the courtiers back in Dillī, when after a few days, reports came in that Bairām Khān was advancing on the city. Preparations were made for war, but that failed to put any of them at ease; there were even a few cowards who started suggesting we had better retreat to Lāhor, or even to Kābul . . . All of them were extremely relieved, when messengers delivered a letter from Bairām Khān, in which he 'respectfully requested to be granted the favour of being allowed a private audience with His Majesty'.

Of all the things I have done wrong in my life, this is probably the one I am most ashamed of: I refused to see him. Māham Anaga and the others had of course warned me against receiving him, arguing that it was a ruse, that I was endangering my life, but that was not the reason. I simply could not bear to see him face to face – I was too afraid of the shame, the guilt, the remorse. . . .

In reply to his request, I sent him an official firmān, ordering him to return to Āgrā, and giving him the permission to turn his attention to the bliss of pilgrimage. Despite Māham Anaga's pleas to the contrary, I did add some friendly words, assuring him that he was like a father to me and dear to my heart, and that I would remit to him whatever extent of land he wished in Hindustān, so that his servants might remit him the proceeds, harvest by harvest, year by year.

Again, Bairām Khān complied with my request and prepared himself for travel. Quietly, he divested himself of his imperial standard, kettledrums and insignia, and sent them to the imperial court. To his supporters, who still tried to convince him to tread the path of rebellion, he reportedly answered:

'This is not what I want to see written in the book of my life!'

He set out to the Panjāb, and proceeded from there through Rājputānā towards Gujarāt, where he would take a ship to Mekkah.

The story would have ended then and there, had I not made a capital blunder – allowing Pīr Muhammad Khān, who had returned to Dillī as soon as he heard about Bairām Khān's dismissal, to follow him to Rājputānā. As he put it, he wanted to go there with a group of cavalry, to 'keep an eye on Bairām' and 'pack him off to Mekkah'.

I should have known much, much better. A man like Bairām Khān might accept injustice, but never an insult. Sure enough, when he became aware of Pīr Muhammad's approach, he promptly turned around to fight. At the first sight of Bairām Khān's Turkomān horse archers, Pīr Muhammad Khān ran like a rabbit. . . .

Much more worried than I cared to admit, I tried to repair the mistake, sending Bairām another firmān, in which I ordered him to continue on his pilgrimage, but it was too late. The matter would now have to be settled on the battlefield.

Bairām Khān and his small army quickly turned east, advancing into the Panjāb. He left his family in the fort of Bathinda, then headed south towards Jālandhar, clearly intending to take the important city of Lāhor.

Hasty preparations were made, and we left Dillī, sending Shams-ud-dīn ahead with a strong and mobile force, to halt or at least slow down Bairām Khān's advance. I followed at the head of the main body of the army.

The unthinkable had happened – the imperial army was marching against Bairām Khān.

Tenth Letter

بیرام خان

Bāirām Khān (I)

Shams-ud-dīn did not waste any time; driving his troops forward, he managed to block Bairām Khān's advance near the village of Gūnācūr, in the area of Jālandhar.

He sent emissaries, in a last attempt to convince Bairām Khān to submit, but it was too late: There comes a time when a man like him will stand and fight.

Morale among the imperial army was low. Bairām Khān's fighting force, though vastly outnumbered, was not to be underestimated – its men were excellent soldiers, devoted to their leader, and commanded by the best general of their age.

Bairām Khān attacked immediately, thus preventing Shams-ud-dīn to deploy any artillery, and taking advantage of the understandable fatigue of our soldiers and animals after their hasty advance. He had divided his small fighting force into two wings: a cavalry vanguard, led by his main lieutenant Walī Beg; and the main group, which he commanded himself and consisted of about fifty excellent fighting elephants, supported by another cavalry force.

Shams-ud-dīn's vanguard cavalry, though clearly superior in number, was quickly routed by the fierce onslaught of Bairām's Turkomāns. Many imperial cavalrymen turned around and fled without a fight, more out of fear than by enemy action.

Bairām Khān did not hesitate to seize the opportunity. He instantly attacked the main body of Shams-ud-dīn's army, which was standing on a small ridge behind a wide rice paddy. In an unorthodox but bold move, he sent his elephants up front, in a direct attack through the rice field, while he and his cavalry came out from behind on the left flank, leaving the rice field on his right.

If things would have worked out as he had planned them, he just might have pulled it off: Shams-ud-dīn's army would have been caught in a deadly pincer, its flank cut off and unable to move, while the centre was being swept away by the elephants.

Fortunately, however, with god's help, his plan failed. The paddy, planted with *shali* autumn rice, happened to be quite deep, and its bottom soil unusually soft; Bairām Khān's elephants, advancing only very slowly, sinking almost up to their bellies into the mud, got bogged down, harassed by clouds of arrows. A number of their leading mahāwats died, and the attack faltered.

Shams-ud-dīn, an excellent soldier himself, was now free to launch a massive counterattack on his right flank, and block Bairām Khān's charge before it could reach his position.

Bairām Khān had gambled and lost – the battle was over for him. Unless he retreated immediately, his forces, much smaller in number than ours, would soon be encircled and annihilated. Only thanks to his generalship and the discipline of his men did he manage to get away with the majority of his army, but he paid a very heavy price for it. Walī Beg, badly wounded in the battle, and several trusted officers were taken in as prisoners, and a number of excellent men fell, while covering Bairām's retreat.

Shams-ud-dīn chased the fleeing enemy for about two kos. Then, he prudently abandoned the pursuit and turned back with his army, joining the rest of the imperial forces, which by that time were encamped at Sirhind.

The news of Shams-ud-dīn's victory was met with elation. A major battle had been won against the great Bairām Khān! Who could still harbour any doubt about the invincibility of my stars? This victory was nothing less than a sign from god Himself!

Our euphoria reached a new climax when Mun'im Khān joined us from Kābul, at the head of a large and well-equipped army.

Sumptuous celebrations were held. Shams-ud-dīn of course was celebrated as a conquering hero and received lavish gifts, including the robes of honour, standards and kettledrums that had once belonged to Bairām Khān, as well as the lofty title of Khān A'āzim. The office of wakīl and the title of Khān Khanān, however, I gave to Mun'im Khān: a ruler is wise to divide power, lest his servant becomes his rival. . . .

The prisoners were dragged before me, chains around their necks and feet. I should have felt joy and pride, but I could not help feeling deeply saddened at the sight of these excellent, brave men who had now become my enemies. I refused to have them executed, in spite of pleas to the contrary: I sent them all to jail instead.

With the exception of Walī Beg, who died of his wounds in prison, all of them were later pardoned, and in time, reinstated as officers of the imperial army. I was right – they all served me well.

After a few more days of leisure and celebration and a brief visit to the city of Lāhor, we moved north towards the Siwāliks, to deal with Bairām Khān: Scouts had informed us that he had withdrawn to the stronghold of Talwāra in the midst of the hills, and was trying to forge an alliance with the local Hindū rājah. As we outnumbered him more than fifteen to one, morale and confidence in our camp was high – there could be no serious doubt about the final outcome.

Defeated enemies never fail to attract would-be heroes, eager to earn themselves a place in history. Sultān Husayn Jalāir, the leader of our vanguard, was such a man. When our scouts first located Bairām Khān's exact whereabouts, he did not want to wait for reinforcements, and chose to attack Bairām Khān, with forces only slightly superior to those of his opponent.

It proved to be a fatal mistake. The battle was an outright disaster: Our vanguard was completely wiped out, with little or no losses to Bairām Khān; and Husayn Jalāir paid for his foolish intrepidness with his life.

All of a sudden, things were not so easy anymore. Our forces were still vastly superior to Bairām's, but this humiliating defeat could change everything. Who was to stop him now from heading further west? What if he escaped into the hills? What if he managed to recruit new allies? He only needed to win over one or two influential amīrs, and the tables could turn very easily!

While we were still having heated discussions about the strategy to be followed, guards announced the arrival of Jamāl Khān, one of Bairām Khān's most trusted officers.

He knelt down, respectfully, but unafraid.

'I have been instructed by Bairām Khān Badakhshāni, to offer Your Imperial Majesty his total and unconditional surrender, and to hand over this letter.'

Mun'im Khān accepted the letter in my stead, and read it out aloud:

Your Imperial Majesty,

Having reached the evening of my life, which I spent almost entirely in faithful service to Your Majesty and his august father, who is nested in the garden of paradise, I now find myself Your Majesty's enemy. Never before has my heart been this heavy and filled with sorrow.

As Allāh Himself and all His angels are my witnesses, I would much rather die in agonising pain than continue war and strife between us! Too many good men have died in a fight which should never have taken place! If Allāh, in His unending mercy, would grant me the bliss of paradise, in spite of my many sins and wrongdoings, I would not dare to enter it, for fear of meeting Your Majesty's revered father, and having to explain to him that I had become Your Majesty's enemy.

I have, therefore, decided that I would much rather die as Your Majesty's prisoner and slave, than go on living in freedom and in conflict with him; therefore, I offer Your Majesty my complete and unconditional surrender.

I humbly implore Your Majesty to find mercy in his heart, and pardon my loyal men and their officers. It would not only be an act of magnanimity, worthy of a noble king, it would also further Your Majesty's interests. They are all experienced and outstanding soldiers, and each and every one of them has, under my personal supervision, taken a solemn oath on the Holy Qur'ān and on the graves of their forefathers, that they will serve Your Majesty until death.

As for myself, I have no other wish but to undergo the sentence Your Majesty will pronounce against me, or to retire to places of holiness and wisdom, and prepare myself to meet my Maker.

There was a long silence.

'Jamāl Khān,' I finally asked, 'why is it that Bairām Khān has decided to surrender now, after having won an important victory against the imperial army vanguard?'

'I do not really know, Your Majesty. All I can say is that after the battle, we brought him the head of Sultān Husayn Jalāir, who had fallen in the battle. He held it in his hands, and looked at it for what seemed like hours.

'"Has it come to this," he said, "that I have to look at the severed head of a man who has been an officer in my own army for years? How many battles has this man fought by my side, only to die as my enemy? This madness has to end, here and now!"

'Some of us still tried to convince him that thanks to his victory against Sultān Husayn Jalāir, he was now in a much stronger position to move to the northwest and return with a much stronger army – but he just put up his hand, and replied: "I am sick of the world and its affairs!"'

The next day, it was announced that Bairām Khān had arrived in person at the confines of the imperial army camp. I had him escorted to my tent immediately.

For a moment, he kept standing at the entrance; he looked unafraid, but immensely tired and sad.

The guards wanted to take his sword from him, but I made a sign to leave him alone. He bowed stiffly, walked a few steps in my direction, and knelt down. He took his sword by the sheath, and handed it to me.

'Your Majesty will do to me what is just,' he said calmly.

I took the sword in both hands, held it in front of me, then pressed the hilt against my heart and forehead, and kissed it, as if I had just received a precious gift from a great king, rather than accepting a rebel's surrender.

'At the battle of Māchhīwāra,[85] this sword has saved my father Humāyūn, may he enjoy eternal bliss in the gardens of Allāh! It is this sword that has slain the mighty Hemū at Pānīpat! No one wears it better than you do, Khān Bābā,' I said softly, handing him the sword back.

---

85. Battle of Māchhīwāra: An important battle in Emperor Humāyūn's ultimate recapture of India.

He accepted it as I had done, with both hands, holding it by the sheath, touching his chest and forehead with its hilt, and kissing it.

It seemed he wanted to say something, but he remained silent. When I saw tears running down his face, I could no longer hold back my own. I rose from the pillows on which I had been sitting, took him by the shoulders, and made him stand up as well. I took the shawl I was wearing around my neck and used it to wipe away his tears and mine.

'Sad and regrettable things have happened between us, these past couple of weeks, Khān Bābā. We must put them behind us. After all, what are a few weeks of misunderstanding compared to so many years of friendship?'

I invited him to sit down next to me, as an exceptional guest of honour, on my own pillows at my right-hand side.

'You have not been taking proper care of yourself, Khān Bābā. I want you to forget all your worries, and dine with me!'

I ordered food and wine to be brought in and told everybody else to leave us alone.

We ate and drank, and exchanged the usual civilities. I inquired about his health and that of his household, and was glad to hear that my lovely cousin Salīmā and his son Abdurrahīm were doing well. Nevertheless, our conversation was interspersed with long, awkward silences.

'It is so sad that all this has happened between us, Khān Bābā. I wish I could undo it all, and start anew.'

'Your Majesty does not need to apologise to me. What has happened was more my fault than his. I should have asked Your Majesty how he wanted to run the affairs of government now that he has reached adulthood. I was a fool to have taken for granted that I could just carry on as if Your Majesty were still a young boy.

'I must confess, it has hurt me deeply to see that Your Majesty has chosen to dismiss me without first talking to me, but I do understand how this has happened. There are more than enough people at the court who will have planted the poisonous seeds of doubt in Your Majesty's heart about my true intentions. But then again, I am to blame as well for the wrong impression I created, and I do understand why Your Majesty acted the way he did. It is Your Majesty's god-given right and obligation to occupy the throne and exercise the powers associated with it. In matters of such high importance, one should never take any chances with people one does not trust completely.'

'I am really very sorry that it had to go this way, Khān Bābā,' I repeated.

'It is probably for the best, Your Majesty. It was Allāh's will. I am profoundly grateful that I can now leave Hindustān, at peace with myself, and assured of Your Majesty's continued friendship and affection.'

'You do not have to leave, Khān Bābā! Why don't you stay here with us? There are so many important tasks you could assume, territories to be administered, enemies to be fought.'

'I am very grateful for Your Majesty's offer, but I would be obliged if he would allow me to continue on my journey to Mekkah. For a long time, it has been my fondest wish to fulfil this most sacred obligation. Is it not written in the Hadīth that the recompense of a well-completed Hajj is nothing less than paradise itself! I really yearn to pray at the Ka'bah, Your Majesty. I want to go and stone the pillars at Mina, I want to stand in the plain of 'Arafāt, and behold Jabal Rahmah, the sacred Mountain of Mercy; I want to drink of the blessed waters of the well Zamzam. I want to travel to the blessed city of al-Madīnah, and pay my humble respects at the holy shrine of the Prophet Himself, peace be upon Him and His household. . . .

'I am fifty-five years old, Your Majesty. At this advanced age, one should not postpone any matters of importance. . . .'

'Who am I to stand between you and Allāh, Khān Bābā? But you have to promise me one thing: that you will come back to Hindustān, as soon as possible! I need good men like you to advise me!'

'*Inshā'allāh*,[86] Your Majesty, I promise. I am happy to know that I will always have a home back here.'

'Well, then, *khudā hāfiz*,[87] and come back soon, Khān Bābā!'

'*Khudā hāfiz*, Your Majesty. May you live a good and glorious life!'

---

86. *Inshā'allāh* (Arabic): If god wills.
87. *Khudā hāfiz* or *khodā hāfez*: God be your protector/guardian; one of many Persian expressions commonly used in Urdu.

Eleventh Letter

بیرام خان

Bairām Khān (2)

Five months had passed since Bairām Khān's surrender. I had returned to Āgrā after a one-month sojourn in Dillī.

Nothing of great importance happened in those first few months. I took appropriate measures to put the government of Kābul in order when I learned that things were not being managed as well as they should, after Mun'im Khān's departure.

There was also a first attempt from our side to take Kashmīr. It was badly prepared, ill-executed, and therefore, failed miserably. It was a disappointment, but I vowed to myself that I would be back some day.

The atmosphere back in Āgrā had clearly changed. I was still not the mighty emperor I would become a few years later, but people had started to respect and fear me more than before. It seemed as if the people at court, and actually the city of Āgrā itself, were quietly preparing themselves for a new, glorious and prosperous era. With my permission, Mun'im Khān took up residence in Bairām Khān's house, and many other nobles started to build pleasant dwellings on the banks of the Jumna.

Then one afternoon in 968, it must have been towards the beginning of Esfand,[88] one of the guards announced that Mun'im Khān was urgently requesting a private audience with me. This did not bode well. . . .

---

88. Around the third week of February 1561, Julian calendar

'I regret to have to inform Your Majesty,' he said, 'that my honourable predecessor, Bairām Khān Badakhshāni, has passed away.'

'What! Is Bairām Khān dead? How can that be? He was not ill, was he?'

'No, Your Majesty. I'm afraid he was assassinated.'

'Murdered? Who did this? I want to know who did it! No matter who it is, I want the filthy son of a bitch executed – no, I want him tortured to death! I want to see him impaled, slowly! I want to see him strangled with his own guts! I want to feed his carcass to dogs!'

'It happened in Pattan, down in Gujarāt. After Your Majesty had graciously pardoned Bairām Khān, earlier this year, he was travelling leisurely towards the coast, where he intended to board a ship to Jeddah, and then move on to Mekkah. On the way, he visited many shrines, mosques and holy places, giving alms to the poor, devoting his time to prayer, meditation, and edifying conversation with learned and saintly mullāhs and hermits. People who were there with him will testify that he really was at peace with Allāh, with the world, and with himself. In fact, they all say, they had not seen him that much contented and at ease in many years. In his conversations, he would often repeat, how much he was looking forward to finally completing the fifth pillar of Islām, and spending the evening of his life in quiet and peaceful retirement, amidst his loved ones.

'Upon arrival in the city of Pattan, the nearest city across the Gujarāt border, the king's local governor, Mūsā Khān Fūlādī, received him with much courtesy and respect. The area of Pattan being most pleasant and agreeable, he decided to stay there for a couple of days to take repose, enjoying the beautiful gardens and ponds.

'On the day of his death, Yawm al Jum'a, the fourteenth of Jumāda al Awwal,[89] he had been enjoying a boat trip on a scenic lake called Sahansa Lang, which has a small island in the middle, with a charming pavilion on it. He and a few of his guards had spent the day on the lake and the islet, and were returning in the late afternoon. They disembarked on the shore, and walked back to the spot where they had left their horses. The

---

89. Friday, 31 January 1561 (Julian calendar)

passable part of the shore is rather narrow and difficult, with boulders and pebble stones, and bushes that obstruct the view.

'There was a small group of five or six Pashto-speaking Afghāns sitting on the beach; one more was standing a few steps away from them. They seemed to be enjoying the view of the setting sun on the lake, and were engaged in what seemed to be pleasant and peaceful conversation. As they were wearing the honourable white robes of pilgrims on the Hajj, Bairām Khān greeted them courteously, and did not pay much further attention to them.

'As he passed them by, the man who had been standing closest suddenly jumped towards him, and stabbed him in the back with a broad-bladed dagger that he had been hiding in his sleeve, yelling, "That's for Māchhīwāra, you pig!"

'The blade missed the heart, but pierced the left lung, the point of the weapon coming out at his breast.

'Bairām Khān must have realised instantly that his wound was fatal. He did not struggle or attempt to strike back, but calmly said, "Allāhu Akbar," and sank to the ground.

'The treacherous, cowardly assassin dashed back to his comrades; instantly, many more of them came out of the bushes where they had been hiding – there must have been about forty of them in total. They came towards Bairām Khān, who was lying on the ground, bleeding to death. Perhaps they wanted to finish him off, or take his head with them, as a trophy.

'One of Bairām Khān's guards, a Qazaqī raider, jumped between them and his master. He killed one of the assailants with his throwing-knife and mortally wounded two more, before obtaining the bliss of martyrdom himself.

'His heroic sacrifice gave Bairām Khān's guards enough time to get their bows ready. Several Afghān pigs instantly paid for it with their lives. The one standing closest to Bairām Khān was fortunate to die a merciful death, taking a direct hit in the middle of the chest, right through the heart. He staggered two more steps, with an expression of disbelief on his face, and collapsed. He must have been dead before he hit the ground. The next two, however, were much less fortunate: both of them were shot through the throat. Your Majesty knows that our archers always try to hit their victims in such a way that they make a lot of noise before they die:

nothing is more discouraging to an attacking enemy than the agony of fallen comrades! Sure enough, these two bastards fell to the ground, their hands clasped in vain around the shaft of the arrow, choking, gargling, their faces twisted in horror and pain.

'As if it had been rehearsed, each one of the next three victims got an arrow high in the stomach, right below the spot where the two halves of the rib cage meet, where even a minor blow causes the most excruciating pain. Provided the arrow has not penetrated too deep, those who have been hit in that spot will die a long and horribly painful death, moaning as if they are vomiting their guts out, until they die of exhaustion.

'The pain of their fallen comrades clearly made the intended impression on the rest of the assailants – their onslaught faltered, and many of them ran away for cover into the bushes. The Turkomān guards pressed forward, intending to take their master into safety, but Bairām Khān, an outstanding soldier until death, stopped them.

'"Leave me," he groaned in Turkī, so the Afghāns would not understand. "Save my family! Make sure they don't hurt my family!"

'He let his head sink back on the pebbles of the beach. He looked at the sky and the lake, and lay still, trying not to cough, seemingly oblivious of his surroundings, clearly resolved to die with dignity, in serene and complete submission to Allāh's will. After a few more moments, he closed his eyes, and stopped breathing.

'The Turkomāns arrived in Bairām Khān's camp ahead of their assailants, just in time to bring everybody into safety, but could not prevent these unwashed, black-hearted Pashtun pigs from completely ransacking and plundering the camp. The guards retreated south, taking four-year-old Abdurrahīm and Bairām Khān's spouses and their retinue safely to Ahmedabād. They had to fight their way back, under constant threat of attack by gangs of Afghāns who were following them. But those filthy pigs learned to keep their distance when a few mornings in a row, they found their guards dead, with purple-black faces, a thin string of hemp around their filthy necks – an unmistakable sign that our raiders had been paying them a nightly visit. . . .'

'And what about the murderer?' I asked.

Mun'im Khān hesitated.

'The son of a bitch got what he deserved, Your Majesty! When he went for his horse, back on the shore of the lake, one of our men put one of these fishbone arrows into him – you know, Your Majesty: those with a long, thin arrowhead and eight sharp little barbs, impossible to pull out. It went clean through the bastard's right kidney, and got stuck in the middle of his liver. It must have taken him many days of horrible pain to die!'

'May his suffering continue in hell, for centuries upon centuries!' I hissed. 'Tell me, Mun'im Khān . . .'

'Yes, Your Majesty?'

I wanted to have him take an oath on the Holy Qur'ān – swear to me that the murderer was indeed dead, as he had described; but I did not dare to ask. Deep down, I knew he had been lying to me, making things up, to make me feel better. Probably, there had not been that many Afghān victims. Probably, the murderer was alive and well. Justice is not always done in this world; as you well know, my son, assassins do not always get what they deserve.

'Tell me,' I said, calming myself down, 'who was this son of a bitch, anyway, and why did he murder Bairām Khān?'

'They say his name was Mubārak Lohāni. His father was among the many thousands of Afghāns killed at the battle of Māchhīwāra – where, as Your Majesty knows, Bairām Khān led the imperial troops to victory when Humāyūn pādshāh recaptured Hindustān. Apparently, he wanted to avenge the death of his father.'

'What happened to Bairām Khān's body?'

'Your Majesty can rest assured – the Khān Khanān was given a decent burial. Some local faqīrs, who had witnessed the incident from afar, took pity on him, and carried his body to the tomb of Shaykh Husām-ud-dīn nearby.'

'I'm glad to hear he was put to rest in a holy place. May Allāh grant him the eternal bliss of paradise! Maybe later, we should have his body brought to a place more nearby. It would be good if I could visit him, and light a lamp on his grave.

'Tell me, where is his family now? I trust they are safe?'

'They are, Your Majesty. They are still in Ahmedābād. I hear they are doing well, under the circumstances. Many good people are helping them out.'

'Have them come to the court as soon as possible. I wish to take all of them under my care.'

'With respect, Your Majesty . . .'
'I want it done now.'
'Yes, Your Majesty.'

For several weeks, I hardly slept at all, haunted by bitter and futile thoughts about what could and should have happened, if only I had done things differently, asking forgiveness, with nothing and nobody to answer me but the silent, black void of the night.

Twelfth Letter

مخفی

Makhfi [90]

From the memoirs of Her Imperial Highness Salīmā Sultānā Bēgam Chaqānīānī, widow of Bairām Khān

مخفی

A small coffer of jewels and gold coins, and the clothes on our backs – that is about all we managed to escape with, when Bairām's guards came galloping into the camp, shouting we had to leave immediately.

Looking outside the pālkī on top of the camel that was carrying me, I could see in the distance those filthy Afghān dogs plundering our camp, tearing down the tents, dragging off everything they got their dirty hands on. A group of about twenty of them started chasing us, probably thinking there were even greater spoils to be gained. They soon changed their minds. Our guards swiftly turned around in the saddle,

---

90. Makhfi: The hidden; artist name used by Salīmā as a poetess.

riding backwards and shooting their arrows like the steppe warriors of old. The first three Afghāns who came too close, paid for it with their worthless lives, and the rest wisely returned to the much easier task of plundering our deserted camp.

I cannot describe the storm of thoughts that rushed through my head. Just one moment before, I had been an important foreign visitor, a high-born Gurkaniyya princess, granddaughter of Bābur pādshāh the Tiger, cousin of the powerful young emperor of Hindustān, preferred spouse of the most wealthy and powerful nobleman of the empire. . . . And now, all at once, I was a nearly destitute widow, a fugitive, fearing for my life and that of my loved ones.

The king of Gujarāt, while allowing us free passage, obviously did not dare to take sides; the emissaries we sent to his court, carrying urgent requests for troops to protect us, came back with polite but evasive promises and prayers. We were on our own, all alone in a foreign, hostile country.

Fortunately, I still had my husband's competent officers and true friends, Muhammad Amīn Dīwāna, and Bābā Zambūr, and their Turkomān and Uzbeg soldiers. I was really moved to see how these men, who could so easily have saved themselves, chose to stay with us, faithful to their fallen master, ready to lay down their lives for us if necessary.

The flight to Ahmedābād was a real nightmare. Particularly for the first few days, we were under constant fear of another attack by the bandits.

But Bairām's men remained on their guard, and made the assailants pay dearly each time they tried to come near us. Our scouts even carried out a number of nightly raids themselves against the bandits. After finding a few more of their men dead in the morning, the Afghāns wisely chose to follow us from a much safer distance.

Down in Ahmedābād, we found a gated house in the northern part of the town, which, according to the reassurances we got from our guards, was safe and easy to defend. There, we waited, and waited . . . hoping to get some kind of reply to the messages we had sent to far away Hindustān. More than once, I thought I would never see it again.

In more than one way, those long months in the relative comfort and safety of the house in Ahmedābād were much worse than the days of hasty flight. Now, there were hours upon hours where I found myself completely alone with my sadness, grieving for the death of my strong, gentle husband.

I spent as much time as possible with little Abdurrahīm. Such a delightful and sweet little fellow, and incredibly bright, too! It was truly amazing to hear how easily he spoke both Persian and Turkī with us, and Hindustānī with the servants.

Despite his young age, it was clear that he would grow up to be a handsome man like his father: the same high cheekbones, the same long face and strong nose.

How often had I envied this wonderful child's mother! How often had I prayed to Allāh that He would grant me the favour of bearing my husband another wonderful son, just like Abdurrahīm! Alas, it was not to be . . .

His son's mother, I was not; but I clearly was Bairām's preferred wife, and I like to think, it was not just because I happened to occupy the highest rank in birth. No, Bairām Khān really loved me, not only as his wife, but also as his friend and companion. It gave me much pride and satisfaction to find that among all his wives and friends, I was the one and only person he would share his plans, hopes and fears with.

Oh, how I cherish the memories of our times together – the long hours of pleasant conversation over dinner; the nights, when we were passionate lovers, his strong hands all over my body, his stern face suddenly full of tenderness. . . .

How I loved watching him asleep in my bed – his lined, tanned face; his hair and beard, with the little gray hairs amidst the black ones. How I loved touching his chest, arms and hands – covered with so much hair, that I used to joke I had married a bear!

Bairām Khān . . . the kind of man I had always hoped I would marry some day: strong and competent, respected and feared by everybody, yet always considerate and gentle towards me. I had wanted to grow old with him, and care for our children and grandchildren, but it was not to be. He was gone forever now . . . not even a grave was there for me to visit. There was nothing left for me to do but to remember him, pray for him, and cry for him.

At last, after months of waiting in sadness and despair, encouraging news reached us from Āgrā: My cousin, young Emperor Akbar, had decided to take us under his care. He would personally take charge of

Abdurrahīm's education, and all of Bairām Khān's family would be residing at the imperial court, under his protection. Much as I resented Akbar for having dismissed my husband, I was grateful for the opportunity to return to a safer place.

And so, we finally left Ahmedābād behind us, and travelled back to Hindustān, this time with a powerful force of three hundred elite cavalry escorting us all the way. We were safe now – nothing but an all-out attack by a large enemy army could pose any real threat to us. Indeed, our assailants were nowhere to be seen, and we arrived safely in Āgrā, after an uneventful, if tiring, passage.

I rode into the daunting red sandstone fort, more or less resigned to my fate, with the prospect of a rather boring, but safe and comfortable life in the women's quarters of the imperial palace, where I would be treated with respect, as a widowed princess of royal blood. There, I would spend the long days, months and years of my life, attending to my toilette and attire, educating someone else's children, playing silly card games with the other women, gossiping, sowing, embroidering, reading, writing, and thinking about what might have been. . . .

The reunion was genuinely cordial. Akbar received us with every imaginable honour – a grandiose feast was organised, and grateful prayers offered to Allāh.

Our guards, who had protected us so bravely during those long months, the soldiers as well as the officers, received most generous rewards – enough gold, in fact, for them to live comfortably for the rest of their lives, and robes of honour, which they seemed to value even more. Akbar, I was happy to see, knew how to appreciate and reward loyalty.

We first assembled in the diwān-i-ām,[91] its courtyard lined with an impressive guard of huge war elephants, rows of lancers and archers, and cavalrymen, all on pitch black, richly caparisoned horses.

As Akbar came in from the balcony and sat himself down on the throne, the elephants bent their front legs, the horses lowered their heads, and all the attendants bowed deep down from the waist, their right hands touching their heads.

---

91. Diwān-i-ām: Hall of public audience

It was the first time since my wedding that I saw my cousin. He had changed quite a bit, and for the better, I had to admit to myself. Despite his youth and the friendly expression on his face, he looked quite imposing, with the natural authority of a true king. He was a grown man now, of medium height, but quite strongly built and broad-shouldered. In accordance with his status, he was richly attired in a robe of red silk, a long string of pearls around his neck, and a rather small, tightly rolled, bejewelled turban on his head. In accordance with the latest fashion, his face was clean-shaven, apart from a moustache. Despite his Persian mother, his appearance was that of a full-blooded Turk. Judging from the portraits, in fact, he and our common grandfather Bābur could have been brothers.

In response to the homage, Akbar nodded and raised his right hand a few times, and remained seated on the throne for a few moments, until the official salutation was over. Then, in sharp contrast with the solemnity of the moment, he quickly came down from the platform, and personally embraced us all, one by one.

'My dear cousin!' he said softly as he took me by the shoulders and held me against him. It seemed to me that he held me just a bit longer than necessary. Was I imagining this, or was there more than just familial affection in the way he looked at me?

There were tears in his eyes as he squatted down in front of little Abdurrahīm.

'My dear little fellow,' he whispered, gently touching the boy's cheek. 'Don't you remember me? I am your uncle Akbar! My, you have grown! Let me look at you! You look just like your father, you know that? Would you like some sweets? What would you like to do? Would you like to take a ride on an elephant with me?'

Abdurrahīm bit his upper lip and looked down.

'Go on, answer, His Majesty is asking you a question!' his mother said.

The child kept looking at the floor.

'Yes, Your Majesty,' he murmured.

'Did you hear!' Akbar asked triumphantly, addressing no one in particular. 'The way he speaks Turkī – just like his father!'

He lifted the child, took him in his arms, and walked across the courtyard, pointing at various things, babbling all the way. They went to see the horses, and then the elephants. Akbar took some sweets out of his robe and had the child offer them to the animals. The little boy seemed enthralled.

'You see, Abdurrahīm? You see the little finger they have at the tip of their trunk?'

He made a sign to the mahāwat sitting on the largest elephant of them all. The man made the animal bend its front legs and sink down on its knees, and jumped off its back. Akbar, still holding Abdurrahīm in one arm, put his foot on the elephant's left tusk, took hold of the rope around its broad neck, and sat himself down, digging in his knees behind the huge ears. He took the mahāwat's spike, clacked his tongue, and made the animal stand again. He steered it out of the courtyard, disappearing for quite a while, and came back in, after what must have been an extensive tour of the premises. Little Abdurrahīm looked proud as a peacock, his eyes big with excitement.

'You did great, Abdurrahīm! You will become a great soldier! Did you like the elephant ride? Would you like to do that again some time?'

Abdurrahīm nodded enthusiastically. All the attendants applauded as Akbar took the child by the hand, and walked him back to its mother.

I looked around the courtyard, and my eyes fell on Māham Anaga. The conniving bitch was watching the scene with a half-hearted smile, trying in vain to hide her jealousy. Several people had told me how she and that lap-dog of hers, Mun'im Khān, had made more than one attempt to convince Akbar that it was unwise and dangerous to have the son of a rebel grow up at the imperial court. I was glad to hear that he had told them in no uncertain terms to shut up.

Fear and anger suddenly came over me. If anything happened to that little boy, I would, so help me Allāh, personally scratch her eyes out!

She happened to look in my direction. She smiled faintly, but I felt her beady little crow's eyes probing into my soul, and I knew, she was guessing what I had been thinking. Just as well.

That same afternoon, about one hour before the evening prayers, one of my personal attendants came into my quarters and handed me a note from the chief eunuch:

His Imperial Majesty,
Abū'l Muzaffar Jalāl-ud-dīn Muhammad Akbar Pādshāh Ghāzī,

*King of Kings,
requests the honour of having dinner
with His dear Cousin,
the High-born Lady Salīmā Sultān Bēgam.*

'Tell His Majesty, I will be honoured,' I said wearily. It was not the answer I wanted to give, but a different one would have been quite unacceptable.

I went to dinner with reluctant resignation, with the prospect of a long, boring evening in the company of a spoilt, conceited young brat. I was pleasantly surprised, though, to see that dinner was served in a large, airy room overlooking the river. It had artfully sculpted stone lattice windows, which allowed the cool, healthy open air to mix with the heady perfumes of the palace. The room was lit by hundreds of candles and decorated with many flowers. Its white-marble floor was almost entirely covered with a number of beautiful Persian and Kashmīrī carpets, all of them in the warmest shades of red. Contrary to what I had expected, Akbar was already in the room when I arrived. I made a slight bow to show him my respect, took off my slippers, and went to sit down on the pillows in front of him. Despite the awkwardness of the moment, the carpet felt soft and pleasant under my bare feet.

I had not planned to eat much, but I did anyway. There were at least fifty different dishes, all of them delicious: succulent mutton, lamb, fowl, and fish from the river, all skillfully grilled on skewers over a low charcoal flame, or simmered in rich, spicy gravy. There were several kinds of *naan* and *roti*, lentils, braised, boiled and steamed rice, eggs, cauliflower, peas with *panīr*, and four or five other kinds of vegetables. Everything was presented on plates and saucers, kept warm with candles. On separate trays, there were also several kinds of sherbets, presented in beakers on crushed ice, and various kinds of fruit, all of which looked delicious.

Akbar made a gesture for the servants to put some of the food on our plates, and sent them off.

He took two silver pitchers out of a large bowl, filled to the brim with crushed ice.

'Here, have some water,' he said, filling the largest of the two beakers on my tray.

'This is very special water, you know, from the Gangā! They bring it here every day, in large sealed earthen jars. It's supposed to be excellent for your health! I don't know whether that is actually true, but I have to say, no water I have ever drunk has a softer, purer taste! And have some wine as well! This one here has been made from the best grapes from Kābul!'

He suddenly looked a bit worried.

'My blessed father always said, it is becoming for members of the royal family to drink wine,' he added apologetically.

I had a sip.

'I'm not sure the mullāhs would agree, but I really hope your father was right,' I said. 'It's really delicious!'

We both started eating. To my pleasant surprise, Akbar was courteous, attentive, and easily kept up a cheerful flow of pleasant conversation. Contrary to what I had anticipated, he did not try to make any amorous advances.

He kept asking dozens of questions, about Gujarāt, about my accommodation in the palace, about Abdurrahīm's education, about music and dance performances I had attended, books and poetry I had read. . . .

I must admit, I was deeply impressed with his amazing knowledge of books. It was very hard to believe that I actually was talking to someone who had never learned how to read. There was not a book or writer he had not heard of, and hardly a poem he could not recite. The only slightly annoying thing about the conversation was his habit of constantly interrupting people. In his eagerness to know and learn everything, he never seemed to have the patience to hear one explanation at a time. Before I had a chance to finish the answer to one question, he had the next one ready. Not that I minded too much. At least it showed that he was not full of himself, but genuinely interested in what other people had to say. At times, though, I knew it did drive the mullāhs crazy. Those who believe they possess the truth do not like to be interrupted. . . .

Noticing that I had finished a few of the items on my tray, Akbar personally spooned out a second helping. The food was delicious, and there certainly was more than enough of it.

'Is this all I get?' I inquired jokingly.

'I'm sorry, would you like something else? I can order anything you want . . . some buffalo meat, maybe . . . even some beef, if you like!' he apologised, clearly quite eager to please me.

'No, don't bother. The food here is more than enough to feed an army! But why would you worry about eating beef or not? You're not a Hindū, and moreover, you are the emperor!'

'Yes, that's right, of course, but you know, eating beef is extremely offensive to the Hindūs, and I don't want to hurt their feelings if I can help it. You see, I do not want to be seen as just another foreign conqueror. Unlike our grandfather Bābur, or my father Humāyūn, I was born here in Hindustān. This is my homeland, and I want all the people living on its soil to see me as their legitimate king, regardless of their religion! That's why I will try to avoid things that are offensive to the Hindūs. Perhaps they will learn to love and respect me if they know that I will not willingly desecrate anything they consider as holy.'

Akbar paused and looked at me. Seeing surprise and disbelief on my face, he insisted, 'Their customs may seem strange and even blasphemous to us, but my teacher, Mīr Abdul Latīf, agrees with me that contempt of any religion is contempt of god Himself!'

What people said about Akbar was true: he had changed indeed. Much as I resented the way he had treated my husband, he was starting to intrigue me.

'I must confess I don't know much about the Hindūs and their customs,' I said, 'but surely, their ways of worship must be an abomination in the eyes of Allāh?'

'I thought so, too, but then I found that it is really not as simple as that,' Akbar said.

'You know, but they are really more similar to us than we think!'

He looked intently at me. I suppose he did so to make sure I was still paying attention, or to guess my thoughts.

'You must have read the tales of the *Thousand and One Nights*, haven't you? You know the stories of Hārūn ar-Rashīd, the great and wise khalīfah of Baghdād, don't you? I've always been fascinated by those episodes where he wanders around in disguise on the streets of Baghdād, observing the people, talking to them, finding out all kinds of things people try to hide from him. Well, a couple of months ago, after Bairām Khān left, I started doing exactly the same thing! Two or three times every month, I slip out of the fort, and spend the better part of a day or night on the streets of Āgrā! Only three of the guards know about it – I had them swear on the Holy Qur'ān that they will keep this a secret.'

'But isn't that dangerous? What if something happens to you? Why do you want to risk your life like that?'

He gave me an amused look.

'You don't have to worry about me, Salīmā! You see, I wear simple, dirty, shabby clothes: Would-be robbers will take me for a poor, wandering traveller, with nothing much worth stealing. Besides, I don't want to brag, but I'm really quite strong, you know – just like our grandfather was! Moreover, I'm a well-trained, experienced soldier, and I'm always armed when I go out: I carry two throwing-knives, concealed in the sleeves of my tunic; I also have a large, broad dagger, hidden under my cloak in my belt behind my back, and even a sword, concealed in my walking stick! No, I can assure you, it will take more than a few robbers to get the better of me. Besides, are we not all in the hands of god? Not a speck of dust will move, unless He wills it.'

'You don't seem to agree?' he asked, noticing that I did not react much.

'I don't know,' I said. 'I have the impression, many people use Allāh's omnipotence to justify their own recklessness. Allāh is almighty, but has He not created us as free beings, at liberty to do as we please? If that is true, then we should accept responsibility for our own acts. If we, for instance, decide to commit a sin, we should not blame Him for it; and neither should we when we get hurt because of our own recklessness!'

Akbar raised one eyebrow in surprise and amusement, and smiled approvingly, slightly nodding his head.

'I must confess, I had not looked at the matter from that perspective,' he admitted. He put his hand to his mouth and stared vaguely at one of the candle flames, thinking about what I had just said.

'Yes, you are quite right,' he admitted after a while, still gazing at the light, 'we should indeed not confuse trust in god with recklessness.'

He paused, and looked at me again.

'But then, neither should we confuse prudence with cowardice!' He smiled, a bit self-righteously, clearly pleased with his own cleverness.

'You know, Mīr Abdul Latīf once told me about the great Ibn Rushd[92] of Al-Andaluz, who used to say that all good things are always in the middle of two extremes. A hero, for instance, stands midway between a coward and a reckless fool, don't you agree? Well, that is where I want to be as well! Bairām Khān has always taught me to do what I have to do, with prudence, but without fear! I do what I think I have to do, and if I have to die, so be it! If it happens, I can assure you, I will spit death in the face, and die like a man, just like he did!'

'And what is so important about wandering around in the dirty alleys of Āgrā?'

'There, at least, I get to know what is going on in my own empire! A king is a very lonely person, you know . . . I live in a fortress, behind high walls, and even when I'm travelling, I am well-protected by powerful armies and surrounded by all the wealth anybody could ever dream off. All of this is keeping me apart from the real life outside – I could just as well be living in a foreign country! I'm completely dependent on other people to tell me what is really going on outside! And now that Bairām Khān is gone, there are very few people I can really count on.'

I could not restrain myself.

'I'm so relieved to hear that you realise that the old wretch Māham Anaga and her entire clique are not to be trusted!'

He sighed.

'Salīmā, you know as well as I do, she has always been like a mother to me. She has fed me; she has risked her life for me when my father was still a homeless fugitive. I share your apprehension about Adham Khān – he has a foul and violent temper, and his ambitions are much greater than his abilities, but how can I blame a mother for loving her son, and wanting the best for him? I really do not want to hurt her feelings, if I can avoid it. But you don't have to worry about me, I've got it all under control!'

'I hope so, Your Majesty. . . .'

---

92. Averroes, (Abū-l Walīd Muhammad ibn Ahmad ibn Muhammad ibn Rushd, 1126–98), Arabian *qādī* and philosopher, born in Cordoba, Spain. His works, translated in Latin, became the highest authority in the West on the philosophy of Aristotle.

'Salīmā, please don't call me *Your Majesty*! I am your cousin, and I want to be your friend . . . your best friend! I know, you must be sad, and you are probably angry with me, because of what happened to Bairām Khān, but I swear to you, I am deeply sad as well about the way things have worked out! I really did not want to see Bairām Khān get hurt, you have to believe me! I really loved him, you know, like a father, and he loved me too!'

'I believe you did not intend any of these dreadful things to happen, but they have, and I would be lying if I said I have not been angry with you for that. However, I have to admit that what you say is true: He did love you, he told me so, repeatedly. He even told me that I should never hold any grudge against you. . . .'

'And, do you, Salīmā?'

'Let's not talk about it anymore.' I stared at my food, trying to evade his look.

'What was it that you were trying to tell me about your wanderings in disguise?' I asked, trying to change the subject.

'Oh, yes, I wanted to tell you about the Hindūs. One early morning, I walked past one of their temples. People came queuing in by the hundreds. In the morning, they have this ritual where the priests go into the sanctuary and "wake up the god" as they say. They wash and dress up the idol inside the sanctuary, and make offerings of food and flowers to it; devotees come to the temple, to see the deity, pay their respects, and pray – they call it *darshān*, if I'm not mistaken.

'As I was standing there, in front of the temple entrance, there was this strange man looking at me.

'"Looking for something, young sāhab?" he asked, in heavily accented but understandable Persian. His smile and the tone of his voice were perhaps a bit mocking, but not hostile, nor unfriendly. He looked very strange indeed: naked to the waist, with long, tangled locks of unkempt hair, ash smeared all over his arms, face and chest. On his forehead, there were three white stripes, and a lopsided, black-and-red eye in the middle.

'"Am I allowed to go inside? I asked. 'I'm a Mussalmān, you know."

'"Yes, I can see that, young sāhab . . . Where are you from?"

'"From Turān. I'm a Turkomān. I'm a cavalry officer in the emperor's army," I replied.

"'So, why are you dressed the way you are, young Turkomān sāhab?'"

'I felt like a thief, caught red-handed.

"'I just want to see how the Hindū people live," I said. "I dress inconspicuously so people don't take too much notice of me. . . ."

"'Eagerness to learn is the beginning of all wisdom, young Turkomān sāhab. Well, if you have come to this temple to learn, and to worship god, you are most welcome to go in with me. Just take off your shoes and come in."

'I took off my shoes, and put them near the entrance, next to a whole row of other pairs. We came into the courtyard of the temple, where there were a number of smaller sanctuaries with images of deities inside. I saw people going from one sanctuary to the other, praying, paying their respects, offering a few flowers or grains of wheat. Some of them were walking around in circles around some or the other deity.

"'You spoke about worshipping god," I said to my guide. "How come you speak of god, as if there were only one? Don't you people claim there are many gods?"

'He smiled.

"'Whether you worship one god, or many, young sāhab, that all depends on your personal development. There are many simple, uneducated people, for whom all the individual Hindū gods are as real and tangible as you and I. Most Hindūs will tell you, however, that the individual gods are concrete manifestations of the One, the hidden, unknowable god, Who upholds everything that exists, this world and the countless billions of other worlds.

"'You see, we are all part of god, young sāhab. You and I, every person, animal and plant, and everything that exists, is part of god, just like a spark is part of the fire, just like a tiny drop is part of the ocean. Eventually, we will all be reunited with Him. Through countless lives, we will eventually progress towards true knowledge, until we attain that divine moment when the soul attains perfect knowledge, truth and bliss, and is reunited with god."

"'If I would want to convert to your religion, what would I have to do?" I asked.

"'We do not try to convert anyone, young sāhab. We do not even claim that there is only one way to god. Countless paths lead to god, and wisdom can be found everywhere – in fact, every path you follow, crooked or straight, will ultimately lead you to Him!

"'You will attain union with god, because ultimately, that is your nature, young sāhab, for your soul is one with god. Think of yourself as a diamond, covered with dust and mud: You appear not to shine at all, but underneath all the filth, you are as clean and pure as you have always been. Through thousands of lives, the dirt that covers you will be removed through the power of wisdom, until you attain your pure self, which is identical with god. Indeed, each and every soul is created by god, is part of god, and is identical with god!'"

Akbar paused, his eyes staring at the flame of a candle.

'Strange beliefs, are they not? Well, maybe theirs is not the right religion. Maybe their way of worshipping is wrong. Still, I don't see why we could not live in peace with them: Do they not intend to serve the same god as we do? Do they not want to live good and decent lives, as we do? As long as they do not harm anyone, as long as they are obedient and recognise me as their king, I think they deserve my protection.'

He looked me straight in the eye, trying to guess what I was thinking.

'Mīr Abdul Latīf, my teacher, always talks to me about the principle of sulh-i-kul, peace for all. He says, this is what a king should try to accomplish. I think he is right, Salīmā. This is my task: I dream of a prosperous and mighty Hindustān, much larger than it is today, its many people worshipping the one true god in their manifold ways, united in peace, under the just rule of our Gurkaniyya dynasty!'

He paused, and mumbled, speaking more to himself than to me:

'I hope and pray that almighty god will grant me the strength and wisdom to succeed.'

I had to admit: Akbar really had changed. It would still take him a few more years before he would actually become the world-renowned, mighty emperor Akbar the Great, but he clearly was no longer the unruly, spoilt brat of before. I would never have thought that a self-indulgent, pleasure-seeking young man like him could be so preoccupied with religion, and so genuinely eager to do the right thing. He was obviously prepared to listen, and learn from other people. I started to understand why Bairām had liked him so much.

'I think you will be a wise king,' I said, and I really meant it. 'May Allāh always be your guide and helper!'

'Thank you,' he mumbled, shyly lowering his eyes and looking down at his food.

I looked through the lattice window. The moon, which had been barely visible near the horizon when we had started eating, was now high up in the sky, casting its silver light on the river. Many of the candles in the room were on the verge of going out.

'It is late, I should be going back to my quarters,' I said.

'Stay a little longer,' he implored. 'You're not tired, are you?'

He poured us both some more wine.

'You know, Salīmā . . .'

His face was turning a bit red. He cast his eyes down, staring at nothing in particular, somewhere in front of the pillows on which I was sitting.

'You know, it's been such a long time since I have been able to talk like this, to anyone. I hope you feel the same way too.'

'I feel very privileged that you have shared your thoughts with me. I must say, it's rather unusual for men to talk to women about serious matters like that.'

'Wisdom can be found everywhere, this much I have learned already,' he answered. 'You are a lady of royal blood, you have read many books, seen many things . . . I would be a fool if I did not value your opinion!'

He looked at me, and his face flushed up again.

'What would you say, Salīmā, if I were to ask you to be my wife? It would make life much easier for you here in the fort,' he added, using the wrong arguments in his eagerness to please me. 'I'm convinced, Bairām Khān would be happy to see that his wife is being taken care of!'

'I would be honoured and flattered, but I would say no,' I said.

'Why, Salīmā? I swear, I would be a good and respectful husband to you!'

'I can take care of myself! I don't want you to marry me out of pity, or to ease your guilty conscience about Bairām's death.'

'Salīmā, I can assure you, that is not the case! Bairām Khān and I parted ways as the best of friends, you must believe me! The bad blood there was between us was not only my fault, really – he must have told you that! And I can assure you, I don't want to marry you out of pity! I love you; I always have! Ever since I was a small boy, I have always found you extremely attractive . . . I have to admit, I was even a bit envious of Bairām Khān when he had the good fortune of becoming your husband . . .'

He paused.

'Besides, and perhaps more importantly, Salīmā, I feel good when you are near me. Tonight, just looking at you, listening to you, I had this feeling of comfort and security – like being near a fountain under a shady tree, in the heat of summer, or near a warm charcoal fire on a cold winter night. No one else has ever made me feel like that . . . not Ruqayyah, although she is a sweet girl and I do like her a lot, and not any of the other girls I've been with either!'

He leaned across the trays and put his hand on mine.

Salīmā, won't you at least consider my proposal? You would make me so happy,' he pleaded.

His hand felt dry and firm. The fingers might have been just a bit longer, but other than that, it looked exactly like a man's hand should, strong and sinewy, with veins showing on the back.

I kept looking at his hand, avoiding his eyes, and heard myself answering:

'I will think about it.'

Five more weeks went by. Akbar made no further attempt to see me in private, but not a day went by without some precious gift being delivered to my quarters. In that brief period, I amassed an entire fortune: earrings, necklaces, anklets, bracelets; diamonds, pearls, emeralds, rubies, textiles . . . all of the most exquisite quality. These were impressive gifts, even coming from a man as wealthy as Akbar . . .

Accompanying the gifts, there would always be something in writing: magnificent, hand-written books, illuminated with sublime miniatures, or sometimes individual poems on a single sheet of paper, about love, the beauty of nature, or the majesty of god. Most of the poems were from the Persian masters, but there were also some of my own—I wondered where he got them from—and there were a few other ones which I had never read, usually quite short, only one or two concise, striking sentences, which I suppose were his own.

All of them were written in the beautiful, elegant Nasta'līq-style handwriting of the head eunuch, followed by a rather clumsy signature at the bottom of the page, just four simple letters, in plain Naskh[93] – probably one of the very few words he had ever learned to write:

اکبر [94]

I saw him every now and then. Most of the time, I would watch from behind the lattices when he was attending to the affairs of state in the diwān-i-ām, or when he was riding out for a hunting trip outside. Gradually I saw the kind of man he was becoming: relaxed and friendly with ordinary soldiers, servants and children; serious and eager to do what was right when he was asked to take a decision about matters of importance.

With each passing day, I found him to be a more likeable person, and I caught myself thinking about him much more often than I cared to admit. How can a young widow remain indifferent to the idea of finding a vigorous new husband, who will care for her and protect her? How can a woman ignore the advances of a man of such incredible power and wealth, when he shows her such courteousness and respect?

Besides, was it not becoming for a pādshāh's granddaughter to occupy the highest possible rank? There was, after all, no denying that the life of an empress is substantially more comfortable than that of a guest, even one of royal blood. . . .

From time to time, I would meet him in the private quarters of the palace, in the presence of his household and attendants, when he was watching some dancers or other kinds of entertainment. We usually did not exchange more than a few friendly civilities, but it was obvious that much more was going on between us. How he could hardly keep his eyes off me; how he would always find a way to sit next to me, to accidentally touch my upper arm, or the bare skin of my hands or feet, allowing his

---

93. Nasta'līq: Cursive Arabic writing, with the letters slanting down from right to left. Almost all Urdu texts are written and printed in the Nasta'līq style.
Naskh: standard horizontal Arabic writing.
94. Akbar

fingers to linger just a bit longer than necessary; and my disappointment, on those rare occasions when he did not succeed. . . .

Then, one afternoon, when he was playing with little Abdurrahīm, carrying him on his shoulders and galloping through the garden, he suddenly came running towards me.

'Salīmā, will you please be my wife?' he asked, still gasping for air, looking up a bit uncomfortably from underneath Abdurrahīm's weight on his neck.

I smiled, and touched his face.

'I will,' I answered.

Thirteenth Letter

ماہم انگہ، ادھم خان

Māhām Anāga, Adhām Khān

Waking up next to Salīmā, in the soft, blue light of dawn . . .

Just looking at her, at the gentle rising and falling of her breathing; looking at her sweet face as the bluish light slowly turns golden; just looking, nothing else, not even reminiscing about the passion of the night before . . .

Just looking, and knowing—not hoping, not thinking, but *knowing*—that everything is perfect. There have been very few moments in my life, where I felt so truly blessed.

Somehow, all my fears, my uncertainties, my hopes and yearnings: they were all gone. I no longer craved or longed for anything. For some strange reason, I just knew, with tranquil certainty that from then on, things would be going my way, and my way only.

Where did this blissful feeling of complete, reassuring confidence come from? Salīmā was, of course, the main reason but there was more to the moment than a mere lover's happiness.

Marrying her was much more than the gratification of lust, more than love, even more than the contentment of finding a great companion: it was an achievement. It was evidence, to myself more than to anybody else, that I had finally taken control over my own destiny.

People around me still failed to see it; perhaps, I had not come to fully realise it myself, but I was becoming the king whom the world would call Akbar-e-āzam, Akbar the Great.

Almighty god has given me many things to be grateful for – so many that I sometimes feel unworthy and ashamed; but Salīma has certainly been among the most precious of my blessings.

She is so much more to me than just another wife of high birth, someone to share my bed and household with. It is not difficult to find girls with fairer faces or slimmer thighs, but she is the best companion any man could ever want. Even later in life, when we had become rather infrequent lovers, she always remained my dearest friend and most trusted advisor. If, among the many wives occupying my harem, I would have to choose one single spouse—as those firanghī priests keep insisting I should—it would, without any doubt, be her.

Not that I would ever agree to even consider such a preposterous idea: Men of property and position—and emperors all the more—should be free to take any number of wives and concubines they please, for that is the way progeny is secured and alliances are forged. It is, moreover, by far the most agreeable and natural way to ease the yearning that god has put in the bodies and souls of men. Had He wanted it otherwise, would He not have made us different?

However, while I never have been, and never will be a man of one single wife, I have to admit, Salīma indeed occupies a special place in my heart. Everything about her is kindness, and balance; wherever she comes, people are charmed by her gentle, caring attitude, and her wise, no-nonsense view of the world. She is unassuming, yet full of natural authority. I love the way she walks, I love the sound of her voice, I feel good when she is around, and perhaps most importantly, I listen when she speaks.

As you might have gathered after reading the extract from her diary that I have included in these writings, it has not been easy to win her over, not at all – she does have a mind of her own! In case you wonder where I got her diary from: She herself read it to me, one evening. By then, we had been married for a couple of years and were reminiscing about our beginnings together, over a nice meal with some good wine. I found it endearing to hear her side of the story, and thought that it might be of interest to you as well.

Yes, she does have a will of her own, and yet, she is, among all my many wives and concubines, the one I love the most. Relationships between men and women are at their best, in my view, when lust and companionship go together. I have never understood why so many men insist on marrying uneducated, subservient, ignorant girls. What good is a woman's body, when it is inhabited by the mind of a child? What use is there for it, outside the bed and the kitchen? Beauty is like good food: when one has taken from it, it ceases to occupy our minds. When the urge of the loins has been satisfied, the silly giggles of illiterate concubines quickly lose their interest. Not so, however, with the companionship of a wife who has something to say!

I suppose, it is with marriage as with the choice of helpers and ministers: The weak invariably prefer to surround themselves with other weaklings – if possible, even worse than they are. Strong, real kings, however, are never afraid to attract strong and talented helpers, who will help them grow and rise above themselves.

Remember this, my son: Surround yourself with the best people – be extremely choosy about who you admit to your service! Empires are not built, nor maintained, with a bunch of nodding yes-men, like that bunch of worthless idiots you had with you at the time of your rebellion, back in Allāhābād! In selecting your helpers, remember the brilliant court of Akbar, where you grew up! Keep in mind the strength and competence of its ministers and army leaders: tough soldiers and brilliant strategists, like Abdurrahīm, and Rāja Mān Singh; sharp administrators and wise advisors, like Todar Mal, Bīrbal, and Abū-l Fazl. . . .

But I am getting ahead of myself. Let me return to the months after Bairām Khān's death.

As I said, marrying Salīmā was a tremendous achievement: as much, or even more so, than the conquest of new territory. I really had to push it through against much opposition, covert and open.

You know I had given orders for Bairām Khān's family to be escorted back to Āgrā, to live there under my protection.

I was vexed to see that preparations for the departure were dragging on interminably. No less than three times, I had to ask Mun'im Khān about the state of affairs. Each time, he came up with some kind of lame excuse: the best troops needed to be selected; the supplies needed to be organised; permission needed to be obtained from the king of Gujarāt for the escort to cross his territory.... While all of this was, of course, necessary, I had the distinct impression he was dragging his feet. He and his associates clearly did not like the idea of sharing the imperial court with others.

Māham Anaga repeatedly tried to talk me out of my plan, with an insistence bordering on the insolent.

'Your Majesty, in his infinite goodness, chooses to forget that Bairām Khān was actually guilty of the loathsome and heinous crime of rebellion! Surely, it is not becoming that the family of a notorious rebel is invited to live with the emperor!

'Your Majesty's magnanimity is proverbial; would it not be more than sufficient if he would give them permission to take up residence in Bairām Khān's former house in Lāhor, rather than bringing them to Āgrā? After all, Bairām Khān was not a member of the imperial family!

'Your Majesty, in his kindness, is running a terrible risk in bringing Bairām Khān's son to court! He is only four years old now, but time flies. In ten to twelve years' time that little fellow may become extremely dangerous! They say, he looks just like his father; I would not at all be surprised if some day, Your Majesty would come to regret his generosity! Your Majesty knows very well that a good number of the amīrs are loyal to themselves before anybody else – it would not be past them to participate in an uprising, if that would suit their purpose!'

In the end, I had more than enough of it.

'I appreciate your concern for my safety, Māhamjī,' I said, 'but the decision is mine, and my mind is made up. I must ask you not to bring up the subject again. And as far as Abdurrahīm is concerned: All those years, Bairām Khān was more than a father to me. It is my duty, and my wish, to see to this child's education, and I will.'

Noticing the bland, unimpressed look on her face, I added: 'It is very important that everybody in the palace realises that this boy is under my personal protection. If anybody, no matter who it is, so much as thinks about hurting him, he will pay for it with his head, and that of his entire family!'

This time, the message was clear. Her face turned all red; she mumbled some kind of excuse, and retired to her quarters. I could not help feeling a bit guilty – little glory is there in threatening an old lady, even if she deserves it....

Then, late in the morning one day, after several more months of waiting, I finally received the message that Bairām Khān's family had arrived safely in Āgrā. I was overjoyed, and nervous at the same time.

When they had rested for a few hours, I officially invited them at the imperial court, and received them with every possible honour.

I did not forget, either, to praise and generously reward their valiant guards, making sure that good care was taken of the families of their fallen comrades. Such matters may seem trivial to you, my son, but they are quite important. Justice and generosity should not be the exclusive privilege of the high-ranked. Ordinary soldiers, who are the backbone of any army, are keen observers – they feel, with unfailing certainty, whether their leader cares for them, or not. Let me tell you, my son: If you have those men on your side, you will be much stronger than what you will be if you settle for an army of mere conscripts. Victories will be won against impossible odds, and rebellions against you will fail before they even have a chance to begin!

I was really moved to see little Abdurrahīm again: What a delightful little fellow he had become! A bit bashful at first, he did not say too much; but I soon managed to win him over, taking him for a ride around the fort, on Dilsankār's neck. . . .

I am still grateful that god has entrusted this boy to my care. Now, forty years later, it brings me such great joy to see how well he has done for himself. I watch the courtiers stepping aside and bowing for the great Abdurrahīm Khān Khanān, the most powerful man in the country, his emperor's iron right-arm, just like his father was before him . . . and I smile, contented. It pleases me to see him go about his duties with that self-evident confidence that is the fruit of competence and success. I take personal pride in his wisdom, power and wealth.

I really hope that Bairām Khān is able to see all this from the hereafter. If he is, I know he is smiling. . . .

The return of Bairām Khān's family to court and my subsequent marriage to Salīmā marked a real turning point in my life. As Māham Anaga and her group were soon to find out, the era of the indolent and docile boy-king, with his all-powerful guardians and advisors, was over for good.

A peaceful transition, however, it was not. In the course of the following months, a number of increasingly serious incidents occurred, which would ultimately lead to their downfall.

My first confrontation with them took place at the occasion of the conquest of Mālwa, which I had ordered near the end of the fifth year of my reign.[95] Remembering Bairām Khān's sound advice, 'A king should always seek conquest and war, lest his army become lazy and ineffective,' I had sent Adham Khān and Pīr Muhammad Khān south of our borders, to annexe this fertile land to our dominions.

At that time, the province of Mālwa was ruled by the so-called 'Shāh' Bāz Bahādūr – if the word 'rule' can be used to describe a useless, wine-soaked life, dedicated solely to music and women.

Bāz Bahādūr himself was the son of a simple Pashtun officer who had served under the Sūr dynasty, and had come to govern the territory in practical independence. His sole interest, however, was to enjoy life – a very common characteristic, quite understandable and maybe even amiable, but extremely dangerous to those who want to succeed in life, my son.

The imperial troops advanced, virtually unopposed, to the capital Sārangpūr, where Bāz Bahādūr put up a battle. Deserted by his best officers, he was easily defeated by the imperial forces, and put to flight.

The news of the victory reached me a few days later. I was, however, displeased to hear that Adham Khān and his crony had celebrated their victory with rivers of innocent blood. Dozens upon dozens of captives had been brought before them, and slaughtered like cattle, while the two imperial captains were cracking jokes. Not even women or children, or old and venerable Sayyids and Shaykhs, holding copies of the Holy Qur'ān in their trembling hands, had been spared.

I do not mean to suggest, my son, that violence is not sometimes necessary. On the contrary, harsh and brutal repression, the expression of justified wrath, will be put to beneficial use, in avenging insulted majesty, chastising the rebellious, and most importantly, in keeping other would-be offenders on the path of obedience. By contrast, however, arbitrary

---

95. March 1561

violence and cruelty will achieve exactly the opposite: More often than not, it will sow the seeds of new and more dangerous rebellions.

What infuriated me even more was the so-called booty that was sent to me: a few mediocre elephants, a bit of silk – that was all. I had been informed that Bāz Bahādūr had possessed untold treasures of gold, jewels, elephants, horses, and a large harem, with hundreds of the most beautiful concubines and dancing girls! Informants told me that Adham Khān had kept them all to himself! Not only was this a breach of the rules: it was an insult, a sign of contempt, and a direct challenge to my authority. If I would let him get away with this, my position would be undermined completely.

I did not hesitate one moment. I saddled up an escort of a few dozen good men, and left for Mālwa. Despite the blazing heat of early summer, we advanced rapidly – so rapidly, in fact, that we arrived way ahead of the fast messengers sent by a worried Māham Anaga to forewarn her son.

Our sudden arrival at Sārangpūr took Adham Khān completely by surprise.

He must have toyed with the idea of eliminating me, seeing that I had only brought a few guards with me. If that was indeed his plan, he had to abandon it soon, when thousands upon thousands of his soldiers, recognising the imperial standards, dismounted and knelt in the dust to salute their emperor.

I greeted the men, saying how glad and proud I was to see them, and congratulated them on their glorious victory.

I did not, however, say a word to Adham Khān, looking coldly past him, as he dismounted and reluctantly kissed my stirrup; I even refused to accept a change of clothes, and ostentatiously drank from my own water skin, ignoring the ice-cooled sherbet he offered me.

'I will retire into Sārangpūr,' I said stiffly, 'kindly have me informed about the spoils taken, so I may adequately recompense you and your men for your bravery.'

The demand clearly took him by surprise.

'Your Majesty . . .' he began, probably wanting to say something about the booty, but he obviously did not find the appropriate words.

'Certainly, Your Majesty,' he mumbled.

He offered me his residence in town, but I said I preferred to sleep in Bāz Bahādūr's palace. Indeed, I had no intention of spending the night anywhere near Adham Khān's harem, providing him with an occasion to avenge his honour. Excuses for treachery are indeed not difficult to find, if one is looking for them. . . .

I spent the night on the highest roof platform, choosing the coolest and least accessible spot, and personally stationing a number of my best men along the approaches.

The next day, we were all quite surprised to see Māham Anaga join us. The spirited old woman had travelled all the way from Āgrā, ostensibly to congratulate her son and her emperor on the conquest of the rich territories of Mālwa. In reality, of course, she was desperate to try to patch things up between us. Despite my anger, I could not help feeling the deepest respect for her – such admirable motherly devotion really deserved much worthier a son. . . .

As I had ordered, the spoils of war were paraded in front of me. I must admit, what I saw went beyond my wildest expectations. Scores of magnificent elephants, the finest horses, cart loads of gold and precious stones, and hundreds of magnificent girls. . . .

To my dismay, I learned that Bāz Bahādūr's harem had been much larger a few days ago. Dozens of girls had been killed by their own guardians when Sārangpūr was about to fall. Most regrettably, among the dead women was the legendary Rūpmatī, Bāz Bahādūr's queen, widely renowned for her beauty. Apparently, she had still been alive when Bāz Bahādūr fled, but had preferred the sting of poison to Adham Khān's greasy embrace.

With Māham Anaga present, both she and her son going out of their way to please me, things went more or less back to normal.

As I had announced, I divided the spoils, keeping, as is becoming, the lion's share for the imperial treasury, and awarding smaller tokens of appreciation to Adham Khān and Pīr Muhammad Khān in recompense of their contribution.

The rewards I attributed to them were just enough not to be openly insulting, but far less generous than what I would normally have distributed among my officers under similar circumstances. The part I gave to Adham Khān consisted mainly of elephants—of the same mediocre kind he had sent to me—plus a bit of gold, and a few girls, chosen from among the plainest ones I could find. Those at the court should come to understand that to loyally serve the emperor is the fastest—and safest—way to acquire wealth.

I stayed in Sārangpūr for one more day, and then headed back to Āgrā, heading the train of spoils.

We had barely left the city when Abdullāh Khān Uzbeg, the senior commanding officer of my escort, came riding next to me.

'Your Majesty,' he said, 'I'm afraid some very disconcerting rumours have come to my ears.'

'Yes, what is it?'

'It is about Adham Khān . . .'

'Yes? Go ahead, tell me, I want to know!'

'They say that Adham Khān kept two beautiful girls for himself when he handed over the property destined to go with Your Majesty's caravan to Āgrā.'

'Is it those two southern girls?'

'I believe so, Your Majesty.'

I knew right away which girls he was talking about. They had instantly caught my attention when Bāz Bahādūr's harem was paraded in front of me: two ravishing Hindū girls, rather tall and slender, very dark-skinned, with splendid big eyes and magnificent, shiny white teeth. The gold of their jewellery and the saffron silk of their sarīs exquisitely matched the shiny colour of their skin. Looking at the grace of their movements when they slowly walked past me, I had, in eager anticipation, been picturing in my mind how I would enjoy their company after a cool bath and a refreshing drink.

I immediately halted the march, ordering a count of the spoils and an inspection of the Sārangpūr garrison.

Outwardly, I kept myself composed and relaxed, but inside, I was boiling with rage.

What would I do to Adham Khān if those girls were found in his possession?

Have him hanged? If it had not been for Māham Anaga, I would not have hesitated.

Have him imprisoned? Banish him? No, that was much too mild a punishment, and besides, it was dangerous: Prisons and places of exile are cradles of rebellion. . . .

What else, then? Ignore the insult, and wait for a suitable time and place to take my revenge? Despite my anger, I decided that that would be my course of action. Even for an emperor, vengeance is oftentimes a dish best served cold. . . .

My suspicions were soon confirmed – the girls were nowhere to be found. Not in the imperial cortege, and neither in the harem back in Sārangpūr.

'Abdullāh Khān,' I said, 'we have wasted enough time here. I want to go back to Āgrā – there are more important matters to be dealt with. But before we go, I want you to find out, discreetly, what exactly happened here!'

'Your Majesty can count on me; I will take a few of these palace servants aside, and ask them a few penetrating questions,' the Uzbeg answered ominously, caressing the hilt of his dagger.

It did not take him long to find out the truth: Māham Anaga, seized by panic at what would happen to her son if he would be caught stealing from the emperor a second time, had bribed one of the female harem guards to kill the two girls and bury them somewhere behind the palace walls. 'Severed heads do not talk', she was reported to have said. . . .

'What are Your Majesty's orders?' Abdullāh Khān Uzbeg asked.

'As I said,' I answered, keeping icy calm, 'we have wasted more than enough time here. We will go back to Āgrā now – I'll deal with this later.'

I headed back as if nothing had happened. Surprisingly, I felt no hatred, no boiling rage, no fear. If anything, I felt relieved, happy to be free at last, free from whatever debts of gratitude I still had towards Māham Anaga, or anyone else for that matter. From now on, I would take other people's advice because I wanted to, not because I owed them anything. From now on, my word, and my word only, would be law.

The journey back to Āgrā gave me ample time to think. Immediately upon arrival, I made my first move.

In an imperial firmān, full of pompous and hollow words of praise, which at times can be the most effective of insults, I relieved Adham Khān of his command and called him back to Āgrā. 'The seditious having been subdued, and the presence of two senior commanders no longer being required', I left the campaign 'in the able hands of my loyal and trusted helper, Pīr Muhammad Khān'.

It was, if I say so myself, a judicious move indeed. Not only was it a clear, if subtle, insult for an army leader to be called back in the middle of a campaign, it also deprived that pig Adham Khān of any independent source of revenue; it would reduce him to what he detested most: a life of idleness and boredom at the imperial court, with lots of bowing and kneeling and nodding, completely dependent on me for his livelihood, and subject to the gloating, mockery and contempt of all the others. For so much was clear: I would make him regret his disloyalty for the rest of his life.

As I expected, Māham Anaga desperately tried to make me change my mind. She begged and pleaded. Her son, in his youthful impetuousness, might have done things displeasing to his emperor, but had not meant any harm. He profoundly regretted his wrongdoings, and would amend his ways. His abilities would be of much greater use to me and my empire, in fighting my enemies. He had no other desire but to serve me and expand my dominions.

Each time, I gave her the same reply, with a gentle and benevolent smile on my face as if I was doing her the greatest of favours: that her son's presence at the head of my troops was no longer required.

Māham Anaga's pleas were taken over, in thin disguise, by Mun'im Khān.

He had to inform His Majesty, with respect, that he was profoundly worried about the military situation in Mālwa. It was his duty to warn His Majesty that it would be imprudent to assume that the major fighting was over. Of course, Bāz Bahādūr had been trounced, but there were disconcerting, disturbing reports that he was forging alliances to win back his lost kingdom. Rumour even had it that Mālwa would be invaded soon by a major enemy alliance. It was to feared that Pīr Muhammad Khān would not be up to the task of leading such a large campaign on his own.

From a military point of view, he was, of course, quite right: To lead a band of marauders is one thing, but to conduct a large-scale military campaign is quite another. The situation in Mālwa, however, was the least of my concerns. If Pīr Muhammad Khān managed to keep the enemy out, so much for the better. If not, I would be back soon!

No, what was really on my mind, was the lack of discipline in my own imperial court. Surely, I had not dismissed the great Bairām Khān only to allow someone else to take his place? One way or the other, they would all have to learn – there was only one man in command: me, and nobody else.

Those who were loyal to me would have nothing to fear, as I honestly intended to be a servant of god in all my actions. Yes, I would be a just ruler, intent on furthering the interests of my dominions and the people living on them; I would actively seek out wisdom wherever I could find it; I would intently and eagerly listen to whatever sound advice was offered to me – but nobody, absolutely nobody, would exercise any power, unless and until and to the extent I had authorised him to do so.

My generals, my governors and courtiers: willing or unwilling, they would all come to understand that their only task, and the only way for them to gain any personal wealth and standing, was to obey me, and faithfully serve the empire. The likes of Adham Khān, and all others who tried to serve themselves, would end up with nothing.

So I told Mun'im Khān that I had the fullest confidence in Pīr Muhammad Khān's martial prowess; and to make sure he clearly understood that I was lying, I added, with the sweetest smile on my face, that I did not want to deprive Māham Anaga of her son's companionship. . . .

The next day, I made my second and final move: I dismissed Mun'im Khān from his office as wakīl, and appointed Shams-ud-dīn.

The firmān announcing the new appointment mentioned that since the task of wakīl was of utmost importance and a heavy burden on the shoulders of the incumbent, it was appropriate that it would, from time to time, be entrusted to someone else. With a thinly veiled insult directed at Mun'im Khān, it added that, because of the threat in Mālwa, it was becoming that the task should now be given to Shams-ud-dīn Muhammad Atga Khān, my devoted foster father, who had proven his valour and talent as a warrior on the battlefield.

This time, Māham Anaga and her followers were wise enough not to again try to make me change my mind, but did the only sensible thing possible under the circumstances: to comply with my orders, without discussion. Avoiding further confrontations with me, they made a brave effort to resume their lives at the court as if nothing had happened, waiting for an opportunity to regain the royal favour once my anger subsided.

It was both amusing and sobering to see how quickly everybody adapted their attitude towards the disfavoured. The signs were subtle, but nonetheless clear: greetings had become less cordial, polite bows of courtesy less deep, orders and requests less diligently executed. Indeed, as I already pointed out to you, my son, a group of people does not behave very differently from a herd of animals. . . .

As I expected, Shams-ud-dīn—may god recompense him for his loyalty!—proved himself an exemplary wakīl: competent, efficient, dedicated, loyal, and unobtrusive. Insensitive to flattery, abhorring gossip and intrigue, he went about his tasks solely at the service and in the shadow of his emperor. The group around Māham Anaga, my informants told me, was consumed with envy. It was exactly what I wanted to hear.

Fourteenth Letter

آجمیر

Ajmir

With Shams-ud-dīn's competent assistance, I seriously devoted myself to my duties as emperor. Following the example Bairām Khān had given me, I made sure nothing escaped my attention, controlling, at random, even the smallest things; present everywhere, making sure everybody realised that their emperor was watching them.

Pleasantly surprising was it to find how easy it all came to me, and even more so, how profoundly happy I felt. I still enjoyed my hunting parties, the cups of wine in the evening, and the sweet companionship of women, but I no longer had to feel guilty over these things, as I was also doing my duty. Only those who are not lazy, my son, can really enjoy the rewards of relaxation. . . .

Despite the frantic busyness of my life and the many uncertainties, my mind was now at peace. As I have done all my life, I put my trust in god, devoting many hours to solitary prayer. Each time I felt uncertain or worried, I would appeal to Him, asking to grant me the strength, endurance, and wisdom I needed.

Most probably under His direct inspiration and guidance, I started to inform myself firsthand about my subjects, their actual living conditions, their opinions, hopes and fears. As you have read in the abstract of Salīmā's memoirs, I followed the great Hārūn ar-Rashīd's example, and started wandering in disguise around the streets and alleys of Āgrā. Gradually, and as I will explain in more detail later, those contacts with the ordinary people helped me understand what god really wanted from me.

One Thursday evening at sundown, I joined a mahfil-e-sam'a[96] around a band of five excellent qawwālī musicians. Together with the other listeners, I abandoned my soul to the entrancing rhythm of the tablā drums, and to the devotion and piousness of the lyrics: *Kirpā karo māhārāj, Muīn-ud-dīn* . . .

The words of the hymn entered my soul like a direct message from god:

Master of all masters of truth, pride of all worlds, crown of the crowns, Muīn-ud-dīn;
With just a wink of your eye, success will be mine;
Your door, the source of my fortune, is given to me by god . . .

Even before the song was over, my mind was made up: I would travel to Ājmīr to pray and meditate at the blessed dargah of that saint of saints, Khwājah Muīn-ud-dīn Muhammad Chishtī,[97] the peace of god be upon him.

A few days later, it must have been in the beginning of the fourth month of the Hijrī year 969,[98] I departed to Ājmīr, accompanied by only a small military escort and a few attendants.

I made sure that Adham Khān, his mother and Mun'im Khān stayed among my retinue: it would not have been prudent to allow them to be out of my sight.

It was the first of many pilgrimages I undertook to that most holy place, where I would find wisdom, clarity of thought, strength, repose, and peace.

---

96. Assembly of listeners
97. See Fifth Letter, last footnote: Khwājah Muīn-ud-dīn Muhammad Chishti (1142–1236), founder of the Chishtiya Sūfī order in India, came to Ajmer from Persia in 1192. Till today, his tomb in the city of Ajmer is an important place of worship, for Muslims and Hindus alike.
98. Mid-January 1562.

Now that I am older, I have come to doubt whether tombs and shrines truly can have the powers that people ascribe to them, but there is no denying: This pilgrimage did bring me all the blessings I had hoped for, and many more. Indeed, if I'm honest, I have to admit that most of the good things in my life have come to me through my association with the Khwājah Muīn-ud-dīn and his sacred legacy.

Already on the way over to Ājmīr, god's grace came over me in plenitude – even though at the time I did not fully comprehend its meaning and extent. It was like the first soft drops of monsoon rain on seemingly barren fields: The land does not seem to change, other than its dust changing into mud, but a few weeks later, it will become alive, lush and verdant, with the promise of crops in abundance.

Crossing into Rājputānā on our journey, it was disturbing to see the villagers fleeing in panic upon our approach. These lands were mine, they belonged to my empire, and yet, it was painfully obvious that its inhabitants had learned to fear their Muslim rulers. I promised myself that the first thing I would do upon my return to Āgrā, would be to prohibit killing and enslavement of civilians in war.

For, as Abū-l Fazl phrased it: 'If the husbands have taken the path of insolence, how is it the fault of the wives; and if the fathers have chosen the road of opposition, what fault have the children committed?'

Mind you, my son: The use of violence is of course necessary in the conquest of new territories and the reduction of its fortresses, for resistance must be crushed with firmness and determination, whenever and wherever it is encountered. However, plunder is not the final purpose of conquest. In order for an empire to grow strong, war must be followed by peace, harshness by magnanimity. The conquered lands must be blended into the empire, through justice and prosperity. Their inhabitants must come to love and respect their new ruler, after they have learned to fear him. The empire, of which they are now citizens, must become to them a source of pride – a safe home, worth fighting for.

Similar thoughts must have been on the mind of the local ruler, Rājā Bihārī Mal of Amber, who had submitted to our authority, and had in exchange been allowed to retain control over the region. Emissaries arrived, carrying exquisite gifts and flowery letters of praise and submission, soon to be followed by the rājā himself, who came in person to kiss my stirrup.

The rājā was a remarkable man indeed. He seemed imposing, daunting, in spite of the humility of his gestures and attitude. He was surprisingly gentle and peaceful, despite his warlike appearance. He was tall, broad-shouldered, and of remarkably strong build for a man of his advancing age. By far the most salient feature of his appearance, however, was the dark, fleshy face under the orange turban. It was dominated, rather than adorned, by the most extravagant beard I had ever seen: a hand's-length long, parted in the middle, then brushed straight sideways and upward. It made his head look at least four fingers wider on both sides, like the mane of a beast of prey.

Despite the singular extravagance of his appearance, he proved to be a rather simple, soft-spoken man, clearly anxious to do what was in the interest of the people entrusted to his care. His black eyes under the bushy eyebrows looked a bit nervous perhaps, but not at all hostile.

He spoke slowly and used whatever Persian words he knew, making it rather easy for me to understand his Rājputānā dialect.

He wished to reaffirm his unwavering loyalty to me – he had been a faithful supporter of my father, who had been a wise man and close to god; and he would continue to support his noble son. All he was asking for was for him and the people of Rājputānā to be allowed to live their lives undisturbed, according to their own traditions, and to serve god in the way their ancestors had taught them. In exchange, I could count on them and their swords to defend the empire and expand its borders.

I assured him that this was exactly the way I saw things myself; that those who remained loyal to the empire would be guaranteed sulh-i-kul, peace for all, even if they did not follow Islām; that it was reassuring for me to know that I could count on the valour and well-known military prowess of the noble Rājpūts. If we, Hindūs and Muslims, would allow ourselves to become enemies, we would destroy or at least severely weaken each other; and in the end, we would both lose. Together, however, we would be invincible.

He looked at me, inquisitively, his eyes slightly narrowed, clearly looking for some kind of evidence or confirmation that I really meant what I said. And indeed, I did: I was and I remain firmly convinced that the land of Hindustān is invincible, if only its inhabitants find it in their hearts to remain united.

Seeing the honesty in my eyes, he smiled, showing two of his upper front teeth: large and bright white they were, and very square, with a large opening in between them. Despite the wild beard and whiskers, he suddenly looked like an eight-year-old.

'I must congratulate His Majesty on the wisdom he has acquired, despite his young age,' he said. 'It is a great relief for me and my people that we will be the allies of a man of god.'

He paused. The smile disappeared, and a kind of sadness came into his eyes. He looked at me pleadingly, as if he were asking for some kind of reassurance.

'Your Majesty, it would be an honour for me and my people,' he said, trying to read my reaction as he was speaking, 'if our pādshāh would do me the honour of accepting my daughter in marriage.'

I bowed courteously.

'I am grateful and honoured by your most kind and generous offer, noble Rājā Bihārī Mal. This marriage will be the symbol of our eternal friendship!'

'You and your family can rest assured that your noble daughter will be treated with the respect due to her high rank,' I added, trying to give him the reassurance he was looking for.

'Your Majesty is most kind. I will . . .'

He swallowed, with some difficulty, as if he was taking some kind of foul-tasting medicine, and then reluctantly finished his sentence.

'I will of course instruct my daughter to make herself fully acquainted with the rules applicable at Your Majesty's court, and to convert to Your Majesty's religion.'

'I am most grateful, but that will not be necessary,' I replied, ignoring the surprise on everybody's face. 'Your daughter will remain free to worship god in accordance with her own traditions, if she so prefers.'

He bowed deeply – this was clearly much more than he had ever expected or hoped for.

'Your Majesty is most wise and just. He can depend on me and my people under any circumstance!'

I nodded my approval, and took him by the shoulders in a friendly embrace, and he reciprocated the gesture. We agreed that the wedding ceremony would take place on my way back to Āgrā, and that Mān Singh, adopted son of Rājā Bhagwān Dās, the heir of Rājā Bihārī Mal, would accompany us to the court as well, and enter the imperial service.

Little did I know that this heir of his would become my greatest general, forging my Muslim and Hindū forces into one, invincible army; fighting and winning close to one hundred and twenty wars for me. . . .

And little did I realise that that bashful young Hindū girl, whom I did not know, whom I had yet to lay eyes on, of whose I did not even quite catch the name,[99] was to become the great qadasī-arkānī Maryam uz-zamānī,[100] mother of the noble Prince Salīm, heir to the Gurkaniyya throne, destined to become the great Emperor Jahāngīr. . . .

Looking back on my life, it was then and there, with that friendly embrace of your maternal grandfather that I founded my empire.

Admittedly, it was my revered father—may he be received in the bliss of paradise!—who gave me my inheritance: a claim to sovereignty over rich and important, if heavily disputed, dominions.

Admittedly, it was Bairām Khān—may he be rewarded in eternity for his dedication and loyalty!—who finished what my father had started. When he took on his task, many powerful enemies were threatening to wipe us out. By the time of his death, he had made us the dominant power in Hindustān – not one of the neighbouring kings could hope to challenge me and survive.

Yes, I do owe my empire to my father and to my faithful atālīq; this much I have to admit. But nobody can deny that it is I who made this

---

99. Surprising though it may be, the name of Akbar's first Rājpūt wife is a matter of some controversy. Apart from the title of honour, Maryam uz-zamānī (i.e. Mary of the age, a title that was bestowed upon her when she gave birth to Salīm), her maiden name is not known with absolute certainty. Popular tradition in India calls her by the name Jodhā Bai or Jodh Bai, which means 'lady of Jodh(pur)'. This is clearly wrong: Akbar never did marry any princess from the Jodhpur area, and certainly never had a wife called Jodhā Bai: Jodhā Bai was, in fact, the name of one of Jahāngīr's wives. The leading opinion among scholars currently seems to be that Maryam uz-Zamānī's maiden name was Rajkumari Hira Kunwari, alias Harkha Bai (that is what the famous author Salman Rushdie calls her in his novel *The Enchantress of Florence*.)

100. Qadasī-arkānī: pillar of purity; Maryam uz-zamānī: Mary of the age (see the previous note).

empire three, four times as large, and gave it its current prosperity and strength.

When I will be dead and gone, Salīm, the empire I shall leave you will indeed be very different from the one my father Humāyūn left me, or the one he inherited from Bābur pādshāh.

Not only is it much larger, wealthier and more powerful but it is fundamentally different too. You see, all the sultāns of Dillī—the Afghāns in Bengāl, Bābur pādshāh, Shēr Khān Sūr, Humāyūn—were foreign Muslim rulers. The population of their dominions remained sharply divided between the ruling Muslim minority, and the subdued Hindū masses, sometimes persecuted, sometimes tolerated, but always despised as a bunch of pagan, blasphemous idol worshippers.

I have done my best to change all that, for I did not want to be the head of the Muslims alone, but of every man and woman living in my empire.

While I may not have been able to fully bridge the gap that exists between the many religions, traditions and denominations in our dominions—will anybody ever succeed in doing that?—I am proud to point out that my reign has truly brought sulh-i-kul. Under my rule, everybody has enjoyed the freedom to serve and worship god according to his own traditions and beliefs, and many have indeed come to understand that all paths, no matter how diverse, ultimately lead to Him, Who is compassionate and merciful to all. Many of the people in our lands have come to appreciate the traditions of the other denominations, and friendships have developed across the boundaries of religion and origin.

I have tried to weave together the many traditions of this land, just like strings of many colours are intertwined and knit together to form a beautiful carpet. I have been able to accomplish that result not only through showing respect for all faiths and traditions, but also and more importantly, through installing a different kind of government. Positions of responsibility in my empire are no longer based on descent, origin, or inheritance, but on dedication and ability. The mansabdārs, who govern my provinces, do so not because they have inherited the territory from their fathers, but in my name and on my behalf, because I have appointed them, and until I choose to relieve them of their duty. The territory under my dominion is no longer a patchwork of fiefs and kingdoms that have surrendered to an invader: It is one empire under the rule of one emperor, who is the sole and legitimate representative of god Himself.

The pilgrimage to Ājmīr went as planned. I spent a few days in the city, praying near the shrines of Khwājah Muīn-ud-dīn and of his saintly daughter Bibi Hāfez Jamāl, visiting the various mosques and seeking the blessings of learned and saintly men. The rest of my time, I spent in solitary prayer and reflection, asking god to help me fulfill my destiny, and to make me His worthy representative on earth.

On the return journey, my marriage to Rājā Bihārī Mal's daughter was celebrated at Sāmbhar. I was happy to find she was quite pretty, a bit frail perhaps, but very graceful and noble-featured.

As could be expected from a princess of royal Rājpūt blood on her wedding day, she was richly attired, heavy gold jewellery adorning every visible part of her body. The parting of her beautiful black hair had been coloured deep red with henna, symbolising her prayers for a long and healthy life for her husband.

Her face, however, was expressionless, her eyes timid and downcast. It seemed she had been crying. I could not help feeling sorry for her – barely fifteen years old, and about to leave her home, her family, and everybody and everything she knew, to be married off to some stranger, and move to a land she had never laid eyes on . . .

I asked Rājā Bihārī Mal to allow my new wife's personal cooks and servants to accompany her to Āgrā, as I wanted to make sure she would be attended to in the way she liked.

Throughout the ceremony and the following feast, I tried to be as friendly and reassuring to her as possible. On our wedding night, I had the wisdom and restraint not to immediately impose myself, but spent the time getting to know her, talking to her the best I could, in Hindustānī. When we were both dead tired, in the middle of the night, I invited her to come to sleep next to me, without touching her.

My patience was rewarded. When I woke up, I was happy to find she was lying next to me, ready this time to become my wife. I kissed her and gently called her 'my love'.

I have continued to do so ever since, even when almost seven years later, god granted me the privilege to create you, my son.

Fifteenth Letter

ماہم انگہ، ادھم خان

Māhām Anāgā, Adhām Khān (2)

We headed back to Āgrā and arrived there on the second of Esfand, or the eighth of Jumādā 'l Ukhrā of the year 969.[101] Twenty-six days later, grandiose festivities were organised to celebrate the beginning of the seventh year of my reign. Despite the exuberance of the feast, I could not help feeling a bit sad: six years already . . . six years had passed, never to come back again. Thus life slips through our fingers, like sand, my son. . . .

Shortly after the celebrations, reports started coming in: The situation in Mālwa was quickly getting out of hand.

Pīr Muhammad Khān had done surprisingly well in the beginning, but then, as expected, had become the victim of his own impetuousness.

After the conquest of Mālwa, he had headed further south, capturing Bijāgarh, again with much—way too much—unnecessary bloodshed. He then invaded Khāndesh, where Bāz Bahādūr had taken refuge. He captured the fort of Asīrgarh and pushed forward all the way to Burhānpūr, destroying and killing everything and everybody on his way.

---

101. Friday, 13 February 1562

But that is where his luck ran out on him. His advance was checked by a coalition of three local rulers: Bāz Bahādur himself, aided by Mubārak Khān of Khāndesh, and Tufāl Khān of Berār.

He hastily retreated towards Mālwa. Having reached the Narmadā after dark, he insisted, against the good advice and repeated pleas of his officers, on crossing it during the night. It proved to be a fatal mistake. In the middle of the river, he was thrown off his horse and drowned – 'the just retribution', as Shaykh Badāonī later phrased it, 'for the sighs of the orphans, the weak, and the captives'.

This was a minor defeat for the imperial army, but a major step forward for me, for a potentially dangerous ally for Adham Khān was now out of the way.

Our army, having lost its commander, headed back to Āgrā, and Bāz Bahādur even managed to temporarily recover his kingdom, but that did not worry me that much. I would be back, whenever I wanted to: My invasion army had not been lost – all it needed was a bit of rest, some reinforcements, and a new and competent general to lead it back into battle.

This, Māham Anaga must have thought, was a chance to redeem herself and that son of hers.

She did do her best to seize the opportunity: The frequency of her courtesy calls increased sharply, and she made more than one passing remark that her son would be overjoyed to get the opportunity to avenge the death of his trusted friend Pīr Muhammad Khān. I merely answered they both could rest assured: Justice would be done.

As I expected, she also sent Mun'im Khān to deliver the same message. Adham Khān, he said, was just itching to get back in the saddle. He would avenge his friend in rivers of blood. He would firmly establish my authority in Mālwa and the neighbouring territories.

I assured him that I had no doubt whatsoever about the truth of his words, and that Mālwa would indeed be restored to the empire.

Whatever hopes they still may have entertained, were thoroughly shattered when I appointed Abdullāh Khān Uzbeg to lead the new invasion into Mālwa.

Predictably, the tough Uzbeg did not disappoint me: In a few weeks' time, he utterly crushed Bāz Bahādur's army and drove him out of Mālwa – this time for good.

The ousted Bāz Bahādūr wandered around for years as a landless fugitive, seeking refuge and support in the sultanates of the south. It was all in vain, of course, for none of the kings of the south wanted to provide the mighty Mughal emperor with a pretext for war.

Eight years later, at Nāgaur, he would finally surrender to me, kneeling and rubbing his forehead in the dust as a repentant sinner, and once more, I would taste the sweetest of victories, which is, to pardon a former enemy. To execute an opponent, is to pay him tribute: it is to admit, that he did constitute a real danger – that he was, to a certain extent at least, a true rival. To show mercy, on the other hand, truly demonstrates one's own power and supremacy.

I allowed him to join my service – just like adding a captured wild elephant to a herd of tamed ones. Truth be told, I have never once regretted my decision – he turned out to be a grateful and loyal assistant, a most valuable enrichment to my court. Many a thing I learned from him – in fact, I know very few people with such thorough knowledge and understanding of music and the arts. It would indeed have been a waste of talent had he been executed.

But let me come back to my story. Abdullāh Khān Uzbeg's appointment was, of course, the deathblow to Adham Khān's ambitions – once again, a clear sign that I had no intention of appointing him to a position of power ever again.

I knew it insulted and angered him beyond words. My informants kept warning me about him almost every day, but I chose not to intervene. In fact, it was exactly what I wanted to hear – I wanted him to stew in his own juice, to resent me, to hate me, and not be able to do one thing about it. To intervene would have been an admission on my part that he still mattered; to ignore him was to confront him with his own insignificance. In the end, he would endure the ultimate of punishments, which is: to despise oneself.

With the wisdom of hindsight, however, I have to admit it was imprudent and reckless of me. He still constituted a real danger – I should have realised that, and acted accordingly. To underestimate an enemy is always a mistake!

Indeed, all this spite and hatred, it was like a festering abscess, waiting to burst – and so it did.

In the hot afternoon of Shanbeh, the fifth of Khordād, or Yawm as-Sabt, the twelfth of Ramadān of the year 969,[102] I was resting in the zanāna, while Shams-ud-dīn and other officials were having a meeting in the neighbouring courtyard, when suddenly, Adham Khān walked into the courtyard with a couple of his personal guards. They went straight to poor Shams-ud-dīn, who, unaware of any harm, courteously rose to greet them. Without any warning, one of Adham Khān's henchmen drew a dagger and stabbed my loyal atga in the chest. He still tried to escape, staggering towards the gate, but the murderers easily caught up with him, and struck him dead before he had taken five steps.

To this day, I do not know what exactly happened. Had the guards been bribed? Were they at a loss as to what to do, as this was apparently some kind of reckoning between prominent members of the imperial court? The fact is, they did not intervene, and Adham Khān ran up the steps to the terrace outside the harem unhindered.

I do not know what he was up to. Most probably, he wanted to kill me as well, or maybe he just wanted to be the first to tell me about my atga's death and appease my anger with some kind of excuse; I guess I will never know.

Fortunately, the eunuch on guard had the presence of mind to shut and bolt the terrace door right in front him, preventing him from entering the zanāna proper.

Meanwhile, I had been awakened by the noise, and came out of my quarters to see what was going on. Rafīq, the old family servant, in panic, pointed through one of the windows at poor Shams-ud-dīn's body in the courtyard.

Without another moment's thought, wearing nothing more than a loin cloth, I grabbed the sword one of the eunuch guards handed to me, and went out onto the terrace through the other door.

There he was.

'You ozgal-i-kuni[103] what have you done!' I shouted, stepping in his direction.

---

102. Saturday, 16 May 1562 of the Julian calendar.
103. Faggot's asshole (Persian). According to some historians, Akbar called him a batchā-i-lada (Persian): young of a dog, son of a bitch; or a babesyā (Hindī), i.e. a catamite, someone in the habit of getting sodomised.

He came towards me, bowing deeply, a phony grin on his face.

'Please wait a moment, Your Majesty,' he said, and took hold of my right arm.

Maybe this was a feeble attempt to overpower me, maybe he merely tried to prevent me from using my sword, but whatever his intentions, he clearly picked the wrong tactic, and the wrong opponent.

I was only nineteen years old at the time, but strong as a bull, and well trained – very few men could hope to defeat me in man-to-man combat. Indeed, god, who is just and merciful and gives in abundance without being asked, has graciously blessed the men of our family with strong limbs, and as you know, I have always found great pleasure in exercising my strength, agility and fighting skills.

Maybe he should have tried to appease my anger; maybe he should have thrown himself at my feet, begging for forgiveness, inventing some kind of excuse for what had happened – I honestly do not know what I would have done. But this insolent attempt to restrain me made me beyond myself with rage.

It did not take me much effort to pull my arm out of his grip, but I did not even bother to use my sword: In one swift move, I hit him straight in the face with my left fist – I could feel the bone in his nose break under my knuckles.

He fell to the ground like a sack of flour, moaning, bleeding heavily – it looked as if he had been hit with a mace. I wanted to go on and kick him to death myself, but decided, in time, that he did not deserve that kind of honour. Regaining my composure, I coldly ordered the attendants to bind his arms and legs with their girdles, and to throw him off the terrace.

'He has violated the sacred area of my home, and entered the confines of the harem, head-first,' I hissed, 'so throw him out of it, head-first!'

My command was executed, but in a rather clumsy way – he landed on his legs, and although he probably did suffer a number of fractures, the fall did not kill him.

'Don't just stand there!' I yelled, still beyond myself with rage, and quite deaf to Adham Khān's desperate pleas for mercy. 'Drag that sack of shit up here again, and throw him off the terrace, again, and again, and again if you must – I want him dead!'

They did not have to do it a third time. This time, he fell on his head; his neck snapped, and the brains dashed out of his fractured skull. For a few more moments, his arms and legs kept on twitching violently, like the wings and legs of a freshly slaughtered chicken. Then, he lay still, his eyes and mouth wide open. Not a pretty sight, but, all in all, a swift and merciful death.

I ordered the bodies of both victim and murderer to be brought to Dillī.

There, Shams-ud-dīn's sons, Yūsuf and Azīz, commenced the construction of their father's tomb, near the sacred dargahs of Khwājah Nizam-ud-dīn and of the divine Amīr Khusrau[104] – not too far from the spot where my own father would later get his final resting place.

Adham Khān's body was to be committed to earth over two kos south of there, in a quiet area near the village of Mehrauli, about three hundred paces west from the beautiful Qutub Minar.[105]

Poor Māham Anaga, who had been ill in her chambers since a couple of days, had heard some rumours that her son had got himself into trouble again; apparently, however, nobody had found the courage to tell her what had happened.

Brave and decisive as always, she asked for an audience, and despite her illness, came to beg my indulgence for whatever her son had done wrong this time.

Upon her arrival, I reluctantly gave orders to admit her in my presence.

When I saw her, a tired, frightened old lady, I did no longer remember her devious, murderous intrigues. I just saw the woman who had taken care of me for so many years when I was a little boy, who had been devoted to me, who had fed me, washed me, clothed me, kept me company and taught me so many things.

---

104. Nizam-ud-dīn Auliya Chishti was a revered Sūfī sage; Amīr Khusrau, a famous Persian poet. The Nizamuddin area still is an important place of pilgrimage in Delhi.
105. 'Axis of Islām', the seventy-three-metre high minaret-tower of victory, one of Delhi's main historical sights. Its construction started in 1193, under Qutub-ud-dīn Aybak, first of the Muslim sultāns of Delhi.

All I saw was an old mother who had loved her own son above everything else, in spite of everything—what else is a parent to do, my son?—and I pitied her deeply.

I did not have the heart to tell her in so many words that her son was dead. Evading her glance, I said, softly, almost apologetically:

'Adham Khān killed the atga – we had to punish him, Māhamjī.'

Pale, her lower lip trembling, she found the strength to reply: 'Your Majesty did well,' and retired. She went straight to her quarters, never to leave them again. She ate and drank very little, and her illness, whatever it was, worsened quickly. Clearly, the will to live had left her. Forty days later, she expired.

I paid homage to her frail old body, and ordered it to be taken to Dillī, to be interred near her son – I even accompanied the bier for a short distance on its way.

I had a beautiful tomb erected above their graves, at my personal expense. If we are capable of showing mercy upon those who have wronged us, maybe god will find it easier to have mercy on us, on the day of resurrection. . . .

The tomb is, if I say so myself, quite a graceful building, with its Afghān-style dome and the octagonal gallery of twenty-four arches, where the people from the neighbourhood come for some cool shade and a quiet stroll in the evening. At dawn and at sunset, its yellow-ochre stones seem aglow with the peaceful, golden light of paradise. . . . May it one day shine on us all, weak and pitiful human beings!

Sixteenth Letter

صلح کل

Ṣulḥ-i-Kul [106]

You have been able to read in Salīmā's diary, my son, how I, after the great Hārūn ar-Rashīd's example, would often leave the palace, in *tebdil*,[107] strolling through the alleys of Āgrā, and mingling with the ordinary people. A wise decision this was, for a ruler should be cognisant of what is on the mind of his subjects.

You have seen how, for the first time in my life, I had a real conversation with a Hindū devotee. If it is true that god directs our lives, there is no doubt in my mind: this was not an accidental encounter – this had been ordained by the Almighty Himself!

Whatever its cause, divine intervention or sheer coincidence, this meeting completely changed my outlook on the country I have been chosen to rule and the people who live in it.

I had always taken for granted that the Hindūs are a bunch of ignorant idolaters – to be converted, if possible, to be repressed, if necessary. During that memorable conversation, however, I came to understand that much wisdom is to be found in their writings, and much sanctity in their ways.

---

106. Peace for all.
107. Disguise

I still see him before my mind's eye: this frail, ash-smeared, skinny old man in his simple loincloth, his friendly, if slightly mocking smile, and his patient, gentle eyes barely visible amidst the wild hair and beard. It seems I can still hear him, explaining patiently and with great clarity, how, in spite of the multitude of gods and goddesses, most Hindūs believe there is only one god, of Whom we are all part, and with Whom we will all be reunited.

'Most Hindūs will tell you, young sāhab, that the many deities are *avatārs*, manifestations of god under a certain aspect. There are also others, for whom these individual deities are just symbols, mere human attempts to describe certain aspects of the ultimate reality in a more understandable language of images and stories. There are even schools of Hindū philosophy that altogether deny god's existence!'

'But how can that be?' I asked. 'Which one of these beliefs is true, according to the holy books of your religion?'

'All of them – and perhaps none of them, young sāhab. As it is proclaimed in our sacred Vedas: *There is One Truth; only men describe it in different ways*.'

'And how would you then describe god?'

'That depends, young sāhab. With my heart, I feel Him near me, a warm, benevolent presence, a loving father Who supports me throughout my existence, and calls me forward towards Him; Who knows me, far better than I do myself, and Who loves me, with a love deeper than anyone is capable of. It is the god from Whom I am separated, and to Whom I will return.

'In my thinking mind, however, he is more distant. There, I understand Him not as a person, but as reality or existence itself. He is the force inside everything and everybody, without which nothing would exist at all; timeless, unborn, imperishable; but also: formless, blind, and, I'm afraid, without any feelings or awareness.'

'But that comes very close to saying that god and the world are one and the same thing, or that there is no god at all!'

'Perhaps, young sāhab. As I told you, there are schools of Hindū thought that deny god's existence.'

Seeing the puzzled expression on my face, he continued:

'Young sāhab, I do not know that much about your religion of Islām and the other religions from the West. However, it seems to me, they are all very much preoccupied with obedience, punishment and reward, and they all follow a similar kind of reasoning:

> One: There is one almighty god, lord and creator of the universe.
> Two: God will reward the good and punish the evil.
> Three: In order to obtain salvation, man must follow god's commands.
> Four: There is only one true faith, which god Himself has revealed to humankind, speaking through one or more prophets and holy scriptures.
> Five: He who fails to embrace this one true faith and does not follow its precepts, will suffer the eternal torments of hell.

'The sanātana dharma, or what you call the "Hindū" faith, young sāhab, is quite different. It is more preoccupied with the attainment of wisdom, you see, and it readily acknowledges that wisdom can be found everywhere. Consequently, it does not claim that there is one single orthodox point of view leading to salvation. It has no central authority, and it allows hundreds of contradictory opinions and practices to coexist. In fact, there is no such thing as *the* Hindū religion or philosophy – there are so many different beliefs and systems of thought in this country that you could never study them all in depth in a single lifetime! Perhaps the only common feature of all these religions is their preoccupation with moksha, liberation, which can, and will be, achieved through wisdom or enlightenment.'

'And how do we attain that perfect knowledge?' I asked.

'In the course of many thousand lives, we create what is called good or bad karma, which is the result of all our thoughts and actions. Everything we do or think has its inevitable consequences, and the lives we are born into, are the result of karma created in previous incarnations. That is why some of us are born as mighty kings, young sāhab. . . .'

He stopped speaking and looked intently at my face. I tried to look as disinterested as possible, but I again had that awkward feeling of being caught red-handed.

He smiled and continued:

'As I said, young sāhab, that is why some of us are born as kings, and others as lowly sweepers. Different as our lives may be, we are all on our way, back to god.'

'So, after death, we are born again, and god punishes or rewards us with a new life, worse or better than the one before?'

'Yes, and no, young sāhab. You see, god does not hate or punish anyone. What happens to us, is simply the inevitable result of our own thoughts and actions.

'You can compare it to the fate of a man standing on top of a cliff, who decides to jump into the abyss below him. If, despite his hopes and prayers, he falls to his death, do you think this is god's punishment for his reckless behaviour? No, young sāhab, the man will fall, because such is the way things are – his death is nothing more than the natural and inevitable consequence of his own action.

'This is how the inexorable law of karma works, young sāhab: Virtuous thoughts and actions produce good karma and lead to knowledge and liberation, whereas bad ones lead to bondage and suffering.

'Another important thought to note here, young sāhab: Does the man from our example fall to his death, because he is a *sinner*? No! He dies because of his ignorance; he dies, because he holds the mistaken belief that prayer will save him from falling. This is another important teaching in Hindū religion: We all sin or create bad karma, out of ignorance.

'There is a beautiful verse in one of the most important of our holy scriptures, the *Śrīmad Bhagvadgītā*, where Lord Kṛṣṇa Himself declares:

> Even if thou art the worst of sinners
> Thou shalt cross the ocean of sin
> By the bark of Wisdom[108]

'So, in the end, will I, a Muslim, get there?'

'Certainly, young sāhab! Lord Kṛṣṇa Himself proclaimed it in the *Bhagvadgītā*:

> Whatever and whichever way men approach Me,

---

108. *Bhagavad Gita*, 4:36.

> Whatever paths they may choose
> Finally lead to Me

'Or, as one of my teachers once phrased it:
As different streams having different sources all mingle their waters in the sea, so the different paths that men take, through different tendencies, various though they appear, crooked or straight, all lead to god.[109]

Live a good life, young sāhab, be a good Muslim – that will be amply sufficient! Serve your god Allāh in humility, and never forget that in your religion, He is called the Compassionate and the Merciful. And maybe try to learn something from us – learn to see and worship Him in everything and everybody you encounter!'

We walked up the stairs of the central sanctuary of the temple. He told me the names of the gods represented by the idols, what they stand for, the symbolism of the objects they hold in their many hands, and the strange animals they are riding.

Some of them I remember: Gaṇeśa, the elephant-headed god, seated on a rat; Śiva, with his trident and his cobras; Durgā, the invincible goddess with the many arms, who rides on the back of a lion; Lakshmī, the goddess of wealth . . . There were many more of them, but I was too busy looking at the people and the temple ceremonies.

'I'm afraid I will not be able to remember all this,' I said. 'I will have to come back some other time, and maybe learn some more about all these gods and what they stand for.'

'Any time, young sāhab! Eagerness to learn is always a good thing. And what is even more important: You are blessed with an open mind – preserve it well!'

He looked at me, still with a friendly smile, but very serious now. It felt as if he were looking right into the depths of my soul.

'Some of us, young Turkomān sāhab,' he spoke slowly, as if tasting every word separately before pronouncing it, 'some of us have the opportunity, to touch the lives of many. . . . Use your life well, young sāhab, and create good karma, for yourself and others around you! Keep looking for your own true destiny; as it is said in our scriptures:

---

109. Swami Vivekananda, quoted by Ed. Viswanathan, p. 9.

> There is a deity residing within you;
> find It out,
> and obey Its commands!'

Before I had a chance to ask him for some further explanation, he joined his hands and bowed his head.

'Namaste, I bow to thee, young sāhab – or rather, I bow to god, Who lives inside you! As they say in your own religion: Khudā hāfiz, may god be your guide and protector! Now, if you will excuse me, I must go back and attend the temple ceremony.'

I touched my heart and forehead, as it is customary among Muslims, and then joined my hands and bowed my head, the Hindū way. 'Khudā hāfiz, and namaste, honourable sir! Thank you for your kindness and words of wisdom!'

I returned to the fort, and went straight to Mīr Abdul Latīf, anxious to hear what he would have to say about all this.

He did not hear me coming in at first, absorbed as he was in his reading.

I almost felt a bit jealous of him. As he was sitting there, the soft, golden light falling into his study, he looked the paragon of wisdom and peace. Everything about him seemed holy and venerable: his eyes under the bushy gray eyebrows, studying the beautiful manuscript on the book-rest in front of him; the long, gray beard under the clean-shaven upper lip; the expression of peace on his pale, lined face; his plain, sallow woolen clothes and turban. The Hindū sage in the temple had been right: There is wisdom to be found everywhere.

He suddenly became aware of my presence.

'Your Majesty! I am so sorry; I did not hear you coming in! How can I be of service to Your Majesty?'

'It is I who owe you an apology, Mīr Abdul Latīf – I did not mean to disturb you in your study. However, I would very much like to hear your opinion about something I have just heard!'

I told him about my wanderings in disguise, after the example of Hārūn ar-Rashīd, and about my visit to the Hindū temple. He listened very intently, smiling approvingly throughout the story.

'I am so very happy to hear that Allāh—praise be to Him—has blessed us with such a wise and noble king,' he said.

He rose to his feet and went to a pile of books and manuscripts in the corner of his study. Unerringly, he took out one paper from somewhere in the middle of the pile.

'Here is a very important document, Your Majesty – from the hand of Your Majesty's illustrious grandfather himself! I have been waiting for an appropriate opportunity to show it to you. As Your Majesty will hear, it is a kind of will and testament, in which Your Majesty's grandfather advises his high-born son, Your Majesty's father, on how to rule this country's diverse populations.'

He proceeded to read the letter to me. I found its message of such importance that I had it read to me in public, hundreds of times – not because I did not remember its contents, for I had very easily learned it by heart, but because I wanted all the mullāhs and courtiers to hear that I was governing Hindustān the way my revered forefathers had decreed it. Indeed, as you know all too well, my son, many are the times I have been accused of having abandoned Islām. . . .

The letter which our illustrious forefather leaves to all his successors, reads as follows:

All praise be to Allāh.
Secret Will of Zahīr-ud-dīn Muhammad Bābur [110]
To his son, Prince Nasīr-ud-dīn Muhammad Humāyūn,
may god prolong his life.

Written for the strengthening of the empire.

O my son, the empire of Hindustān consists of various religions – domination and sovereignty whereof has been bestowed on you by the grace of the almighty.

It is appropriate that religious bigotries be wiped off the tablet of the heart, and justice meted out to each religion according to its own tenets.

Specially, abstain from the sacrifice of cows, as this would tend to win the hearts of the people of Hindustān, and the populace of the country would be loyal to the royal favours. The temples and places of worship of whatever religion under the royal authority, may not be desecrated. Such

---

110. Will of Bābur, quoted by Professor R. Nath, in *India as Seen by Bābur*, p. 21-2.

218   The Emperor's Writings

justice may be adopted, that the king may be pleased with the rayyat,[111] and the rayyat with the king.

The advancement of Islām is better achieved with the weapon of obligation than with the sword of tyranny.

Overlook the dispute between the Sunnīs and Shī'as, since such weakness persists in Islām. Establish administration with the rayyat of various communities in accordance with the four principal elements so that the body of the empire may be free from different diseases.

The model work done by his Late Majesty Temür Sāhib Qirān should always be kept before the mind, so that you may become mature in the work of administration.

Written on the first of Jamādī 'al-Awwal 935.[112]

Mīr Abdul Latīf looked at me as if to make sure I had clearly understood.

'Your illustrious grandfather was right, Your Majesty: The most important, overriding principle that should guide any king of Hindustān, is sulh-i-kul.

'You see, Your Majesty, Hindustān is such a large country, its populations so diverse that a way needs to be found to allow all these peoples to live together – if not in complete harmony, then at least in peace and mutual respect. A Muslim king who would try to impose Islām by the sword, would do himself, and Islām, a disservice. In the eyes of the Hindū masses, he would never be more than a foreign invader, a conqueror to be opposed or at most endured, but never a king to be loved and respected. On the other hand, many more people will find the path towards the light of Islām under the guidance of a just, benevolent and tolerant sovereign, who is the true king of everybody – Muslims and non-Muslims alike.'

'Reverend master, are you then in agreement with that Hindū sage, who said that in the end, all religions are the same, and all will lead to salvation?'

---

111. Rayyat: Subjects
112. 11 January 1529

'Yes and no, Your Majesty. Let there be no misunderstanding: In my opinion, the religion of Islām is, without any shadow of a doubt, the ultimate and most perfect of all religions, and the holy Prophet Muhammad—eternal peace and blessings of Allāh be upon him and his household!—is the true seal of the prophets, Allāh's ultimate messenger.

'However, there should be no doubt: Divine revelation has been given to all humankind. The Holy Qur'ān says so itself, in various instances! For example, it is written: Mankind is a single nation. So Allāh raised prophets as bearers of good news and as warners, and He revealed with them the Book with Truth.[113]

'It is also written: For every nation, there is a messenger.[114] And also: There is not a people but a warner has gone among them.[115]

'From time to time in history, the cool, limpid, soothing, life-bringing waters of the bottomless ocean of mercy that is Allāh, have washed over the arid shores of humankind. The pools that have stayed behind, are the various religions revealed through the prophets. Through human error and sin, many of these pools have dried out or got polluted over time, and there is no doubt in my mind that among them, the religion of Islām is the deepest, the purest and the ultimate: indeed, it is the fulfillment and culmination of all other religions! However, we should never forget the divine origin of others' religions. We should respect and revere the holiness in them, and compete with them in doing good deeds, without allowing them to lead us astray or confuse us with error.

'Therefore, Your Majesty, while I remain profoundly convinced that Islām is superior to any other religion, I believe that where possible, we should be at peace with other religions, for they, too, have been inspired by the All-Merciful. Wherever you turn, there is the face of Allāh!'

'Is it then your opinion that non-believers will be allowed to enter paradise as well?'

'It is, Your Majesty. There is no doubt in my mind that eventually, everybody will attain paradise – Muslims and non-Muslims alike! Allāh

---

113. Qur'ān, 2:213
114. Qur'ān, 10:47
115. Qur'ān, 35:24

will reward the good and punish the evil, no matter where it comes from. The Holy Qur'ān states that 'he who has done an atom's weight of good will see it; and he who has done an atom's weight of evil will see it'.[116] However, the purpose of Allāh's chastisement, terrible as it may be, is not to torture us, but to purify our souls. Indeed, as it is written, Allāh 'has ordained mercy on Himself!'[117] Even the worst of sinners should not despair of the mercy of Allāh!'[118] For mercy did He create all men'!'[119] Yes, I am firmly convinced that hell, however long it will last, will cease to exist at some time. I do have to warn Your Majesty that many learned and respectable men will disagree with me. The highest-ranking Muslim scholar in Your Majesty's empire, Makhdūm-ul Mulk, will probably tell you that hell is eternal, or that only Muslim sinners will ultimately be released from it, but I believe he is mistaken: Allāh's wisdom and mercy are limitless!

'Allāh does not deal out punishment in anger or revenge; the recompense He gives is but the natural result and consequence of our own actions, and will lead to salvation and unity with Him.

'No, there is no doubt in my mind – all human souls, even those of the worst of sinners, and even those of non-Muslims, shall ultimately be released from hell when they are ready for their new and blissful existence in paradise!

'This is already clear from the Holy Qur'ān, which states that those in hell will abide there forever, *illā māshā'allāh:* except as Allāh pleases. The gift of paradise, in contrast, is truly eternal, a gift never to be cut off!

'This reading of the Holy Qur'ān is corroborated by the sayings of prophets and other venerable traditions. For instance, 'Umar, the second khalīfah—may his grave be holy—has declared: 'Even if the dwellers in hell may be numberless as the sands of the desert, a day will come when they will be taken out of it'. And the wise and learned Bukhārī—the peace of Allāh be upon him—has written: 'Surely, a day will come over hell when there shall not be a single human being in it'!

---

116. Qur'ān, 99:7,8
117. Qur'ān, 6:12,54
118. Qur'ān, 39:53
119. Qur'ān, 11:119

'So, you see, Your Majesty, I do not think that all religions are the same, but I do believe that what that Hindū sage said, was in fact true: All paths, straight and crooked, will ultimately lead to Allāh, because, in His endless mercy, He will forgive all sins and admit everyone in His presence.

'Ours should, therefore, be a religion of peace, tolerance, and humility before Allāh, Your Majesty. While our faith is undoubtedly the best of all religions, we should be ready to acknowledge goodness and truth, wherever we encounter it, for Allāh has given truth and wisdom to all peoples of the earth. We should at all times remain humble, for our knowledge and insights, however brilliant, will always remain incomplete and imperfect. Indeed, human knowledge and wisdom, however sublime, when compared to the divine wisdom, is like the flame of a candle to the light of a million suns. To Allāh alone belongs the beautiful name al-Haqq!'

'So, what you are actually saying, honourable master, is that contempt of religion, any religion, is really contempt of god Himself?' I asked.

For a moment, Mīr Abdul Latīf seemed to be hesitating.

'I have never phrased it so strongly, but yes, I suppose you are right, Your Majesty.'

That afternoon, my son, I had, for the first time, a clear vision of the Hindustān I wanted to create. Not the Hindustān of the Lodhis and the Sūrs, not even that of Bābur or Humāyūn. Not the Hindustān of Muslim conquerors ruling their Hindū vassals. No, in my mind's eye, I saw a prosperous and mighty Hindustān, its many people worshipping the one true god in their manifold ways, united in sulh-i-kul, under their one true emperor, god's shadow on earth.

I hardly slept that night, hoping and praying that almighty god would grant me the strength and wisdom to succeed.

The next morning, before dawn—the colour of the sky in the east was barely starting to shift from black to dark blue—I ordered Hairan to be saddled, the finest and fastest Irāqī stallion in my stables, and rode out, strictly forbidding anybody to follow me. The guards and servants were not even surprised: I had done this before, one morning in the times of the long siege of Mānkot, when, after a sleepless night, my mind was filled with darkness of thought, and I needed to get away from it all.

As Abū-l Fazl phrased it: 'His Majesty felt constrained by the presence of shortsighted men; he became averse to the servants of fortune's threshold and separated from them, and issued an order that no one in his retinue should be in attendance on him. He even sent away his grooms and suchlike persons, so that the solitude of his retirement might not be contaminated by the crowd'.

Indeed, I desperately wanted to be alone.

I left Āgrā behind me and headed east, towards the light of dawn, taking the direction of the hunting grounds, far away from any village or settlement. At first, I merely went at a brisk trot, but as soon as the ground became visible enough, I made Hairan run as fast as he could, until his flanks were soaked with sweat, and flocks of foam were flying from his mouth.

I halted in the middle of the wilderness and jumped off Hairan's back. The horse immediately galloped away and disappeared from sight, but I made no attempt to stop him or call him back.

I looked at the landscape around me. The sun was still behind the horizon, yet everything was turning copper-red with its first glow.

Suddenly realising that I was running late for salāt as-subh,[120] I hastily performed the required ablutions – with clean sand, as is allowed for those who do not have any water at their disposal. I took off my upper tunic, spread it on the ground as a prayer mat, and started my morning prayers, facing west towards Mekkah.

When I had finished, I rose to my feet, slowly turned around and looked at the landscape and the sun, the rim of which was now above the horizon, setting everything aglow with its golden light.

Despite the balmy air, I suddenly started shivering. In a way I cannot describe, I was overwhelmed with the unspeakable majesty of god, the awesome, daunting lord of all worlds, to Whom this giant, golden sun is but a tiny spark, and the mightiest empires of men are but passing specks of dust in the winds of time.

---

120. First ritual prayer, to be prayed in principle before dawn, between the moment when a thread of light is visible on the horizon, and the actual rising of the sun. It is usually performed as a 'missed prayer', upon waking.

It was as if I was standing before the divine throne, powerless, alone, naked and exposed in all my pitiful smallness, yet comforted by a loving, all-forgiving mercy, softer and gentler than moonlight. Tears rolled down my cheeks, and I fell to my knees before the sun, touching the ground with my forehead, as in salāt prayer.

After a few moments of wordless prayer, my soul had become completely peaceful. I sat myself down, cross-legged, facing the sun, my arms stretched out and resting on my knees, the palms of my hands upwards – the way I had often observed Hindū wise men meditating. In that position I stayed, thoughtless, motionless, I cannot say for how long, but when I opened my eyes again, the sun had reached the height of at least three men, and the air had started to shimmer with its heat.

I looked at the landscape around me again. The magic was gone, but I felt rested and peaceful and strong as never before, my soul filled with tranquil happiness.

I suddenly noticed that Hairan had returned after his escapade; he was standing at about ten paces from me. I just held out my hand, and he readily came to me. I softly touched his muzzle, patted the flank of his neck, and jumped back in the saddle. At a leisurely pace, we headed back to Āgrā.

I suddenly realised that this was the first time I had ever prayed while facing the sun; my back was turned towards Mekkah, but I did not feel guilty about it at all. Clearly, I had felt the daunting but sweet presence of god, Who is everywhere: inside man's temples, mosques and churches, and, maybe even more so, outside of them.

Countless times have I tried—and thankfully, often succeeded—to relive the blissful magic of that moment, meditating on a stone slab in the sun, or praying while looking at the light of a fire.

Light, fire, and the sun. . . . Indeed, the Parsīs are right: No manmade object better symbolises god's gentle yet awesome power, or the ineffable mystery of His magnificent creation. Not the Hindū statues and temples; not the holy books of the Jews, Muslims and Sikhs; not the qibla in the mosques; not the Christian crosses and bells, or the golden halos of their icons.

Light, fire, and the sun: gentle and terrifying are they, like god Himself. . . .

Without light, we cannot see, yet it can strike us with blindness; fire gives warmth to our homes and taste to our food, yet will reduce anything to ashes. The gentle, golden sun will call forward the crops from the earth, yet it is able to turn our fields into lifeless deserts and render fruitless the labour of our hands . . .

I know that evil tongues—including your own, my son—have tried to use my prayers and meditations against me. 'The emperor has abandoned Islām,' they whispered behind my back, 'he has adopted the wicked ways of the pagans. . . .'

You would know better than that! Never have I worshipped anything or anybody but god! All my life, I have been, or tried to be, His faithful servant, in complete submission to His Majesty – and what else is Islām, but submission to god?

One thing, however, I have come to realise: that all religions are but human attempts to understand god. Some may be better than others, but none of them is perfect, for no human being is perfect. Indeed, as Abū-l Fazl has quoted me saying: 'Each person, according to his personal condition, gives the supreme being a name, but in reality, to name the unknowable is vain . . .'

God—eternal praise be upon Him—will always be the One who defies human explanations. He is al-awwal, the first; al-ākhir, the last; al-aḥad, the One; al-wāhid, the unique; and always, akbar, the greater.

Greater is He, greater than any human mind could ever comprehend; and those who claim to know or possess Him, are in error.

Seventeenth Letter

سلطنت

Saltanat [121]

Thus ended my youth, Salīm my son, with the long overdue and well-deserved execution of a rebellious courtier, and the dawn of a great vision – that of a strong, prosperous and united Hindustān, ruled with firmness, generosity and justice by its rightful emperor.

Merciful god, who gives in abundance to whom He has chosen, has graciously made this dream of mine come true, and given me more than I could ever hope for, even in my wildest dreams. With His powerful help, I have removed all obstacles, and established what is probably the wealthiest and most powerful empire on the face of the earth – more than three times larger than that of my illustrious grandfather Bābur, at the height of his power!

Rarely, if ever, has the world seen an empire like the one you are about to inherit, my son. No enemy could ever hope to conquer it, if you maintain your vigilance. On the contrary, if you apply yourself to your task, and keep using your power in accordance with god's will, He may well allow you to expand our borders much further!

---

121. Saltanat: Kingship; empire.

Soon, very soon, you will find yourself on the throne, my son. I beseech you: Do not take your task lightly, for power is a precious treasure – lost more easily than gained!

Do remain on your guard, amidst and despite all the wealth and luxury that surround you, for they will distract you from what is important. You are of course welcome to enjoy the pleasures of life, for after all, they are god's merciful gift to man in this world – but only with moderation! Pleasure and repose, my son, are to be enjoyed like food. They are necessary to restore body and mind after work and exertion; but when taken in excess, they will bring nothing but sickness and ruin.

You know I am speaking the truth, Salīm – you know it, from your own experience: Desire enslaves the mind, and he who wallows in it, shall never attain success! How could you ever hope to rule over other people, if you are unable to control your own self?

Just read the history books, and observe, how sloth and greed have been the ruin of so many mighty kings! Preoccupation with pleasure and wealth softened their spirit, made them hungry for compromise, when they should have prepared themselves for war. I implore you, my son, in the name of our glorious ancestors, never allow this to happen to you!

The throne is a lonely place, Salīm my son. He who occupies it, needs to be strong, and watchful. He must realise that he is locked in a golden cage – dependent on others to tell him what is going on outside, and to act on his behalf.

Indeed, it is through the work of other people that you will succeed, or fail; therefore, nothing is more important than the selection of your ministers and advisors.

What the books say about this is so true: 'Rulers tend to get the advisors they deserve'. The easiest way indeed to assess a ruler's ability, is to look at his courtiers: Competent kings will always choose skilled assistants, and inept rulers inevitably pick the incapable ones. Never forget this, Salīm: A true king has no use for flattering yes-men; what he needs, is a group of strong helpers, resourceful, hard-working, ambitious, and loyal – loyal enough to warn him, respectfully but unequivocally, if they believe he is making a mistake.

However, no matter how competent your officials are, and no matter how deep your affection and trust, you always need to keep a close watch over them, and make frequent and unexpected examinations into their conduct – for, as the saying goes, opportunity makes the thief!

A king must, above all, be an astute observer, an excellent judge of character. Ask yourself what people think deep down inside behind their servile faces, my son; find out what it is that really drives them, and what is holding them back. Do you remember that pun, the one that Rājā Bīrbal so fondly used? 'The difference between truth and lie is the distance between the eye and the ear, because what we see with our own eyes is true, but what we hear with our ears usually is not!' So very true, indeed. . . . The best way to find out the truth, is to keep asking questions, a lot of them, all the time. In particular, ask people for their advice, for: Counsel is the mirror of the mind!

On the other hand, be extremely careful about what you say to whom, my son. Resist the temptation to confide in people. As the saying goes, a secret is merely something divulged to only one person at a time. . . . A king is wise not to reveal his inner thoughts – let him be an alert and careful listener, rather than a smooth talker!

Trust your old father, Salīm: I have seen and done it all, I know every trick in the book; I know the dangers and the pitfalls. Trust me, my beloved son, for I wish you nothing but well. Try to learn from this, the story of my life! Observe how I have dealt with the many challenges I had to face, so that you may be prepared to face your own when the time comes!

Looking back at the long years of my reign, my son, there have been—in my recollection at least—three periods, quite distinct from each other.

First, there were the eventful years of my now distant youth, which I have just finished describing to you: starting with the hasty enthronement of a young boy prematurely made emperor, and ending with the execution of an unruly foster brother who turned out to be a murderous rebel.

Most people tend to look back on their own youth with a degree of wistfulness. They remember the vigour of their body when it was still young, free from diseases and infirmities; they remember the seemingly limitless promise of an unspoilt future. In the light of the evening sun, the road behind them seems to be paved with gold. . . .

I, for one, do not share such rosy views of the past. No, my youth was not a period I am proud to remember. I do not have much liking for the spoilt young weakling I, or he, was at that time – torn as I, or he, was between jealousy and gratitude, between guilty laziness and burning but impotent ambition.

Should I write 'I', or can I write 'he'? A man is, of course, the only one responsible for his own past actions, but if he manages to rise above his own self, and becomes an entirely different person, can he not take pride in that, and distance himself from those past mistakes? People can change, if they want to, Salīm, and so can you!

With god's help and guidance, I *did* change; I did manage to take control of myself and my surroundings, and came out much, much wiser and stronger, firmly resolved to fulfill my destiny: to become, with god's grace and blessings, His shadow on earth.

It has not been easy – on the contrary, it has taken me many years of hard toil, many worries, and endless fighting against powerful enemies, outside and inside my realm. Many a strong man in my place would have been driven to despair; but with god's help, I succeeded.

Looking back, the second part of my reign can be summarised as four decades of conquest, triumph and ever-growing power and wealth—forty years the world will remember as the magnificent reign of Akbar-e-āzam,[122] as people have come to call me—and rightfully so, I have established one of the greatest empires the world has ever seen; and I have ruled over it, supreme, and alone.

Alone, indeed. There is only one god in the universe, and likewise, there can only be one pādshāh. So much I learned from Adham Khān's rebellion: A king should suffer no rivals! To be sure, I have continued to seek the advice and support of many good people, and appointed them to positions of high power and responsibility, but never again have I allowed anyone to challenge my authority. Never anyone, except you, my son. . . .

But now? Now, my only son has become my most dangerous rival, and I, for all my power and wealth, find myself a lonesome, tired old man.

---

122. Akbar-e-āzam: Akbar the most glorious, the great(er). *Āzam* – greater, most important, magnificent, most glorious – is the comparative/superlative of *azīm* – mighty, glorious, magnificent.

My invincible armies, the untold treasures I possess, the sweet, soft-breasted girls in my zanāna: they are all at my disposal, but somehow, they bring me little comfort. I tremble when I think that what I have built over forty glorious years is now in grave danger.

Every night, I lie wide-awake, my heart full of grief and sorrow, my face wet with tears, when I think of all those good people who were part of my life and have now passed away: two of my three sons; and so many old friends, near and dear to my heart. Where are they, my friends and loved ones? Where have they gone, my years of glory? They have slipped through my fingers, like water, or desert sand. . . .

Countless hours have I spent, praying to god, almighty and merciful, that He would enlighten your mind, and bring you back to me. Countless times I have relived your insolent acts of rebellion – foaming with rage, weeping like a child, or both . . . I do not think you realise how much you have hurt me, Salīm; if you did, I am sure you would not have behaved the way you have. Oh, how I wish I could undo everything that has come between us!

But I should not dwell upon those sad thoughts. First, I must finish what I have undertaken: I must go on, and tell you my story – after all, is it not through stories that we learn best? I must tell you about my reign, and make you reflect upon what it is to be a king, to rule an empire, to determine the destiny of entire peoples. . . .

Here and there, you will have noticed, I have thought it appropriate to include a few court archives, or extracts from other people's private writings, which I have managed to copy, or have reproduced from memory as accurately as I could. Not only does this save me the trouble of writing down everything myself: it will oftentimes serve my purpose much better, for is it not sadly true, my son, that people tend to believe and value the advice of strangers more than that of their own kin? It will be so much more convincing if you see that what I say and think is shared and supported by people you respect.

Those who study the history of my reign will see an incessant series of wars and military campaigns, against numerous enemies, inside and outside the empire. Close to one hundred and twenty major battles were fought during those long years, my son. I do not think it is necessary or useful for me to recount them all; you can read about them in the history chronicles. I will refer to a number of them when I think it is necessary for you to understand the context, or convenient for me to make a point. What is more important for you to study, my son, is the life I have led as the supreme ruler, so that you may follow my example, learn from my mistakes, and more importantly, correct your own.

Part II

ظهر

123. Zohr: Noon

Eighteenth Letter

رفع حجاب

Rāf-ē-Hējāb[124] (J)

In the name of Allāh, the compassionate, the merciful.

Private Notes
On the youth, coming of age, and rise to absolute power
of His Imperial Majesty, Jalāl-ud-dīn Muhammad Akbar-e-Āzam[125]
May Allāh be well pleased with him;
May Allāh grant him a long, healthy and prosperous life;
May Allāh expand his territories, and put all his enemies to shame!

Written for the edification of posterity,
during these months of Muharram and Safar of 981,[126]
in this, the eighteenth year of His Majesty's glorious reign,

by Mīr Abdul Latīf, his humble teacher.

---

124. Removal of the veil
125. Akbar the Great
126. May–June 1573

On the seventh of Shawwal of the year 954,[127] the fourth day of the fourth month of the fourth year of young Prince Akbar's life, it pleased his august father, Emperor Jahānbānī Jannāt-Ashyāni Nasīr-ud-dīn Muhammad Humāyūn—may Allāh be well pleased with him—to ordain the start of his son's formal education.

The tutor carefully selected for this lofty and most noble task, was Mullāhzāda Mullāh Asām-ud-dīn Ibrāhīm, an experienced teacher and a man of profound knowledge, great wisdom, and irreproachable piety.

His Majesty the emperor, eminently knowledgeable himself about the celestial sciences, and well versed in the mysteries of the stars, had personally selected the precise and exact auspicious hour on which his son was to meet his tutor for the first time, and receive his first scholarly introduction into the many domains of knowledge that are appropriate for a king and a servant of god to be acquainted with.

However, when that critical moment had arrived, the young prince was nowhere to be seen: He had gone out to play! Search parties were sent out in every direction, but he was nowhere to be found. Only hours later did he return, still in much too playful a mood to apply his mind to any learning.

Alas! To Emperor Humāyūn's bitter disappointment, this first day proved to be a bad omen for the entire remainder of his son's scholarly upbringing: Prince Akbar did not seem to care much for education, and used every pretext to go horse riding or hunting, or engage in other outdoors amusements.

Truth be told, the prince did excel in all kinds of physical activities and martial arts, showing great agility and strength for his age, and was able to wrestle down boys two or three years older than him. Over the years, he developed impressive fighting skills with sword, battle-axe, mace, spear, and lance; and revealed himself an outstanding marksman, with bow and musket alike.

The prince also showed a truly extraordinary aptitude with animals – not only with horses, camels and dogs, but also with wild animals like falcons and chītahs, and in particular, elephants, which he handled with

---

127. 20 November 1547 (Julian calendar)

amazing confidence and skill, as if he was one of their regular caretakers. Under his touch, the most vicious bull elephant would, as if by magic, turn into the meekest of lambs! The young prince would also spend many hours in his teacher's dovecot, growing almost as fond of pigeon-flying as his tutor was.

Not to say that young Prince Akbar did not show any interest in other, more serious matters. He would fondly listen to lessons in religion, poetry, or the art of counting; particularly attentive was he when his teacher told him the stories of the great kings and warriors of old.

However, when it came to the all-important skills of reading and writing, he did not seem to be able to apply his mind to mastering them.

Despite all the desperate efforts of his tutor, he kept on confusing the various letters:

Rā ر with Zā ز and Zhā ژ; Zāl ذ with Dāl د;
The loops in Hēh, in its four forms (ه ه ه)with the loops in the middle forms of Fēh ف, Qāf ق, and Ayn ع;
Fēh ف with Qāf ق and Vāv و;
Ayn ع and Ghayn غ;
Hamza ء with Initial Ayn ع;
Sād ص and Zād ض; Zā ظ and Tā ط

final Nūn in its two forms ن ں with final Yēh ى;
the four letters derived from Jīm: ج چ خ ح;
those derived from Bēh: ت ب ث پ; and so on.

While this kind of confusion is of course perfectly normal in the mind of a beginner, it only seemed to grow worse over time, and so did Prince Akbar's diligence and zeal. At first, he had at least shown *some* willingness to cooperate, but after a few weeks, he lost all interest, and flatly refused to listen to any more reading lessons.

His most august father, himself a man of such eminent learning, was extremely displeased with his son's lack of progress, and dismissed the unfortunate teacher Asām-ud-dīn Ibrāhīm, reproaching him bitterly to have squandered his son's precious time with pigeon-flying and other trivial amusements, rather than with science and study.

Prince Akbar's second teacher was Maulānā Hakīm Bāyazīd, an eminent physician and descendant of one of the astronomers of the great Ulugh Beg. While hopes were very high, alas, this good man too utterly failed to make any progress. He was dismissed by the time the prince reached his eighth birthday.

Emperor Humāyūn was bitterly disappointed, not to mention increasingly worried, about his son's future. He personally tried to convince him of the importance of reading and writing, this art being the basis of all further learning and knowledge. Prince Akbar, however, cleverly replied that the most noble Prophet Muhammad—Allāh's peace and eternal blessings be upon Him!—had been illiterate as well.

Feeling helpless, Emperor Humāyūn decided to put his trust in Allāh and the stars: He ordered lots to be drawn, in order to decide who of three eminent scholars would become his son's teacher.

Fate appointed Maulānā Abdul Qādir, whose efforts, thanks to Allāh, met with more success. As far as reading is concerned, he did not fare any better than his predecessors; however, after a few days, he wisely chose to follow a completely different course. Giving up all further attempts to teach the prince how to read and write, he started introducing him to a variety of books and scriptures, reading aloud extracts, and subsequently discussing with him the content of what had been read.

To everybody's amazement and relief, Prince Akbar turned out to be quite fond of these new lessons! With amazing ease, he learned by heart lengthy passages from the Holy Qur'ān and the Hadīth, and many beautiful poems of such well-known Persian and Arab masters as Farād-ud-dīn Attār, Jalāl-ud-dīn Rūmī, Sanā'ī, Hāfiz, and Jāmī.

Even today, as an adult, he continues to do so. No matter how occupied he is, whenever his lofty duties allow him a moment of leisure, he will ask for books to be read to him. Over the years, he has achieved such high level of knowledge and understanding that he is able to sustain a learned conversation on almost any subject of interest, quoting from the most varied sources of wisdom. Anyone who does not know him would readily swear that reading is his favourite pastime!

He has ordered the collection of a library of thousands upon thousands of books—in Persian, Arabic and Hindī, and also in Sanskrit, Turkī, Kashmīrī, and even Greek!—about every imaginable subject, religious and profane.

Works he believes will be of particular interest to him are translated into Persian, so that he may personally acquaint himself with their content. He has thus recently asked the learned Maulānā Abdul Qādir of Badāon to supervise the translation of the *Māhabhārata,* which, as everybody knows, is one of the most important ancient scriptures of the Hindū religion.

He also greatly appreciates the beauty of the books he commissions, and a great number of renowned illustrators and masters of calligraphy are permanently employed at the imperial court: men like Maulānā Bāqir, Mīr Husayn-i-Kulankī, Muhammad Amīn of Masshad, Maulānā Abdul-Hay, Maulānā Daurī, Maulānā Abdurrahīm, Nīzamī of Qazwūn, Alī Chamman of Kashmīr, Nūr-ul-Lāh Qāsim Arsalāh, and, last but not least, of course, the incomparable Muhammad Husayn of Kashmīr, deservedly honoured with the title of zarrīn-qalam.[128]

Indeed, despite his illiteracy, His Majesty greatly appreciates the beauty of writing and has no problem whatsoever in recognising the various styles – Kūfic, Ma'qalī, Suls, Tanqī, Muhaqqaq, Naskh, Rayhān, Riqā, Gubār, Talīq and Nasta'līq; but still, he will angrily dismiss any attempt to teach him the skill of reading for himself. . . .

Clearly, it has been Allāh's will—praise be upon Him alone!—to use our emperor's glorious example as a sign to the self-righteous and the conceited, and show them that true wisdom does not depend on books, but is a divine gift that resides in the hearts of His servants!

When Prince Akbar was thirteen years of age, Emperor Humāyūn elevated him to the lofty rank of governor of the Panjāb, and appointed Lord Bairām Khān, Sipahsālār of the imperial army and Khān-i-Khānān, as his son's new atālīq. His teacher Maulānā Abdul Qādir, having expressed the pious and commendable wish to depart to Mekkah and dedicate the rest of life to study and prayer, was granted leave to retire.

To my great joy and surprise, the honour of teaching the young prince then befell me, Abdul Latīf of Qazwīn, son of Mīr Yahyā, of the Sayfi Sayyids of Qazwīn. Quite an unexpected honour it was, for a poor and humble mullāh, just arrived at the imperial court as a destitute fugitive from Persia. . . .

---

128. Zarrīn-qalam: Golden pen

Indeed, the many bitter enemies of my revered father having convinced the authorities at Esfahān that our family was dangerous, because of our adherence to the Sunnī tradition, we were all sentenced to be imprisoned, pending an investigation into charges of treason. My aging father, too old and too infirm to flee, quietly awaited the Shāh's soldiers, ready to die with dignity and in quiet resignation to the divine will. May it please Allāh to reunite us both in paradise! As for me, obeying my revered father's command, and with Allāh's help and protection—praised be He!—I managed to bring my family to safety.

We fled to Gīlān, and from there, further east, into Hindustān. The Mughal governor at the frontier, aware of Emperor Humāyūn's keen interest in matters of philosophy and religion, graciously awarded me a letter of recommendation, and we travelled on to the imperial court in Dillī, accompanying a trading caravan on its way over there.

Like the lord governor had predicted, we were well received indeed: Emperor Humāyūn, himself a man of admirable knowledge and learning, clearly enjoyed the company of scholars. We were given comfortable and spacious living quarters, and almost every day, I had the honour of being invited to join His Majesty and other learned men in stimulating conversations on many an interesting subject.

I knew the emperor was pleased with me; but still, my sudden appointment as his son's personal teacher came to me as a complete surprise. Honoured and privileged as I felt, I was also terrified that I would not be equal to a task of such eminent importance.

Emperor Humāyūn, however, was most kind and encouraging:

'Do not be too modest, honourable Mīr Abdul Latīf – I have full confidence in your abilities! Your family's reputation, as men of great piousness and learning, is well known. Your exquisite command of the Persian language, your acquaintance with both the Shī'a and the Sunnī traditions, your vast knowledge of religion, literature and science, will make you the ideal teacher for my son!'

Having thus been appointed to such a lofty and important office, I implored the support of Allāh, and applied myself, to the best of my knowledge and abilities, to teach Prince Akbar what I thought a future emperor needs to know. I of course prudently continued the successful practice of my predecessor, reading to the prince from books about many a subject, discussing with him at length the content of what had been read, and comparing it with other sources of wisdom.

Most encouraging it was to see, how Bairām Khān himself would also devote much of his time to the education of His Majesty, placing greater emphasis, of course, on matters of warfare and military governance of newly conquered dominions. He taught the prince about the battles fought by the Seal of the Prophets, Muhammad (Allāh bless him and his household!), and the conquests of his able successors, the right-guided Khalīfahs. He thoroughly instructed him in the history of the great empires and dynasties of the Umayyads, Abbāsids, Mamlūks, Buwayhids, Sāmānids, Ghaznavids, Hamdānids, Fātimids, and Seljūqs. Prince Akbar would listen fondly to all those stories about the great soldiers and kings, such as Iskāndār the conqueror; or Salāh-ud-dīn Yūsuf Ayyūbī, sword of Islām, liberator of Jerusalem; or Sultān-i-Rūm Mehmet the second, conqueror of Istanbul – and in particular, of course, to the famous deeds and accomplishments of his own glorious ancestors: Chingīz Khān the great; Amīr Temür the Iron; and Bābur pādshāh the Tiger.

Then suddenly, quite unexpectedly, Emperor Humāyūn, a strong and vigorous man in the prime of his life, received the divine summons to leave behind this fleeting earthly life, and enter the realm of eternity.

A strange irony of fate it was that he should die while obeying Allāh's commandment: Responding to the muezzin's call to salāt al-maghrib, he fell down from the stairs of his library, where he had been standing on the observatory roof, talking to his astrologers. . . .

Fragile, so fragile is human life! Verily, to Him alone we belong, and to Him we return! Like it is written: *Lā hawla, wa lā quwwata, illā bi-Llāh* – there is no power nor strength, save in god! All our weapons and treasures, all our might: they are of no avail; all our strivings and endeavours: they will remain futile, unless Allāh supports them!

Soon after Emperor Humāyūn's unexpected demise, Bairām Khān, who had remained in charge of the affairs of state as His Majesty's atalīq, confirmed my appointment as the young new emperor's teacher. He and I would continue His Majesty's education, guided by the same principles as before.

A difficult, but gratifying, task it was. Despite His Majesty's often unruly behaviour and his continuing refusal to learn the skill of reading and writing, he would frequently surprise and delight us with his remarkable and unsurpassed memory and his broad knowledge about matters of religion and of this world alike. I clearly sensed that inside this unruly, pleasure-seeking, restless youth, there was true greatness of soul, and majesty, waiting to develop and emerge.

≈

The first few years of His Majesty's reign were fraught with the gravest of dangers. Being myself a man of the pen rather than the sword, I must confess that in those days, I have more than once despaired of the empire's survival, surrounded as it was by such a multitude of mighty enemies.

Bairām Khān, however, acquitted himself admirably of his heavy responsibilities. Plying himself to his task with competence and dedication—and aided, no doubt, by the almighty hand of Allāh Himself—he managed to overcome the many challenges that were facing him.

≈

Nothing in this world stays the same; young boys become adults, and pupils become teachers. . . . When His Majesty had reached the age of seventeen, he rather abruptly dismissed Bairām Khān as his guardian, and personally assumed the reins of government.

Those were bad and troubling times . . . times of mistrust, estrangement, rebellion and sin; but fortunately, also of forgiveness and reconciliation; and of true friendship, lost, but found again.

I do not want to dwell on these unfortunate events, as they bring back sad and painful memories. Besides, it is not necessary for me to recount them here, as they are still fresh in everybody's memory, and an extensive account of them can be read elsewhere. I do want to emphasise, however, that His Majesty and Bairām Khān parted ways as the best of friends, with no bitterness left between them – except, perhaps, for that regretful sadness we all feel in our hearts when we look back on the moments in our lives where, we know, we should have acted otherwise.

Bairām Khān was offered a new and high-ranking position, in accordance with his merits and abilities. However, in view of his advancing age, he chose to decline the offer and expressed the pious wish to acquit himself of the sacred duty of the Hajj. Although reluctantly, His Majesty did grant him permission to leave his dominions, but not until after Bairām Khān had promised, that upon his return from Mekkah, he would again join His Majesty's service.

With a warm embrace, he bade me farewell: 'Inshā'allāh, my learned friend. We will meet again, in a few years! Take good care of yourself – I look forward to many more nights of your learned and edifying conversation!'

Alas, it was not to be: Allāh, Who is just and all-knowing, granted him the bliss of martyrdom, shortly after his departure. . . .

Why did it have to end like this? Why was it so ordained that such a great and noble man had to lose his life at the hands of a filthy Afghān murderer?

I do not know . . . I have tried to resign myself to the thought, that nothing happens without good reason, and that it is futile for us, weak and ignorant creatures, to look for the reason behind the dispensations of Allāh's omnipotence – praise be to Him under all circumstances!

But whatever motive divine providence may have had for allowing Bairām Khān to leave this transitory world, one thing is certain: his death did help His Majesty to find the strength and courage to dedicate himself entirely to the task of government.

Within a remarkably short space of time, His Majesty's character appeared to have undergone the most profound change. Although still very much a seeker of pleasure, fond of hunting, sports and rough amusements, and indulging far too often in the drinking of wine and other inebriating concoctions, he did no longer run away from his duties, but applied himself to his task with commendable zeal and diligence. It was, as the chroniclers have phrased it so aptly, as if he had 'emerged from behind the veil'.

Alas, not everybody understood the sign of the times. . . .

With Bairām Khān out of the way, the clique around Māham Anaga, and that worthless son of hers, Adham Khān, thought they could control our young emperor and take advantage of his inborn kindness to serve their own selfish interests. Sadly mistaken were they, indeed!

≈

With the death of Adham Khān—may Allāh forgive his sins!—the atmosphere at the imperial court changed markedly: Everybody tried to keep as low a profile as possible, and anxiously awaited His Majesty's next initiative.

It was of course widely expected and feared that the emperor, in furious and justified anger at Shams-ud-dīn's murder and the attempt on his own life, would wipe out the entire Māham Anaga clique, guilty or innocent. In any case, it seemed to be beyond any doubt that at least the main conspirators would be duly executed, as a stern but just warning to any other would-be rebels. The only question was: How far would the emperor go?

In the same line of reasoning, everybody was expecting the atga khail, or 'foster-father horde', as Shams-ud-dīn's family was commonly called, to become all-powerful at the imperial court. It will be remembered that Shams-ud-dīn was the emperor's foster father on account of his marriage to Jī Jī Anaga, and that his sons (among whom was the highly ambitious and rather unruly Azīz), therefore enjoyed a position of high prestige and influence at court as the emperor's *kokas*, foster brothers – united with him, as the expression goes, by a river of milk.

Maybe, so it was speculated, Shams-ud-dīn's elder brother, Mīr Muhammad Khān Khalān, would be appointed as the new wakīl? Or maybe the other brother, Sharīf Khān? The elder son, Yūsuf Muhammad, a hopeless drunkard, was an unlikely candidate, but Azīz, the younger one, was strong and dynamic, and the emperor liked him – had they not played together when they were still young boys?

All these worldly-wise speculations proved to be sorely mistaken. All of Shams-ud-dīn's relatives, after having been judiciously placated with the sight of Adham Khān's bloodied corpse, were given lucrative and important, but far-away fiefs and military assignments in remote border regions. Rather than rising to absolute power as generally expected, the atga khail had thus, tactfully but effectively, been removed from court!

As for Mun'im Khān: To be sure, he had been Māham Anaga's main supporter and trusted friend since many years, and was widely regarded as the real ringleader behind Shams-ud-dīn's murder – nobody believed there was even the remotest chance for him to escape death.

Similar thoughts must have crossed his own mind, for he attempted a hasty and desperate, if futile, escape – westward, to Kābul probably, or Persia perhaps. A detachment of the imperial guard tracked him down without too many difficulties, and arrested him, in a small village not far from Āgrā. The soldiers dragged him from a shabby peasant hut, crazy with fear, trembling, sweating, pleading, weeping. . . .

To his great relief and utter astonishment, however, the captain of the guard treated him with respect and courtesy. The soldier—stiffly but with consideration—announced that His Majesty, the emperor urgently requested Mun'im Khān's presence in Āgrā. It was His Majesty's wish to reinstate him as wakīl of the empire, and bestow on him the lofty title of Khān Khanān, he explained.

Everybody—I am embarrassed to admit, I was no exception—stood amazed at such extraordinary generosity, and thought it was a serious mistake.

It was the emperor's lack of experience, people said – a sign of weakness, a dangerous error of judgement. . . . It would soon become apparent, however, that His Majesty was neither weak nor confused. In fact, he was quite the contrary!

Mun'im Khān's fear quickly returned when he saw the cool reception that befell him upon arrival at the Āgrā fort. The guards treated him with cool politeness – more, so it seemed, like a high-ranking prisoner than like a guest of honour. Without even a private moment to freshen up or adjust his clothes and appearance, he was escorted to the emperor's presence.

'That will not be necessary. His Majesty is quite anxious to see you,' the captain of the guard answered, when Mun'im Khān timidly asked for leave to retire to his private quarters. 'We have orders to escort you to the diwān-i-ām.'

Mun'im Khān was terrified. No private interview with the emperor, as one would expect, would be the privilege of a high-ranking official. A public audience, in front of dozens of courtiers, who would hear every word and witness every deed seemed more likely? This did not bode well at all. . . .

'Mun'im Khān, I am so pleased to see you are in good health,' the young emperor said softly as Mun'im Khān bowed before the throne. There was, however, no smile on his face to match the kindness of his words.

A long and awkward silence followed. Mun'im Khān, who did not dare open his mouth, kept staring timidly at the floor in front of him.

'I was grieved to hear that you had left Āgrā so suddenly,' the emperor resumed, a sad expression on his face.

Silence again. No one as much as blinked an eye.

'People are actually telling me that you were trying to run away from me, Mun'im Khān – I just could not believe them at first! Tell me, is this really true?'

There was utter disbelief in his voice and facial expression, as if the very thought was unimaginable.

'No, Your Majesty.' Mun'im Khān's voice was barely audible.

'You were not? Well, what exactly were you up to?'

'Your Majesty,' Mun'im Khān stammered, sweating profusely, 'I wanted to visit my son in Kābul . . .' He hesitated.

'I am an old man, Your Majesty, and it has been such a long time since I have seen him,' he added, a bit more forcefully, as if on the verge of believing his own lies.

'You wanted to visit your son, did you? And so, you left Āgrā fort, just like that, with little or no baggage, and without taking your leave of me? I somehow find that hard to believe, Mun'im Khān! I'll tell you more: I am actually starting to believe that it is true what people are saying! Be honest now: You were fleeing, were you not?'

Mun'im Khān bowed his head, afraid to say anything.

'Well?'

'Yes, Your Majesty . . .'

'Go on.'

'I was scared, Your Majesty. I swear, Your Majesty, on the Holy Qur'ān: My conscience is clear, there is nothing I have to reproach myself . . . but I was afraid that I would be blamed for Shams-ud-dīn's death.'

'And, should you not be?'

'As Allāh is my witness, no, Your Majesty – I am innocent!'

'Are you going to tell me that you regretted Shams-ud-dīn's murder? That you opposed it, tried to prevent it? Do you seriously expect me to believe that?'

'I can assure Your Majesty, I swear . . .'

'How very convenient, was it not, to have a hothead like Adham Khān around, to do the dirty work for you?'

Mun'im Khān was now bathed in sweat and trembling with fear. It seemed the emperor's eyes were wandering off to the courtyard behind him, to the sinister line of rocks on which criminals and traitors are executed, their skulls cracked like walnuts under the front leg of a war elephant. . . .

'I beg Your Majesty to have mercy on me, I swear I am innocent!' he yelled.

Again, a long and awkward silence. The emperor looked at him, his face expressionless, inscrutable.

'Maybe you are . . . and maybe you are not. Maybe you did not actually *tell* Adham Khān, in so many words, to commit that murder, but I'm certain you have not said or done anything to stop him either! Am I mistaken, Mun'im Khān?'

Mun'im Khān bit his upper lip. It was futile to deny the truth.

'On the contrary, you did everything you could, to poison his soul, to make him jealous of my poor atga, did you not?'

Mun'im Khān bowed his head. Obviously, it was all over for him now.

A faint smile came over the emperor's face.

'Thank you for being honest with me at last, Mun'im Khān. Would you mind passing me that beaker of sherbet?' he asked, pointing—with his foot—at the tray placed in front of the low, pillow-covered throne on which he was sitting.

The sherbet was well within the emperor's reach, and there were, of course, more than enough servants around to comply with any request he might have had. This was clearly a deliberate insult, and its message was equally obvious: In the presence of the emperor, even the Khān Khanān is a servant.

'Go ahead, have some,' he said, nodding at the bowl of sherbet with unexpected amiability. 'You must be thirsty from all that travelling around in this heat!'

Mun'im Khān scooped out a small portion, and took the beaker in both hands.

'Quite delicious,' the emperor said, smacking his lips, 'exactly the way it should be: the ice crushed, but not molten, the lime and mango juice well mixed and seasoned, not too sweet, not too sour, with just a pinch of salt. . . .'

He paused, gazing dreamingly at the beautiful silk ornaments above his head, seemingly absorbed in the contemplation of their beauty and the agreeable taste of his refreshment.

After a while, he again cast his eyes on Mun'im Khān and abruptly stopped smiling. For a few moments, he just stared at him, expressionless, unblinking, like a snake observing its prey. Then, his eyes seemed to relax again.

'The past, Mun'im Khān, we cannot change, but the present and the future are ours, don't you agree?'

'Yes, Your Majesty.' Mun'im Khān was still holding his beaker, clumsily, in both hands, too scared to take anything from it.

'I could of course keep myself occupied for a few weeks with the elimination of everybody whoever opposed Shams-ud-dīn. I guess, many people would expect me to do just that, don't you think so?'

He again looked at Mun'im Khān, his eyebrows raised, as if he expected an answer. 'The important question is – would that actually help the empire? Would it make us stronger?'

He took another sip of his sherbet, and stared absentmindedly at the battlements of the outer walls.

'An empire should be fighting enemies *outside* its borders, not waste its good men and resources on internal strife, Mun'im Khān. So much remains to be done, so many battles are still ahead of us, and the empire needs experienced and loyal men. The only question is – are you one of them, Mun'im Khān? Will I be able to count on you?'

'I swear on the Holy Qur'ān, Your Majesty, I am your most loyal servant! Your Majesty can rely on me! Allāh is my witness, may I die in agonising pain if I should lie!'

'You will, if you do, Mun'im Khān – of that, you may rest assured!' The emperor burst out laughing, followed by all those present, the soldiers in particular. He abruptly stopped and raised his hand, with a vague, tired gesture. The clamour stopped immediately.

'I have lost my wakīl,' he said gravely, and paused. 'I have lost my wakīl, and I need to appoint a successor for him – someone experienced and reliable, someone who will keep me well informed; a man who can represent me when my duty requires my presence somewhere else; who can lead a campaign for me, when I am involved in another.

'You do have the right experience, Mun'im Khān, and you have sworn a solemn oath—an oath on the Holy Qur'ān—that I can count on your unwavering loyalty, have you not?'

'Yes, Your Majesty! Your Majesty can count on me! May Allāh bless Your Majesty!'

'Go then, do your duty, remember your oath, and do not disappoint me again!'

Mun'im Khān wanted to say something else, but the emperor cut him off with a friendly smile, accompanied, however, by a vague gesture of his hand, betraying impatience and irritation.

'You must be tired from all your travails, Khān Khanān. You have the permission to retire.'

Mun'im Khān clumsily put down the beaker he had been holding in his hands, its content molten and still untasted, and slowly made his way out of the diwān-i-ām, stepping backwards all the way, and bowing deeply with every step. The emperor did not even bother to watch him leave. He made a gesture to one of the court scribes to call forward the next visitor. For the rest of the afternoon, he went about his customary activities, as if nothing had happened, passing judgement on the disputes that were brought before him, and listening, with undivided attention, to reports from the provinces.

How much had we all underestimated our young emperor! In just a few months' time, he had managed to transform his court beyond recognition – from a pit of gossiping, self-serving courtiers, into the obedient following of a truly supreme ruler.

Nineteenth Letter

رفع حجاب

Rāf-e-Hējāb (2)

Part One
From the private notes of
Mīr Abdul Latīf

Rather than a mistake or a sign of weakness, Mun'im Khān's appointment proved to be a true masterstroke. The highest office in the empire was now in the hands of a mediocre yes-man, competent and experienced enough to be an emperor's assistant and messenger, but much too weak and scared to harbour any dangerous ambitions of his own.

It must be said that he has learned his lesson well. Ever since that faithful day when he got pardoned, he served His Majesty with unwavering, exemplary loyalty, in grateful obedience, and to the best of his abilities – limited though they may be.

'Yes, I know, he may not be the most brilliant of my generals, nor the most competent administrator,' His Majesty confided in me a few years later, on one of those rare occasions when he did elect to share his private views with anyone, 'but it has been a real blessing from god that I was not able to find a better minister at the time! I think you will agree with me, my revered teacher and trusted old friend, that it would neither have been wise, nor safe, for me to appoint a strong and ambitious man in a position of that importance. Of course, I did need all the help and good advice I could get, but could I really afford to leave my army in the hands of someone harbouring a burning ambition of his own? No, my friend – better a weak wakīl than a dethroned emperor, wouldn't you agree?

'Besides, even if I *had* managed to find a minister who was competent as well as loyal—someone like Bairām Khān, for instance—may Allāh be well pleased with him—would that have been such a good thing? To be honest, I do not think so! You see, my trusted old friend, now, the people have come to respect me. I like to think that most of my subjects honestly love me, but even those who do not: at least they all *respect* me. Suppose I had had a strong wakīl at my side, someone like a Bairām Khān: would they have respected me as much as they do now? Wouldn't they have thought that everything I accomplished was really my wakīl's work?'

Although I fully understood the reasoning behind His Majesty's decision, I must confess it made me quite worried at first: I was afraid that he would slip back into his old bad habits, or that he would succumb to the obvious temptation of surrounding himself with nothing but docile flatterers devoid of any talent or vision. But Allāh be praised, my fears have proven entirely unfounded. Indeed, it must be said: Rarely, if ever, has the world seen a king of such natural authority and majesty, or a court of such magnificence!

We are now, as I am writing these lines, living in the eighteenth year of His Majesty's reign. Thirty years of age is he ... a strong, healthy man in the prime of his life. No king could be more impressive to behold, nor more worthy of praise and obedience: ruler over a vast empire, powerful and wealthy beyond imagination, a paragon of majesty, wise and balanced, exuding confidence, benevolence, strength, and magnanimity! With advancing age, as he has become more self-assured and at ease about himself and his divine task in this world, his manner has become ever more refined, affable, and imposing alike.

The common soldiers truly idolise him. They admire his courage and strength, and will fondly tell each other the well-known stories of his heroic deeds – like when, only eighteen years old, on foot and single-handedly, he killed an attacking tigress with just one blow of his sword; or when, one year later, during a hunting trip, he took on a gang of armed robbers, personally leading the charge, driving his elephant Dilshankar straight through the wall of the house where they had taken cover. He took no less than *seven* arrows in his shield, but he did not care! The men know bravery when they see it; they know their emperor would never ask them to do anything he would not dare do himself! As he casually walks among their ranks, a bit bow-legged like most of them, from so many long hours on horseback, he truly is one of them. He touches their hearts when he inquires about their wellbeing and that of their families, addressing them, one by one, in their native Persian, Turkī or Hindī.

And it is not only the soldiers who adore him. He has a truly extraordinary ability to adapt himself to his audience. While always maintaining his dignity, he is, as it has so aptly been phrased in the chronicles, 'great with the great, and lowly with the lowly'. Especially with the common people, his manner is particularly endearing: if ever there was a monarch deserving of the title gharīb-parwarī,[129] it is indeed our beloved Emperor Akbar! Always showing them kindness and indulgence, he would readily make time to hear their petty requests. He will smilingly accept the small gifts they offer him, raising them above his head, and then holding them to his bosom with conspicuous gratitude – in stark contrast to the casual disdain with which he receives even the most lavish gifts when he esteems the giver's pride to exceed his merit.

His conversation will, in general, be reassuringly pleasant, polite and kindly; yet, he radiates awesome power and majesty, and his innermost thoughts will usually remain hidden, behind a faint, inscrutable smile. The way he moves, the way he keeps himself; the power of his dreamy eyes, when they suddenly fix their gaze and peer right into your soul . . . As the chronicler phrased it so aptly, 'everything about him is in such perfect accord with royal dignity, that anybody would instantly recognise him as a great king'.

At times he does have a quick, not to say violent, temper. Occasional outbursts of wrath can put him beside himself, as occurred, for instance,

---

129. Gharīb-parwarī: Cherisher of the poor; Persian expression, commonly used when addressing superiors.

when he had his rebellious foster brother, Adham Khān, summarily executed. Such occasions, however, have become quite rare. As a rule, he will be forgiving and understanding, and he possesses such complete mastery of his emotions that he will seldom be seen otherwise than as gentle, pleasant, and perfectly at ease.

In the administration of justice, he sincerely aspires to be fair to everyone, in accordance with what he believes is the true will of Allāh. Unlike his father Humāyūn, who could ordain the harshest punishment for even the most trivial of offences, he strives to be magnanimous as well as equitable, and not to let his personal feelings interfere with his judgement.

It is true: Predominantly in the early years of his reign, there have been a few occurrences where, in anger and indignation, he has pronounced a harsh and brutal sentence, which he later came to regret. Once, for instance, he had found a guard asleep at his post, and in his anger, had him thrown off the fortress ramparts. On another occasion, one of his senior palace servants had his feet cut off, for robbing the shoes of a poor man.

In both instances, it can of course not be denied that the convicts had been guilty of grave offences. Indeed, is it not the essence of a sentry's duty to remain wakeful and protect those entrusted to his care? And what could be more hideous and despicable, than a well-paid courtier who misuses his position to rob a poor person of the last of his meagre possessions, when he himself has more than ample means to live in comfort? Still, being kind-hearted and of noble disposition, His Majesty later felt much remorse at the severity of his verdict, and he decided to protect himself as well as his subjects from any such rash decisions in the future. He ordained that henceforth, whenever he would sentence an offender to death or to the mutilation of a limb, he should be reminded three times before the sentence would actually be carried out. Is this not the clearest evidence of exceptional wisdom and greatness of soul? How many other examples are there, of kings so desirous of justice that they have willingly restricted their own power? Thanks and eternal praise be to Allāh, that He has blessed us with a king of such noble disposition!

But let me return to the events after Mun'im Khān's reinstatement. As it should be, life at court was now revolving entirely around His Majesty's person. After what had happened to Adham Khān, there was no one reckless or foolish enough to try and push himself to the fore; from that day forward, not a single decision would be made without His Majesty's personal involvement and consent.

Not that he suddenly started behaving like a tyrant – our beloved emperor has always been among those few enlightened rulers who understand that true power seldom needs to resort to brutality! On the contrary, I have the impression that the mightier he has become, the more willing he is to listen to good advice. He is eager to attract to his service the very best people available. Over the years, a multitude of new faces has thus made its appearance at the imperial court. Today, without a shadow of a doubt, it has become the most exquisite centre of arts and learning in the whole world, home to a most impressive score of outstanding soldiers, administrators, scholars, poets, painters, architects, artisans and musicians. Verily, is this not the hallmark of true greatness in a king: that he has the prudence to seek good advice, and the wisdom to put it to use?

Easy as this may sound, it is not – not at all! The self-absorbed and conceited will always be tempted to believe that they can manage without any help, whereas the lazy and the weak will allow their advisors to rule in their stead. Alas, both kinds of mistakes have been the ruin of many a powerful empire, but fortunately, our emperor has found the wisdom to avoid them both! Indeed, many of his men are of such outstanding and extraordinary ability that people have come to call them 'the gems of Emperor Akbar's court'.

Among His Majesty's most competent helpers, mention should first be made of Rājā Todar Mal, erstwhile an unknown, humble Hindū scribe from Lāhor, but now the most trusted and powerful of His Majesty's ministers. Despite the modesty of his manner, his presence is daunting. Conversations tend to fall silent wherever his tall, sinewy figure appears; the piercing black eyes in his stern, bony face constantly seem to be probing his interlocutors' motives and honesty.

The story of Todar Mal's rise to power is as simple as it is remarkable. Immediately after Adham Khān's well-deserved execution, His Majesty, gravely concerned about the declining stream of revenues to the imperial treasury, decided to attract an expert to rectify the situation – a most appropriate measure, for there is nothing more important to the prosperity and survival of an empire than a well-stocked treasury. His eye fell on old Khwājā Phūl Malik, the eunuch who had been working for several years at the court of Shēr Khān Sūr's son Salīm Khān, earning himself the lofty title of I'timād Khān,[130] on account of his formidable reputation as an outstanding and incorruptible administrator.

As usual, His Majesty's choice proved to be excellent. The old eunuch and his helpers worked day and night to put the imperial court's affairs in order: counting all the stocks, verifying every revenue account, and sending inspectors to the farthest corners of His Majesty's dominions. Their efforts soon met with remarkable success: After only a few months, the stream of revenues to the imperial treasure more than doubled! And as it was so aptly phrased in the court chronicles, a stone fell on the glass of great men's reputations: 'Quite a few local officials were found guilty of embezzlement. All of them were summarily dismissed and heavily fined; a few of them, guilty of the most flagrant outrages, had their arms duly shortened,' as the chronicler put it so eloquently – a warning that did not miss its effect on their successors!

Like all wise and capable men, old I'timād Khān had the good foresight to avail himself of the assistance of skilled helpers, regardless of their background. Among them was Todar Mal, this taciturn Hindū scribe who, on account of his outstanding competence and sense of duty, soon managed to attract His Majesty's attention. Exceptionally quick-witted, as will so often be observed in members of the Hindū race, he showed himself so amazingly proficient in the art of calculation, and gifted with such limitless capacity for hard work that very soon, the most delicate and difficult assignments were entrusted to him. After a few years, to the surprise and envy of many, he was appointed as I'timād Khān's replacement when the latter retired from office. The palace was rife with gossip: a common Hindū, appointed to one of the highest positions of the empire! Unbelievable as it sounded, it was but the first example of many.

Another extremely influential Hindū at His Majesty's court and a remarkable, rather arrogant character, is a Brāhmin from Kālpī originally called Mahesh Dās. They say he came from an extremely poor family

---

130. I'timād: (Person in whom one has placed one's) reliance, dependence, confidence, etc. Hence: support(er), help(er).

with very few credentials, but nevertheless, thanks to his obvious literary talent, he managed to be admitted into the imperial service as a poet. Truth be told, the man is extremely bright, and as good with words as Todar Mal is with numbers; but his mind is more playful, and he is gifted with a special, rather irreverent wittiness, which His Majesty seems to appreciate very much. So much so, that this formerly unknown and destitute Hindū vagrant can now call himself a rājā – Rājā Bīrbal, holder of the lucrative jāgīr of Nagarkot!

Two of His Majesty's most senior and powerful army commanders are Hindūs as well – I am of course referring to Rājā Bhagwān Dās and Rājā Kūwar Mān Singh, the two Rājpūt leaders who accompanied the princess of Amber after her marriage to His Majesty. Bhagwān Dās is Rājā Bihārī Mal's own son, and therefore, His Majesty's brother-in-law; Mān Singh, in turn, is Bhagwān Dās's highly talented nephew, adopted son and heir. Both commanders are highly skilled warriors, strong, proud, and like most Rājpūts, utterly fearless. In view of their obvious talent and valour, His Majesty not only allowed them to lead their own Rājpūt soldiers, but also put them in command of large contingents of Muslim troops as well. This, in turn, alas and of course, has not failed to arouse the bitter envy of many others . . .

Yes, His Majesty's remarkable tolerance and sympathy for the Hindū race was—and still is—provoking many bitter comments, which undoubtedly he must have heard many times through his spies and informers. Yet, he seem to care precious little about them. On the contrary, he appears to be quite determined to make his court the true reflection of his empire and its inhabitants, regardless of their religion, and will do whatever is in his power and seize every opportunity to further mutual understanding and appreciation between the various traditions and religions of Hindustān.

Sometimes, I have the impression that his desire is not merely to promote peace among his subjects, but that he actually wants to unite them, to blend them together into a whole new people. Even his outward appearance and attire seem to symbolise this idea. Unlike his father and most Muslim noblemen, he does not wear a full beard; instead, he is clean-shaven, except for a moustache, in the fashion of his Turkish ancestors. In contrast, however, his hair is not close-cropped, as the Muslim custom dictates, but he has allowed it to grow long, like the

Rājpūts do, and has it tucked inside a tightly rolled turban of a rather peculiar model, neither Muslim nor Hindū, but a kind of combination of both. That turban, by the way, is becoming quite fashionable nowadays, as many young men are overeager to demonstrate their allegiance.

The emperor's patronage of the arts is another case in point. In every kind of art or craft, he favours, promotes and rewards the blending of Muslim and Hindū styles – 'sulh-i-kul in stone and paint', as he likes to call it.

The buildings he commissions are of a novel and quite pleasant style, aptly called 'Hindustānī', as it is nowhere to be found outside His Majesty's dominions. It freely combines the shapes and ornaments of both traditions: Persian-style arches, domes and lattice-work, with beams, pivots, niches, pillars, terraces, eaves and chhatris,[131] as can be seen in Hindū palaces and temples.

Likewise, in music and painting, Muslim and Hindū traditions are happily joined together. The painters, musicians and artisans the emperor has attracted to his court come from literally everywhere, and every background. There are Hindustānīs, Bengālīs, Gujarātīs, Kashmīrīs, Persians, and Turānīs;[132] there are Hindūs, Jains, Pārsīs, Sunnīs, Shī'as, and Sūfīs; all beliefs, religions and denominations, all united in the service of the emperor. His Majesty requires them to live and work together, and encourages them to influence each other and learn from each other. 'The language of god is beauty,' he says. 'It is god's will that people learn to appreciate each other's art and music!'

This remarkable attitude of universal tolerance and sympathy – where does it come from? With all due modesty, I think I can state that the many conversations His Majesty has had with me, have greatly influenced his thinking. Strange as it may sound: I, Mīr Abdul Latīf, a trembling, feeble old man on the verge of death, find myself among His Majesty's most intimate confidants! Many an ambitious courtier must have wondered in envy why such a great honour should befall *me*, of all

---

131. Umbrella-shaped cupolas, usually resting on four pillars, used as ornaments on walls, terraces, minarets, etc.
132. Turān: Central Asia, north of the Hindu Kush; more specifically, the territory called Transoxania, i.e. the land between the Syr and Amu Darya Rivers.

people: I am a man of the pen, not the sword; precious little do I know or care about commerce, the administration of estates and dominions, and other such worldly matters. I am a man of books, a humble seeker of wisdom without any other personal ambitions or aspirations. Yet, it is not science or poetry or philosophy that has been bringing His Majesty to my study so often: it is his remarkable and ever-increasing interest in everything pertaining to god and religion.

For a person of such young age, and certainly for a man in his lofty position, his interest in these matters is truly exceptional. Every day, he spends several hours in solitary prayer and meditation, his mind solely preoccupied with the adoration of the almighty. Rarely has there been a king so eager to rule in complete obedience to the divine will.

Already around the age of fourteen or fifteen, his sharp and far-seeing mind became preoccupied with the discord and strife caused by religious divisions. No longer satisfied with the bigoted certainties offered by the mullāhs, he took interest, I am proud to say, in the humble insights and views I had to offer him on the subject. I have indeed given these matters much thought – more often than I care to remember, as I have been a victim of bigotry myself throughout the early years of my life. Back in Irān, my family has been persecuted because of our adherence to the Sunnī tradition, whereas here in Hindustān, the Sunnīs regard me with utter suspicion because I am Persian. . . . After much painful reflection on these matters, I have come to the conclusion that a king's primary duty towards Allāh, and at the same time the greatest gift to his people, is to guarantee sulh-i-kul, security and peace for all, regardless of their religion. It is a principle that our young emperor soon made his own, with commendable zeal and enthusiasm. With surprising, not to say disquieting speed, he developed in these matters a policy of his own, which, to my knowledge, makes him absolutely unique among Muslim rulers of any era.

Take his betrothal to the princess of Amber, for example. One could argue that there were logical, political motives behind this union; and of course, there is no doubt that his decision to marry the noble Maryam uz-Zamānī was inspired by his desire to secure the loyalty of the powerful Kacchwaha Rājpūts of Amber, without which there would have been little hope for him to subdue the rest of Rājpūtānā and neighbouring Gujarāt. And in itself, his marriage to a Hindū princess was not really a novelty:

Several other Muslim rulers before him had accepted in marriage the daughters of Hindū rājās as a token of their submission. In all those cases, however, the new spouse, and usually all her relatives as well, immediately converted to Islām. Not the princess of Amber, however! Not only was she put under no pressure whatsoever to convert: the emperor even had a Hindū shrine built especially for her inside the imperial palace, so that she would be able to continue to worship according to her own religion! Similarly, His Majesty is extending to his new in-laws—Rājā Bihārī Mal, Bhagwān Dās, Mān Singh, and all the others—exactly the same honours, favours and distinctions as he would convey to Muslim relatives by marriage, even though they remained, quite openly, devout Hindūs.

Hindū noblemen, openly performing their infidel rites inside a Muslim ruler's palace with pride and impunity; a Muslim sultān, treating Hindūs like intimate friends or next of kin . . . it is all unheard-of, and in the eyes of many, absolutely outrageous. I must confess: even among the moderate-minded, including myself, it is regarded with concern. Is His Majesty not taking things too far? Why is he making it so hard for himself? Why all this effort to achieve an impossible friendship, when mere peace is sufficient? I'm sure he realises all this, but he obviously does not care. He has a task to fulfill, a calling, a destiny: He seems determined to create, slowly but surely, an entirely new Hindustān, in which the difference between Muslims and non-Muslims will simply be blotted out.

As far back as the days of Adham Khān, during the conquest of Mālwa—possibly under the influence of his Hindū wife or her Rājpūt relatives—he already issued an explicit ban against the enslavement of the inhabitants of conquered territories, even of prisoners of war.

'We do not wish to lay waste to the lands that are added to our dominions,' the firmān stated, 'we do not merely want to conquer them, we wish to rule over them in justice and in accordance with the will of Allāh, so that they may prosper. From now on, it is therefore forbidden to deprive the dwellers of those lands of their freedom.

Undoubtedly, this was a prudent and wise measure, intended to temper the army commanders' lust for plunder, and to stop them from depriving the land of its main source of wealth: the people who labour its soil.

While the regulation was a complete surprise to most courtiers, and consequently, much talked-about in the corridors of the palace, there seemed to be no disagreement about it.

About one year later, however, the emperor suddenly decided to abolish the pilgrim's tax, which since time immemorial had been levied on the visitors of Hindū shrines. He had witnessed the tax being collected during one of his hunting trips, and in the spur of the moment, without paying any heed to the objections of his courtiers, decreed that it was to be abolished forthwith.

'It is contrary to the will of Allāh to impose taxes on people whose sole intention is to worship Him, even if their form of worship is erroneous,' he stated.

This time, there was much less understanding among the courtiers. What in Allāh's name could have possessed the emperor to show such indulgence towards those idol-worshipping infidels? To what possible avail could that be? How did the emperor think he would compensate the loss of revenue to the imperial treasury? Yes, it might help him to forge and strengthen his alliance with the Rājpūts; but surely, he must realise that this kind of behaviour is not at all helpful in showing the Hindūs the error of their ways!

Incomprehension turned into profound indignation when in the course of the year 971—it must have been around the month of Rajab[133]—he took the ultimate step, abolishing the jizya on Hindūs.

As every educated person will know, the Holy Qur'ān stipulates that ahl al-kitāb, or 'people of the book'—that is to say, people who worship god but do not recognise the Holy Prophet Muhammad to be His messenger—are entitled to protection of the Muslim rulers, and will remain free to worship according to their own ways, erroneous though they may be, provided they pay the tax called jizya. In the days of the Prophet—peace be upon him—ahl al-kitāb referred to the Jews, and to the adherents of the Nazaryah sect, who call themselves Christians.

After the conquest of Hindustān by the armies of Islām, however, it was the consensus among the ulamā, that the Hindūs, provided they submitted to their Muslim rulers, could be considered as ahl al-kitāb

---

133. Early 1564.

as well, since their scriptures, full of error though they may be, profess that ultimately—above and beyond the countless multitude of gods they worship in their temples—there is only one god. Similarly, also the Pārsīs can be considered as 'people of the book', rather than mere pagans or disbelievers.

It should be noted that this interpretation is in perfect accordance with the Holy Qur'ān, which clearly states that several divine revelations have been made that are not explicitly mentioned it its text. In Sūrah 10:47, for instance, it is clearly stated that every nation has its messenger, whereas Sūrah 10:78 proclaims: We sent messengers before you; of some, we have related to you, and some we have not related to you.

The Hindūs were thus to be considered as 'people of the book', and the jizya had been levied on them right from the advent of Islām on their lands.

And now, this tax was simply abolished, as if it were the most trivial of matters! Was it any wonder that this measure raised endless controversy and bitter resentment among the Muslims?

Although a strong proponent of sulh-i-kul myself, I must confess that even I feared that this time, His Majesty was taking things too far: Rather than promoting peace and understanding among his subjects, was he not taking the risk of creating a dangerous rift between himself and all the Muslim amīrs and ulamā? Several times, I tried to discuss the matter with him, but he refused to listen, merely stating, kindly but firmly, that his mind was made up.

But the debate could not be avoided. Only a few days after the imperial firmān had been issued, Abdullāh of Sultānpūr, better known under the lofty title of Makhdūm-ul Mulk,[134] the highest-ranking of all the ulamā in the empire, requested a private audience with him. To refuse to see him would have been quite unthinkable, and so, a private audience was granted in the diwān-i-khās, no one being in attendance but His Majesty, Makhdūm-ul Mulk, and myself.

For those not familiar with His Majesty's court, I should maybe explain that Makhdūm-ul Mulk, rightly or wrongly, has earned himself the reputation of being the most learned legal specialist in the empire.

---

134. Guide of the kingdom.

Already in the days of Shēr Khān Sūr, he had been appointed as the ruler's legal advisor, with the most lofty titles of Makhdūm-ul Mulk and Shaykh ul-Islām, position and titles, which he kept after Emperor Humāyūn's return to power.

Emperor Humāyūn held him in high esteem, and entrusted him with the instruction of his son in Islāmic law. Prince Akbar, deeply devout and god-fearing himself, would even hand him his slippers, as a sign of respect.

It would be wrong for me to deny or belittle Makhdūm-ul Mulk's vast legal knowledge. I must confess, however, that I do not like him much. He is, may Allāh forgive me for saying so, a bigoted, greedy man, who has all too frequently misused his position, persecuting people he had a personal grudge against, under the pretext of defending orthodoxy, and accumulating fabulous personal wealth in exchange for sometimes dubious legal opinions.

The audience started in a tense atmosphere. Waiting for the guards to escort Makhdūm-ul Mulk into the diwān-i-khās, the emperor seemed to be nervous, but did his best not to show it to me. He sipped absentmindedly from his lime sherbet, and stared at the ceiling. We waited in silence.

When Makhdūm-ul Mulk came in, the emperor put his beaker down and courteously rose to greet him – a great honour indeed. However, he did not step down from the low platform on which he had been seated: instead, he bowed down to give his guest a formal but distant embrace, barely touching his shoulders.

'Honourable and learned Shaykh ul-Islām! It is, as always, a pleasure to see you! I trust you and your family are doing well?' the emperor smiled. His gaze seemed to fix itself on Makhdūm-ul Mulk's well-fed belly.

'Subhān Allāh,[135] Your Majesty, we are all in good health, thank you!' replied Makhdūm-ul Mulk, his fingers nervously playing with the tasbīh[136] he usually carries with him.

---

135. Subhān Allāh: God be praised.
136. Tasbīh Persian name for the *subhah*, i.e., the 100-bead Muslim rosary.

'And what brings you here, honourable Shaykh ul-Islām?' asked the emperor, wasting no further time on formalities. 'Judging by the worried look on your face, it must be bad news! Is there a legal dispute that requires my urgent attention?'

Makhdūm-ul Mulk took a deep breath to summon up his courage.

'May Your Majesty forgive my impertinence, but I think it is my duty to convey the grave concern Your Majesty's recent firmān has caused.'

'So? And what firmān might that be?' The emperor's face remained inscrutable, his voice perfectly calm.

'The abolishment of the jizya. With all due respect, I must humbly beg Your Majesty to reconsider, and to repeal this measure.'

Still, the emperor's face remained completely expressionless, showing neither anger nor sympathy.

'I'm afraid you will have to explain this to me, Shaykh ul-Islām. What is the motive behind your request?'

'We are all very much afraid that this generosity, which, in itself, is of course, highly commendable and a sign of the nobility of Your Majesty's heart, will turn itself against Your Majesty's best interest!'

'And why is that? And who is *we*? Who says so? Is this your opinion, or someone else's?'

'Begging your pardon, Your Majesty, but everybody says so: the amīrs, the ulamā . . . We are all extremely concerned that this measure will substantially reduce the treasury's revenues, and hence, weaken Your Majesty's empire!

'And what is even worse, it will weaken the position of Islām in these lands! Those Hindū idolaters need to know their place! If we start treating them the same way as the true believers, they will never learn to see the wickedness of their ways! We should not forget that their numbers are much higher than ours! There will be no limit to their arrogance!'

'Are you implying that it is my *religious* obligation to impose the jizya upon them?'

'Well, yes, Your Majesty . . . the Holy Qur'ān says so explicitly:

Make war upon such of those, to whom the scriptures have been given, as believe not in Allāh or in the last day, and forbid not that which Allāh and his apostles have forbidden, and who profess not the profession of truth, until they pay jizya out of their hand, and they be humbled.'

The emperor appeared wholly unimpressed.

'I am aware of this sūrah, but thank you for reminding me, Makhdūm-ul Mulk. Answer my question, if you please: Is it your legal opinion that I have an obligation, under Sharī'ah law, to impose the jizya on the Hindūs?'

Makhdūm-ul Mulk was starting to feel uneasy now.

'Well, Your Majesty . . .'

'As far as I'm aware, honourable Shaykh ul-Islām, the jizya is not really a *religious* tax, is it?'

'Begging Your Majesty's pardon, but I'm afraid I have to say it is – the jizya is to be imposed on non-Muslims, never on Muslims, and it is explicitly mentioned in the Holy Qur'ān, as Your Majesty knows. Therefore, it is most certainly a religious tax . . .'

'I'm afraid I must insist, Shaykh ul-Islām. I do not think it is . . . Honourable Mīr Abdul Latīf, what is your opinion about this?'

I understood what the emperor was aiming at, and could not help admiring his cleverness.

'Yes, I see what Your Majesty means: the jizya *is* a religious tax; but indeed, it is not really a tax *on* religion – it is a compensation for the protection offered to non-Muslims, and for their being exempt from compulsory service in the armies of the Muslim rulers.'

Makhdūm-ul Mulk wanted to say something, but I did not let him interrupt me.

'That is precisely why non-Muslims who pay the jizya are referred to as ahl al-dhimmah, "people under protection", and that is precisely why whole categories of non-Muslims are actually exempt from jizya, including all the females, the males who have not attained maturity, the elderly, the crippled, the blind, the slaves, the monks, and so on – am I right, Shaykh ul-Islām?'

'Yes, but . . .'

'It is a tax, to be levied on any able-bodied non-Muslim man, who is able to fight, but exempt from serving in the Muslim army and allowed to live under its protection. You will recall that well-known story about the noble Khalīfah 'Umar—may Allāh be well pleased with him—who once saw a blind dhimmī[137] begging, and finding that the poor man had to pay the jizya, not only exempted him from it, but ordered a stipend to be paid to him, from the khalīfah's treasury, for the rest of his life. . . . And I do not need to remind you, honourable Shaykh ul-Islām, that there are several examples in Muslim history where non-Muslims assisted their Muslim king in his battles, and in exchange, were exempted from the jizya!'

Makhdūm-ul Mulk tried to hide his anger, and said nothing. The emperor nodded approvingly. 'I think you are quite right, Mīr Abdul Latīf. So, we all seem to agree, that if I require the Hindūs to fight in my armies, they in turn can ask me to exempt them from jizya. Am I right?'

We both nodded in agreement, the two of us equally astonished to hear our emperor engaging in a legal dispute with such depth of knowledge.

A long silence followed, the emperor looking pensively into his beaker of sherbet again. He took a long sip, put the goblet down, rose to his feet, came down from the platform, and put his hands on Makhdūm-ul Mulk's shoulders.

'This is why I am in such dire need of learned and wise men like yourself, to help and support me, honourable Shaykh ul-Islām! Your wisdom and learning are known and respected throughout this empire and beyond! When you speak, even the most learned, wise and proud of men start to listen attentively! You know the subtleties of the law, you recognise error when you see it – I need you to help me explain all these things to our men! The amīrs are not wise and learned like yourself, Shaykh ul-Islām; they are easily misled in matters of law, falsafah[138] and religion. Learned men like you must help them to see the truth and the wisdom behind their emperor's policies!'

He kept looking Makhdūm-ul Mulk straight in the eye, his hands still on his shoulders. Finally, he let go of him, and went back to sit on the pillow on the platform.

'Explain to them, Shaykh ul-Islām,' the emperor continued, the expression on his face again composed and neutral, 'that I have exempted the Hindūs from paying the jizya because I do not want to exempt them

---

137. Dhimmī: Protected person (non-Muslim)
138. Falsafah: Philosophy

from serving in my armies! Explain to them, how important it is for the future of the empire, to secure the loyalty of the Hindūs, and of the powerful rulers of Amber in particular!

'Surely, everybody knows how tough these Rājpūts are: not at all peaceful and docile like most other Hindūs, but a strong and proud warrior race, never conquered before by any Muslim invader!

'Just suppose—Allāh forbid!—that all of Rājāstān that is to say, Amber in the west, Jaisalmer in the east, and Mewār in the south, would unite against us: It could take us maybe ten years or more to defeat them, and even if we are victorious, it would deplete our forces considerably! And what would we have gained? We would have nothing more than what we currently have, and in addition, we would have become vulnerable to an invasion from other enemies, the rulers of Bengāl for example, or the sultanates of the Deccan. If, however, we manage to convince the Rājpūts to fight on our side, no power on earth will be able to stop us! We can turn Hindustān into the mightiest and wealthiest empire the world has ever seen!'

The emperor again paused for an uncomfortably long time, as if to allow his words to sink in.

'But if we do want the Hindūs to fight for us,' he continued, 'it is necessary that they see us as their allies, and even better, as their brothers. They need to see me as their legitimate emperor – not as their conqueror, not as a foreign ruler to whom they have reluctantly agreed to pay tribute. Yes, the noble princess of Amber is now married to me, and that is an important first step, but only the first step! It is essential that I make them feel part of the empire, not just at peace with it! They must feel at home in my dominions, they must feel as safe and comfortable in Āgrā, as they do in Amber!'

'I know, Shaykh ul-Islām, their way of worshipping is strange and abhorrent to many devout Muslims. But is it not for Allāh to judge them? Who else but He alone is the lord of the day of judgement? Does not the Holy Qur'ān itself speak of many religions? Is it not written:

> To every one of you, we have appointed a right way and an open road. If Allāh had willed, He would have made you one nation; but that He may try you in what has come to you. So be you

forward in good works; unto Allāh shall you return, all together; and He will tell you of that whereon you were at variance.[139]

'Besides, I am profoundly convinced that, Allāh willing, the Hindūs will find the way towards Islām much easier, if they consider us as their friends. For all their errors, they are a god-fearing people, and open to other ways of worshipping than their own. I am convinced that many of them will soon be attracted by the austere beauty and simplicity of Islām, as compared to their own elaborate rituals. You have to help me, Shaykh ul-Islām, help me explain all of this to our people! You have to make them see, that their emperor is furthering the cause of the true religion!' The emperor intently looked at his guest's face, trying to ascertain the effect of his words.

'I will, Your Majesty!' Makhdūm-ul Mulk hastened to declare.

The emperor nodded in appreciation, and again remained silent for a few moments. Gradually, an expression of sadness came over his face, and he resumed, in a soft, but distinctly ominous tone of voice:

'It is never pleasant for a king to hear that his policies are the subject of discussion and criticism, Makhdūm-ul Mulk. I am grateful to you for your honesty, but people should realise, that it has hurt my feelings, and caused me great pain and distress to hear that they have been questioning my devotion to Allāh. You may reassure them that so far, I am willing to consider this as the empty-headed babble of courtiers with too much time on their hands, the kind of idle gossip that will unfortunately be there wherever human beings are gathered together. . . . Let them make sure, however, not to give me any cause to question their loyalty!

'And, lest they forget, remind them of their oath! Remind them, that Allāh Himself has invested me with His authority! Make sure they understand, that disobedience against their emperor is, in fact, an act of rebellion against the order established by Allāh Himself!

'Can I count on you to help me, Shaykh ul-Islām?' The emperor's voice was barely audible now, but somehow, ominously threatening.

Makhdūm-ul Mulk nodded hastily. Beads of sweat covered his forehead.

---

139. Qur'ān, 5:51

'Your Majesty can count on me!'

'Thank you in advance for your most appreciated help, Shaykh ul-Islām – I am most grateful,' the emperor nodded.

As in an afterthought, he added:

'And Shaykh ul-Islām, I am deeply touched by your concern for the imperial coffers. However, let me put your mind at ease: There are other ways of filling the treasury than extorting a meagre jizya from a score of poor peasants. No, if I really want to increase the empire's wealth, I probably need to add a few new dominions to it; I need to convince neighbouring kingdoms to join me, or at least, pay tribute to me – not to extort more money from the common people! Besides, as the excellent work of I'timād Khān and Todar Mal shows, many dignitaries of the empire have been rewarding themselves, more than handsomely I would say, with monies that actually may be due to the imperial treasury. It seems to me that if revenue is lacking, I should perhaps look into that matter first . . .'

He looked his guest straight in the eye for a few moments, then allowed his gaze to wander off.

'You have our permission to retire, Shaykh ul-Islām. Thank you again for your support.'

Makhdūm-ul Mulk was now soaked with sweat. He mumbled something about being grateful, and made haste to get out of the diwān-i-khās, stooping, stepping backward, and bowing as deep as his fat belly would allow him.

For a while, the emperor kept staring at the door, his face turning more and more angry, until he lost his composure, throwing his goblet on the floor, suddenly foaming with rage, and looking at me in great anger, as if I were responsible for Makhdūm-ul Mulk's behaviour.

'Who does this pompous, insolent bastard think he is, anyway? What is keeping me from having him hanged? Can you tell me that?'

'That is not possible! I must urge Your Majesty to remain calm!'

'And why would that not be possible? Am I not the emperor?'

'Your Majesty knows this as well as I do: A Muslim king is required to rule in accordance with the law of Islām. A conflict with the ulamā would undermine Your Majesty's authority, because enemies of the empire would find in it an ideal excuse to legitimise rebellion!'

My words were clearly not to the emperor's liking, but thankfully, he realised I was right.

'Besides, I fully understand the displeasure, but Your Majesty has handled this incident impeccably! The great Hārūn ar-Rashīd could not have done it any better! And I have to say, I admire Your Majesty's profound knowledge and insight in matters of law and government!'

In spite of himself, the emperor smiled.

'I did have a few good teachers, my old friend. . . . Besides, it is my duty to think about these things!'

He paused.

'We did set him straight, didn't we?'

'You did, Your Majesty, indeed you did!'

'Well, let us hope that that will be the end of this discussion!'

'Let us hope so indeed,' I said, smiling sheepishly, and realised how feeble that sounded. But as much as I hated myself for it, I did not know what else to say – for the very simple reason that in my heart, I did not believe the problems would go away at all . . .

The emperor clearly sensed my embarrassment.

'It is getting late, and you must be tired, Mīr Abdul Latīf! Thank you again for your much-appreciated help and guidance! I wish you a restful night. Khudā hāfiz, my old friend!'

'Khudā hāfiz, Your Majesty! May Allāh be Your Majesty's guide, guardian and protector!'

I returned to my quarters, took a sleeping potion, and went straight to bed. Despite my ardent prayers, my night was distressful, and sleepless.

Part Two

هندوستان

Hindustan

Mīr Abdul Latīf's anxious foreboding proved to be, alas, quite justified, my son. As I re-read his comments, it is as if I see myself in that distant mirror: ingenuous, worriless, naive amidst the evident, looming danger. How could I be so blind? It was as clear as day, to everyone who cared to open his eyes: Sooner or later, my preoccupation with religious matters was bound to lead to dissidence and conflict. I guess I knew it all along but refused to see it. Whatever the consequences, I would have it my way.

There were, as Mīr Abdul Latīf perspicaciously observed, practical as well as religious considerations behind my attitude. I genuinely and honestly desired to know the divine will and to lead my life in submission to it; and at the same time, I was profoundly convinced that sulh-i-kul was the best, if not the only, way to guarantee the prosperity and stability of my dominions.

I already pointed out to you that with that policy of tolerance, I was following in the footsteps of my august father and grandfather, both devout but broad-minded Muslim rulers, who had little interest in, or tolerance for, religious strife. In fact, as far as the Sunnī–Shī'a divide is concerned, my father Humāyūn, although a Sunnī himself, had every reason to be favourably inclined towards the Shī'a. As you know, his favourite spouse, my mother and your grandmother, is a Shī'a, like most Persians; his iron right-arm and my faithful atālīq, Bairām Khān was a devout Shī'a as well; and last but not least: Had it not been for the Shī'a troops which the Shāh of Persia had so graciously put at my father's disposal, he could never have regained his throne from the Afghān usurpers. Consequently, whenever confronted with strife between his Sunnī and Shī'a followers, my father would say: 'We all worship the one true god, and we all recognise the Holy Prophet Muhammad as His messenger; let each man worship Allāh according to his own tradition and to the best of his abilities, and leave the judgment of his brethren to the almighty!'

My father and my grandfather also consciously strove to live in peace with the Hindūs, leaving them free to live according to their own traditions, without trying to forcibly convert them to Islām. Indeed, they both understood quite well that the cause of Islām is much better served through a policy of peaceful coexistence, than through the wanton destruction of temples and shrines.

Thus, with sulh-i-kul, I was following the example of my tolerant and enlightened ancestors. But as Mīr Abdul Latīf astutely observed: I wanted much more than that. My dream was—and it still is—to bridge the religious divide, to create an entirely *new* Hindustān, a truly united land that would rise above the differences between its inhabitants. The more I thought about it, the more convinced I became: It was my destiny and my duty to unite Muslims and non-Muslims, to forge them into one nation! How exactly I would go about it, was not fully clear to me yet, but I had every hope that dialogue and reason would bind together what tradition and ignorance had separated.

I know, my son, I have been hopelessly naïve, and it nearly cost me my throne. But do not be mistaken: No ruler of Hindustān can afford to ignore this issue! Unless his subjects live together as brothers, or at least as friends, they will continue to waste their strength in attempts to subdue one another, or to break free from them. But just imagine, my son, what it will be like, when Hindūs and Muslims realise that they are hairs on the same head, eyes in the same face! No power on the face of this earth will be able to resist their might!

Well then, my son, read, and observe, how your father built his empire; how he almost lost it, and how he won it back. Think, and reflect on what I did right, and where I went wrong; think about how you will preserve and expand what your father left you.

Twentieth Letter

فتح ، شورش ، ملک

Fāth, Shuresh, Molk[140]

Consider this map of Hindustān, my son.

When my father died, there was not even a definite territory I could call my own: I had nothing more than a long stretch of land along the Jumna and Gangā rivers, supported by a few garrisons; surrounded, however, by many powerful enemies.

Little more did I have, than a disputed title; my hold on the country was, at best, precarious. When Hemū's army chased Tardī Beg's troops out of Āgrā and Dillī, most people, including the majority of our own army leaders, believed that we would be driven back to Kābul, back to where my grandfather had started his conquest.

Seven years later, at the time of Adham Khān's death, that map looked very different indeed. The Panjāb was mine, all the way down to the city of Multān and the territory between the Sindh[141] and the Sutlej rivers. I firmly held the fertile basin of the Jumna and the Gangā, from high up in the Himālayas, all the way east to Allāhābād. Towards the south, my borders were secure: I held Gwālīor and Mālwa, and, thanks in part to

---

140. Conquest, rebellion, kingship
141. Sindh: Indus

my marriage to your mother, I also controlled a vitally important part of Rājputānā: from the left bank of the Chambal up to, and including, the sacred city of Ājmīr, where the shrine of the venerable Khwājah Muīn-ud-dīn is honoured by so many. Moreover, my alliance with your mother's family had assured me of the loyal support of the strongest and bravest of the Rājpūt kings.

In seven years' time, I had thus become the most powerful ruler in Hindustān. Across the Khyber Pass, the territory of Kābul also belonged to me, although I must admit that in reality, it was ruled in practical independence by my younger half-brother Muhammad Hakīm and his conniving but competent mother.

The fortress of Qandahār, unfortunately, had been re-occupied by the Persians, around the time we took Mānkot from Sikandar Sūr. We could not do much about it at that time, as we had more than our hands full with our many rivals in Hindustān. I swore, however, that in time, Qandahār would be mine again.

All in all, I could be quite satisfied with what I had achieved: Bābur's vast and wealthy dominions were mine again – with a minimum of vigilance, no one could ever hope to dethrone me. I could, indeed, look forward to a life of leisure and luxury.

But that was neither my hope, nor ambition. Would I have been a worthy son of Chingīz and Temūr if I had decided, at barely twenty years of age, to spend the rest of my life sitting in a single palace? No, my son: A king worthy of that name should be intent on conquest when he has the chance, for to conquer new territories, is to honour god; and to rule over them with justice and wisdom, is a way of serving Him!

Besides, just look at the map, my son: The territory that I held, the one Bābur had conquered before us – look how inherently vulnerable it is! Yes, I could have held on to it; but sooner or later, in my lifetime or that of my successors, we would have found ourselves at war with our neighbours. When two strong countries are not separated through natural borders, it is, in the long term, inevitable that one will conquer the other. . . .

Hindustān's northern border is well protected by the formidable wall of the Himālaya and Hindū Kush mountains, but in order for it to be completely safe, it clearly needs to include control over Kashmīr.

North of Kābul, it is important to retain sufficient control over the unruly mountain tribes, and if possible, we should also hold Balkh and Badakshān, with the cities of Qundūz, Balkh and Mazār-i-Sharīf. Remember this, my son: Until we finally subdue the Uzbeg Khāns—may god punish them!—the Amuya River[142] should be the border between us and them! Only if our armies are firmly established on the southern banks of Amuya, can we hope that one day, when the time is ripe, Samarqand and Bukhārā will once again be ours!

Towards the west, any major attack from Persia can easily be prevented, if we keep a tight grip on Kābul and Qandahār: for he who controls those two cities, controls Hindustān's 'western gates'.

Further south, it is self-evident that the entire course of the Sindh, including the territories of both Multān and Thatta, inherently belongs to Hindustān. In addition, to safeguard our western border, we should control at least the easternmost mountain ranges of Baluchistān.

Having thus secured Hindustān's northern and western borders, another look at the map will make it clear that an independent Gujarāt in the west and Bengāl in the east would sooner or later lead to war.

Indeed, without these territories, Hindustān remains land-locked and vulnerable. To defend its borders, and even more importantly, to keep control over the profitable trade with the outside world, it also needs to annexe those neighbouring territories. But he who wishes to conquer Gujarāt, first needs to control the fortresses of Rājpūtānā.

Those were my considerations when, at age twenty, I found myself in charge of my grandfather's empire. I wanted it to be powerful, prosperous and independent, but realised, that for this to happen, I would sooner or later need to bring Rājpūtānā to cooperation, and then eliminate the neighbouring rival sultanates of Gujarāt and Bengāl.

Once those goals would be achieved, it would only be a matter of time before the smaller sultanates of the Deccan, the firanghī coastal establishments, and the rest of the southern tip of the continent, would eventually become ours.

---

142. Oxus or Amū Dāryā River

At the beginning of the ninth year of my reign, near the end of the month of Esfand,[143] I thus made my first and still modest move, against the kingdom of Garha-Katanga or Gondwāna.[144]

That territory was then governed by Rānī Durgāvatī, a descendant of the famous Hindū dynasty of Mahobā, on behalf of her young son Bīr Nārāyan.

As she and her son had repeatedly and defiantly refused to submit to my authority, I sent Āsaf Khān with an army to subdue them.

Against our overwhelming numbers, many of Rānī Durgāvatī's twenty thousand soldiers deserted her before even the first shot was fired. But despite the hopelessness of her situation, she refused to yield, and made a gallant stand with the remainder of her forces, near the town of Narhī.

As Abū-l Fazl would phrase it, 'gallantry and foolishness are sometimes hard to distinguish'. Her army was no match for ours, but in spite of this, she kept on leading her men with remarkable bravery, seated on a mighty war elephant, until she was herself disabled by two arrow wounds. Choosing death rather than disgrace, she stabbed herself to the heart, and died nobly on the battlefield. Two months later, Āsaf Khān marched on to her capital Chaurāgarh, where, pointlessly courageous like his mother, Bīr Nārāyan chose to offer battle, and was slain as well.

It is truly sad that two people of such outstanding nobility and valour should have died – I would have gladly appointed them as governors over vast and rich territories, made them powerful and wealthy, married them into my family . . . but they did not want to listen to reason. They failed to see the sign of the times: those who oppose me, have only one of three choices – submit, flee, or die.

Rich spoils of gold, pearls, jewels and over a thousand elephants fell into the greedy hands of Āsaf Khān who, despite what had happened to Adham Khān, could not resist the temptation, and kept a large part of the booty for himself. Although my informants had told me about it, I chose, for now, to ignore the insult. I had, so I thought to myself, more urgent and important things to do, and did not want to waste any time before attacking the formidable enemy, Rājpūtānī strongholds of Chittor

---

143. Mid-February 1564
144. An area in the current state of Madhya Pradesh.

and Ranthambhor, control of which was indispensable, if I ever wanted to annexe Gujarāt.

To my surprise and utter dismay, however, I was suddenly prevented from pursuing this important work of conquest. For the better part of three years, I found myself fighting in every part of the empire, trying to suppress, among others, the dangerous revolt of my own Uzbeg army leaders.

Looking back on the course of events, I think I have finally understood what moved these former friends and allies of mine to suddenly rise in arms against me.

Firstly, it should be remembered that the Uzbeg war chiefs who had helped my father and me to recover the throne of Hindustān, were not really interested in a place to settle down. They were adventurers, on the lookout for a war to join, thirsting for excitement and easy spoils. Their alliance with us was only temporary, and their loyalty to my family, lukewarm at best. In fact, their ancestors and fellow countrymen up in the lands of Turān were and are our family's hereditary enemies: Let's not forget that it was Uzbeg Khān who drove my grandfather Bābur from his ancestral lands! History, my son, is a convenient source of inspiration for those looking for excuses. . . .

Secondly, the Uzbegs—bigoted Sunnīs all of them!—had always resented the appointment of Persian Shī'as and Hindū infidels to positions of high authority. Religious fervour, even more than history, can be quite convenient an excuse for the pursuit of selfish interests. . . .

As long as I had kept the Uzbeg nobles near me, as long as we were fighting the same battles, it was relatively easy to keep them under control. However, in sending them off to remote regions, far away from the imperial court, I had made a grave mistake: Distance, my son, breeds estrangement, and estrangement breeds rebellion. . . .

Indeed, it was a dangerous mistake, and one that could have been avoided. I should have recalled them much earlier, assigned them to other tasks – then maybe none of this would have happened.

But it did happen, and indeed, with the wisdom of hindsight, it is easy to see how, for instance, it turned a trusted officer and excellent soldier like Abdullāh Khān Uzbeg into a rebel.

You will remember that back in the days of Adham Khān, I had sent him to recapture Mālwa after that region had been lost because of

Pīr Muhammad Khān's bungling. And sure enough, he led a brilliant campaign, and recaptured Mālwa in no time.

But then, once the battle is won, distance and greed start doing their poisonous work: the soldier becomes a governor, the governor sets up a sumptuous court of his own, and suddenly, the emperor seems far away. . . .

How easy it seems, to keep part of the imperial revenues for oneself; and when that first embezzlement appears to go undiscovered, how tempting it becomes, to go on stealing, more and more. How far away is the emperor, when his messengers take several days to reach you; how easy it is, to keep them waiting for several days before you send them back, with polite but evasive and noncommittal replies. Unfortunately for him, however, Abdullāh Khān Uzbeg grossly underestimated the resolve of his emperor, and the perceptiveness and competence of his emperor's ministers.

As usual, indeed, Todar Mal had been quick to draw my attention to the growing irregularities in the revenues coming from Mālwa, and the evasiveness of its governor's letters. And as usual, I had been equally quick to react: On Yeksanbeh, the twenty-first of Tīr of the ninth year,[145] I left Āgrā at the head of a powerful expeditionary force, and swiftly headed south to Mālwa.

He grips the world who hastens, my son. The rebels were taken by complete surprise by our rapid advance, and we overtook their main force near Māndū before they had the time to organise their defence.

A rather disappointingly small number of them were killed; the rest fled in disarray into Gujarāt, from where, after a short while, they were thrown out by the local king – to whom I had sent a letter, demanding their immediate expulsion. Their small remaining fighting force completely disintegrated, while Abdullāh Khān Uzbeg himself had seemingly vanished from the face of the earth. It later appeared that he had made his way to Jaunpūr up north, where he placed himself in the service of the local Uzbeg officers, who, as I will now relate, had ventured onto the ruinous path of rebellion themselves as well. But god spared me the grief of having to punish my old comrade myself. He died of

---

145. Sunday, 17 July 1564 (Julian calendar)

natural causes before the Uzbeg rebellion was finally, and quite literally, crushed.

Having thus defeated Abdullāh Khān Uzbeg, I headed back to Āgrā by the middle of the month of Mehr,[146] looking forward to a period of repose and leisure.

I thoroughly enjoyed the taming of a large herd of magnificent wild elephants, which I had managed to capture along the march, and ordered the building of a beautiful hunting palace—aptly called Nagarchain, or Amānābād[147]—about two and one half kos south of Āgrā. The reconstruction of the Red Fort was making excellent progress as well.

It was, so I thought, an outstandingly auspicious time for me. Indeed, how to describe my elation and relief, when I learned that one of the slave girls in the zanāna, a good-looking Persian girl with whom, months back, I had spent a few pleasant afternoons, was pregnant, and was expected to give birth in a few months!

I was overjoyed: Until then, not one of my many wives had ever borne me a child, and I was getting worried that maybe, for some reason, god had decided that I was to remain childless . . . and behold! Now, three months before the beginning of the tenth year of my reign,[148] twin sons were born unto me!

I of course ordered grandiose festivities to be held, and publicly announced that the children would be called Hasan and Husain. By choosing the names of the sons of the Prophet's daughter Fātimah and her husband Alī, names that are respected throughout Islam and popular with the Shī'a even more than with the Sunnī, I again made it clear to everyone that I did not wish to make any distinction among the various religious beliefs and denominations.

Alas! Soon after the festivities, the court physicians came to warn me that the two children were not in good health. Their mother's constitution had clearly not been strong enough to bear two children at once; as a result of that, neither of them had received sufficient nourishment from

---

146. Early-October 1564
147. Abode of peace
148. Late 1564

their mother's womb; their weight was far below what was considered healthy for a newborn child.

The best and strongest wet nurses in the empire were brought to the court; every three hours, the children were given drops of strengthening elixirs, prepared by pre-eminent physicians, from the most exquisite ingredients; continuous prayer services were held; the best astrologers were called upon to make powerful charms and incantations – but alas, it was all to no avail. In less than a month, my two little sons were dead!

I still see their pitiful little bodies before me, smaller than the length of my forearm; their tiny faces, which had been bright-red at birth, now pale as candle wax; their innocent little eyes and mouths slightly opened, as in silent protest against what had happened to them. . . .

I tried to console myself. I told myself, it was a good sign that at last, sons had been born unto me; that I was still young; that I would, with god's help, father many more children; that what had happened was just the way this world is, that many children die at a tender age; that maybe god had wanted to spare me the grief of seeing two sons, born on the same day, grow up to be each other's bitter rivals, and see my life's work ruined. . . .

But no matter how hard I tried, I could not convince myself – this was a terrible disaster, and a very bad omen. What I had thought to be an auspicious period in my life, now suddenly was full of pain, darkness and menace.

Unfortunately, my misgivings proved to be correct – misfortunes, indeed, rarely come singly. . . . Soon after my two sons' death, I found myself confronted with a second, and far more dangerous rebellion of the Uzbeg officers.

This time, the main instigator was Alī Qulī Khān, the competent army leader who, nine years before, had earned himself the title of Khān Zamān at the battle of Pānīpat. With him were his brother Bahādūr Khān; uncle Ibrāhīm Khān, governor of Surhurpūr; and Iskandar Khān, governor of Awadh.

Having grown suspicious about the Uzbegs after Abdullāh Khān's earlier misconduct in Mālwa, I had ordered Iskandar Khān Uzbeg to come to Āgrā – I wanted to probe their intentions, and assure myself of their continued loyalty and support.

My suspicions unfortunately proved to be justified. Iskandar Khān blatantly disobeyed my orders, and fled to Jaunpūr, taking Ibrāhīm Khān of Surhurpūr with him. Under the leadership of the Khān Zamān, the three now broke out in open rebellion, defeated our local troops at Nīmkhār, and besieged the fortress of Mānikpūr in Oudh.

I immediately sent out Mun'im Khān to block any further rebel advance to the west, and crossed the Jumna myself at the head of a large army three months later, on Panjshanbeh the thirteenth of Mordād of the tenth year.[149]

The situation was grave, and I could not afford to take any further risks. It gives me no pleasure to recall this, but after many sleepless nights, I saw no alternative but to order the private execution of my cousin Abū-l Qāsim Khān, the son of Kamrān, my father Humāyūn's treacherous brother and bitter rival.

Three months earlier, the evening before he left Āgrā at the head of our vanguard, Mun'im Khān had asked whether he could see me in private.

Wasting no time on further introductions, he said, 'I regret that I must advise Your Majesty to urgently rid himself from his cousin Abū-l Qāsim!'

'What makes you say that, Khān Khanān? Abū-l Qāsim has done nothing to hurt me; as far as I am informed, he keeps himself occupied with hunting and reading and similar innocent pastimes!'

'Possibly, but failing to eliminate Abū-l Qāsim, leaving him behind in the imperial palace while Your Majesty is far away, is to provide the insurgents with an ideal opportunity to justify their rebellion!

'Your Majesty should not forget, that Your Majesty's father Humāyūn and his brother Kamrān were most bitter rivals! Who knows, one day Abū-l Qāsim might be tempted to claim the throne for himself! More importantly, as long as he is alive, he is a godsend to those who wish Your Majesty ill: He is just what they need to give their rebellion an appearance of respectability, and to spread discord in the imperial camp! In him, they have found an alternative king to whom they can pledge their allegiance. I must insist, it is too much of a risk to let him live!'

---

149. 24 May 1565

He paused and added, timidly, 'I know Your Majesty is honest and righteous, and it is difficult for him to do what he believes to be unjust. And indeed, for all we know, Abū-l Qāsim is still innocent of any wrongdoing. Sometimes, however, innocent blood needs to flow in order to prevent even greater bloodshed; sometimes, an injustice is the only way to serve the greater good! Sometimes, we cannot choose between good and evil; sometimes, alas, we have to choose between two evils, and the best we can do, is to choose the lesser one . . . I am convinced that Abū-l Qāsim, in Your Majesty's place, would act the same way: for such is the burden of kingship, Your Majesty, that it sometimes requires the hardest and most bitter sacrifices . . .'

For a moment, I looked at Mun'im Khān's innocent eyes, thinking to myself, how much I had been underestimating the old fox. Much as I disliked what he had been saying, I appreciated his frankness and loyalty. I nodded and thanked him for his wise and honest advice.

The rest of the day and night, and all the following weeks, I could think of nothing else. Much as I hated to admit it, I knew Mun'im Khān was right. I considered and re-considered all the alternatives, looking for a way out. But no matter how hard I tried, I could see no solution. The empire was in grave danger; could I allow myself to squander my forefathers' inheritance, all for the sake of one innocent man?

Abū-l Qāsim's execution, I am relieved to say, was swift and painless; he was dead before he realised what was happening to him. But no matter how much I tried to console myself, that it had been the only way out, that being in my place he would have done exactly the same, I could not help feeling deeply sad and guilty. There was no way I could argue or explain it away: Abū-l Qāsim's death was a sin, a sin for which, on the day of judgement, I will need god's infinite mercy and forgiveness.

Ever since Abū-l Qāsim's death, I have often wondered: Does power necessarily lead to sin? Is it possible to be a king and to live a life of absolute righteousness? To be honest, my son: I do not know. All I know is that it is very difficult, and that I, although I did try, have not succeeded. May god, Who is the ultimate justice and mercy, and Who knows the predicaments and weaknesses of His creatures, graciously forgive me!

The preparations for the campaign being completed, I headed east. I was joined by Mun'im Khān's troops at Kanauj. We immediately marched on to Lakhnau, causing Iskandar Khān to hastily flee that city, whereupon the Khān Zamān, alarmed at the rapid advance of the imperial forces, abandoned the siege of Mānikpūr, and fled eastward.

After a few further skirmishes of little importance, I managed to corner him near Allāhābād, and prepared myself for battle.

Having seen the might of my army, and clearly fearing, rightly so, that he was no match for me, he sent a messenger to Mun'im Khān, asking for clemency, and offering submission.

His letter talked about unfortunate misunderstandings, recalling the unwavering loyalty with which he had served my revered father and me, he appealed to the unbreakable bonds of brotherhood that had united us on the battlefield, and similar words to that effect.

What was I to do? Could I forget the major role the courageous Uzbegs had played at Pānīpat? Was I going to waste so many good soldiers in a fratricidal struggle when so many cities and fortresses still remained to be conquered?

I decided to forgive and forget, and extended a general amnesty to the Uzbegs, leaving it to Mun'im Khān to work out the terms and conditions of the truce. Among others, it was agreed that all Uzbeg forces would remain north of the Ghaghara or Gogra River, until I had returned to Āgrā.

Being in the eastern part of the empire, I took the opportunity of visiting the Hindū holy city of Varānasī, on the Gangā River. I spent a few leisurely days there, fascinated by the sight of the colourful crowd of pilgrims, priests and Hindū sādhus, many of them stark naked and smeared with cremation ashes, with no other possessions on this earth than a begging bowl and a small trident, symbolising Lord Śiva. I was captivated and horrified at the same time, at the sight of the many funeral pyres on the ghāts, and the omnipresent smell of scorching human flesh.

My rest and tranquility were short-lived, however. No sooner had I reached Varānasī than Khān Zamān's Uzbegs violated the terms of the truce, again crossing the Gogra and menacing the cities of Ghāzīpūr and Jaunpūr.

I immediately turned back and attacked them on several fronts, easily routing them wherever I found them. It was clear that they had grossly underestimated both my prowess at using mobile cannons and smaller field guns on the battlefield, and the impeccable discipline and fighting skills of my Rājpūts.

Again impressed at the speed and overwhelming force I was capable of, the Khān Zamān re-opened negotiations for peace, promising complete submission and unwavering loyalty.

It clearly was a mistake, but I allowed myself to be persuaded yet again. My troops were weary of the long and exhausting campaign and the many forced marches, and I longed for the tranquility of Āgrā and Salīmā's companionship. Once again, I forgave the rebels, and reinstated them in their positions. On the twenty-fifth of Esfand,[150] I headed back to the capital.

Things appeared to go well at first. There were no more reports of any disturbances, and the stream of revenues from Jaunpūr showed no irregularity.

Alas, it proved to be the quiet before the storm. Eight months later, I received the perplexing notice that my half-brother Muhammad Hakīm had left Kābul and was crossing the Khyber Pass at the head of a large invasion army. Almost simultaneously, I learned that in Jaunpūr, the khutba was now being read in Muhammad Hakīm's name: the Uzbegs had encouraged him to invade Hindustān! It was, so they said, every good Muslim's duty to fight the emperor, as the emperor had turned Shī'a, or maybe even Hindū. . . .

Beside myself with rage, I immediately marched north into the Panjāb, to repel Muhammad Hakīm's invasion. It did not take long before I had the incompetent weakling on the run: After a few minor skirmishes, all of them disastrous for his forces, he meekly headed back across the Khyber Pass, without offering battle.

I would have gladly pursued him, all the way to Kābul if necessary, and finished him off, once and for all, but unfortunately, that was quite impossible, for I realised all too well that I could not afford to leave Hindustān as long as the treacherous Uzbegs had not been properly dealt with.

To make things even worse: While still in the Panjāb, I received an alarming message from Mun'im Khān that back in Āgrā, the Mīrzās had broken out in open rebellion as well.

---

150. 6 March 1566

As you will probably know, my son, the Mīrzās are distant cousins of ours. They are descendants of Temür's second son 'Umār Shaykh Mīrzā, whereas we descend from Temür through his third son Mirān Shāh. Their ancestors had joined my grandfather Bābur's service, but apparently that did not prevent them from harbouring their own ambitions.

Their whole family had joined the uprising: Muhammad Sultān Mīrzā, Ibrāhīm Husain Mīrzā, Muhammad Husain Mīrzā, Mas'ūd Husain Mīrzā, Āqil Husain Mīrzā, Ulugh Mīrzā, and Shāh Mīrzā. They roamed plundering through the countryside, and at one moment even threatened Dillī.

Alas, the sparks of rebellion had set off a devastating forest fire, threatening to engulf my entire empire.

I immediately headed back from the Panjāb towards Āgrā. Upon my arrival, however, I was relieved to find that Mun'im Khān had already done excellent work: He had attacked the rebels head on, managing to capture Muhammad Sultān, and chased the others into Mālwa. This allowed me to focus my attention to the Uzbegs. On the twenty-fifth of Ordībehesht of the twelfth year,[151] I left Āgrā at the head of my troops, and marched east.

Finding upon arrival that the enemy had crossed over to the south bank of Gangā, with a view of proceeding west towards Kālpī, I, as a chronicler put it, 'displayed my customary zeal and contempt of personal danger': I swam the elephant I was riding right across the swollen Gangā River. About fifteen hundred brave men crossed the river with me, while the main body of my troops, under Rājā Bhagwān Dās and Khwāja Jahān, proceeded further west.

For the last time, the Uzbegs had made the mistake of underestimating me. Nearly all of them had been spending the better part of the night carousing, getting dead-drunk, and had posted far too few sentries. At dawn on the twenty-eighth of Khordād,[152] despite the weakness of my forces, I carried out a surprise attack on their camp.

I had placed musketeers and bān rockets at three carefully chosen locations, and ordered them to fire no less than half of all their ammunition in the first attack. It all went as I expected – the Uzbegs,

---

151. 6 May 1567
152. 9 June 1567

bewildered by the devastating fire from all sides, and seeing the imperial standards, assumed that the entire army had fallen upon them, and fled without offering battle. A few kos further west, as planned, they ran into the main body of our troops. There was nowhere to run; all they could do, was to surrender, or fight.

They attempted to break out of the encirclement, concentrating their entire fighting force on the point where they thought our formation was the weakest, away from the imperial standards: the Rājpūt foot soldiers. It was their last and fatal mistake. The Rājpūts' discipline was impeccable; they held their ground, and our well-aimed rocket and mortar fire caused deadly carnage in the enemy ranks. A final, beautifully executed charge of Irānīs and Turkomāns on the right flank and Rājpūt elephant drivers on the left finished them off, with very few losses on our side.

The Khān Zamān had fallen in battle, while Bahādūr Khān, who had been captured alive, had been beheaded immediately after the fight. I was a bit disappointed when my soldiers brought me the two severed heads – after all their lies and treachery, I would have gladly watched their skulls cracking under Dilshankar's front legs.

No, this time, I was no longer in any mood for clemency. A few of the surviving younger officers, who could still be of use for my army, had their lives spared; the rest were herded together in a circle, and trampled to death by my war elephants – killed, as Abū-l Fazl aptly put it, 'under the feet of the elephants; or rather, under the weight of their sins and ingratitude'. The great Uzbeg rebellion, the gravest menace I had to face since Pānīpat, had been—quite literally, as I said—crushed.

In triumph, I headed back to Āgrā, where I dispatched Shihāb-ud-dīn Ahmad Khān to Mālwa, to deal with the Mīrzās. Upon his arrival, they fled in disarray into southern Gujarāt, where, for some time at least, they would find refuge. There were no more rebels left to fight. At last, I was free to fulfill my destiny: to build a united, powerful, invincible Hindustān.

Twenty-first Letter

راجاستان

Rājastān

I guess most other people in my situation would have been more than glad to take a few months' rest after so long a campaign and so many hundreds of kos of marching and fighting in the blazing sun.

But not me. I felt elated and restless, eager to make up for the time lost. There was so much to be done, so little accomplished. . . . Never before had I felt so alive, so proud of myself, and so impatient.

Pānīpat and the other earlier battles – they had really been other people's work. But this major campaign had been conducted by me alone, and I had proven—to myself even more than to others—that I was a truly gifted soldier, a worthy son of Temür and Chingīz Khān. It was I who had decided when to march, when to strike camp, where to deploy which troops and weaponry, how to secure their supply, and when and where to attack. It was I who had known how to drive them on when hardship was making them battle-weary. And, maybe most important of all: It was I who had forged all those separate and rivalling groups into one united army; it was I, who, through my personal courage and prowess, forever earned the respect of my men; for the first time, Hindūs and Muslims truly had a common leader.

I could hardly wait to move on and start in earnest with the hard work; the kind of hard work that is indispensable to make any worthwhile dream come true – never forget this, my son!

I have already pointed out to you that for Hindustān to be powerful and prosperous, it needs to be in possession of Gujarāt, and that in order to achieve this, it must control at least the major roads and fortresses of Rājāstān.

Through my marriage to your beloved mother, through my prowess in battle, and thanks to my tolerance and fairness in matters of religion, I had earned myself the unwavering loyalty and friendship of the powerful rājās of Amber; they had become my closest friends and most trusted allies; their brave fighting forces had become the backbone of my army. It was high time the other Rājpūt leaders followed suit.

However, it soon became apparent that regrettably, this goal would not be achievable without war.

The Rānās of Mewār prided themselves as the greatest among all the kings of Rājāstān; they were said to have taken a solemn vow never to 'sully their blood' by giving a princess of their family in marriage to a Muslim.

That in itself did not bother me all that much – I had more than enough wives, and could easily do without a Mewārī bride. What I did want to secure, however, was loyalty – an unconditional recognition of my sovereignty. And here, their attitude had at best been half-hearted.

It is true that Rānā Uday Singh did send his son Sakat to my court as a conciliatory gesture, but it is equally true that he refused to attend on me in person – he even refused to pay me a simple visit to show his friendship and respect! Worse than that, there was clear evidence that he had actually helped the Mīrzās in their uprising!

This was clearly an attitude I could, and would not, tolerate. I wasted no further time on parleys and negotiations: The treachery of the Uzbegs had made me weary of talks and treaties with unreliable opponents. It was time my neighbour learned that those who refuse to be my allies, thereby become my enemies, and must suffer the consequences.

I stayed in Āgrā no longer than strictly necessary to prepare for this new and major campaign. I allowed myself but little leisure, but I did take a few hours to inspect the work of the court painters and sculptors, and meet with a few new artists recently admitted to the court. Among them, I met a talented young poet, named Abū-l Faizī, son of one Shaykh Mubārak; little did I realise that I had just made the acquaintance of the elder brother of the man who, some years later, would become my most influential courtier: Abū-l Fazl.

The preparations for the campaign made good progress, and on Sehsanbeh the twenty-seventh of Shahrīvar of the twelfth year,[153] barely two months after the final suppression of the Uzbeg rebellion, I marched south into Mewār, heading straight for its capital, Chittor.

Our advance through the countryside was unopposed. Rānā Uday Singh, a spineless weakling, 'the unworthy son of a worthy father', as chroniclers have aptly described him, like a coward left his capital under the command of his army leader Jai Mal, and ran to hide himself in the Arāvallī hills.

On the tenth of Ābān,[154] we pitched our camp—three kos long it was!—in sight of the western cliffs of Chittor, and started preparing ourselves for a lengthy siege. The heavy mortars (needed to hammer breaches in the fortress' massive walls) were cast on the spot; it would have been much too cumbersome and time-consuming to take them along with us.

It was not going to be easy. Even today, so many years after its demise, Chittor remains dauntingly impressive. It is really a heavily fortified, steep cliff, rising abruptly from the surrounding plain, about one-tenth of a kos high. Its length from north to south is a daunting one and one-third of a kos; at its broadest point, it is over a quarter kos wide; at its base, it is no less than three and a quarter kos in circumference!

Upon arrival, I ordered an immediate frontal assault from the north-east and north-west, to test their defences – hoping that maybe, if we managed to surprise and overrun them at the point of attack, we could avoid the loss of time and effort of a protracted siege.

Unfortunately, the defenders were well prepared, and well led. Two attack waves of ours were repulsed with heavy losses, and I had no alternative but to withdraw my troops beyond the range of the enemy guns, and to start the encirclement of the hill.

It took us more than a month of hard work before we finally succeeded and had Chittor completely sealed off. As of then, no one

---

153. 9 September 1567
154. 23 October 1567

could approach, enter or leave it without our permission. The noose was around their neck; now came the long struggle to pull it tight.

Direct assaults having proven costly as well as pointless, we began the long, cumbersome travail of digging sābāts, which, as you know, are large ditches, protected against enemy projectiles by heavy logs of wood covered with rawhide. The excavation works were executed under the competent direction of Rājā Todar Mal and Qāsim Khān, the master builder of the Āgrā Fort.

I ordered the sābāts to be built wide enough for horses to advance through them in rows of ten, and deep enough to be ridden through by a man, spear in hand, seated on the back of the largest elephant bull. While this was, of course, quite time-consuming, it would make the final assault much easier and less costly.

Again it was painfully apparent that our enemies were determined, well-led, and amply stocked with gunpowder and projectiles. As soon as the sābāts came within reach of their fire, they did whatever they could to hinder them, pounding them with nearly incessant musket and cannon fire. Despite the movable ramparts we used to protect our workers, heavy casualties were inflicted upon the ranks – sometimes as many as one hundred in a single day!

In spite of this stiff resistance, we continued to make progress, albeit annoyingly slowly. Every day, the sābāts inched closer towards the foot of the hill, like fat, giant snakes, slowly crawling towards their victims, waiting for an opportunity to strike.

As we edged closer to the foot of the cliff, we managed to inflict more and more losses on the defenders. Through loopholes in the sābāt roof and the movable bulwarks, our musketeers fired incessantly at the defenders on the ramparts, forcing them to take cover more and more. I personally spent several hours every day in the sābāts myself, firing one musket after the other while my attendants busied themselves reloading. It will be no surprise to you that I did more than my fair share of the killing: I have been shooting muskets since the age of five, and countless hunting parties have made me an excellent marksman: When I get a clear shot, I rarely miss, and moreover, I seem to have that innate hunter's talent, to be able to guess where the game—or in this case, the opponent—is going to show himself.

Despite the cover provided by the bulwarks, standing in the sābāts was quite dangerous. One time, I was nearly hit by a cannon ball that went smashing through the sābāt roof and killed several of my men. But I refused to move into safety, despite the pleas of my officers to do so. If you want your men to respect and admire you, my son, if you want them to go to the gates of hell for you, show them that you are not afraid of risking your own life. If god wishes to keep you alive, he will.

At long last, the time had come, or so it seemed: One of our sābāts had reached the foot of the hill. Under Qāsim Khān's direction, workers began digging a deep shaft, in which gunpowder charges would be set off to bring down Chittor's wall.

Everything seemed to go as planned. The charges were placed, the fuse was lit – there was a massive explosion, causing a landslide which took part of the wall with it. The breach was only ten paces wide – not as wide as I had hoped, but sufficient for the storm troops to force their way through. On Todar Mal's orders, they launched a massive assault.

Alas! What we did not realise was that *two* charges of gunpowder had been placed, which, unfortunately, had not gone off simultaneously. As our assault troops were rushing towards the breach, the second charge exploded. A few dozen defenders standing on top off the crumbling ramparts were killed as well, but by far the majority of victims belonged to our own camp. Over two hundred of my men, including some of the best and bravest, perished in the blast. I was forced to call off the attack and witness how the defenders quickly repaired the breach and erected new defences. Hearing their laughter and insults, I swore to myself that I would make them pay dearly.

The next few weeks were spent in building new sābāts and further weakening their defences. However, despite our hard work and the daily losses inflicted on the defenders, they still showed no real sign of weakness. Still no sign of their ammunition running low, no sign of shortage of food or manpower. . . .

I managed to resist the urge to order another frontal assault, but I must admit, I was getting extremely impatient – a state of mind besiegers need to avoid, for impatience leads to impetuousness, and impetuousness to costly mistakes.

The time I did not spend fighting in the sābāts or consulting with Rājā Bhagwān Dās, Mun'im Khān, Todar Mal, Rājā Mān Singh and the other army leaders, I spent in prayer, asking god to help me.

The days passed by without any real progress being made, and losses on both sides continued to be heavy. Much as I hate to admit it, there were times, in the middle of the night, when I started fearing that god was on my enemies' side. Nevertheless, I did not give up praying, pledging myself to visit Ājmīr as soon as god would grant me victory, and perhaps more importantly, promising Him that I would use my power only to serve Him.

Then, in the afternoon of the thirteenth of Esfand[155], the tide finally turned. As usual, I was standing in the sābāt, when I suddenly saw on the ramparts a tall man in heavy hazār mīkhī[156] armour, directing the enemy troops. I did not know who he was, but shivers went down my spine. I felt like a hunter who has finally managed to track down an elusive, man-eating tiger, after days of searching in the jungle.

I asked for my favourite gun Sangrām and patiently waited for the man to appear again. I do not know how long I waited, not making a single move, hardly blinking an eye. Then at last, my patience was rewarded – there he was, exactly where I had been expecting him, right in front of my gun.

It was not more than a fleeting moment, but I can still see it in my mind's eye, as if frozen in time: the sunrays on the man's shining armour, the blue sky, and Sangrām's black barrel.

I squeezed the trigger, and felt Sangrām's butt slamming into my shoulder, my ears deafened by its thunder. Amidst the rising gunpowder smoke, I saw the man being knocked backwards as if he had been struck by lightning – I must have hit him full in the chest. The chaos on the ramparts and the frantic yelling and screaming confirmed my suspicion: He must have been a very important man.

Less than an hour later, reports started coming in that most defences had been deserted, and that large fires were burning in several places inside the fortress. 'These must be jauhar pyres,' Rājā Bhagwān Dās

---

155. 23 February 1568
156. Hazār mīkhī: Thousand nails

explained. 'Your Majesty must have killed the enemy commander, Jai Mal Rathor. When the leader has fallen, the battle is lost, and his men prepare to die. The women will jump into pyres, lest they should fall into enemy hands.'

His words were soon confirmed. The man I had killed was indeed Jai Mal Rathor, the leader of the garrison, and, as usual, the death of the leader had sealed the fate of his army.

I seized the opportunity and ordered coordinated attacks on several points throughout the night. Musket fire kept the ramparts clear, while heavy mortars hammered the walls and new gunpowder charges were brought forward. Just before the break of dawn, we had again breached the wall, and the assault troops stormed in, thirsting for booty and revenge. I followed right after the first attack wave, amidst a large group of battle elephants.

A few thousand enemy soldiers still staged a few valorous, if utterly futile, attacks. It seemed as if they were more eager to fall in battle than to win it, and we, of course, obliged them. After about an hour, the last resistance broke down. A few dozen survivors made their last stand around Patta, Chittor's second-in-command; after a brief struggle, they were all trampled to death under my elephants.

At last, the fortress was mine. Contrary to my usual practice, I ordered all adult male prisoners to be killed on the spot. No more soft-heartedness this time – it had been more than enough! They had angered and insulted me by their stubborn resistance and the loss of so many of my best men; I want to teach their coward king a lesson. After this long and costly siege, killing the able-bodied men was plain, absolute necessity if I wanted to break Mewār's fighting capability. Their king was still around, hiding in the Arāvallīs like a coward, but probably waiting for an opportunity to raise a new army and come back to fight me. Most of Chittor's regular soldiers had perished in the battle, but much of the fighting had been done by the farmers who had taken refuge in the fortress. If I had spared their lives, I probably would have had to fight them again some day!

No, I do not apologise for the 'slaughter of Chittor', as some have chosen to call it; it was the well-deserved retribution of treachery and rebellion, and more importantly, it was the only way to avoid future bloodshed among my own troops.

No, I do not regret the massacre; the only thing I do regret is that I failed to kill them all: A few hundred of them managed to escape, passing themselves off as my own troops, driving their women and children bound in front of them as if they were their prisoners.

I ordered Chittor to be vacated, its massive gates to be unhinged and transported to Āgrā as war trophies, and strictly forbade any repairs to its ramparts and defences. Until the end of time, the fortress will remain there like I left it, daunting but powerless and emasculated, a tribute to the power of its conqueror.

Harsh as my verdict may have seemed to some, history has, once again, proven me right. As you know all too well, my son, this would not be the last time that the Rānās of Mewār would be making trouble for us. Uday Singh, that spineless coward, kept hiding in the hills until his death; his son and successor Pratāp, however, clearly had inherited more of the fighting spirit of his forefathers and would give us more than one headache.

Without Chittor and the other fortresses, however, he never posed any serious threat to us; indeed, without Chittor, the Rānā of Mewār is nothing more to us than a nuisance, a gadfly, a small stone in our boot, annoying enough to make itself felt from time to time, but not enough to bother to stop and get rid of it.

I entrusted the government of the conquered territories to Āsaf Khān, one of my trusted officers, and left Chittor on the eighteenth of Esfand,[157] heading straight to Ājmīr, as I had promised god I would.

Eager to show my gratitude and humility before His all-powerful Majesty, I covered most of the forty-eight kos[158] on foot, and spent several hours on my knees before Khwājah Muīn-ud-dīn's sacred tomb, thanking almighty god for the many favours He had so graciously bestowed on me throughout my life, and asking Him for His continuing guidance and protection.

Back in Āgrā on the third of Ordībehesht,[159] I went to work immediately: Despite the upcoming summer heat, I was eager to start the final campaign against the remaining Rājpūtānā fortresses.

---

157. Saturday, 28 February 1568
158. 120 miles, or 192 kilometres
159. 13 April 1568

Much to my regret, I found myself forced to postpone these plans, when I learned that the Mīrzās had again been carrying out raids into Mālwa. I sent Ashraf Khān at the head of a strong cavalry force to chase them out, and stayed behind in Āgrā, using the hot summer months to supervise the ongoing construction work and reflect on matters of government.

The three Uzbeg rebellions, the invasion of Muhammad Hakīm and the troubles with the Mīrzās had made me think.

It seemed that the larger an empire gets, the stronger it becomes in comparison to its neighbours, but also, the more vulnerable to internal strife and disintegration. Is this really inevitable? And if not, what can be done to avoid it?

In complicated matters like this, it is always useful to hear what other people have to say; and in this respect, I have found that a conversation among people of different backgrounds and experience will often lead to the best insights. I therefore decided to meet with Mun'im Khān, Rājā Mān Singh, Todar Mal, Bīrbal, and Mīr Abdul Latīf. Knowing how sensitive some people—Hindūs in particular—are about eating together with people of another caste or creed, I invited them to join me after the evening meal.

We met in an open room on the eastern ramparts of Āgrā's Red Fort, overlooking the Jumna River. The breeze from the river felt delightfully refreshing and comfortable after another hot summer day.

I ordered trays of ice and cooled drinks to be brought in, and told the servants to leave us alone.

As I expected, Todar Mal and Mīr Abdul Latīf drank nothing but water, and Bīrbal and Mān Singh had some sherbet, while Mun'im Khān and I were indulging in a few beakers of wine.

'I should probably not be drinking any wine,' Mun'im Khān admitted, more to himself than to us, 'but it is lovely on a summer evening. . . .'

'Indeed it is, Khān Khanān! And I would not worry too much: Allāh—eternal praise be upon Him only—is prepared to forgive much worse sins than that,' I agreed, taking a sip. It tasted, as I expected, delicious.

'Nice and cool, crisp, not too sweet. . . . Ah, my friends, evenings like these are the raisins of life, don't you agree? A cool breeze, some wine, and pleasant conversation – is this not what life is all about? Remember the great Hāfiz's verse:

> *Hermits the flowing spring approve;*
> *But poets the sparkling bowl enjoy:*
> *And, till he's judged by Powers above,*
> *Hāfiz will drink, and sing, and toy!'*[160]

Mun'im Khān applauded; Mīr Abdul Latīf and the Hindūs smiled and nodded courteously, although it was not clear from the expression on their faces what they were really thinking.

'Anyway,' I said, forcing myself to get down to some serious talk, 'much as I am tempted to start a conversation about the merits of wine and the meaning of life, this is not why I have invited you here tonight. Tell me, my trusted friends, what do you think of what has happened these last few months? Do you think we can now rest assured that we have overcome all dangers?'

Mun'im Khān was the first to break the ensuing silence.

'I believe we do, Your Majesty,' he said pensively. 'Indeed, we have been attacked on many fronts; the situation has been quite perilous, and many a mighty empire might have collapsed under similar circumstances, but under Your Majesty's able leadership, we have overcome all adversities, and actually, we have come out much stronger! The army is without a shadow of a doubt the mightiest fighting force I have ever seen; not only is it large and well-equipped; it is cohesive, loyal, battle-hardened, and extremely effective!'

He stole a passing glance at Todar Mal and Mān Singh, and continued:

'One would never expect an army consisting of so many different factions to hang together the way it does, but it does! All the men—Turks, Persians, Rājpūts—they are all devoted to Your Majesty!'

He paused, and took a good mouthful of wine.

'And what is perhaps even more important,' he added, 'I do not want to flatter, but Your Majesty clearly is the most able army leader of his time! The speed with which Your Majesty moves his troops, the way he

---

160. Quoted by James Morier (1824), p. 126.

ensures their supply, the discernment and perspicacity with which he deploys them, the judicious use of rockets, musket fire and mortars – I have never seen such soldiership, not even in the days of the great Bairām Khān, may Allāh be well pleased with him! Indeed, Your Majesty is the Iskandar of his age, the worthy son of Chingīz Khān and Amīr Temür the Iron!'

Much as I appreciated Mun'im Khān's words—after all, as Abū-l Fazl cleverly observed: 'of all lies, flattery is the most effective!'—it was not quite the advice I was looking for.

'I have to thank you for your kindness, Khān Khanān! It is most encouraging to hear such words of appreciation from an experienced soldier like yourself! However, my mind is still not at ease: What pains me, is the treachery we have experienced. The Mewārī resistance, I can still understand – these people were misguided, they did not know me, they considered me as a foreign invader! But the Uzbegs, the Mīrzās – they have been my comrades in arms for so many years! Am I such a weakling, or such an animal that people rise up against me as soon as I have turned my back?'

'No,' Mīr Abdul Latīf exclaimed. 'I am convinced that this is not Your Majesty's fault!'

He paused, looking for words to express his thoughts.

'It is clearly not a matter of how Your Majesty reigns over his subjects; on the contrary, Your Majesty is a promoter of peace, prosperity, and justice, and the people are well aware of that!'

'That is very true,' said Mān Singh. 'Just look at the support we got from the villagers around Allāhābād! After the battle, they actually helped us in hunting down the remaining Uzbeg stragglers – they even brought us their heads! Would they have done that if they liked the Uzbegs better than us?'

'That is exactly what I mean,' Mīr Abdul Latīf said. 'These uprisings have nothing to do with Your Majesty's government – only with the sinful ambitions of local governors! It is a matter of greed, pride, conceited arrogance – not of government!'

'It may be a matter of greed and pride and arrogance,' Bīrbal admitted, smiling faintly, 'but precisely for that reason, it *is* a matter of government!'

'With all due respect, honourable Mīr Abdul Latīf,' he added, raising his hand as the old teacher wanted to interrupt him, 'government is not only a matter of righteousness and living in accordance with god's will; it is the art of achieving a perfectly organised empire, using less-than-perfect people!'

'You are so right, master Bīrbal,' Todar Mal concurred, with unusual enthusiasm. 'Human nature cannot be changed, but human behaviour certainly can be! As the saying goes, it is opportunity that makes the thief, and indeed, it is my experience, that people who know that they will be subject to thorough control, will think twice before they start stealing, no matter how selfish and greedy they are!'

'Precisely,' said Bīrbal. 'Human greed is like a fast-growing weed; it needs to be trimmed and cut back constantly, lest it overgrows everything – and even better is to not allow it to take root! More often than not, local governors are left in possession of their jāgīrs for decades; is it then any wonder that they start behaving like they own the land? With each passing year, they feel more and more like kings, who by coincidence happen to have pledged allegiance to a faraway emperor!'

'And how would you propose to change all that, master Bīrbal?' I asked, smiling, in spite of the insolent frankness of his tone, rather amused to hear how much his reasoning was similar to my own.

'Governors need to be Your Majesty's representatives – nothing less, but also, nothing more,' Bīrbal answered without hesitation. 'They should be transferred to other stations, on a regular basis, so that they do not start behaving like the owners of the land they have been assigned to!'

'And perhaps even more importantly, Your Majesty,' Todar Mal added, 'they should not be allowed to pay themselves from the revenues of their jāgīrs! Governors should be dependent upon the emperor for their personal wealth; they should receive a salary in accordance with their merit!'

'I think this is very sound advice,' I agreed. 'You are right, if I would have called back the Uzbegs to Āgrā much earlier, if I would have divided the Mīrzās and moved them to different jāgīrs in time, maybe none of this would have happened!'

'Tell me something, my friends,' I added, as in an afterthought, 'in your opinion, are there any other governors in the empire whom I should be calling back right now?'

I looked at them, one by one, and noticed how Mun'im Khān was evading my glance.

'Well, any ideas?'

Mān Singh answered in Mun'im Khān's stead: 'It probably is rather delicate for the Khān Khanān to say this, Your Majesty, but the family of his honourable predecessor, Shams-ud-dīn—may god receive him in his mercy—I fear they may one day pose a risk to Your Majesty. Not that I have any reason at all to doubt their loyalty, but one should not forget that all of them hold important jāgīrs in the Panjāb, that they have very strong family ties, that they live only a few days' travelling distance from each other.... Again, I have no reason whatsoever to doubt their loyalty, but having heard Bīrbal's and Todar Mal's words: If I were in Your Majesty's position, I would consider assigning them to different jāgīrs....'

'Thank you for your wise and honest advice, Rājā Mān Singh. I will most certainly give it due consideration,' I answered, nodding in appreciation.

My trusted advisors had said exactly what I had been thinking and planning myself, but—and remember this, my son—when difficult decisions have to be taken, it is always preferable that the people around you have reached the same conclusion by themselves: This will avoid much idle gossip afterwards....

As it was past midnight already, I thanked them again for their advice, bade them all a good and restful night, and retired to my quarters; but it was several hours before I finally fell asleep.

As I lay awake in the night, I pondered over the conversation with my advisors, and in particular, on the cleverness and perspicacity of Mān Singh, Todar Mal and Bīrbal. I could not help wondering—it was not the first time, nor would it be the last—how it had been possible that so smart and competent a race like the Hindūs had been overrun so easily by a handful of Muslim invaders.

The only plausible answer I could and can come up with—other than divine intervention, of course—is that the Hindūs were defeated because they had allowed themselves to be divided. Had there been a Hindū Akbar at that time, the invaders would never have stood a chance – the few survivors would have brought back tales of such horror that no foreigner would ever again have dared to invade Hindustān!

It is our task, my son, to see to it that such an invasion will, indeed, never happen again.

≈

Things went entirely as planned during the remainder of the year.

The Mīrzās and their band of marauders were easily driven back into Gujarāt; and Shams-ud-dīn's family members were called to Āgrā, where, as Abū-l Fazl would phrase it, they 'obtained the favour of kissing the threshold of the sublime court', and were all assigned to different jāgīrs elsewhere in the empire, far away from each other. Only my foster brother Azīz Koka, who resided most of the time at court anyway, was allowed to keep his fief in the Panjāb.

I do not know, nor care, whether they guessed the reason behind their reassignment, and whether or not it suited their convenience. I did see to it, though, that they were more than handsomely rewarded for their loyal service, and showered with honours. Loyalty, my son, is a matter of mutual benefit. . . .

Finding thus my borders secure and the affairs of the empire in good order, I could at last direct my efforts towards the further conquest of Rājāstān.

On the twenty-ninth of Bahman,[161] I pitched camp before Ranthambhor, the great stronghold of the Hāra clan, vassals of the Rānās of Mewār.

Ranthambhor being not much smaller than Chittor, I had resigned myself to another protracted siege. Sābāts were dug, and fifteen huge mortars were dragged all the way to the top of the steep hill facing the stronghold.

After several weeks of siege, however, my mortars had been causing such destruction that Rāi Surjan Hāra, the chief of Būndī and commander of Ranthambhor, sent us two of his sons as emissaries, asking for negotiations to be opened.

Rājā Bhagwān Dās and Mān Singh were allowed to enter the fortress to negotiate on my behalf. At first, I did not want to let them go – it would have been a disaster to lose my two most important allies and army leaders over a single fortress, but in the end, they convinced me that they

---

161. 8 February 1569

would be quite safe, since, as one chronicler aptly put it, 'courtesy among Rājpūt chiefs is never laid aside, even in times of war'.

It did not take them long to reach an agreement. On the eleventh of Farvardīn of the fourteenth year,[162] barely six weeks after the start of the siege, I made my triumphant entrance into the fortress.

Though I had been harsh towards Chittor, I was very lenient towards Ranthambhor. In exchange for the surrender of the fortress and his pledge of loyalty, Rāi Surjan Hāra was offered lucrative and prestigious jāgīrs elsewhere in the empire: He was first given an important command in Gondwāna and then appointed governor of the holy city of Vārānasī – a great honour and privilege for any Hindū. In addition to that, the Rāi and his family were offered exceptionally favourable terms and conditions: They would be allowed to keep their capital forever; they were exempted from sending me a bride, and their wives and female relatives were under no obligation to participate in the bazārs organised in the imperial zanāna; their temples would not be touched; they could beat their kettledrums in the streets of Āgrā as far as the gate of the imperial fortress; they would be allowed to enter the diwān-i-ām completely armed, and were under no obligation to prostrate themselves before the throne; their horses would not be branded with the imperial dagh;[163] their troops would never be placed under a Hindū commander other than a Rāi of Būndī, and would never be asked to cross the Hind.

I had, of course, ample reasons to be lenient. Ranthambhor in itself was worth paying a high price for, but even more important was the message it sent to the other Rājpūt chiefs: that I was the most generous and grateful of friends, but ruthless and lethal to those who chose to be my enemies.

The message did not fail to come across. Four months later, the strong fortress of Kālinjar, the siege of which, years before, had cost the life of the formidable Shēr Khān Sūr, surrendered to my troops without offering any serious resistance. Its leader, Rājā Rām Chand Bāghela, who had already demonstrated his obedience by sending Tānsēn to the imperial court, was granted an important jāgīr near Allāhābād.

---

162. 21 March 1569
163. Dagh: A flower-mark branded on the forehead.

Without a single additional shot being fired, the powerful rājās of Jodhpūr, Bikāner, and Jaisalmer made their submission in the year that followed. Rājāstān was finally mine. My troops were able to move about it freely, from Amber to the Thar Desert, and from the Panjāb to the borders of Gujarāt.

Even more importantly, its inhabitants no longer saw me as a Muslim invader, but as a loyal ally, a benevolent and equitable protector, with whom they gladly associated themselves. What had been a hostile and dangerous wilderness, I had turned into my power base.

Only the dethroned Mewārīs stubbornly remained behind in their Arāvallī hills. I let them. Of what use would it have been to waste more blood, treasure, and above all, time, on the conquest of an isolated hill range of little or no value, when my troops could go unhindered wherever I wished to send them?

No, I had more ambitious plans, and could hardly wait to carry them out.

≈

Thus commenced what, my son, I now see as the happiest period of my life. A golden time it was, with a past to be proud of, and a future to look forward to. God had blessed me in such abundance that at times, it made me feel guilty. Everything, absolutely everything I ever wanted or hoped for, was given to me. I was twenty-five years old, healthy and strong, and well under way to become one of the mightiest kings the world had ever seen; but above all, my son, god had finally blessed me with what I started to fear would never happen: the birth of a strong and healthy little boy, of whom the astrologers predicted that he would become a learned, wise, just and powerful king – you, my dear son.

Twenty-second Letter

سیکری

ṢİKRİ (I)

Part One
From the private notes of
Mulāzim Hakīm[164] Alī Gilanī,
Jālīnūs-uz-Zamānī,[165]
personal physician of His Majesty the Emperor

The day after the mortal remains of the unfortunate newborn Princes Hasan and Husain had been committed to their final resting place, I received a summons to present myself at His Majesty's private quarters.

With grave concern, I obeyed. I knew His Majesty to be just and kind; yet, it would not have been the first time that an unfortunate occurrence,

---

164. Mulāzim: Personal attendant. Hakīm: Physician.
165. Jālīnūs-uz-Zamānī: Galen of the age; honorary title referring to the famous physician and philosopher Claudius Galenus of Pergamum (c. 130–c. 200), whose teachings have dominated medical science in the Muslim and Western world for centuries.

while solely due to the divine will, is blamed on a poor hakīm's alleged incompetence. . . .

I was escorted to that spacious open room on top of the ramparts, overlooking His Majesty's beloved Jumna River. As I entered and performed the taslīm,[166] I was surprised to see that there were no guards in attendance. Clearly, His Majesty wanted the conversation to remain strictly private.

'Thank you for joining me, Hakīm Alī,' he said, pointing at a pillow at the foot of the low platform on which he was sitting. Although courteous, he was less friendly than usual – he seemed sad and preoccupied, if not irritated.

'Pray sit down. I wish to talk to you about the death of my unfortunate sons, may Allāh smile upon them.'

It was as I had feared, I thought to myself – the emperor was clearly displeased with me: He was blaming me for what had happened. My throat felt dry and painful, as if an invisible hand was slowly choking me.

'I can assure Your Majesty . . .' I stammered, but the emperor stopped me with an irritated gesture.

'Yes, I know, you have done your very best to save them, and I appreciate all your efforts,' he said impatiently.

I bowed, staring at my feet, afraid to look up.

'I know that what has happened cannot be undone, Hakīm Alī,' he added, in a softer tone of voice. 'What I want to hear from you, is: What, in your opinion, has been the exact cause of their death?'

Again, I bowed, trying to hide my relief.

'The two little boys—Allāh bless their souls!—were twins, Your Majesty. Twins are always more at risk than single children, especially if their mother is not strongly built. You see, Your Majesty, the blood in a frail woman's womb is often insufficiently abundant to nourish two children. And indeed, when all the nourishment has been consumed, the womb will expel the children, causing them to be born with immature organs. Quite often, the lungs will be too small to properly air the body, causing it to overheat; also, in many cases, the stomach is unable to hold and digest sufficient quantities of food . . .'

---

166. Taslim: Formal bow.

'So, other than the will of Allāh, it was their mother's frailty that has caused the children's death?'

'Other than the will of Allāh, yes.'

'Tell me, could sickness or death of newborn children also be due to the constitution of the father?'

'On rare occasions, yes, Your Majesty . . . although I have to emphasise, this is quite rare.'

'And such was not the case here?'

'Most certainly not, on the contrary!'

'What makes you so sure about that, Hakīm Alī?'

'The fact that twins have been conceived, is in itself clear evidence of the presence of abundant and strong, well-formed sperm, Your Majesty.'

The emperor looked pleased, but remained clearly unconvinced.

'May god give that you are right, Hakīm Alī. But still, I cannot help feeling worried. I have bedded hundreds of women in my life; and do you realise that up to now, not a single one of them has given me any children? Do you realise, that Hasan and Husain were the two first sons ever to be born to me? How is this to be explained? If my sperm is, as you say, strong and well-formed, why has it failed so far to engender any offspring?'

'This can still be a coincidence. I really do not think there is anything wrong with Your Majesty's constitution – the elements are clearly well in balance, as is apparent from Your Majesty's complexion, pulse, and all other vital signs. There is little advice that I could give Your Majesty to improve his current good health – other than what Your Majesty already does: eating and drinking in moderation, sleeping well, and exercising his body sufficiently for it to remain vigorous, without exhausting its strength.

'There is, maybe, one additional advice that may be wise to follow, and that is: moderation. For the gestation of children, it is of course advisable to have intercourse, but it may be recommended not to maintain too high a frequency. Especially in vigorous young men like Your Majesty, where abundance of red blood causes great appetite for all things which provoke the senses, all too frequent visits to the women's quarters will cause the sperm to overheat, and diminish in quantity. A pause of a few days will allow it to properly mature and absorb the right balance of the four elements, so that it attains both the right quantity and quality.

'But I should again emphasise: No matter how strong and healthy a man is, and even if his sperm is of optimal strength, intercourse will not always lead to pregnancy – in fact, I would say that pregnancy is the exception, rather than the rule!'

'Is that so, indeed? And why is that, Hakīm Alī?'

'I'm afraid this is a rather lengthy explanation. I should first point out, that the natural order of things has clearly been ordained by Allāh, who, in His endless wisdom, compassion and mercy, provides us with what we need – even if we do not always realise it.

'Indeed, intercourse and the delicate pleasure it provides, is certainly among Allāh's most generous blessings. When performed with reasonable frequency, it is, without any doubt, quite wholesome, and clearly contributes to a healthy balance in both body and mind. Moreover, it will generally increase the affection between husband and wife, thus strengthening the bonds of marriage and the harmony of family life.

'As Your Majesty knows, the male organs necessary for procreation are two. There is, of course, the virile member, which in healthy individuals is able to penetrate the female body and expel the semen towards the entrance of the womb. The male sperm contributes two things: form and life force; the female blood provides two things as well: nourishment, and the mother's form.

'It is true that women have two white glands inside their belly, and it is true that they are able to produce a form of transparent sperm. All men of learning, however, agree that this female sperm does not contain any life force. It is only produced when the woman is enjoying the intercourse. It may seem quite remarkable, but it should, in fact, be no surprise that two such similar organs and excretions can have such entirely different functions in males and females: Suffice it to think of the example of female breasts, which will produce milk, whereas male breasts are devoid of any practical function.

'I should first point out to Your Majesty, that the female body, being substantially colder in nature than that of a man, inherently needs less red blood for its functioning, and therefore will from time to time expel this excess blood, or, in case of pregnancy, use it to feed the child.

'The blood the woman does not need for her own body, is diverted to the womb, where it will be stored for a few weeks, to serve as nourishment for her child, should she become pregnant.

'The exact time during which the womb will be fertile is impossible to establish beforehand. However, it can be said with reasonable certainty that immediately after the woman's period, there will not yet be enough new blood present to allow an unborn child to grow. If, on the other hand, intercourse occurs too late in the cycle, the blood will have started to turn rancid and no longer suitable as food for the unborn child.

'I do beg pardon for this lengthy explanation, but it will be clear that it is very well possible for a healthy man like Your Majesty to have intercourse with many women, without pregnancy occurring. It is just a matter of coincidence!'

'Coincidence, and the will of Allāh, I suppose?'

'The will of Allāh, indeed. The best Your Majesty can do, in my humble opinion, is to pray to Allāh, and to ask for His powerful protection and guidance.'

Part Two
From the private notes of
Mīr Abdul Latīf

With the conquest of the great Rājpūt fortress of Chittor, His Majesty's power had reached a new high point in his life. Yet, he seemed more restless and ill at ease than ever before.

'If I may be forgiven for saying so,' I ventured to observe, after he had been listening quite absentmindedly to a few Hadīth[167] which I had been reading to him, 'Your Majesty seems preoccupied. Is there anything I could be of assistance with?'

The emperor smiled wearily.

'Thank you for your concern, Mīr Abdul Latīf, but there is little or nothing you can do about it, I suppose. . . .'

He looked at me, as if asking for confirmation.

'You know,' he explained, 'when it comes to the empire, everything has been going my way, and the future looks bright. Inshā'allāh, it will not be long before Rājpūtānā will be mine entirely, and I am currently taking a number of important new measures of government, which will strengthen my hold over the lands that belong to me. But I have to tell you, Mīr Abdul Latīf, I have been saddened, deeply saddened, by the death of my two sons,' he said, suddenly looking intently at me, as if I had anything to do with it.

'Tell me, my honourable teacher and friend: What will become of this great empire I have been building, if there is no one to leave it to?'

'It seems to me, Your Majesty should not worry too much about this – after all, Your Majesty is still very young!'

'You know as well as I do, Mīr Abdul Latīf, that life is fleeting, like the waters of a mountain river – you cannot hold on to it . . . it passes you by as it pleases!

'One day, you are strong and healthy; the next, they carry you to your grave, killed by a sudden onslaught of fever, or a hunting accident . . .

---

167. Hadīth: Traditions or sayings of the Holy Prophet Muhammad.

Only Allāh is the giver of life and death, and we should not assume to be ours what belongs to Him only! What kind of king would I be, if I would not worry about the future?'

'I stand corrected,' I admitted. 'Still, Your Majesty should not give up hope! Your Majesty should put his trust in the help of Allāh – He is always there to help and protect us, even if at times, He will put our strength and resilience to the test! When the time is ripe, our prayers will be answered!'

'I do hope you are right, Mīr Abdul Latīf, but I cannot help feeling worried. I do not know how many women I have had over the last few years' but I still do not have any children! Poor little Hasan and Husain were the very first children born to me! How is this to be explained? How many times have I not seen simple farmers in the villages, poor devils who can barely afford to marry one wife, and still, they are blessed with five, six and more children, whereas I, with hundreds of wives and concubines, have none! No, I must confess, Mīr Abdul Latīf: I fear, that for reasons known only to Him, Allāh has ordained that I should remain childless. . . .'

'I can only say that Your Majesty should put his trust in Allāh. Even if we do not always understand His reasons, what He ordains is for the best, for He alone is the all-knowing, and His compassion and mercy are limitless. Those who put their trust in Him, will never be disappointed!'

'And do you believe that He has ordained, for some or other strange reason that I should remain without offspring?'

'I do not know, but I am inclined to believe that if Your Majesty has not had any sons up to now, it is only because the time has not yet been auspicious. In due time, Allāh will answer Your Majesty's prayers, this I strongly believe!'

'I pray you are right, venerable master . . . I would not mind waiting, for years if need be, if only I knew that in the end, all would work out for the best – but nobody seems to be able to give me a straight answer! I have of course asked the astrologers, many times, but as usual, their answers have been vague and inconclusive. Also, back in Ājmīr, at Khwājah Muīn-ud-dīn Muhammad Chishtī's sacred tomb, nobody has been able to help me!'

'Now that Your Majesty mentions Khwājah Muīn-ud-dīn: Not so far from here, in the town of Sīkrī, lives one of his descendants – Shaykh Salīm Chishtī. People say that he has inherited the wisdom and holiness of his saintly forefather; they say that Allāh answers each and every one of his prayers, and that he is able to foresee the future!'

'Then I will visit this holy man as soon as possible, and ask him for his blessings! Will you accompany me, Mīr Abdul Latīf, or do you think it will be too strenuous a journey for you? After all, you are an old man, and I would not want you to fall ill!'

'It is not so far away, Your Majesty. It will be an honour and a privilege to accompany you!'

The messengers we had sent ahead had done their work: By the time we arrived in Sīkrī, the whole town had trooped together. The village elders knelt in the dust before the emperor, pointing at the humble but well-intended offerings the inhabitants had prepared: food, carvings in wood and stone, carpets, woven fabrics, simple jewellery, and the like.

As always, the emperor went out of his way to put the simple village people at ease, eating some of their food offerings, and accepting their meagre gifts with conspicuous enthusiasm and gratitude, as if the most precious treasures of the world had been offered to him. He more than returned the favour, for he ordered his soldiers to distribute gold coins – each one worth more than anything the villagers had ever laid their hands on.

After this friendly exchange of civilities, for which His Majesty took ample time—no less than an hour, without in any way showing his eagerness to see the shaykh—he was finally escorted to the holy man's dwelling by the village elders.

Any person familiar with today's glorious city of Fatehpūr Sīkrī would barely have recognised the town as it was in those days. It was no more than a small village at the foot of the hill, next to the bed of the Khari Nadi, the seasonal river which now has been dammed to form the beautiful lake that ensures the city's water supply.

The small hut in which the saint spent his days in hallowed silence and seclusion was outside the town, on the slope of the rocky hill which runs lengthwise along the river bank, and on which the current imperial city has been built. In those days, however, it was all barren wilderness, and—apart from the occasional visit he got from his next of kin and from pilgrims asking for his blessings—the old shaykh lived there, alone and secluded, far away from the noise of the town.

At the foot of the hill, the emperor dismissed his escort; he and I ascended, on foot, the narrow rocky path leading to the hut.

Upon our approach, the shaykh came out of his hut – a tall, sinewy man, still surprisingly strong and healthy despite his nearly ninety years of age. There was still black hair in his wiry beard and eyebrows, and the surprising swiftness of his movements revealed that in his youth, he must have been a man of considerable strength and agility.

He walked a few steps in our direction, bowing woodenly, rather ill at ease as it would seem.

'*As-salām aleikum*, honourable Shaykh Salīm Chishtī,' the emperor said, bowing his head and touching his heart, ill at ease himself as well – indeed, how does an emperor greet a saint, and how should a holy man salute his emperor?

'*Wa-aleikum salām*,[168] Your Majesty,' the shaykh answered, again bowing as deeply as he could. 'It is indeed an unexpected and undeserved honour for me, to meet so great and powerful a king, but I'm afraid my scanty dwelling is quite unworthy to receive such a noble visitor,' he proceeded, pointing apologetically at the hut.

'It is I who has to thank you for receiving me, honourable murshid,[169]' the emperor answered, 'for I am in dire need of your wise counsel, your blessings, and your prayers.'

'I am entirely at Your Majesty's disposal,' the shaykh answered, touching his heart.

'Allow me to present my teacher, the honourable Mīr Abdul Latīf,' the emperor proceeded. 'It is he who gave me the good advice to consult you.'

'It is a privilege to meet you, sāhab,' the shaykh said, bowing again, and looking at me inquisitively from beneath his bushy eyebrows.

We arrived at the hut. The shaykh went in and came back with his prayer mat, offering it to the emperor to sit on. To me, he offered his

---

168. As-salām aleikum: (The) Peace (be) with you; Wa-aleikum salām: and with you, peace. Formal Arabic greeting, also used in Persian and Urdū.
169. Murshid: Guide, master.

winter mantle, but I politely declined, and sat myself down in the dust, as he did.

A small tandūr, a water pot, a few pieces of crude earthenware, and a few books on two small wooden stands – that was, apparently, all he possessed in this world. . . .

'This is really all I need,' he said, guessing my thoughts. 'In gratitude for my blessings and prayers, the simple people who come to visit me bring me some vegetables, some flour, ghī, dāl – those are the only gifts I accept. Indeed, what would I need gold, silver or jewels for? What more could I want than the things I already have? I enjoy peace and quiet, I eat the honest and wholesome foods of the people of the land; and if for a day or two, I have nothing to eat, I just go without it, like they do. Since long I have given up eating meat, and I do not miss it at all. The Hindūs are right, you know: One does not need to make one's body a grave of animals in order to remain healthy. On the contrary, I find that vegetable food brings calmness, wisdom, and peace of mind.'

'How do you spend your days, revered master?' I asked.

'I pray, and I read,' he answered. 'I have the Holy Qur'ān, the Hadith, and a few poems of Rumī and Hāfiz at my disposal – there is more than enough in those writings to fill a thousand lifetimes!'

'I do not see any qalam,[170] ink, or paper, revered master? Surely, mankind would benefit from your wisdom if you would commit your thoughts to writing?' I asked.

'I must confess, I have thought about it,' the shaykh said, smiling faintly, 'but if I am honest, sāhab, I must admit there is little, if anything, that I could write, that has not yet been written before – much more eloquently than I could ever express it! To what use would it be, to add yet another volume of paraphrases and repetitions to the vast libraries that have already been written? No, I am content, sāhab, just to sit here, and to give, to whoever comes to ask me for it, whatever little wisdom I have to offer. Verily, this is what I believe Allāh has destined me to do.'

'I suppose it is mainly Muslims who come to see you?' the emperor inquired.

---

170. Qalam: Wooden writing pen, usually made of reed, used in Arabic and Persian calligraphy.

'On the contrary, I would say, Your Majesty: I think I am even more popular among the Hindūs!'

He paused and smiled.

'You know, that is the way the Hindūs are: They see Allāh as a huge, immeasurable mountain, and all the world's many religions as different paths leading up that same mountain. Different though all these beliefs may be, in a sense, they are all equal, since all of them will ultimately lead to the same summit. The individual path a person is destined to follow, is determined by birth; and birth, in turn, is determined by previous lives; ultimately, however, every person, nay, every living being, is destined to be reunited with Allāh, that is what they believe.

I have often been favourably impressed by their god-fearing attitude. Each time, I am moved to see the respect and devotion with which they kneel before the Holy Qur'ān, even if they do not know Its sacred message.'

'Do you not try to convert them to Islām, venerable shaykh?'

'In the beginning, yes, I did. I tried to convince them that their beliefs were erroneous and displeasing in the eyes of Allāh. But now . . . I have given up on that. I confine myself to answering any questions they may have, and offering them my blessings and prayers whenever they ask me for them. It is my experience that the frugal life I lead greatly appeals to them, much more than any learned reasoning that I may have to offer.

'I do not condemn them, I do not argue with them; I leave it to Allāh's limitless wisdom and mercy to judge their hearts and minds, and to guide them unto the right path, if He so chooses. Indeed, some of them do come back to me, asking for my help to become true Muslims; but even if they keep on worshipping the many gods of their forefathers, I do not mind. They all show such deep respect and devotion that I believe this is what Allāh wants me to do: to lead a simple life, to offer prayers and blessings, and through my example, incite all those who visit me, to worship the one and only true god, the lord of all worlds, the first and the last.

'Your Majesty may be familiar with the saying: The mosque and the temple divide, but the Sūfī shrine unites. How very true, indeed! As long as we preach, condemn and divide, we are creating fear, resistance, hatred and strife. But as soon as we bow and kneel down, together, in silence before Allāh's unspeakable majesty, we realise that we are all united in our smallness before Him.'

The emperor, visibly impressed, nodded enthusiastically.

'This is exactly how I see things as well, respected shaykh! I strongly believe it is my duty to provide sulh-i-kul, peace and security to all, and thus, to unite all people in peace and security under god – that, I believe, is ultimately the best way to promote the sacred cause of Islām!'

'Indeed. One just needs to think about the example of Ājmīr, where thousands upon thousands of Hindūs and Muslims pray together before the tomb of my illustrious forefather Khwājah Muīn-ud-dīn, may Allāh be well pleased with him! How many Hindūs have not found the path to Islām, standing before that sacred shrine? Indeed, if one looks at the history of Hindustān, Islām has invariably made the greatest and most lasting progress when it succeeded in uniting the people in peaceful prayer, without trying to forcibly convert them!'

The shaykh paused, looking at the emperor with a fatherly smile.

'Hindustān is blessed with so noble-minded and wise an emperor! Clearly, Your Majesty has been chosen by Allāh to achieve great things!'

'I pray to Him that you are right,' the emperor said.

'Your Majesty should not worry – Allāh is with him! I know Your Majesty is concerned about his succession, because he does not yet have a son to whom he will leave the empire. But let me put Your Majesty's mind at ease: not one, but three strong and healthy sons will be born unto him, and all three will reach the age of adulthood!'

'You make me very happy, honourable Shaykh Salīm Chishtī – may Allāh fulfill your wonderful prophecy! I hope you will forgive me for asking, but are you really sure that I have nothing to worry about – that indeed, three healthy sons will be born unto me?'

'This is my strong belief, yes.'

'Is it your strong belief, or is it what you have actually seen in the future?'

'I have to admit, I do not really see the future, Your Majesty. Every morning, I pray to Allāh, that He may be my guide; I ask Him to steer my tongue, and make it an instrument of righteousness and truth.

'When people then come and ask me about their future, I merely say what I think, what comes through my mind – that is all. I do not pretend to have any power of my own: I merely ask Allāh, that He may use me, and that is my only ambition – to be Allāh's humble instrument. Just like the chisel and the hammer have no merit or ability of their own, but are destined to shape great things of beauty in the hands of the artisan, I merely wish for Allāh to use me as He deems fit to do.'

'I must confess, I have never thought about it this way, but indeed, this should be every man's ambition: to be nothing but a willing tool in god's hands,' the emperor agreed pensively. 'If you would allow me to come back on what you just said, honourable Shaykh Salīm, about the sons you say will be born unto me: Is there any other advice you can give me in this respect?'

'What does Your Majesty mean?'

'I mean, do you know which one of my many spouses and concubines will become the mother of my firstborn? Often have I prayed, that my son would be born out of Princess Salīmā, for I appreciate her wisdom, and like me, she is a descendant of the glorious house of Temür!'

After a few moments hesitation, Shaykh Salīm replied: 'Make your firstborn a son of Hindustān, Your Majesty.'

Part Three
From the Memoirs of Her Imperial Highness Salīmā Sultānā Bēgam Chaqāniānī

مخفى [171]

Barely three months after Akbar had returned from his visit to Shaykh Salīm Chishtī of Sīkrī, the imperial court was buzzing with rumours that the princess of Amber was with child: She had not had her period, she was feeling sick every morning, and it was a well-known fact that the emperor had been visiting her quite frequently, ever since his return from Sīkrī.

After a few more weeks, the slight but visible swelling of the princess' belly proved that for once, the rumours had been right.

I have to confess that at first, I felt quite jealous of her. How ardently had I prayed that I would become the future emperor's mother? Was I not Akbar's favourite? Was I not a descendant of Temūr? Knowing, however, that nothing in this world happens unless Allāh wills it, I forced myself to banish these unworthy thoughts from my mind, and to resign myself to the divine will.

Having given the matter more ample thought, I came to understand and appreciate Allāh's reasons: It was actually a very good thing, for the empire and for our family, that the mother of Akbar's successor was not a Gurkaniyya princess, but a Hindū of noble Rājpūt blood.

Indeed, Akbar's extraordinary power had been, to a large extent, the result of his ability to unite Muslim and Hindū forces under his victorious banners. And now, his son and successor was also Rājā Bihārī Mal's own grandson, and Rājā Bhagwān Dās's nephew! Indeed, this young Gurkaniyya prince would have royal Rājpūt blood flowing through his veins – no longer a foreign ruler would he be, but a true son of Hindustān!

---

171. Mākhfī

Yes, this was a good thing; and besides, I knew my duty as a Gurkaniyya princess. I would do what I had promised Akbar that night by the river: I would be a loving mother and teacher to his son and heir.

Akbar's initial joy at his spouse's pregnancy was soon overshadowed by understandable worries. Was this indeed the first of the three sons the shaykh had promised would be born unto him? What if it was a girl? And if it was a son, how to make sure that what had happened to poor little Hasan and Husain would not happen again? The princess of Amber was a frail woman – how to keep her and her child in good health? Should he postpone the planned campaign against the fortress of Ranthambhor and stay behind with her?

After much deliberation and consultation of every teacher, physician, and astrologer he could find, Akbar decided that his pregnant spouse was to go to Sīkrī, where she and her servants and midwives were to reside until after the delivery. This, so he reasoned, 'would avail her of the utmost benefit of the saint's orisons'.

With great dispatch, a nice house was built for her, spacious and comfortable, on the flank of the hill overlooking the riverbank. As soon as the construction works had progressed sufficiently, she and her retinue moved to Sīkrī, where I went to visit her a few times during her pregnancy. Each time I saw her, doing so well, enjoying the tranquility of the village and the frequent visits of her friends and relatives, far away from the crowded zanāna and all its meddling and gossip, it was difficult for me not to start feeling jealous again. However, I did my very best to hide my feelings – from her, as well as from myself.

Under the protection of Shaykh Salīm Chishtī's blessed prayers, everything went well. At noon on the eighteenth of Shahrīvar of the fourteenth year,[172] in the middle of the season when the gentle rains bring life in abundance to the countryside, Rājā Bhagwān Dās's frail daughter gave birth to a remarkably strong and healthy boy, of whom the astrologers immediately predicted that he would grow up to be a just, mighty, world-adorning king of kings, who would walk in his illustrious father's footsteps.

---

172. Tuesday, 30 August 1569 (Julian calendar)

The fortunate mother received the lofty title of Maryam uz-zamānī,[173] whereas the newborn prince himself was given the name Salīm—Shāhzāda[174] Sultān Muhammad Salīm, to be complete—in grateful recognition of the holy man's prayers, and in an effort to ensure his lifelong protection and blessings. Akbar, however, rarely if ever called his son by his official name: Even when he had grown taller than his own father, he would always affectionately call him Shaykhu Bābā.[175]

A healthy son and successor! Akbar was truly overwhelmed with joy. He came to visit his little son in the zanāna as often as he could, holding, kissing and cuddling him all the time.

Akbar was, for that matter, not the only one to be so fond of the little boy: The prince grew up as everybody's darling, mine in particular; a good-humoured, funny and bright little boy he was, who made the dull zanāna suddenly seem full of life.

It is always amazing to see how quickly a child will change during the first three years of his life, but Salīm was truly remarkable. He seemed to literally drink in everything he saw and heard. By the time he was three, he spoke not only fluent Persian, the common language of the imperial court, but also quite passable Turkī, which he often heard Akbar, Ruqqayah, Aunt Gulbadan and me speaking among ourselves; and excellent Hindī, which he picked up from his mother and the many zanāna servants.

Salīm's remarkable sense of beauty, for which he is so renowned today, manifested itself at a very early age. He could hardly speak when he would already be pointing at every painting and drawing he saw, crowing 'Look, pretty, pretty!'

For hours on end, he would sit in the artisans' workshops, amusing himself with paper, paint, brushes, ink and qalams – drawing flowers and animals, and 'writing' pages upon pages of letters, many of them remarkably harmonious and shapely, coming from the hand of such a small child.

---

173. Mary of the age.
174. Shāhzāda: Son of a shāh; prince.
175. 'Daddy shaykh'; dear little shaykh.

It was a surprise to no one that when, at the age of four years, four months and four days, he received his first formal instruction in the art of reading and writing, Salīm revealed himself as a bright and diligent student, and it must be said that Akbar, despite his own inability to read and write, never failed to encourage his son in this respect. Quite often, he would ask Salīm to read him some poetry; and knowing most of these poems by heart, he actually proved himself quite able to help his little son with his reading practice!

Apart from his son's scholarly education, Akbar of course took a lively interest in his development as a soldier, personally teaching him how to handle guns and swords. He would enjoy himself for hours, wrestling with his little son and in the end, allowing himself to be vanquished. He was also extremely satisfied to see that Salīm, although more prudent and considerate than most children, proved to be utterly fearless, just like his father.

So proud he was of his little boy! Each time he saw me, or his mother Hamīda, Aunt Gulbadan, Ruqqayah, or another family member, he would never fail to talk about him:

'Have you seen how strong he is? Mark my words, he will grow up to be taller and stronger than I am! Don't you agree, he is exceptionally smart for a boy his age? Have you heard how well he speaks Turkī, although he hardly ever gets a chance to practice? A true prince of the house of Temür, so much is clear! His ancestors would be really proud of him!'

Akbar's joy and pride were equalled by the immense gratitude he felt towards the holy saint to whose blessings and prayers he owed this good fortune. Salīm was barely two months old when Akbar decided that Sīkrī was going to be the seat of the new imperial residence. Indeed, so he reasoned, was it not clear that Sīkrī was a most auspicious place? Was it not there that Bābur had inflicted a crushing defeat on the rānā of Mewār? Did not Bābur name it Shukrī,[176] because of that victory? Was it not clear that the good Shaykh Salīm Chishtī's sacred presence had brought more of god's blessings on this place? Was it not there that Prince Salīm had been born?

---

176. Shukrī: Thanks

I tactfully tried pointing out to him that it would take considerable time and treasure to turn that sleepy little farmers' town into the grand city he was envisaging. Was that kind of money not better spent on Āgrā?

Akbar wanted nothing of the kind. The great kings before him had built grandiose new cities, and so would he. His capital would be Sīkrī – or Fathābād, the city of victory, or Fatehpūr Sīkrī, as it would soon be called, the magnificent capital of Akbar the Great.

Twenty-third Letter

سیکری

Sikri (2)

Blessed, I was truly blessed.

The successor I had prayed for so ardently—you, my dearest son—had been born unto me at last; and those mighty fortresses of Rājāstān, which for centuries had defied so many a powerful invader: they were all mine.

It seemed there would be no end to my good fortune, for barely two months and twenty days after your birth,[177] my son, the zanāna was gladdened by the birth of your sweet and lovely sister, Shahzadi Sultān Khanam; and barely had we celebrated her birth, when it became apparent that yet another of the imperial concubines was with child.

Verily, one blessing after the other was befalling me. Clear as day it was now, clear for everyone to see: I was god's chosen. The common people called me Akbar the fortunate; and 'as lucky as Emperor Akbar' was quickly becoming a commonplace expression. And indeed, could I deny it? Had I not been given more than I, or any other human being, could ever deserve or reasonably hope for?

What was I to do, in the face of all this undeserved divine generosity? Little could I do to repay god; I could only pray to Him, offer Him my

---

177. Sunday, 20 November 1569 (Julian calendar) – the tenth of Jumādā ul-Ukhra 977 A.H.

devotion and gratitude, implore His continued blessings, and pledge, from the bottom of my heart, that I would fulfill, to the best of my ability, the lofty tasks He would choose to put upon my shoulders.

In pursuance of the solemn vow I had taken before you were born, my son, I set out as soon as possible to the sacred city of Ājmīr, eager to place my forehead on the cool white marble of Khwājah Muīn-ud-dīn's holy shrine.

Although escorted, as usual, by an impressive cortege with hundreds of horse archers and richly adorned, mighty war elephants, I covered the entire distance on foot, the whole ninety-one kos,[178] every single step of the way, showing everyone the kind of man I was: the invincible emperor and sovereign ruler of men; yet, a humble pilgrim before god.

I arrived in Ājmīr on Panjshanbeh, the twenty-first of Esfand,[179] and stayed there until shortly before the celebration of the fifteenth anniversary of my enthronement, spending my time in prayer and administering justice and charity.

As usual, around that time of year, my thoughts went out to my unfortunate father, dead and gone, fifteen years already . . . I decided not to return directly to Āgrā, but to travel to Dillī instead, to pay my respects at his tomb, the construction of which, according to the reports I had received, was now complete.

I had visited the site before, and had seen several drawings of it, made after its completion; yet, when I arrived, I could not help being overwhelmed by the mausoleum's beauty and magnificence. The tranquility of the surrounding gardens, the grandeur of the tomb, its perfect proportions – verily, I thought it was as I had promised Bairām Khān it would be, one of the most magnificent buildings the world had ever seen; a sublime resting place, worthy of a king of kings; more beautiful, more harmonious, more imposing, I am sure, than even Temür's tomb at Samarqand.

To be laid to rest in the perfect harmony and tranquility of a building of such exquisite proportions, somehow, made death much less intimidating. Later, I thought to myself, in due time, I would personally

---

178. 228 miles, 365 kilometres
179. Thursday, 2 March 1570 (Julian calendar)

concern myself with the construction of the mausoleum where, one day, my own body would find its last resting place.

But there would be plenty of time to worry about that later. Now, I wanted to live – live my life to the fullest, and rise to true greatness, for god's benevolent smile was upon me; I felt His strength in every part of my body; and my head was teeming with plans and ambitions.

The imperial cortege unhurriedly made its way back to Āgrā. As usual, I amused myself with grandiose hunting parties – many of them in the middle of the night. I really had come to enjoy the excitement of nightly hunting parties: the confused shouting of the drivers in the darkness, the breakneck cavalcades in pursuit of the fleeing deer, with nothing but the pale moon and flickering of torches to light the way.

Back in Āgrā, I celebrated the birth of the second of the three healthy sons that the good shaykh had promised would be born unto me: Your dearly beloved and now so deeply regretted brother Murād had beheld the first light of day at Sīkrī, on Chāhārshanbeh the twenty-seventh of Khordād of the fifteenth year, the third of Muharram of 978.[180]

I was truly elated. Another son had been given to me, another healthy boy! Once again, he had been born unto me in the good town of Sīkrī, under the protection of the venerable shaykh's prayers! This, so I thought, could hardly be a coincidence; it strengthened my resolve to take up residence in that most blessed place, so that its auspiciousness might continue to protect me and my family.

I ordered the most elaborate festivities to be organised, and large amounts of treasure to be distributed among the people: I wanted everybody to share my pride and joy.

From the farthest corners of the empire, governors and nobles travelled to Āgrā to offer me their congratulations. I gladly took this opportunity to strengthen the ties of loyalty and friendship that united them to me, making sure they became equally impressed by my power and wealth, as by my kindness and generosity. As I pointed out to you before, my son, a subject's faithfulness is like a delicate jewel: The precious but tender pure gold of his love, affection, and gratitude needs to be strengthened by the alloy of harder metal. If possible, the people should

---

180. Wednesday, 7 June 1570 (Julian calendar)

love and admire their emperor for his righteousness and generosity – but never should they stop fearing his power.

≈

Two more carefree, leisurely years slipped by, nearly unnoticed.

I spent most of that time travelling about the empire. Indeed, it is not wise to always stay in the same place, my son: An emperor's moves and whereabouts should remain unpredictable; his subjects should realise that in a few weeks' or months' time, he might be there to personally investigate their dealings.

To render thanks to god for Murād's birth, and to beseech His continued guidance and blessings, I of course travelled to Ājmīr first, where I supervised the repairs and enlargement of the fortress, and the construction of beautiful buildings for the imperial court and pleasant dwellings for its members. Imposing and graceful buildings, my son, are an excellent way to remind the people of their emperor's might and generosity.

About two months later, I headed northwest, to Nāgaur, which as you know, is located about halfway between Amber and Bikāner. As I had done in Ājmīr, I commissioned several important building works, including the embellishment of its famous seventeen-mouthed fountain.

It was there that I tasted the intense satisfaction of receiving the formal submission of the powerful rājās of Bikāner and Jaisalmer, who had sent high-ranking ambassadors to pay deference to me and to offer me their princesses in marriage as a sign of their loyalty and friendship. Rājāstān was mine!

It was also at Nāgaur, that Bāz Bahādūr, the former king of Mālwa, came to kneel before me, rubbing his forehead in the dust like a repentant sinner. For eight years he had been wandering around as a fugitive, vainly seeking support, avoided like the plague by everyone: Nobody dared to provoke the wrath of the 'mighty great Mughal!'

I of course graciously pardoned him, and gave him an appointment at my court. As I told you before, my son: To kill an opponent, in a way, is to honour him – it is to acknowledge, that to a certain extent at least, he was a true rival. To pardon him, however, is to demonstrate your own supremacy, and to emphasise his insignificance. And thus it happened that the once so proud and recalcitrant king of Mālwa ended up eating the bread of charity from his former enemy. Bāz Bahādūr would spend the rest of his life as one of my courtiers, entertaining me with his poetry and music – for which, I have to say, he was quite talented.

Shortly before the sixteenth anniversary of my enthronement, the imperial court travelled further north, crossing the Sutlej River into the Panjāb. I visited the shrine of Shaykh Farīd Shakarganj at Pākpattan, and from there went to the district of Dibālpūr, the jāgīr of my foster brother Mīrzā Azīz Koka.

I have to say, I did not fully like what I saw: Azīz did receive us with what appeared to be unfeigned enthusiasm, but there was something rather arrogant in the lavish openhandedness and the conspicuous display of brotherly love with which he received me.

Not that I had any doubts about his loyalty – a new Adham Khān, he was certainly not. Conceitedness, however, is never a good quality, in any man, much less in a courtier.

However, one must make do with what one has. . . . And after all, Azīz was my foster brother, whom I had known since infancy, united to me by a river of milk. . . . Moreover, he was a brave and competent soldier, and I needed men like him.

I therefore, forced myself not to pay too much attention to his familiarities, and concentrated instead on strengthening our mutual friendship. Throughout my stay, I spent as much time with him as possible. I invited him to join me on hunting trips, and we spent many hours eating and drinking together, sometimes all through the night.

It was reassuring to hear how enthusiastically he supported my plans for further expansion of the empire. When I informed him of my desire to add the wealthy territory of Gujarāt to my dominions, he could hardly wait to gird himself to battle.

'Gujarāt is a real quagmire,' I said, chewing on a succulent piece of lamb his cooks had prepared for us. 'There are currently no less than seven would-be kings fighting with each other over its throne!'

'That land and its people indeed deserve much better, Your Majesty,' Azīz nodded in agreement. 'They need order and justice, which only Your Majesty can give them!'

'Are you saying, my brother, that it is actually my duty to intervene, and to annexe these lands to my dominions?'

In his excitement, he forgot all formalities.

'If not your duty, then certainly your right! Remember, your father once ruled over Gujarāt – that alone makes your claim on it as good as anybody else's! Besides, don't forget that at this time, the Gujarātīs are weak, because they are busy fighting each other; but just imagine what would happen, if one day, the whole territory would fall into the hands of one strong king? You simply cannot afford to have such a wealthy and powerful neighbour at your doorstep!'

Despite the impertinence of his tone, I very much liked what he was saying – those were exactly my own views about the situation.

'Thank you for your advice, my brother,' I said. 'I knew I could count on you.'

'You just say the word, and my men and I are on our way,' he exclaimed, jumping up excitedly, and knocking over, in the process, his beakers of water, sherbet and wine! 'When do we attack?'

'Your zeal is highly commendable, my brother, but I think we should be patient. Let us wait a bit longer for the opportune moment!'

'Wait? What on earth do we have to wait for? Surely, you are not afraid that we will not be able to deal with them?'

I choked back my growing vexation at his insolence, and replied, in the friendliest tone I could force myself to:

'Haste is the enemy of wisdom, my brother. I think we should allow them a bit more time to wear each other down. Why exhaust ourselves, if they are doing the job for us?'

'As Your Majesty commands. I do beg Your Majesty's pardon.'

It finally seemed to have dawned on him that his tone had been out of line. Seeing his embarrassment, my anger melted away, as quickly as it had risen.

'A few months from now, we will attack, my brother. Let us spend that time well! Your troops appear to be in good condition; keep them well occupied, and make sure you have ample supplies of gunpowder, rockets and cannon. And we need to spend some time on our battle plan. Gujarāt is vast, and the great number of rivalling fiefdoms complicates the situation. We will need to split up our forces, but make sure that they remain well coordinated.'

'As Your Majesty commands. Your Majesty can count on me.'

Satisfied with what I had seen and heard, I continued my journey, and travelled further north, to Lāhor, where I administered justice and 'disposed of the affairs of the country under the guise of hunting', as Abū-l Fazl would politely phrase it.

From there, I returned to Āgrā, passing again through Ājmīr, and sojourning at Sīkrī for a few weeks.

I was happy to see that the buildings I had ordered were making excellent progress. The sleepy little town of yore had changed beyond recognition: On the rocky ridge, where there had been nothing but wilderness; palaces, mosques, courtyards, towers and gates were rising up everywhere, like young greens in the monsoon season. The Khari Nadi had been dammed, as I had ordered; the ensuing lake was starting to form, and looked wonderfully inviting.

The venerable old Shaykh Salīm Chishtī was the first among the town elders to come out to greet me, although I noticed he was walking with difficulty, and seemed to be in pain. He bowed, bid me welcome and thanked me, politely and profusely—a bit too politely and too profusely, I thought—for the undeserved honour I had bestowed on their undeserving and insignificant, humble little hamlet.

I could not help smiling: The old man, so my informants told me, had been wandering around the construction site, shaking his head, and sighing that he wished the emperor had been a little less grateful to him.

I took his hands in mine, dismayed to feel how frail they had become since the last time we met.

'Do not worry, revered master,' I said. 'You will see, I will make this a place of splendour and piousness!'

He gave me a long, scrutinising look. After what seemed to be an eternity, he seemed to be reassured. He smiled and raised both his hands in blessing.

'Verily, Your Majesty is the greatest of kings. May Allāh bless and protect him! I will pray for Your Majesty – both here, and from beyond my grave!'

'Khudā nakhāsta, revered master![181] I pray to Allāh, that He may grant you many, many more years among us – we are in such dire need of your guidance and wisdom!'

---

181. God forbid (Persian).

'Your Majesty is most kind to say this, and I am touched by his friendship, but he knows as well as I do that it is neither possible, nor desirable for me to go on living much longer. I am a weak, old man; my time has come to leave this transient world. More than nine decades have I lived on this earth, Your Majesty – twice or thrice the life span of most people! Would it not be ungrateful, nay, unworthy, if I were to ask Allāh for more?'

His eyes wandered off and looked at the village of Sīkrī.

'It gives me great comfort to know that I have spent a long and happy life in this village, in the service of Allāh and the many people who have sought my help; it fills me with joy and pride to know that my name will be remembered by generations to come when the silsilah[182] is recited after the Friday evening prayers. But I have lived enough; I am old and tired, and I long for the sacred silence of the grave, where, in the comforting presence of Allāh's blessed angels Munkar and Nakīr, I will prepare myself for the Last Day. From there, if it pleases Allāh, I will pray for those who will come after me, and blissfully await the sound of the Angel Isrāfīl's trumpet.'[183]

Barely a few months later, the old man passed away. One morning, he was found lying on his prayer mat, his eyes half open, still staring at the Holy Qur'ān that he had been reading. The holy book was opened—it can hardly be a coincidence—in the middle of Sūra Yūnus. The last thing the shaykh's eyes saw in this world, must have been Āya 56:[184]

It is He Who gives life, and causes death,
and to Him you shall return.

---

182. Unbroken chain of Sūfī masters, reaching back all the way to the Holy Prophet Muhammad. All Sūfī orders trace their spiritual lineage to Muhammad through his son-in-law Alī, except for the Naqshbandi order, which traces its lineage through Abū Bakr, the Prophet's father-in-law and first khalīfah of Islām.
183. According to the Muslim tradition, Isrāfīl is the angel who will announce Judgement Day, whereas Munkar and Nakīr are the angels who interrogate the deceased and prepare them for the final resurrection.
184. Qur'ān 10:56. Yūnus, the title of Sūra 10, is the Arabic name of the Biblical prophet Jonah.

I ordered his body to be laid to rest in the middle of the sahn-i-ibādat,[185] opposite the Jama Masjid. Within a matter of days, his sacred tomb became a place of refuge for seekers of wisdom, help and consolation from all over the country; for indeed, the good shaykh is praying for us, even from the yonder side of the grave.

185. Sahn-i-Ibādat: Sacred complex.

Twenty-fourth Letter

مخفى

Makhfi

From the Memoirs of Her Imperial Highness Salīmā Sultānā Bēgam Chaqānīānī

I have always enjoyed travelling: a change of air, a different landscape, the busyness of the encampments – all welcome distractions, after long months at the court, where every day is drearily similar to the previous and to the next one.

Not that I have any reason to complain, and I really do not want to sound ungrateful – after all, who would not want to live in a spacious palace, completely safe and well protected, warm and comfortable in winter, cool in summer; with every convenience and luxury one could ever imagine: beautiful gardens, water basins and fountains, exquisite food, beautiful clothes and jewellery, and scores of servants to attend to one's every wish?

I enjoy looking through the curtains of the pālkī, watching the changing landscape, and even more so, the people in the villages. I like to watch them, leading their simple lives, tilling the land, tending their animals, preparing their food. Little or no possessions do they have, and very few moments of leisure, apart from the time they spend praying at their shrines, and eating their frugal meals together. Yet, it always strikes me, how despite their poverty, the squalour and the dirt in which they are forced to live, they do not seem to be unhappy. I guess, provided their crops do not fail and their family and their animals remain free from disease, they have all they need to be happy – indeed, what else does one really need, but freedom from hunger and disease, and the companionship of loved ones?

I remember, during the first few years of my marriage, when we accompanied Akbar on one of his many trips, I used to be so fascinated by the village life. Through the curtains, I saw the women, caring for their children, chatting with their mothers, sisters and friends, and I often wondered what my life would have been like, if I had been born among them . . . if I had been a simple farmer's only wife rather than one of the emperor's consorts.

One of many wives, indeed . . . Akbar's favourite, no doubt; the only one who has his ear, most certainly; but still, just one of many. . . .

Again, I certainly do not want to complain, and I would not want to trade places with anyone. And after all, is that not the only relevant answer to the question of whether one is happy or not: whether one would like to be someone else? Still, it will not come as a surprise to anybody, that life in a powerful emperor's zanāna is far from simple . . . How could it be, with over five thousand women living together inside a heavily guarded, walled city?

Not more than a mere three hundred of these five thousand women have ever shared Akbar's bed: his nikāh and mut'ah[186] wives and concubines, plus the occasional pretty dancing girl that has managed to catch his attention. The rest of them are all employed in the service of the zanāna: from the well-dressed personal maidservants of the bēgams, to the ragged cleaning women scavenging the sewers and latrines.

Indeed, every aspect of life is taken care of by females: cooking, cleaning, lighting, gardening, maintenance . . . everything. Even the guards inside the zanāna walls are all women: tough, strong and heavily

---

186. Nikāh: official marriage. Mut'ah: Temporary marriage, in principle allowed under Shī'a law only.

armed female warriors from Turān and Afghanistān, recruited and trained especially for this purpose. They will take orders only from the emperor himself, and in his absence, from their own officers, who, in turn, answer to the emperor or the khwājasara.[187] The zanāna has but one gate connecting it to the rest of the imperial palace, and that gate is strictly guarded, every hour of the day and night. No male—not even the mukhanni[188] soldiers—will ever venture inside its enclosure, unless they have the emperor's express authorisation.

Even among Akbar's officially wedded wives, there are many who will hardly ever get to see him in private. This should be no surprise either: Most of his marriages have been concluded with the sole purpose of sealing an alliance with the new bride's family. If she has the misfortune of being rather plain-looking or otherwise uninteresting to him, she will not often meet him face to face after the marriage has been consummated! Most women inside the zanāna are thus forced to lead their lives without any male companionship; and this, in turn, will sometimes lead to friendships that—how shall I put it?—transgress the boundaries of sisterly affection. . . .

Be this as it may: I do not mean to imply that Akbar treats any of his wives with neglect or disrespect. Indeed, he is most generous to all of us: The highest-ranking women are paid staggeringly high salaries, of over one thousand rūpaē[189] per month! In fact, Akbar's three most important spouses—his first wife Ruqayyah, Salīm's mother, and I—receive no less than 1,610 rūpaē every month! Taking into account that many people survive on less than one rupiyah per month; that an average family in Āgrā (husband, wife and four children) can live quite comfortably off a mere five rūpaē per month, and that an entire tola[190] of pure gold will cost no more than ten rūpaē, it will be clear that all of us enjoy what the common people would call fabulous wealth.

And Akbar's generosity does not end there: On the occasion of both our solar and lunar birthdays, or other festive occasions, or even

---

187. Khwājasara: The highest officer of the harem administration.
188. Mukhanni: Eunuchs
189. Rūpaē: Plural of rūpaya, rupee
190. 1 tola = 11.66 grams

for no particular reason at all, he will surprise us with lavish, not to say extravagant gifts of jewellery, clothes, perfumes, works of art, and the like. From time to time, he will organise a bazār inside the zanāna, where women offer their embroideries and handicrafts for sale. On those occasions, he will always be in an excellent mood—kind and courteous to every single one of his wives, his favourites as well as the others—and will smilingly allow himself to be seduced into paying inordinate sums of money for the smallest trifles.

Akbar's openhandedness enables us all to pursue whatever interests we have, and he allows us every freedom to do so.

Many highborn ladies, including his mother Hamīda Bānū Bēgam and his good-natured aunt Gulbadan, are spending fortunes on the construction of mosques, schools and other charitable projects. Humāyūn's other widow and first-wedded wife, Hājī Bēgam, has busied herself deservingly with the construction of her late husband's magnificent mausoleum back in Dillī.

Salīm's mother, on her part, appears to have inherited a singular talent for trade – all the more surprising, since this kind of activity, to my knowledge, has never been a tradition in her Rājpūt family, certainly not among the women! Anyway, as a pastime, she buys and equips scores of sea-going ships, has them laden with spices, silk and other goods, without ever leaving the zanāna! Using a network of correspondents in various cities and seaports, she sells her merchandise to local and foreign traders from all over the world—Gujarātīs, Sindhīs, Persians, Arabs, and fīranghīs[191]—often at twenty times the price she paid for it herself! Over the years, she has thus amassed a fortune of such immenseness that it would dwarf the treasury of many a king! Akbar strongly encourages her in her endeavours, and will never fail to ask her about her undertakings. He is of course aware that she does not need the money, but all the same, he keeps paying her the same salary and buying her the same extravagant gifts he gives to his other spouses of the same rank.

I have to say, despite her being a Hindū and coming from an entirely different background, I have grown quite fond of her over the years. I really enjoy the way she talks – an incessant stream of good-humoured

---

191. Fīranghīs: 'Franks', i.e. western Europeans.

babble (in quite faulty, but incredibly fast Persian, interspersed with lots of Hindī), about the most diverse subjects, ranging from bath oil and shoulder massage, to the equipment and crewing of ships!

Many times has she offered me the opportunity to join her in her undertakings, but I have always politely declined. Even though my personal wealth is much smaller than hers, I have more money than I could ever reasonably spend in ten lifetimes, and I have to say, I am not at all attracted to the tension and excitement that apparently is involved in trading activities. Every so often, I hear her complaining about ships lost at sea, or merchandise ruined or stolen, but it never seems to put her off for more than a few hours. Every day, she prays and makes offerings to her elephant-headed god Gaṇeśa—to remove all the obstacles, she says—and to goddess Lakshmī, for wealth and prosperity. Nothing but superstitious nonsense, of course; but so far, it seems to have worked quite well! Akbar may be right after all: Allāh does not really mind under which form we worship Him. . . . Anyway, this much I know: Trading is not for me, and it never will be. I am really a book person: I just love reading, and writing, the rustling of a well-cut qalam on paper. . . . When the interests of our family do not require my attention elsewhere, I prefer to spend most of my time in the well-stocked library I have been able to build for myself over the years. As far as poetry is concerned, I am proud to say that it can rival the imperial book collection!

Akbar likes to join me there, and often asks me to read to him from my collection. I must admit: I do enjoy these conversations very much.

Even after all these years, he keeps amazing me with his wit and knowledge – it is hardly imaginable that a man of such erudition is unable to read! Without a single mistake or hesitation, he will recite entire pages of Jalāl-ud-dīn Rūmī, Sanā'ī, and Hāfiz – and never fail to flatter me with extensive quotes from my own work as well. . . .

What flatters me even more, though, is that he will always consult me about the affairs of state: new conquests he envisages; appointments he intends to make; firmāns that he wants to issue; disputes he needs to settle; roads, bridges, mosques and fortresses he wants to have built. The final decision is and remains, of course, entirely his; but he will always carefully consider my opinion.

There are, to my knowledge, only three women Akbar will ever share his plans and concerns with.

First and foremost, I am proud to say, there is me: If I am to believe his often-repeated assurances, I am and remain his favourite, and without a doubt, his closest confidante. My opinion clearly matters to him, and when he senses there is something I do not agree with, he will go to surprisingly great lengths to convince me and win me over to his point of view. He says he sees me as a co-heiress of Bābur's legacy, and appreciates what he calls my 'wisdom and sound judgement'. How many times has he not taken me into his confidence, about the government of the empire, the merits of his ministers, and, let's not forget, his relationship with his sons?

Second, though certainly not nearly as close to Akbar as I am, comes Salīm's mother. Akbar of course highly respects and reveres her, as the woman who has borne him his first-born son and heir, but also clearly appreciates her experience and quick wit. As mentioned above, he is extremely interested in her trading activities, and even more so, in the information she has about the foreign traders she deals with. He will also often ask her opinion in matters pertaining to the Hindūs: their religious sensitivities, the relationships and rivalries among their innumerable castes and clans, and the like.

And then, of course, there is Hamīda Bānū Bēgam, Akbar's own mother. Each time they meet, he will show her the highest respect: He will go out of his way to make sure she does not have to walk to meet him; he will personally help her dismount from her pālkī; he will even perform the taslīm for her, and bend down to touch her feet as a sign of respect, before putting his arms around her shoulders to embrace her. On her part, she is visibly pleased with these lofty gestures of honour—bestowed on nobody else in the empire!—and she is justifiably proud of the incredible power and wealth her son has been able to amass in such a short period of time.

Yet, their relationship is certainly not the easiest. Truth be told, she is not the easiest person to get along with, either: very hard to please, moody, and used to getting her own way in everything. They say that when she was only fifteen years old, it took her parents over forty days to convince her to take Humāyūn's marriage proposal into consideration!

Despite her admiration for Akbar's unequalled success, Hamīda does not at all approve of her son's unusual tolerance in religious matters.

While she understands his reasons to forge an alliance with the Rājpūts, she abhors the presence of Hindū shrines and priests in the imperial residence; she loathes the idea of her son joining his Hindū wife while she is worshipping the idols in her temple; she does not at all approve of her son participating in Holi, Diwālī and the other Hindū festivals, and much less, of him wearing a Hindū tikka on his forehead on those occasions!

And while she still appreciates to some extent the reasons behind his friendly attitude towards the Hindūs, the presence of firanghī priests at the imperial court is a real thorn in her flesh. That he has invited them to his court to find out more about the plans and ambitions of their rulers, is one thing; but it is quite another to make them permanent residents in the imperial palace; to allow them the freedom to try and convert good, honest, pious Muslims to their blasphemous errors; and not to silence them, when their foul-reeking mouths are hurling the worst insults at the Holy Prophet Muhammad, the blessings of Allāh be upon him – how on earth is it possible that he allows this to happen?

'I really do not know what has possessed Akbar,' she often grumbles, 'to entertain those self-righteous, conniving, infidel bastards at his court! How is it possible, that my son, a Muslim king, tolerates all these outrageous insults of the Holy Prophet in his presence? If I could have my way, I would have these slithering snakes beheaded, and all those other Nasrānīyah[192] infidels thrown back in the sea, where they came from!'

In the beginning, she tried several times to make Akbar change his mind, and he in turn has tried to explain his motives to her – but neither of them has been very successful.

Indeed, sincerely pious and god-fearing though he may be, Akbar is highly unorthodox in his religious practice. He knows all too well that many people are taking offense at this; he knows that behind his back, people are accusing him of betraying the sacred traditions of Islām; yet, he does not seem to care at all.

I remember one afternoon when we were having sherbet together. Akbar's mother told him to his face the fact that 'many good Muslims'

---

192. Nasrānīyah: 'Nazarean', i.e. worshipper of Jesus of Nazareth; Arabic term for Christian.

at the court were scandalised at their emperor praying with his back turned to Mekkah.

He merely smiled, and replied:

'I think I know who those "good Muslims" are, Mother.... Please tell Makhdūm-ul Mulk, and all the others who gossip, that their comments remind me of that story about a Sūfī pilgrim who was found sleeping by the roadside in the Arabian desert, with his feet pointing in the direction of Mekkah. A mullāh who happened to pass by, shocked and outraged at what he saw, rudely kicked the pilgrim awake, and shouted: "You dirty pig! Are you not ashamed of yourself, carelessly sleeping like this with your filthy feet pointing towards the holy city of Mekkah?"

'Upon which the Sūfī replied: "I am so sorry that I have offended you, honourable sāhab, and I do beg your pardon most humbly. However, if you kindly could point out to me, where in this world Allāh is not present, I will gladly point my feet in that direction!"'

Akbar smiled, visibly pleased with his argument. Then, his expression hardened.

'Revered Mother, next time you see the right honourable Shaykh ul-Islām, please tell him that I do not, have never, and will never worship the sun, the moon, fire, or anything or anybody but Allāh Himself! Tell him, that I fully realise that the sun is but an insignificant spark compared to Allāh's unspeakable majesty. But when I see the awesome, mysterious power He has put in fire and sunlight, I cannot but kneel humbly before Him Who has created all these wonders, next to which, all the treasures of kings pale into insignificance!

'Revered mother, rest assured that I am a devout servant of Allāh. But it seems I can hear His voice much more clearly in the silence of the desert, than amidst the noisy rituals of men. I feel His presence much more intensely when I look at the sun, the mountains, the moon and the stars, than when I sit in the grandest man-made house of worship, and certainly much more than when I am forced to listen to the pompous, self-righteous talk of Makhdūm-ul Mulk and the likes of him!'

The thorny subject of religion is now avoided altogether between Akbar and his mother, and whenever they meet, he will make sure to invite aunt Gulbadan, Ruqayyah and me to join them, so that he does not have to keep the conversation going all by himself. Hamīda, in turn, rather than living at her son's court, where she is constantly disturbed by so many things she does not approve of, prefers to live on her own. Most of the time, she resides in a beautiful palace in Dillī, where she runs her own household, with just a few of her close friends and confidantes to keep her company.

But in spite of all their differences, I have to emphasise, there is much tenderness and mutual respect between them, and whenever the need arises, they will stand shoulder to shoulder to further the interests of our family.

And Akbar clearly trusts and values his mother's wisdom and capabilities. For instance, at the time when he was leading his army to Kābul, to crush the rebellion up there, he has not hesitated to appoint her—her, and not one of his generals or ministers—as the provisional governor of Dillī; a responsibility of which, by the way, she acquitted herself admirably.

Yes, women do play an important role in Akbar's life: He loves and reveres his mother; he is a gentle, caring and attentive husband; he respects us, much more than most other men respect their wives and mothers. Sooner or later, however, we all have had to resign ourselves to the facts: he is not a one-woman man. He will never be the obedient son his mother would have liked him to be, and I fear he has never felt, for me or for anyone else, that kind of burning passion the poets write about, the passion that makes one forget all the others, and even one's own self. . . .

No, I may as well face the facts: I am not the love of his life; I am merely one of his best friends, who also happens to be a woman he feels attracted to. I hasten to add, however, that this in itself makes me quite special, for real friends, that is to say, people he will readily share his inner feelings with, he has but very few.

Now that Akbar is getting older, and so much more predictable than before, things have settled down considerably in the zanāna. We all know where we stand, and over the years, we truly have become one family – with its fair share of gossip and petty quarrels, no doubt, but, fortunately, with plenty of warm-hearted friendship as well.

It has not always been like that, though – not at all! At the time I married Akbar, the zanāna was a real cesspool of jealousy and strife of the worst possible kind! The breast of men has no milk, they say in Arabic – meaning that men have no mercy, whereas women do. . . .

I don't know who invented this nonsense, but nonsense it is: There is nothing more nasty on the face of this earth than the mind of a jealous woman. Gossiping, spying, intriguing . . . what pastime could be more interesting to a group of women who have little else to keep them busy? And to make things worse, maids and servants eagerly join in with their mistresses' quarrels, and they do whatever they can to stoke up the fire. Most of them run a secret but flourishing trade in all kinds of charms, spells, amulets, potions, salves and the like – magic charms and perfumes to awaken the emperor's desire; spells to secure his continuing love and devotion; potions to promote the buyer's pregnancy and to make sure her child will be male and healthy; amulets to avert the evil eye; and curses to destroy the influence of rivals, to make them unattractive and their wombs barren, to cause their offspring to be stillborn, or at the very least, female.

I remember as if it was only yesterday: A few days after my wedding, I had hardly taken up residence in the imperial palace, when I had this short but laden conversation with Ruqayyah – normally the nicest person one could imagine, and actually one of my very best friends.

'So sweet of the emperor that he has taken pity on you after everything that happened to your husband,' she said, in a compassionate tone of voice, and feigned sadness on her face.

'Yes, my cousin and I have always been very close,' I replied, with an equally friendly smile, which I hoped would look as condescending as possible.

Better to be envied than pitied, the saying goes, and there is much truth in that indeed. All the same, it is not very pleasant, to sense the bitterness, the rancour and jealousy in the words of people you always had a liking for.

But whether Ruqayyah and the others liked it or not, it was soon evident for everyone to see, that Akbar had not just married me out of pity. The first few months after the wedding, hardly a night went by without him sharing my bed, his passion clearly awakened by a new body to explore – a body, as he smilingly confessed, about which he had often fantasised when he was younger. Akbar has always been a vigorous, passionate and attentive lover, and it would be a lie for me to pretend that I am insensitive to this kind of attention: A woman who claims not to care whether or not she is attractive to men, is, in my opinion, either dishonest, or abnormal.

I do not think, however, that I ever fooled myself into believing that I would remain the only woman in his life; although, I have to admit, that the first time he went with a new girl, I had my share of the feelings Ruqayyah must have had when I came to the court.

It was one late afternoon in the zanāna courtyard. Akbar had ordered a dancing performance of a new group of artists, which had recently been brought to the court and trained by Tānsēn. All of Akbar's spouses had been invited, and as usual, I sat next to him. He had already indicated that after the performance, he would like to accompany me to my quarters, if I wanted to receive him.

It was a truly festive occasion. We all received lavish gifts of exquisite clothes and jewellery; various kinds of excellent food and drink were served, and the performance, which went on for several hours until well after dark, was spectacular. All the dancers and musicians were very talented and the performance was outstanding. Akbar enjoyed it tremendously, and it soon became obvious that he was taking a lively and more than musical interest in the leading dancing girl, who, much as I hate to admit it, was quite pretty.

I watched him throughout the performance, clapping his hands, laughing, staring shamelessly at the girl's plump, wiggling breasts and shaking hips. She, in turn, clearly aware of his attention, openly smiled at him.

I would have slapped her in the face, have her flogged, but what could I do? What indeed, but smile, and pretend to be amused? I spent the rest of the afternoon keeping up appearances, smiling, chatting, hoping no one would notice my anger and disappointment, knowing all too well that that hope was quite in vain, for by tomorrow morning, the entire zanāna would know that Akbar had spent the night with that vulgar slut instead of me.

I managed to remain outwardly calm and relaxed, but retired to my quarters as early as I decently could, making some vague excuse about being tired and having had too much to eat. I ordered my servant to bring me an ice-cooled pitcher of wine. I drank, goblet after goblet, almost the entire pitcher, but rather than giving me the lightheartedness I was looking for, it made my mood even more sombre.

It did help me fall asleep, but not for long. I woke up in the middle of the night, with a pounding headache and a sour, burning stomach. I called the servant to bring me some lightly salted lassī, which quickly eased the heartburn, but I did not manage to go to sleep again. I lay wide awake the rest of the night, getting angrier with the hour – angry with that arrogant dancing whore; angry with Akbar, and with all men: insensitive, selfish pleasure-seekers, every one of them; vulgar, and unworthy.

I must have finally dozed off around dawn, for it was already late in the morning when a servant came in to wake me, handing me an invitation from Akbar's mother to join her for the noon meal.

I bathed and dressed hurriedly and went to Hamīda's quarters. She received me as usual, courteously but rather formally, conscious of her rank.

We chatted for quite a while, about the summer heat, the deplorable quality of the newly arrived fruit, Hamīda's building projects, and similar harmless but hardly relevant subjects. However, it was quite obvious that she had not just invited me to talk about a fruit and the weather. Throughout the conversation, she kept observing me askance, scrutinising every expression on my face, keenly observing how much—or how little—I was eating of the food in front of me.

'You don't seem to be very hungry, my dear,' she said. 'Are you feeling unwell?'

'I had too much to eat yesterday, and did not sleep very well,' I confessed.

'It must be all that wine that you keep on drinking,' she said, making no attempt to hide her disapproval. 'I know what you are going to say, Salīmā. Akbar, Humāyūn, Bābur, the entire Gurkaniyya dynasty, and, for that matter, all those other Chagatai savages: They have always thought rather casually about drinking wine and spirits; but true believers should not forget that Allāh has repeatedly warned us in the Holy Qur'ān against the dangers of drinking wine. And who are we to think that His commandments do not apply to us? Yes, I know what you're going to say, Allāh is compassionate, merciful, and all-forgiving – He knows our weaknesses, better than we know them ourselves! And no, I do not think that people like you, who do drink, will be punished in hell . . . not for long, anyway. But do you believe that He would warn us against all these things, just for the sake of forbidding them? No! He forbids them for our own good, He knows what is best for us; and those who submit to His will, will never be disappointed!'

She made an impatient, dismissive gesture, as if annoyed with her own nagging.

'Anyway, I did not invite you here to talk about the dangers of drinking; I want to talk about you, and Akbar, and our family.'

She suddenly smiled kindly, and put her hand on mine.

'You did very well last night, my child! I have carefully observed you, and you did not once show how much Akbar's attention for that dancing girl was annoying you. You acted as if you did not care at all, and indeed, that is exactly the way you should feel about it!'

She looked at me inquisitively, trying to guess what I was thinking.

'Listen to me, Salīmā! Don't let a trivial incident like this get to you, for that is all it is: a trivial incident! Yes, Akbar has slept with a dancing girl, so what? That is the way he is, and, for reasons known to Allāh alone, that is the way most, if not all, men are! Don't make yourself unhappy, fretting about things that are of no importance and that you cannot change, anyway! Believe me, we all have been through this, Salīmā – sooner or later, we all have! Do you think my late husband Humāyūn—may Allāh receive him in paradise!—ever stopped sleeping with dancing girls after he married me? Of course not!

'Still, as you know and everybody knows, he always held me in the highest respect! I have always been his favourite – he would go out of his way to please me, and hardly ever has he done anything that I did not approve of!

'And that is exactly the kind of influence you have on Akbar, Salīmā – perhaps even more than I had on Humāyūn! He listens when you speak, he values your opinion more than that of his most prominent ministers and advisors; indeed, more than that of his own mother!'

She stared pensively at the lamps in the back of the room, a bitter smile on her face.

'Salīmā, an attractive woman is a plaything to them, a toy they have got to have as soon as they cast their eyes upon her – but that they grow tired of very soon once they have it! That a man wants to sleep with you, does not make you special at all, my child: What does make you special, is that you are his companion, that he listens to you!'

She suddenly leaned over to me, and took me by the shoulders. I was surprised to see tears in her eyes.

'Think about it, Salīmā,' she insisted. 'Think about who you are! You are not some vulgar concubine whose livelihood depends on her prowess in bed! You are a queen, a queen of imperial blood, a Gurkaniyya princess, descendant and heiress of Bābur the Tiger and Temür the Iron!'

She let go of me, and leaned back on her pillow.

'There are many ways to be an emperor's wife, my child,' she proceeded, with resignation in her voice, and a feeble, rather scornful smile on her face. 'Admittedly, there is only one woman who can lay claim to the title of first-wedded spouse, but what is that other than an empty title? Does it not make her solitude even harder to bear, when willingly or unwillingly, she has to make room for other, younger, prettier companions?

'Indeed, enviable it is to be his favourite – to be the one who ensnares him with her charms, and makes him drunk and foolish with lust. Alas, more often than not, that triumph will be short-lived; for what is more common than a woman's body? And what body is more attractive than the one yet to be possessed?

'No, my child. By far, the strongest is she, who has managed to gain her husband's friendship and confidence, for friendship and confidence are lasting sentiments, and they do not depend on base attractiveness. Even when the weakness of old age will have completely extinguished the fires of carnal lust in his decaying body, he will still be capable of friendship, trust, and loyalty!'

She again leaned over to me, and gently touched my face.

'And, of course, the most powerful and enviable is the woman, who combines it all: the high-ranking spouse, who is also his favourite lover, his best friend, and the mother of his successor! Every day, I pray for you, my child! I pray that this may happen to you; that you may become the mother of Akbar's first-born son and successor: There is no other woman in the entire empire who would be a more suitable queen mother! You are cultivated and wise, my child; noble blood flows through your veins, and you have your husband's ear!

'Think about the influence you have on the future of the empire, and don't let your mind be distracted by silly preoccupations of trivial importance!

'Suppose, just for the sake of the argument, that Allāh, in His wisdom, should decree that some other woman is to become the mother of Akbar's successor. Just imagine, that the child would be born from the womb of one of the Hindū wives, khudā nakhāsta! Then, it would be even more important that you remain Akbar's favourite: the child's education would depend on it!'

She was right, of course, but that was not much of a consolation. It took me several days to regain my peace of mind. Allāh may have created people as reasonable creatures, but it takes more than reason to convince the heart. Jealousy is like black, bitter ink, its stains much easier made than washed out. . . .

≈

Fortunately, Akbar made it rather easy for me to forgive him.

The day after my meeting with Hamīda, he sent me a message, asking me whether I would allow him to join me for the evening meal.

While friendly and courteous as always, he seemed rather tense. Clearly determined to avoid any awkward silence in the conversation, he talked incessantly, about every imaginable subject – every subject, indeed, except women. Much more serious than other evenings, he spent quite some time discussing the affairs of state: his courtiers, disturbances in the empire, measures he intended to take, and the like. Knowing my interest in the arts, he also talked about paintings he had ordered, buildings he had commissioned, poetry, and music – painstakingly avoiding, however, any reference to the virtuosity of the music performance two days earlier; much less, to the merits of the plump-breasted dancing girl that had ruined my evening.

Near the end of the meal—it was deep in the night already and we were both getting tired—he suddenly asked:

'Salīmā, would you like to come with me on a hunting trip tomorrow?'

'I need to get out of the palace for a few days,' he explained, before I was able to answer. 'I need some peace and quiet, and a bit of exercise: horseback riding, walking, swimming in the river, eating in the open air . . . would you like to come with me?'

I again wanted to answer, but he quickly went on, as if to prevent me from saying no.

'Besides, I would really like to spend some time alone with you, Salīmā; I need someone to talk to, a friendly face, someone who understands me, someone to give me some honest advice. . . . There are important things I want to talk to you about, and we never seem to have enough time on our own in the palace!'

As usual, Akbar had now made it virtually impossible for me to refuse. He has a way of getting what he wants, without actually giving direct orders . . .

But I have to confess, I really loved the prospect of getting out of the palace for a few days.

We left at dawn on the next morning so that we could travel to the hunting grounds in the wilderness, while it was still cool enough. At my explicit request, I did not travel in a pālkī, but spent the entire day riding next to Akbar, on an exquisite Irāqī white mare, one of the finest horses in the imperial stables, strong and fast as the wind, but very good-natured and docile. Before mounting her, I fed her a few greens and some sweets, talking to her, patting her neck and gently caressing her soft muzzle, to allow her to get used to my scent and the sound of my voice. The animal seemed to develop an instant liking for me, and I was eagerly looking forward to riding her for a few days.

We left Āgrā, accompanied by a strong escort of about two hundred horse archers, who would act as game drivers if Akbar wished to hunt, and protect us against any conceivable danger—human or animal—along the way.

Following us was a small train of not more than five pack animals and about twenty servants. Clearly, Akbar wanted this to be a very simple excursion, not one of those grandiose expeditions his hunting parties usually turn into, and intended to camp in the open, not in the luxurious, city-like camps that normally are built wherever he stays.

I was appropriately dressed for the occasion, in a white hunting-costume, quite similar to the clothing the nomad Arabs usually wear. As long as we travelled in sight of the escort, I covered my face with the long trailing piece of my turban, but as soon as we were riding through the open country, Akbar ordered the escort to distance themselves about one hundred and fifty paces from us, so that we could enjoy some privacy, and I could unveil my face.

It felt a bit odd at first to be in the saddle again: I had not been on horseback since my youth in Kābul. But fortunately, riding is one of those skills that are never lost, once acquired. Before long, I found myself racing against Akbar – extremely satisfied to find that my mare was as fast as his stallion.

'Well, that was real Turkish blood at work,' he panted out admiringly, after a long gallop at breakneck speed, where despite a few attempts, he had not really managed to shake me off. 'I very much doubt if there is any woman in Hindustān who can ride like this! Clearly, my dear wife and cousin, the blood of Chingīz Khān and Temür the Iron is flowing in your veins, as it is in mine!'

'This is a magnificent horse you have given me,' I said, not knowing how else to react to the compliment. 'It is truly a pleasure to ride her!'

'She's a beauty, indeed, and she seems to like you a lot – as if you have worked with her for years! Well, from now on, she is yours, Salīmā . . . I would know of no better mistress for her!'

I thanked him, quite pleased with such a precious gift, but thought to myself, with some regret, that I would have little opportunity to really enjoy her – quietly riding in a courtyard is really not the same as galloping in the middle of the wilderness. . . .

Akbar must have sensed what I was thinking.

'We should do this much more often, Salīmā – then you will have more opportunity to really enjoy her! Life in a palace can get tedious, don't you agree?'

'Indeed, it can be,' I snapped, maybe a bit harshly. 'I must say, I often envy you men – your lives may be more dangerous than ours, but also, so much more exciting!'

'Well, yes, but . . .'

'Anyway, I thank you for this!'

'There's hardly any need for that. It is I who am obliged to you, that you agreed to come with me!'

He turned astride in the saddle, looking intently at me.

'You know, I really like being with you, Salīmā! Of all the people in the world, you are the only one I really feel closest to . . . you know that, don't you?'

Before I could answer, he continued:

'You know, it is really true what they say: No lonelier place is there in this world, than the throne! Power creates distance, you know: There is hardly anybody I can really talk to, the way normal people can. Of all the people in the world, you, Salīmā, you are the one that is closest to me! We share the same blood, you are not afraid of me as most other people are, and I know of no other woman as learned and wise as you are!'

I smiled faintly and looked down, not knowing how else to react.

'I also want to tell you, Salīmā, how impressed I am, and how much I appreciate you looking after little Abdurrahīm the way you do!

'I really like that little fellow, you know, and I want the very best for him! It's unbelievable how much he knows for a small boy his age! He is perfectly fluent in Turkī, Persian and Hindī; he knows all the classics; he quotes from his father's writings – and all that, thanks to you, because you have taught him!

'And not only will he, thanks to you, most certainly grow up to be a wise and learned man, but I believe he will be a great soldier as well, just like his father!

'I've watched him wrestling with other boys. He is fast, strong and brave, and not at all afraid to hurt himself! And have you noticed how well he handles that wooden sword I've given him? I'm telling you, Salīmā, if he continues growing up like this, I will make him as rich and powerful as his glorious father, may the peace of Allāh be upon him! I know there have been regrettable misunderstandings between Bairām Khān and me, but I will forever be grateful for what he has done for me, and I will take care of his son, as long as I live!'

'You are a good man, Akbar,' I murmured, fighting back my tears. 'I am grateful that you are honouring my late husband's memory, and I really appreciate how much you are taking Abdurrahīm's future at heart! May it please Allāh to send His angels to comfort Bairām Khān in his grave, and tell him how well his little boy is doing!'

'Allāh karē,'[193] Akbar nodded in assent, piously raising his hands upward.

---

193. May it please Allāh; may Allāh do so.

He steered his horse next to mine and leaned over to me, putting his hand on my arm and gently touching my cheek with the back of his middle and forefinger.

'Every day, I pray, Salīmā, that Allāh may give me a strong and healthy son, one just like Abdurrahīm, a son who will one day be my successor . . . and each time, I pray, that he may be born from you, for there is no one in the entire empire who would be a more suitable mother to my son! But if, khudā nakhāsta, he is not . . . if he is to be born from another woman, you must promise that you will help me raise him as if he were your own! Regardless of the womb that has carried him, you have to be his mother, Salīmā! There are things that only you can teach him – you can tell him about the great deeds of his ancestors, you can teach him to speak perfect Turkī as well as Persian and Hindī; you alone can see to it that he grows up as a real Gurkaniyya prince and a worthy emperor of Hindustān!'

In spite of the gravity of the moment, I could not help but smile, wondering whether perhaps Hamīda had spoken to him.

'Well, will you, Salīmā?'

'Of course, I will be honoured to do so,' I said, putting my hand on his, and leaning over to kiss him on the lips – something he was clearly not expecting, and was highly pleased by.

'When the time is there,' I continued, 'it will, Inshā'allāh, be my privilege and sacred duty to help your son to grow up to be a great king! You may rest assured that I will teach, help and protect him to the best of my ability!'

'Thank you, Salīmā. You have no idea how much this means to me,' Akbar said softly, putting his arm around my shoulders and kissing me tenderly on the lips.

We travelled for the better part of the day, deeper and deeper into the imperial hunting grounds, taking only a few hours' rest at high noon. We must have been at least nine or ten kos from any inhabited area when, in the late afternoon, Akbar ordered the camp to be set up, on a beautiful, broad stretch of sandy shore, next to a wide river bend.

The soldiers secured the area, posting guards all around the encampment on both sides of the river, at a distance of about two hundred paces from us. Again, we were perfectly safe, yet far enough from the soldiers to be on our own the way we wanted to.

A comfortable tent had been set up for us, but we decided to have our food outside, on the sand, enjoying the balmy evening and the changing colours of the sky and the water. When the sun was almost down, the servants started lighting maybe a hundred oil lamps, scattered all over the sand. We sat down in front of a simmering charcoal fire, similar to the one, a bit further, on which the servants were preparing our food for the evening: bread, vegetables and meat in gravy, prepared in the tandūr and other pieces of meat, deliciously seasoned and carefully roasted on skewers above the glowing embers.

On two occasions, Akbar had shown us an example of his remarkable riding and hunting prowess. First, while chasing a large deer that had been driven towards us by the soldiers, he killed his prey with a single spear thrust between the shoulder blades. The next time, he shot a small antelope with his bow, at a distance of at least thirty paces, while riding at a full gallop. He hit the animal behind the left shoulder, right through the heart, killing it before it even hit the ground. The arrow shaft had gone in all the way up to the quills. I knew this was merely to show off his tact to me and the soldiers – do men not often feel the need to behave like that in public? Still, I could not help being impressed, and proud to be married to so strong a man. Clearly, it was no coincidence that Akbar was held in such high respect by his soldiers.

When we had almost finished eating, Akbar ordered the servants to bring us two more pitchers of wine and two of Gangā water, in buckets of crushed ice—a luxury he would rarely do without—and we spent another hour or so in pleasant conversation, indulging in the deliciously cool drinks.

When I assumed a different sitting position, I must have inadvertently twisted my face into a painful grimace.

'Anything wrong?' Akbar inquired.

'My legs are a bit stiff, from that day on horseback – it's much more than I'm used to,' I confessed.

'Let's take a walk by the river. Nothing like a leisurely walk to get rid of cramps and stiffness!'

He took me by the hand and helped me up. We walked towards the river, and he put his arm around my waist. We strolled for a while, looking in silence at the star-lit sky and the moon's silver reflection on the water. I thoroughly enjoyed the feeling of the cool wavelets and the soft river sand under my bare feet.

Behind a small bush, where he was sure the guards could not see us, Akbar stopped, gently pulled me towards him, and started kissing me, softly at first, then, full of passion, caressing my back and neck, and softly running his fingers through my hair. Suddenly, he lifted me up and carried me, as easily as he would carry a small child, to our tent.

There, in the soft light of the oil lamps, we spent a nearly sleepless, wonderful night – one that I will never forget, for the rest of my life.

≈

My strong, dear husband! So formidable and awe-inspiring to the mightiest of the mighty, so kind and just towards the weak, so warm and gentle towards me! How often have I observed him through the stone-lattice windows of the zanāna, and admired him for the natural, self-evident ease with which he carries the heavy burden of his high and mighty, divine office!

They say that as a young boy, he was lazy, moody and unpredictable.

If that is indeed the case, he has clearly mended his ways since the time he reached adulthood. Nothing in the empire escapes his attention and involvement; never once does he forget that he is the emperor; and never once does he neglect his obligations towards Allāh.

Yes, unlike many people to whom religion remains confined to the prescribed daily prayers and a weekly visit to the mosque, disconnected from their daily life and work, Akbar will never once forget god.

He may be king of kings, builder of empires, conqueror of lands, subduer of nations; but deep down, he has the soul of a faqīr, a saintly errant, desiring nothing else but to plunge his soul in the silent depths of the divine.

And like most of this kind of people, Akbar seems to care very little about the generally accepted practices. Hence, his highly unorthodox way of praying, and his remarkably tolerant attitude towards non-Muslim religions that is treated as offensive by his own mother and so many other good Muslims.

I have always been astounded at the calm resolve with which Akbar has been able to impose his will while dealing with these thorny matters. During the first years of his reign, he was still relatively careful in his utterances and practices. But now, with all the rebellions crushed and the neighbouring kingdoms conquered, he makes no scruples whatsoever about doing exactly as he pleases: praying according to strange rituals of his own; organising nightly debates about religion, with him as arbitrator; allowing infidels to worship according to their beliefs even at the imperial court, and granting them the same rights and privileges as Muslims.

I suspect there is more than one reason why he is doing this: He does intend to promote peace and understanding among his subjects, no doubt; but he also wants to make it clear that on this earth, the ultimate authority is his, and his alone. Regardless of their religious beliefs, whether they worship god in a mosque, a Hindū temple or a Nasrānīyah church, his subjects cannot be loyal servants of god if they do not serve their lawful emperor.

This is Akbar's ultimate message to everyone: The imperial court is the axis of the world; the emperor is the centre, the middle point around which everything revolves; he, and only he is the authorised exponent of the divine will; he stands above all mullāhs, ulamā and priests, of whatever belief or denomination; he is the bridge between god and men, the source of all power and majesty; he wants his throne to be like the sun – radiating with justice, benevolence and kindness, but also with awesome power, and unattainable majesty.

In every respect, Akbar is the embodiment of kingship itself – benevolent, charming, endearing, lovable; but also imposing, unattainable and daunting.

Everything about him commands respect and awe: the way he dresses, walks and sits; his square-shouldered, strong and muscular build; the ease with which he controls the most unruly animals; his loud and thundering voice, which at times can be so enchantingly soft and warm.

I really admire the way he handles visitors and supplicants of all kinds, listening intently to what they have to say, his head typically dropping slightly towards the right shoulder, his face either expressionless, or smiling faintly. Whatever the subject, whatever the time of day, and no matter how long he has been sitting in the audience hall, he will always respond with extraordinary acuteness, lucidity and wisdom.

As a rule, he will be remarkably kind and forgiving towards even the worst transgressors. It would be foolish, however, to mistake his generosity for weakness. Though he may be warm-hearted, he can be quite ruthless and lethal when crossed.

His innermost thoughts will usually remain hidden, behind an inscrutable mask of courtesy and majesty. He may be the most open, friendly and accessible king and husband one could imagine; yet, he remains a mystery, even to his closest friends and family. Rarely, if ever, will he reveal his true feelings to anyone . . . except, maybe, from time to time, to me, and to Abū-l Fazl, when he was still alive.

'No lonelier place is there in this world, than the throne,' he often complains. I do believe he honestly means that, and I think I perfectly understand that strange, deep sombreness that so often befalls him, despite the incredible power he wields.

For along with all his incredible might, comes the daunting, god-given task to put it to good use; and also, utter loneliness, for although he can and will ask other people for their counsel, in the end, the decision—and the responsibility before Allāh—will be his, and his alone. No matter how friendly his smile, how kind his manners, there is a deep moat between him and the people around him – a moat, or some kind of glass wall, behind which everyone can see him, but no one can come near him.

A strange feeling it is indeed, to be married to a man of this stature. It is certainly a privilege, to be able to counsel and assist him, to know him more intimately than anybody else does. Yet, it is not always easy, having to share him with an entire empire, and to have to carry with him the burden of duty.

Despite and amidst the wealth in which we both live, and the comfort provided to us, we are never on our own, never at ease. Both of us have a duty to fulfil: to preserve and protect the heritage of our ancestors, and to provide a future for our posterity, so that when we die, we can render an account to Allāh of how we have served Him with our lives.

In more than one respect, I share Akbar's solitude. If we would have been born as common people like simple farmers, maybe, or city merchants, or countryside nobles living in a remote region, our marital life would have been altogether different. A tighter bond would have united us; I think we would have been inseparable companions.

Now, alas, I am merely an occasional visitor in his life – as he is in mine.

He is and remains the great king and conqueror, Akbar-e-āzam; and I am and will always be mākhfī, 'the hidden'.

Such is life: We were born alone, and we will die alone. . . . Our family and friends, our spouse, our children – they are but fellow travellers, whom we meet along the way; and the higher and mightier we are, the more we walk alone.

Twenty-fifth Letter

گجرات

Gujarāt (1)

Gujarāt . . . its unfettered independence had been a thorn in my flesh for quite a long time; but the path leading to it was clearer for me, now that Rājāstān and Mālwa were mine, and it was in dire need of a just ruler, one who could give it order, peace and justice.

The kingdom had fallen prey to utter chaos and anarchy. The rebellious Mīrzās, driven out of Hindustān, had made themselves masters of the southern part of the country, whereas in the north, Muzaffar Shāh III, the nominal king—himself a prince of doubtful legitimacy, as one chronicler aptly put it—had become a mere puppet in the hands of rivalling nobles who had partitioned the country among themselves.

One of them, I'timād Khān, cornered by an alliance between Muzaffar and one Shēr Khān Fulādī, sent me an urgent message, begging me to intervene, and to reclaim the rightful inheritance of my most noble and august father, and thus bring to the country of Gujarāt the justice, peace and prosperity enjoyed by the lands fortunate enough to live under the protection of the commander of the faithful, His Majesty Jalāl-ud-dīn Muhammad Akbar Pādshāh Ghāzī, emperor of Hindustān, shadow of god on this earth.

This was all the encouragement I needed. To conquer Gujarāt was my right; it was my manifest destiny. Thus, on the twenty-first of Tīr of the seventeenth year,[194] the imperial army left Sīkrī and headed east.

Underway, in the sacred city of Ājmīr, it was my pleasure to supervise the arrangements for yet another imperial birth: One of the concubines in the zanāna, a young Afghān girl, whose blue eyes, fair complexion and slender waist had caught my attention nine months earlier, was with child, and would, so the physicians informed me, not be able to continue on the journey with the rest of the imperial cortege.

She and her retinue were stationed in the house of the venerable old Shaykh Dānyāl, himself one of Khwājah Muīn-ud-dīn's successors and the most prominent attendant of the sacred shrine. I decided that if she would give birth to a boy, I would call him Dānyāl, in honour of his esteemed protector.

Day after day, I went to the shrine to pray, asking god for the safe and successful birth of another healthy and strong son, and invoking His almighty help and guidance in the war I was about to fight.

The remainder of my time, I used to my advantage, inspecting the troops, surveying the final preparations for the invasion and discussing marching routes and battle plans with my army commanders.

Out of precaution—lest Muhammad Hakīm or anyone else would try to take advantage of my absence—I decided to send a sizeable force up north, to the Panjāb. Under the command of Bīrbal and Yūsuf Khān, they were to reinforce the Lāhor garrison and beat back any would-be invader.

For the attack on Gujarāt itself, a powerful cavalry force of ten thousand was to ride ahead, while I myself would follow two weeks later with the rest of the army. The strength and mobility of this advance guard and the distance between my two fighting forces would allow me to keep fully abreast of the strength and whereabouts of the enemy forces, and adapt my battle plans accordingly.

On the thirty-first of Mordād,[195] the vanguard rode out of Ājmīr. Among them, a good number of my best officers, including Khān Khilān,

---

194. Wednesday, 2 July 1572 (Julian calendar)
195. 12 August 1572 (Julian calendar)

Ashraf Khān, Shāh Qulī Khān Mahram, Shāh Budāgh Khān, Saiyyid Mahmūd Khān, Qulij Khān, Sādiq Khān, Shāh Fakhr-ud-dīn, Haidar Muhammad Khān Akhta Begī, Qutlaq Qadam Khān, Muhammad Qulī Khān Tūqbāi, Kharram Khān, Beg Nūr Khān, Beg Muhammad Khān, Muhammad Qulī Khān, son-in-law of the commander, Khān Khilān, Mīr Alī Khān Sildūz, Saiyyid Abdullāh Khān, Mīrzāda Alī Khān and Bahādur Khān. I myself marched forth on the twentieth of Shahrīvar,[196] at the head of the remaining troops.

Apart from a disturbing, but altogether insignificant, incident in southern Rājāstān, where I had to crush and exterminate a band of rebels—loyalists of the rānā of Mewār, no doubt—who had made the fatal mistake of trying to hinder my vanguard, my advance into enemy territory was quite uneventful. In fact, the whole voyage seemed more like a leisurely excursion than an arduous army campaign.

One day, while we were hunting on the way to replenish the supply of meat for the troops, Citr Najan, my best hunting leopard, was chasing a deer, when suddenly a ravine appeared in front of them. The deer leapt into the air, a spear and a half high, and managed to cross the ravine. To our astonishment, the chītah, in its eagerness to catch its prey, did not even slow down before the forbidding obstacle. With a giant, lightning jump, it cleared the ravine, and, going on at the same breathtaking speed, caught and killed the deer. All cheered and praised Allāh, for this was, so everybody acknowledged, a very good omen.

A good omen it was, indeed: Only a few days later, I received the news that my beloved third son Dānyāl had been born in Ājmīr, on the twenty-eighth of Shahrīvar, the first of Jumādā 'l Ula 980,[197] and was in excellent health – Shaykh Salīm Chishtī's prophecy had been fulfilled.

When the messenger brought me these good tidings, I dismounted from the elephant I was riding, knelt down in the direction of Mekkah and, pressing my forehead in the dust of the road, rendered thanks to the almighty.

I did not return to Ājmīr to pray at Khwājah Muīn-ud-dīn's shrine—there was a war to be fought and the advance guard counted on my

---

196. 1 September 1572 (Julian calender)
197. 9 September 1572 (Julian calender)

support—but did decide to strike camp for a few days, spending many hours in prayer at the local mosques, and organising, as is customary, splendid feasts in celebration of the birth of the new prince. Generous gifts were distributed to all the people in the area; as Abū-l Fazl phrased it so elegantly: 'The coin of liberality was poured into the lap of the world'.

I ordered that as soon as Dānyāl would be a month old, he was to be sent to Amber, to be entrusted to the care of Rājā Bhagwān Dās's spouse – yet another sign of the bonds of friendship and loyalty that united us.

After the festivities, I hurriedly proceeded further south; it was time for me to reclaim the throne my father had once occupied.

As we neared the border, the reports about the various rival Gujarātī factions were most encouraging indeed. Muzaffar Shāh, the Gujarātī king, struck with panic on hearing about the approach of the mighty imperial army. He deserted his capital Ahmedābād, leaving his former ally Shēr Khān Fulādī in charge of its defence. The latter, however, had himself deserted the city immediately thereafter. He was now heading south, to the region of Surat, where, no doubt, he was hoping to find new allies.

I ordered the army to proceed straight on to Ahmedābād, but first sent Rājā Mān Singh with a body of troops in pursuit of Shēr Khān Fulādī's two sons. According to our informants, their father had sent them to the area of Pattan, to shift their family and goods to places of safety; they were now heading south, to rejoin their father. As I expected, Mān Singh routed their force without too much trouble. The two brothers managed to escape in the wilderness, but their valuable baggage fell into our hands.

On the twenty-sizth of Ābān,[198] I finally crossed the Gujarātī border, and marched triumphantly into the city of Pattan, hailed and cheered by the local people as their liberator. I was showered with flowers and gifts, and the town elders, who had come to pay their respects, thanked divine providence that they could now peacefully eat their bread in the comforting shadow of His Majesty's kindness.

For a few days, we struck camp before the gates of Pattan.

---

198. 7 November 1572

Not without some apprehension, I invited young Abdurrahīm to join me for a short trip to lake Sahansa Lang, on the shores of which, thirteen years before, his father Bairām Khān had met his untimely death, at the filthy hands of a stinking, cowardly Afghān assassin.

The delightful breeze and peaceful atmosphere around the blue waters of the lake seemed almost unreal. This was a place of repose, a place to make one's peace with god and the world – not a place for a good man to die!

I looked at Abdurrahīm, who was strolling up and down the shore, squinting against the sun. He said nothing.

In silence, both of us absorbed in our own thoughts, we proceeded to the shrine of Shaykh Husām-ud-dīn, where Bairām Khān's body had been laid to rest by the local people.

The shrine was located in the immediate vicinity of the main mosque, and was, as usual, surrounded by a tranquil courtyard where pilgrims gather before and after prayers. In its sacred shadow were a few simple graves, and our guide pointed to the most modest of them all. There, under a small nameless headstone, the great Khān Khanān of the Mughal empire had been laid to rest.

We stood in silence before the grave. How terrible is death, I thought, how unjust to reduce a life, so filled with greatness and nobility, to the impotent, numb silence of a nameless stone!

I bowed respectfully and started praying aloud in Arabic, as once Bairām Khān himself had done at the foot of my father's casket in Sirhind:

> *Peace be upon you, O dwellers of the grave!*
> *May Allāh grant you and us protection!*
> *We pray to Allāh for security, for ourselves and for you.*
> *You are those who have gone before us, and we are following you.*
> *We will meet you, if it pleases Allāh.*

The words sank into my soul. O god, I thought, may it please You that one day, Bairām Khān and I may be reunited! What kind of paradise can it be, O god, if we are to be deprived of the company of our friends and loved ones?

I knelt down, put my hands and forehead on the grave for a few moments, and remained there, in silence. When I rose to my feet again,

I went to stand next to Abdurrahīm, and whispered softly, in Turkī, my eyes full of tears: 'God's peace be upon you, forever and ever, my faithful friend, my strong atālīq, my trusted guide, my beloved second father! See, your son and I have come from afar, to pay our respects, and to tell you, that we have been taking good care of what you have left behind for us. Standing on your shoulders, noble Khān Khanān, we have seen far, and our arms have been victorious: Chittor, Ranthambhor, Kālinjar: they have all fallen, they are ours, and we promise you, that is only the beginning!'

I paused, and put my hand on Abdurrahīm's shoulder.

'Behold your son, my friend – see what a strong and handsome young man he has become! You would be proud of him, my friend – a full-blooded Turkomān warrior he is, just like his father! You should see him on a horse – he rides like the devil, he can spear an apple and fire a musket at full gallop!

'He will go far, this son of yours: He is only seventeen, but already one of the best commanders in the army! And this I promise you, my friend, on your grave and on my own life, I will take care of him!'

All the time, Abdurrahīm had said nothing, his head bowed deeply, staring at the headstone, his eyes glistening with tears.

When it was time for us to leave, he knelt down, kissed his father's grave and put his hands and forehead on it, as I had done; he then came back to me, fell to his knees, and kissed the edge of my cloak.

I made him rise to his feet again, and patted him on the shoulder.

'Henceforth, you will be the protector of your father's grave, Abdurrahīm. From now on, the city of Pattan and its surroundings are your personal jāgīr!'

'Your Majesty is most kind,' he answered, 'and I swear to god that I will be worthy of this confidence!'

He hesitated for a moment and said, apologetically:

'With Your Majesty's permission, I would at some time in the future wish to move my father's remains to a resting place nearer to Your Majesty's capital. You see, Your Majesty . . .'

'Of course, my young friend! Nothing would please me more than to build for your father the tomb a man of his stature deserves! As soon as you decide when and where, I will see to it that it gets done!

'Let me tell you one thing, though – your father said exactly the same to me, when I was your age, standing in front of my own father's casket: "To take care of your father's grave is highly commendable; but by far the most important thing you can do for him, is to live a life that will make him proud"!'

He bowed deeply and wanted to sink to his knees again, but I took him by the arm.

'Let us go back to the camp, Abdurrahīm; we have work to do! There are many enemies to fight before Gujarāt is ours!'

The next day at dawn, we broke up camp and headed further to Ahmedābād.

On the march, I tasted the satisfaction of accepting the submission of the fugitive king, Muzaffar Shāh – my scouts had found him, hiding in a cornfield, scared to death.

He fell to his knees, his face streaming from every pore, mumbling flowery phrases of abject flattery – about daring to approach the sacred dust of Your Majesty's feet, and being granted the privilege of making it the salve of his weary eyes, and of placing his entire submission and complete devotion at the foot of Your Majesty's throne. After some time, I managed to interrupt his rambling and put him more or less at ease, stating that if he remained faithful to his promise, I would, in turn, not be unmindful of his loyalty. To demonstrate my friendship, I immediately set an example of justice: Since his camp-followers had insolently plundered their sovereign's personal belongings, I had them rounded up and brought before me; those found in possession of plunder were crushed to death under the feet of my elephants, and the goods restored to its rightful owner. The times of lawlessness were over.

A few days later, I'timād Khān and his allies came to make their submission as well. It seemed that at least for the moment, there was nobody left to oppose us in the north of Gujarāt. On the ninth of Āzar,[199] we marched in triumph through the gates of Ahmedābād, without a single shot being fired.

Provisional arrangements were made for the government of the new province: I appointed my foster brother Azīz Koka as governor of the

---

199. 20 November 1572

country northwest of the Māhī River, whereas I'timād Khān, whom I wished to give the benefit of the doubt, was made responsible for the southern part.

After a few days, on the twenty-seventh of Āzar[200] to be precise, I left Ahmedābād and headed south towards the coast, to the port of Khambhat,[201] where, for the first time in my life, I beheld the ocean.

I was myself surprised how deeply impressed I was by its vastness and awesome beauty. I had heard descriptions of the sea quite often, and so I knew what to expect: a vast body of water, stretching as far as the eye can see, its waves glistening in the sun. . . . Yet, the actual sight of it moved me to tears. It was as if god Himself deigned to show me a glimpse of His own mysterious Being: daunting, unfathomable, all-powerful; yet at the same time, gentle, inviting, and of unspeakable beauty.

Before anything else, I wanted to feel what it was like to travel on those mighty waves. With a few of my officers and the local Gujarātī garrison commander, I boarded a ship which, according to the commander's repeated assurances, was the fastest one in the entire port. As I wished to go far out, and the wind was blowing straight from the sea onto the shore, we had to sail close to the wind, as the sailor at the helm called it. Crisscrossing into the sea at a sharp angle, its sails pulled taut, the ropes creaking under the pressure of the wind, the ship took us deeper and deeper, until the shoreline was nothing more than a vague yellowish stripe at the horizon. All around us, there was nothing – nothing but deep-blue, glistening water, more beautiful in colour than the most precious emerald or sapphire any amount of money could buy; nothing but the pounding of the waves against the hull of the ship, the salty droplets on my face, and the piercing, angry shrieks of dozens of white, long-beaked birds, sailing in the blue sky above us.

Not without regret, I ordered the boat to return to the port. With the wind and the waves now right behind us, we suddenly went at breathtaking speed, faster, it seemed to me, than the fastest horse.

Back on shore, I asked the local commander, a tall, thin man with a lined, tired and worried-looking face, to show me around town. He was,

---

200. 8 December 1572
201. Cambay

he told me, born in Sind, from a family of Arab merchants who had taken up residence there. Being, as he described himself, more a man of the sword than of learning or commerce, he had, when still a boy, obtained his father's permission to join the army of the king of Gujarāt, and risen from the ranks, until his appointment as head of the local garrison. He seemed a simple, honest man, and I very much appreciated the orderly state in which he had kept the city entrusted to his care.

Despite the recent wars that had scourged the land, the port was bustling with activity. Merchants from nations and lands near and far—Gujarātīs, Marathīs, Rājpūts, Hindustānīs, Sindhīs, Baluchīs, Farsīs, Arabs, Turānīs, Syrians, Turks, and even firanghīs,[202]— were trading wares of all kinds, shouting, negotiating and bargaining frantically, with no other interpreter at their disposal than the gestures of their hands and fingers.

It was the first time I ever laid eyes on firanghī merchants. To my surprise, most of them did not look that strange at all. They all had brown eyes, and not a single one of them had the red or yellow hair I had so often heard about; their skin, though fair, looked quite tanned. They looked more like Turks, I thought, if it would not be for their strange attire: black trousers, sleeveless vests, and wide shirts, all of very poor quality, and weird-looking hats of various, ridiculous-looking shapes.

'A lot of people here, from all around the world, it seems,' I said, pointing at the multitude of merchants amidst their wares. 'I see you have even firanghīs visiting your port; do you see many of them here?'

He grimaced with contempt; for a moment, I thought he was going to spit on the ground.

'Much more often than I care to, Your Majesty. These infidel dogs are everywhere these days!'

'You do not seem to like them very much . . .'

'I hate them, Your Majesty. Which decent person would not?'

'Surely, you are not afraid of them? They come from far away, their numbers are small; how could they ever constitute a threat to us?'

He looked down and mumbled:

---

202. Firanghī: 'Frank', European, Caucasian

'Your Majesty is right – I should not presume to talk on things about which I know nothing. I beg forgiveness.'

'Speak freely. I want to hear what you really think, not what you think I wish to hear; a wise king should avail himself of the experience of the people he meets – how else can his own wisdom increase?'

He put his hand on his heart and bowed deeply.

'Allāh be praised, it is very true what they say about Your Majesty: we are blessed with a truly great king, wise and just! May Allāh grant Your Majesty a long life, and may all Your Majesty's steps be fortunate!'

He paused, looking for the appropriate words to express his concerns.

'Your Majesty is wiser than I am, and despite His young age, much more experienced. I have no other desire in my heart but to serve Your Majesty to the best of my abilities, and if necessary, lay down my life for him. But since I have been expressly commanded to voice my opinion, I feel it is my duty to warn Your Majesty against those accursed firanghīs, for I am convinced that they are extremely dangerous; yes, I am even afraid that some day, they may pose a threat to Hindustān itself!'

'You are exaggerating, old man,' I thought to myself. How could a handful of foreign adventurers ever pose a threat to a kingdom as vast and mighty as mine?

Probably guessing what I was thinking, he insisted:

'Perhaps I am just getting old; maybe the sombreness of old age is impairing my judgement. In fact, I hope from the bottom of my heart that I am mistaken. But I have been living on these shores for many years, and I have seen these firanghīs – Purtugēsh, they call themselves, for there appear to be many separate nations of them . . . I have seen them increase both in numbers and arrogance, year after year, and what I have seen, worries me exceedingly.

'When they set up their colonies and trading posts, they will sometimes ask the local king's permission, but as soon as that is granted, they behave like the place is their own property. Quite often, in places where local authority is weak, they will just steal the land, or as they say, take possession of it in the name of His Christian Majesty, the king of Purtugal – as if that accursed infidel had any rights here!

'Once they have established themselves somewhere, these Purtugēsh are like lice, flees, or warts – almost impossible to get rid of! For example, only a few days sailing south of here, on the Konkanī coast beyond the country of the Marathas, they have managed to carve out an entire kingdom for themselves – Goa, they call it. Sultān Adīl Shāh of Bijapūr in the Deccan has repeatedly tried to chase them from the territory, but his forces have been repulsed, time and again; the only thing he has been able to achieve with the help of Allāh, is to keep the infidels confined to the coastal area.

'It is well known how these Purtugēsh have wreaked havoc among the innocent people of that once so peaceful region. They have exterminated every Muslim in the area – man, woman and child. Not a single believer is left alive in the entire country, and only very few have managed to escape with their lives into neighbouring regions. The infidels even enlisted Hindū mobs to do their dirty work for them, offering a reward for every Muslim's head.

'The Hindūs' treachery did not do them much good. However, no sooner had the Muslims been eliminated than the Hindūs found themselves reduced to abject slavery, and all of their temples and shrines razed to the ground. Forcefully converted to the firanghī religion, if they are found or merely suspected of having remained loyal to their old faith, they are forthwith imprisoned, tortured for weeks on end, and forced, under unspeakable pains, to betray all their friends and relatives. Then, they are roasted to death on slow-burning pyres!

'That is what makes these firanghīs so dangerous: They are bigoted fanatics. In spite of their utter lack of civilisation, they seem to be absolutely convinced that they and their blasphemous religion is destined to rule the entire world, and that other people and religions are only there to be converted or eliminated. For us Muslims, they feel only hatred; for the Hindūs and the other idolaters, nothing but contempt!

'Your Majesty has pointed out that their numbers are few and that they therefore do not pose a threat to us. Of course, that is right: Not a single one of their ports and fortresses could withstand an all-out attack by Your Majesty's forces. Still, I fear that that would not solve the problem. These firanghīs are like flies on a lion's head, vultures on a carcass, crows on a freshly seeded field: They can be chased away . . . only to come back a few moments later. Unless, by the mercy of Allāh, we could kill them all, those who escape will always find an easy retreat into the sea, from whence they came. And here, I am sad to say, lies our greatest weakness.

Their ships are faster than that of any Muslim nation, be it Gujarātī, Persian, Arab or Turkish, and the guns mounted on them carry much farther. Because of this, they control with impunity the traffic on the high seas between here and the port of Jeddah. Muslim pilgrims on the sacred Hajj are now compelled to avail themselves of firanghī passports, full of Nazariyya crosses and blasphemous drawings of the prophet Īsā and his saintly mother, upon both of whom be the peace of Allāh. Those who refuse to pay these scandalous ransom monies, are sure to be attacked and sunk by Purtugēsh warships. Is it not an outrage that for the fulfillment of one of the most sacred obligations of Islām, honest Muslims need to obtain the permission and assistance of infidel pirates?'

I thanked him for his advice, weary of the sombre tidings he had brought me. This was all grossly exaggerated, I thought. What did I care about a handful of infidel sea-rovers and petty merchants? Deserted regions—the sea included—will always be infested with robbers and hoodlums of all kinds: a nuisance, but hardly worthy of a king's attention! Surely, I had better things to do than to go equip a fleet – there were more dangerous enemies to be dealt with on land!

With the wisdom of hindsight, however, I have to admit, my son, that the old Gujarātī commander was probably right: Sooner or later, we will have to deal with these firanghīs. Do not trust them, my son! And ask yourself the question: When the sultanates of the Deccan will have been brought to heel, what should be our next objective? The answer will of course depend on the situation at that time, including our relationship with the rulers of Persia and Turān, and the strength of their armies.

However, should we at that time not seriously consider to build ourselves a strong fleet, to at least command the seas around us? He who rules the waves, rules more than a wasteland of water, my son: He rules the highway connecting the entire world! He who dominates the seas, has unlimited access to knowledge and wealth, and thus, to power.

There is still time, of course: The firanghīs' numbers are low, and we could crush them like bugs if we chose to do so; but we should keep an eye on them, and not let them become too strong, nor too rich. No foreign power should exist, unless it be safely separated from us through formidable and easily defensible borders.

Nothing would have pleased me more than a long, leisurely sojourn at the seaside, enjoying the cool breeze; the reports I kept receiving, however, were too alarming to ignore.

Ahmedābād and the north seemed to be under control well enough, but further down south, the Mīrzās—Ibrāhīm Husain in particular—persisted in their rebellious ways, determined, so it seemed, to defy me.

Ibrāhīm Husain was marauding around Barodā, barely two days' marching from Ahmedābād, practically under my nose; Muhammad Husain still held the important port of Surat in the south, and Chāmpāner, east of Barodā, was occupied by Shāh Mīrzā.

Not one of these arrogant bastards had the khutba read in my name; not one of them bothered to send any gifts to the imperial threshold; conciliatory letters remained unanswered. It was high time these dogs were taught a lesson. If they chose to refuse my hand offered in friendship, I would, as a chronicler aptly put it, 'show them my mailed fist!'

In my indignation and youthful impetuousness, however, I almost made a fatal mistake. Rather than taking my time and crushing them one by one, as I could have done quite easily, I insisted on dealing with all three of them at once.

On reaching the outskirts of Barodā, I dispatched Sayyid Mahmūd Khān Bārha with about half of my army towards the Mīrzās' main stronghold Surat, down south near the mouth of the Tapti River. Another strong force under Shābāz Khān, was to head west, and take Chāmpāner.

I stayed behind near Barodā with the other army leaders, with little more than a personal guard—two hundred, all in all—to protect us.

However, when I learned that Ibrāhīm Husain's gang had been spotted nearby, moving north, no doubt in an attempt to escape the advance of the imperial army, I did not hesitate for one moment, and headed as fast as I could to the Māhī River, to cut off his escape.

My forces were of course much too small to give battle to any opponent worthy of that title, but I stubbornly refused to hear my officers' desperate pleas: I did not want to be sensible, I did not want to be prudent. I refused to wait for reinforcements to arrive from Chāmpāner; I would deal with that band of rabble myself.

Reaching the banks of the Māhī, we found that the enemy, over one thousand strong, had already crossed the river, and was camping in the small town of Sarnal, about two kos east of Thasra.

Against better judgment, I attacked immediately. Without any further scouting or preparation, without even giving any command, I drove my mount through the ford in the river, and scrambled up the steep bank on the other side, forcing Mān Singh, Bhagwān Dās, Todar Mal and the others to do the same.

Ibrāhīm Husain, seeing this wild bunch crossing the river and approaching the town, hurried out of it from the other side, looking for space to deploy his superior force. We, of course, pursued him as fast as we could, in an effort to prevent him from doing so.

Like so many other Gujarātī towns, however, Sarnal was surrounded by a maze of narrow roads and tiny fields, all fenced with thorn bushes and prickly-pear cactus – more unsuitable terrain for a cavalry battle was hardly imaginable.

This state of affairs had two consequences. The most important and advantageous one was that the enemy was unable to exploit his numerical superiority and move around to encircle us. On the other hand, the fight amidst this maze of bushes and thorns bore no resemblance to an orderly battle; it was little more than a vulgar, man-to-man street fight between two rivalling gangs.

Man-to-man, indeed. Behind the front—or so I thought—I was looking for higher ground from where to better direct the battle, when suddenly, I found myself face to face with three enemy troopers.

I do not know whether they realised whom they had in front of them, but from my shining armour and the magnificent caparison of my horse, they must have guessed that I was an important man. Keen on plunder and reward, they fell on me. The two swordsmen riding in front attacked me left and right, while the third one, carrying a long lance, came out from behind them and started wheeling around me.

I pranced my horse and threw myself upon the two swordsmen. I had to disable at least one of them, or they would have me completely surrounded in no time. Both my opponents, however, were experienced warriors. One parried my sword-thrust with his shield, and the other skilfully avoided my horse's flashing forehoofs; they had been thrown back, but not defeated. From the corner of my eye, I saw the lancer closing in on me from the right. I was about to turn around to face him, and try and fend off his attack, when he was suddenly struck in the middle of the stomach by a Rājpūt javelin. He dropped his lance, grabbing, in vain, the shaft of the spear, and fell to the ground. I heard the thunder of hoofs behind me and saw a tall, bearded Rājpūt warrior in hazār mīkhī armour galloping towards us: Bhagwān Dās had come to my aid.

With remarkable agility for a man of his stature, the rājā tore his spear out of his dying victim at full gallop, and stormed forward, shouting his Lord Kṛṣṇa's name 'Gopāl!' from the top of his lungs.

I turned around to fight the two remaining enemies, but they seemed to have realised that they now stood two against two. They quickly turned around and made haste to save their skin; we, from our side, were prudent enough not to take any further unnecessary risk, and returned to the troops.

The battle, meanwhile, had been taking a favourable turn. The enemy's front lines had been scattered by the sheer ferocity of our attack, and in the fighting that followed, their bunch of marauders, man for man, proved to be much inferior to our own elite troops. After their front men had been cut down like grass, the next row was seized by so much panic that they started to flee, hindering the others in their advance. That, in turn, led to further panic and confusion, which our men did not fail to exploit, chasing them wherever they went and cutting them down by the dozen. Ibrāhīm Husain himself, regrettably, managed to escape under the cloak of darkness.

The next morning, we returned to our camp and reunited with the reinforcements arriving from Chāmpāner. The two hundred men who had fought so valiantly were covered with rewards, and Rājā Bhagwān Dās was honoured with an amīr's banner and his personal kettledrums, an honour never before bestowed on a Hindū.

The battle of Sarnal has been hailed as one of my most glorious victories, and I have to say, my son, I was quite proud of it myself in those days.

Looking back on it, however, I have come to realise it was maybe the worst mistake of my reign, a wholly unnecessary act of foolish recklessness, which could easily have cost me my life and my throne. My whole empire could have ended then and there, in that insignificant skirmish, because of my stubbornness and daredevilry, and a number of excellent men, including Rājā Bhagwān Dās's own brother Bhupat, paid for my vainglory with their lives.

It does not please me to admit this to you, my son, but I feel I have to. It is my duty to warn you against such dangerous and foolish mistakes.

Chance does favour the reckless sometimes, but a wise king owes it to himself and to the thousands depending on him, to keep at all times his cool-headedness. Chroniclers and poets may love pitched battles and great deeds of valour, but a wise king knows that what counts is not battle, but victory.

Twenty-sixth Letter

گجرات

Gujarāt (2)

With most of the Mīrzā rabble gone from the area—or so I thought—only Surat remained to be conquered; it was time we got this over with. At dawn on the last day of the solar year—a uniquely auspicious moment, according to the astrologers' calculations—we left Barodā, and leisurely travelled south, hunting and administering justice underway.

Eleven days later, we reached the outskirts of Surat, where we joined the men of our vanguard, who, I was pleased to find, had not been idling away their time: The area had been successfully pacified, the city surrounded, and its supplies cut off. The only thing left to do, was to smoke them out.

Sure enough, after barely six weeks of fighting, the defenders were forced to capitulate. Much to their surprise and relief, I spared their lives. Only the garrison commander—a former officer in my father's army—had his tongue cut off, in just retribution for his insolence and faithlessness.

The whole incident would not even be worthy of further mention in these letters, were it not for the encounter I had on that occasion with those famous Purtugēsh.

We had just started the siege operations against Surat, when Todar Mal came to see me, a worried look on his face.

'Your Majesty,' he said, 'our informants tell me that a huge war fleet has arrived in the port of Damān, the firanghī stronghold on the southern border of Gujarāt. They say there are over twenty large battle ships, and dozens of smaller boats, packed with soldiers!'

'Do we know what their intentions are?'

'No, Your Majesty. The firanghī army has gone ashore, but it has not moved from the port.'

'Then I suppose they will be sending us an emissary soon. If not, we will send them one, and find out what they are up to. Make sure we have plenty of scouts everywhere, and that we are not taken by surprise in case they want to attack us!'

Indeed, the next day, an emissary arrived, carrying a letter written in surprisingly fluent Persian, in which the humble servants of His Christian Majesty the king of Portugāl presented the mighty king of Hindustān their respectful greetings and sincere wishes of good health, peace and prosperity.

As the country of Cambay—apparently the name they gave to Gujarāt—had now been annexed to Hindustān's dominions, there were urgent matters of high importance that needed to be discussed, and they would therefore be extremely grateful, if His Majesty would kindly send them an ambassador, who would be received with all the respect due to his lofty rank, and to whose personal safety they pledged their souls.

'Whom shall we send?' I asked, casually looking at Todar Mal.

'With Your Majesty's permission, I will go,' he answered without hesitation.

'I was hoping you would say that, my friend – no one in the entire army is smarter than you. Keep your eyes and ears wide open, and be sure to tell me everything! May god protect you.'

In the company of the firanghī messenger and a small retinue, Todar Mal rode out. Two weeks later, he was back, in good health, and accompanied by a small firanghī delegation. I immediately invited him to my private quarters.

'I must say, I was quite impressed, Your Majesty! I counted twenty-two large war ships, many of them bigger than any ship I have ever seen, with scores of powerful cannons – these firanghīs are definitely a force to be reckoned with! However, that being said, they received me with full honours, with flags raised and cannon shots fired to salute me upon my arrival, and made my stay as comfortable as possible.

'I have met with their viceroy several times. He is the highest representative of their king in these lands. He too was extremely courteous, and did his utmost to convince me of his people's friendly intentions. They truly seem quite eager to avoid any conflict with us, Your Majesty.'

'Why then this war fleet?'

'It appears they have been misled by the Mīrzās, Your Majesty. The Mīrzās had sent them a message, begging for their help, and urging them to come, in their own interest – under the pretence that Your Majesty's armies were marching on Damān. Upon their arrival, however, the Purtugēsh quickly found out that 'the Mīrzās were a spent force', as their viceroy phrased it. They clearly do not wish to get caught up in a war that is not theirs; in fact, the viceroy told me that the Purtugēsh welcome the return of law and order to the country of Gujarāt, and expressed the hope that we would live together in peace and prosperity.'

'And what was your reply?'

'I told him that our emperor was a just and peace-loving sovereign, who favoured mutually beneficial commerce and trade between the people on this earth, and to my knowledge, did not object against the firanghīs establishing a few trading posts on the coast, provided they would not try to expand their dominions inland. I also told him that it had greatly pleased our emperor to hear about the valuable role the Purtugēsh fleet is playing in the protection of peaceful merchants and pilgrims against pirates at sea. In short, I assured them they would have nothing to fear from our emperor, as long as they remained a factor of peace, stability and prosperity in the region.'

'Well said, Rājā Todar Mal! What was their reaction?'

'They seemed to be quite relieved, Your Majesty. They reassured me that they fully recognise Your Majesty as the lawful sovereign of Gujarāt, and that they wished to live in peace. As a sign of their good faith, they have pledged to withdraw their fleet to Goa, and have sent one of their senior officers to accompany me. He wishes to offer Your Majesty a few gifts as a token of their respect and friendship.'

'Excellent. I will receive him at once.'

António Cabral—that was his name—was a tall, strong man in his late thirties, with a trim, well-kempt, manly beard, long black curly hair, and honest eyes, looking unafraid, neither friendly nor hostile.

Apart from a plain white shirt and an elaborate kind of lace shawl around his neck, he was dressed in stern black clothes of rather mediocre quality. On his head, he wore a strange but jaunty hat, with a curly, waving feather. Upon approaching me, he took it off, bowed, and repeatedly brushed the ground with it – to all appearance, the way the firanghīs pay their respects.

An excellent soldier, that I saw at a single glance: He was self-confident without arrogance; fearless, yet composed and courteous; a man in control of himself and open to others, ready to make peace if possible, and war if necessary. I would have engaged him in my own army without a moment's hesitation.

It soon became apparent where the surprisingly elegant Persian letter had come from: The interpreter for the firanghī delegation, a puny little man of distinctly unfavourable appearance, with a moth-eaten, thready beard, and pockmarked, oily, quite unsavoury-looking skin, proved to be a native Iranian!

His suit of clothes, though entirely black and made of the same inferior cloth, was quite different from those worn by the other members of the delegation: It consisted of a long, ankle-length robe with a high collar and a short black shoulder mantle, and a strange-looking, wide-brimmed black hat; his only ornament was a simple necklace with a large wooden cross, on which was affixed a brass figure, representing the crucified, agonising body of Īsā ibn Maryam, or Jesùs, as the firanghī call him. Not only was this man a convert to the Nazariyya sect; he had actually become a Christian priest – a member, so I found out later, of the most influential and learned elite among the firanghī priests: the Society of Jesùs, or the Jesuitas, as they commonly call themselves.

Had I been aware of all this, I would probably have spent much more time with him, to learn some more about the firanghīs and their religion, but I had more pressing obligations and no time to waste: There was a war to be fought, and I wanted to get on with it as fast as possible.

Fortunately, Todar Mal's assessment proved to be correct: The Purtugēsh, although clearly intent on conquest and expansion, as any ambitious nation should be, clearly understood that peace with the 'great Mughal', as they apparently called me, was in their own best interest.

Cabral explained at length that the Purtugēsh were a seafaring, merchant nation; that their home country was much smaller and less populous than Hindustān; that their main interest in this part of the world was to find spices and other wares to trade, through which they would be able to increase their wealth and power, which in turn would help them hold their own with the rival nations of Firanghīstān, primarily the Shpanyol, the Ingrēsh, the Olandēsh, and Fransēsh.

I, of course, wanted to learn more about all this. Cabral readily answered my questions, but I soon found myself completely lost in an intricate maze of countries, regions, warring Christian sects, rivalling kings, high priests and noblemen, all with barbarous, unpronounceable names no one in Hindustān or Persia had ever heard of. Firanghīstān, so much was clear, was not a unified region, and—fortunately for us— neither were its inhabitants.

The peace treaty between us and the Purtugēsh was quickly agreed to and signed: We would not attack their coastal settlements, they would not interfere in the ongoing hostilities, nor try to expand any of their settlements inland; and their warships would continue to protect the Muslim pilgrims on their way to Mekkah.

As a token of their friendship and respect, they offered me a number of valuable and interesting presents, among which an intriguing painting, representing the exotic landscape of their home country, as well as a Purtugēsh sword and musket, which highly evoked my interest.

The sword was straight-bladed, long and narrow – a weapon clearly designed primarily for thrusting from a certain distance: It was obviously not very suitable to hack or hew with, and too long, in my judgement, to be effective in close combat. However, the steel it was made of was of the finest quality, and its intricate and elegant knuckle guard looked both ingenious and effective. The musket, though oddly shaped and rather unhandy, had the most perfect steel barrel I had ever laid my eyes on. These firanghīs, unsophisticated though they looked, proved to be real masters in the art of metal foundry and forging. As Todar Mal had phrased it: 'a force to be reckoned with. . . .'

As I wrote in the beginning of this letter, the further conquest of Gujarāt posed no real problems. Surat capitulated in a matter of weeks, and up north, Azīz Koka inflicted a crushing defeat on the last remaining enemy army in the area. Muhammad Husain Mīrzā, Shāh Mīrzā and a few survivors fled into the Deccan; peace and calm had returned to the region – or so I thought.

On the twenty-third of Farvardīn of the eighteenth year,[203] I started out on the long journey back to Sīkrī, which, so I decreed, would henceforth be named Fathābād, city of victory. About a month later, however, while I was inspecting the construction works over there, I overheard two Hindū masons calling it Fatehpūr or Fathpūr. I immediately thought to myself: this is the true name for my city! Places in Hindustān with names ending in 'bād' have been founded by Muslim rulers, and names ending in 'pūr' refer to Hindū origins – everybody knows that. My capital, however, would be special: This would be a truly Hindustānī city, uniting Hindū and Muslim building styles, and combining, in its name, a Muslim concept with a Hindū ending.

I stopped using the name Fathābād; from that moment on, it was Fatehpūr Sīkrī I talked about, and the people, of course, duly followed suit.

But let me return to the events following the victory in Gujarāt. On the way back, a messenger from Multān brought me the happy tiding that Ibrāhīm Husain Mīrzā, was dead at last.

After the battle of Sarnal that arch-rebel had made his way up north and had managed to rake together another bunch of thieves and robbers of the worst kind, with which he set out to plunder some defenceless villages in the Panjāb. Fortunately, the local governor reacted swiftly, and surprised the rabble near Multān. In the ensuing battle, the rebels were all but wiped out, and Ibrāhīm Husain's younger brother Mas'aūd and many other ringleaders taken prisoner.

Ibrāhīm Husain himself once again managed to escape, but got severely wounded a few days later in a skirmish with a gang of Balūchīs. He was tracked down and marched off to the capital with the rest of the survivors. Unfortunately, I was deprived of the satisfaction of having him executed: His wounds proved to be so severe that 'the bond between his perverse spirit and his vile body was dissolved', as Abū-l Fazl phrased it

---

203. Thursday, 2 April 1573 (Julian calendar)

so elegantly; upon my arrival, the troops presented me with his severed head.

The surviving rebels were paraded in front of me, sewn up in the rotting hides of asses, hogs and other unclean or ridiculous animals. Most of the prisoners—worthless hoodlums, anyway—were of course executed on the spot. A few of them, however—the ones who seemed innocent or useful—I chose to pardon.

Among those few was young Mas'aūd, who, in an excess of zeal, had been brought before me in a truly pitiable state, more dead than alive, and with his eyes sewn up. The boy's face was a ghastly sight, black and blue from the beatings he had taken, his cheeks full of gore, his eyelids swollen around the nasty black thread that held them shut. . . .

'Is it not becoming and appropriate, that a traitor's eyes be downcast with shame?' the governor joked, a triumphant grin on his face. The troops seemed to greatly appreciate the pun, but I did not. What joy, merit, or glory is there in the suffering of a barely seventeen- or eighteen-year-old kid, whose only crime is to be a rebel's brother?

I ordered his eyes to be opened and his wounds to be dressed by my personal hakīm; after his recovery, the boy was to be enlisted in the army. The unfortunate lad, who, no doubt, had expected to die a horrible death, fell to his knees, sobbing barely intelligible words of gratitude.

Looking at him, I knew I had done the right thing; I felt peaceful, and good about myself. Mercy is not an easy virtue, my son, a delicate plant, hard to cultivate, but its fruits taste much sweeter than the grapes of wrath. . . .

Were it not for the unpleasant surprise that fate had in store for me a few weeks later, I would have had the fondest memories of my return to Fatehpūr Sīkrī.

After those strenuous months of war, I of course enjoyed the leisurely life at the court: the cool, umbrageous buildings, the splashing fountains, the exquisite food, the ice-cooled wine, the sweet companionship of beautiful women, and all those other luxuries, but the reason for my joy went much deeper. I was truly elated; I felt as if god's gentle light was shining straight into my heart, for in every thing and every detail, I knew myself to be blessed. I was strong and healthy; I was the happy father of three healthy sons; in barely a few years' time, I had become the mightiest and wealthiest king Hindustān had seen in many centuries, and everything seemed to indicate that this was only the beginning!

Surely, all of this was no coincidence – it could not be. After all, not even a single leaf will fall from a tree, unless god wills it! No, even though I was just an ordinary mortal like the rest, even if I had little personal merit, it was now obvious, beyond a shadow of a doubt: I was—I am—god's chosen instrument on earth, entrusted with a special mission.

Yes, the more I thought about it, the more certain I became: God Himself had given me a sign, when, on the very day of my triumphant return, amidst the interminable series of congratulatory speeches by enthusiastic courtiers and flattering sycophants of all sorts, He caused my attention to be caught by the remarkable words of a humble shaykh I had barely heard of.

The whole afternoon, I had been sitting in the diwān-i-ām, receiving gifts, and listening, with a mixture of pride and boredom, to the flowery words of praise of dozens of visitors, who had come from far and wide to congratulate me on the conquest of Gujarāt. In overblown metaphors, one more lofty and far-fetched than the other, I was told that all the treasures, glory and power of this world pale into insignificance when compared with the all-gracious and refulgent presence of the pearl of royalty, the gem of magnificence, the fountain of justice and benevolence, quintessence of all earthly perfection, His Majesty, the great king of kings Abū-l Muzaffar Jalāl-ud-dīn Muhammad Akbar Pādshāh Ghāzī, commander of the faithful, double-bladed sword of Islām, terror of infidels, lion of lions, tower of strength, refuge of the sinners, cherisher of the poor, and many more of such niceties.

Amidst all that came, this humble shaykh, whom I knew only vaguely, and who had been allowed to present himself at the court, through a letter of recommendation from my foster brother Azīz.

Mubārak of Nāgaur was his name, a rather poorly dressed, tired-looking man in his late sixties. Time, worry and deprivation had worn deep wrinkles down his cheeks, which his scanty beard was unable to hide; his eyes, however, were unusually lively, quick, and piercing.

He was accompanied by his two eldest sons: Abū-l Faizī, whom I knew as a talented poet, since he had been employed at the imperial court since the days of Chittor, and another, rather chubby young man, not much older than twenty, with a clean-shaven, round face, and the same keen, smart eyes as his father. In his hands, he was nervously fingering a bundle of closely written pages.

From the corner of my eye, I noticed that Shaykh Mubārak's presence at the court was clearly not to the liking of Abdullāh of Sultānpūr, the highest ranking of the ulamā, better known under the lofty titles of Makhdūm-ul Mulk and Shaykh ul-Islām; the greedy fat pig who, years before, had had the insolence to oppose me when I decided to abolish the jizya tax on the Hindūs.

'Most learned and honourable Shaykh Mubārak, it is indeed a pleasure to see you! We have heard so many good things about you lately,' I lied, noticing with glee that my words did not miss their intended effect on Makhdūm-ul Mulk's conceitedness.

The shaykh bowed deeply; hiding his trembling hands in his sleeves, he composed his features, and proceeded:

'Words fail me, Your Majesty, to express my and my sons' joy and gratitude, to be granted the undeserved honour and privilege to stand before Your Majesty's august presence. I probably do not need to introduce to Your Majesty my elder son, Abū-l Faizī, whose verses have met with Your Majesty's favour, and who is enjoying the privilege of living at the imperial court, in the comforting shadow of Your Majesty's kindness.

'This here is my younger son Abū-l Fazl, who has chosen to lead a life of study like his father; despite his young age, he has achieved a depth of knowledge and learning, which, if I say so myself, ranks him among the wisest philosophers in Your Majesty's dominions.'

This was quite a bold statement to make, and it did not fail to catch my attention. Shaykh Mubārak proceeded:

'We possess but few earthly goods, Your Majesty, none of which are worthy to be presented to a king; knowing, however, Your Majesty's lively interest in matters of religion and science, we venture to place at the foot of Your Majesty's throne these few writings by my son Abū-l Fazl, which perhaps Your Majesty will deign to have examined at a more suitable moment: It is a treatise, which Your Majesty may find of interest, on the most noble and holy Āyat 'l Kursī.'[204]

---

204. The 'verse of the throne', the 256th verse of the second chapter of the Holy Qur'ān.

Just as I expected, I thought to myself, a bit disappointed: The man merely seeks employment for this other son of his! Still, my interest had been awakened: If this young man was half as good as his father claimed he was, it would indeed be interesting to meet him some time.

'Thank you, Shaykh Mubārak,' I answered. 'We have indeed a great interest in the limitless world of books and the furthering of knowledge, and shall be interested to acquaint ourselves with your son's insights.'

'Your Majesty's kindness and wisdom are boundless,' the Shaykh mumbled, his forehead almost touching his knees.

I now expected to see the three of them bowing their way out, but to my surprise, Mubārak resumed his talk:

'I am aware that Your Majesty's time is precious and limited – that he has more pressing and important matters to attend to, than to listen to the inept stammer of a poor old man. Nevertheless, I would be most grateful if Your Majesty would allow me to express my profound gratitude and joy, that it has pleased Allāh to send to Hindustān the true khalīfah, next to whom the reign of the great Hārūn ar-Rashīd, of happy memory, will pale into insignificance!

'In less than twenty years, this world will witness the advent of the thousandth lunar year since the Holy Prophet Muhammad—eternal blessings of Allāh be upon him and his household!—led his followers to al-Madīnah, obeying Allah's command. Yes, the thousandth year of the Hijrī Era draws nigh, and we have every reason to believe that what has been foretold about the end of time, is now about to manifest itself!

'Eternal praise and gratitude be to Allāh! In the noble person of Your Majesty, He has given us the noble khalīfah we, His humble subjects, are yearning for, not only to rule over us, but to be our spiritual guide in the critical times ahead. May Allāh's blessings rain down on Your Majesty in abundance!'

The *true khalīfah*? The end of time? The spiritual guide of the people? Maybe the old man was just a sycophant like all the others, but I have to admit, his cryptic statements had roused my interest, and I was quite anxious to learn more about them.

However, those things would have to wait: These were no matters to be discussed in the diwān-i-ām, in front of dozens of nosy courtiers. I thanked the shaykh for his good wishes, and told him that I would soon require his and his son's presence in private audience.

I spent most of that night in ardent prayer, that god would grant me wisdom, and continue to guide my steps.

≈

My worldly duties, however, left me but little time for profound reflection. There were building works to be supervised, revenues to be secured, justice to be administered – and on top of all that, as I will relate more extensively in another letter, the situation in Bihār and Bengāl suddenly required my urgent attention. The days flew by in frantic busyness.

Just when things seemed to calm down a bit, alarming reports came in from Gujarāt – the country was again aflame with an unexpectedly violent and dangerous new insurrection. In the south, Muhammad Husain Mīrzā had come back from the Deccan with a large army – how he had been able to raise one so fast, I will never know. His hordes invaded the area of Surat and occupied Khambhat, chasing out the local imperial garrisons. Together with Shēr Khān Fulādī's sons, and a local Gujarātī warlord named Ikhtyār-ul Mulk, he was now threatening Ahmedābād itself!

What was I to do? The Gujarātī invasion army had been disbanded, most troops had returned to their jāgīrs, or had been sent east to Bihār. To call them back, to reconstitute and equip an entirely new invasion army would take several weeks, and the march back down to Gujarāt, at the very least, another month or so: Ahmedābād was over two hundred kos[205] away – trading caravans needed two full months to cover that distance!

There was clearly no time for all of this. If these reports were accurate, we stood to lose the entire Ahmedābād garrison, and Azīz's life was in danger! The best I could do, so I thought to myself, was to head back immediately, as fast as I could, with whatever troops I had available: I would still be able to join forces with Azīz, and I would at least have the advantage of surprise.

In a matter of two days, I hastily assembled a striking force – barely three thousand cavalry; not nearly enough, but all hand-picked, battle-

---

205. 500 miles, 800 kilometres

hardened, excellent men, and generously equipped at the imperial treasury's expense.

Of course, well-meaning friends and advisors begged me to wait:

> They say, the enemy has over twenty thousand men, Your Majesty! If, Allāh forbid, the Ahmedābād garrison would be defeated before Your Majesty's arrival, or if they fail to break through the encirclement, Your Majesty's forces will be outnumbered seven to one! Should we not consider building up a larger force before attacking – even if this would mean the temporary loss of Ahmedābād? At the very least, Your Majesty should think of his own safety! Let these three thousand be the vanguard, Your Majesty can follow later, with a larger force!

I know it was all meant for the best, but I wanted nothing of it. This was something I wanted to take care of myself – the Mīrzās had defied me one time too many.

'The hoofs of my own horse will be the first to cross the Gujarātī border,' I swore, making sure to repeat this oath several times in front of the troops: In times of trouble, there is no substitute for the king's personal example.

Thus it was done. We left Fatehpūr Sīkrī on Yawm al-A'had, the twenty-fourth of Rabi ath-Thani of 981,[206] speeding through the country despite the blazing, infernal heat, covering over twenty kos[207] per day, on camel and horseback. Barely nine days later, we were standing on Gujarātī soil.

I sent scouts down to Ahmedābād to warn Azīz: We would press on as fast as possible and attack the enemy's rear; this would allow him to break through the encirclement, and crush the rebels between hammer and anvil.

Unfortunately, however, it did not quite work out that way.

Azīz, suspecting an enemy ruse to lure him into the open, stayed safely behind Ahmedābād's ramparts. The enemy, on the other hand, did not take any chances. Hearing the rumours about the advent of an

---

206. Sunday, 23 August 1573 (Georgian calendar)
207. 50 miles, 80 kilometres

imperial army, Muḥammad Ḥusain Mīrzā left his ally Ikhtyār-ul Mulk behind to block the gates of Ahmedābād with five thousand men, while he rode out, at the head of fifteen thousand, determined to check our advance at the Sabarmati River.

I have to say, it was quite an unpleasant surprise, to descry in the distance on the other side of the river, not the imperial standards, but the detested red banners of the Mīrzās, and a strong enemy host, complete with dozens of war elephants.

Impetuous and stubborn as I was, I nonetheless refused to listen to prudence or reason, and driving my horse through the river, ordered the attack even though there was no sign yet of Azīz and his men, and even though the enemy clearly outnumbered us, five to one at least.

The rest, as you know, my son, is history: It was quite a pitched battle, but against all odds, we won – collecting over two thousand enemy heads on the battlefield, against a loss of barely one hundred of our own men.

How was this possible? Was it sheer luck, as some of my critics probably whisper behind my back? No, definitely not! Was it divine assistance, as eager courtiers claim it was? It is quite tempting to believe so, but the truth, I'm afraid, is far less spectacular or miraculous.

I won the Ahmedābād battle, against vastly superior numbers, my son, because, if I say so myself, I understand the iron laws of warfare, and know how to make them work for me.

You will remember, no doubt, the wise lessons Bairām Khān taught me, back in Jālandhar, when I was still a young boy: Since, all other things being equal, god favours the larger army. The entire art of warfare is to influence and change the circumstances of battle; it is to understand the advantages and disadvantages of your own and the enemy's situation, and then, to do whatever you can to exploit both.

Contrary to what people think, my decision to attack was not merely a matter of impetuousness or daredevilry. I simply *had* to attack before the enemy had the chance to fully draw out his own troops. Even more importantly, I had to lure him into a fight on the narrow stretch of flat land near the bank of the river. Remember Bairām Khān's wise lesson: When a large army is forced to fight on a narrow, restricted battlefield, its numbers are an impediment rather than an advantage, because they will slow it down and hinder it in its movements; a small army, on the contrary, should try to use its greater mobility and the element of surprise, so that, when and where it strikes, it can effectively outnumber its opponent.

Perhaps even more decisive in this case, was the difference in the fighting spirit and ability of the men. I had myself a small but effective force of hand-picked, battle-hardened soldiers, each and every one of them devoted to their emperor, ready to follow him to the gates of hell. The Mīrzā army, by contrast, impressive though it looked, was nothing but a bunch of hoodlums out for plunder: adventurers, robbers, mercenaries – worthless cannon fodder, nothing more.

It was as if I heard Bairām Khān's voice again: Even more important than weapons, defences and equipment, is the fighting spirit of your men. Each army may have its number of heroes, but the vast majority of the soldiers on the battlefield will be just ordinary men, afraid to die, naturally inclined to avoid the heat of the battle and to flee from danger. An ordinary soldier, when left to himself, will feel the urge to run away, or in contrast, to attack prematurely, in an instinctive effort to get everything over with as quickly as possible. He will discharge his bow or musket in the general direction of the enemy, without taking proper aim, thereby wasting and reducing his own army's striking power. When his army suffers a setback, he will flee in panic, and thereby allow himself and his comrades to be slaughtered like the meekest of sheep.

How very true! The most important battle to win, my son, is that of the mind: A commander needs to overcome the natural weakness of his own men, and exploit that of the enemy.

If I say so myself, that is exactly what I did.

I divided my troops into four fighting forces: Turkomān horse archers on both flanks; heavily armed, unflinching Rājpūt shock troops in the centre. Behind the front line on both flanks, I positioned my best marksmen, ordering them not to fire at random into the enemy host, but to carefully target the enemy leaders and their bravest soldiers. Around my person, I only kept a bodyguard of two hundred of the best men on the fastest horses, enough to escape unharmed if things would turn against us.

As I said, it was a pitched battle. Our men, though far better and braver than the enemy, were initially pushed back and nearly overwhelmed by the enemy's superior numbers. To make things worse, my horse got hit by a musket bullet and collapsed. This very nearly cost us the battle: For a moment, the men thought I had been killed, and our battle lines started to falter. Fortunately, I was back in the saddle of another horse, just in time to prevent a complete rout. Seeing me alive and well, the men took heart and attacked with renewed courage.

After some time—truly endless it seemed—my strategy finally started bearing fruit. With deadly effectiveness, my archers and musketeers had been picking out the enemy leaders; and the Rājpūts were now making deep, bloody inroads in their ranks.

Muhammad Husain Mīrzā, realising that his army was on the verge of collapse, pushed forward to encourage his men, when suddenly, one of his elephants, seized with panic of an exploding rocket, wreaked havoc in his own rearguard. The ensuing panic was the end for him; his battle lines collapsed completely; everywhere, his men were fleeing in disarray, slaughtered by the hundreds by our victorious troops. Muhammad Husain himself, wounded in the melee, was captured alive.

The battle was over. Our men were resting by the river bank, apart from a few who had been assigned the task of collecting the enemy heads, and digging graves and building funeral pyres for our fallen heroes.

Suddenly, a few of our scouts (a prudent commander always keeps a number of those on the lookout – don't you ever forget that, my son!) rode in the camp to warn me that another army was advancing against us. I first thought it was Azīz and his garrison, but for the second time that day, we were in for a most unpleasant surprise: This was the other enemy army under Ikhtyār-ul Mulk, who, probably alerted by an emissary, had come to his ally's aid. I quickly had Muhammad Husain beheaded, and ordered the battle lines to be formed.

Our men, thank god, remained calm. Disciplined and orderly, they took their positions, and advanced towards the enemy.

The enemy soldiers, from their side, were seized with panic, horrified at the sight of Muhammad Husain's bleeding head on a Rājpūt lance, and the tower of heads in the making in the background.

They did not even try to put up a decent fight: Even before our men had reached their front lines, the entire enemy host had been transformed into a panic-stricken herd of cowardly sheep. Our men butchered them with virtual impunity – I do not think we lost a single soldier in the entire engagement.

Ikhtyār-ul Mulk desperately tried to save his vile carcass, but Sohrāb Turkmān, one of my best scouts, spotted him, hunted him down like a falcon catches a rabbit, and, as Abū-l Fazl phrased it so elegantly, 'relieved his shoulders of the burden of his head'.

Thus, after barely a few hours of fighting, the rebellion was utterly crushed. There was a brief moment of panic when, to the men's bewilderment, a third army arrived at the scene, but this time, thank god, it was our own Ahmedābād garrison under my foster brother Azīz.

We joyfully reunited with our brethren and had a great feast on the river bank. As for the enemy, this time, the Mīrzās had tried my patience once too many. Contrary to my habit, I decided to set an example. I personally ran my spear through the piece of scum that had slain Rājā Bhagwān Dās's brother in the battle of Sarnal, and ordered the summary execution of all the others.

I stayed in Gujarāt no longer than was strictly necessary. Leaving the governorship of the province in the hands of Azīz, I gave Todar Mal the special assignment to busy himself with the organisation of revenue and tax collection – a task of which, as usual, he would acquit himself admirably: Only a few weeks later, the incoming revenue from Gujarāt would swell, from the disappointing trickle it had been before, into an impressive and incessant stream of wealth, with which I could fund my further plans and ambitions. The province was finally mine.

We finished our tower of heads—one of the highest I ever built, a stern warning to the rebellious and the seditious—and marched back north.

Barely three weeks later, on the eighth of Jumādā ath-Tania,[208] I rode, spear in hand, through the gates of Fatehpūr Sīkrī, amidst the cheering crowd. I had been absent from the capital for forty-three days.

It was, and so the historians keep telling me, the fastest and most impressive campaign in history. No one, not even Iskandar the Macedonian or the great Chingīz Khān, had ever won so complete and decisive a victory in so little time, against so distant and powerful an opponent.

Thus, my son, ended the rebellion of the 'proud' Mīrzās. . . .

---

208. 5 October 1573

So true it is, what Abū-l Fazl wrote about them in his chronicles: 'From the height of presumption, they cast themselves into the abyss of ruin'. They could have had so much, but they wanted it all. They could have lived carefree lives of ease and luxury; I would have allowed them to share in my power, wealth and glory; as kinsmen of the emperor, the entire world would have held them in the highest esteem; but they chose to throw it all away.

Who remembers them now? Who is there to pray for their souls? Who will light a lamp on their graves? Their fortunes, their names: gone and lost forever, in the dust of time.

Twenty-seventh Letter

ابو الفضل

Abu-l Fazl

From the private notes of Mīr Abdul Latīf

High noon, this day of Chāhārshanbeh, the second of Ābān of the eighteenth year of His Majesty's glorious reign – or, to put it in more traditional terms: the sixth of Jumādā ath-Tania[209] of the year 981 of the Hijrī era.

It is unbearably hot, and although I cannot sleep, I feel tired, very tired; tired, like I never felt before in my life. Alas, judging by the alarming decrepitude of this old, aching body, this eighteenth year of His Majesty's glorious reign will also be the last one of my life on this earth. . . .[210]

---

209. 6 October 1573

210. Chāhārshanbeh: Wednesday. Ābān: The Persian solar month of Scorpio (23 October – 22 November). The date corresponds to 14 October 1573 on the Julian calendar (24 October on the present-day Gregorian calendar).

Mīr Abdul Latīf died about two weeks later, on Saturday, 31 October (fifth of Rajab, 981).

My eyes are blurred by a grayish, milky haze, a kind of dirty mist which seems to be growing denser by the day, and which not even the midday sun is able to dissipate. A few more months, weeks maybe, and I will have gone completely blind. Each time I move, my wrist is tortured by a nagging, crippling pain, and my fingers feel so cramped and wooden, that I barely manage not to drop the qalam. I, who have written thousands upon thousands of pages of fleeting, harmonious, flawless Nasta'līq script, find myself clumsily scratching the paper, smudging it with shaky, barely legible scrawls and scribbles, so disgracefully awkward and square that I feel deeply ashamed of myself. Only a few years ago, if I would have caught a beginner bungling like this, I would have reprimanded him severely. . . .

Verily, Allāh is wise and compassionate, even when the fate He sends us seems harsh—confronting us with the impotent feebleness of old age—He leads us onto the path of humility, which every man must tread, before he can enter paradise.

It is, indeed, not hard for me anymore to feel humble: My body is almost literally falling apart, like a decaying cart under its own burden. I realise, with calm, ice-cold certainty: These are the last pages I will ever write, for the day of my return to the ultimate reality behind the veil of this transient world is near.

Am I afraid to die, now that I feel death's black shadow over me? I really wish I could answer that question with a simple, unequivocal 'no'. An old and supposedly wise man like me should be prepared to leave this world, not merely resigned to his fate, but actually looking forward to it! With shame, however, I have to admit, to myself if to no one else: I am not.

I do realise, of course, that I have little reason to complain: Mine has been a good and fulfilling life, longer and much more comfortable than most could ever dream of. I have provided amply for myself and my family, I have been able to pursue all of my interests, and I enjoy the respect and esteem of the greatest men on earth. And surely, I will be man enough to face the pain and discomfort of death with courage and dignity: Whatever the final hour will bring me—exhaustion, nausea, shortness of breath—I pledge I will bear it with supreme equanimity.

My mind, however, is not at ease. Day and night, I keep wondering: Are they really true, all those things I learned and taught all my life? Will

Munkar and Nakīr[211] really come to visit me in my grave, to prepare my soul for eternity? Will I be worthy of Allāh's clemency, will He spare me the horrible tortures of hell? Will I be allowed to behold His unspeakable majesty, and the everlasting bliss of paradise?

No matter how hard I try to chase them away, those nagging words of Khayyam's irreverent verse keep coming back to haunt my brain:

می برکف من نه که دلم در تاب است
وین عمر گریزپای چون سیماب است
دجیاب که آتش جونی آب است
هشدار که بیداری دواب خواب است

> Come with old Khayyam, and leave the wise
> to talk – One thing is certain: life flies;
> One thing is certain, and the rest is lies:
> The flower that once has blown, forever dies.[212]

No matter how hard I try to banish it from my mind, I simply cannot repress this blasphemous thought: When I'm dead, I'm gone; I will simply cease to exist; my mind will descend into the abyss of annihilation, it will disappear into the motionless, pitch-black darkness, where there is no light, no sound, and no movement; it will sink into the void, where there is neither joy nor sadness; where there are no hopes, no prospects, no plans, no memories, not even regrets.

It is not the first time my mind is plagued by doubts of this kind, but never before have they been so compelling. Never have they drawn

---

211. 'The unknown', and 'The repudiating': the two angels who are said to visit the dead in their graves, 'to interrogate them as to their belief in the Prophet and the true religion preached by him'.

212. Abū-l Fath 'Umar al Khayyam' (1047–1123): Iranian mathematician, astronomer, philosopher, and one of the most famous Farsi poets of all time. The verse and its poetic English translation by Edward Fitzgerald is quoted by Yavar Dehgahni in the Lonely Planet *Farsi (Persian) Phrasebook*, p. 99.

A more literal (albeit, arguably, less catching) translation is:

Mey bar kaf e man neh ke delam dar tāb ast	Bring me wine, for restless my mind is,
Vin omr e gorizpāy chon simāb ast	And like mercury this fleeting life is;
Daryāb ke ātash e javāni āb ast	Youth's fire: behold, mere water it is;
Hoshdār ke bidāri ye dolat khāb ast	Beware, fortune's watchfulness: sleep it is.

so nigh to certainty, bitter and pitiless. Soon, Mīr Abdul Latīf will be no more; the only thing that will remain of him are these words. A few awkwardly scribbled pages, and my name: that is the only immortality I can aspire to.

I must admit, in spite of everything, it is a flattering and even somewhat comforting thought that some of the things I have said, done and written, may live on in the minds of people who will come after me – just like the words of so many writers and philosophers are alive in my own mind. Thoughts, indeed, are like contagious diseases: They keep on spreading, even when their first victim is long dead and buried. Thoughts live forever, even if their thinkers do not.

But alas, I will not be there to take pride in them: Nothing will be known to me, for there will no longer be a knower. Like a splashing drop of water that has fallen back into the ocean, I will no longer be separate: Utterly unified I will be, one with the blind and deaf force that we call god. I will become an unknowing part of that silent, mindless power, that creates and destroys, inexorably, majestically, awesomely, terribly, without knowing or caring, without love, or hatred, or any other feeling. I will be one with the all-encompassing, inescapable cycle of life and death, the vortex that was, is, and will be, the great happening, the ultimate union of everything and nothing, fullness and void, motion and stillness, the eye of the storm where nothing at all is moving.

All of this would not be so terrifying – after all, have I not been dead or non-existent before I was born, for countless thousands of centuries? Why would the non-existence that follows life be more terrible than the one that precedes it? And what is the difference between non-existence and dreamless sleep?

But then again, there are these other moments, terrible and agonising, when I fear the consequences of my own thoughts: What if I am mistaken? What if everything that has been written is literally true? Does my lack of faith not make me a murtadd, worse even than a kāfir,[213] doomed to eternal hellfire? Is it not written that kufr is the only sin that Allāh cannot and will not forgive, because it refuses Him and His mercy? Is it not said that every sinner will sooner or later be released from hell –

---

213. Kāfir: infidel, person in a state of kufr (unbelief in god, blasphemy). Murtadd: Apostate, person who has abandoned Islām.

every sinner, except the kāfirūn, who will be punished in all eternity? Have we not been warned, by generations upon generations of learned and pious men, that salvation depends entirely on the inscrutable will of Allāh, Who guides aright the good and leads astray the wicked? Is this not corroborated in the Holy Qur'ān itself?

Have I indeed been led astray? Has my doom been inscribed on the eternal tables of divine wrath? Am I to be damned for all time?

Alas, if I were to ask the opinion of the sour, bigoted men of the law—Makhdūm-ul Mulk and the likes of him—they would, no doubt, leave me little hope. . . .

But could Allāh's divine justice really be that harsh? Is it possible that a compassionate and merciful god could destine some of His own creatures for eternal suffering?

Surely, if He is all-knowing, if not a speck of dust moves in the entire universe without Him being aware of it; if not even the most fleeting or hidden thought escapes His attention – surely then, He must know that I would never reject Him? Surely, He must know that my poor, feeble mind never intended nor wanted to rebel against Him, that it was merely the helpless victim of questions – haunting, nagging questions that kept coming back, questions it found itself incapable of answering, yet unable to avoid? Surely, if Allāh knows all my sins, will He not also understand my weaknesses, and will He not appreciate my good intentions, however inept they may be?

If my wise and trusted friend Hakīm Alī Gilanī were here with me today, he would surely tell me that I worry too much. In fact, he would probably smile, shake his head, and say something like:

> Do you not think, my learned friend, that Allāh is greater than all the worries and cares of a compunctious old scholar like you? Have some wine, my old friend, and get some rest; you will feel much better!

Maybe I should follow that advice, and order myself some wine, and maybe a bit of opium-laced rosewater as well. For a while at least, it will ease the pain in my bones. And who knows, it may give my poor, tormented head a few moments of peace.

Alī Gilanī—Allāh bless him!—is quite right, of course: Medicine, taken in moderation to treat an illness or ailment, is hardly harām[214] – a harmless, minor transgression at most. Why else would Allāh have put them at our disposal? Just a few beakers, an hour or two of pain-free repose – what a world of difference they make to a weak old man! I truly feel a bit stronger, and my wrist and fingers, thank god, are much less cramped and painful. I may yet be able to take advantage of the cool of the night, and get some more of this writing done.

Some more of this writing . . . sometimes I wonder why I am so eager to get this finished – for whom and wherefore am I writing all this?

First and foremost, I guess, I am doing it for my own comfort: It helps me to compose my fleeting thoughts, to discipline my wandering mind, to come to terms somehow with my ending life and my impending death. . . .

And pretentious though it may sound, I also hope that these scribbles of mine may be of some significance to posterity.

Admittedly, they will not be of much interest to my family. My sons, I'm afraid, will have little use for the anxious musings and speculations of an old man. They are doing quite well, they have their families, their means of sustenance, their occupation and position in life. They have come to know their father as a wise, learned, irreproachable man, a paragon of decency and respectability. Let them keep the pious image they have of me, and by all means, let them keep their unquestioning faith in god, if they still have it, for it is a source of great comfort and stability in life. Let them light a lamp on my grave as custom requires, and pray for my salvation, but let them not be troubled by my doubts and weaknesses – that would neither be necessary, nor desirable.

I do hope, however, that my musings may be of some interest—maybe even of some practical use—to other people. Blasphemous though my thoughts may sound to some, they may actually be of some comfort to people whose mind is plagued by doubts akin to my own, people who lust too much for knowledge beyond human comprehension.

His Majesty, for one, may find my notes of particular interest. In fact, if I am honest with myself, it is His Majesty whom I had in mind when

---

214. Haram: Forbidden, unclean

I was writing these pages. They will be my personal legacy to him – our last falsafeh[215] conversation, so to speak.

There is no grave risk that he will be shocked or led astray by my doubts. In fact, I sense that his beliefs are not at all dissimilar from my own. He has a restless, inquisitive, free-thinking—some would say, 'irreverent'—mind; and never have I known a man of the world with such keen interest in philosophical issues, so eager to explore the mysteries of existence and the intricacies of religious doctrine.

'Discourses on philosophy have such a charm for me that they distract me from all else,' he once confessed in public. 'I sometimes have to forcibly restrain myself from listening to them, lest I should neglect the necessary duties of the hour!'

How many hours, indeed, have we not talked about religion, the afterlife, truth and the way in which it can be ascertained? He never seems to tire of those kind of subjects! Whenever he has the time—and sometimes even when he does not—he will call to his presence a few what he calls 'interesting' people, freethinkers like Bīrbal and me, and indulge in learned, congenial, often wine-soaked conversation, sometimes right through the night, about the teachings and doctrines of all kinds of religious creeds and sects.

Who will take my place in those debates when I'm dead? I do not know, but it is comforting to know that, through my writings, His Majesty will, from time to time, still remember his old teacher.

Not that I claim to be indispensable – the graveyards are full of indispensable people! Nevertheless, the matter is not without importance. I have always taken great pride in the influence I have on His Majesty. To name but one example: The principle of sulh-i-kul, which so strongly guides his opinions and policies, is entirely the result of the conversations he had with me. The idea that others could ever have a similar influence on him does not appeal to me at all, but what can I do? Like all other mortals, I will have to reconcile myself to the facts. . . . And truth be told, there are many good men among His Majesty's courtiers, and I am confident he will be wise enough, even without the help of his old teacher, to decide for himself what is valuable and what not.

---

215. Falsafeh: Philosophical

I will not present these notes to His Majesty myself – he would, bless his soul, insist on sending me hordes of healers with potions and salves and incantations, and I wish to be left in peace during these last months of my life. No, I think I will entrust them to Hakīm Alī Gilanī, a good friend, and above all, a man of confidence, who has seen much and spoken little, a real physician if there ever was one. I will wait no longer. Tomorrow, I will ask him to come and pay me a visit. It would be foolish for a sick old man to postpone a meeting with his hakīm.

≈

Such an obliging, courteous, amiable man! I only sent him a small scribbled note, requesting a meeting with him in the course of the following week, but considerate as always, he presented himself at my quarters within an hour.

We exchanged a few civilities, whereupon he proceeded, with that mixture of sympathy and firmness so typical of physicians, to take my pulse, examine my eyes, palpate my stomach and the like. His ear to my chest, he listened, at length and with badly dissimulated concern, to the impotent shallowness of my breathing, and the feeble, irregular beating of my weak old heart, but said nothing.

'What ailments exactly are you suffering from, honourable master?' he inquired, trying to sound as casual as possible. I gave him a brief description of the most relevant of my complaints: my fading eyesight, my general feeling of weakness and exhaustion, and the sometimes excruciating pain in my wrist and fingers. Visibly relieved to retreat to more familiar terrain, he eagerly started commenting on the latter:

'Inside your wrist,' he explained, 'there is a kind of sheath, a fine tunnel so to speak, through which the tendons lead from your forearm to your hand. In many elderly people, those tendons tend to swell, especially when performing tasks requiring the same repetitive movement for an extended period of time, for instance as you do when you are writing. As far as those aching fingers are concerned, you clearly suffer from an inflammation of the joints, also quite common in the elderly, that is causing those painful knobbles. Well, I'm afraid there is no real cure for these ailments, my honourable master and friend. . . . The best you can do, is to take plenty of rest – I would advise you to do a little less writing, or better still, to call in a good scribe who can take dictation from you, rather than trying to write everything yourself. Another advice: Keep your hands warm at all times, and soak them in hot water whenever you can.'

He went through the leather bag he had brought with him, and took out a small box filled with dark brown granules.

'If the pain becomes too severe, you can take some of this medicine: one or two grains will suffice to alleviate the pain; three or four will help you go to sleep. Be careful, though: Never take more than four grains at a time, and do not use them too often. Make sure you drink plenty of water.'

He paused, looking for the right words.

'As far as your eyesight is concerned . . . it is rather hard to predict how that will evolve, revered master. You may experience increasing difficulties in recognising details, faces and expressions. I will not lie to you. Without adequate help, this may eventually lead to blindness. However, it is still possible to remove the clouded lens from the eye and restore much of the eyesight, but let us hope that it will not have to come to that. Oftentimes, and may Allāh grant that this will be your case, the disorder progresses very slowly; you may be able to keep the eyesight you currently have. If you have difficulty reading, I can give you a specially polished magnifying glass – when you put it on the text you are reading, it will make the letters appear much larger and more legible.'

I put my hand on his arm.

'Allāh be praised, that He has granted me the privilege of making your acquaintance, my learned friend! I am truly grateful for your help. Now tell me, if you will: How much longer do I have?'

'I don't know what you mean, honourable master. . . .'

'I do not have much longer to live, do I?'

'I have found nothing abnormal for a man your age,' he answered evasively.

'I know you mean well, my friend, but I need to know the truth,' I insisted. 'Be honest with me now: How much longer do I have?'

'If there is one thing you have to avoid as a physician, unless you absolutely want to make a fool of yourself, it is to predict how much longer someone has got to live,' he retorted with a nervous chuckle.

He looked at me, and his face turned grave and sombre again.

'The hour of our death, revered master, is known to Allāh alone. But you have asked me to tell the truth. Well, I will not lie to you: As you will have experienced yourself, your heart is what can be expected in a man of your venerable age; its beat is a bit irregular and weak. I will give you a tonic to strengthen it. In a few days, you should feel better. Let me assure you, though: Your condition is not at all uncommon in elderly people – I have seen people live for many more years, with a heart much weaker than yours!'

'But you have seen many others dying from a condition less severe than mine, have you not?'

He hesitated. With a faint, wistful smile, he slowly nodded, acknowledging defeat.

'I must admit, I have, revered master.'

'Thanks for being honest with me, my friend. Do not worry, you have merely confirmed to me what I have known myself for quite some time now. And rest assured, I have not called upon you to find a cure that I know does not exist – I have lived a long and happy life, and have every reason to be grateful.

'No, my health is not the main reason I have asked to see you. I would, if you would be willing to accept, like to ask you to take care of a few practical matters for me after I'm gone.'

'Of course, you can always count on me, revered master! But I pray to Allāh that many more years will come to pass before I am called upon to fulfill my promise!'

'May it please Allāh, indeed, my good friend. Thank you so much for your appreciated help! Well, let me explain a few things to you.'

I conveyed to him a few practical matters regarding my estate – mainly instructions on how to divide it in equal parts, what to give to which child, and the like. Hakīm Alī took due note of them. I went on to talk about my life, about the modest yet significant role I played in the development of His Majesty's thinking, and about my desire to leave for him my memoirs.

He appeared quite interested and eager to cooperate.

'Could I have the honour of reading a few pages, revered master?'

I handed him a few pages talked of the emperor's early youth and my appointment as his teacher. He read them intently, his eyes never once leaving the paper.

'This is really fascinating!' he exclaimed after a while. 'I am convinced His Majesty will be very pleased, not to say deeply moved, to hear the voice of his revered teacher reaching his ear through these writings! It will be an honour and privilege for me to be of assistance to you in so important an endeavour, revered master!'

He paused.

'But why and how, may I ask, did you decide to entrust your writings to me, revered master? Surely, there are many men at the court, well-versed in matters of philosophy and government, much more than I am?'

'Whom better to trust than one's own physician?' I answered. On an impulse, I gave him the papers I had been writing the night before.

No sooner had I handed them over, I wished I had not. To what use was it, to add those private musings to my memoirs? Had I not better destroyed them?

But what was done could not be undone. I nervously looked at Hakīm Alī's smart eyes flying over the lines, halting here and there to decipher a clumsily written word.

When he had finished reading, he looked at me, with what seemed a mixture of compassion and admiration.

'Revered master, I am profoundly convinced the emperor would be elated if you would be prepared to share these notes with him,' he said softly. 'As you so rightly point out, he does have an inquisitive mind, and his interest in matters of religion and philosophy is, indeed, truly remarkable!'

His smile broadened.

'And I have to say, I am most honoured to read that you think me worthy of your trust, venerable master! However, as you say yourself: I really do think you worry too much – way too much! Your scrupulosity is of course to your credit, but I am sure you are taking it too far!'

He paused, looking for an argument that would convince me.

'Suppose, for the sake of the argument, revered master, that a man like me would suddenly find himself sitting on Allāh's throne of judgement, and that a learned and wise old man like yourself would be brought before me by the angels of death. Suppose the angels of death would testify against you:

As it is our mission, we have questioned this wretched man's soul, and we have found, beyond doubt, that he is an infidel. His faith weighs less than a grain of desert sand! There is nothing that he does not doubt – absolutely nothing, not even Your very existence, O lord of all worlds! Outwardly, he may have observed the fast of Ramadān and given alms to the poor, he may have prostrated himself five times per day, but the only prayer he is capable of without lying, is nothing more than two blasphemous lines: My god, if there is One; save my soul, if I have one . . .

'What do you think would be my answer to them, revered master? 'Do you really think I would be so pitiless to say:

I gave this man a long life among the true believers, yet he failed to serve Me. In doubting My existence and the truth of the glorious Qur'ān, he has gravely sinned, and I am deaf to his supplications. Throw him in the flames of hell – eternal suffering will be his fate!

'Do you really think I would condemn my own creature to eternal suffering, on account of a mere mistake? Of course not! To eternal suffering, I would not even condemn the vilest murderer! Punish him, I would; for centuries if necessary, but in the end, after a certain amount of time, he would have expiated his sins and my wrath would subside!

'And as far as you are concerned, revered master, my answer would be:

I know of this man's doubts and errors, and I know he made them out of ignorance, not out of ill will. Throughout his life, he has honestly tried to be true, good and kind. And behold, those who serve truth and justice, are true servants of Mine. Go, and show this righteous man his well-earned place in paradise!

'Consider, revered master: If this would be my mindset, if this would be the attitude of a sinful, limited man like me, how much more will it not be the position of Him Who is perfect, without a single blemish, the source of all holiness, compassion and mercy? How could Allāh, who is nothing but goodness, ever desire the suffering of a pious, holy, gentle old man like yourself?'

I wanted to answer that I was neither pious nor holy, but he quietly raised his hand.

'I am not a learned philosopher like you, venerable master, but as your physician let me tell you something; in my opinion, most, if not all, of those scruples and concerns of yours have to do with your melancholic temperament, more than with anything else!'

'What do you mean?'

'People like you, venerable master, people whose temperament tends to be dominated by an excess of black bile, are studious and pensive in nature. They are sensitive, kind and considerate, creative in poetry and arts, but they also tend to be overly worried and preoccupied. Their character is noble and humble – more humble, in fact, than is good for their own health; they are often highly critical of themselves, and dissatisfied about their own abilities and achievements. In some cases, they may suffer from such oppressive sorrow and sadness about themselves and the condition of the world that it will render them completely listless.'

He paused and smiled reassuringly.

'What you need to do, is to go out more, revered master! Try to go for a brief walk every day, preferably in the cool of the morning. Movement of the limbs promotes the formation of new red blood, which is the natural antidote to black bile; and sunlight helps to brighten the mind. And have a pitcher of wine from time to time – if possible, in the company of friends; friendly company is one of the healthiest and most potent medicines that exist against excessive bile – both black bile, which causes sombreness, and yellow bile, which induces anger. Above all, never be ashamed to laugh. Healthy laughter promotes the flow of wholesome juices; it opens the mind, makes it free from the prejudices that imprison it. What better remedy against sombreness and solitude, than pleasant conversation between kindred souls?

'And speaking of kindred souls, revered master, there are two learned men I would very much like you to meet. With your permission, I would like to invite you to an evening meal, where they could make your acquaintance. I am sure that it will be quite an interesting evening, for all of us!'

'Well, I always enjoy meeting new people and learning new things,' I said.

'My entire life has been devoted to study, and the more I have learned, the more I realise how precious little I know. I will therefore accept with both hands whatever new wisdom I can find! A Yahūdī[216] scholar from Tehrān once told me that their main book of learning—a compilation of thousands upon thousands of pages of commentaries called *Talmud*—has the first page missing; only to remind the scholars in all their haughtiness, that no matter how much knowledge they claim to have acquired, they have yet to arrive at page one! How true, how very true. . . .'

'Words of great wisdom, revered master!'

'Indeed . . . in fact, the older I get, the more I find that wisdom is everywhere – if only one cares to look! Now tell me, who are these two men you want me to meet?'

'Shaykh Mubārak of Nāgaur, and his younger son, Abū-l Fazl.'

'Mubārak, the father of Abū-l Faizī the poet? The man who was presented at the court after His Majesty's return from the first war in Gujarāt, through intercession of His Majesty's foster brother Azīz Koka?'

'Indeed, revered master. He seems to have made an excellent impression on the emperor. Do you know him, by any chance?'

'We have never spoken, but by reputation, I know him quite well. I hear he is a man of great learning. However, he got himself into serious trouble with Makhdūm-ul Mulk!'

'So? How did that happen?'

'Around the year 960, during the Afghān rule, Shaykh Mubārak, like so many others at that time, became convinced that with the approach of the thousandth year of the Hijrī Era, the advent of the glorious lord of the latter days, sāhab i zamān[217] imām mahdī, was, or is, imminent.'

'What is your opinion about that prophecy, revered master?'

'What shall I say? Only Allāh knows the truth. According to an oft-quoted prophecy, the latter days of Islām will be marked by a general decadence in faith and morals, until the advent of the imām mahdī, who will restore the true faith in its pristine glory. Through his profound teachings, every living human being will be led to true Islām, and

---

216. Yahudi: Jewish
217. Lord of the age

an empire of righteousness will be established, after which the day of judgement will dawn.

'I have to say, it is not altogether implausible to believe so. Leading collectors of the Hadīth, including Nisā'ī, Abū Da'ūd, Muslim, and Bayhaqī, have confirmed that the Prophet once said:

'"Muhammad Mahdī shall be of my family, and of the descendents of Fātima."[218]

'And Ahmad, Abū Da'ūd, Tirmizī, and Ibn Mājah, state that the prophet at some other time said:

'"When of time one day shall be left, Allāh shall raise up a man from among my descendents, who shall fill the world with justice, just as before him the world was full of oppression." And again, "The world shall not come to an end till the king of the earth shall appear, who is a man of my family, and whose name is the same as mine."

'Since a few decades, many people have started to believe that the coming of the mahdī is near. There are others who claim that he has already come into the world as the twelfth imām of the Shī'a, who mysteriously disappeared and is believed to lead a hidden existence since then. To be honest, I do not know what to believe about all this. I only know that since time immemorial, there have always been self-declared prophets from all creeds, claiming that the end of the world is near, and there have always been scores of people to follow them. Anyway, Shaykh Mubārak was among them. He became a follower of the infamous Shaykh Alā'ī.'

'Who was that, revered master?'

'Surely, you must have heard of him? He was one of the many mahdī preachers that appeared in Hindustān around that time. The son of a Bengālī teacher, a saintly man of great learning who had settled near Āgrā after his return from Mekkah, spending a life of teaching and prayer, Alā'ī himself clearly took after his father. Right from the early years of his youth, he appeared to combine the learning of a lawyer with the rigour of a saint. After his father's death, numerous pupils started gathering around him.

'Then, a few years later, under the influence of Mahdī teachings, he suddenly forsook all worldly goods, distributing all his possessions—even

---

218. Fātima: The Prophet's daughter; wife of Alī

his books!—among the poor, turned faqīr, and joined a wandering group of fanatics. The members of the fraternity gave up all work, as it is said in the Holy Qur'ān: "Let not men be allured by trade or selling to give up meditating on Allāh". They roamed the countryside, praying, preaching, and eking out their frugal meals in exchange for blessings.

'Every day, after each of the five obligatory prayers, they would be preaching in the villages, warning people about the end of time and the advent of the promised mahdī, urging them to repent and devote their lives entirely to god. Their ranks were increasing every day, and soon, they found themselves strong enough to interfere with municipal matters, inspecting the bāzārs, armed to the teeth, and removing by force all articles which they considered forbidden, in defiance of the local magistrates if necessary.

'Shaykh Alā'ī's dubious fame soon reached the ear of the Afghān king Islām Shāh, who summoned him to Āgrā. Although the king was resolved to put him to death as a dangerous hothead and ringleader, he became so charmed and impressed by Alā'ī's saintly words about the vanities of this world and the ignorance of those who call themselves learned, that he let him live. To the amusement of the nobles and generals at the court, Alā'ī effortlessly defeated and put to shame the court ulamā who tried to challenge him. Among his victims was even the great Makhdūm-ul Mulk himself! Alā'ī's reputation spread like wildfire, and day after day, new converts were joining him – among them, Shaykh Mubārak.

'However, Makhdūm-ul Mulk and the ulamā, who felt their positions threatened, refused to give up. After some time, they managed to convince the king that all these mahdī teachings were nothing but dangerous and sinful Shī'a heresy, utterly incompatible with established Sunnī doctrine. Before long, Alā'ī and his followers found themselves banished from the court, a command they made haste to obey, for the great king Islām Shāh was notorious for his severity, not to say cruelty, towards the enemies of the true faith.

'A few years passed by, when, rather unexpectedly, Islām Shāh found himself compelled to quell some disturbances in the Panjāb, and marched north. Up there, he again came across Shaykh Alā'ī. When the king saw him, he said: "Say that you recant, and I will not trouble you".

'But Alā'ī did not want to listen to reason, and started arguing against his sovereign, who, to keep up the appearance of authority, ordered him whipped. Rather unexpectedly, this mild punishment proved fatal to Alā'ī, who had been recovering from an attack of the plague. The whip ripped open one of the sores on his back. Only a few hours later, he died, burning with fever.

'The downfall of the troublemaker Alā'ī was a great victory for the court ulamā, and vigorous persecutions of all mahdī preachers and disciples was the result. The harassment abated after the return of Emperor Humāyūn, who always had shown much tolerance and sympathy towards Shī'a doctrines. After Lord Bairām Khān's downfall, however, the persecutions started again: Emperor Akbar was still young and inexperienced at the time, and in matters of law, he would unquestioningly defer to the opinion of the ulamā.

'Thus it came to pass that Makhdūm-ul Mulk, one afternoon, taking advantage of His Majesty's youthful inexperience, obtained from him an order to prosecute one Shaykh Mubārak—whom His Majesty did not know—as one of the worst mahdī heretics, an infidel who was not only damned himself, but led others into damnation.

'As I said, this is something the emperor would never allow to happen today. Ever since Makhdūm-ul Mulk tried to oppose him on the abolition of the jizya tax on Hindūs, he profoundly distrusts the ulamā, and has taken the administration of justice firmly into his own hands. He will never condemn anybody, unless he has personally been convinced by the evidence!

'Anyway, to continue my story: When Shaykh Mubārak heard about the new persecutions, he wisely decided to flee from Āgrā, leaving only a few humble belongings for his enemies to wreak their revenge on. In despair, he applied to Shaykh Salīm Chishtī of Sīkrī for protection, but the good shaykh, knowing the wickedness of men, wisely advised him to head further west, and to leave, for a while at least, His Majesty's dominions.

'Thus he did. He fled to Gujarāt, where he lived a simple and frugal, but satisfying, life in the company of the pious, earning a modest living as a teacher. After the conquest of Gujarāt by the imperial armies, however, Mubārak found himself again living within the borders of His Majesty's dominions. He decided not to flee again, but approached the newly appointed governor, His Majesty's foster-brother Mīrzā Azīz Koka. He told him the story of his life, and implored his good offices.

The generous-minded Governor Azīz Koka, convinced of Mubārak's innocence, provided him with a letter of introduction to the imperial court.

'That is when I saw Mubārak and his younger son for the first time in the flesh: during the audience in the diwān-i-ām. I must say, although His Majesty did not have much time, he seemed to be quite pleased and impressed with Mubārak's speech, and with young Abū-l Fazl's scholarship; and the fact that Makhdūm-ul Mulk hates them, is, I suspect, all the more reason for the emperor to be interested in them!'

'That is what I suspect as well, revered master. I have met them a couple of times, and they seem to be exactly the kind of people whose company the emperor enjoys: learned, intelligent, and free-thinking. I am convinced we have not seen the last of them at the court!'

'It would be interesting to make their acquaintance,' I said.

'It will be my pleasure to have this arranged,' he answered.

≈

That very same evening, he invited us to his residence.

The conversation started a bit stiffly, as can be expected when people meet each other for the first time, although Shaykh Mubārak went out of his way to please me and show his respect. In phrases most flowery, he rendered thanks to Allāh that He had preserved him to that day; that it was an honour, a pleasure, as well as a privilege to be allowed to pay his most humble respects to the man, nay, the mastermind, who had personally educated and formed the greatest monarch of all time; that I was the north star of the wise; the Aristatalis[219] of the Iskandar of the age; the beacon of wisdom guiding the ships of power, and many more words to that effect – all vastly exaggerated and quite undeserved, of course, but they pleased me more than I care to admit. Alas, even a supposedly wise old man cannot remain indifferent when his vanity is thus gratified. . . .

Under the influence of the late hour, the pleasant conversation between learned men of obviously kindred spirits, and a truly exquisite repast, washed down with many a beaker of ice-cooled wine—which, as

---

219. Aristatalis: Arabic for Aristoteles (Aristotle).

Hakīm Alī Gilanī kept assuring us, was medicine for elderly people and therefore not really harām—we soon found ourselves chatting with each other like old acquaintances. Although slightly inebriated, having drunk much more than I am accustomed to, I did not fail to notice how cleverly Hakīm Alī was steering the conversation towards the subject he knew I would find of great interest.

'I had an interesting discussion the other day, with an acquaintance of mine,' he said, 'about our emperor's remarkable—some would say, disturbing if not outrageous—tolerance towards the non-believers. Abolishing the jizya tax, building Hindū shrines in his palace for his Rājpūt wives, and the list goes on; people say he even worships the sun, like a superstitious pagan! No one dares to speak out openly of course, but many of the ulamā are whispering that the emperor has gone much, much too far – that he has actually forsaken his duty as a Muslim ruler! Tolerance is one thing, they say, but should a true Muslim not be promoting Islām, much more than he currently does? It would seem he actually favours the Hindūs above the true believers! One would almost say, he is turning pagan himself! Should a true Muslim not try to lead his fellow men to the one true path? Is it not every Muslim's task to encourage virtue and forbid the wrong? And is that not the very essence of a Muslim king's task?'

'This is all nonsense! Of course, the emperor is right to be so tolerant,' young Abū-l Fazl exclaimed with unexpected vehemence. 'In matters of religion, there should be no compulsion – the Holy Qur'ān says so explicitly,[220] and besides, is the cause of Islām not much better served by tolerance and kindness, than by repression? Islām is a religion of peace! Where possible, and unless we are forced to fight in self-defence, we Muslims should be at peace with the others; we should compete with them in holiness, justice and good deeds – that is by far the best way to win over new converts. According to the sixteenth Sūrah of the Holy Qur'ān, those who seek to please Allāh will be guided by Him to *paths of peace*! And let us not forget that as-salām, peace, is one of god's most beautiful names!'

---

220. Qur'ān, 2:256

'I wholeheartedly agree with you, my young friend,' I said, 'but what would be your answer to those who state that good Muslims should shun the company of infidels, lest they be led astray or confused with error?'

'There is no doubt in my mind,' answered Abū-l Fazl imperturbably, 'that the religion of Islām is the best and purest of all religions. In fact, it is the essence, the fulfilment and culmination of true religion! Nevertheless, we should remind ourselves that Allāh has allowed the other religions to exist, and that He has sent messengers to all the peoples of the earth. While all other religions are less pure than our own, we should not forget that divine revelation is at their origin, and we should not be surprised to find people among them, who, by divine mercy, have attained the highest degrees of wisdom and holiness!'

'Is it your opinion that there are infidels who will be allowed to enter paradise?'

'It is, revered master. In fact, I am convinced that ultimately, everybody will attain paradise – Muslims and non-Muslims alike!'

'Even idolaters, guilty of shirk?[221] Even atheists, who have denied Allāh's existence?'

'Even they.'

'And what would you say to those who disagree with you, quoting the words of the Holy Qur'ān itself: Verily! Allāh forgives not the sin of setting up partners in worship with Him, but He forgives whom He pleases, sins other than that; and whoever sets up partners in worship with Allāh, has indeed strayed far away?[222] And what to think of the stern warning in Āyāt 91 of the third Sūrah: Verily, as for those who are bent on denying the truth – not all the gold in the world could ever be their ransom! It is they for whom grievous suffering is in store; and they shall have none to succour them?[223] Is it not written that shirk is the gravest of all sins, that no sin surpasses it in terms of gravity, severity and enormity? Is it not written that to lead a virtuous life is of no avail to those who commit shirk? Is it not written that Allāh may pardon all

---

221. Shirk: Polytheism; belief in more than one god.
222. Qur'ān, 4:116
223. Qur'ān, 3:91

His servants' transgressions, but their refusal to submit to Him and Him alone, never?'

Abū-l Fazl's expression remained unperturbed.

'Exactly! All this is of course true, but it really concerns those who consciously, knowingly and willingly reject Allāh, not those who have merely erred in good faith, nor those who repent. And sooner or later, even for the greatest sinner, there comes a time when he will see the error of his ways, repent for his sins, and attain salvation!'

I was growing more and more fond of this bright young man. Still, I wanted to put him further to the test.

'And how, my young friend, do you reconcile what you just said with the fourth Sūrah, Āyāt four and fourteen? Is it not written that Allāh leads astray whom He pleases and guides whom He pleases; He is the mighty, the wise,[224] and that He leads the wrongdoers astray; Allāh does whatever He pleases?[225]

Young Abū-l Fazl was still not in the least impressed. He merely smiled and said:

'Revered master, you touch upon a much-debated, thorny question indeed: How to reconcile Allāh's omnipotence, His omniscience, His providence, His justice, and His mercy? Learned men of all generations—including the four of us present here tonight—no doubt, have agonised over this problem: On the one hand, Allāh is omniscient; He knows the past, the present, and the future; He therefore knows in advance whether a person will sin or not. He is also omnipotent, and therefore, nothing comes to pass, unless He wills it. But if He knows everything beforehand, and if nothing in this world happens unless He wills it, does this not imply that He actually *causes* evil; that He actually *wants* people to sin; in fact, that He has created many of them, merely for the purpose of punishing them in all eternity?

'On the other hand, however: How can that be compatible with His divine justice and mercy? How can it be called just, to punish an impotent, helpless creature, that has done nothing else than what it was predestined to do?'

---

224. Qur'ān, 4:4
225. Qur'ān, 4:27

He paused and looked at me.

'Go on, my learned young friend – I am very interested to hear what you have to say about this!'

'A paragon of wisdom and learning like yourself, revered master, is of course well-acquainted, much more than an inexperienced student like myself could ever be, with all the subtleties, complexities and intricacies of the debates between the various schools of falsafah: the Murjites, who set faith above works and emphasise the divine love and goodness; the Qadarites, who affirm, and the Jabarites who deny, that men are responsible for their actions; the Mu'tazilites, who build their theology on the basis of reason, rejecting the qualities of Allāh as incompatible with His unity, and predestination as contrary to His justice; and finally the Ash'arites, the classical scholars of what many consider to be orthodox Islām, who have formulated the doctrinal system that underlies the creed of most men of the law like Makhdūm-ul Mulk.[226]

'However subtle all their lines of reasoning, all these different schools have, in the end, managed to come up with only two answers to the seemingly unsolvable problem of evil in a world created by an almighty and good god: Either that we have an inadequate understanding of divine justice; or that we underestimate god's compassion and mercy. Either we believe that god exercises jabr, absolute compulsion; or we accept that He has given us tafwīd, delegation of power and responsibility. Personally, I vastly prefer the latter solution!'

He paused. I noticed how his father was smiling and nodding in approval.

'As far as the first group is concerned,' he continued, 'there are, indeed, many scholars who emphasise the inescapability of god's inscrutable will. Their reasoning is clear enough: Allāh can do what He pleases, and everything He wills, comes to pass. Therefore, everything in this world, good and evil, must exist by His will – the faith of the believer, as well as the irreligion of the wicked. As it is said in the *Mishkātu'l Masābī*,[227] with bone-chilling clarity: When Allāh resolved to create the human race, He

---

226. Reynold A. Nicholson, *The Mystics of Islam*, pp. 5-6.
227. *The Niche for Lamps*, a well-known compilation of Sunnī tradition, based on the work (AH 737) of Shaykh Walīyu-ud-dīn and Imām Husain al Baghawī.

took into His hands a mass of Earth, the same whence all mankind were to be formed, and in which they after a matter pre-existed; and having then divided the clod into two equal portions, He threw the one half into hell, saying, "These to eternal fire; and I care not"; and projecting the other half into heaven, adding, "And these to paradise; I care not."'

He paused again, slowly shaking his head.

'But what kind of paradise would that be? What kind of justice? What kind of divine compassion and mercy? There would be no virtue, no wickedness, no acts good or reprehensible, no true punishment or reward; only the arbitrary, inescapable will of a stern, inscrutable god, who takes pleasure in burning one individual for all eternity, amidst red-hot chains and seas of molten iron, and granting another the bliss of eternal paradise, just because He wills it? No, that is impossible! That is not the infinitely good god Who has spoken to us in the Holy Qur'ān!'

He stopped speaking, apparently awaiting my reaction. I nodded encouragingly.

'Go on, my young friend; what is the solution to this problem, according to you?'

'I have given this much thought, revered master, and I have come to the conclusion that the key to understanding this transient world and the Qur'ānic message, lies with the concepts of divine mercy, and human freedom!'

'What do you mean?'

'Allāh is the compassionate and merciful lord of the worlds; every creature enjoys His divine rubūbiyat,[228] in accordance with its own nature. On every single one of them rests the protective eye of Allāh's providence, and there is none who is denied His blessings![229]

'Us, human beings, Allāh has graciously put at the head of His magnificent creation, and moreover, He has blessed us with the most precious of gifts – reason and freedom! We can decide for ourselves what kind of person we will be! All the faculties with which we have been endowed are but weak and imperfect reflections of the perfect and infinite

---

228. Rubūbiyat: Providence (literally: tender and caring nourishment).
229. Quote from Mawlana Abul Kazam Azad's *Opening Chapter of the Qur'ān*, (transl. Syed Abdul-Latīf), ed. Islamic Book Trust, Kuala Lumpur, 2001, pp. 20-21.

attributes of the divine being. Of course, circumstances must determine the extent of our responsibility, which may be almost negligible in some cases, and extremely grave in others, but anyhow, we have been given a choice to decide.

'No, Allāh does not cause us to sin, He merely allows us to do so. All the Qur'ānic references to god's "letting man go astray", in my opinion, have to be understood against the background of what is written in the second Sūrah, Āyāt 26 and 27: None does He cause to go astray save the iniquitous, who break their bond with god. Is it not written, in Āyāt 44 of the tenth Sūrah, that Allāh does not wrong mankind at all, but mankind wrongs itself? Is it not written, in Āyāt 182 of the third Sūrah, that Allāh is not in the least unjust to the servants?

'No, god does not forsake anyone, except those who actually *choose* to be forsaken; that is to say, those who consciously, knowingly and willingly decide to reject Him.'

I could not help smiling and nodding approvingly. This wise young man had come to exactly the same conclusion as I had, so many years ago.

'And those who refused to worship Him during their lives? Those who adored idols? Those who have denied god's existence?'

'As soon as they see their errors and regret them, they will be forgiven,' Abū-l Fazl answered without hesitation.

He looked at me, verifying the effect of his words. His quick, beady, black little eyes seemed to be piercing right into the depths of my soul.

'Allāh will accept everyone,' he continued, 'even those who have nothing to offer Him but their desire to be saved. And sooner or later, even the most obstinate, unrepentant sinner will see the light and will thus be saved! Indeed, in the words of the Holy Qur'ān Itself: Allāh has ordained mercy on Himself!![230] Even the worst of sinners should not despair of the mercy of Allāh![231] For mercy did He create all men[232]!

'I once heard a Sūfī preaching,' Abū-l Fazl continued, 'in a way of reasoning quite similar to that of the Hindūs. He said that since Allāh is the one and only ultimate reality, the human soul is necessarily

---

230. Qur'ān, 6:12,54
231. Qur'ān, 39:53
232. Qur'ān, 11:119

an integral part of that divine reality. Human souls are part of god, but have become separated from it at birth – in the same way that a splashing drop of water is, for a brief moment, separated from the ocean it came from. The drop is still essentially the same as the ocean, it still consists of the same water, and yet, it utterly lacks the ocean's awesome power and majesty, because it has become separated from it: "Seventy thousand veils," said the Sūfī, "separate Allāh, the one reality, from the world of matter and sense. And every soul passes, before its birth, through these seventy thousand. The inner half of them are veils of light; the outer half, veils of darkness. For every one of the veils of light passed through, in this journey towards birth, the soul puts off a divine quality; and for every one of the dark veils, it puts on an earthly quality. Thus the child is born weeping, for its soul remembers its separation from Allāh, the ultimate reality. And when the child cries in its sleep, it is because its soul remembers something of what it has lost. Otherwise, the passage through the veils has brought with it forgetfulness (nisyān); and for this reason man is called insān. He is now, as it were, in prison in his own body, separated from Allāh by these thick curtains."[233]

'Verily, Allāh has blessed you with much wisdom and a brilliant mind, my young friend,' I said to the young man I now knew would soon become my successor as the emperor's closest confidant; 'I will put in a good word for you with the emperor.'

≈

It is hot and sticky in the room; that wretched pain in my wrist and fingers is back, and it is almost unbearable. Breathing is painful and tiresome; it feels as if someone has put a heavy stone on my chest.

It will not be long now – not more than a few days. The time has come to put down the qalam, and await what is to come, in prayerful resignation.

---

233. After a quote from a Rifā'ī dervish cited by W.H.T. Gairdner, *'The Way' of a Mohammedan Mystic*, (Leipzig, 1912); quoted by Reynold A. Nicholson, *The Mystics of Islam*, (London, 1914, republished by Arkana, London 1989, pp. 15-16).

May the lord of all worlds have mercy on this poor old man, and may He grant wisdom to those who remain behind. Soon, old Mīr Abdul Latīf will be no more. His soul will effortlessly glide back through the seventy thousand veils, and beatifically succumb to the ultimate reality behind them. Gone will be all the delusions that have kept it prisoner in this transient world; gone will be, in the first place, its own self. Nothing of him will remain behind in the world of the living – nothing, but a few words, and a name.

> *The flower of yore, withered in the sands:*
> *As name only it stands;*
> *A naked name is what remains the bereft,*
> *Naked names is all we have left.*[234]

---

234. Stat rosa pristina nomine; nomina nuda tenemus: The closing words of Eco's *Nome della Rosa*.

Twenty-eighth Letter

بنگال، موار

Bengāl, Mewār

As I already mentioned to you in the twenty-sixth letter, my son, Gujarāt was not fully mine yet, when the situation in the east, in Bengāl and Bihār more in particular, suddenly demanded my urgent attention.

Up to that moment, those territories had never been a primary concern of mine. Traditionally, they had always been more or less dependent on the sultāns of Dillī, and that situation did not change when I came to power and defeated Sikandar Sūr: The Sūrs who ruled over Bengāl made haste to swear allegiance to me.

In the ninth year of my reign, power in Bengāl was seized by the Afghān Tāj Khān Karanānī, a former army leader of Shēr Khān Sūr; however, both he and his successor and younger brother Sulaimān, were wise and prudent enough never to provoke me, and fully recognised my authority. All over Bengāl, the khutba was read and coins were struck in my name, and sumptuous gifts were sent to the imperial court on a regular basis.

However, when Sulaimān died—'much regretted by his subjects,' the chroniclers say—the problems started. Sulaimān's elder son Bāyazīd, who had succeeded him, was murdered a few months later by Afghān army leaders, who raised his treacherous younger brother Dā'ūd to the throne.

Dā'ūd, 'a dissolute scamp who knew nothing of kingship', as one chronicler fittingly described him, thus inherited his father's vast treasure and powerful army, but alas, not his wisdom. Taking advantage of my absence, he forsook the prudence of his predecessors, and shamelessly assumed all the dignities of independent royalty, ordering coin to be stamped and the khutba to be read in his own name. Soon, he pushed the insolence even further, attacking and destroying the imperial frontier fort of Zamānīyā in the Ghāzīpūr district.

When I heard about these intolerable disturbances, I ordered Mun'im Khān, who had stayed behind in Āgrā during my absence, to chastise the rebel forthwith.

Mun'im Khān hastily assembled a striking force and marched east, towards Patna. After the first skirmishes, however, he was approached by Dā'ūd's chief minister Lodī Khān, who, with lavish gifts, flowery compliments and solemn oaths of friendship and submission, sought to placate him. Old Mun'im Khān, well in his seventies and weary of the hardships of travelling, was more than glad to end hostilities, and granted peace on exceedingly lenient terms.

When I heard the news, I immediately decided to send the more level-headed Todar Mal with additional reinforcements. I imagine that Mun'im Khān did not appreciate the covert reproach I thus made him, but I thought it necessary, and alas, I was soon proven right: Dā'ūd, demonstrating the viciousness of his nature, rewarded his faithful minister by confiscating his goods and having him executed, and entrenched himself in the fortress of Patna. We had to start all over again.

Mun'im Khān, ashamed and angered, laid siege to the city. Soon thereafter, however, fearing that he would provoke my anger if the siege dragged out too long and realising that his force was not quite up to the task, he sent a message, imploring me to take personal charge of the campaign.

So I did. On the fourth of Tīr of the nineteenth year,[235] I left Āgrā at the head of a powerful army, accompanied by excellent army leaders like Rājā Bhagwān Dās and Mān Singh. The monsoon season being at its height, the rivers were dangerously swollen. In order not to waste any

---

235. Tuesday, 15 June 1574 (Julian calendar)

time, I insisted on travelling by boat – this would enable us to speedily transport the cannons and other heavy material, which otherwise would have got stuck in the mud of the rain-soaked roads.

Twenty-six days later, I reached Vārānasī, where I stayed for three days, deeply fascinated, once more, by this ultimate fusion of sublimity and horror – one big tangle of death, decay, depravation, holiness, beauty, fragrance, stench, all blended together. Heavenly and hellish, fascinating and repulsive, strange and familiar at the same time – the strange, noisy rituals; the colourful, swarming mass of pilgrims, priests and holy men; the ominous smell of funeral pyres mingling with the fragrance of incense; and next to all this frantic busyness, the eternal, unperturbed tranquility and majesty of the golden Gaṅgā. . . .

I proceeded from Vārānasī and anchored near Sayyidpūr, where the Gumti River flows into the Gaṅgā. On the same day, we were joined by the rest of the army, which had travelled by land. The ladies and children were escorted to Jaunpūr, while I advanced at the head of the army to the infamous ferry at Chausa, where, thirty-five years before, my father had been defeated by Shēr Khān Sūr. This time, however, the omens were better, for upon arrival, I received a dispatch, announcing that the fortress of Bhakkar in Sind had just been added to my dominions.

Apart from the sad loss of one of my most exquisite prize elephants, we managed to bring the army safely across to the southern bank of the river, and we proceeded to Patna, where we arrived on the twenty-second of Tīr.[236]

It must have been a painful surprise to Dā'ūd, to suddenly see the imperial army, complete with heavy cannons and war elephants, setting up camp near his gates. Never before in the history of Hindustān had a major battle been fought in the middle of the monsoon: It was thought impossible for a large army to cover any large distances before the beginning of the month of Ābān.[237] And yet, there I was . . . god favours those who act, my son!

After careful scouting of the surroundings, I decided to first reduce the small fortress of Hājīpūr on the other side of the river, as this

---

236. Saturday, 3 July 1574
237. Ābān: The Persian solar month of Scorpio (23 October – 22 November)

appeared to be of importance to the supply of the enemy garrison. The detachment I sent to accomplish this task did excellent work. Despite the difficulties caused by the wild and dangerous river—over one kos wide in that season!—and the tough resistance of the defending Afghān garrison, our men successfully stormed the fort. The heads of the enemy leaders were thrown into a boat and brought back to me, and I of course did not fail to forward them to Dā'ūd, 'as a hint of the fate that awaited and in due course befell him', as a chronicler so aptly put it. With the heads, I sent Dā'ūd a personal message, challenging him to meet me in a man-to-man combat.

As I expected, the coward did not have the guts. That same night, he and his garrison sneaked out of the city and fled, as fast as they could, back to Bengāl. I pursued the fugitives myself, all the way up to Daryāpūr. Regrettably, they managed to escape, but we did return with a fabulous amount of booty, including 265 prize elephants.

With Patna and Bihār now firmly under control, I decided to return to Dillī, leaving an army of twenty thousand under Mun'im Khān and Todar Mal to complete the annexation of Bengāl. The towns of Sūrajgarh, Monghyr, Bhāgalpūr and Kahalgām fell in quick succession, and after our scouts had taken out the enemy defences, Mun'im Khān marched triumphantly through the fortified Teliyāgarhī Pass, right into the Bengālī capital Tāndā, which he took, with little enemy resistance, on the thirteenth of Mehr.[238] Dā'ūd now left Bengāl and fled into Urīsā, while our forces continued their advance, easily establishing imperial authority in Sātgāon, Ghorāghāt and Burdwan.

After some months, however, tensions were starting to grow in our camp. The soldiers, exhausted after such a long and strenuous campaign in the heat and humidity of the Bengālī marshes, were dying to get back home, and the morale among the army leaders was not much better. Todar Mal had the greatest difficulties to convince the aged and weary Mun'im Khān to leave the relative comfort of the Bengālī capital and pursue the campaign into Urīsā.

Through his informants, Dā'ūd must have heard about the growing battle-weariness and discord in his opponent's army. He saw his chance

---

238. 25 September 1574

and marched against our slowly advancing troops, his army clashing with ours near the village of Tukaroi, three-and-a-half kos south-east of Dāntān in the Midnapūr district.

Unfortunately, Mun'im Khān found himself compelled to engage before he was fully ready for the battle. The result was that his fighting force, consisting almost entirely of cavalry, had far too few cannons to support it. Dā'ūd's general, Gujar Khān, cleverly exploited this, and opened the battle with a massive elephant charge. His strategy very nearly worked: Our vanguard and centre were completely scattered by the irresistible mass of charging elephants; one of our senior commanders was killed, and Mun'im Khān himself, severely wounded, barely escaped with his life.

Defeat would have been inevitable, had it not been for Todar Mal's tenacity and skill. Leading our left wing, he wheeled around the flanks of the attacking elephants, killing several enemy mahāwats and wounding many of their elephants. He then fell on the enemy with such vehemence that their right wing was routed and driven off. The rest of our troops now took heart, regrouped and launched an all-out attack on the Afghān centre and right flank.

The death of the enemy general, Gujar Khān, decided the battle; the Afghāns fled in disarray, and our men, eager to avenge the losses they had sustained at the onset, pursued and slaughtered them by the hundreds. To paraphrase Abū-l Fazl's words, Mun'im Khān's wounds and lacerations were healed by the balm of conquest. He ordered all the prisoners to be brought before him, and had their bodies separated from their souls; the collected heads, so I was told, served to build eight sky-high minarets on the battlefield.

Dā'ūd and the surviving Afghāns fled to the fort of Katak,[239] where, on the first of Ordībehesht of the twentieth year, coinciding with the first of Muharram of 983,[240] he made his submission to Mun'im Khān, handing over his nephew as a hostage.

Once again, Mun'im Khān, eager to put an end to the strenuous campaign, allowed himself to be talked around, and again, Dā'ūd got

---

239. Katak: Cuttack
240. 12 April 1575

away with overly generous peace terms, including the governorship over much of Urīsā.

Todar Mal, smelling deceit and foul play, openly opposed the treaty and refused to sign it. Alas, he would soon be proven right.

A few weeks later, Mun'im Khān headed north, to quell some disturbances in the Ghorāghāt region. Ignoring the advice of his officers, he insisted on moving his capital from Tāndā to the ancient capital Gaur, which, so he had heard, abounded with the finest buildings. Unfortunately, the persistent rumours about pestilence in that region proved to be true. Hundreds of officers and men perished – so many of them that the living no longer bothered to bury the dead, and just threw their comrades' corpses in the river.

Mun'im Khān, gravely ill himself, retreated back to Tāndā, only to die upon arrival. May god almighty receive him in His mercy!

Pending the arrival of new instructions, the officers appointed a new leader among themselves. The new commander, however, was not strong enough to maintain discipline. Everybody only thought of getting his booty out of pestilent Bengāl as soon as possible. In utter indiscipline, the army retreated to Bhāgalpūr in Bihār.

The treacherous Dā'ūd, who, owing to Mun'im Khān's ill-considered leniency, had been left in command of substantial forces, did not scruple to again take advantage of the situation and reoccupied the whole of Bengāl, including Tāndā and the Teliyāgarhī pass. It was his last and fatal mistake.

When I got word of this vexing news, I sent Khān Jahān, governor of the Panjāb, to deal with the situation. At Bhāgalpūr, he intercepted the retreating Bengālī army. With the able help of Rājā Todar Mal, who had arrived from Fatehpūr Sīkrī carrying my personal instructions, he managed to bring the men back to their duty.

Khān Jahān invaded Bengāl and, to Dā'ūd's surprise and dismay, quickly recovered the important Teliyāgarhī pass. Joining forces with Muzaffar Khān, governor of Bihār, he gave battle to the enemy near Āk Mahal or Rājmahal as it is now called, and after a pitched battle, defeated and captured him.

This time, Dā'ūd's promises and pleadings were to no avail. When I was barely one day's march outside of Fatehpūr—I had decided to travel to Bengāl and take personal charge of the campaign—I had the great pleasure of receiving my enemy's severed head. I had it put on a stake, and returned in triumph to the capital, where great feasts were organised, and, to put it in Abū-l Fazl's words, 'waves of largesse quenched the thirst of the needy'.

Bengāl was finally mine – although I must confess that imperial authority remained confined mainly to the cities. On the countryside, local Hindū and Afghān landlords would, to a large extent, continue to lay down the law for many more years. Indeed, it would be in those accursed, bug-infested marshes that only a few years later, the most dangerous rebellion against my authority would break out.

≈

Before Dā'ūd finally met his doom at Rājmahal, I also found myself compelled to deal once more with my old enemy, the rānā of Mewār.

As you know, after the fall of Chittor, the coward Uday Singh had fled to the Arāvallī hills, where he set up a new capital and ruled the surroundings. I had let him be – at the time, the conquest of wealthy Gujarāt was of much greater importance and urgency to me. Of what use would it have been, to waste more blood, treasure, and above all, time, on the conquest of an isolated hill range of little or no value, when my troops could go unhindered wherever I wished to send them? Thus, I had allowed Uday Singh to live undisturbed in his hills, and he meekly stayed there until his death, without giving us any further trouble.

Regrettably, however, his son and successor Pratāp, had inherited more of the pride and the fighting spirit of his forefathers. As the chronicler phrased it, race feeling taught him to hate the foreigners, ancestral pride to despise them, and high martial spirit, his grandfather's legacy, to resist them. Slowly but surely, he started to recover some of the land that once had belonged to his ancestors. It is true that without Chittor and the other fortresses, he was nothing more than a local nuisance; nevertheless, I thought it prudent to deal with him before he could pose any serious threat.

Towards the end of Farvardīn of the twenty-first year, early Muharram of 984,[241] I sent Rājā Mān Singh with an army from Ājmīr. Three months

---

241. April 1576

later, on the tenth of Tīr,[242] their advance was opposed by Pratāp's forces at the entry of the Haldīghāt Pass.

Truth be told, Pratāp and his men fought with remarkable valour. Wave upon wave, clan upon clan charged the imperial lines with utter contempt of death. But despite their bravery and the few hundred casualties they managed to inflict on us, they were no match for the firepower of the imperial army with its many field cannons and gun swivels, mounted on the backs of camels and elephants. Pratāp, though seriously wounded, managed to escape to the hills, saved by his swift and faithful steed Chetak, and the exhausted imperial cavalry horses were unable to catch him.

Despite the victory, I was very vexed when I learned that Pratāp had managed to escape. Alas, I was right. Although he was forced to retire deep in the wilderness, and one by one, his strong places fell into our hands, later in his life, during the thirteen years that I was obliged to transfer my capital up north to the Panjāb, he again managed to recover much of his lost territory.

Even today—due to your culpable laziness and disobedience, as you well know, Salīm!—his son Amar Singh has yet to be brought to heel. It is time you took care of this matter for good, my son. The rānā of Mewār may, as I said before, be nothing to us, nothing more than a nuisance, a gadfly, a small stone in our boot, annoying enough to make itself felt from time to time, but not enough to bother to stop and get rid of it; but his insolence is a stain on our armour, an insult to our honour. It is about time we dealt with them, my son. Promise me, that in due time, you will.

---

242. 21 June 1576

Twenty-ninth Letter

إبادت خانه

Ibādat-Khāna (I)

Supreme lord and master of a vast and mighty empire, stretching from mountains to mountains and from ocean to ocean, with no one left to challenge me, and therefore no need to busy myself with my army's smaller campaigns, I now enjoyed a period of relative calm. Outside of the many hours I still kept scrupulously devoting each day to the affairs of state, I finally found the leisure to occupy myself with my favourite pastime – religion, falsafah, and Kalām.[243] I ordered the construction, on the palace grounds, of the ibādat-khāna or house of worship, a sacred meeting place dedicated solely to the study of god, where the most learned scholars of Hindustān and beyond would be invited to join me in learned reflection on the divine mysteries.

What was I hoping for? That every religious divide would be bridged by respectful dialogue? That the light of reason would erase all differences? If I ever did, it did not take me long to awaken from that dream. . . . As Hakīm Alī Gilanī put it so perspicaciously in the notes you are about

---

243. Kalām: Theology, the study of god and the divine attributes. Literally, kalām means 'speech', hence ilm al-Kalām, the study of divine speech, i.e. the science of the knowledge of god, His eternal attributes, His word, His power, etc.

to read, my son, I could, and maybe should, have known that his entire effort, however praiseworthy the motives behind it, was doomed to failure: Far from uniting people's views, the debates seemed to merely exacerbate the existing differences. In the end, the open-minded did become more enlightened, the tolerant more tolerant; but the bigots, even more hostile and fanatic.

In spite of their sad failure, however, the debates in the ibādat-khāna proved to be of paramount importance in the history of the empire, and you would be wise, my son, to study them carefully! Observe, my son, how an innocent quest for religious truth quickly turns into a thinly veiled, most bitter row over the very foundation of our kingship; and observe, my son, how my and your throne is built, to no small extent, on the labour of those two people you seem to respect so little – the erudite old Shaykh Mubārak and his brilliant son Abū-l Fazl.

≈

From the private notes of Mulāzim Hakīm Alī Gilanī, Jālīnūs-uz-Zamānī, personal physician of His Majesty the Emperor

Much has been said, and no doubt, will be said, about our beloved emperor's religious convictions and policies. A man's inner beliefs remain a matter between him and Allāh, unless and until, through his own words and deeds, he makes them a public issue. All the more so, when the man in question is no one other than the emperor himself!

Whatever people may have to say about His Majesty's orthodoxy, no one can deny that he is, and always has been, an honest, god-fearing seeker of the truth; and since he is an honest *seeker* of the truth, rather than one who claims to have found it, he is tolerant of, and interested in, all creeds and opinions, and fond of the company of the wise, be they Muslim faqīrs, Hindū yogīs, or whatever other kind of sage or priest. 'A king, yet the slave of dervishes', is what he likes to call himself.

From his father Humāyūn, who profoundly disliked the strife between the Sunnī and Shī'a sects, he inherited a profound distrust of all kinds of fanaticism and bigotry. This innate pragmatism has strongly been encouraged and further developed by his wise teacher, the right honourable and greatly lamented Mīr Abdul Latīf. It was indeed wise old Mīr Abdul Latīf—may Allāh be well pleased with him—who taught His Majesty that a king's primary duty is to ensure sulh-i-kul, peace and prosperity for all his subjects, and that the cause of Islām is usually much better served through peace and tolerance, than by the sword.

It was no great surprise to me, thus, when in the month of Ramadān of 982,[244] His Majesty suddenly issued orders for the construction of the ibādat-khāna. The best and brightest minds of the empire would be invited to that sacred place, to join their emperor in pious and learned discussions on the divine mysteries and man's duties towards the creator.

The new building was to be erected in the palace gardens, near the former abode of Shaykh Salīm Chishtī; more precisely, at the spot that had been the dwelling of one of the Shaykh's most prominent disciples, the renowned ascetic Abdullāh Niyāzī of Sirhind. The emperor ordered the ruined hermitage to be rebuilt, and a domed hall, of considerable dimensions and graced by appropriate ornaments, as described by a chronicler, to be built around it.

At the outset, only Muslims were invited to the debates. There were four groups of them, to wit: the amīrs or leading nobles of the empire; the ulamā, learned specialists of Sharī'ah law; the sayyids, descendants of the Holy Prophet Muhammad through his daughter Fātimah and Ali—may Allāh be well pleased with them; and finally, to phrase it in the words of Abū-l Fazl: 'Sūfīs of clear heart, absorbed in beatific visions': a diverse group of shaykhs, faqīrs and other holy men, who by virtue of their ascetic and pious life, their prayers and studies, were reputed to have attained a special communion with god.

At first, everybody was allowed to go and sit wherever he pleased in the building. This state of affairs, however, led to such acrimonious, not to say ignoble, quarrels over who should take precedence over whom, that quite soon, the emperor found himself obliged to assign separate quarters to each group: the shaykhs were to sit in the northern section;

---

244. January 1575

the southern side was reserved for the ulamā; the sayyids sat west, and the amīrs, east.

Evil tongues say that it was then and there, in the course of those heated debates that the emperor lost his faith and ceased to be a Muslim. That is blatant nonsense – His Majesty never renounced Islām, neither publicly nor privately. His complete and utter devotion to god is undeniable. The truth of the matter is that throughout his life, he has become more and more profoundly convinced that in the eyes of Allāh, *all* religions lead to Him. As a result of that, he has always been a generous supporter of religious devotion in all its expressions – Islām in the first place. How else is it to be explained, that he allowed his favourite wife, her highness Salīmā Sultānā Bēgam, his aunt Gulbadan and several other highborn ladies of the imperial family to leave the safety of the court for several years and undertake the hazardous voyage to Mekkah? That he revered with such deep respect and devotion the Prophet Muhammad's petrified footprint, which the ladies brought back to the court upon their return? That he desperately yearned to become a Hajjī[245] himself, and could only be persuaded with great difficulty that god required him to stay with his subjects? That he donated such large sums of money from the imperial treasury, to pay for the pilgrimage of poor Muslims who lacked the means to pay for the voyage themselves? No, the emperor never abandoned Islām, and never ceased to be what he has always been – an exceptionally pious devotee to the almighty.

It is true, though, that the debates in the ibādat-khāna did change him profoundly, in more ways than one. It was there that his personal outlook on religion took its final shape – remarkably tolerant and freethinking, bordering on the downright heretical. Those personal views and insights, in turn, ended up estranging him completely from religious authority in general, and from the court ulamā in particular.

As a privileged witness of—and at times an active participant in— these discussions, I believe I do have an unbiased view of His Majesty's personal views. Following the example of my deeply regretted master and friend Mīr Abdul Latīf, I have decided to describe them as honestly and accurately as possible: the Testimony of an honest eyewitness may

---

245. Hajjī: Person who has completed the Hajj or sacred pilgrimage to Mecca.

be of importance to posterity, and in fact, I believe it is actually what His Majesty is expecting from me.

I remember as if it was only yesterday that late afternoon, a few days after the demise of my old friend Mīr Abdul Latīf. Having obtained a private interview with the emperor, I had presented him with his old teacher's private diaries. Even more enthused and interested than I had expected, he immediately cancelled all other activities scheduled for that day, and urged me to start reading.

He listened with undivided attention, at times amused and visibly flattered by his teacher's praise for his astuteness, wisdom and nobility of character, at times moved to tears by the memory of his old friend.

'How good it is to be able to listen to him once more!' he sighed, wiping the tears from his eyes. 'It is as if he is actually reaching out to us from yonder side of the grave, to endow us with his wisdom and guidance!'

He took the papers in both hands, kissed them, and held them to his forehead, as the most sacred of writings.

'Never in my life have I regretted this much that I never learned to read myself,' he continued after a pause, wiping his eyes and looking at the closely written pages. 'How fascinating is the world of writing! Is it not like a sort of heaven, where the thoughts of the dead are preserved, even if their authors are long gone; where their wisdom is held in safekeeping, in hallowed silence, at the disposal of the living for guidance and inspiration?'

He paused, staring again at the papers with glazed eyes.

'I only wish there was someone to continue Mīr Abdul Latīf's memoirs,' he said, without looking at me or even raising his eyes from the papers.

'I know,' he continued, still talking more to himself than to anyone else, 'the imperial court has its own scribes, but official chronicles are not the same than the candid observations of an honest and astute observer . . .'

'Forgive me, honourable Hakīm Alī,' he said, suddenly raising his head after another long silence, as if awakening from a dream. 'We will need to continue this conversation some other time. There are a few urgent matters I need to attend to with Rājā Todar Mal.'

He thanked me again for my visit and bade me a good and restful night – the audience was over. Mumbling words of gratitude and respect,

I bowed myself out of the room and retired to my quarters, not daring to ask whether I had to take his final observation as an order, a personal request, or a casual remark.

That same night, I started taking these notes, with the intention of presenting them to His Majesty at an appropriate occasion.

That moment, I believe, has arrived. Two days from now, we will be celebrating His Majesty's fortieth solar birthday,[246] an age at which it is appropriate to take stock of one's life, to look back at what is in the past, and to make plans for the remaining years ahead. I have no doubt, it will appeal to His Majesty's pensive nature.

So many things have happened in those nine years since Mīr Abdul Latīf's passing! The arrival at the court of those two insolent firanghī priests; the acrimonious squabbles between lawyers, priests, sages and hermits of all sorts; the covert but growing opposition of the ulamā, and the masterstroke, with which the emperor managed to rein in their power; the Bengālī uprising and Muhammad Hakīm's invasion, when suddenly, the mighty throne of Hindustān seemed to be shaking to its foundations; His Majesty's brilliant campaign and easy triumph, followed by a series of bewildering innovations: a new calendar, far-reaching new laws on religious freedom; and then finally, the creation of a new religious society – many people say, an entirely new religion, a religion that aspires to replace or unite all others. . . .

What to think of all this? Amidst all this confusion, it is good to pause for a while, and examine these remarkable occurrences in their proper perspective.

≈

Where to begin? I have always had a lively interest in falsafah and religion; I have read extensively on the subject; I pride myself to be one of the few of my classmates who managed to learn the entire Qur'ān by heart by the time we were fifteen, but I can by no means pretend to be an expert on either law or tradition. I have chosen the path of science. From a tender age, it has been my calling to study the wonders of god's creation, and to put to use whatever modest knowledge and skill

---

246. Sunday, 11 November 1582

I managed to acquire, in the fight against disease and human suffering. I neither have the ambition, nor the ability, to recount and discuss in exhaustive detail all the matters that were discussed; yet, it would be wrong to underestimate their significance, and I will try to summarise them to the best of my abilities.

I of course do not know all of what His Majesty's expectations were when he decided to have these wretched debates organised. To a certain extent, it was a personal pastime: It amused him to invite learned men to debate in his presence, just like he could have ordered dancing girls, musicians or acrobats to perform before him.

But it was much more than a whim or intellectual entertainment. It was, on the one hand, a pious god-seeker's honest attempt to attain a deeper understanding of the object of his veneration; and it was, on the other hand, an emperor's attempt to strengthen his empire, for indeed, I believe His Majesty harboured the secret hope that under his mediation, all religions would be united or at least reconciled.

In the latter ambition, he was bound to be sadly disappointed. Far from uniting people's views, the debates seemed to merely exacerbate the existing differences. In the end, the open-minded did become more enlightened, the tolerant more tolerant; but the bigots, even more hostile and fanatic.

In hindsight, His Majesty could and maybe should have known that his entire effort, however praiseworthy the motives behind it, was doomed to failure. Debates between parties who claim to own the truth can, alas, never lead to any solution. Experience shows that everyone who attempts to unite or reconcile hostile religions, ends up creating another sect. He is bound to fail for one simple reason, namely, that the worst enemy of truth is not error, not even falsehood; but *conviction* itself. Nothing is more resistant to new insights than a convinced mind; deaf and blind to anything outside itself, it is like a clenched fist, unable to grasp anything, unless and until it finally resigns itself to opening up.

Although he never publicly said so, at least not to my knowledge, the debates in the ibādat-khāna must thus have been, right from the start, a bitter disappointment to our beloved emperor.

I have already described the shameful bickering between the four groups of attendants about precedence at the meetings, but that was only a foretaste of the squabbling and the strife that was to come.

As was to be expected, the fighting started in real earnest, with bitter arguments and accusations back and forth between Sunnī and Shī'a. The latter, of course, accused the Sunnī of having betrayed the Prophet and his family, and martyred the Prophet's grandsons. The Sunnī retorted that the Prophet had never ordained that his successors should be chosen among his own descendants, and that the Shī'a devotion to Alī and his would-be successors, the Shī'a imāms, was nothing but ilhād,[247] outright heresy. Indeed, argued the Sunnī: The Shī'a tenet that their imāms are sinless channels of the divine light of the Prophet (Nūr Muhammadī), puts these imāms on practically the same level as Muhammad himself, and at least attributes to them a status of prophethood, in blatant contradiction with divine revelation, which clearly states that Muhammad, and Muhammad alone, is the seal of the prophets.

The argument soon became so heated that the emperor ordered them to speak in turns, without interrupting each other. Alas, this hardly helped to soothe the tempers. The Sunnīs, who were given the floor first, started arguing among themselves, on the question whether Shī'as are still to be considered Muslims. Only a minority was ready to concede that the Shī'a are Muslims, albeit guilty of ilhād. The majority maintained that the Shī'a have placed themselves outside Islām, and that they are, at best, entitled to the status of ahl al-kitāb, people of the book, like the Yahūdīs and the Īsāwīs.

When the emperor then gave the floor to the Shī'a representatives, they—after establishing the legitimacy of the claims of Alī and his party—maintained, on the contrary that it was the Sunnī who had placed themselves outside Islām, for, so they claimed, he who dies without knowing the imām of his age, dies an unbeliever. Soon after that, they, too, lost themselves in endless quarrels amongst their own factions and sects: the majority Ithnā'asshariyyah, or twelve-imām Shī'a, the Zaydī, or five-imām Shī'a, the Ismā'īlī seveners, the Khārijites, and so on.

After some time, the emperor grew tired of all this. He asked the participants to refrain, for the time being, from further debates on the Sunnī-Shī'a divide and invited them to instruct him in what he hoped would be a less controversial subject: Sharī'ah law and jurisprudence.

---

247. Ilhād: heresy (literally, 'deviation'); heretics are called malāhidah in Arabic.

Soon, we found ourselves entangled in a cobweb of rules, regulations, principles and precedents, which, as the emperor did not fail to remark, seemed to be mainly preoccupied with rather trivial formalities.

How should nāmāz be said? Should one lean on one knee or both? Should the word amīn be pronounced softly or audibly? Is it permissible to say nāmāz for the dead? What is the validity and merit of a prayer for which the prescribed formalities have not been followed? What kind of prayer is one allowed to say *before* having performed the necessary ablutions? What is the validity of a prayer said while standing up or walking?

In the beginning, the emperor seemed amused, rather than bored or irritated, by the unexpected complexity of these matters. Then, however, the inevitable incident occurred.

One evening, the ulamā had debated at length among themselves about the necessary ablutions before prayer: 'There is no question that a bath is necessary when an emission of semen has occurred, but what if there has only been arousal? What if a few drops of lubricating slime have leaked and stained the clothes, although no effusion of semen has occurred? What if a man—or a woman—experiences arousal in the bath? Will that in itself turn the washing water napāk?'

'It seems to me,' the emperor casually remarked after a while, an amused smile on his face, 'that a man and a woman who want to make love, better take their bath *before* they lie together – they will find each other's body so much more enjoyable! And I have to say, I fail to see how and why the emission of so tender a fluid would suddenly render a man unfit to pray to his creator!'

No one dared to react, and the debate went on as planned. The next day, however, the emperor's informants warned him that the palace was rife with gossip, confusion and controversy. Certain ulamā—no doubt, Makhdūm-ul Mulk and his clique were behind this—were spreading the rumour that the emperor had been mocking the precepts of religion; that he wanted to abolish the law, or at least introduce bid'ah;[248] and many other reproaches to the same effect.

Fortunately, Shaykh Mubārak managed to quickly put the issue to rest.

---

248. Bid'ah: Unauthorised innovation in religious matters.

'It has come to His Majesty's attention,' he stated at the next assembly, 'that the recent debates in this very ibādat-khāna have given rise to misunderstandings and confusion – not among the wise like ourselves, of course, but among the uneducated, the simple-minded, and those of malicious intent!'

There was a long, uncomfortable pause. Mubārak was keeping his eyes averted, but it did not escape anyone's attention how the emperor's inscrutable gaze rested, one by one, on each of the ulamā – gauging, as it were, the very depths of their conscience.

'As men of wisdom, my friends, my brethren,' Mubārak continued, suddenly in a much gentler, amicable tone, 'as men of learning who have dedicated our lives to the study of Allāh's message, it is our task to light the torches of wisdom in the darkness of error; we, my brothers, have to be beacons of light in the tortuous caves of confusion.

'Now, the question before us is quite simple: Is there a contradiction between the recommendation to bathe before the act of mating, and the precept to do so afterwards? Of course not! We all know, that to bathe after semen has been emitted, is to comply with a religious rule. But what is the purpose of that rule? Evidently, it has little, if anything, to do with bodily cleanliness: Its main purpose is to remind us, that in prayer, our full and undivided attention, our entire mind and soul, should be with god, and God alone. On the other hand, the recommendation to wash *before* making love is of another kind: It is a practical piece of advice, based on reason, on considerations of personal hygiene and bodily comfort; it is a conclusion to which every right-minded person will arrive, when reflecting on the act of mating.'

'The obligation to wash *after* lying with a woman,' Mubārak summarised, 'is thus a *religious* guideline, pertaining, not to intercourse, nor to hygiene, but to *prayer*; whereas the recommendation to wash *before* sleeping with her, is *practical* guidance pertaining to human life, a simple conclusion of factual experience, common sense, and *reason*. Is one recommendation right, the other one wrong? Of course not – both are true, and both are respectable, for both have their origin in god, the benevolent creator Who has given us both reason and revelation, and Who is the source of all truth. And god being the foundation and essence of all truth, how could one aspect of it ever contradict another? Impossible! god is merciful, and He is One – inside Him is no contradiction, and to state the contrary would be blasphemous!'

After this allocution, the gossip and rumours died down quickly. Whether it was thanks to Mubārak's persuasiveness, or out of fear for the emperor's spies, I choose to leave that aside. The important thing, I thought to myself, was that an open conflict had been averted.

Alas, how could I be so naïve? Did I not sense the brooding hatred behind the slick, courtly manners? How could I fail to recognise the insidious disease, the slowly festering abscesses under seemingly healthy skin? Clearly, it was only a matter of time, before the next one would erupt. . . .

≈

On the tenth of Rajab of the year 987 of the Hijrī Era, the twenty-first of Shahrīvar of the twenty-fourth year of His Majesty's reign,[249] a solemn declaration was issued, bearing the signatures and seals of the highest-ranking jurists and scholars of the empire: Abdullāh of Sultānpūr, Makhdūm-ul Mulk; Shaykh Abd-un Nabī, sadr us-sudūr;[250] Qadī Jalāl-ud dīn Multānī, qādī ul quzāt,[251] sadr-i-jahān, muftī general;[252] Ghāzī Khān Badakhshī, who had no rival in the science of falsafah and kalām; and Shaykh Mubārak of Nāgaur, the most learned man of the age, who was in fact, as we have seen, the real author of the text.

In one masterstroke, thanks to young Abū-l Fazl's ingenuity, the power of the ulamā had been broken: This fatwāh officially and unequivocally established the emperor's position as final arbiter in all issues, religious as well as governmental. It formally acknowledged that the rank of imām-i-ādil is superior to that of any mujtahid[253] or interpreter of Muslim law, thus solemnly recognising the emperor as the true highest authority, and

---

249. Wednesday, 2 September 1579
250. Sadr us-sudūr: High official under the wazīr (minister of finance, treasurer) presiding over the diwān-i-rishālat, a lucrative office dealing with religious foundations and stipends to scholars.
251. Supreme judge
252. Legal functionary entitled to issue legal opinion (fatwā).
253. Mujtahid: highest legal authority, entitled to make original decisions of canon law (rather than merely applying precedents already established).

in fact, giving him the ultimate authority and virtually unlimited power in all matters.

The text of this declaration, which evil tongues have ventured to call the infallibility decree, goes as follows:

> Whereas Hindustān has now become the centre of security and peace, and the land of justice and beneficence, a large number of people, especially learned men and men of the law, have immigrated and chosen this country for their home.
>
> Now we, the principal ulamā, who are not only well-versed in the several departments of the law and in the principles of jurisprudence, and well acquainted with the edicts which rest on reason or testimony, but are also known for our piety and honest intentions, have duly considered the deep meaning, firstly, of the āyāt of the Holy Qur'ān:
>
> 'Obey Allāh, and obey the Prophet, and those who have authority among you';
>
> and secondly, of the genuine Hadīth:
>
> 'Surely the man who is dearest to Allāh on the day of judgement is the imām-i-ādil; whosoever obeys the amīr, obeys Thee; and whosoever rebels against him, rebels against Thee';
>
> and thirdly, of several other proofs based on reasoning or testimony: We have agreed that the rank of sultān-i-ādil is higher in the eyes of Allāh than the rank of a mujtahid.
>
> Further, we declare that the sultān of Islām, amīr of the faithful, shadow of god in the world, Abū-l Fath Jalāl-ud-dīn Muhammad Akbar Pādshāh Ghāzī (whose kingdom god may perpetuate!) is a most just, a most wise, and a most god-fearing king.
>
> Should, therefore, in future, a religious question come up, regarding which the opinions of the mujtahids are at variance, and His Majesty, in his penetrating understanding and clear wisdom be inclined to adopt, for the benefit of the nation and as a political expedient, any of the conflicting opinions which exist on that point, and should issue a decree to that effect, we do hereby agree that such a decree will be binding on us and on the whole nation.

Further, we declare that, should His Majesty think fit to issue a new order, we and the nation shall likewise be bound by it – provided always that such order be not only in accordance with some āyāt of the Holy Qur'ān, but also of real benefit to the nation; and further, that any opposition on the part of his subjects to such an order passed by His Majesty shall involve damnation in the world to come, and loss of property and privileges in this.

This document has been written with honest intentions, for the glory of god and the propagation of Islām, and is signed by us, the principal ulamā and lawyers, in the month of Rajab in the year nine hundred and eighty-seven.

Few weeks later, Abdullāh of Sultānpūr (Makhdūm-ul Mulk) and Shaykh Abd-un Nabī (Sadr us-sudūr) received the license to leave His Majesty's dominions, in order to obtain, as had been their ardent and pious desire, the sacred blessings of the Hajj. Escorted by armed guards, they were hastily marched off to the Gujarātī coast and put on the first available ship headed for Arabia.

Not a living soul was left in the entire empire to challenge our emperor's supremacy. At least, so it seemed.

Thirtieth Letter

إبادت خانه

Ibādat-Khāna (2)

From the private notes of Mulāzim Hakīm Alī Gilanī

With Makhdūm-ul Mulk and Abd-un Nabī out of the way, and the remaining ulamā reduced to respectful obedience, there was—or so it seemed—nothing or nobody left to prevent His Majesty from pursuing his intellectual curiosity. Not surprisingly, he ordered the religious debates to be reopened; and equally not surprisingly, be it to the utter dismay of many, the meetings were no longer restricted to Mussalmān scholars and indeed, no longer focused on the subtleties of the laws of Islām. 'My object, O wise mullāhs,' the emperor declared to the assembly, 'is to find out and disclose the principles of genuine religion, trace them to their divine origin, and thus ascertain veritable truth!' A more ambitious goal is hard to imagine, but he seemed quite confident it was achievable.

In a few months' time, Fatehpūr Sīkrī became a unique meeting place for dozens of scholars and holy men of all kinds – the more eccentric, the better, it seemed. Half-mad, rambling, 'illuminated' Sūfīs; daunting Pārsī fire priests; Hindūs – sādhus and savants of all kinds and denominations, their bodies and faces smeared with cremation ashes, or painted with patterns and colours of ominous extravagance; austere, white-clad and even stark-naked Jains, mouths and noses permanently covered with cloth, sweeping the ground in front of their feet, in a commendably scrupulous, if futile, attempt to avoid killing even the smallest, vilest, most insignificant of insects: all these extraordinary characters were invited to the palace, covered with gifts and honours, as if they had been emissaries of the mightiest kings on earth. In the emperor's august presence and under his personal protection, they rubbed shoulders with the orthodox ulamā and their mortal enemies, the black-robed firanghī fanatics. Verily, for all their mutual hatred, the latter two so strongly resembled each other in their strictness and their contempt of all the others that more than once, they seemed to be one and the same.

For hours in a row, His Majesty would converse with these men, questioning them about their practices and convictions, and inviting the others to comment on what they just heard. And strangely enough, although not one of these conversations ever led to any conclusion; although each one of them seemed to raise more questions than it answered, His Majesty never seemed to tire of them.

I neither have the ability, nor the intention, to try and compile a learned treatise on all the strange teachings and doctrines thus expounded to our emperor during these long months – my mistakes would be manifold, and my readers needlessly distracted. It is, however, of the utmost importance that I at least try to recount a few of them, for it is quite impossible to understand the history and present condition of His Majesty's empire, if one does not at least have some knowledge of the influence these remarkable debates have had on him.

Before pursuing this matter, however, I should say a few words about His Majesty's growing and, I have to say, rather disconcerting, interest in the firanghīs.

Ever since he first met with their emissaries, down in Gujarāt, he had been favourably impressed with them: the quality of their firearms, their self-assured (not to say arrogant) manner, and their soldiery discipline. These people and the far-away places they came from obviously fascinated him, and he wanted to find out everything there was to know about them, their strange habits and their erroneous but intriguing beliefs.

Ibādat-Khāna (2)   433

Early in the year 986,[254] he decided to send a well-travelled army officer—a Yemenite by the name of Habībullāh—on a fact-finding mission to the firanghī settlements down in Goa. The envoy was entrusted with ample funds, and accompanied by a group of craftsmen, ordered to carefully study and copy any paintings and artifacts they could lay their hands on.

The mission returned later that same year, laden with a wealth of the most exotic objects. Worthy of particular notice was a man-sized wooden box, containing a series of metal pipes, which, when air is pumped through them, make the sound of many flutes playing together. There were also works of art: sculptures and paintings, admittedly of a completely different style than those made by Persians or Hindūs, but skilfully crafted and quite beautiful nevertheless. Most of the paintings represented the prophet Īsā[255] and his saintly mother Maryam (upon both of whom be peace), or some other firanghī saint. The emissaries also brought back several suits of clothes in the firanghī fashion, both male and female; and a set of strange utensils, including some small iron claws, which they use to have their food, and a number of tiny, hard-wooden pots, burnt and charred on the inside, mounted on a hollow reed. The inside of these little pots, about the width of a man's thumb, is filled with smoldering herbs, the smoke of which is inhaled, reportedly to improve digestion and overall health.

The emperor was visibly pleased to see all these remarkable objects brought before him.

'You have done well; I am most pleased with you and your team!' The emperor made a gesture, upon which generous amounts of gold and silver were distributed among the emissaries. 'Kindly betake yourself to the diwān-i-khās in one hour,' he added. 'I would be quite interested to hear in private what you have to say about these people!'

An hour later, as ordered by His Majesty, Habībullāh presented himself at the diwān-i-khās, where Rājā Man Singh, Rājā Todar Mal, Rājā Bīrbal, Abū-l Fazl, and I had also been invited to attend the meeting.

---

254. 1578
255. Jesus Christ

'So,' His Majesty said, 'those are some quite remarkable objects you brought back with you! Now, do tell me more about these Purtugēsh: I gather you are quite impressed with what you have seen in their settlements? What are these people like? Speak freely; tell me everything – the good as well as the bad!'

'To be quite honest, Your Majesty, the impression they gave me is mixed, at best. Indeed, they seem to be skilful in a few areas: Their ships are enormous, their weapons are made of excellent steel, and their paintings are quite beautiful, I have to admit; but overall, they are nothing but arrogant, barbarian infidels!'

'Are they, really? And what makes you say that? What is it about them you dislike so much?'

'Everything, Your Majesty!'

'Indeed? I must confess, you are arousing my curiosity! And what is it about them that is so barbarous?'

'To start with the simplest example, Your Majesty: They do not write from right to left like the believers do, but from left to right, in strange, rounded scribbles, which seem more like signs of black witchcraft to me than normal decent writing. Just like the letters of the noble Qur'ān have been given to mankind by Allāh Himself, this kind of writing could only have come from the evil one!'

'Their writing may be different, but does that necessarily mean it is inferior to ours?' the emperor inquired, a gently mocking smile around his lips. 'Do not the Hindūs write from left to right as well? The characters they use are also quite different from ours, but I hear from those who have cared to learn their script that it is actually quite skilfully conceived, and indeed, easier to read than ours, because all the sounds that are heard in speech are represented in it, whereas in ours, only the most important sounds are written!'

'Your Majesty is right, of course,' he admitted reluctantly, though clearly unconvinced. 'But I just wanted to point out to Your Majesty, how different these people are from us. Their writing may or may not be equally legible as that of the Hindūs, but it is most certainly much less orderly, and utterly devoid of any grace or beauty. And everything else one knows about these people leads one to believe that it must be much inferior indeed.'

'And again, what makes you say that?'

'One only needs to look at the abominable way they dress, Your Majesty! While we believers take pride in ample, graceful clothes, made of precious fabrics, theirs are usually plain black, made of the cheapest, coarsest of cloth, and tightly fitted around their bodies – textile must be a scarce commodity indeed, in the barbarous lands where they come from! They are not ashamed to show themselves in public with their heads disrespectfully uncovered, their hair often long like that of unveiled women, and, more often than not, uncombed, unwashed and disgustingly greasy. They are not even ashamed of wearing trousers, so tightly fitted around their legs that one can see the shape of their private parts! And their manners! On those rare occasions where one of them is invited to enter the dwelling of a believer, he will not even have the elementary decency of taking his boots off: He will actually soil and defile his host's carpets with the dirt of the street!

'And that is only one example. Their lack of morals and civilisation is even more apparent from the way they treat their women. In this respect, they are scarcely better than mindless animals! Female beasts do not hide their faces; neither do firanghī women. Male and female beasts herd together and share the same stables; so do the firanghīs. And not only do the women show their faces to whoever chooses to look at them, they freely meet and converse with men who do not belong to their own family! It is not hard to imagine that their cities must be little else than giant brothels!

'And the list of these abominations goes on and on, Your Majesty. Without any shame or apprehension, these godless savages will eat the most unclean animals, of all shapes and kinds, no matter how repulsive: absolutely everything, from swine to turtles! When they kill an animal they are about to eat, they do not care to pray or return thanks to Allāh, nor do they observe whatsoever rule of cleanliness or piety. Is it not true, that any Muslim worthy of that name will pray at least five times a day, and will on that occasion carefully wash his head, hands and feet? Even the Hindūs, ignorant idolaters though they may be, meticulously observe all kinds of rules of cleanliness and decency; but these accursed firanghīs do nothing of the kind. More shameless and filthier a race is scarcely imaginable! Even when they pray, they do not bother to wash, and neither when they eat. To eat their food, they use those small iron claws, and maybe just as well for them, for if they would use those dirty hands of theirs, they might actually poison themselves!'

'And what have you learned about their religion?'

'They claim to be god-fearing people, Your Majesty, but one will hardly ever see them praying. A few times a week, they go to their churches and worship images of Īsā ibn Maryam[256] and other prophets – most of them false, of course. As Your Majesty knows, they claim that the prophet Īsā—upon whom be peace—is in fact god himself! When they feel safe enough, they will never miss an occasion to curse the blessed Prophet Muhammad, calling him an impostor, a fraud, or worse! Towards the Hindūs, they feel nothing but contempt, and towards us Muslims, nothing but hate and fear. I am sure they would kill every last one of us, if they had the chance!'

'Like we would probably do with them, if *we* had the chance,' the emperor mused, clearly unimpressed. 'Speaking of killing, tell me more about the strength of their army, the way they are organised . . .'

For the next two hours or so, the poor commander found himself under an intense bombardment of questions about the dimensions and strength of the firanghī battlements and fortifications, the make and calibre of their guns, the number of warships, horses and men at their disposal, their equipment, and so on. The good man did his best, but there is only so much that one can find out during a few weeks. . . .

When it had become clear—painfully clear—that no further information could be obtained from the commander, the emperor thanked him again most kindly, and gave him leave to retire, with another purse of gold as an additional reward for his efforts and loyalty. The commander, visibly relieved, bowed himself out.

Despite the courtesy of the emperor's manner, it was obvious that his curiosity had not been fully satisfied.

'It may well be,' he mused, talking more to himself than to us, 'that these firanghīs are barbarian infidels. But if I look at all those things Habībullāh brought back with him, if I look at the quality of their steel, the make of their ships and their guns, it seems to me that these

---

256. 'Īsā ibn Maryam: Jesus, son of Mary

firanghīs, ill-mannered though they sometimes may be, are in possession of a wealth of knowledge well worth acquiring!'

A few days later, as coincidence would have it, a remarkable story was brought to His Majesty's attention. A report came in from the governor of Bengāl that two firanghī priests had been travelling through the country, preaching and trying to win converts to their religion. And apparently, they had been saying some quite remarkable things. Īsā, or Jesùs as they called him, teaches us that it is our duty, not only to forgive but to love our enemies, as much as we love ourselves; justice and honesty are due to everyone, whether friend or foe. A few Purtugēsh merchants, who had been embezzling tax monies due to the imperial treasury, had been publicly and severely reprimanded by the priests. They were reported to have said: 'Give to the emperor, what is due to the emperor, says the lord! To steal from the king, even if it is a foreign king, is to break god's law!'

True or not, this story greatly impressed His Majesty. On more than one occasion, he mused that a religion which so unreservedly condemns dishonesty, even when practiced against an alien government, surely must possess values and morals of a truly exceptional nature!

From that moment, the firanghīs never seemed to leave his mind. Day in, day out, he would talk and speculate about them. And as nobody at the imperial court was able to satisfy his insatiable curiosity about the firanghīs and their homelands, history, customs and religion, queries for more information were sent to every corner of the empire. When it was reported that there were two Purtugēsh in Bengāl, a sailor named Pedro Tavares, who had found employment in the Bengālī ports, and an aging priest called Juliano Perreira, both men were summoned to render themselves to Fatehpūr Sīkrī without delay.

They were received with courtesy and generosity. Hardly a day went by without one or more private audiences, during which His Majesty would inundate them with questions. It seemed like every day, he found new reasons to invite them, more questions to ask, but the more information he managed to obtain, the less satisfied he became. Especially the explanations about the Nazariyya religion seemed to fall disappointingly short of his expectations. Surely, with surprising vehemence for such a meek and amiable man, the old priest kept fulminating against the Holy Prophet Muhammad (upon whom be the blessings of Allāh!), calling him a fraud and an imposter, and the Holy Qur'ān a heap of lies, but the information the old man was able to convey about the fundamental doctrines of his own faith was rather scanty, and quite confusing.

One god, consisting of three distinct divine persons? The Father, causing the Son to be born as a mortal man, from the womb of the blessed Virgin Maryam? God the Father requiring his own son to be tortured to death, in remission of the sins of mankind? Īsā, or Jesùs, one person with two natures: entirely man and entirely god?

No, none of this seemed to make much sense. And yet, entire nations were convinced about the truth of these stories! The old priest, by his own admission, a man of greater piety than learning, found himself unable to answer the emperor's many questions. But down in Goa, he said, there was a famous school, the 'College of Saint Paul'; it had been founded by a special order of very wise and learned priests, the Pādres Jesuitas. Each and every one of these pādres our priests had acquired a vast amount of knowledge during many years of hard study; they would most certainly be able to answer any remaining questions His Majesty might have, and, god willing, would lead him to salvation.

Thus it came to pass, late in the month of Āzar of the twenty-third year,[257] that yet another emissary was sent to Goa, carrying a highly unusual letter: one requesting the leaders of the Order of Saint Paul to send a delegation of learned men with books to Fatehpūr Sīkrī, as the emperor wished to be instructed in their faith.

The imperial emissary arrived in Goa few months later, and the letter he was carrying was received with understandable elation: The Purtugēsh must have immediately started fostering grand illusions about converting the mightiest monarch on earth, and creating a great firanghī empire in the East. . . .

Hasty preparations were made, and three of the priests, set sail for the port of Damān on the southern border of Gujarāt, from whence they set out to travel overland, via Surat, Sarangpūr, Narwar and Gwālīor, to Fatehpūr Sīkrī.

As the eldest of them was taken quite ill with a persistent and rather severe indisposition of the bowels, the pādres were able to make but slow

---

257. December 1578

progress. Then at long last, near the end of the of the twenty-fourth year, on the nineteenth of Esfand,[258] the first two of them finally arrived at the imperial court, to be followed a few days later by their ailing colleague.

The emperor, who had been impatiently awaiting their arrival, received them with every possible honour. So eager was he to see them that he had them brought to his presence immediately.

He was quite impressed with the valuable presents his visitors had brought with them. Of particular value was a beautiful painting representing the blessed Virgin Maryam (called Marīah by the pādres); His Majesty took it in both hands with great respect, bowed and placed it above his head. He then ordered it to be taken immediately to his private quarters and fixed high on the wall – high, as it would, so he explained, be quite unbecoming for him to look down on the Blessed Virgin.

The pādres then presented him with a set of eight voluminous books, bound in white parchment. This, they explained with great pride, was the precious and world-famous *Biblia Polyglotta*,[259] containing the entire holy scriptures in Hebrew, Aramaic, Syriac, Greek and Latin, a work of exceptional scholarship! His Majesty took each of the volumes in his hands, respectfully kissing them and placing them on his head. He then asked which volume contained the injīl.[260] They pointed it out to him, upon which he again took that book in his hands, kissed it, and placed it over his head. Noticeably and understandably impressed and pleased with these signs of deep and sincere reverence, the pādres must have thought that it was only a matter of time before the emperor would convert to their faith.

As is customary with important visitors, the emperor ordered lavish amounts of gold to be handed to them as a welcome gift. To his surprise, however, they politely but firmly refused to accept it.

'The revered Pādre Rodolfo Aquaviva and I are profoundly touched by Your Majesty's kindness and generosity,' said the oldest one of the two,

---

258. 28 February 1580
259. 1100 copies of the famous *Polyglot Bible* were printed between 1568 and 1573 on the presses of Christopher Plantin in the city of Antwerp (Antwerpen) in present-day Belgium.
260. Injīl: The Gospel or New Testament

a squat little man of about forty, who, though he had introduced himself as Pādre Francisco Henríquez, did not look like a firanghī at all. 'We would not want to appear ungrateful towards Your Majesty; but to accept such valuable gifts would be a breach of the solemn and irrevocable vow of poverty that we have taken when we indued these humble garments to dedicate our lives to the Lord Jesùs the Christ, our Saviour. The only things we are allowed to accept for ourselves, is food, shelter, and bare sustenance. Your Majesty should rest assured, however, that we are most obliged by his kindness, and that he is in our constant prayers.'

Henríquez went on to explain that he had been born from Persian parents on the island of Hormuz,[261] as Hasan, son of Alī. Orphaned at the age of ten, he had been taken into the care of Īsāwī priests living in the firanghī fortress on the island. They had given him his Christian name, delivered him from the darkness of error, and guided him to the shining light of truth: the Gospel of Jesùs the messiah, god's only-begotten son.

Such was his gratitude that at the age of eighteen, he had expressed the desire to join the holy Society of Jesùs, and to take the fourfold vow of chastity, poverty, obedience, and unquestioning loyalty to his holiness the holy father, the head of Christianity. His mission had brought him to various Purtugēsh settlements in the area, and finally to Goa, where he busied himself with priestly tasks and the education of children. Since he was the only pādre able to understand and speak the Persian language, he had been selected to accompany his two learned brethren on this important mission to Fatehpūr Sīkrī, and—until such time as they would have acquired sufficient fluency themselves—to act as their interpreter.

The leader of the mission, he explained, was the young priest standing next to him: Pādre Rodolfo Aquaviva, who came from a very important family of so-called Condes, which are high-ranking amīrs among the firanghīs.

Aquaviva, who had heard his own name and understood he was being introduced, bowed stiffly. Despite the man's young age—he must have been barely thirty—it somehow did not come as a surprise to me that he had been appointed as the head of the mission. His pale, ascetic,

---

261. Hormuz: Iranian island in the Persian Gulf, occupied by the Portuguese from 1515 to 1622.

unsmiling face had the determined expression of the soldier, or the fanatic; and in his dark, rather deep-sunken eyes smouldered the fire of passion.

His Majesty, much taken with his new visitors and eager to get to know them, entertained them until well after midnight. As is his custom when something catches his interest, he inundated them with questions, skipping constantly from one issue to the other.

The two of them exchanged a few sentences in what I suppose was Purtugēsh, a quite incomprehensible language, full of strange nasals and 'sh' sounds. Once again, I observed with disquiet the feverous, hostile expression on the young priest's face, as he set out to enumerate his arguments.

What would you say is the greatest difference between the Īsāwī and the Mussalmān?

'Your Majesty, the difference between those two could not be greater. It is the difference between day and night, light and dark, truth and lie, salvation and perdition!' Henriquez answered.

'Really? Do we not all worship the same creator?'

'Perhaps, Your Majesty; and indeed, there is only one god. But unfortunately, the moors have been led astray by the lies of an imposter: We Christians worship the true saviour of mankind, Jesùs the Christ, the only-begotten son of god, whereas the moors worship the liar and imposter Muhammad, or Mahomet as the firanghīs call him.'

'You are mistaken, Pādre! We Muslims do not worship Muhammad – he was a mortal man, like all of us. We do respect and honour him as the seal of the prophets, but we do not *worship* him – that would be contrary to his own teachings! Nothing and no one should be worshipped except god himself, that is what Islām says!'

'That may be so, but the Muslims consider Muhammad as the final messenger of god, and the so-called Qur'ān as god's own word, and those tenets are false, entirely false!'

'You claim that Muhammad was a false prophet?'

'We do, Your Majesty we do; and the Holy Scriptures provide ample and irrefutable evidence to that statement!'

'Really? But our ulamā state exactly the contrary! They say that those very same scriptures clearly predict the advent of Muhammad!'

'We can assure Your Majesty, that this is either a blatant lie, or a sad mistake, and we will have no difficulty in proving this!'

'Really? I will be most interested to hear your arguments! But tell me, do you really think Muhammad was a liar? Do you think he tried to deceive people? Do you not think he honestly believed he was god's messenger?'

'Maybe he did, maybe not. But this much is certain: If he really did believe he was a prophet, he was, at the very least, in error – in grave, guilty, sinful error! Rather than humbly accepting the true word of god as he should have, he fell prey to his own conceited vanity, and thus allowed himself to be led astray by the demons of his own pride!'

≈

The following day saw the arrival of the third of the firanghī pādres: one António de Montserrat, a broad-shouldered, red-haired giant of about forty-five years of age, with a wide, rutty face and a broad, fleshy nose, a mouth full of yellow, crumbly teeth, and a bushy red beard. Like his brethren, he was dressed neck to toe in a long, black robe, and on his head, he wore that strange, wide-brimmed black hat of theirs. His illness had left him exhausted and emaciated, but it was obvious that when in good health, this must be a man of considerable bodily strength. In pleasant contrast to his strong build, the expression on his face was one of quiet self-assurance, inner peace, and kindness.

As he is accustomed to do, His Majesty bade his newly arrived guest a cordial welcome. With unfeigned concern, he kept inquiring about his health, urging me and the other court physicians to see to it that the honourable pādre would get the best possible care.

During further introductions and the usual exchange of civilities, Pādre Henríquez happened to mention that Pādre António was a Catalán, a native of Catalunya, a region in Firanghīstān, about a week's travelling north-east of Purtugal. To my surprise, His Majesty appeared to be highly intrigued by this seemingly trivial information.

'How is it to be explained,' he asked, 'that of the three priests who travelled from Goa to Fatehpūr Sīkrī, not a single one seems to come from the country of the Purtugēsh?'

'I can assure Your Majesty, that is merely a coincidence,' Henríquez replied after briefly consulting with Aquaviva. 'You see, Your Majesty:

Firanghīstān has many kingdoms, but the holy church instituted by our Lord Jesùs is one and universal. The priestly order to which we belong, the Societas Jesu, includes members from all nations, and the bonds of love and brotherhood unite us, even if the countries where we came from would be at war with each other. Ultimately, we all take our orders from the supreme leader of the holy church: the holy father in Rūm, the pāpa, the true representative of the Lord Jesùs on earth. In fact, even our kings, at least those who are true believers, recognise the holy father as their supreme leader, and in fact, it is from him that they receive their crown.'

'Really? How interesting! So the pāpa is a sort of high priest, but also the supreme ruler of all Firanghīstān? But if I understood you correctly, you said that not *all* the firanghī kings recognise the holy pāpa as their superior?'

'There are indeed a few who do not, Your Majesty, but those are nothing but despicable heretics, renegades who have put themselves outside the church! All the truly faithful recognise the holy father as the spiritual leader of Christianity!'

'You say the *spiritual* leader? Not the actual *ruler*?'

'The spiritual leader, indeed, Your Majesty. The holy father does not have great armies at his disposal, but no true believer could ever ignore his admonitions, for he is Jesùs' appointed representative on earth!'

'I see,' the emperor mused. His eyes wandered off and he looked absently at the floor in front of him, ostensibly lost in thought.

After what seemed quite a long time, he looked up again and resumed the conversation, now busying himself with the personal comfort of his guests, ordering they be provided with ample and comfortable living quarters, worthy of the highest-ranking ambassadors. Without them even asking for it, he also assigned a spacious room which they were free to furnish as a small church, or Capela as they seem to call it.

The weeks came and went, and as was to be expected, the presence of the firanghī pādres and the growing influence they seemed to have on our emperor was the subject of almost every conversation at the imperial court.

The emperor, however, did not seem to care. On the contrary, he would seize every occasion to visit the pādres or to invite them to his presence, paying them great respect at every occasion, even though he clearly did not always agree with what they said. Each time he entered the Capela, he would bare his head, kneel down, and make the sign of the cross as they had taught him, showing great reverence for the crucifixes, pictures, relics and all the other religious objects and ornaments. He could spend an hour or more in silent prayer in front of a portrait of Īsā, or in front of what the pādres called the god-lamp, a small oil lamp behind red glass, representing, so they explained, god's immanence: His ever-enduring, wakeful presence among us.

Sadly, but not unexpectedly, rumours and speculations about His Majesty's imminent conversion to the Īsāwī cult started spreading like wildfire.

The emperor's closest confidants and the noble of heart of course understood that he was merely attempting to express his respect, his belief in the sacredness of all religions. The firanghī pādres, however, in their conceited arrogance, eagerly allowed themselves to confuse politeness and respect with agreement, and consideration with conversion; whereas the ulamā from their side mistook tolerance for ilhād, piety for bid'ah, and openness of mind for kufr.[262]

What neither of the two camps seemed to realise, was that the harder they tried to win the emperor's favour, and the more radical and fanatic their arguments, the less convinced he became. He was looking for the truth; they wanted to teach him their doctrine. He wanted to unite, conciliate, bring together; they only wanted to accuse, condemn and exclude. He wanted to free people's minds; they only wanted to enslave them.

As I said before: there is little point in trying to recount in detail all those interminable, and, I'm afraid, quite pointless disputes.

Every day brought more of the same unsettling spectacle: the pādres and the ulamā ever more impatient and irritated; the debates between them increasingly acrimonious; the emperor courteous and respectful, but less and less convinced; and the tension at the court palpably rising.

I find it hard to imagine that His Majesty was not aware of this, that he did not sense the impending danger. If he did, he chose to ignore it – probably assuming he was invulnerable.

It very nearly cost him his throne.

---

262. Bid'ah: forbidden 'innovation' in religious matters; kufr: infidelity.

Thirty-first Letter

إبادت خانه

Ibadat-Khana (3)

So much knowledge, so much learning; so many hours of deep-delving arguments and intricate, hairsplitting logic; and yet, so little progress. . . . Every argument, every exchange of views only deepened and widened the chasm between the participants. The seeds of respect and understanding that I had attempted to sow in people's minds had born me nothing but the acrid, venomous fruits of hatred and fear. I had failed, and failed miserably.

And yet, just like even the darkest night is followed by the first glimmer of dawn, it was amidst utter failure that I finally came out victorious. Precisely at the moment where it was painfully evident that no amount of religious debate would ever lead to a conclusion, it became clear to me that it is always possible for people to live in peace and in obedience to god, provided their king correctly understands the task he has before him.

You see, my son: A king cannot erase or reason away the differences between his subjects and their traditions; but he can and must surpass them, transcend them, rise above them. Like the sun shines down on the world without making any exception or distinction, a king must stand above all distinctions. He must lead and serve his people, while he himself answers to no one but that one god with many names: the true, the good and the beautiful.

446 🏴 The Emperor's Writings

Read the following two accounts, my son, and understand that it is your duty to rule over all your subjects in fairness and equality, no matter how irreconcilable the differences between them are. Read, and see for yourself how eloquently, brilliantly, and compellingly this has been worded by Abū-l Fazl, my faithful friend and helper, whose quicksilver mind and golden tongue are now forever silenced, through your fault. Read, my son, and understand how much you owe to this man you hated so much. Read, and realise that when you ascend the throne, history will never recognise you as a good and just emperor, unless and until you take at heart the wise counsel of Abū-l Fazl.

From the Archives of the Imperial Court of Hindustān:

Allocution by Shaykh 'Ālim[263] Qutb-ud-dīn Jalesarī

Your Most August Imperial Majesty,
Shadow of God, King of Kings,
Invincible Commander of World-conquering Armies,
Paragon of Wisdom,
Pious Follower of the Path of God,
Truth-loving Fountain of Justice,
Benevolent Cherisher of the Poor

It is not without hesitation, and dare I say, a certain apprehension that I have accepted my right honourable brethren's plea to present to Your Majesty the opinion of the Muslim ulamā, after the vile attacks we have been forced to witness and undergo these past few days. Not because all those firanghī lies and falsehoods would have caused me to entertain the slightest doubt whatsoever – neither about the truth and excellence of Islām, nor about the blatant error and falsehood of the Nazariyya creed.

No, if I did hesitate to accept this honourable task, it is because I was afraid of being unworthy of it, of finding myself inadequate, not learned or smart enough to come up with the right arguments to convince Your Majesty and the rest of this honourable assembly. May Allāh—the lord of all worlds, the one to Whom nothing is impossible, the one to Whom

---

263. Ālim: Singular of ulamā – Muslim theologian, Islamic jurist. Qutb-ud-dīn of Jalesar was one of the ulamā present during the religious debates.

belong, among many others, the glorious names of al-mu'izz, al-muzill, and al-fattāh[264]—graciously come to my assistance, compensate for my many shortcomings, enlighten my spirit, and quicken my tongue!

I have Your Majesty's kind permission to speak frankly, without any fear of reprisal; and knowing Your Majesty's honesty and most noble disposition, I will not hesitate to do so. Like the firanghī infidels, I will indeed not mince my words. However, I am proud to be able to reassure Your Majesty and this assembly: I will not need to resort to the kind of insults and abuse the firanghīs have poured over the heads of the believers, for truth is with us, and our arguments are solid.

I must confess to Your Majesty that hardly any sleep has comforted my weary eyes this past week: such was my indignation, not to say my outrage, at the scandalous, hideous, unspeakable insults these misguided, perverted infidels have been heaping upon the sacred religion of Islām, and upon Allāh's holy messenger, Muhammad – eternal peace and blessings be upon him and his household!

After a few nights thus spent wide awake in futile and impotent rage, I finally managed to repress my anger, and I brought myself to consider, as calmly and methodically as possible, all their hollow, baseless arguments. And now, with Allāh's help, I do hope I will be able to offer Your Majesty a decisive and compelling refutation – based, as much as feasible, on reason only, as this seems to be the only kind of argument Your Majesty is willing to accept in the framework of these debates.

Upon closer examination of the murky stream of nonsense the firanghīs have been pouring over our heads, it becomes blatantly clear that they hardly ever manage to come up with *any* argument based on reason. Instead, they call upon what they claim to be divine revelation, quoting a number of uncontrollable statements from the Injīl, the Tawrāt, the Zabūr[265] and other sacred writings, all of which are supposed to prove that the blessed prophet Īsā ibn Maryam—upon whom be peace!—was

---

264. Al-mu'izz: The honourer – he who makes one glorious, gives dignity, and treats one with kind respect. Al-muzill: The dishonourer, he who puts the sinners to shame. Al-fattāh: The opener, he who eliminates all obstacles and brings the solution to all problems.
265. Tawrāt: The Books of Moses or Pentateuch (Torah); Zabūr: The Psalms of David.

actually a god-man, and that his mission on this earth has been predicted in the books of divine revelation.

When we from our side counter their arguments, quoting from the Holy Qur'ān, they flatly deny its divine origin, and do their utmost to discredit it and the messenger to whom it has been revealed. Arrogant or stupid enough to ignore the Holy Qur'ān's unique and undeniable beauty and matchless poetic perfection, they maintain that it is not the word of god, but the malicious invention of a conceited liar, or at the very best, a collection of misguided, delusional ramblings of a devil-possessed lunatic; they say it is a primitive, tribal creed, favouring divorce, indecency, promiscuity and lasciviousness – even in paradise. They have the audacity to maintain that the Holy Prophet Muhammad, far from being god's ultimate messenger and the saint we know him to be, was nothing but a lewd, illiterate robber, who was merely inventing so-called divine messages to serve his own selfish purposes. The god-man Īsā ibn Maryam, in contrast, was the seal of perfection, who led a life of holiness, chastity and self-effacement, and whose divine mission was blessed and endorsed by god through many wonderful miracles – none of which, they hasten to add, have ever occurred during Muhammad's life.

Behold, Your Majesty and distinguished members of this honourable assembly, the entire foundation of the Īsāwī reasoning: a series of blatant lies, outrageous insults, and gratuitous allegations, clearly and entirely unfounded and unproven, but supposedly sufficient to reject the final message of god, and to replace it with a set of blasphemous old wives' tales, about a triune god entering into a piece of bread, and more of that kind of nonsense!

But enough said about this pagan nonsense! Even merely summarising it makes me sick to the stomach! The more important question tonight is: How do we get out of this impasse? For alas, an impasse it is: If one party says, 'Black, for my Holy Book says so, and your book is false,' and the other one replies, 'White, for my Holy Book holds the truth, and yours is full of lies,' how are we to decide between them?

Fortunately, the creator has gifted us with reason. And while human reason in itself, I mean reason without revelation, is of course not sufficient to discover the whole truth, it does suffice amply to demonstrate, beyond any reasonable doubt, the truth of Islām and the errors of the Īsāwī creed.

I humbly thank Your Majesty and the honourable members of this assembly for their patience and kind attention, and will now proceed to conclude.

In the beginning of this allocution, I have indicated that human reason, as such—human reason without divine revelation, that is—does in itself not suffice to irrefutably *prove* everything it knows to be true. For example, if I would state that everything we experience in our lives is nothing but an illusion, created in our minds by an evil spirit who wants to deceive us, then it will be impossible for anyone in this room to actually *prove* that I am wrong. You can show me that nothing in our lives supports such an outrageous proposition. You can cleverly point out to me that if everything is an illusion, my own proposition must be an illusion as well. But you can never actually *prove* that it is completely excluded that what I say could be true.

However, when you wholeheartedly submit to Allāh, when you accept that in His infinite goodness, He will not mislead you in this way; the existence of the world becomes self-evident again, and your mind will finally come to rest.

In this case, this distinguished assembly is being confronted with an argument most bitter between two religious traditions. Both claim to be entirely and literally founded on divine revelation; both deny the validity of the other party's scriptures. One side cannot actually *prove* that the other is wrong. However, when thus confronted with two alternatives, reason and common sense will help us to indicate where the truth lies, and in this case, they will be able do so beyond any reasonable doubt.

Consider, Your Majesty and distinguished members of this honourable assembly: On the one hand, the Īsāwī summons to believe in a nonsensical story about a triune god with a virgin wife; in delivery of sin, which evidently never took place, and a blasphemous pagan rite where one is invited to eat and drink the flesh and blood of god Himself – as if the eternal god had a human body with blood, and would want us to behave like cannibals!

What a painful contrast with Islām, where there is nothing but clarity, purity, and sacred simplicity. There is only one god; He is one; and there is no other like Him; He begets not, and is not begotten. He is the sovereign creator of everything and everybody (including Īsā, peace be with him!); He is the eternal and sovereign lord of the universe, and blesses those who submit to Him.

Your reason and common sense, I trust, will not find it too difficult to choose between the dark and the light, the blatant error and the manifest truth.

I therefore rest my case.

For my fellow Muslims, I pray that Allāh may keep you, and forever be your guide; and I take my leave from you with the words of the Holy Qur'ān:

> *Say: He is Allāh,*
> *The one and only;*
> *Allāh, the eternal, absolute;*
> *He begets not, nor is He begotten;*
> *And there is none like unto Him.*[266]

And for the non-Muslims, and for those whose vision is clouded by needless doubt, I pray that the compassionate and merciful may open your hearts and minds, dissipate the clouds that blind you, guide you unto the right path and lead you towards the truth.

Eternal praise be unto Him, the first and the last, the eternal lord of all worlds and of the day of reckoning; and uncountable salutations and prayers be upon His messenger, the seal of the prophets, the lord of apostles, Muhammad!

Dīn-e-Illāhī

'Well, what do you make of this, my wise and learned friends?' I asked Bīrbal and Abū-l Fazl, as we were sitting together in a private room after Qutb-ud-dīn Jalesarī's remarkable allocution. 'I have to say, I found tonight's plea rather convincing, but I am anxious to hear what the two smartest men in the empire have to say about it!'

'Your Majesty is too kind,' Abū-l Fazl said, bowing his head and touching his heart. 'If Your Majesty is in agreement, perhaps it would be interesting to hear Rājā Bīrbal's comments first; since he is neither

---

266. Qur'ān, 112, 1-4.

an Īsāwī, nor a Muslim, his opinion will be more unprejudiced than my own.'

'Excellent advice, as always, my friend! Pray go ahead, Rājā Bīrbal. Tell us what you think!'

'I don't know, Your Majesty,' Bīrbal answered hesitatingly. 'I should perhaps not speak of other people's religions, or venture to comment upon ways of thinking in which I have never been properly instructed. Besides, I really would not want to hurt anyone's feelings. . . .'

'Do not be afraid to speak your mind, my friend! We are interested to hear what you think, not what you think we would like to hear!'

'Well, Your Majesty,' Bīrbal continued, still somewhat ill at ease, 'to be completely honest with you, in these past few weeks, while hearing those long and bitter arguments back and forth between the firanghī pādres and the ulamā, the thought that most often crossed my mind was: "Why are all you Westerners so bigoted? Can't all you fanatics see that god—whatever He, She, or It may be—must be greater than all your petty differences?"

'I am of course no authority on Islām, and I know even less about the Īsāwī creed, but the more I hear these people arguing, the more I realise there is hardly any difference between them!'

'What makes you say that? After all, they hardly agree on anything!'

'Well, in my mind, both of them are right, and both of them are wrong, in exactly the same way. I mean, both of them have given to this world a set of scriptures of profound wisdom, and art of truly exquisite beauty; but both of them seem equally misguided in their bigotry. Whence this destructive fervour, this zeal, this urge to condemn and eradicate everything that does not come from their own tradition? Well, I am proud to say, that is not the way most Hindūs think about these things!

'For example, all of us have a special devotion towards a certain deity, Lord Śiva for instance, and usually that is because of the caste, the village, the family in which we were born. But that does not stop us from visiting, with equal respect and piety, temples dedicated to Lord Vishnu or any other deity; nor does it stop us from praying at the shrines of Sūfī saints, or baring our heads and feet in an Īsāwī church! The reason is that we realise that all religions, with all their different deities, saints and rituals, are merely human attempts to get in touch with the same greater, unspeakable, mysterious reality, which greatly surpasses all comprehension.

'Your Majesty and Shaykh Abū-l Fazl may be familiar with a passage from one of our sacred scriptures, the *Bṛadāraṇyaka Upaniṣad* – an often quoted conversation between the devotee Vidagdha Śākalya and the old sage Yajñavalkya:[267]

> "Tell me, Yajñavalkya, how many gods are there?"
> "As many as are mentioned in the ritual invocation within the laud to the all-gods: three and three hundred, and three and three thousand."
> "Yes, of course; but really, Yajñavalkya, how many gods are there?"
> "Thirty-three."
> "Yes, of course; but really, Yajñavalkya, how many gods are there?"
> "Six."
> "Yes, of course; but really, Yajñavalkya, how many gods are there?"
> "Three."
> "Yes, of course; but really, Yajñavalkya, how many gods are there?"
> "Two."
> "Yes, of course; but really, Yajñavalkya, how many gods are there?"
> "One and a half."
> "Yes, of course; but really, Yajñavalkya, how many gods are there?"
> "One."'

Bīrbal paused and took a long sip from his beaker of sherbet, closing his eyes as he slowly savoured it, as if all the wisdom of the world was contained in that single mouthful of ice and lime.

'As I said, Your Majesty: I am by no means an expert on Islām, and much less the Īsāwī religion, but it seems to me that both of them are attaching an inordinate importance to *orthodoxy*, to the acceptance of a well-defined, specific set of *beliefs*. For instance: "The Holy Qur'ān is eternal and uncreated, a part of the eternal divine attribute of speech, and it has been revealed to the Prophet Muhammad, the seal of the prophets,

---

267. *Bṛadāraṇyaka Upaniṣad*, 3.9.1. Based on the Oxford World's Classics edition, translation by Patrick Olivelle.

by the Angel Jibriel"; "Īsā is God the Son, who became man to die for our sins"; "He and the Father and the Holy Ghost are the three persons inside the one god"; "Maryam the mother of Īsā was a virgin"; and so on, and so forth. The slightest doubt about any of these statements puts one outside the community, subject to persecution in this world and eternal damnation in the next. Why are they so stubbornly unable to accept, as we Hindūs do more easily that there are many ways to god, many ways, including Īsā, *and* including Muhammad? We Hindūs believe that god is inside everything and everybody. There is, if you will, a spark of god inside all of us; a divine spark, which is destined, sooner or later, to return to its origin. We therefore accept that there are as many paths to god as there are living beings; and that the divergences between the individual beliefs are not so important. Does it really matter that much if I believe that Īsā was a saintly prophet, rather than a pre-existing son-god, if I acknowledge that what he taught was a message of wisdom, holiness and love? For us Hindūs, the divine penetrates everybody and everything, and all holiness, wherever it comes from, is part of god!'

He took another sip, closing his eyes as he had done before.

'I am afraid this is all the wisdom I have to offer, Your Majesty. . . . To me, all religions are fundamentally equal: All of them are different paths towards the same mountain top, different rivers flowing to the same ocean, separate pools of water, all reflecting the light of the same moon. That is why the adherents of one religion should never despise the others – on the contrary, they should engage in respectful dialogue and endeavour to learn from one another, and thus move nearer to god!

'For example, living at Your Majesty's court, I have come to realise that Islām is probably closer to the truth than most Hindū religions in its rejection of caste differences; the message of forgiveness and brotherly love that Īsā taught is certainly an example to all other creeds; and both Muslims and Īsāwīs have much to learn from us Hindūs when it comes to tolerance of diversity. All religions reflect their own facet of the truth, just like a diamond, with its many facets, reflects the same sunlight in a thousand shades of colour!'

'Wholesome food for thought have you given us, my friend! Thank you for your wise counsel and truthful observations – if only there were more people like you! Well, Shaykh Abū-l Fazl, how about you? What is *your* opinion about all this? You have not said anything tonight, and that is quite unlike you, if you do not mind my saying so!'

'I do beg Your Majesty's pardon,' said Abū-l Fazl, an amused smile on his face. 'If indeed I did not say too much until now, it was because I have been overwhelmed by so many conflicting thoughts and impressions.'

'Well, we are anxious to hear about them!'

'Let me start by briefly commenting upon Qutb-ud-dīn Jalesarī's allocution today. Like Your Majesty, I have been quite impressed! Quite honestly, if I had to write a refutation of the Īsāwī creed myself, I could not have done it any better! And I have to say, I fully agree with his analysis. For the past few weeks, I have been listening with great interest, an open mind and deep respect to the firanghī pādres. Beautiful and fascinating though their Injīl is, my conclusion is that their teachings are, quite simply and quite evidently, not true. I am convinced that the prophet Īsā—upon whom be peace—was a saint, a man of exceptional holiness; but all this talk about trinity, incarnation, atonement, resurrection and so on, utterly fails to convince me! It is really too far-fetched, incoherent, and contrary to reason to be believable! No, as beautiful and moving as the Injīl may be, and as much as I have come to respect the prophet Īsā—peace be upon him—I could never be an Īsāwī. I'm afraid I must side with 'Ālim Qutb-ud-dīn Jalesarī on this issue. In this respect, I am and remain a Muslim!'

'In this respect only?' I asked, scrutinising the expression on his face, trying to gauge his thoughts. 'Are there any other respects, in which you do not consider yourself a Muslim?'

Abū-l Fazl looked somewhat embarrassed. 'Probably very few people in this world are entitled to consider themselves true servants of the almighty,' he answered with an evasive smile. He reached for his beaker of wine and took a long, slow draught, in an obvious attempt to gain some time.

'What makes one a good Muslim?' he resumed, smacking his lips. 'And when does one cease to be one? How much deviation is allowed, before one becomes a murtadd? These are important questions, to which, alas, not all Muslims will give the same answer. . . .

'But if Your Majesty allows me, I would like to come back to this a bit later. Before expounding my own personal religious views and doubts, which are anyway neither important nor orthodox, I would first like to state how wholeheartedly I agree with what Rājā Bīrbal has said just now!

'Like Rājā Bīrbal, I profoundly believe that all Hindustānīs—Muslims and Hindūs and all the others—should live together in this land like brothers. We should accept and even cherish our differences, and should take every opportunity to learn from each other! If we are all different, it is because we all have something different to give to the world; if god had wanted us all to be the same, He would not have made us what we are! It is clearly His wish, that we should live together in peace, emulating each other in wisdom and good deeds. And praise be to the almighty, that it has pleased Him to bless us with a king, the wisdom of whom the world has not witnessed since the great and wise king Sulaymān ibn Dā'ūd,[268] peace be upon him!'

'My dear Abū-l Fazl,' I said. 'Much as I enjoy hearing such flowery words of praise—was it not you who once told me that of all lies, flattery is the most effective?—I have to tell you that you are, alas, not putting my mind at ease. Yes, like you and Rājā Bīrbal, I am convinced about the value of all religions; like you, I hoped and believed that dialogue between them would bring us all closer to god. In fact, that is exactly why I have ordered the ibādat-khāna to be built; that is exactly why I have invited representatives from all creeds and denominations to join me in that sacred quest. Yet, if I am honest with myself—as I would urge you to be as well—I have to admit, that so far, these debates have been a bitter disappointment to me. And I often ask myself the question: Have I been able to influence anybody at all? Has anybody changed his mind as a result of this dialogue? If anything, I have the impression that on the contrary, the fanatics have only become more fanatic!'

Abū-l Fazl nodded in agreement and pensively looked down, putting his hand to his forehead.

'Let me first assure Your Majesty,' he answered after a rather long pause, 'that I speak the truth when I express my admiration! There is no doubt in my mind that Your Majesty's reign is a shining example to mankind, to be studied and followed by the righteous and the wise of all times, for thousands upon thousands of years! Your Majesty's justice,

---

268. Solomon, son of David.

kindness and tolerance is comfort and shade for the wise; soothing balm on the aching souls of the humble and the downtrodden; wholesome food and drink for those who hunger and thirst after peace, justice, and truth!

'Like Your Majesty, I have given this matter much thought and reflection these past few months, and much to my regret, I have come to the sad and distressing conclusion that it cannot be resolved – at least not entirely, not entirely satisfactorily. This conclusion, however deplorable, should come as no surprise. By definition, any true faith is intrinsically fanatic: After all, any strongly held conviction or persuasion, religious or other, necessarily implies that in the mind of the believer, only that particular belief is right, and all the others are wrong. Where there is no doubt, there is no tolerance. . . .

'Alas! As we have witnessed during these debates in the ibādat-khāna, it seems we will have to resign ourselves to the fact that no amount of dialogue, no appeal to conscience or reason will ever have the power to bring all the religious fanatics together. On the contrary, as Your Majesty pointed out, it appears that any contact between bigots, far from promoting any mutual understanding, only helps to exacerbate feelings of contempt, fear and hatred. In fact, many of them reject the very idea of a debate between religions! I remember that my father once showed the writings of one of his own teachers, an old man strongly opposed to any kind of contact with unbelievers. This is what it said:

> The possessor of the truth must not expose himself to the blindness, folly and perversion of those whom it has pleased Allāh to leave in error. Idle conversation can never lead to desirable consequences; for Allāh knows what He wants, and if it suits Him that the infidel or the murtadd find the right path, He needs the help of no one to bring about this miracle. One should therefore hold silence useful, and know that speaking to unbelievers, through exposing the person of the believer, is inappropriate and often even sinful.

'Discouraging, is it not? I have often wondered: Why does it have to be like this? Why are there so many bigots? Why is it so much easier to teach people to despise each other, than to accept and appreciate the differences between them?

'I think that at least part of the answer is that fanaticism has one major advantage – it makes life so reassuringly simple! How comforting, how heartening it is, to be able to say: "God is almighty, god is all-knowing, I am His faithful servant, and all the others are not!" No need to think anymore, no need to seek the truth, no need to form a personal opinion about anything; everything is crystal-clear – there is black and white, right and wrong, friend and foe, the saved and the damned, us and the others! How convenient it is to find oneself on the right side! And when in doubt or when challenged, the answer is sure to be found in the holy scriptures. . . . Whether they truly are of divine origin, I do not know, and to be honest, Your Majesty, I very much doubt it. But one thing I do know: They have never failed to yield an appropriate quotation, every time anybody wanted to justify a crime!

'Reason, alas, provides no solution either. Many in the past have tried to establish religion on a sound basis of reason – a magnificent and commendable endeavour, no doubt; but alas, one that is doomed to remain fruitless. Indeed, in my experience, the honest application of reason excites the very doubts it intends to satisfy! It may amuse the quick-minded and bring tranquility to the wise; but it will, without fail, give grave offence to those who cannot bear to see their certainties being undermined.

'Things thus being as they are, the task of a king appears to be quite difficult indeed: How is he to deal with this regrettable state of discord and strife? Is there a way he can convince—or force—his people to live together in peace, if not in friendship and harmony?

'There are, in my humble opinion, only two—or three—alternatives available to him: To impose one religion at the expense of the others; or to be tolerant, either through allowing other religions next to the official one, or through decreeing universal tolerance and freedom for all religions, regardless of their origin.

'As far as I am aware, most kings will favour their own religion. Driven by religious fervour, political considerations, or both, they will proclaim their own faith as the religion of the realm – a clear way of ascertaining their authority. As far as the unbelievers are concerned, their situation varies greatly. In most civilised countries, particularly those under Muslim rulers, other religions are tolerated, and their adherents protected; sometimes, they may even rise to high office! But there are many other kingdoms, particularly in the lands of the Īsāwīs, where all the dissenters are banished, and sometimes even killed!

'Sure enough, as the Purtugēsh experience shows, it is still possible to build a powerful nation on the basis of a single religion, but at what price? Rivers of blood and tears, and the loss of half the population! A kingdom thus founded on bigotry and hatred has to literally eradicate all its dissenters; it has to cut them out, like a poisonous canker; failing to do so, sooner or later, it is bound to fall prey to the monster of hatred it has itself created. In doing so, it is bound to lose many of its best and brightest. . . . Compare this sorry state of affairs to the peace and prosperity in a country where, under the guidance of a wise and just king, there is peace for all!'

'Sulh-i-kul, as dear old Mīr Abdul Latīf used to say. . . .'

'Sulh-i-kul, indeed, Your Majesty! Not always the easiest or the simplest way to govern, but certainly the best, and in my opinion, the only one that truly pleases god: *Khudā solh ast*!'[269]

'But as you rightly point out, that is neither simple, nor easy. . . .'

'It certainly is easier to be the king of a land with only one nation, one language, and one religion,' Abū-l Fazl admitted, 'but will a truly great empire not always have several nations living together on its soil? And while diversity may indeed pose a challenge, it is also a source of richness! Look at the human body – our hands are different from our feet; our eyes, ears and all other organs have their own shapes and their own tasks to perform. This is beneficial, and even necessary. Just imagine how difficult it would be for us to walk if we would have four hands and no feet! Similarly, it is a good thing that an empire is home to different nations, for each of them will have their own strengths and skills to bring to bear!'

'On condition that they agree to live in peace!'

'Indeed, Your Majesty. An empire, ruled by its sovereign, can be compared to a body, ruled by its head. It is not good that the members be divided among themselves; on the contrary, they all have to work together, and execute what the head has ordained! This is the god-given

---

269. God is peace.

task of the king – to be the head of his people, to bring oneness to the multitude!'

'And how do you suggest a king should accomplish this?'

'By ruling exactly the way Your Majesty does!'

'You always were a shameless flatterer, my friend!'

'May Allāh strike me down, may I die in agonising pain if I lie! I swear to Your Majesty, this is not flattery; this is my honest and well-considered opinion!'

'I am honoured, my friend, but I do fear you think me to be wiser than I actually am. . . . Anyway, tell me, how would you describe the way I rule my empire? What makes it so different from, for instance, the way my grandfather Bābur ruled over it, or my father Humāyūn, or, for that matter, his rival Shēr Khān Sūr and so many others?'

'I would say, it is the difference between the seed and the plant, the mine and the jewel, the unploughed land and the field in crop! It is true that all the three rulers Your Majesty just mentioned have endeavoured to reign with justice, and were tolerant towards their Hindū subjects. But not one of them had Your Majesty's broadmindedness and vision! Not one of them actually dared to *abolish* the difference between Hindūs and Muslims; not one of them took such drastic measures to rule out arbitrary punishment. Your Majesty is the mightiest king on this earth, but he uses his power to *serve*: to serve god, and to serve his people. Truly, this is what makes an empire prosperous: when the people submit to their emperor, and their emperor submits to god.'

'I agree, my friend, but this begs the question – how to serve god when there are many religions? How to bring about unity, when dialogue only seems to deepen the rift between the various creeds?'

'This is where I would like to come back to what Rājā Bīrbal said earlier this evening: All those differences between the various creeds do not really matter, for inside all religions lies a common core of human decency, and this is sufficient to build a peaceful and harmonious society.'

He reached for his beaker and took a sip from his wine.

'Your Majesty asked me a few moments ago, whether I considered myself a Muslim. I do. I certainly am nothing else. I have the highest respect for my Hindū brethren, but I have no use for their deities and rituals; I respect the prophet Īsā, but I could never believe what the firanghī pādres urge us to accept as true. Yet, I very much doubt if a man like good old Qutb-ud-dīn Jalesarī—Allāh bless his soul—would still consider me to be a true Muslim, if he knew my private thoughts on religion!'

'Would he not? And what might those thoughts be?'

'Well, Your Majesty, to be honest, I think that most religious people take themselves too seriously. I think they are much too eager to ascribe to god all kinds of thoughts and intentions that are really their own. They confound the mountain and the mirror in their hands; they confound reality with the constructs of their own minds.'

'You mean to say that religions are mere concoctions, fabrications, figments of the imagination?'

'To a large extent, yes, Your Majesty. However, that does not mean to say that they are all deliberate lies, nor that there would be no value in them – quite the contrary!'

He took another sip of his wine.

'How shall I explain this best? Your Majesty is of course aware that most religions state that we are created in god's image; in fact, I think the opposite is true. The image that most people have of god is a reflection of their own hopes and fears, an attempt to make sense of a harsh and unpredictable world. Even if we have every happiness and luxury in life, we fear we may lose our loved ones, that we may become poor, or ill; and in the end, we are certain to die. Death, in fact, is the only absolute certainty in life. We know we have to die, and yet, we long for eternity. And so, we imagine ourselves a god, Who will make everything right, even if this life has been full of suffering and disappointment – a god Who will reward the good and punish the bad, Who will make the limited and fragile lives of ours perfect and eternal.'

'So you actually think that god does not exist?'

'To be honest, I do not know, Your Majesty. I think He does exist, but I do not know what He is like – whether, as Rājā Bīrbal expressed it, god is a He, a She, or an It. It may be that He is like the Injīl or the way the Holy Qur'ān describe Him, but I often wonder whether He might the same as the blind, awesome force of nature, the force that creates and destroys, that makes the lion and the lamb, the nightingale and the cobra, all with the same imperturbable indifference. . . .'

'Do you mean a bit like some people describe Lord Śiva of the Hindūs?'

'Indeed, Your Majesty. As I said, I do not know. But then, I do not think it makes that much of a difference.'

'Does it not? But if there is no personal god, and if god is just a blind force, then there is no good and bad, no morality. . . .'

'With all due respect, Your Majesty, that is what most religious people say, but I do not think it is actually true. Let me try to explain what I mean. The true, the good, the beautiful – these are the names of god, but are they not also deeply human values? Are they not universal principles we all feel we should try to remain faithful to, because they are important in every human life? If I honestly try to serve the true and the good in my life, what practical difference does it make whether I believe that these are *human* realities, or, in fact, aspects of an eternal, almighty, ineffable god? Siding with the right honourable Rājā Bīrbal, I would venture to say: There is *no* practical difference. Indeed, this is a wise insight for which we remain very much indebted to our Hindū brothers. Hindūs have no problem allowing hundreds and hundreds of different concepts of the deity – even including outright atheism! Their sages have understood that all these human theories are bound to remain imperfect attempts to describe a reality which anyway surpasses our understanding.

'Similarly, does it matter whether I believe the Holy Qur'ān is of divine or of human origin? What practical difference does it make whether I believe it has been dictated word for word by the angel Jibriel, or whether it gradually arose in the mind of a prophet – that is, a human being who was overwhelmed by the true, the good and the beautiful? Personally, I am inclined to believe the latter is true, but that does not make my respect for the Holy Qur'ān and the Prophet any less! The Holy Qur'ān was, is, and will remain, in my mind at least, one of the, if not *the*, most beautiful and holy scripture that has ever been written. In an unparalleled, sublime way, it expresses truth, goodness and beauty, and in that sense, it is for me, without any doubt, the word of god.'

'I must admit, my honourable friend,' Bīrbal said, 'thoughts like these have crossed my own mind as well.'

'And mine,' I agreed.

'I would have been surprised if they had not, Your Majesty. In fact, I think there are very few intelligent people who do not have these kind of doubts. But then again, does it really matter that much? I think—no disrespect intended, Your Majesty—that the debates in the ibādat-khāna, fascinating as they were, have clearly demonstrated that it is impossible for one believer to convert another. But fortunately, that is not necessary! All of us do not have to believe in the same ideas to be able to live together! Of one thing I am certain – if god does exist, He is big enough for all of us. How exactly we see Him, is not that important. The only thing that really counts is that we serve Him through goodness and truthfulness. Behold, the common religion that unites us all: dīn-e-illāhī, submission to that one god, and obedience to the one emperor, who is god's representative, and whose task it is to serve god through peace and justice!'

'Dīn-e-illāhī . . . the religion of the one god, the religion that peacefully unites all others, without forcing itself on them. . . .'

Thirty-second Letter

کابل

Kābul

I believe it was Abū-l Fazl who once told me—or was it Shaykh Mubārak?—that all virtue holds the middle between two extremes. A soldier's bravery, for instance, holds the middle between cowardice and futile recklessness; generosity stands in between stinginess and extravagance. The same goes for self-confidence – too little of it will make you fearful and weak; too much will make you reckless and irresponsible.

Much as I regret to admit it, at the time, the latter was my problem. In my defence, I do want to point out, and I'm sure you'll understand me, my son, that it is not easy to remain levelheaded when surrounded by lofty buildings and untold wealth; it is indeed difficult not to get overconfident when the world is at your feet; it is hard not to start believing in the flowery words of praise that people are pouring on your head, day after day. . . .

Thus it is inexcusable, but perhaps understandable, that when early in Esfand of the twenty-fifth year,[270] Todar Mal came in to inform me that a number of local zamindārs in Bengāl were refusing to pay their taxes, I

---

270. February 1580.

was not overly alarmed. Little did I realise that only a few months later, I will be facing the most dangerous rebellion of my reign with powerful enemies rising up in arms against me in the three corners of the empire: Bengāl and Bihār in the east, the Panjāb in the northwest, and Gujarāt in the southwest.

As I said, it all began with what seemed to be a simple tax-collection issue. Suspecting that the local governor Muzaffar Khān Turbatī had possibly been a bit overzealous or heavy-handed, I sent Todar Mal to appease the parties involved and remove the causes of discontent. I did not give further attention to the matter, until a few weeks later, truly alarming reports started reaching Fatehpūr Sīkrī. All conciliation attempts had proven to be unsuccessful, and every day, a new local zamindār was joining the mutiny.

To make matters worse, the newly-appointed qādī of Jaunpūr, Mullāh Muhammad Yazdī, had the audacity of issuing a fatwā, condemning the emperor's 'religious innovations'!

How convenient, is it not, when Sharī'ah becomes an excuse not to pay taxes? The rebellion, then 'legitimised', spread like wildfire, into Bihār, Urīsā, Ghāzīpūr, Banāras and Allāhābād, and the outnumbered local imperial garrisons suddenly found themselves confronted with an all-out war.

Alas! The beginning of the campaign was an outright disaster for the imperial army. The Bengālī mutineers crossed the Gangā at Rājmahal, where they joined forces with the rebels from Bihār, and defeated the local imperial forces led by the brave governor, Muzaffar Khān, who was captured and, sadly, put to death, after what reportedly were the worst imaginable tortures. May the delights of paradise be the eternal reward for his loyalty!

Rājā Todar Mal, now in peril of death himself, with forces much too small to take on the enemy, was of course unable to avenge him. But despite the grave danger, he staunchly refused to flee back to the safety of Fatehpūr Sīkrī, and retreated to the fortress of Monghyr, where he and his men were besieged by the rebels.

I was just getting ready to head east myself and cool my anger with towers of heads, when I received an even more disturbing dispatch: The rebels had started reading the weekly khutbah in the name of my half-brother Muhammad Hakīm, a worthless, drunken sot to be sure; but allegedly and conveniently, an orthodox Muslim. . . .

Gone were all my lofty musings, my profound speculations about god and universe, my grandiose plans for a dīn-e-illāhī to unite all religions. Gloomy thoughts were racing feverishly through my head. What had started as a rather trivial dispute over taxes and local autonomy, had assumed the pretense and legitimacy of jihād! Years of toil and labour, my family's honour, and my own were at stake. I simply could not afford to make any further mistakes! Seething with impotent rage, I called an urgent meeting with Rājā Mān Singh, and Amīr Shāhbāz Khān, one of my senior army generals in Fatehpūr Sīkrī.

'I hear that those Bengālī mutineers—may Allāh punish them in this world and the next—are reading the khutbah in Muhammad Hakīm's name! Can you believe this? These dogs actually have the audacity to recognise that worthless idiot, as pādshāh of Hindustān! What do you suggest we do about this?'

'Your Majesty,' said Shāhbāz Khān, 'intolerable an insult though this may be, the greatest threat clearly lies in the east. Vast and rich territories are in enemy hands, and many of them are experienced army commanders, unlike Muhammad Hakīm, who has never led a campaign before. My suggestion is, that we quickly march east in force, and defeat our most powerful enemies first!'

'You may be right, my friend,' said Mān Singh, 'but just suppose Muhammad Hakīm does invade the Panjāb while we are tied up far away in Bengāl! If he ever manages to get his hands on the treasures of Lāhor, Dillī and Āgrā, all is lost! Even with the fall of Lāhor alone, our position would be precarious!'

'And what do you suggest we do about it, honourable rājā? That we go to the Panjāb to fend off an invasion that may never come? And what if those Bengālī rebels attack us in the rear? Have you ever thought of that?'

'With all due respect, honourable amīr, you may be right that your solution may win us the battle of Bengāl more quickly, but I fear it may actually cost us the war over Hindustān!'

I realised that both of them were getting angry, and raised my hand – this was no time for us to be divided.

'Thank you, my good friends, those are exactly the ideas that have been going through my own mind as well. Let us not lose our coolheadedness here, for you are both right: Amīr Shāhbāz Khān correctly points out that the strongest enemy is in the east, but Rājā Mān Singh is right when he says that the greatest danger to the throne actually looms across the Khyber Pass. If ever the treasures of Lāhor, Dillī and Āgrā would fall into Muhammad Hakīm's hands, it could, god forbid, be the end of the entire empire!

'No, we simply have to find a way to deal with both threats at the same time!

'Here is what I think: In the east, the most urgent thing is to *contain* the enemy – making sure we keep fighting in *his* land, not on our own. I therefore suggest, Amīr Shāhbāz Khān, that you immediately march east, with all your troops. I will send an urgent dispatch to my foster brother Mīrzā Azīz Koka to join you as soon as possible with another strong contingent. He will be a formidable ally. Like yourself, he is an experienced soldier who adores a good fight. . . . Try to get a message across to Todar Mal – tell him to hold out at all costs. And once you have been able to relieve the pressure on him, concentrate your efforts on the Teliyāgarhī Pass first. As I said, the most important thing right now is to contain them. I promise you, we will take care of them later!

'Mān Singh, my noble brother and trusted friend, I would like you to secure the Panjāb. In case Muhammad Hakīm does attack, show him and his Afghān rabble what Rājpūt courage is capable of! Make sure they do not get past Lāhor – I promise I will start following you as soon as I can, and together, we will crush this vermin, once and for all!'

I will not bore you with the details, my son, but the events soon proved the soundness of my reasoning. Encouraged by the support of the Bengālī rebels, Muhammad Hakīm prepared for war. Two scouting expeditions led by his generals Nūr-ud-dīn and Shādmān were repulsed with relative ease by our border garrisons, in the month of Āzar of the twenty-fifth year;[271] a few weeks later, however, Muhammad Hakīm himself attacked in force, with his entire army.

---

271. December 1580

He crossed the Sindh and headed straight towards Lāhor, where fortunately, his advance was brought to an abrupt halt, thanks to Rājā Mān Singh's staunch resistance. Muhammad Hakīm, who clearly counted on a general uprising in his favour, was sadly disappointed to find that nobody in the Panjāb was prepared to join him – not the Rājpūts, not the Sikhs, not the local Muslims. When he learnt that Emperor Akbar himself was not safely occupied in far away Bengāl as he had hoped, but was actually advancing against him, he beat a hasty retreat; indeed, such was his panic that four hundred of his men perished crossing the Chinab River.

Meanwhile, I had left nothing to chance. Personally busying myself with the campaign preparations, I had in no time managed to assemble a force of truly overwhelming strength – no less than fifty thousand cavalry, over five hundred prime war elephants, and a host of foot soldiers and cannons. Each soldier had received eight months' pay in advance: Never forget, my son, that army loyalty, in the first instance, is based on sound treasury!

On the twenty-ninth of Bahman,[272] this huge, magnificent army headed northeast, with amazing speed and precision. The Purtugēsh pādres, travelling with us, were astounded at the perfect organisation of the supplies for such an immense number of people and animals. At each stopping place, accommodations were excellent and supplies ample, everything had been prepared in every possible detail by disciplined as and courteous purveyors. They had paid in advance and more than in full, for every item – and I mean in freshly minted, unadulterated, pure gold and silver, painstakingly, up to the last stalk of straw. The villagers, of course, were left in peace, their elders and temples respected, their women untouched, just as I learned it from Bairām Khān when I was young; however, I tried to be even more gentle, generous, and reassuring to them.

Soon, the army's well-deserved reputation started to precede its advance. Everywhere on its line of march, the villagers gathered from far and near, gazing at the awesome magnificence of this army, and cheering their generous and benevolent emperor.

---

272. 8 February 1581

Near the town of Sirhind, scouts brought me the happy tiding that Muhammad Hakīm had taken to flight, head over heels. But that did not change my decision. This time, I chose to chase that bastard all the way to Kābul, and make him eat dust.

After advancing via Kalānaur and Rohtās, the imperial army reached the mighty Sindh River, which was crossed with understandable but no less irritating difficulty and loss of time. To make things worse, the Hindū commanders had the greatest trouble persuading their men to cross over to the 'unclean' lands on the other side. I did my best not to lose my temper, but I had no time to lose. I needed a quick and decisive victory, I could not afford to have my forces tied down in a protracted siege of a big city like Kābul! Much to my relief, Rājā Mān Singh, who had managed to restore order and discipline among his Rājpūts, saw it my way. He volunteered to ride ahead with a fast and powerful vanguard of twenty thousand cavalry to catch the rebels before they reached the city. Murād, barely eleven years old, insisted on riding with him. So full of fighting spirit was the lad that he kept pestering me until I finally let him have his way.

We then headed towards the Khyber Pass. I hardly allowed myself the time to enjoy the majestic landscape, and spent my days conferring with the army commanders and devising battle plans, preparing for every conceivable eventuality.

I did not need to wait much longer. Ably guided by the scouts, Mān Singh caught up with Muhammad Hakīm's army, and attacked it, with neither hesitation nor mercy. With god's help, it did not take him long to inflict on the enemy a defeat, so crushing and bloody that Muhammad Hakīm did not have a glimmer of hope left of making a stand at Kābul. Scared to death, he fleed to the mountains further west. My plan had worked perfectly.

And thus, on the twenty-ninth of Mordād of the twenty-sixth year,[273] the great imperial army of Hindustān proudly marched through the wide-open iron gates of Kābul, and I made my triumphant entry into his grandfather's ancient capital. Awe-struck at the sight of my magnificence and power, the inhabitants received me with humble reverence and every

---

273. 10 August 1581

possible honour, but visible dread for they wondered if they would be punished with executions, rape, plunder and punitive taxes.

Fear quickly turned to relief, and then enthusiasm, when for the first time, they saw for themselves the kindness and clemency that a great and just emperor is capable of. Leaving everything and everybody in peace, I distributed alms to the poor, and with unfeigned albeit conspicuous piousness, I rendered myself immediately to the great Alī Masjīd, where I humbly removed my armour, turban and boots, and performed the required ablutions, slowly and thoroughly. Barefoot and in plain white clothes like the humblest of worshippers, I entered the musalla and prostrated myself in front of the mihrab,[274] where I remained for a full hour, kneeling on a simple rug, in silent prayer, thanking god for my victory.

Anxious to get back to Fatehpūr Sīkrī, closer to the dangerous war in Bengāl, I stayed in Kābul for only seven days – just the time required to settle the affairs of local government. I officially appointed Bakht un-Nissah, Muhammad Hakīm's sister and my own half-sister, wife of Khwājah Hasan of Badakshān, as governor over the province, leaving her clear and written instructions – that I entrust the government of Kābul and Badakshān to her *personally*; that I will take it back, if and when I please; that I do not care if Muhammad Hakīm, whose name I never want to hear again, returns to Kābul or not; but that she should warn him, that in the event of any new acts of misbehaviour, he should no longer expect the kindness and clemency shown to him now.

Indeed, he never bothered me again. For the rest of his life, he confined himself to the only thing he was good at – drinking himself to death. When in the month of Tīr of the thirtieth year,[275] he died, barely thirty-one years old, I did not have a single rival left. For the rest of my life, I will think, say and do as I please.

After crossing the Khyber Pass, the Sindh and the great rivers of the Panjāb once again, I triumphantly made my way back to the capital. On

---

274. Musalla: Prayer hall. Mihrab: Niche in the wall, indicating the direction of Mecca.
275. July 1585

the twentieth of Āzar,[276] I arrived at the gates of Fatehpūr Sīkrī, where grandiose feasts were held to celebrate the victory.

Meanwhile, in the east, the tide had turned. The rebels besieging Todar Mal had taken to flight upon Azīz Koka's arrival; Bihār, Allāhābād, Jaunpūr had been recovered by the victorious imperial armies. The back of the insurrection was broken – slowly but surely and thoroughly, Bengāl and the eastern provinces would be pacified.

≈

The victorious imperial armies were still busy mopping up the last pockets of resistance in the rebellious east, when a new and equally dangerous revolt broke out in the opposite corner of the empire: Gujarāt. Nothing to do with religion this time, but all the more with taxes. Disgruntled local zamīndārs, eager to 'throw off the imperial yoke', suddenly found themselves a ringleader when the former Gujarātī king, Muzaffar, who was captured during the conquest of Gujarāt but had managed to escape, reappeared from his hiding place. He promised them the moon – lucrative jāgīrs, treasure, freedom from taxes, high offices, glory, honour . . . and they were foolish enough to believe him. Soon, he succeeded in bringing together a sizeable force, and cleverly took advantage of the temporary weakness of the imperial garrisons due to the retirement of the former governor Sihāb-ud-dīn and his replacement by his successor I'timād Khān. Against vastly superior numbers, Ahmedābād fell to the enemy, and a few weeks later, Qutb-ud-dīn, the loyal governor of Barodā, was also defeated and treacherously killed when he surrendered after having been promised a safe-conduct out of the country. All of Gujarāt, except the city of Pattan, had fallen to the enemy.

I reluctantly started making preparations for another major campaign, when it was announced that Abdurrahīm had requested a private audience with me.

'Your Majesty,' he said with that tone of firmness and resolve that so strongly reminded me of his father, 'I would like to request the honour of leading an expedition to punish the Gujarātī traitors.'

---

276. 1 December 1581

'Thank you, Abdurrahīm, but do you not think I should go myself? The whole of Gujarāt is breaking away! This requires a major campaign!'

'Your Majesty's wish is my command, of course. However, if I may be so bold as to say this, I do believe Your Majesty's presence is required here, in the centre of the empire! It is true, our troops in Bengāl are doing well, but the war is not over yet! Moreover, with two wars going on in two opposite corners of the empire, it may be wise to keep a large contingent of troops in the centre, to be prepared against any eventualities. With Your Majesty's permission, I will go. I will take only five thousand men, and raise extra troops with Your Majesty's allies in Rājpūtānā. I will ride fast! The rebellion will be crushed in no time, Your Majesty can count on me!'

'Maybe,' I said, looking at the determined expression on his face with an amused smile. Those cheekbones, that long, bony nose, the fire in those black eyes – how he reminded me of his father!

'Your analysis of our situation is of course quite correct, my young friend. But my question is – can I *afford* to stay back here, or to allow you to leave with such a small force? You are only twenty-eight, my friend; I do admit that you have won your spurs in many battles, that you are bright and brave; it is for that reason that I have decided to make you Salīm's atālīq, just like your father, the great Bairām Khān—may Allāh receive him in paradise—was my own atālīq when I was young. I like and respect you, Abdurrahīm; but can you run such a major campaign, so far away? Will you indeed be able to raise all those extra troops you need? Let me tell you what your father taught me: "All things remaining equal, god favours the larger army"! I hear that Muzaffar, that filthy dog, has no less than forty thousand cavalry at his disposal! Forty thousand, do you realise what that means? That is a force to be reckoned with, my young friend! Do you really think you can handle that?'

Abdurrahīm looked at me, at a loss for words at first, trying to hide his impatience. 'The grave where the bones of my father rest is in danger of being desecrated by enemy occupation, Your Majesty,' he said softly, bowing his head. 'I humbly request Your Majesty's permission to go there and fight for its liberation. If, with Allāh's help, I succeed, I will be able to kiss my father's hand in paradise without shame; and if I fail, I swear that Your Majesty will find me amidst the corpses of the fallen!'

I put my hand on his shoulder.

'I am happy to see, my young friend, that the great Bairām Khān lives on in his son. Go with god – may He bless and keep you!'

I was wrong to doubt him. Abdurrahīm proved to be as resourceful, bold and brave as his illustrious father once was. Advancing rapidly through Rājpūtānā, he allied himself with the good Motha Rājā,[277]—may god bless him—and other local Hindū and Muslim zamīndārs, including Abū-l Qāsim Bunyād, Rāi Durgā, Tulsī Dās Jādūn, Khīzr Āqā, and Mīān Bahādūr.

Abdurrahīm's force—small in number, but of excellent quality—crossed the Gujarātī border, and came upon the rebel army at Sakhej, southwest of Ahmedābād, on the sixth of Bahman of the twenty-eight year.[278] The enemy had an overwhelming force of forty thousand cavalry and about one hundred thousand foot soldiers, against Abdurrahīm's mere ten thousand cavalry and five hundred elephants. Many imperial officers begged him to retreat, but Abdurrahīm refused to yield, and went on to attack. Protecting his right flank against the town walls, he used the same bold and daring tactic his father had used against Shams-ud-dīn – a massive elephant charge in the centre, combined with a furious cavalry attack on the left, in a deadly pincer movement. Only here, there were no rice paddies to slow down the elephants; and the enemy was literally crushed between hammer and anvil. Abdurrahīm's furious onslaught wreaked havoc on the enemy's centre. The elephants, headed by the vicious old bull Shermār, penetrated deep into the enemy ranks, and trampled them by the dozen. At the same time, Rāi Durgā, with elite Rājpūt and Turkomān cavalry, slammed into their right flank and prevented them from manoeuvring. In less than a quarter of an hour, Muzaffar's great army was on the run, leaving behind several thousand dead.

Abdurrahīm pursued him to Khambhat, and from there, north to Barodā and Nāndod, where he inflicted on him a second and final defeat, again with several thousand dead. Muzaffar managed to flee the carnage and went into hiding until his capture, a few years later. Seeing

---

277. The 'fat rājā': Udai Singh of Jodhpūr, father-in-law of Jahāngīr, grandfather of Shāh Jahān.
278. 14 January 1584

no escape, he slit his own throat, sparing me the trouble of ordering his execution.

When the good tiding of this new great victory was brought to me, I did not hesitate one instant: Abdurrahīm ibn Bairām Khān, the brave young officer who once came to my court as a shy four-year-old orphan, was appointed Khān Khanān, lord of lords, head of the imperial armies – just like his father was before him. I felt shivers down my spine when the draft text of the firmān was read out to me for my approval. High up above in god's sweet heaven, I knew that the great Bairām Khān, my faithful atālīq, was smiling.

Thirty-third Letter

دینِ الاحی

Din-e-Illahi

From the private notes of Mulāzim Hakīm Alī Gilanī

Something about His Majesty has changed after his triumphant return from Kābul. He seems pensive and rather quiet during the celebrations, and he spends quite a lot of time on his own: horseback riding, aimlessly strolling around the palace gardens, meditating on a stone in the pale light of dawn. Obviously, he is brooding on something.

Then suddenly, in rapid succession, things start to happen.

Mullāh Muhammad Yazdī, the qādī of Jaunpūr, the pompous windbag who was so eager to support the rebels with his ill-considered fatwā, is invited to present himself at the sublime threshold, along with his colleague, the qādī of Bengāl. No official reason is mentioned in the firmān, but there can be little doubt: The emperor wants them in the court to account for their treacherous attitude during the rebellion. But those expecting to witness a sensational trial, are bitterly disappointed indeed; the two learned mullāhs perish underway to Fatehpūr Sīkrī, when the boat carrying them suddenly and inexplicably capsizes.

And this is only the first of a series of similar incidents. The following weeks, several of the leading mullāhs suddenly expired from mysterious illnesses, met with fatal accidents, got killed in roadside robberies, or disappeared from their homes, for reasons unknown, and in unexplained circumstances.

There probably are not too many people around who have the slightest doubt, that all these unfortunate incidents are, in fact, nothing less than clandestine executions, ordered by the emperor himself, most probably to spare himself the inconvenience of lengthy public trials. In fact, this is what *everybody* believes, but the few who dare to voice their suspicions, do so sparingly and privately.

The emperor, for his part, seems wholly unperturbed. Not a single comment on the rebellion; not a word about the dead mullāhs, neither in public, nor in private as far as I know. He goes about his duties calmly, as if nothing had happened. The qādīs and other dignitaries who have died or disappeared are casually replaced with new incumbents, usually after a brief private audience with the Khān Khanān, or, in some cases, with the emperor himself.

Whether it has all been planned like this or not, the result is strikingly effective: In a few weeks' time, law, order and discipline are restored; peace and tranquility return to the land. Never again will a mullāh dare to pass judgement on the emperor's policies, not even in private. No more doubts, no more arguments, no more criticisms – the emperor is the undisputed imām-i-ādil,[279] the true khalīfah. He is god's viceregent on this earth, the ultimate authority in all matters, temporal and spiritual. No Makhdūm-ul Mulk, no Shaykh ul-Islām: Henceforth, the emperor is the mujtahid,[280] high and unattainable on the sublime throne of Hindustān. Emperor Akbar reigns, and he reigns alone, in his own way – justly and independently; respectful to all, subservient to none.

With no one left to criticise, let alone challenge him, once again he indulges in his favourite intellectual pastime – religion. He seems to have lost interest in formal public debates, of which he convenes but few;

---

279. Imām-i-ādil: The just leader, the sovereign.
280. Mujtahid: highest legal authority, entitled to make original decisions of Islamic law (rather than merely applying precedents already established).

however, private audiences are granted almost on a daily basis, sometimes through the entire night. He seems truly insatiable in this quest for knowledge and wisdom; and the more unworldly and mysterious his interlocutors and their teachings, the more they seem to evoke his interest and respect.

With unfeigned piety, he participates in arcane Pārsī fire rituals, performed by an old mūbid[281] named Ardsher and his younger colleague, Dastūr Māhyārjī Rānā from Nausari in Gujarāt. Such is the emperor's interest and zeal, that he orders a perpetual sacred fire to be lit and maintained in the palace.

To the dismay of some, but with the consent of many, the Hijrī lunar calendar falls into disuse at the court. Events are henceforth recorded using the Persian solar calendar, with the chronology starting in the year of His Majesty's accession to the throne. 'All religions have their own way of recording time, and there is nothing wrong with that,' explains the emperor, 'but just like there is only one god, and only one sun shining down on all people, there is only one emperor, and it is only becoming that he uses an era common to all his subjects.'

Every day at dawn, noon, dusk and midnight, the emperor now publicly worships the sun – either directly, outside, in the open air, or through the symbols of fire, and light. With devotion and respect, he kneels down before every sacred fire, wherever it burns, be it the Pārsī shrine, the Hindū temple, or the Īsāwī church. He issued orders that henceforth, each evening when the lamps are lit, all courtiers are to rise to their feet and bow their heads, 'for to light a candle is to commemorate the rising of the sun, and the sun is the sacred symbol of god's eternal majesty and the compassion with which He sustains His creation'.

One would be inclined to conclude from all the above that the emperor has become a confirmed Pārsī fire-worshipper, but that would not be entirely accurate, for the Parsi mūbids are clearly not the only people to enjoy his favour and attention.

Sitting on the balcony of his private quarters, he listens, night after night, weeks on end, to the teachings of a feeble old Brāhmin priest named Debi. The old man, by his own express request, is hoisted up the

---

281. Mūbid: Zoroastrian priest

wall of the imperial residence in a cot of thick hemp ropes, as 'it would be impossible for him to set foot in a mlechcha[282] home, albeit the palace of a king most high: The rules of Brāhmin purity, the old man explains apologetically, are a matter of age-old rituals, and alas, not of human politeness. . . .'

The emperor does not seem to mind the insult. Tears are glistening in his eyes, as he listens, with baited breath, to the tales of the *Mahābhārata*, and to the old priest's profound comments on the thousand names of the great Hindū gods Vishnu and Śiva.[283] His scribes are ordered to take due note of every single word, so that he may have them read out to him whenever he desires.

The Hindū religion is clearly at the forefront of his mind, and the subject of many a learned conversation.

'Tell me, Shaykh Abū-l Fazl, Rājā Bīrbal,' he enquires one evening, 'you who are so learned and wise . . . when you hear those names of the Hindū gods Vishnu and Śiva, when you compare them to the beautiful names of Allāh in the Holy Qur'ān – what is the difference between them, according to you?'

'There is none, really . . .' said Abū-l Fazl after a brief pause. 'None that matters, anyway!'

'Well said, my brother, very well said!' said Bīrbal enthusiastically. 'There really is no real difference between them – or rather, the difference between them is only apparent. It is of course true that many of the Hindū names, like Candrāpīda (having the moon for diadem), Trilocana (three-eyed); Nīlalohita (blue-blooded), Jatin (of matted hair), and so on, are quite different from the divine names used in Islām, as the names I mentioned refer to Hindū imagery. But what to say about the other names, the ones referring to the essence of god, like Puskara (the nourisher), Dhyānādhāra (object of meditation), Aparicchedya (the inexplicable), Parātpara (greater than the greatest), Anādīmadhyanidhana (with no beginning, middle or end), and so on? All those names are, just

---

282. Mlechcha: Non-vedic, barbarian, impure, unclean.
283. The names of Śiva are found in the Hymn of Thousand Names, *Śiva Purāna*, Kotirudrasamhitā, Chapter 35; those of Vishnu, in the *Mahābhārata*.

like in the Holy Qur'ān, attempts to describe, in feeble human language, the infinite, unspeakable reality behind this fleeting world!'

'I think so too,' agrees the emperor. 'When it comes to outward appearances, no two religions would seem more different. Yet, in essence, they are both the same!'

The Brāhmin priest is just one of many venerable teachers introducing the emperor to the many branches of the Hindū tradition. Particular mention should be made of Hīravijaya Sūri, Bhānuchandra Upādhyāya, and Vijayasena Sūri, three venerable Jain monks residing on the palace grounds, who seem to exert a remarkable influence on the emperor.

Heeding the imperial summons to come to the court to instruct him in their faith, the three old sages have walked all the way from Gujarāt to Fatehpūr, politely declining the comfortable transportation provided for them. Upon their arrival, they have of course been received with every possible honour, but once again, they have kindly turned down all the treasures offered to them in recompense for their efforts. The three will accept nothing but a jar of plain, unchilled water, and one frugal meal every day, from which not only meat and fish are strictly banned, but also any carrots, onions, leeks, garlic, and any other kind of vegetable growing under the ground – harvesting plants that grow under the ground, so they explain, may cause harm to some small worms or insects.

With patience and kindness, the old savants initiate His Majesty in the teachings of the noble Mahāvīra, the great hero, the world-relinquishing venerable one, twenty-fourth and last of the great jinas,[284] who achieved ultimate liberation or moksha at the end of a life of veracity, control, penance, goodness, and absence of any kind of violence, whether in thoughts, words, or deeds. The noble and humble Mahāvīra, who spent the entirety of his blameless life fasting and meditating, naked and possessionless, 'indifferent alike to the smell of ordure and sandalwood, to straw and jewels, dirt and gold, pleasure and pain, attached neither to this world nor to the one beyond, desiring neither life nor death', until, in his seventy-second year, his soul effortlessly left his mortified body, to rise upward, to the very top of the universe. There, it dwells, motionless and absolutely free, for all eternity. . . .

---

284. Jina: Victor, conqueror

To follow the great Mahāvīra's saintly example, so the teachers explain, is man's true and only road to liberation; and on that road, the most important commandment of all is ahimsā, the absolute and complete avoidance of any violence, whether of body, speech or mind. The virtuous will *never* kill nor cause to kill, not even the vilest and lowest of creatures, not even the most vicious of enemies; he will refrain, under all circumstances, from lying, stealing, illicit intercourse, and attachment to worldly possessions; he will avoid negative thoughts of any kind, and maintain equanimity at all times.

Never will he tread on wet soil, lest he might inadvertently kill even the smallest worm or insect; never will he light a lamp or fire of any kind, lest unsuspecting insects be attracted to its deadly glow; he will refrain from any farming activity requiring soil to be ploughed, lest a worm or insect, no matter how despicable or insignificant, be killed or injured in the process.

Visibly touched by these saintly teachings, the emperor proclaims: 'The duties of the throne will, alas, at times compel a king to leave the path of ahimsā; nevertheless, for the sake of his own soul and the wellbeing of his subjects, he should endeavour to tread it as much as possible!'

Thenceforth, he refrains from hunting; he abstains from meat, onions, leeks and garlic, and rarely takes more than one meal a day. On more than one hundred days per year, the killing of animals is prohibited throughout the empire, and the slaughter of cows is banned altogether, as it would be in a Hindū state.

Indeed, the emperor's interest in all things Jain or Hindū seems to be growing every day. 'So that the wisdom of the *Mahābhārata* may become accessible to all', he orders it to be translated from Sanskrit into Persian, under the reluctant supervision of Maulānā Abdul Qādir Badāonī, an orthodox Muslim scholar. Hindū symbols, customs and rituals become commonplace at the court: Holi, Dīwālī, Navarātri, Durgā-Pūjā, and all the other feasts are celebrated as they would be at the palace of a Hindū king. Sometimes, he actually dresses like one, complete with a bindu on his forehead, and a thread around his wrist. He seems to belong to all religions, and to none. As Abū-l Fazl expresses it with his usual discernment and wit: 'The emperor is Pārsī in his rites, Hindū in his food, and Sūfī in his heart'.

'Of one thing I have become firmly convinced over these last few years, my friends,' the emperor himself testifies one evening, over some wine. 'At the core, all religions are the same! All creeds of course have their own shar'a, their own rituals and prayers, which may be very different from other traditions; but at their core is the same dīn, the true spirit of religion, the actual devotion to the highest deity, which dwells in the souls of all people of good will. And after all, is that not what really matters? What else does god expect from us, but to honour Him with our lives? Will He not recognise true devotion wherever He finds it, even in the humblest prayer? And conversely, will He not recognise lies and hypocrisy, even under the most elaborate and orthodox of rituals? No, my friends, there is no doubt in my mind – true religion is one, as god is one. Was it not the great poet Ibn Arabī who once said: "My heart is a mosque, a church, a synagogue and a temple"? As a human being, I was born in one particular tradition; but as the emperor, as the guardian of sulh-i-kul, I must protect and embrace them all!'

And then, in the month of Bahman, towards the beginning of the twenty-seventh year,[285] it all becomes official: The emperor solemnly promulgates dīn-e-illāhī, the religion of the one god, the one religion peacefully uniting all others. Thus, the firmān states, 'honour will be rendered to god, peace will be given to the peoples, and security to the empire'.

Or, as Abū-l Fazl observes in the *Ā'īn-i-Akbarī*, with the usual flattery:

> Whenever, from lucky circumstances, the time arrives that a nation learns to understand how to worship truth, the people will naturally look to their king, on account of the high position he occupies, and expect him to be their spiritual leader as well; for a king possesses, independent of men, the ray of divine wisdom, which banishes from the heart everything that is conflicting.

Up to this day, I do not know—in fact, I would very much doubt that anybody does—what His Majesty's motives were at the time when he decreed this. Was he actually hoping that the masses of Hindūs and

---

285. Early 1582

Muslims would convert, by the hundreds of thousands, to his mysterious new religion? Or did he merely intend to establish a religious order of his own, a fellowship similar to the Sūfī orders, but open to like-minded people of all backgrounds, Muslims and non-Muslims alike? Was it a symbolic gesture, to show the people of Hindustān that they are all one people, in spite of all their differences, and that their emperor belongs to all of them? I cannot be sure.

In any case, there never is any pressure on anyone to join the new society; no attempts are being made to win any converts; no doctrines are issued to disprove or supersede any others; and membership remains limited to a rather small number of devoted courtiers, eager to please their emperor, and proud to belong to his inner circle.

But the common people, blissfully unaware of palace intrigues and philosophical arguments, illiterate and ignorant though they may be, seem to understand him. From far and wide, Muslims and Hindūs alike, they flock to the lofty court of their great prophet-king, longing to dwell, if only for a few moments, in the auspicious shadow of his kindness, hoping to obtain a magic token of his blessings – a flask of his washing-water, perhaps; or an earthen drinking-cup that has been taken to his blessed lips; a scrap of paper upon which he has breathed; maybe a shred of cloth that has actually been worn on his body.

And while he never claims to be the saintly gurū the people believe him to be; he visibly enjoys the reverence shown to him. Patiently smiling, he listens to their inept stammering; with great kindness and respect, he touches their foreheads, breathes upon their newborns' little round heads, and accepts their humble, petty gifts as if they were the most grand treasures this world has to offer.

And the people watch their king praying devoutly, in the direction of the sun, or in front of the Pārsī fire; or in the Hindū shrine, respectfully kneeling in front of a lingam; or in the mosque, facing the qibla on a simple prayer mat; or in the capela, bareheaded, an Īsāwī cross on a chain around his neck, on bended knee before an image of Īsā or the Virgin Maryam. Everywhere, their emperor prays with the same unfeigned devotion and humility, and the message he conveys is clear – all your different creeds are equally respectable, and behold: I, your emperor, belong to all of them.

'It pains me to hear, honourable pādres, that you wish to leave this court and return to Goa. Is there anything I can do to make you change your mind? I am in need of your wise teachings, your blessings and prayers!'

'My brethren and I are most grateful for the kind hospitality Your sublime Majesty has been kind enough to bestow upon us,' replies Pādre Rodolfo Aquaviva, in heavily accented but otherwise impeccable, formal Persian—it keeps amazing me how quickly and thoroughly he has been able to master our beautiful language!—'but I believe that regrettably, our task here at Your Majesty's lofty court has come to an end. Our humble services are required elsewhere.'

There is a long pause. The emperor's countenance remains gentle, calm, and as usual, inscrutable.

'I will not deny,' Aquaviva proceeds, 'that my brethren and I will leave Fatehpūr Sīkrī with great sombreness in our hearts, for despite the kindness we received from Your Majesty, we have, alas, failed to guide him to the light of truth and salvation. We can only hope and pray, that our preachings will be like the seeds of grain, lifeless seemingly, buried for years in dry, barren ground, only to re-emerge as healthy green sprouts, when conditions have turned more favourable. . . .'

'So you hope that I may yet become a true Cristião, as you call it?'

'That is indeed our most ardent prayer, Your Majesty.'

'And you actually think that unless I get baptised, my soul will be lost forever?'

'Alas, not only do I think so, I *know* so. Outside Christ our lord, there is no salvation!'

'But I respect Him, I pray to Him, I allow His churches to be built and His message to be preached in my cities, I keep His effigy in my private quarters . . .'

'That is of course excellent, Your Majesty. But alas, I am afraid it is not enough.'

'And why not?'

'Your Majesty respects Him as a prophet, not as what He truly is: the saviour of the world, god incarnate Himself. Your Majesty does pray in our church, but with the same zeal, he also prays in Mohammedan mosques and heathen temples. Your Majesty kneels down before the His effigy, but he does the very same before the Mohammedan Koran, or before the most scandalous, pagan idols!'

'So, honourable pādre, if I understand you correctly, the greatest objection you have against my demeanour is not so much my lack of respect towards Īsā—god's peace be upon him—but the tolerance and deference I show towards other religions?'

'Not so much Your Majesty's *tolerance* of other creeds but rather, Your Majesty's failure to *choose* between them! Religion is not a matter of some noncommittal intellectual entertainment, but one of *choice – fundamental* choice, between truth and falsehood, light and darkness; the choice to stand *with* the lord, or against Him – there is no middle way, no neutral ground! Like all other human beings, Your Majesty *must* choose! And to put it bluntly – what Your Majesty calls respect for all religions, equals allegiance to none, and rejection by all!'

'You are forgetting your manners, pādre!' exclaims Abū-l Fazl, losing his usual composure. 'Need I remind you, that you are a *guest* in His Majesty's palace, that you—'

'Shaykh Abū-l Fazl, let the honourable pādre speak his mind, by all means,' the emperor interrupts him in a warm and friendly, but decisive tone. 'This is precisely why I invited the pādres and all these other wise men to my court – that I might learn from all creeds, that I might behold the treasures of wisdom they have acquired!'

Suddenly, there was silence in the court. For a while, the emperor just stares at the ceiling, then suddenly looks into Aquaviva's eyes.

'But that is exactly your problem, is it not, honourable pādre? You believe it is unthinkable that true wisdom could be found anywhere outside your own creed, do you not?'

For a few moments, Pādre Aquaviva seems to be at loss for an answer, looking at the emperor with what I would call reluctant admiration. After a while, he regains his composure.

'Alas, Your Majesty,' he says, smiling bitterly, 'that is not *my* problem, it is *yours*!'

Abū-l Fazl again wants to say something, but the emperor gestures him to remain calm.

'Alas, Your Majesty,' Aquaviva proceeds, 'alas, the devil never sleeps. . . . Temptation and evil readily present themselves to the unwary, in the guise of wisdom and profundity. . . .'

'So, according to you, honourable pādre, what I call wisdom is actually the work of the devil? You say that it is inherently wrong to study *any* religion – other than your own Cristianismo, that is?'

'The word of our Lord Jesùs is clear: "I am the way, and the truth, and the life; no man comes to the Father, but by Me!"

'As far as the pagans and the heretics are concerned, our duty is to love and pity them, while hating the error of their ways. Our duty is to reprimand them, to teach them the lord's way, and lead them to the light – not to make common cause with them!'

'And whom do you hate most, pādre? The Hindūs or the Muslims?'

'As I told Your Majesty, we do not hate the nonbelievers. They are human beings like us; they are our brothers, and as such, we love them. But with equal firmness and resolution, we have to reject the error of their ways!'

Aquaviva no longer tries to hide his anger and contempt.

'Your Majesty may have me killed, he may have me tortured, but I must and I will speak! Let me warn Your Majesty – his soul is in grave, grave danger! Your Majesty takes pride in his interest in the Hindūs, the Jains, the Pārsīs and whatever those misguided fools may be called. Well, he should not! He should run away from them! It is dangerous, foolish, not to say sinful, to study their so-called *religions*! Nobody can expose himself to the mystic babble and satanic rituals of paganism, without the dark forces behind them trying to take possession of his soul! Beware, Your Majesty, beware, be very afraid – behind those idols stands nothing but the demonic power of evil! Their true maker is Satan, the fallen angel!'

The emperor smiles wryly.

'You seem quite eager to attain martyrdom, pādre, but I'm afraid I cannot oblige you – you are my guest, you see . . . and besides, I will never hurt anyone for his beliefs – only for his *acts*, and only when I have to. But leaving that aside, I have to admit that what you have been saying here is quite disturbing to me, and let me tell you: I refuse to believe it! Why would god, Who is infinite goodness and mercy, condemn the honest prayers of His own creatures? Why would He deny His blessings to people who are so ardently looking for them?

'Alas, honourable pādre, I can only pray that you are mistaken, for I find it impossible to believe that god is as harsh as you describe Him to be. May god be merciful to both of us, pādre, and may He be your protector and guide on your journey.'

'I will pray for Your Majesty.'

'As I will pray for you, honourable pādre.'

≈

A few months later, we get news from Goa. It was to be expected, but still, it comes as a surprise – young Pādre Rodolfo Aquaviva has been killed by an angry mob of Hindūs, for burning down one of their temples.

The emperor seems strangely moved when he hears the news.

'What a pity,' he sighs, slowly shaking his head. 'Such a waste of youth and devotion! Let us pray for him, my friends, and for his victims.'

Thirty-fourth Letter

ظهر

Ẓöhr [286]

Life is a strange thing when you think about it. It is either *not yet*, or *no more* – we always seem to be craving some unattainable future, or bewailing a bygone past. And the gems of life, those rare moments of real, perfect happiness, where there are neither wants, nor regrets . . . how quickly do they lose their lustre as soon as we realise that they too are bound to come to an end? All pleasure lusts for eternity; every moment of human happiness craves that one treasure that cannot be found in this world – permanence. . . .

I am exaggerating, of course. Life is a precious gift, to be cherished and enjoyed, an exciting adventure, to be lived to the fullest! Still, what I just wrote is true – when I was young, I was *not yet* as powerful as now, *not yet* the father of a son; but now that I am emperor and powerful, I find that I *no longer* have the strength of my youth, I *no longer* am the centre of my son's world; and with wistful dismay, I remember the many good friends of yore who have, alas, passed away for good. Why is it only when we stop to look back, when it is too late, that we fully realise what treasures we had, when we had them?

---

286. Noon

Somewhere along this long and winding road of my life, *it* must have happened; somewhere in between, I was at my highest peak, but I was too busy to realise it. It was but a fleeting moment, impossible to take hold of or hold on to, like the exact time when the sun reaches its highest point – one moment, the shadows are still shortening; the next, slowly but surely, they start to grow longer again.

Only now, now that the dusk of my life is drawing near at alarming speed, do I realise – dīn-e-illāhī was my high noon, the high point of my life.

Dīn-e-illāhī was everything my reign stands for. It was the living proof that I truly answered to no one – no one but god. All my enemies lay down in the dust; no governor or ulamā could even dream of any authority, unless I had decided to delegate it to him. Kings of neighbouring regions could only hope that their lavish gifts and letters of abject flattery and pledges of eternal friendship would convince me to let them keep their independence. The common people, of all castes and creeds, loved, admired, not to say worshipped, their emperor – so powerful, so just, so obviously blessed by god.

At the time I decreed dīn-e-illāhī, I was thirty-nine years of age, strong as a bull, free of any bodily ailment. My zanāna was a haven of merriness and opulence, a heaven on earth, where I loved to retire – not only, and not even primarily, to enjoy one or the other pretty young dancing girl and her shapely curves. It was the one place where I felt truly at home and at ease, free for a few hours from any commitment, enjoying the always enriching companionship of my strong and wise Salīmā; of my sweet Ruqqaya and her good-natured gentleness; and of your charming mother, smart, witty, with her quicksilver mind.

At the time I decreed dīn-e-illāhī, you were thirteen, my son, and what pride and joy it was for me to see you and your two younger brothers growing up so well! You were actually growing taller than me, and incredibly strong for your age, and skilled with horses and weapons, and extremely bright, too – fluent in Persian, Turkī, Hindustānī, and Arabic; good with numbers; a gifted painter and an even better calligrapher, blessed with a steady hand and a keen, observing eye. Never had an empire seen a more promising young crown prince.

You were thirteen, my son, exactly the age I was when my father died. . . . The thought confronted me, for the first time, with my own death. What if something were to happen to me? It was without hesitation that I decided to appoint Abdurrahīm as your atālīq – just like, twenty-six years before, I had been entrusted to his father. What better teacher and guardian could I have given you, than this skilled warrior, this accomplished scholar, this competent governor, this noble and loyal friend? When I saw you in his company, on horseback among the soldiers, or sitting down under the palace arcades, studying battle tactics on a piece of paper, it was as if I saw myself again with Bairām Khān, and I was at peace. If, god forbid, I were to die unexpectedly, the two of you would make it. You, and Abdurrahīm Khān Khanān, with Todar Mal, Bīrbal, Abū-l Fazl, Bhagwān Dās, and Mān Singh; you, at the head of this invincible alliance of Rājpūts and so-called 'Mughals' – who in this world could ever hope to challenge, let alone defeat you?

Once again, I thanked god that it had pleased Him to put your revered mother on my life's path. My fortunate alliance with her and her family had more than doubled my power, and it had allowed me to father the best imaginable successor, for in your veins, my son, flows the blood of Chingīz Khān and Amīr Temür, harmoniously blended with that of the mighty Hindū kings of yore! I resolved to further strengthen the ties between our two families. And what better way to forge an alliance, than through the bonds of blood? Two more years, and you would be old enough to marry a Rājpūt princess yourself, just like I had done; god willing, we would soon find ourselves blessed with a new generation of true Hindustānī princes – strong, noble and wise, who would, in grateful remembrance of their grandfather, preserve, protect and enhance what I had built.

Yes, the time of dīn-e-illāhī was truly the high point of my life and my reign. Ironic, is it not, that the high point of one's life can at the same time be a failure?

To be sure, thanks to my policies and my personal example, Muslims and Hindūs are now living together in prosperity, security, peace, and oftentimes unfeigned friendship – and that is an accomplishment I take great pride in. Regrettably, if understandably, I have failed to achieve anything *more* than that. Disappointingly few people have ever cared to join the emperor's 'new religion' – only a few good friends, plus the inevitable number of ambitious sycophants, but it has utterly failed to appeal to the masses. On the contrary, rather than uniting people, dīn-e-ilāhī has been a source of much controversy and misunderstanding, and it very nearly estranged me from some of my best friends.

It angered Azīz Koka, my faithful but rather bigoted and quite hotheaded foster brother, to the point that he left and sailed for Mekkah, without asking my permission! I am happy to say, though, that two years later upon his return, I found him quite eager to make amends. He even became one of the most fervent dīn-e-illāhī disciples – the merchants of Mekkah had fleeced him so thoroughly that his Islāmic ardour had cooled off. . . .

Mān Singh too was not happy with the new cult. And god bless him, he even had the courage to say it straight to my face, when I was having a drink with him and Abdurrahīm. I brought up the subject of them becoming dīn-e-illāhī murids,[287] upon which he suddenly retorted, with thinly veiled irritation: 'Forgive me, Your Majesty, but I do not know what you mean by me becoming your murshid. If it is my willingness to lay down my life for you, have I not given you more than sufficient proof of that? But if it refers to religious faith, I do not know what it is you want to achieve. I am a Hindū, to be sure. If you command me to become a Mussalmān, I am prepared do so. But I know of no other religion than these two!'

Yes, much as I hate to admit it, my son, dīn-e-illāhī was probably a mistake. I do realise that now, and I have no illusion that its rituals will survive me when I'm dead and gone. But what is an emperor to do when he has made a mistake, my son? If he can repair it, he should of course do so, but sometimes, trying to fix things only makes them worse. There was simply no going back; it would only have added to the confusion. And so, I continued to lead dīn-e-illāhī ceremonies and accepted a few disciples, but I made no further attempt to convince or convert anyone. And while the cult and its ceremonies will probably die with me, one thing I hope will never die – the thought that all people are brothers; that all their religions, in the eyes of god, are one; and that the emperor, who is the servant of god and the guardian of his people, should stand above all creeds and denominations.

---

287. Murid: Disciple of a Murshid (Sufi master)

Yes, my son, in spite of its imperfections and ultimate failure, the promulgation of dīn-e-illāhī was truly high noon, my sun was at its zenith. From then on, slowly, imperceptibly, but inexorably, the shadows would start lengthening again.

Thirty-fifth Letter

سلطنت

Saltanat

It was a muggy afternoon in the height of summer of the thirtieth year,[288] when a messenger from Kābul brings me the happy tiding of Muhammad Hakīm's death. Unexpected news it was, but hardly surprising; ever since his humiliating defeat two years ago, he had busied himself with little else than drinking himself to death, an endeavour in which, at the age of merely thirty-one, he appeared to have finally succeeded. The last of my would-be rivals is rotting in his grave, and I am alive, at the height of my power, strong and invincible. Gone are all the whispers and muttering behind my back; the mere mention of my name suffices to turn the stiffest knees into puls.

The moment I heard the news, my mind was made up: I decided to go up north.

People were surprised, as usual, at the rashness of my decision, but I had my reasons. For one, I did not want—rather, I could not afford—to take any chances. Reports had come in that the Uzbegs had taken possession of Balkh and Badakshān, the country across the mountains north of Kābul, south of the Amuya River. That in itself was vexing

---

288. 1585

enough, but the situation could have quickly become much worse, since the buffer between ourselves and the Uzbegs had gone, and the dangerous void Muhammad Hakīm's death had left in Kābul. If I had not been careful enough to fill it quickly, the Uzbeg bandits would have marauded our northern mountain passes. Kābul itself, god forbid, could have been in danger one day!

You see, my son, kingship is rather like a game of chess – you should always think a few moves ahead; you should constantly be on your guard for chinks in your armour, for weak spots that a shrewd opponent might use in an attempt to shift the balance of power.

I had to quickly make my countermove: That old fox Abdullāh Khān Uzbeg Bukhārī, may god exterminate his seed through mine, was not to be underestimated. Ever since he sat on the throne of Turān, he had been struggling to expand his dominions southward, at the expense of the shāh of Irān. Frankly, I didn't care what he did to the Persians – in fact, the more the Uzbegs and the Irānīs fought each other, the better I liked it! But now that the old Uzbeg bastard had gotten himself a foothold across *my* northern border, things were different and unpredictable. What if he patched up a peace deal with the Persians, to attack *me* for a change? No, I simply could not afford to keep on living at ease, hundreds of kos away down south in Fatehpūr Sīkrī, when that wily jackal was loitering about my northern border. I decided I had to go up there myself, in full force, and make it crystal clear to that bastard, that any false move from him will have dire and immediate consequences; he needed to understand that if he chose to challenge me, he had absolutely nothing to gain, but much—if not everything—to lose!

I have to say, my presence up north, while necessary to keep the Uzbegs at bay, had its distinct advantages, too. I was finally able to busy myself with the conquest of that exquisite gem that I had been longing to add to my crown for so many years: Kashmīr. Countless poets have sung the praises of its landscape, the majesty of its snowcapped mountains, the lushness of its green gardens, the breathtaking beauty of its limpid blue lakes and the freshness of its fast-fleeting rivers. . . . Besides, and more importantly, is Kashmīr not our natural border? Is it imaginable, is it conceivable that I would leave such an important land in the hands of a foreign ruler? Never! Kashmīr belongs to Hindustān; it is mine! And besides, I had more than enough of its pompous little kinglet Yūsuf Khān, a worthless buffoon who had been ignoring my orders, while trying to placate me with vague promises and halfhearted signs of friendship. It was time to put an end to his charade.

Less than a month after the news of Muhammad Hakīm's death, the imperial court was ready to leave Fatehpūr Sīkrī. I took a last stroll around the grounds, paid my respects at Shaykh Salīm Chishtī's tomb, admired once more the Pānch Mahal's[289] fiery-red outline against the black monsoon clouds; sat myself down on the stairs of the Buland Darwāzā[290] for a while, and watched the bees swarming about their nests, high up in the mighty arch of the gate. Deep in my heart, I realised – this was not a goodbye, but a farewell; this will never again be my capital.

To my own surprise, I felt neither sadness nor nostalgia to leave this city that I had built with such zeal. Actually, I found myself quite eager to leave – I guess I had grown a bit tired of the place; or maybe not tired but perhaps disappointed. The bursting of the dam, two years back, and the interminable difficulties with the water supply had made it painfully clear to me, that this is, alas, not the place to sustain a large population.

A farewell to Sīkrī it was, then. The affairs of state would keep me in the far north for no less than thirteen years, and by the time I finally return to the area for a hasty visit, I found it as I expected – the imperial residence untouched, like new. It looked beautiful and imposing as ever, but the surrounding area was deserted, all its shops and houses in pitiful decay. Fatehpūr was no longer the lively city of my time; it had become a monument. That was its destiny – to stand there on that lonely hill, for all generations to come, a testimonial to its maker, a symbol of the Hindustān he created. Muslim-style arches and domes, combined, blended and unified with Hindū pillars, terraces, and chhatris – sulh-i-kul in stone.

The imperial cortege—several kos long it was, thousands upon thousands of elephants and horses and guns and oxcarts and pack camels—set itself in motion and slowly wound its way northward. As

---

289. The five-storey open palace at Fatehpūr Sīkrī.
290. The High (or 'Great') Gate, built by Akbar to commemorate the conquest of Gujarāt. It is reportedly the highest gateway in the world.

we rode through the gate, I did not look back – not even once. Looking back never makes much sense, my son. Do we not live in the present, and is the future not our destination? The past is there to be built upon, not dwelt upon!

Barely three months after leaving Fatehpūr, we set up camp near the town of Attock, where the Kābul River runs into the mighty Hind. Not a very comfortable place, but truly an ideal base for operations. From here, I could oversee the entire north; from here, my troops could be in Kābul, or Kashmīr, or both places at the same time in a matter of days.

Together with my army leaders, I took stock of the situation, and I was relieved to find that it could have been much worse. True, the roads around the Khyber Pass and the Sulaimān Hills were infested by unruly Afghān tribesmen (the work of Uzbeg instigators, no doubt), but Kābul itself, thank god, was safe. The new governor appeared to have everything under control; there was no unrest, no sign of any Uzbeg incursions. Kashmīr, as I expected, begged for peace, while preparing for war. I was no longer interested in a negotiated settlement with them. This time, I was not to be fobbed off with a few fair words – this time, they *will* submit to me, completely, entirely, unequivocally!

It probably serves little purpose, my son, to recount in detail all the tribulations of the conquest. Besides, is the outcome not known beforehand? Of course, there are a number of setbacks; snow and ice hinder our advance; enemy resistance is at times stiffer than anticipated. But the final outcome is never in doubt – it may take us one year, two years, three maybe, but in the end, the Kashmīrīs' knees will bend, their haughty necks will bow.

Thus it happened. A mere eight months after my arrival at Attock, the victorious imperial army under Rājā Bhagwān Dās marched into Srinagar; the insubordinate Yūsuf Khān and his son had but one alternative – unconditional surrender. This time, however, I did not show them my usual leniency. No public reconciliation, no appointments to high office, no fat stipends – they were carted off to Bihār, where they remained imprisoned like common criminals for over a year, after which I assigned them to humble positions well below their rank, a just retribution for their insolence and a warning to all other would-be rebels. Their proud kingdom was history; without too much ceremony, it was annexed to the empire, not as a separate sarkar as everyone expected, but as a mere suba, joined to the sarkar[291] of Kābul. Thus fare the insolent, the disobedient, the vainglorious. . . .

If the campaign against Kashmīr, at first sight a major war, passed off rather smoothly, in any event easier than expected, the operation against the Yūsufzāi and Mandār Afghān tribes, supposedly a routine job, turned into an outright disaster – a disaster that could and should have been avoided, were it not for my own stupid mistake.

The start of the operations was successful enough. Simultaneously with the attack on Kashmīr, I ordered a punitive expedition into the Afghān mountains under commander Zain Khān. In accordance with his orders, he invaded the tribal territories with a two-pronged attack – one via the Bājaur territory to the west, and the second one due north into the Sāmah plateau between the Kābul and the Suwāt rivers. After duly chastising any opposing brigands, he crossed the Suwāt and occupied the town of Chak-darah, where, entirely in the correct manner, he built a stronghold from where he could further harass the tribesmen and pacify the country. So far, everything went smoothly. As his forces had been exhausted from the strenuous marches in difficult terrain, he sent a messenger back to Attock to ask for reinforcements. Even at this point, everything was okay. But then, I made a stupid, and alas, fatal, mistake. A number of my courtiers—bored by the tranquil life in the camp, I guess—had started quarreling among themselves for the honour of leading the reinforcement troops. I should of course have dismissed them right away; the Afghān mountains are no place for inexperienced courtiers to dabble around in. But because they all kept pestering me, and since the campaign had been going quite well so far, I finally gave in and let them have their way. In fact, there were so many candidates that the dispute had to be solved by drawing lots. Fate appointed Rājā Bīrbal, together with Hakīm Abū'l Fath. The next day, after a night of celebrations, they rode off, proud as peacocks.

I must have been out of my mind to allow two inexperienced courtiers, a physician and an administrator, to lead an army into an Afghān-infested country! And an even worse, unforgivable blunder it was to send them off without clear instructions. Learn from this, my

---

291. Sarkar: Province; suba: district.

son – a king, no matter how rich and mighty, should *never* slacken his vigilance!

What exactly happened? Where did it all go so terribly wrong? I can only rely on the accounts of those who returned. . . .

Barely had Bīrbal arrived at Chak-darah with his reinforcements than ignoble disputes broke out between him and Zain Khān – the former, believing himself to be the latter's superior, too proud to acknowledge the better judgement of an experienced soldier. Zain Khān maintained—quite correctly, of course—that the fortress should be held in strength, while the Afghāns were further reduced in a series of punitive raids. Bīrbal, on the other hand, insisted, with unusual stubbornness, that it was not at all necessary to occupy the fortress, and that they should make their way back to the base camp in Attock. To make things worse, Bīrbal—again with highly unusual obstinacy for a man of his intelligence—refused to withdraw through the rather broad and much more easily surveyable Malākhand Pass as Zain Khān recommended, but instead resolved on going back through the Karakar and Malandarāi passes. It was a big, big mistake – one that, alas, cost him his life. The retiring army, though grievously harassed by the Afghān tribesmen, had held its own in the narrow Karakar defiles; but when it reached the Malandarāi Pass further south and again found itself under attack, the withdrawal degenerated in a humiliating and disastrous rout, a headlong flight where every man tried to save his own skin, without putting up even a semblance of resistance. Zain Khān and Hakīm Abū'l Fath survived the disaster, with a little over half of the army; but a full eight thousand men, including poor Bīrbal himself, were slaughtered like cattle.

The chronicler wrote, truthfully, that I 'shed tears most bitter, and was unable to eat or drink or sleep for days on end'. It is true: I was absolutely devastated. Not only because I grieved the loss of a dear old friend; not only because I had not even been able to give his body a proper cremation according to Hindū and dīn-e-illāhī rites; but also because I felt so terribly guilty and ashamed . . . ashamed at having been thus humiliated by a bunch of ragged, unwashed Afghān dogs.

Of course, I made them pay dearly for it. They had shed the blood of a Hindū courtier; Hindū warriors would shed theirs. Todar Mal, later followed by Mān Singh in the west, went into the tribal areas, and beat the Afghāns the only way Afghāns *can* be beaten – by fighting them on his own terms, not theirs. Remember this always, my son – mountain men are not to be fought in the caves and crevasses where they try to lure you into. Do not waste your time and effort in heroic but pointless and dangerous marches through their treacherous defiles! You have to fight them methodically, patiently, determinately; you have to harass them day and night, starting from a number of carefully chosen strong points, near river crossings, road junctions, mountain pass accesses and the like, where you have ample supplies and they cannot dislodge you. Strongholds are the stepping stones of conquest, my son. As Abū-l Fazl phrased it so aptly, 'they protect the timid, frighten the rebellious, and please the obedient'. If you hold enough fortresses, you can do as you deem fit, with impunity – burning and plundering the villages of the rebellious, while showering favours on the obedient. Then, gradually, with the lapse of time, brutal slaughter can be replaced by, or complemented with, discreet consultation with battle-weary village elders. Confronted with the choice between slaughter and bribery, even the closest alliances are bound to fall apart! Thus, through a judicious mix of wrath and mercy, bravery and stealth, the toughest mountain tribes can be checked, then reduced, and finally, brought to obedience and calm.

As I said, Todar Mal, after availing himself of an appropriate number of well-placed fortresses, harried the eastern mountain tribes so brutally that they were soon begging for peace; and near the Khyber Pass, Mān Singh inflicted on the western tribes a defeat so crushing that it took them years to recover from it. Our roads were safe again, the mountain passages cleared, and order restored.

Order, or at least a semblance thereof, for who knows what evil broods in the grim darkness of the Afghān soul? Right to this day, the border tribes have never really been conquered, only pacified. Remember that, my son, and beware of the Afghān tribesmen! Never underestimate them, never let down your guard! Know that the Afghān is mean and tough, hardened by icy cold and blazing heat and endless fighting; that he is haughty, and proud; and that his mind is a cauldron of bigotry, rancour, spite, deceit, and betrayal. The Afghān is to be controlled carefully, my son: suppressed if necessary, befriended if possible; but never, never to be trusted.

But enough said about that unwashed vermin. Let me return to matters more weighty – the building of that mighty empire that you are about to inherit, my son. Let us examine together, if you will, where I succeeded, and where—through your fault, alas—I failed.

≈

The following years of my life—I mean the period roughly between the thirtieth and the forty-third year, between the annexation of Kashmīr and my return to Āgrā—constitute, in hindsight, what one could call the afternoon of my reign. To be sure, vast and rich and crucially important territories were added to the empire – Sindh, Baluchistān, Qandahār, Berār, Asirghar, and Ahmadnagar fell into my hands. But those conquests were like afternoon sunshine where the air keeps getting hotter for a few hours, even though the sun is already sinking lower in the sky; but inexorably, the white heat turns golden, and the golden turns red, and amidst and despite all the simmering heat, the lengthening shadows forebode the darkness of the night. My dominions were still expanding, I had never been more powerful, but I somehow derived little satisfaction from it. Every new conquest seemed less gratifying, less glorious, more cumbersome than the one before; and for the first time, I felt the true curse of old age – loneliness. I lost many of my most trusted, life-long friends, and with growing despair, I had to witness how my three promising, wonderful sons, rather than making me proud like before, were becoming a cause of grave concern, and disappointment most bitter.

Thirty-sixth Letter

تنهای عصر

Tanhāyi-e-'Aṣr[292]

After the successful campaign in Kashmīr and the long-overdue punishment of the Afghān rabble, the northern borderlands were safe again. Safe enough, anyway, for me to retire to the more cultured comfort of Lāhor, which was to remain my capital city for the next thirteen years.

From thence, I further built and consolidated the mighty empire you will now be ruling, my son. Observe carefully, how I got what I wanted – through war and conquest, of course; but equally and at times more importantly, through carefully worded correspondence and elegant conversation, artfully blending courtesy with thinly veiled threats. Take it from me, my son – the sweetest victory is bloodless; you taste it when treasure and territory fall into your hands solely because of the power of your name.

I told you that kingship is a bit like a game of chess. Well, in fact, the entire decade was really a gigantic game of chess between me and Abdullāh Khān Uzbeg. A game with very high stakes indeed – the entire balance of power in the northwest depended on it. A game that, I am proud to say, I won brilliantly – to the extent that any such game *can* be

---

292. Silence of the late afternoon.

won, for history never ends, and what was won by one generation can, alas, be squandered by the next, my son. . . .

In hindsight, it was not so difficult. I used the Uzbegs to wear down the Persians, and then the Persians to chastise the Uzbegs; and while the two were at each other's throat, I quietly helped myself to the spoils. . . .

If we consider Hindustān and its neighbours Irān and Turān, my son, those three, to a certain extent, are balancing each other out – none of them could ever hope to conquer one of the others, unless through an all-out war that would probably take decades, and probably even ruin the victor as badly as the vanquished. But do not let yourself be lulled to sleep, my son – that balance, seemingly so obvious and unshakable, is precarious at best! Internal strife, and the loss of an important region can turn the tables quickly!

Just cast your mind back, if you will, at the time when your great-grandfather Bābur was still young. Look how things have changed since then – in the span of barely one lifetime!

At the time your great-grandfather was a young man, there weren't three rivals in the region – there was only the mighty Persian empire, stretching from the great Euphrates River to the Hindū Kush Mountains, vast, inexhaustibly wealthy, and powerful. What could such an Empire possibly have to fear from a handful of petty kingdoms and sultanates in faraway Hindustān, or from the Uzbegs, with their army a hundred times smaller than its own? Little, if anything!

And yet, barely a few decades later that situation looks quite different indeed. Persia's wealthy western provinces—including the eternal city of Baghdād itself—have been lost to the Turks of Rūm (I've been told they call themselves 'Osmāniyye' – Devlet-i Āliye-yi Osmāniyye,[293] no less!); and the northwestern borders are under constant threat of invasion by the ever more arrogant Uzbegs.

Learn from this, my son; observe how, in just a few decades, a magnificent, invincible empire has been brought to the brink of collapse. All it has taken, is a few shortsighted weaklings on the throne, a few spineless drunks, learned idiots, too preoccupied with feasting and

---

293. The Sublime Osmān State, or Ottoman Empire.

paintings and poetry to recognise how much their armies are antiquated and in need of cannons. . . .

Anyway, the whole thirty-first year, I found myself involved in lively correspondence with my two quarreling neighbours – the tremulous, half-blind, old Persian king Muhammad Shāh Khudābanda, and his ruthless, land-hungry Uzbeg adversary. It was not difficult to see what has been behind all the lavish gifts and pledges of everlasting friendship they both keep sending me – they both want my support, or at least my neutrality, in the longstanding feud that divided them.

If I would follow my heart, I would of course combine forces with the mild-mannered old Shāh, and crush the Uzbegs, once and for all. After careful consideration, however, I chose not to. What good would it do to strengthen the Persians? Who can say that the next Shāh will not one day turn against me? And why should I be wasting my time on the other side of the Hindū Kush when there is so much left to do in Hindustān proper? No, I just stayed put; and from behind the safety of my borders, I watched them weakening each other, while I was free to do what I wanted.

Before long, the Uzbegs invaded the Persian northeast and quickly seized Herāt, Sistān and Mashhad from the ill-prepared Persians. Humiliated and powerless, the old Shāh had no alternative but to abdicate in favour of his sixteen-year-old son Abbās, whose first worry was to stay alive amidst a quagmire of strife and court intrigues.

I have to say, the boy managed admirably. If he had not been a potential enemy of ours, it would have been quite enjoyable to observe how brilliantly he succeeds in restoring order and rebuilding his empire!

But let me first come back to the situation in Hindustān. As I said, as long as the Persians and the Uzbegs kept each other occupied, I had my hands free for my own projects, and it was an opportunity I did not intend to miss.

My first target, of course, was Sindh, the region along the Hind River between Multān and the sea. The local ruler, Mīrzā Jani Beg, stubbornly refused to pay homage to me. What was that arrogant fool thinking? Did he really believe that I will allow the Hind River, the river to which Hindustān owes its very name, to remain separated from it? Is it at all thinkable that I would leave the Panjāb's natural access to the sea, the beautiful cities of Hyderābād and Thatta, the fertile plains around the lower reaches of the river, and my own birthplace Umarkot, in foreign hands?

I didn't waste my time on futile negotiations; when amicable overtures were of no avail, I sent down Abdurrahīm with an army, to bring him to reason. Jani Beg attempted to resist, but of course, he was no match for Abdurrahīm. Jani Beg had finally learned his lesson. Meekly surrendering all his cities and fortresses to Abdurrahīm, he travelled to Lāhor to prostrate himself at my feet.

I had half a mind to have him executed, or at least thrown in jail, but when I saw his honest, rather pleasant face, I changed my mind, and decided to give him another chance: I let him go back to his native region to be its governor. As usual, my instinct did not fail me; for the remainder of his life—which, alas, ended prematurely in a drinking bout a few years later—he served me faithfully, fighting at my side in the Deccan, and becoming a confirmed dīn-e-illāhī adept.

Now that Sindh was mine, I was able at last to consolidate all the other southwestern regions. In the beginning of the fortieth year, my forces invaded Baluchistān and quickly captured the fortress of Siwi in the Kirthar Mountains, southeast of Quetta; barely two months later, the jewel of the crown fell into my lap, when the Persian governor of Qandahār, fearing an imminent invasion by the Uzbegs, delivered the city into my hands. With glee, I heard the reports coming in – no sooner had my troops taken the city and manned the territory's borders, than the Uzbeg hordes withdrew, tail between their legs. . . . Amusing, is it not? The more power one has, the less one needs to use it! The entire land of Qandahār had been annexed to the empire, and an Uzbeg invasion repelled, without the shedding of a single drop of blood, by the mere awe and dread of the name Akbar-e-āzam!

With Sindh, Baluchistān and Qandahār firmly in our hands, we could finally rest assured that the northern part of our empire was safe, behind well-nigh impregnable natural borders, and its two entrance gates, Kābul and Qandahār, well guarded.

But do keep an eye on that border, my son, for behind it looms our young friend Shāh Abbās, and you can be sure that he has not forgotten that Qandahār was once his. Beware of him, my son; know that he is smart, ruthless, and vengeful. I know he is preoccupied with Baghdād before anything else, but once he recaptures it—and there is no doubt in my mind that he will, someday—he will be knocking at your door.

Do not underestimate him! Just think about how judiciously, carefully, and ruthlessly he has managed to rebuild his power, in barely ten years' time! Just look at how cleverly he dealt with the Uzbegs! As I said, were he not so dangerous, it would actually have been quite fun to watch . . .

Swiftly dealing with any would-be rivals—that is to say, having them blinded, poisoned, or strangled—he quickly patched up a peace deal with his powerful adversaries in the west, ceding them some additional territories; and while the Osmāniyye Turks were revelling in their easy victory, he quietly availed himself of a few firanghī advisors. With unremitting zeal, he strengthened and reorganised his armed forces, similar to the model of his Osmāniyye opponents. Cannon foundries were built everywhere; hundreds of thousands of muskets were fabricated; ample supplies of gunpowder were stockpiled all over the land. Behold, my son, how god favours those who act – barely ten years after his father's humiliating defeat, Abbās's victorious armies washed over the Uzbeg occupants like a tidal wave; only a handful of maimed and blinded survivors were allowed to stumble back to Bukhārā, and bring Abdullāh Khān Uzbeg the tiding that his grandiose plans had failed. A few years later, the old jackal died, in the certain knowledge that there was no one of value to succeed him. Gone were the dreams of a great Uzbeg Empire . . .

With Abdullāh Khān Uzbeg out of the way, his forces decimated by Abbās, and his successor an impotent weakling, I was strongly tempted to march north, to Samarqand – where the bones of our great ancestor Temür the Iron are resting; Samarqand, the priceless jewel that was stolen from my grandfather by the Uzbeg usurpers. But then again, I thought to myself: What does this have to do with me? Why would I spend the remaining years of my life in lands where I have never set foot – lands where, reportedly, winters are long and cold, the soil barren, good food scarce, and the women ugly? Growing old is about losing options, my son. When a man is past forty, he should not waste his time on dreams, on things that *might* have been, or on new projects that may take lifetimes to finish. At my age, and very soon, at your age as well, a man needs to be practical. He should make up his mind about what he wants in his life, and then finish what he started, not waste his time on pursuits that are not his own. Samarqand can wait, my son; what you and I need to do, is not to waste our strength in faraway regions, but to unite all of Hindustān, from the Himalayas to the southern ocean and the island of Lanka; and then, to make it the mightiest and wealthiest empire on earth. Let us complete what I started; and if we do that well, the seed of our seed will be able to busy itself with the conquest of foreign lands. By all means, let us be ambitious; let us dream of a Hindustān that stretches deep into the north and far across the ocean; but let us first build it, make it strong, and make it one.

Having thus made up my mind, and in the knowledge that the north is safe, I decided to move back to Āgrā. I was growing old—fifty-six already, how time flies!—and so much remained to be done! The operations in the Deccan were not progressing as fast as they should; I needed to move much closer to the action, maybe even get involved myself – it has been too long since I had stood on a battlefield.

Alas, little did I realise that my last adversary was not to be some recalcitrant Deccan ruler, but my own firstborn – you, my son.

≈

Where did it all go so terribly wrong? It is difficult, not to say impossible, to pinpoint a specific moment, but for a while, I have been tempted to think that all my misfortunes started with Bīrbal's death at the beginning of the thirty-first year. To be sure, Kābul was safe at the time, the conquest of Kashmīr was going well, I was in excellent health, and with three bright sons, my succession was assured; still, no matter how much I tried to console myself, I felt Bīrbal's death was a bad omen, a very bad omen. Never before had my plans been thwarted so brutally, and so unexpectedly; never before had I felt so utterly humiliated; never before had it been even imaginable that a high-ranking official of Akbar the Great's court could be killed by a bunch of Afghān rabble.

Was my lucky star waning? Was the hour of my death drawing near? No matter how well the astrologers did their best to convince me of the contrary, doubt kept lurking in my mind for quite a few months.

I was wrong, of course – there is no such thing as a 'lucky star'. And even if there were, we should never allow ourselves to be intimidated, much less ruled by it. I know I am repeating myself, my son, but it really cannot be emphasised enough: God favours those who *act*! Things never just happen to us; things are what they are, either because we *make* them so, or because we *allow* them to be so. True, many events and occurrences around us are of course not under our control; but we do decide how we react to them! I would say that only one-tenth of our lives is determined by what happens to us; but nine-tenths, by how we react to it! Just look at the story of my own life: Could I not have rested on my laurels, after Sikandar Sūr surrendered to me at Mānkot? Surely, there is more than enough wealth and luxury in the Panjāb and central Hindustān; who knows what a cushy, carefree life I could have had! But then again, just suppose that I would have chosen that leisurely path: Hindustān would have been exactly like its neighbours – exactly like all the petty kingdoms I have later subdued and annexed to my dominions. But I chose not to rest on my laurels, I *acted*; I did not take life as it came to me, I *changed* it. And behold, my son, how god had rewarded my resolve: I was now more powerful than the Persian Shāh or the Uzbeg Khān; I was, most probably, the most powerful ruler on this earth. Not because it was pre-ordained, but because I *acted*, because I took advantage of the opportunities that offered themselves to me.

These were the thoughts that were going through my head as I travelled back to Āgrā, and reflected on the thirteen years I had spent up north. I had seen no evidence of lucky or unlucky stars. The years had come and gone, and life had gone its way, as it had before, as it always has, with its ups, and its downs – and more often than not, with lots of hard work to bring about the former, and courage and determination to overcome the latter. Much as the astrologers had toiled and ciphered and done their utmost to sound learned and wise and complicated, they had failed to predict any of the important events, other than the ones that were already clear from looking at the earth, rather than at the sky.

Much had happened to me during those thirteen years. Of course, I had had my share of challenges and setbacks, but more numerous and important had been my blessings.

True, my dear old friend Bīrbal had been slain needlessly—a victim, not of god's disfavour, but of his own arrogance and my error of judgement—but his death had been duly avenged, and vast territories had been added to the empire, making me the most powerful ruler in the region, if not the world.

True, the loss of Bīrbal had, alas, not been my only bereavement, as both Todar Mal, my faithful help and stay, and my strong brother in arms Rājā Bhagwān Dās had both died in the thirty-fourth year, barely one week from each other; and four years later, the wise old Shaykh Mubārak had passed away as well. But thank god, the pain of their loss had been more than alleviated by the birth of three healthy grandsons – Khusrau on the twenty-fourth of Mordād of the thirty-second year,[294] Parvez on the nineteenth of Ābān two years later,[295] and Khurram[296] on the twenty-fifth of Dey of the thirty-seventh year.

Khusrau's birth in particular had been a cause of great rejoicing. Not only was he your firstborn, not only did he ensure the continuity of our dynasty, but the fact that he was born to your first-wedded wife, the princess of Jodhpūr, god bless her, again reinforced the bonds of kin and friendship that unites us with the Rājpūts. Never forget this, my son: The unity of Amber and Āgrā, Muslims and Hindūs, is the basis of our power.

Yet, as I reflected on all this on my way to Āgrā, my heart was heavy. And it had little to do with divine blessings or lack thereof, but with time, the inexorable passing of time. Whether I chose to admit it to myself or not, I had become a white-haired, aging man, and my three sons were now grown men living their own lives.

At the time I left Fatehpūr Sīkrī, I was forty-three and at the top of my strength, and everything and everybody revolved around me. You and your two brothers were merely sixteen, fifteen and thirteen; and you were good, promising children, all three of you – a bit over-indulged perhaps, but nevertheless smart, strong, and always respectful towards their father.

By the time I decided to return to Āgrā, those three wonderful sons, alas, had changed beyond recognition, into conceited, quarrelsome, indolent drinkers, well on their way to become total failures. And what was even more worrisome – the brotherly love and friendship that once

---

294. 5 August 1587
295. 31 October 1589
296. 5 January 1592. Khurram was to succeed Jahāngīr in 1628 under the name of Shāh Jahān, and to achieve worldwide fame as the builder of the Tāj Mahal.

had united you had given way to barely hidden mistrust and resentment. Abū-l Fazl and the other courtiers did their best to spare my feelings, but they could not hide from me that the entire court was rife with scandalous rumours – rumours that you and Murād were already looking for allies in the war of succession that would surely break out the moment I would have laid down my weary head; that the three of you were living in constant fear of assassins and poisoners.

I of course ignored the rumours, and meanwhile did my best to talk some sense into the three of you. It truly pained me to see the kind of men you had become – you, secretive, inscrutable, calculating, venomous like a snake; Murād, loud and moody and superficial; Dānyāl, shy and visibly scared. I really tried everything, from fits of rage to friendly conversation; but whether I kept you in the palace, or entrusted you with important, faraway missions, nothing I said or did seemed to have any effect; all I got was evasive answers and vague promises; all I achieved was that you became even more estranged from me and from each other.

One late afternoon, as I was watching a flock of birds in the pale blue sky, the stark, bitter truth suddenly dawned on me – my years were numbered, and there was nothing I could do about it. Another five, ten, twenty years maybe, and I would be dead; and my sons were getting themselves ready for it. I might as well face it: The world no longer revolved around me; or if it did, it was more like a flight of grey vultures hovering high above some wounded animal, waiting for it to collapse.

≈

Thirty-seventh Letter

موراد، اسیرگڑھ

Murād, Asīrgaṛh

Have you ever observed a cavalry charge getting bogged down in a marshland, Salīm? With every step, the horses lose power and speed; and in a few moments' time, what starts as a thundering, overwhelming assault turns into impotent plodding. Well, that is exactly how I have felt ever since I left Lāhor – bogged down, powerless, not by enemy action, but by my own flesh and blood. . . .

If everything would have gone the way I planned, our borders would now extend at least fifty kos further south than they currently do. The khutbah would have been read in my name in every mosque of Ahmadnagar, Bijāpūr and Golconda. And who knows, our victorious armies would probably be making their way by now to the southernmost tip of the continent! Alas, it was not to be . . .

It really is a crying shame that I will have to die before the Deccan has been fully unified with the empire. A region of such vital importance, still in the hands of a few petty local kings . . . the very idea is an insult to our power!

For decades, Deccan independence has been a thorn in my flesh. Hindustān can never be complete without the Deccan. But with it, everything becomes possible. With the Deccan, it is only a matter of time before the entire continent is ours! Think about it: Even the arrogant

Purtugēsh will be brought to heel: Once they become our neighbours, there will be no alternative for them but to recognise our sovereignty and pay dearly for our hospitality, or be thrown back into the sea where they came from.

As early as during the wars in Gujarāt—when, alas, I had too many other things on my hands—I had been sending envoys to Khāndesh and Ahmadnagar to invite them to join me. But their submission had only been temporary, and halfhearted at best. On the contrary, some of them (that filthy rat Burhān Shāh of Ahmadnagar, not to name him) had been insolent enough to call upon my help when they needed it to defeat their local enemies, and then ignore me as soon as they got what they wanted! In the summer of the thirty-sixth year,[297] I decided to give it one last try. I dispatched four missions, to Khāndesh, Bijāpūr, Ahmadnagar, and Golconda, under the leadership of Shaykh Abū-l Faizī. Patiently, I waited, and waited, but the vague reports I kept receiving gave me little hope. Two years later, alas, my worst misgivings were confirmed – he came back with a meagre fourteen elephants and a handful of jewels as a so-called token of friendship; not only had the bastards refused to submit or pledge allegiance, they had not even deigned to treat my emissaries with the respect due to their rank! This time, I really had more than enough.

I sent Abdurrahīm at the head of an army, and instructed Murād— who was at the time governer of Gujarāt—to join him, and subdue the enemy. The two imperial armies met at Chandur and crossed the border virtually unopposed, laying siege to the fortress of Ahmadnagar already on the fifteenth of Dey of the fortieth year.[298] Things seemed to be going all right, but in fact, they were not – not at all. Disconcerting reports kept coming in, about bad blood between Murād and Abdurrahīm – the former reportedly too drunk and arrogant to take advice from a more seasoned warrior, and the latter too proud and stubborn to keep his mouth shut. Murād, so it was reported, even went as far as to openly and insultingly question his own father's judgement. 'The old man really must be senseless,' he was reported to have said, 'to be sending a goddamn Shī'a to fight against Shī'a rebels!' I seethed with rage when I heard about

---

297. August 1591
298. 26 December 1595

it. The nerve! Who did he think he was? Lucky for him that he was so far away, or I would have unleashed my fury on him.

Anyway, my army leaders seemed to be more preoccupied with their own private feuds than with the war they were supposed to fight. Little wonder then, that in the face of Ahmadnagar's stiff resistance—quite heroic resistance, I am told—they quickly patched up a peace deal with the enemy, whereby the siege was lifted in exchange for the territory of Berār.

I was beside myself with rage when I heard the reports. Who were they to conclude a peace agreement I had not authorised? Did they think that I was paying for a major military campaign to be contented with a mere border region? But there was little I could do, being so far away. With the distance between Āgrā and the Deccan, dispatches back and forth took over a week to arrive; all I got was a few polite letters with vague reassurances, while the disturbing rumours about drunken misbehaviour and violent rows, continued unabated.

The dispatch I received in late Esfand of the forty-second year was the drop that made the cup run over. The rebels had broken the peace treaty, and Abdurrahīm—not a word about Murād—had fought them at Ashti near Supa on the Godavari River. The enemy army had been much stronger than expected, and an indecisive victory had been the result: Abdurrahīm had managed to rout them, but his own losses had been so heavy that he had been unable to pursue and annihilate the fleeing rebels.

This time, I had enough of all this bungling. I sent down Abū-l Fazl to assess the situation, and bring Murād back to the court. Alas, it was too late. . . .

I still remember as if it were yesterday, Abū-l Fazl's messenger presenting himself, a blue handkerchief around his wrist. The ominous blue handkerchief could only mean one thing – someone very close to the emperor had died, someone so close, that the messenger did not dare to speak his or her name. I managed to remain outwardly calm and did not move a muscle of my face, even as I felt the gazes of the entire court upon me. Inside my head, however, thoughts were racing feverishly: Who had died? Was it Abdurrahīm? Abū-l Fazl himself? Was it, god forbid, Murād, my own flesh and blood?

I looked around the crowded diwān-i-ām, causing those who had been staring at me to quickly avert their eyes. As I expected, you were prudent enough not to show any emotion. Standing tall, arms crossed, features composed, you confidently looked at the messenger and waited for him to deliver his message. I knew what you were thinking: 'If it's Abdurrahīm, that's too bad, but I don't really care; and if it is Abū-l Fazl or Murād – so much for the better!'

'You bring us sad news?' I asked the messenger.

'Alas, Your Majesty, I do,' the man answered timidly.

'Well, tell us what you have to say.'

'I carry with me a letter from the honourable Shaykh Abū-l Fazl, Your Majesty.'

'And?'

'The honourable shaykh profoundly regrets to inform Your Majesty, that unfortunately, His Imperial Highness the Shāhzāda Sultān Murād has passed away, after a brief illness.'

I heard myself answering, in a surprisingly calm and steady voice: 'We will discuss this in our private chambers.'

I rose from the throne, and went inside the palace. Few moments later, in the seclusion of the diwān-i-khās, I sat myself down again and resignedly listened to the messenger, my dry eyes staring aimlessly at the floor below the throne platform.

Hesitatingly, almost inaudibly, he proceeded to read out the letter. Behind Abū-l Fazl's usual euphemism and flowery language, the painful, humiliating truth soon became evident – Murād had drunk himself to death. For months in a row, he had been living like a pig, blind drunk from the morning till the evening, neglecting all his duties except for a few undignified arguments with Abdurrahīm. In the end, it had become so bad that his friends had to spoon-feed him two full cups of araq every morning before he was able to do anything, because his hands were shaking so badly! Nothing anyone said to him seemed to help; in the end, he would drink over thirty cups per day, and hardly eat anything, until he became completely bedridden. The letter remained discreetly silent as to how exactly he died; but it was clear that it had been amidst a hell of sweat, filth, and vomit.

I dismissed the messenger with an impatient wave of hand. For what must have been at least an hour, I just sat there, alone in the empty diwān-i-khās, staring at the floor. Much as I blamed myself for it, I found myself unable to cry, or even to feel anything. My son, dead? It was so unreal, it somehow did not seem to get through to me. I tried to picture him in my mind's eye, but all that came to me were a few fragments – the sound of his disturbingly loud voice, which, as Salīmā cautiously told me one day, sounded exactly like my own; the irritation I felt when time and again, he would show up late when I sent for him; his remarkable prowess with guns and horses; his disturbing laziness and lack of interest in anything other than eating, drinking, treasure, and women.

Then, I thought of him as he had been when he was fifteen, sitting on his horse as if he had been born on it, galloping at breakneck speed while shooting well-aimed arrows at a straw puppet. A hot, burning tear—the first one of many—came running down my face, as I realised that my son's life was over and done with, that it was utterly impossible to do anything about it. A young life that could have been full of greatness had come to an abrupt end; an end so stupid, so shameful, so unnecessary, that I wanted to stamp my feet and shout in rage; but I knew that nothing I would say or do would change anything. There was nothing but the empty hall, and my silent, bitter tears.

Except for the most urgent matters of state, I hardly left my private quarters the following days, spending my time sitting listlessly on my bed or pacing up and down, thinking, brooding. Not that it was of any help or use. It was as if some infernal mill in my head kept churning out the same thoughts, over and over and over. How could Murād do this to himself? How could a strong young man throw away his own life like that? Was it my fault? Should I not have gone down there myself and tried talking to him? He brought this on himself! I gave him everything, a life of wealth, power and luxury, and he squandered it all away! Perhaps—god forgive me for even thinking so—it was for the best. Who knows what would have happened if he would have survived me? He was ambitious, an excellent soldier, and far too proud and hot-tempered to live the life of an obedient courtier to his brother. Perhaps god Himself had intervened here, to spare Hindustān the scourge of civil war, a war that would have ruined everything I worked for all my life! No, who was I kidding? Did I really think that god—if He existed—would be bothered with men's thrones and successions? No, what happened, happened. Nothing I said or thought or did would change anything about it.

After a few days, Hakīm Alī Gilanī requested a private audience, which I granted reluctantly. With that well-meaning meddlesomeness so typical of men of his profession, he suggested that it would be better for my health if I went out more, got some air . . . I grumpily told him to leave me in peace, but deep down, I knew he was right. The next day, I made up my mind: I would go to the Deccan. Take charge of operations myself. It would be good to hear the roar of cannon again, the shouting, the thunder of hooves. . . .

And so, on the twenty-ninth of Tīr of the forty-fourth year,[299] barely two months after Murād's death, I headed south, to Khāndesh and Asīrgarh, to pick up where my son had left off.

≈

Asīrgarh . . . merely writing down the name of the wretched place makes me furious! If I could, I would even erase it from my memory. What should have been my last and most glorious conquest, became a most embarrassing, disgraceful spectacle – all because of you, Salīm.

As you remember all too well, I left you in charge of Āgrā while I was away; I ordered you to make yourself useful meanwhile, and lead a campaign into southern Rājāstān to bring the rānā of Mewār to heel. Knowing your indolent nature, I kind of suspected that not much would come from the Mewār campaign, but how could I expect the kind of treachery you were up to?

While you and that bunch of useless sycophants you call your friends were cooking up evil plans, I unsuspectingly headed south, where I reached the border of Khāndesh near the end of the solar year. Upon my arrival, I found that the local ruler Mirhan Bahādur and most of his forces had taken refuge in the fortress of Asīrgarh. I quickly seized the opportunity. Bypassing the fortress, I marched further south to the capital Burhanpūr, which I took, virtually unopposed, on the twenty-first of Farvardin of the forty-fifth year.[300] Abdurrahīm and Dānyāl were sent ahead further into Ahmadnagar, where they surrounded the capital, and took it by storm on the seventh of Shahrivar,[301] imprisoning the local king

---

299. 10 July 1599
300. 31 March 1600
301. 19 August 1600

and his family, and putting to the sword the defending garrison of about fifteen hundred. Meanwhile, I had laid siege to the fortress of Asīrgarh. It is there that, alas, things started to go seriously wrong.

You have to know that Asīrgarh is at least as strong a fortress as Chittaur, its ramparts high up on well-nigh inaccessible cliffs, with the added difficulty that all the ground around it is solid rock, preventing the construction of sābāts. It has its own potable water from numerous wells and reservoirs inside its walls, and supplies sufficient to feed the entire defending garrison for over ten years. As the ramparts could not be stormed, and I did not have enough heavy cannons at my disposal to breach the walls, I found myself stuck. I sent an embassy to Goa, with a message that if the Purtugēsh valued my friendship, they would quickly come to my aid with a number of their heavy guns.

As I waited in vain for the Purtugēsh—they were apparently not so eager to help me conquer the South and thus become my neighbours— and was devising alternative plans to either bring in additional artillery from up north, or found extra cannons and mortars on site from locally available bronze and iron, most disturbing dispatches came in from Āgrā, and alarming letters from Salīmā and my mother: Shāhzāda Salīm, they wrote, was in open rebellion against his father. He had attempted—in vain, fortunately—to seize the treasuries in Lāhor, Dillī and Āgrā. He had raised an army of over seventy thousand cavalry and taken Allāhābād, where he had set up court as an independent king.

My own son, a traitor? I could hardly believe my ears, but alas, it appeared to be true. What was I to do? I could not bear the thought of having to run back, tail between my legs, with Khāndesh still unconquered, but then again, could I afford to stay away from my capital with a major rebellion going on? I urgently needed to get back, and talk some sense into you.

I thus hastily proceeded to secure the last but regrettably most inglorious victory of my life. Through the intermediary of a few local nobles, secret negotiations were opened with the leading defenders. As I hoped and expected, gold and silver bribes quickly proved to be far more effective than steel and gunpowder. After a few weeks, Asīrgarh opened its gates, and without a single drop of blood having been shed, the imperial standard flew over the ramparts.

I paid a hasty visit to the newly conquered fortress, but found little joy in the sight, however magnificent and impressive. What was supposed to have been my ultimate victory was in fact a smudge on my immaculate armour.

Thus ended, in disappointment most bitter, my inglorious Deccan campaign. As quickly as my honour permitted me, I headed back north to secure my capital from my own son. My firstborn, the one I had so ardently prayed for, was threatening my treasure, my throne, and possibly even my life.

Part III

شام [302]

---

302. Shām: Evening, dusk

Thirty-eighth Letter

الآحاباد

Allāhābād (I)

From the Memoirs of Her Imperial Highness
Salīmā Sultānā Bēgam Chaqānīānī,

مخفی

The late afternoon of Yawm as-Sabt, the sixteenth of Shawwāl, 1011,[303]
The ninth of Farvardīn, this forty-eighth year of Akbar's reign;
On the road to Allāhābād, about twenty-five kos east of Āgrā.

Allāh be praised, the messenger has returned, at last – and there is even a personal letter from Salīm!
 The reception was cool but courteous, the messenger says.

---

303. Saturday, 19 March 1603

Salīm was drunk, as usual, and did not say much; but even so, he did offer him food and refreshments and a place to rest, before sending him back to me, with the letter.

'Tell Her Highness, she had better save herself the trouble,' he said, 'but if she persists in her resolve to see me, it will be an honour and a privilege for me to receive her as my guest.'

I must say, the tone of the letter is rather encouraging: formal and polite, of course, as can be expected from a king writing to his stepmother, but definitely not unfriendly.

'Most honourable and chaste lady, whom I cherish and revere as I do my own mother,' that is how he addresses me!

He profoundly regrets, he says, that the unfortunate differences between his august father and himself have caused me such distress, that I have thought it necessary to undertake so strenuous a voyage.

Deplorable though the quarrel with his revered father may be, he fears there is very little that I can do about it: I must see that it is his duty to follow the path he has taken – the path he profoundly believes to be in full accordance with Allāh's will.

He is concerned about my health and comfort, he says; he wonders whether it would not be wiser for me to return to the safety and convenience of Āgrā. Not that he does not wish to see me – on the contrary, and I know that he has always had the highest respect and deepest affection for me. If I do choose to come, as he suspects I will, for he knows I have the character and perseverance of my glorious ancestors, he will be most honoured and pleased to receive me with the highest honour, and he is very much looking forward to this opportunity of seeing me again.

He urges me not to hesitate to call upon him, if there is anything I should need during my voyage. He suspects his most noble father will have provided me with ample supplies and a strong enough escort to guarantee my comfort and safety, but again, he would be glad to be of assistance should I so require.

He will for now bid me farewell, and express the wish that Allāh may be my guide and protector.

The 'unfortunate differences between his august father and himself... a deplorable quarrel'... Is that all he has to say about the dreadful things he did? Taking possession of the fortress of Allāhābād, seizing the imperial treasure there, raising an army of over thirty thousand cavalry, and even striking coin in his own name – what is that, if not open rebellion? And what to say about the cowardly murder of Abū-l Fazl?

I have never seen Akbar so enraged—enraged and devastated at the same time—as when they told him that his best friend and most trusted confidant had been butchered by a gang of robbers, led by some petty local warlord, paid and instructed by his own son. . . .

Salīm always detested Abū-l Fazl – so much I knew. I knew he was jealous of him, he resented and feared him for the influence he had on Akbar. But who could have imagined that he would be capable of such atrocity? What kind of son has his father's best friend murdered in cold blood? How vengeful can one get, to throw the poor man's head in the latrines, leaving it there to rot under the excrements, and making sure your father gets to know about it?

Still, not all is lost. Despite his grief and anger, Akbar has managed to resist the urge to launch his armies against Allāhābād. Anyone else, he would have crushed like an ant, but punishing his son is clearly something different altogether. Furious though he may be, he will always put the interests of his empire first!

And Salīm? He yearns to be king, he longs for a court of his own – so much is certain. So far, however, he has avoided any direct confrontation with the imperial army, and he does continue to speak about his father with utmost respect. He may call himself the 'king of Allāhābād', but never has he gone so far as to reject or deny his father's overlordship.

No, all is not lost – not yet. With Allāh's help, I may still be able to talk some sense into him, and show him that it is not only his duty, but also in his own best interest to reconcile himself with his father.

Yes, I will put my trust in Allāh. With His support, nothing is impossible! I pray to Him, that He may grant me the wisdom to find the right words, and to Salīm, the openness of heart to hear them.

Thirty-ninth Letter

الآحاباد

Allāhābād (2)

From the Memoirs of Her Imperial Highness Salīmā Sultānā Bēgam Chaqānīānī

Yekshanbeh the fourth of Khordād, this forty-eighth year of Akbar's reign,[304] about two hours before dawn.

Allāh be praised a thousandfold, I have succeeded! Salīm has agreed to return to Āgrā with me!

Our conversation has, of course, been neither pleasant nor easy, but I have to admit, he does listen to reason, after all. He's a fickle, hotheaded drunkard, no doubt, and his mind has obviously been poisoned by that worthless bunch of profiteering flatterers he calls his advisors, but deep down, there is honesty and strength in him, a nobleness of character that, however imperfectly, reminds me of Akbar.

Salīm is quite smart, actually – in many respects, smarter and more talented even than his father! Unfortunately, he misses Akbar's perseverance and resilience, but then, who does not? And anyway, does

---

304. Sunday, 15 May 1603 (Julian calendar)

he have to be exactly like his father, in order to be a good king? Is it always necessary to be an exact copy of one's predecessor? I would argue, it may be preferable for a country that a conqueror be succeeded by a peacemaker, a wise man by a smart one, a visionary by a pragmatist. . . . No, with Allāh's help, Salīm can be a good and just emperor, I am sure of that.

It was as I expected; the reception that befell us was lavish beyond imagination – clearly intended to impress, if not intimidate.

After two days' travelling from Allāhābād, we were met by a powerful, well-equipped cavalry force, much larger than any escort that could be considered necessary under the circumstances. Although I took care not to show it too conspicuously, I was truly overjoyed to see that Salīm had come in person to greet me. He actually seemed to be quite eager to please me, calling me his revered mother, and showing me every possible honour, although he did avoid being alone with me. 'We will have ample time to talk when we arrive, revered mother,' he would answer evasively each time I tried to start a private conversation with him.

We continued our way to Allāhābād in great pomp. When the cortege was about one kos from the city gates, Salīm rode ahead with his men – to bid me an official welcome upon my arrival, he explained. I followed at the head of my retinue, seated in a beautiful pālkī, on the towering back of one of Akbar's most impressive elephants.

Upon our arrival at the fortress, an impressive fighting force bade us welcome, with rows upon rows of heavily armoured war elephants and beautifully caparisoned horses, rolling kettledrums, and blaring trumpets.

I rode through the gates and entered the fortress. Dozens of well-dressed courtiers were awaiting me in the diwān-i-ām, bowing deeply as I entered, their right hands touching the ground. I did not deign to wave or nod or otherwise acknowledge their presence: I would have nothing to do with that worthless bunch of sycophants Salīm called his 'court' . . . despicable liars and profiteers, every single one of them, who had estranged him from his father for their own profit!

The diwān-i-ām, though smaller than the one back in Āgrā, was well laid out and quite impressive. Just like at Akbar's court, there was a large shaded area along the palace wall, covered by an elegant roof, its arches artfully sculpted and adorned with beautiful silk curtains, and its floor covered with precious Kashmīrī silken carpets. In the wall was a balconied platform, supporting an impressive throne, perched above the crowd. On the throne sat Salīm, laden with pearls, a bejewelled sword in his hand, broad-shouldered, manly, imposing, and indeed, of eminently royal countenance. I must admit, I did feel somewhat intimidated. This was not a welcome at the residence of some local governor, not even one of royal blood – this was truly the court of a mighty king receiving a foreign ambassador.

I resolved, however, not to show how impressed I was – definitely not in front of Salīm's courtiers! After all, was I not the emperor's preferred wife and his official ambassador, invested with an imperial mission? Was Salīm's rank not that of a local governor – lower than mine? Ignoring the servants who had come to help me get down from my mount, I merely opened the curtains of the pālkī and remained seated on the elephant – higher than Salīm's throne. Keeping my face expressionless behind the transparent veil that covered my head, I kept silent, waiting for him to greet me.

'My heart is overjoyed, revered mother!' Salīm said with a slight bow. 'It is a great honour indeed for my court and the entire city of Allāhābād to receive the visit of such a highborn and most noble bēgam!'

'I am glad to see you in good health, my son!' I answered with a brief nod and a faint smile. 'I bring you your noble father's most affectionate greetings! He has instructed me to give you this robe of honour, made of the finest silk and embroidered with gold thread; he has worn it upon his own person for a full day! He also wants you to have this fine Irāqī stallion, faster than the wind, strong and fearless; and this war elephant, which is the pride of the imperial stables; his name, most appropriately, is Fath-i-lashkar.'[305]

'Words fail me to express my gratitude and joy at these tokens of my noble father's affection and generosity, revered mother,' Salīm answered, touching his heart and bowing his head. Was he being facetious? Or did he actually mean what he said? I could not be sure.

'I bring you his tidings, my son, and there are indeed matters of the highest import we need to talk about – in private of course,' I answered.

---

305. Fath-i-lashkar: Victory of the army

I briefly looked down upon the bunch of sycophants at the foot of the throne, with what I hoped was conspicuous disdain.

Salīm seemed to hesitate for a moment, then nodded in approval. 'I look forward to continuing our conversation in private, revered mother. I hope you will find your quarters comfortable – please, do not hesitate to ask if there is anything you require.'

We dismounted. Palace servants guided me and my retinue to the zanāna, where I found that an entire wing had been vacated to accommodate us. Food and drink, flowers, exquisite silk, soothing balms, precious perfumes – everything had been provided for in abundance. I took a bath and had something small to eat, then took a brief stroll around the grounds. The zanāna was smaller than the one at the Āgrā Fort, but just as comfortable, and I have to admit, even more refined. The rooms and hallways abounded with beautiful works of art, from all over the world it seemed; the colours and patterns of the carpets and curtains had been combined judiciously and with exquisite taste. This was truly the dwelling of a lover of beauty.

I instructed the servants to inform Prince Salīm that I was ready to meet with him. He did not keep me waiting. Servants carried me in a comfortable sedan chair to his private quarters, where he was waiting for me, sitting cross-legged on a cushion in a comfortable, lamp-lit room. Next to him was a precious, gem-encrusted box, a large jewel case so it seemed.

Salīm rose to his feet to bid me welcome, embraced me and respectfully bowed down to kiss both my hands. We sat ourselves down, facing each other, a silver tray with fruits and sweets between us. He ordered the servants to bring us some ice-cooled water, sherbet, wine and some more duātasha arraq[306] – a yellowish, unsavoury-looking liquid, of which he would from time to time gulp down a large mouthful, without any obvious enjoyment though, judging by the rather painful grimace on his face each time the stuff was making its way to his stomach.

He looked a lot less impressive than back in the diwān-i-ām a few hours before. He had been drinking, that much was certain – the room reeked of it. His eyes were reddish, watery and dull; from time to time,

---

306. Duatasha arraq: Twice-distilled spirit

however, when something annoyed him, they would narrow to slits, and suddenly start glowing, like the eyes of a tiger about to strike.

He did his very best to look relaxed and in control. Each time I mentioned his father's name, though, he would give away his nervousness, inadvertently shuffling on his cushion, belying the confident, disdainful smile around his lips.

'Serve us our drinks and leave us,' Salīm ordered the two servant girls who were waiting near the door.

'I think I will just have some lime sherbet,' I said, and the girl standing closest to me made haste to attend to my wish. Salīm merely pointed at his beaker, nearly empty by now. The other servant replaced it with another one, filled it to the rim with some more ice-cooled arraq, and put an entire pitcher of the stuff in a bowl of ice in front of him. Before the girls had left the room, he had taken another sip.

'You have to stop drinking so much of this, Salīm! Have you forgotten what it has done to your poor brother Murād, may Allāh have mercy on him? And still, you and your brother Dānyāl continue drinking, as if nothing has happened! Why are you both so keen on destroying yourselves that way?'

'I appreciate your concern, most noble bēgam and revered mother,' Salīm answered stiffly, 'but I can assure you that I am in excellent health!'

'Salīm, why won't you listen to me? Hakīm Alī has told me all about the dangers of heavy drinking! Do you realise, that . . . '

He impatiently raised his hand.

'As I said, revered mother, I do appreciate your concern, but you can rest assured, that I have everything under control! Besides, I must assume that you have not been travelling all this way, just to talk to me about my drinking habits?'

'You are right, I have not. I have come to ask you to come back to Āgrā with me, Salīm! This dreadful feud has to stop!'

'Feud? What feud?'

'Don't play the innocent, Salīm! You have been openly rebelling against your father for over two years now!'

'Rebellion? As far as I'm aware, there is no armed conflict between my father and me!' Again, that cold smile and that dangerous flicker in his eyes.

'What other name is there for your outrageous behaviour? Your father leaves Āgrā to go to war against the Deccan sultanates, and he leaves you in charge of the capital. He orders you to take an army to Rājāstān, to bring the rānā of Mewār to heel. And how do you repay his trust in you? You head back before even reaching Ājmīr! You do not listen to Mān Singh; you even refuse to go and see your own grandmother when she asks you to, and you try to steal from the imperial treasury, in Lāhor as well as in Āgrā! And when that attempt fails, you head east, and take Allāhābād!'

'I wanted to be left in peace. . . .'

'To be left in peace? You call this *peace*? Seizing the local treasury—thirty lakhs of rupees, no less!—spending it shamelessly on your own comfort and glory, and setting up your own court? Appointing confidants of your own and replacing your father's officers, everywhere from Kālpī to Bījāpūr?

'No apology, no word of gratitude, no sign of respect, nothing! On the contrary, you have the insolence of having coins minted in your own name – nothing short of a declaration of independence! What do you think your father would have done to you, had you not been his son? He would have crushed you like a bug! But still, out of love for you, he holds his peace. He sends you his best advisor, his most trusted helper, his best friend – hoping that this man will be able to talk some sense into you. And what is your reply? Not only do you refuse your father's hand in friendship, you have the audacity to have his closest friend ambushed and murdered by some dirty roadside robber chief!'

'I hear indeed that Shaykh Abū-l Fazl was killed in a skirmish with Rājā Bīr Singh of Orchha. There must have been some kind of enmity between those two. . . .'

'Do you deny that it was you who sent that unwashed bandit to kill your father's friend?'

'I wrote to him saying that Shaykh Abū-l Fazl's coming to Allāhābād was displeasing to me,' Salīm admitted with a phony smile. 'I am sure Bīr Singh must have had my best interests at heart, when he attacked the Shaykh's retinue. . . .'

'People say, you even had the poor man's head thrown in the latrines!'

'Do they? Well, if I did, I did well, and I had every reason to!' shouted Salīm, suddenly seething with rage. 'When I think of all the crap that has come out of that pig's mouth, no place could be more appropriate for it!'

'How can you say this, Salīm? And how could you do such a terrible thing? He was your father's most trusted friend!'

Salīm did not answer immediately. I could see the muscles around his jaw moving as he struggled to restrain his anger.

'Trusted, most certainly! But my father's friend, he was not!'

'What makes you say that?'

'Abū-l Fazl has never been anyone's friend! Never has he served anybody or anything but his own private interests! Filling his own coffers was the only thing he ever cared for! He was a shameless opportunist, who cleverly offered my father the jewels of flattery – but at what heavy price!'

'Do you really think your father is a fool who can be taken in by flattery? Well, trust me, he is not! He is an excellent judge of character – you don't get to be as mighty and powerful as he is if you pick the wrong helpers! Of course he knows that Abū-l Fazl was a shameless flatterer – most courtiers are, by the way, and your own in the first place! But very few people are as competent and hard-working as Abū-l Fazl was – the poor man worked like a dog for your father! And yes, your father did reward him handsomely for it. So what? Don't you think it is normal that a hard-working minister with so many important responsibilities gets rewarded for his faithful service? How about your own helpers: Do you not pay them a handsome salary? Of course you do! Well, I am certain, they are not half as competent or hardworking as Abū-l Fazl was!'

Salīm smiled.

'You may rest assured, revered mother: I know my father is no fool. I may have many shortcomings, but blind or dishonest, I am not. And yes, I'll admit to you that Abū-l Fazl was smart and hardworking. But let me tell you, for all his qualities, the empire is much better without him!'

'But why?'

'I think you know why, revered mother.'

'But I really do not. Why don't you tell me?'

'Revered mother, I somehow find that hard to believe! Everybody knows how wise you are, and everybody knows that you are my father's preferred wife. I really find it hard to believe that you did not see how Abū-l Fazl deliberately estranged me from my father and my brothers!'

'I really don't know why you think this? I have never heard him say anything of the kind!'

'Of course not, he would be more subtle than that! But that has not stopped him from being effective – highly effective!'

'I'm sorry, I do not have the faintest idea what you are talking about! You keep speaking in riddles!'

Again, that angry flicker in Salīm's eyes. For a few moments, he said nothing, just looking intently at me, trying to read my mind. He must have come to the conclusion that I actually meant what I said, for he resumed, in a much softer tone of voice:

'Revered mother, I trust you are familiar with Abū-l Fazl's chronicle, the *Ākbar Nāmā*,[307] are you not?'

'I am.'

'And you have read it, I suppose?'

'Yes, I have, several times! I agree it abounds with flowery phrases and flattery, but does that not prove Abū-l Fazl's loyalty?'

'Have you not noticed, revered mother, how often, or rather, how *seldom* he makes mention of me or my brothers? Just think about it: hundreds upon hundreds of pages of chronicles, and hardly a word about the emperor's own sons! And you know what is even worse? He actually does not *need* to talk about us, because we hardly ever got to play any role of significance!'

'Aren't you exaggerating a bit, Salīm? Has your father not entrusted you—all three of you—with many important missions?'

'Has he, indeed?' Salīm sneered. 'Well, we have been sent on a few campaigns, yes – campaigns of little importance, when *he* had better things to do! But have we ever been involved in any matters of real import? Never!'

He gulped down some more arraq, closing his eyes, with a painful grimace on his face until the liquid had reached his stomach.

---

307. *Akbar Nāmā* and *Ā'Īn-ī-Akbarī*: Chronicle and detailed description of Akbar's institution, both written by Abū-l Fazl.

'Revered mother, let me give you another example to prove my point. You are of course familiar with the Nau Rathan or Navaratna, the nine gems of Emperor Akbar's court, are you not? As you know, it is the title of honour the people of Hindustān have given to my father's preferred advisors and friends. Most of them are dead now, but they are still quite famous for the high esteem in which they were held, and for the influence they had on my father. And who were those famous nine gems? The list of names will of course include Abdurrahīm Khān Khanān and Rājā Mān Singh, my father's best army commanders, and Todar Mal, Bīrbal and Abū-l Fazl, his trusted administrators. The list will usually include Abū-l Faizī, the poet, Tānsēn, the famous singer and musician, and one or two religious advisors. The names of those advisors tend to differ, depending on whom you ask, but those who know my father, will always include old Shaykh Mubārak in the list. Hah! Can you imagine? One of the greatest empires the world has ever seen has practically been *ruled*, for decades, by a lowborn, babbling old shaykh, and his two fat, conniving sons! Allāh be praised that they are dead and gone at last, all three of them – at least they will no longer be poisoning my father's ear!'

I wanted to say he was exaggerating, but he impatiently smacked his flat hand on the cushion.

'Don't try to deny it! You know very well it is true! These three flatterers have even talked my father into creating that ridiculous new religion of his! The poor man probably does not even realise what a fool he has been making of himself! But these three bastards, rather than advising him correctly, rather than telling him what is really going on in his dominions, actually encouraged him in this nonsense! And you know why? To protect their own privileges and to line their own pockets, that's why!'

'I don't like all this dīn-e-illāhī nonsense, either,' I admitted. 'But you are wrong to think that Abū-l Fazl was ever unfaithful to your father, or that he tried to estrange him from you! Moreover, can it be denied how exceptionally smart and hardworking he was? He and Mubārak have been absolutely invaluable to the emperor in his disputes with the mullāhs!'

He smiled wryly.

'Yes, I'll admit to that. He was smart and hardworking, and yes, my father loved his wit, his freethinking attitude and his contempt for the mullāhs; but much more importantly, Abū-l Fazl gave my father exactly the one message he adores to hear – that he, Emperor Akbar the Great, is absolutely unique, indispensable, and irreplaceable! And meanwhile, he cleverly took advantage of my father's vanity to make himself indispensable, and keep *me* out of government affairs! As I said before, he offered him the jewels of flattery, but made him pay dearly for them!'

'Keeping you out?'

'Let me ask you a simple question, revered mother. Has my father ever asked my opinion or advice? Has he ever involved me in any of his decisions? Have I ever been his confidant? Never! All my life, I have been following his orders, as if I were some third-rate officer. And why is that? Because all these years, Abū-l Fazl has subtly but effectively been keeping me out!'

'And how is he supposed to have done that?'

'Oh, as I said, he went about it quite subtly! In the first place of course, he would try to keep me away from the court as far as possible – never missing an opportunity of having me sent off on some or the other campaign in some or the other faraway region!'

He pouted his lips and imitated Abū-l Fazl's mannered, servile way of speaking. 'Oh, Your Majesty, this would be an excellent experience for His Highness the Shāhzāda!'

'And then, with the crown prince safely out of the way, good old Abū-l Fazl finally had free play! Of course, he knew very well that I hated his guts, and that his game would be finished as soon as I ascend the throne! And so, subtly, cleverly, he began sowing seeds of doubt in my father's mind, with veiled hints that I am really not fit to succeed him. He rarely missed an occasion to glorify Dānyāl's wisdom or Murād's soldiery skills, but when it came to me, he merely mentioned my "keen eye for the arts", as if I were some stupid harem concubine! Or he would point out "how wonderful it is that Abdurrahīm is just like his father, so courageous, so strong, so wise" – while I, of course, am not! Likewise, he never got tired of saying that Khusrau, Parvez and Khurram have "their grandfather's greatness in them" – something he would, of course, never say about me!

And behind my father's back, he was even less subtle: belittling, disparaging, criticising me in front of everyone who cares to listen! Every amīr, every army leader was given to understand that "the shāhzāda sadly lacks his father's wisdom and insight, that maybe it would be better if His Majesty would appoint one of his grandsons to succeed him", and so on, and so forth. . . .'

Salīm's face was now flushed with anger. He gulped down what was left in his cup, filled it again, and took another large mouthful.

'Clever little plan, wasn't it?' he continued. 'You just plant the seeds of doubt and confusion, and quietly let them do their poisonous work in the emperor's mind . . . "Does Salīm really have what it takes? If not, who else does? Murād was probably the best and the strongest of the three, but sadly, he has passed away, and the doctors say that Dānyāl is heading the same way if he doesn't stop drinking . . . What to do? Should I not appoint my eldest grandson? Khusrau is a fine young man – stronger, healthier, brighter, more disciplined, no drunkard like father and uncle . . ."

'And while the emperor tossed and turned and wondered and worried, Abū-l Fazl, of course, was in high spirits! As long as Salīm is far away, as long as the emperor does not appoint him as his successor, he is powerless! And of course, there was nothing to fear from Dānyāl either – drunk all the time, meek and docile, or from the grandsons, who are still young and perfectly malleable. If one of them got appointed, there would have been no more worries for Abū-l Fazl! He must have thought he could have been the new young emperor's atālīq, advisor, wakīl perhaps . . .

'Well, I spoiled that neat little plan of his, didn't I? That son of a bitch thought he could just come over here to insult me in front of my court, and drag me back to Āgrā by my ear, didn't he? Thought I would never dare to lay a finger on him, didn't he? Well, he was wrong!

'Yes, I know my father is furious, but I don't care! At least, I gave that conniving bastard what he deserved – at least, he will not be there to reap the rewards of all his slander and intriguing! And so what if my father wants to appoint someone else as his successor? To hell with it! Let him appoint whomever he wants! I am sick and tired of grovelling and begging and minding my step and sitting and waiting! I'm thirty-three years old – old and wise enough to start making my own decisions, and I want some respect!'

He grabbed the silver bowl of sweets on the tray in front of him and flung it at the wall. It clanged against the stones with a terrible noise, but not one of the servants dared to show her face and come in to clean up the mess.

For what seemed to me like an eternity, he just sat there, clenching his teeth, breathing heavily, staring at the dented empty bowl and the sweets scattered all over the floor.

Finally, he seemed to calm down. He looked at me, his features surprisingly composed and peaceful again.

'I really appreciate your concern for me, revered mother. I am truly grateful that you travelled all the way to see me, and I deeply appreciate your efforts to restore peace between my august father and myself, but as you can see, it is better that he and I go our separate ways. Allow me to express my gratitude, and offer you one of the most valuable treasures of my library – I bought it a few years ago from an Esfahānī merchant. I know it will be in excellent hands if I give it you!'

He bent over towards the jewel-encrusted case next to him and handed it to me. I took it in both hands—it was quite heavy, as I expected—and put it on my lap. I opened it; inside was a magnificent book, artfully bound, with hundreds of pages of exquisite calligraphy, illustrated on every single page with beautiful miniatures.

'Jalāl-ud-dīn Rūmī – your favourite poet, is he not? Well, I want you to have this, revered mother, as a sign of my appreciation!'

I wanted to protest, tell him it was too much, but he did not let me speak.

'I have but one more request, revered mother – when you get back to Āgrā, please tell my august father that I want no quarrel with him. Tell him, he can appoint whomever he pleases as his successor on the throne of Hindustān. Tell him, I only desire to be left in peace.'

I slowly closed the jewel box. Thoughts were racing frantically through my head. What was I to say?

'Thank you, my son,' I answered, slowly, word for word, trying to buy myself more time to think, 'this is really beautiful, but I cannot possibly accept it!'

'Why not?'

'Books are supposed to be a source of enjoyment, Salīm. I could never lay my eyes on this book, beautiful and valuable as it is without feeling deeply miserable – it would always remind me of the worst failure of my life! No, if you want me to accept it, you will have to come back to Āgrā with me!'

He ignored the question, and bent forward to help himself to a few almonds.

'You *have* to come back with me, Salīm! Can't you see you are bringing ruin on yourself, your father, the empire, and our entire family? Yes, I know what you're going to say: you want no quarrel with your father, you want to be left alone. Can't you see that is impossible? Your father has toiled and laboured his entire life to build this empire; he would rather die a thousand deaths than see it fall apart! If you want to be on your own, he will give you the governorship of Allāhābād or Bengāl or whatever, but he will *never* agree to a partition of the empire, you have to realise that!

'And let me tell you another thing, Salīm. Whether you were right or wrong about Abū-l Fazl—I think you were terribly wrong, but that's beside the point now—whether or not he was the devious intriguer you say he was, he was still your father's best friend! You broke your father's heart, Salīm – he was devastated! He didn't eat or leave his bedroom for days! In these last few years, he has lost all his closest friends and confidants – Bīrbal, Todar Mal, Rājā Bhagwān Dās, and now, you have taken Abū-l Fazl away from him!

'But all is not lost, Salīm! Think about it – in spite of all the grief and anger you caused him, your father has not renounced or disinherited you, yet! And why do you think that is? Partly, because in spite of everything, he still loves you, he still cannot bear the thought that his long-awaited first-born son, the one he had such high hopes for, has become his enemy!

'But there is another, even more important reason – above all, your father wants to protect his life's work, his empire! Put yourself in his shoes; what would you do, if you were him? Sure, you could disinherit your unruly first-born son, have him banished, imprisoned, killed even. You could appoint someone else, but who? Dānyāl, perhaps? Would you take that risk? Dānyāl is a fine person, refined, well-educated, but would you entrust the future of your empire to a hopeless drunkard with one foot in the grave? You could appoint your first-born grandson, and sure, Khusrau is a talented young man, but will he be able to keep your empire together when you are dead and gone? Dānyāl will feel past over; when they are older, Parvez or Khurram, at least as competent as their brother, may want to try their luck; Salīm himself may yet be back to claim his birthright, and all of them will have their ardent supporters. Before you know it, the empire is plunged in civil war! The winner inherits a weakened, deeply divided land; and when Kashmīr, Bengāl, Gujarāt or other regions try to break away from him, he is well-nigh powerless to prevent it! Can't you see, Salīm? Your father does not want to fight you, but he will, if you force him to! So do yourself a favour: Come back to Āgrā with me, and make amends – you have nothing to lose, and everything to gain! Don't plunge yourself and the empire in a disastrous fight, which you will lose, and no one will win!'

'You seem to be quite sure that I would lose that fight, revered mother. . . .'

'I am, and if you are honest with yourself, so are you, Salīm! You know your father is a better soldier than you are!'

'I am nothing!'

'You are not worse nor better than your father, Salīm, just different, very different! In some respects, your father is indeed much stronger than you. He is a veteran warrior with a record of victories that remains unsurpassed; he is disciplined and dedicated, and he has an unequalled capacity for hard work. In many respects, however, you are more talented than he is. You are an outstanding scholar, an accomplished writer, you speak many languages. . . . You do not need to be another Akbar to be a great emperor, my son: just try to be the best Salīm you can be!'

Salīm smiled faintly. 'I can see, revered mother, why my father is so fond of you. But are you really sure? Will he be able to forgive me, after all the bad blood between us? Who says he will not have me thrown in prison, or worse?'

'No, Salīm, that will not happen! As I told you, in spite of everything, your father loves you very much; you're his first-born – he would never hurt you! And even more importantly, he would never endanger the empire for which he has toiled and fought so hard, all his life! Come with me, my son, it will be so much better for everyone!'

'Just suppose that I do go back to Āgrā with you, I can't just disregard everything that has happened, can I? Should I apologise for what happened? Should I beg his forgiveness?'

After a few moments of reflection, I answered: 'No. Let the past be the past. Don't ask for his forgiveness, but show him your loyalty and affection, show him you're pleased to be back and reunited with him. Impress him. Bring him gifts – lots of gifts. Gifts so lavish that they surpass his wildest expectations! And let us go there together, as a family. On our way to Āgrā, we will humbly ask your revered grandmother to accompany us. Don't you see? He would never do anything to displease her – not in a matter of this importance!'

Salīm reached for his arraq, then changed his mind. He poured himself a large beaker of lime sherbet and began sipping at it, staring aimlessly at the wall.

After what seemed an eternity, he put the beaker down, and looked at me, a faint, amused smile around his lips.

'You are wise and clever, revered mother. And I must say, you do know my father – probably better than he does himself! All right then, I will put my fate in your hands, and follow your advice. Let us head back to Āgrā.'

Fortieth Letter

الآحاباد

Allāhābād (3)

You were offering me seven hundred and seventy elephants, and twelve thousand golden mohurs! I could hardly believe it when the messenger read out Salīmā's letter to me. This was not a courtesy gift; this was complete and entire submission, surrender even; this was your hand, offered in true reconciliation. You truly cannot imagine, my son, how profoundly relieved and happy I felt.

The big day had arrived. You and your retinue would be arriving at noon.

Noon finally came. I could hardly conceal my emotion when you entered through the gate, accompanied by Salīmā—glowing with pride, and rightfully so—and your noble grandmother. We had not seen each other in four and a half years, but you had not changed much. A bit thinner you were, perhaps, your face a bit paler; but you looked strong as before, and noble, and I felt proud of you. I rose from the throne, descended from the platform, and walked in your direction, several steps - an exceptional mark of honour, and the clearest possible sign of my fatherly affection and goodwill. You amply returned the compliment, kneeling down with utmost reverence. I cannot begin to tell you how elated I felt when I took your hands in mine, made you stand up, put my arms around you, kissed you on both cheeks, and in front of the entire court, placed my turban on your head, recognising you publicly as my heir and successor. Everything would turn out for the best, after all. We would do great deeds together, you and me.

It did not take more than a few days to make me realise that it was, alas, an illusion. The few private conversations we had were forced and halting, your answers evasive, your eyes furtive. All we had left to offer each other, was a few bland civilities, and long, awkward pauses.

We both knew what was standing between us: not so much the stolen treasury, not your half-hearted rebellion, but the one thing neither one of us spoke about – the murder of Abū-l Fazl, for which you could offer no apology, and I, no forgiveness.

No matter how often I resolved, usually after yet another night-time conversation with my wise and sweet Salīmā, to put it all behind me, I could not help mulling it over and over in my mind: how I had sent him a letter telling him about your misconduct; how, faithful as always, he had immediately promised he would travel from the Deccan to Allāhābād and bring you to reason; and how he had been murdered in a cowardly manner, on your orders at that, by some filthy local hoodlum, one Bīr Singh of Orchha.

Poor Abū-l Fazl! He never was a man of the sword, yet he—bravely, foolishly—chose to die like one. He had been forewarned by informants. He could have escaped, he could have taken proper precautions, a much stronger escort, but he did not listen to reason. Early in the morning of the thirty-first of Mordād of the forty-seventh year,[308] a day that will forever be among the blackest in the history of Hindustān, he and his retinue of barely a handful suddenly found themselves under attack by five hundred heavily armed horsemen. But he did not flee. On the contrary, he 'preferred an honourable death over a life in shame', he is supposed to have proclaimed. How naïve, how stupid can one be? What good does it do, to die for nothing? Did he really think that god—if He exists—cares about heroes, that He offers them some kind of special protection? What is bravery against vastly superior numbers?

---

308. Thursday, 12 August 1602

My poor old friend never stood a chance. Before he could kill or wound even a single enemy, the assassins speared him like a hunted animal.

They robbed him of his possessions, cut off his head, and took it to Allāhābād, to collect their blood money. It is said that when you saw the severed head—and you have given me no reason to believe otherwise—you ordered it to be tossed in the latrines.

What pained me most was that I had been unable to avenge him. The shame of Bīrbal's death had quickly been erased with piles of Afghan heads; but for the death of Abū-l Fazl, it seemed there was only impotent rage. The troops I had sent to Orchha to bring me that bastard Bīr Singh had failed: though wounded, he had managed to escape. Poor consolation, that everything he owned had been confiscated. As soon as I would be gone, the bastard would have no trouble getting into the new emperor's good graces. . . .

The more I thought about what had happened, the angrier I got. Why this needless, cowardly murder? What had I ever done to deserve this? What kind of son kills one of his father's most trusted helpers? What kind of a man denies the dead a decent burial?

I thought to myself – was this the kind of man to be ruling Hindustān? But what if I disinherited you? For all your faults, you were too much of a man to accept that. There would be civil war, most probably the breakup of the empire! Could I risk ruining everything I worked for? Not even poor Abū-l Fazl would have wanted me to do that!

Thus, we went on, you and I. Officially reconciled, but estranged from each other more than ever before. Between us stood a past that neither one of us could forget, and that, as far as I was concerned, tasted more bitter by the day. I resented you for having been such a terrible disappointment to me, and you, I am quite certain, resented my living too long and standing in your way. Apart from a few official court sessions, we saw very little of each other; you spent most of your time in Fatehpūr Sīkrī; and I avoided you as much as you did me.

One thing did please me – at least, you were not idling away your days. My informants told me you were still drinking, but within limits, and that you spent much time meeting with the old amīrs, and with the firanghī priests. Ostensibly, your conversations with the former were about Sharī'a law, and with the latter, about the life of the blessed Virgin

Maryam, whose effigies you seemed to hold in particular reverence; remarkable subjects, for a man who cares so little about religion. . . .

It was all too clear what you were up to – you were forging the alliances you would need in the fights to come – against me, against Khusrau, or anybody else. And I have to say, those were smart moves you made: The amīrs would readily believe you were their best guarantee for the protection of Islām, and the firanghīs again had high hopes that they would yet be able to convert the 'great Mughal'. . . . If I had not been so worried about the future and the obvious rivalry between you and Khusrau, your astuteness really would have amused me. It seemed you were made of the right material, after all.

The monsoon went by; weeks of reflection with the soothing rustle of the pouring rains outside finally brought me calmness and resolve. I would give you additional responsibilities, involve you more in the affairs of state, give you a chance to prove and redeem yourself. You would go to southern Rājāstān and force the arrogant rānā of Mewār into submission, like I had ordered you to do before I went to the Deccan.

I should have known better. You of course did not refuse to execute the order, but it was crystal clear you had little appetence for a war in some faraway hills, where little plunder was to be gained, and more importantly, where you would be unable to keep things under control at the court, should anything happen to me. After weeks of procrastination, delays, extravagant demands for all kinds of completely unnecessary reinforcements, you made your move. You wrote me a letter – elaborate, flowery, abjectly flattering and servile, but no less clear. You assured me of your ardent desire to fulfill my wishes, but esteemed it your sacred duty to inform me of your presentiment that the time was inauspicious; you implored the favour of a private audience with me, and permission to return to Allāhābād where you felt you would be of better service to me.

I gave up. What would we possibly have to say to each other? What good would it do to have another meeting full of idle talk that would only make me angry? I gave you the desired 'permission to attend to matters in Allāhābād', adding that you should feel at liberty to return to the court at any time.

You finally had what you wanted. On the twenty-ninth of Ābān, you left Fatehpūr Sīkrī, crossed the Jumna near Mathura, and went back to

Allāhābād. Utterly disappointed as I was, I have to admit it did please me to hear that you had organised the most brilliant festivities upon your arrival, celebrating our reconciliation. At least, you were kind enough to keep up appearances.

My relief was, alas, short-lived. Each report I received was more unsettling than the previous one. The only news I seemed to get were stories about drunken depravity, vicious cruelty and excesses of all kinds.

I underwent the celebrations for the beginning of the forty-ninth year in the most sombre of moods. To what end had been all my hard work? What was to become of my Hindustān?

Forty-first Letter

دانیال

Dānyāl

I was in Salīmā's bedroom, late in the afternoon on Shanbeh, the twenty-fifth of Ordībehesht of the forty-ninth year.[309]

She was sitting next to me on the bed, her arm around my shoulders; neither of us knew what to say. I was wiping the tears from my burning eyes, but fresh ones kept welling up, no matter how hard I tried to restrain them.

The messenger from the Deccan had left two hours ago, but I kept hearing his halting voice in my head, over and over again: 'I profoundly regret to have to inform Your Majesty . . .' He did not have to finish his sentence. There was that blue handkerchief, again that dreadful blue handkerchief, that could only mean one thing: His Imperial Highness Shāhzāda Sultān Dānyāl had passed away; Dānyāl, my youngest, my gentlest, my wisest, was dead.

'When did this happen?' I tried to maintain my composure, but my voice was hoarse and barely audible.

'One month ago, Your Majesty.'

'How?'

---

309. 5 May 1604 of the Julian calendar (Saturday, 15 May 1604 CE).

'His Highness passed away in his sleep.'
'What was wrong with him?'
'The hakīms say it was his heart, Your Majesty.'
'Leave us alone,' I ordered. All the guards and courtiers instantly left the diwān-i-khās.
'His heart, you say? Just like that?'
'I do not know, Your Majesty.'
'Don't lie to me!'
'The hakīms said it was caused by excessive drinking,' he admitted hesitatingly.
'Drinking? What do you mean, drinking? I had given explicit orders that my son was *not* to have *any* wine or arraq, under *any* circumstance!'
The man bowed his head and looked down at his feet.
'Speak up, man, or I'll have you hanged!'
'I beseech Your Majesty, have mercy on me! I am innocent! I know nothing! I only know what I overheard other people say!'
'And what did they say?'
'That His Highness felt terribly sick without drink, Your Majesty; that he was sweating, trembling, shaking, unable to eat anything . . . That he bribed his friends and servants to get him his daily ration of wine and arraq – they smuggled it in, in phials hidden in their turbans and clothes, and even in musket barrels! After a few draughts, His Highness would always feel much better, but he still had no appetite for any regular food. They say that the last month of his life, he was completely bedridden and hardly able to eat anything at all. He had become dreadfully thin, but his belly kept bloating. The white of his eyes was yellow, his face ashen. He grew weaker by the day; in the end, he passed away in his sleep. . . .'

I wanted to yell at him, demand from him the names of those responsible, but I could not utter a single word. I just sat there, staring in front of me, unable to think or even feel anything. Finally, I found the strength to tell the terrified messenger he could go – I even had the composure to award him the customary reward for messengers who have travelled from afar and have dutifully acquitted themselves of their task. When he had left, I rose from the throne and went into the palace gardens. Despite the muggy heat, I kept wandering aimlessly through them, for I do not know how long, numb and dazed in my head. Finally,

I went back inside the zanāna. On seeing a painted portrait of Murād and Dānyāl when they were little, my eyes filled with tears at last; my shoulders started shaking uncontrollably, and I heard myself howling like a wounded animal.

For I don't know how long, I just stood there in front of that wretched painting, sobbing like a child. Then, I heard the soft shuffle of women's slippers behind me, and Salīmā's voice whispering: 'Come with me, azīzam!'[310] She put her arm around my shoulders and led me to her quarters, where we sat ourselves down on her bed.

'Dānyāl,' I whispered. 'Dānyāl, my youngest, my gentlest . . . Why? How could this happen? Where has it all gone so wrong, Salīmā? Where have *I* gone wrong?'

'Stop torturing yourself, Akbar! This was really nobody's fault – least of all yours!'

'You're very kind, Salīmā, but . . .'

'Listen to me, Akbar, this was *not* your fault! There is nothing you could have done, even if you would have known everything beforehand!'

'Why?'

'Dānyāl was very sick, and so was Murād! That is what the hakīms say, and that is what I believe. Short of locking him up, and making absolutely sure his guardians could never be bribed, there is nothing you could have done to prevent this. Sooner or later, he was going to drink himself to death.'

'But why? Why did he do this to himself? I must have warned him a thousand times, and so did Hakīm Alī, and so many others! Each time, he would promise and swear on the Holy Qur'ān that he would never drink anymore, and each time, he would fail to keep that promise!'

'As I said, the hakīms say it is a disease, really. Alcohol is a very dangerous thing – it is with good reason the Holy Qur'ān warns us against it! There may be people who do drink a lot but still manage to keep things under control— just look at yourself, for instance—but many others are not so strong. . . .'

'Tell me what to do, Salīmā! What in god's name *can* I do? Two of my three sons are dead, and I tremble for what is happening to the

---

310. Azīzam: My love

one I have left! Ever since he has gone back to Allāhābād, the news I'm getting is nothing less than shocking! Oh, my god! What have I done to deserve this?'

'Is Salīm drinking himself to death too?'

'No, not yet, at least I don't think so, but that won't take long, if he goes on like this! I hear he's hardly ever sober – he drinks from morning till the evening, not to mention all the opium he takes! It is as if he's actually adamant on destroying himself! And everybody is terrified of him – all those excesses are affecting his mind, of course!'

'What do you mean?'

'He has become downright insane, Salīmā! Fickle, moody, unpredictable, cruel beyond belief! Do you know he had one of his men *flayed alive* in front of him, for some minor, trivial offence? Can you imagine? They say that for more than half an hour, he calmly watched him being flayed, without as much as blinking an eye!'

'What!'

'Yes, it is . . . let me tell you, Salīmā: In the forty-nine years I spent on the throne, I have pronounced a number of death sentences, but I can honestly say that it was almost always with reluctance that I resorted to it – because I had to; because there was no other way! Yes, I'll admit that on a few occasions, I did give the order in furious anger, with vengeful pleasure even; but never, never have I ordered that kind of torture on anyone, not even for the most heinous of crimes!'

'I'm still having trouble believing that Salīm would be capable of a gruesome deed like that! Are you sure this story is actually true?'

'Alas, Salīmā, I am – I have it from several dependable sources! And to be honest with you, I really don't know what to do anymore! What will become of the empire with a man like that leading it?'

'Will you disinherit him?'

'I have not decided yet, but yes, I very well may! In fact, I think I would have disinherited him a long time ago, were it not that I was frightened at the thought of what will happen after I'm gone. . . . if there is a full-fledged war? What if the whole country falls apart?'

'You still have time to decide, Akbar. Don't allow anyone to pressurise you into taking a decision you don't want to take! You are strong and healthy; Allāh willing, you may yet have ten, fifteen, maybe twenty more years to live! By that time, your grandsons will be grown men, and you will know what to do!'

I smiled, in spite of myself. She spoke like a true granddaughter of Bābur!

'Yes and no, Salīmā. You are right that I still have time, and yes, I do intend to use it well, but I'm afraid I will have to make up my mind much earlier! Camps are already starting to form among the amīrs! And they make no secret of it! Azīz and Mān Singh, for instance, have given me to understand, more than once, that they would much rather like to see Khusrau on the throne. . . .'

'That's not hard to see why: Khusrau's mother is Mān Singh's own sister, and Azīz Koka is Khusrau's father-in-law! If he gets appointed as your successor, their power and influence would be assured!'

'Precisely. But don't underestimate Salīm – he has some very powerful supporters too! All the ulamā are behind him, and most of the Turkomān amīrs!'

'Why is that?'

'Well, for one, he's supposed to be a much better Muslim than I am, and more importantly, he has all the laws and traditions on his side! The Chagatai Turks of old would never allow a son to be enthroned to the prejudice of his father! And that's not all – there are also quite a few Rājpūt nobles supporting Salīm. Don't forget he is married to a Rājpūt princess too, and don't underestimate the internal rivalry among the Hindū nobles: There are many among them who would only be too glad to supplant Mān Singh if they could! So you see, my dear, if it does come to a fight, Salīm will be far from powerless! And he is not taking any chances: I hear he's been in correspondence with the Purtugēsh of Goa. . . .'

'With the firanghīs? Those unwashed infidels?'

'That is not as strange as it sounds, Salīmā. They have first-rate guns, and though their numbers are small, they are excellent soldiers; they would be formidable allies in any war!'

'So, you think he would actually take firanghī soldiers into his army?'

'Of course! Why do you think he has been so conspicuously devoted to the Virgin Maryam for the last few years? Why does he collect dozens of her effigies? As far as I know, he has precious little interest in religion! He does love firanghī paintings, but more importantly, this interest in the

Blessed Virgin enables him to spend a lot of time with the firanghī pādres, giving them hope—quite false, I'm sure—that he may one day convert to their religion! Just think about what would be in it for the Purtugēsh, if they could put the next "great Mughal" in their debt. . . .'

I took off my turban and slowly rubbed my forehead and the back of my neck, in a vain attempt to ease the throbbing pain in my head.

'You see my problem, Salīmā? If I appoint Khusrau, or one of my other grandsons, there will be civil war; maybe I will be able to prevent it during my lifetime, but it will certainly break out when I'm gone, and that would be an absolute disaster! Not only will kindred blood be spilt—which is terrible enough—but no matter who wins this civil war, he will inherit a weakened and deeply divided land. How long do you think it will take, before the Uzbeg Khān, or the Persian shāh, or some or the other ambitious zamīndār tries to take advantage of this weakness?

'So you see, my dear, there are hardly any options I have left! If I do not appoint an official heir, if I just leave things to run their course as they are today, I'm effectively condoning the partition of the empire I fought for all my life, undermining my own authority, and sowing the seeds of lawlessness and war. If I die while Salīm is still in Allāhābād, Khusrau and his supporters will almost certainly disavow him, saying that he forfeited his right to the throne because of his rebellion. On the other hand, if I do appoint Khusrau, it is almost certain that Salīm will either go to war to claim his birthright, or declare independence and split up the empire.'

'Is there a solution to this?'

'There is, but only one: Salīm *has* to come back, and he *has* to submit to me, unconditionally! Only when we reconcile, only if he shapes up, can I appoint him as my successor! Only when he is officially appointed according to the laws and customs of our family, will he have the necessary authority and the support of the amīrs!'

'And if he does not? What if he refuses to come back?'

'Then, I will need to take other measures.'

'Would you fight your own son?'

'Don't you see that I have no other choice? Either Salīm submits to me and I forgive him and I appoint him as my successor, or I *have* to disinherit him and ask him to leave the empire. It's one or the other. I simply cannot allow things to go on like they are today – it would ruin everything I worked for, all these years!'

'I'll go to Allāhābād. I'm sure I can talk some sense into him! I've done it before.'

'No, Salīmā! No more pleading, no more negotiating, no more playing games! There's a limit to my patience! This time, I'll go there myself – and at the head of an army!'

'Surely, Akbar . . .'

'I'm at the end of my patience, Salīmā! He will come with me to Āgrā, or he will have to fight me!'

And thus, my son, while still mourning the loss of your youngest brother, I once again prepared for war. Not to conquer the Deccan, as I had planned; not to invade Persia or the lands held by the Uzbeg Khāns, as I once had hoped; but to fight my own flesh and blood.

There was, as usual, the frantic busyness everywhere of soldiers and animals and supplies; but this time, none of the anticipation, none of the almost joyful excitement that precedes any great campaign. No prospect this time of land or booty or glory; only the looming menace of bloodshed and destruction; this time, there was absolutely nothing to gain, and everything to lose.

With every gun I inspected, every elephant, every horse, every soldier I saw passing by, the anger gnawed itself deeper into my soul. Such useless waste of a fine army! And all this because of one arrogant, spoilt drunkard who called himself my son! Who did this ungrateful bastard think he was? A true son, worthy of that name, would be proud to expand his father's dominions! But this good-for-nothing was actually squandering them, ruining decades of hard work; unashamedly disobeying, nay, betraying, the father to whom he owned everything, desecrating the memory of his noble ancestors!

Staunchly and with grim determination I continued the preparations, deaf to your mother's and Salīmā's pleas, ignoring the worried letters your grandmother kept sending me. This time, you would come to heel, if I had to drag you to Āgrā!

Alone in my quarters every evening, however, I waited with dread for the moment I would have to go to bed. For I already knew the unbearable, horrifying sight that would come to haunt me in my dreams: the sight of my victorious army, bringing me your severed head.

Forty-second Letter

سلطنت

Saltanat

From the Memoirs of Her Imperial Highness Salīmā Sultānā Bēgam Chaqāniānī

مخفی

No matter what I told Akbar, no matter how much I begged and prayed, he just would not listen.

'Why do you insist on going there yourself?' I pleaded. 'And why do you need an army to go and see Salīm? I know his behaviour has been unacceptable, but has he actually rebelled against you? Can't you just tell him to come to the court? You are the emperor; would he disobey a direct order from you?'

Akbar—if he deigned to answer at all—would silence me with curt statements like 'enough is enough', or 'Do you really think I'm going to let him destroy everything I worked for all my life?' Pressing letters from his ailing mother, who feared the ruin of the grandson she had always been so fond of, remained unanswered. Amidst the heavy monsoon rains, Akbar doggedly prepared himself for war.

After a few weeks, his forces encamped on the other side of the Jumna, at about two kos from Āgrā, fully equipped, Akbar was ready for battle. But as he was about to march off, he suddenly found himself plagued and hindered by all kinds of incidents and accidents. His camp was inundated and partly destroyed under a deluge of rain; the barge he wanted to travel in got stuck on a sandbank in the middle of the river, but these setbacks did not change his resolve. The astrologers, who understandably had been seeing in every incident as many an evil omen, were told, in no uncertain terms, to shut up; Akbar's mind was made up. He marched off, at the head of his powerful, invincible army.

He had not gone far, when the news reached him that his mother's illness had become critical. At first, he decided to continue his journey, but when the report was reconfirmed, he felt bound to abort the campaign. By the time he arrived at her bedside, he found her barely conscious and unable to speak. Five days later, on the seventeenth of Shahrivar,[311] at the age of seventy-seven, the old empress passed away.

Akbar seemed to be profoundly disturbed by her demise – more deeply than I expected, to be honest, for he and his mother had never been really close: His policies in religious matters had never met with her approval. But death heals many differences. . . . As a sign of mourning and filial piety, he took off his turban, shaved his head—even his whiskers and eyebrows—and fasted for several days.

Hamīda Bānū Bēgam's body was washed, shrouded, and placed in a bier, which Akbar personally helped carry for a considerable distance. The body was further conveyed to Dillī by a relay of noblemen, to be laid to rest at the side of her husband, whom she had outlived for more than four decades.

Something seemed to have broken inside Akbar after his mother's death; he did not pursue his planned march on Allāhābād. After a few listless days, during which he hardly appeared in public and spent his time aimlessly walking in the gardens or brooding in his private quarters, he unexpectedly accorded a private audience to Mīr Sadr Jahān, an orthodox mullāh and one of Salīm's confidants – exactly the reason why the man had never been taken into Akbar's confidence.

---

311. 29 August 1604.

The audience lasted for a full two hours. When it was over, the mullāh, carrying two sealed firmāns with him, hastily packed a few belongings and left for Allāhābād. Nobody knows what was written in the firmāns, but it is not hard to guess: One of them, most certainly, was an official letter written by the court scribe, informing Salīm of the passing of his grandmother, and inviting him to the court to share in his father's mourning. The second one, most probably, must have been a personal message to Salīm, warning him that if he did not immediately present himself at the court, Akbar would officially disavow him and appoint Khusrau as his successor.

Whatever was in the letter, it certainly did not miss its intended effect. Soon after Mīr Sadr Jahān's arrival in Allāhābād, Salīm started the journey to Āgrā, ostensibly with the intention of offering his condolences for the death of his grandmother. On Jom'eh, the twenty-eighth of Ābān,[312] he arrived at the court, accompanied only by a small escort, having left his troops at a considerable distance from the city limits, as Akbar had ordered him to do.

The reunion was markedly stiffer, more formal than the previous one, but still, reassuringly warm and friendly. Salīm was welcomed with full honours, in the presence of the entire court, and after a brief but friendly exchange of civilities, invited to join his father in the zanāna.

When Salīm came in, I rushed towards him to embrace him, but stopped when I saw Akbar's face. He was beside himself with rage; I had never seen him like this. He grabbed Salīm by his clothes, dragged him into an empty room, and started hitting him straight in the face, four, five, six times, as hard as he could, with the back and the flat of his hand.

'You bastard,' he shouted, completely beside himself, his face all red, 'who do you think you are? Is this how you repay me? Is this how you show your gratitude for everything I have done for you? Disobeying my orders, sullying your hands with innocent blood, and for the rest, putting me to extreme shame and drinking yourself to death? What kind of a man are you, anyway? If you hate me so much, why don't you go ahead and fight me? Where are your seventy thousand horsemen? Too much of a coward to use them? Afraid of failing miserably?'

---

312. Friday, 9 November 1604.

He went on like this for I don't know how long, literally foaming at the mouth with rage, showering Salīm with bitter reproaches, mocking him for being a spineless coward, and threatening him that if he would ever dare to disobey him again, he would kill him with his own bare hands. Neither I, nor anybody else dared to say anything. As for Salīm, he just stood there, his turban knocked off his head, his eyes downcast, mute; he was sweating profusely and disgracefully reeking of drink.

At long last, Akbar seemed to calm down a bit. His features composed again, he gave orders to call in Hakīm Alī Gilanī and the court physicians.

'My son is ill,' he said in a surprisingly soft voice. 'He needs to be cured.'

Salīm was to be locked up in small living quarters, under the care of the physicians. He was not to receive any visitors, and not to communicate with anybody other than the physicians, in writing or otherwise. Under no circumstances was he to receive any opium, wine or arraq of any kind. 'If anybody dares to give him any wine or opium,' Akbar added, suddenly shouting again, 'I will personally rip his guts out!'

The following days passed by in unbearable tension. Except for the daily meeting, Akbar did not show himself in public at all. However, he clearly kept busy. In a matter of barely two days, Salīm's army was entirely disbanded, his horses and elephants accommodated in the imperial stables, and his main supporters incarcerated. It was eerily silent at the court; except in strictly private conversation, Salīm's name was only mentioned in whispers, if at all. It was said that the forced abstinence from drink and opium had made him critically ill. Hakīm Alī Gilanī and the other physicians did not move from his side, but official news was sadly lacking.

After ten days—which seemed like ten months—rumours were suddenly buzzing about that the emperor had visited his son! He had personally brought him some opium, a beaker of opium-laced rosewater on ice! I dismissed the story as just another rumour, but Allāh be praised, it proved to be true: Soon, Salīm reappeared in public at his father's side. The forced abstinence seemed to have done him much good. He seemed to be in good health, though he had visibly lost weight and looked quite pale.

As if nothing had happened, life at the court retook its normal course.

≈

Father and son are officially reconciled now. In accordance with his rank, an entire wing of the palace has been vacated for Salīm and his zanāna. His supporters have gradually been released from prison. In official ceremonies, he occupies the first place, closest to Akbar's throne. When his father does not require his presence, he busies himself with his favourite pastimes: reading, writing, and collecting paintings. People say he drinks quite a lot and uses opium every day, but he seems to keep himself under control.

Officially reconciled they are, but close to each other, they are not – not at all. They never speak in private, and they clearly avoid each other's presence as much as possible; the slumbering enmity between them is almost palpable.

I am so worried . . . what is to become of us? No matter how strong and healthy Akbar still is, he is a white-haired old man; how long does he have to live; and what will happen when he is gone? Will he confirm Salīm as his successor, will he yet appoint Khusrau? The entire court is rife with rumours.

≈

Forty-third Letter

شام

Ṣhám

The entire court was rife with rumours, indeed. There was strife, and enmity; rivalling factions were forming, alliances were being forged and broken; one could almost smell the putrid stench of civil war. Alas, there was little I could do about it. The tiger may roar, but the vultures keep hovering above his prey, patiently waiting until he is gone. No one would dare to make a move as long as I was alive, but no man lives forever. . . .

The best thing, the only thing I could do, was to prepare for the future the best I could. And I think I have. Before I leave this earth, I will make sure that you are firmly in the saddle, my son.

For I have made up my mind – you, and you alone, will be my successor. Not because of the outcome of the prize fight between your prize bull Girānbār and Khusrau's champion Ābrūp: I have ceased to believe in silly omens like that a long time ago. No, not because of that stupid elephant fight, and not even because of Khusrau's intolerable misbehaviour afterwards. I will appoint you, because it is the law – the god-given law of nature, and the law of our ancestors. It is proper and becoming that a father should be succeeded by his elder son, and it is indispensable that this law be respected and adhered to by everyone, lest the empire would become ungovernable.

And thus we have come to the end of these writings, my son. This is my last letter to you, and it will have to be a brief one, for I am exhausted by the loss of blood, and I desperately long for a bit of opium to numb the burning pain in my entrails. Tonight, the sun will be setting on Akbar the Great; tomorrow, it will rise over Jahāngīr. . . .

So, you are about to become emperor, my son. Do not take this lightly, but do not be afraid either. You are smart, my son, and so learned! If you resolve to take your task at heart, I am confident that you can, and will be, a great king, one that will be loved and remembered by his subjects as a just and benevolent ruler.

Just promise me one thing: that you will not get your laziness get the better of you, and settle for a life of smallness and self-indulgence. Our task in this short life is to leave the world a better place than we have found it; and from those who have received much, much is expected. To be an emperor is a great privilege, but for that very same reason, it is also a crushing responsibility: A king's burden is heavy, and his office full of labour.

When I see this thick stack of papers, and think of all the work that has gone into it, I wonder whether it has been worth all this effort, and all those sleepless nights? After all, why would you need to read the story of *my* life in order to lead your own? And who am I to tell you that you have to follow my example in everything? In this world, we walk alone; the book of our life is ours to write.

Fortunately, there are many kinds of good books, and there are many ways to be a good emperor – you just have to find your own, my son. Think about it: You can be remembered as Jahāngīr the great, the just, the wise, the magnificent – it is up to you to make it happen! You should live your life in a way that posterity would say what you want them to say about you.

What I hope these letters will have shown you, is that your father, the loud, overbearing, demanding emperor you have admired, feared, and at times hated, was but a man. A man like you, with his own strengths and weaknesses, hopes and fears; a man, who often succeeded, but sometimes also made mistakes; a father also, who at times may have been too harsh, too distant, too unattainable, but who never stopped wanting the best for his sons. This is my hope, my deepest wish, Salīm: that these writings may help to bring us together, even if it will only be after my death.

I have felt a bit better this afternoon, thanks to the opium, but I know, it has been the last flicker. Even if I would stop taking the poison, I am beyond help now. My time has gone by, the hourglass of my life is running empty.

When this letter is finished, I will call in Karīm, the old servant, god bless him. I will instruct him to bring all these papers to the archive, and put them in their secret hiding place. You can rest assured – never will he mention this to anyone, under any circumstance. He is discrete and devoted, and he would rather die than disobey me. When he is back and I am certain that everything has been done according to my instructions, I will finally treat myself to that opium I have been craving for, and tomorrow, I will have you called to my bedside. I will bestow on you the imperial turban and sword, and give you my blessings; all I have to do after that, is to close my weary eyes, and die.

Do not worry, my son: I am ready for it. Sickness and old age have their own and quite effective way of reconciling one with death: Old friends pass away, one by one; the eyesight starts to fail, the sense of hearing becomes less acute, and in the limbs creeps a leaden heaviness, which makes one yearn to lie down and rest.

Soon, I will return to my maker. What will it be like? What will He be like? What kind of existence, if any, will await me beyond the grave? I honestly do not know. Makhdūm-ul Mulk and the likes of him were right to warn me about this kind of thinking: My frantic quest for the truth, if anything, has made me more confused than I was before. All the effort I have put into falsafah and kalām, all those countless hours of heated debate and refined conversation may have made my ignorance much more articulate, but I have to admit, they have utterly failed to bring me any closer to any real knowledge or certainty.

May god forgive me if I am mistaken, but I very much doubt that He will be like the master of the day of judgement, of Whom the mullāhs speak, or Pādre Rodolfo Aquaviva's sweet but stern Jesùs.

I hope I will behold His countenance as an unspeakably beautiful, gentle, radiant light, compared to which all earthly majesty pales into insignificance, and in front of which all questions, all worries, and all longings blissfully disappear. But I must admit: The doubts that dear old Mīr Abdul Latīf had before his death have been haunting my own mind ever since. Sometimes, I wake up in the middle of the night; and in those wretched hours, when one's thoughts tend to be as black as the nightly sky, I tremble with fear. What if I was wrong? What if Aquaviva was right, or the mullāh clique? What if god punishes me for my misbelief? But then, in the limpid clarity of the morning sky, I know better. How could a god, who is infinitely good, be as limited and narrow-minded as a few self-righteous fanatics would want Him to be?

Be all this as it may, there is only one thing that I do know with absolute certainty: I am about to die. And when I am dead, what remains of me will become one with the world again, just like all the waste I excreted and the air I breathed out during my life is now part of something else. Part of my body will remain inside a marble tomb, turning first into a loathsome, stinking, rotting mass, and then into a pitiful heap of dry, brittle bones and dust. But the many other specks of matter that once belonged to my body, that I once inhaled or ingested, will continue to pass in and outside other things. They will become flower petals, desert dust, ants and god knows how many hundreds of thousands of other things and creatures, large and small, beautiful and ugly; for countless millions of years, they will be part of the great dance of the all-encompassing, unknowable Natarāj. . . .

Maybe, probably, that is all there will be to it. Maybe my soul will simply perish with my body, and be gone forever; it will be lost in an endless, dreamless sleep, unaware that it ever existed. Of course, some of the thoughts that inhabited my mind, some of the words that I have spoken during my life, will live on in your mind, my son, and in the minds of your own sons, and later, unbeknownst to them, in the sons of your sons and so many other people. Many of the things that I held dear will thus continue to exist, thanks to what I have said and done. Maybe, probably, that is the only kind of immortality I can aspire to. But even if that is the case, that does not make my life unimportant. If thanks to my life, the world after me will become more enlightened than the world I was born into, I will have contributed to goodness, truth and beauty, which is nothing less than god Himself.

Farewell then, my dear son. Praise be to god, that you will be there tomorrow, to help me close my eyes in peace. Light a lamp on my grave from time to time, pray a few fātihas[313] for the peace of your old father's

---

313. The Sūrah al-Fātiha is the opening chapter of the Holy Qur'ān.

soul; and take good care of Hindustān for me – she deserves and needs a wise ruler!

May god be your guide and protector always. And many, many years from now, after you have led a wonderful and fulfilling life, may it please Him to reunite us in paradise.

Epilogue (1)

From the Memoirs of Mulāzim Hakīm Alī Gilanī

On Doshanbeh, the twenty-first of Mehr of the fiftieth year, corresponding to 20 Jumada-l-Ula 1014,[314] the day after the elephant fight, His Majesty was suddenly taken ill with an attack of severe stomach cramps.

I was not overly alarmed at first. Loose bowel movement is a way for the intestines to cleanse themselves of harmful elements; and knowing His Majesty's strong constitution, I felt rather confident that his body would soon start to heal itself. For the first few days, therefore, I did not give him any medicines; I just ensured he got enough of the right liquids and nourishment. I advised him to abstain from fatty and spicy foods, from raw fruits and vegetables, and sharp-tasting condiments other than salt. I told him to regularly eat small amounts of plain boiled rice and curds; and to drink plenty of strengthening fluids, including broth made from lean meats and vegetables; plain Gangā water without ice; and tea with moderate amounts of mint leaves, cinnamon, cloves, saffron, and if necessary a bit of opium, to ease the bowel pains.

But His Majesty's condition failed to improve. As mild herbs seemed to have little effect, I administered stronger astringents, which indeed stopped the diarrhoea, but alas, badly worsened his overall condition:

---

314. Monday, 23 September 1605 (Julian calendar)

Within a few hours, he developed a dangerously high fever, accompanied by severe belly cramps, stabbing flank pains, and—perhaps the most alarming symptom of all—the utter inability to pass water.

I stopped the astringents and gave him herbal infusions which relieved the kidneys and brought down the fever, but soon after that, the diarrhoea returned. The next day, it worsened to acute dysentery, with quite alarming and increasing amounts of blood in the stools.

Truly a strange illness it was. His Majesty's condition would sometimes improve without any apparent reason, then worsen again most dramatically. More than one courtier has suggested that the emperor was poisoned. I, too, would have sworn that some kind of poison was involved, had that not been completely excluded, for I solemnly swear that I had taken all possible precautions to protect His Majesty: Not a single grain of rice, not a crumb of bread, not the tiniest drop of water was offered to him, unless in my presence, and after it had been tasted by three different people, the last one always being myself. Moreover, if poison would have been involved, how was it to be explained that the course of the illness was so strangely irregular? Why would any would-be assassin have bothered to administer poison in varying, non-lethal doses? A few people have suggested that the emperor might have accidentally poisoned himself – that he had mistakenly eaten poisoned food which he had destined for someone else. That is, of course, an entirely preposterous idea. If the emperor had wanted to eliminate someone, he would not have needed to resort to poison! Moreover, if he would have accidentally poisoned himself, he would have died in a matter of hours or days, not weeks. I know of no poison that would produce symptoms like that. No, any way I look at it, I am convinced that His Majesty died of natural causes.

A disease, but which disease, and how to cure it? In my desperate attempt to find a treatment, I worked tirelessly, consulting all the books I could lay my hands on: at-Tabarī's *Paradise of Wisdom*; al-Kindī's *Manual of Medicines*; Ibn al-Baitar's *Study of Medicinal Herbs in the East*; Hunain ibn Ishaq's *Greek and Roman Medicine*; Ishaq al-Isrāilī's treatise on fever; Musa ibn Maimun's *Kitāb al-Fusul*; Ibn Rushd's *Kitāb al-Kullijat*; Ibn Sina's *al-Qānun fi al-Tibb*; Ibn Zuhr's *at-Taisir*; the *Kitāb al-Hawi* and *Kitāb al-Mansuri* of ar-Rāzī, and the insightful discussion of intestinal diseases in Alī ibn al-Abbas' *Kitāb al-Malaki*. I spent many sleepless nights, studying and praying. Setting aside all unwarranted pride, I decided to consult the Hindū physicians Mahadev, Bhima, Narayin, and Sijav hoping that their Ayurvedic knowledge could be of help here. In my despair, I even gave my permission to try some of their nārāyana powder, and fruits bitten by a furious cobra.

Alas, it was all to no avail. Every herb, every potion, and every remedy we tried, only seemed to worsen His Majesty's condition. There we were, the most learned and experienced physicians in the empire, surrounded by all the knowledge of the entire world, and utterly powerless against what had seemed a simple case of indisposed bowels.

'Stop worrying so much, Hakīm Alī,' said His Majesty, noticing the sombre preoccupation on my face, in spite of the care I took to keep it hidden from him. 'Are we not all in the hands of god? I want you to know that you have served me well, and that you have given me the best possible care!'

He was obviously in a lot of pain and discomfort at times; yet he seemed strangely cheerful and patient – as if he actually welcomed his predicament! The only thing I could do was to stand by and watch, trying to alleviate the pain and ease the cramps with moderate amounts of opium. Day after day, I watched, in impotent despair, how he grew weaker and weaker.

As his condition worsened, the imperial court soon became rife with gossip and speculation about the succession. Such, alas, is life. . . .

The supporters of Prince Khusrau, headed by his father-in-law, the Khān-i-Azam Mīrzā Azīz Koka and Rājā Mān Singh, were in favour of placing the young prince on the throne and excluding his father Salīm from the succession. Prince Khusrau, they argued, was a pious young man, his body youthful and strong, his character noble, his conduct exemplary and his record unblemished; his father, in contrast, was a capricious weakling, an opium addict and a hopeless drunk! Besides, was he not thirty-six years old already, and had his two younger brothers not died from exactly the same vice as his? How much longer could he hope to live?

It was a heated argument, but in the end, a majority among the amīrs, strongly supported in their opinion by Shaykh Farīd-i-Bukharī and other legal scholars, rejected the proposal.

'On what ground could we allow the son to take precedence over his father?' they argued. 'Would that not be contrary to natural justice, and to the laws and customs of the great Chagatai nation? If we allow Prince Khusrau to occupy the throne, how will we ever establish an appropriate and accepted order of succession? How could we hope to prevent war between Khusrau's supporters and those of his father, or, for that matter, those of one of his brothers? It could mean the ruin of the empire, the ruin of everything we all worked and fought for!'

These arguments, in the end, managed to convince the assembly. Anxious to prevent civil war, they all pledged to support Prince Salīm, provided he would be prepared to swear two solemn oaths: first, that he would not punish or injure any of Khusrau's supporters, nor hold any grudge against them; and second, that he would protect the religion of Islām.

So he did; and, it must be said – he honoured both promises.

Adequate security measures were taken in agreement between the amīrs and army leaders. A strong Rājpūt force was sent to guard the imperial treasure, and the prince's personal guard was strengthened with a contingent of fearless elite soldiers from all corners of the empire.

He was unusually relaxed and cheerful that day; he seemed to be in slightly better health than the days before, and spent the remainder of the afternoon and evening in pleasant conversation, in the company of Abdurrahīm Khān Khanān, Rājā Mān Singh and other trusted friends.

The following morning, however, his condition had suddenly worsened dramatically. He was hardly able to speak, his breathing had turned alarmingly shallow, and his eyes were sunken deep inside his skull. Again, I would have sworn that poison was at work, were it not that His Majesty, on his own request, had spent the night alone, and that Rājā Mān Singh, Abdurrahīm Khān Khanān and the other attendants who had kept him company the day before were clearly above any suspicion.

He sent for his son, together with Abdurrahīm Khān Khanān, Rājā Mān Singh and the other leading amīrs.

The prince, who had up to that moment not found the courage to visit his father, possibly out of fear that he might be rejected as heir to the throne, presented himself immediately. Mumbling a respectful greeting, he humbly remained standing at the door, and prostrated himself, his forehead touching the floor.

The emperor smiled weakly and began moving his lips, trying to speak, but no sound came from his mouth. Signalling his son to come nearer, he looked at him for a while, faintly nodding his head in approval, smiling, his eyes moist with tears. He put his hand on his turban beside him, and gestured that the prince should put it on his own head. He then pointed at Jannāt-Āshyānī's sword hanging near the bed, and had his son gird himself with it.

Looking at the amīrs in the room, he slowly turned the palm of his right hand upward, and pointed in the direction of the prince. All bowed deeply to show their respect and loyalty to their new emperor.

Emperor Akbar gave his son a last look, and made a weak gesture for him to leave the room and let him rest. The prince respectfully took his father's hand, kissed it and placed it on his own heart and forehead, and then slowly went out of the room, walking backwards, bowing deeply all the way, tears streaming down his cheeks. The emperor watched as his son left the room, reclined on the pillows, and closed his eyes. He had completed his last deed as Emperor of Hindustān.

Outside the imperial apartments, the amīrs and other members of the imperial court took turns kissing the ringed hands of their future new emperor, who received the honours in silence, smiling faintly, his eyes still glistening with tears.

It became eerily silent in the palace. The rumours about the succession had died down and given way to whispered speculations about the dying emperor's condition. Contrary to everybody's expectations, Prince Salīm was rarely to be seen. I saw him once very briefly from afar, the same night he had received the imperial sword and turban, outside the imperial archives, carrying a stack of documents. It must have been a confidential matter that preoccupied him, for normally the prince would take along a servant to carry his books for him. Anyway, I saw that he pretended not to have noticed me, and thought it wise to do likewise. In the following days, he spent most of the time in his private apartments, alone.

Meanwhile, the emperor's condition further worsened. From the moment he had appointed his son as his successor, he refused all food and drink, apart from a few drops of water to comfort the dryness of his mouth. It was as if, after the example of the Jain monks he so admired, he had now decided to hasten his death through fasting. He grew weaker by the hour, and though obviously in a lot of pain at times, a weak, peaceful smile hardly ever left his lips.

As is customary, the faithful amīrs and mullāhs present at his bedside constantly repeated the Shahāda, inviting His Majesty to demonstrate his agreement with it, for the Prophet—peace and blessings of Allāh be upon him and his household!—has affirmed that he who dies with the sacred Shahāda on his lips, will surely enter paradise. It vaguely seemed the emperor did try to pronounce the first sentence, Ashadu an lā ilāha illā-Llāh, I declare that there is no god but god, but I am not sure. After a while, his lips stopped moving altogether and he seemed to lose all interest in his surroundings. His eyes glazed over, and stared into the flames of the candles.

Towards the later afternoon of Shanbeh, the 7th of Ābān[315], it seemed he had lost consciousness.

His deep-sunken eyes were still open and kept on gazing at the candles, but I do not think there was any light left in them. They just remained wide open, moving nor blinking, staring from the darkness of their sockets into the void of death. Only a few irregular intervals of deep, rattling breathing, with long pauses in between them, indicated that there was still a spark of life left in his emaciated body.

Towards the middle of the night, in the early hours of Yeksanbeh the eighth of Ābān[316], his breathing became ever more shallow, and the pauses in between grew longer and longer, until, without any apparent transition between life and death, he breathed no more. I put my ear to his chest, and found that his brave heart had finally stopped beating.

I closed his eyes, and we all prayed, as is customary on such sad occasions, the last verses of the Sūrah As-Sāffāt[317]:

Glory to You, my Lord
The Lord of Honour and Power!
Free is He from what they ascribe to Him!
And peace on the Messengers
And Praise to Allāh
The Lord and Cherisher of the Worlds.

---

315. Saturday, 19 October
316. Sunday, 20 October
317. Qur'ān 37:180-182

On an impulse, I took his right hand in mine, kissed it, held it to my face and wetted it with my tears. My voice broken and shaking, I sobbed:

'Farewell, Your Majesty, farewell! May Allāh keep and protect you, and may it please Him to reunite us in paradise!'

We bathed and washed the dead body twice with clear, cold water, then rubbed it over with lime, salt and camphor. Even I was surprised to see the pitiful state his martyred body was in. The disease had literally wasted him away. His strong arms and legs, his broad shoulders: all the muscle was gone, nothing seemed to be left but pale, wrinkled skin over bones and sinews. With his fallen-in cheeks and the black-blue rings around his deep-sunken eyeballs, his face hardly bore any resemblance to the imposing countenance of the strong bull of a man we had known before.

As is customary, we bound the feet together, placed the arms alongside the body, put a stone slab on the stomach to prevent any bloating, and clothed the body in simple white linen.

The next morning, in accordance with time-honoured Sunnī custom and the teachings of the Prophet, the mortal remains of our beloved emperor were taken to their last resting place.

A gap was broken in the sandstone wall of the fort, and the chārpāī was carried out; Prince Salīm and his sons took it upon their own shoulders and carried it as far as the Diwān-i-Ām. From thence, all the great amīrs and courtiers, each and every one of them anxious to receive the honour of carrying His Majesty's mortal remains, followed each other in quick succession, taking the body out of the fortress. The entire court, heads and feet bare, followed the body to the tomb at Sikandra, two kos to the north, where our emperor's body was placed in the beautiful mazār[318], still under construction at that time, which he had designed himself.

I have to say, the building is exactly like the great king whose mortal remains it houses: open to light and air from all directions, bringing together many different styles; aspiring to belong to all traditions, yet, belonging to none in particular.

---

318. Mazār: Tomb, mausoleum.

Belonging to all traditions, and thus, to none.... Was our beloved emperor still a Muslim when he died? Had he turned Pārsī as people say, or Hindū? Was he guilty of Ilhād, had he become a Murtadd?

I have given this matter much thought, and have come to the conclusion that he lived and died as a true believer—albeit admittedly a highly unorthodox one—and that whether or not one can still call him a Muslim, depends more on the outlook of the beholder, than on the piety of our emperor.

What gives me the right to say that he remained a true believer? First of all, because he believed in god's unity and worshipped Him all his life, with all his heart and soul. Second, because he never converted to another religion. He highly respected the Hindūs and the Jains, to the point of rejecting the slaughter of animals and believing that there might be some truth in the idea of transmigration of souls, but he had no use for any of their gods and statues and rituals; he liked the Pārsī fire symbols, but did not find much use in their concept of god; he revered the Prophet Īsā and his saintly mother—upon both of whom be peace!—but found it impossible to accept the obvious nonsense of a triune divinity, the virgin birth of a god-man, and all those other errors and superstitions.

What made him unorthodox, to the point of incurring, not entirely undeservedly, the reproach of being a heretic and an unbeliever? I think his worst heresy from the point of view of Islām was the rather low esteem in which he held the Prophet Muhammad and the Holy Qur'ān: in his eyes, they were merely a prophet and a sacred scripture among others. The constant quarrels between the ulamā had convinced him that the Muslim law and religion were far from indubitable, since there were so many differences between the scholars themselves. In the Ibādat-Khāna, he had been looking for unity and insight, but had found nothing but confusion and disagreement.

In the end, his concept of religion was a rather simple one. There is but one god, and all must worship and honour Him, and allow other people to do so in the way they prefer. All must subdue evil passions and practice virtue. All must be led by reason, and not merely bow to the authority of any one man or tradition. Differences in creed or ritual are of little importance: The people of the land should be united under their king, whom god has placed above them, and whose duty it is to serve god through bringing justice and prosperity to the people entrusted to his care.

Was Emperor Akbar a Muslim, or a kāfir? Bīrbal once said: 'Our emperor is a Hindū in his food habits, a Pārsī in his rites, and a Sūfī in his heart.' As far as I am concerned, he was like the Sikh Gurū Nānak, or the great poet Kabīr – both men denied they were either Muslims or Hindūs, for such names seemed useless to them. As Kabīr sang so eloquently:

Hindūs call Him Rām, Muslims Khudā
Kabīr says: whoever lives, should not bother about this:
Ka'bah becomes Kashi, Rām becomes Rahīm.

Abdul Haqq, the great scholar, ending his book on the lives of great Muslim saints, wrote that his father, when still a child, had asked his own father, whether Kabīr had been a Muslim or a Hindū. The grandfather replied that Kabīr had been a Muwahhīd, a believer in the unity of god. His father then asked whether a Muwahhīd was a kāfir, or a Muslim. Upon which the old man replied: 'To understand this is difficult; you will understand when you grow up.'

Allāh willing, one day, when it grows up, the world will understand.

On the southern entrance of Emperor Akbar's tomb, there is an elegant inscription, written by the famous calligrapher Abd al-Haqq, son of Qāsim as-Shirāzi:

'These are the Gardens of Eden. Enter them, to live forever.'

And there is no doubt in my mind: The gardens of paradise will forever be the abode of our beloved emperor. Allāh, the omnipotent ruler of all worlds, the supreme lord of the past, the present and the future; He who is greater than anything conceivable or imaginable; He who defies any description or limitation; He who is merciful, compassionate and all-forgiving: He will smile upon our good emperor. He will mercifully forgive all his sins, doubts, errors and shortcomings; He will make his grave wide and pleasant, illuminate it with the splendour of His soft-shining light, and fill it with the sweet companionship and gentle conversation of His angels.

And on the day of the Resurrection, He will call him forward, among the best of His faithful servants, to share in the eternal, unspeakable bliss of paradise.

Epilogue (2)

From the Memoirs of Father António Machado S.J., Superior of the Jesuit Order in Agra, Member of the third Jesuit mission to the court of Akbar the Great

(...)

Thus ended the mighty emperor Akbar . . . His funeral was astoundingly, disgracefully simple and austere. No pomp, no circumstance of any kind, no ceremonies, no chants, no hymns, no eulogies. Back in Castilla, or any other Christian country, even a simple peasant would have gotten a more dignified funeral than this! Akbar's corpse, placed on a plain wooden bier, was carried off to the mausoleum with indecorous haste, and as soon as it had been placed in the tomb, everybody immediately left the grounds. It seemed they all wanted to get away as quickly as possible from the burial place of a man they knew was damned forever.

In spite of everything, I pity the old emperor, for I do believe there was much nobility in his soul. Unfortunately, his vainglorious pride and arrogance prevented him from dying in the state of grace. Stubbornly refusing to accept our lord and savior Jesus Christ, in spite of all the evidence, in spite of all the prophecies, in spite of the countless many hours of patient instruction he received, in spite even of a personal letter from His Holiness the pope of Rome himself, he rejected the one true religion, and in doing so, damned his immortal soul, and brought irreparable ruin upon countless others. He was guilty of Adam and Eve's original sin – which is not, as many people believe, the sin of lust and lasciviousness, but the even more dangerous evil of Superbia, $ὕβρις$[319]: supercilious, conceited, sinful pride, the arrogant delusion that man himself is the ultimate judge of right and wrong. It was that pride, that same arrogant, damnable pride that made Adam and Eve yield to the Serpent's temptation and eat the Forbidden Fruit.

It saddens and angers me to think about what might have been, and what has been lost by the stubbornness of that one man. Blinded and misguided by his own worldly power, Akbar thought that he could find 'true religion', all by himself. In the end, it brought him nothing, nothing but confusion, error, and sin; it made him a skeptic and a misguided muddlehead, who, in his eagerness to show respect to all religions, put himself outside every single one of them. With that, he not only endangered and finally damned his own immortal soul, but also that of so many millions of his poor, misguided subjects, who might have found the light of our lord Jesus Christ, if only their emperor had shown them the way. Their error remains on his head, and there can, alas, be no doubt about it: it has earned him the eternal flames of hell.

One week after Emperor Akbar's death, on Sunday, the 6th of November of the year of our lord 1605[320], shortly after sunrise, Prince Salim ascended the imperial throne in the hall of public audience at the Red Fort.

The imperial crown, which had been crafted in the days of Akbar after the crown worn by the great kings of Persia, was brought to him. He put it on his head, and as an omen auspicious to the stability and happiness of his future reign, kept it there for a full hour. The so-called khutbah was read in his name for the first time.

---

319. Greek *Hubris*, Latin *Superbia*: Pride, one of the cardinal sins.
320. Father Machado uses the Gregorian calendar (the current Common Era), which was proclaimed by Pope Gregory XIII and took effect in most Catholic states in 1582, in which 4 October of the traditional Julian calendar was followed by October 15 in the new one. Britain and her colonies only adopted the Gregorian Calendar in the year 1752, when Wednesday the 2nd of September was followed by Thursday the 14th.

As a formal sign of his accession, he assumed the title of Jahāngīr, which in Persian means 'seizer of the world'. To seize the entire world, his courtiers said, was his destiny. May almighty god preserve us from such disaster!

(...)

Epilogue (3)

جهانگیر

Jahangir

From the memoirs of
Shaykh Bishotan ibn Abdurrahmān ibn Abū-l Fazl Allamī,
Mansabdār of Seven Thousand Zat and Three Thousand Suwar[321]
In the service of His Majesty Shihāb-ud-dīn Muhammad Shāh Jahān[322] Pādshāh, May Allāh perpetuate his reign and expand his dominions;
Son of Shaykh Abdurrahmān Afzāl Khān[323],
Grandson of Shaykh Abū-l Fazl Allamī,
Great-grandson of Shaykh Mubārak Allamī,
May Allāh receive them and all their ancestors in His infinite Mercy,
(. . .)

---

321. Mansabdār: Commander in the imperial army. The words Zat and Suwar indicate the rank, and refer to the (theoretical) number of cavalry and auxiliary cavalry under the incumbent's command.
322. Shihāb-ud-dīn: Flame of faith; Shāh Jahān: King of the world. Shāh Jahān, grandson of Akbar, third son and successor of Jahāngīr, became famous as the Mughal emperor who commissioned the universally admired Tāj Mahal.
323. Abdurrahmān, son of Abū-l Fazl, was born in the Hijrī year 979 (1571 CE).

It was in the late hours of the night, on one of those occasions, when too much wine and loud conversation makes men careless, and their questions impertinent.

I must have been twenty or twenty-one years old at the time. The breeze was pleasant, the moonlight soft. We were sitting together in the inner courtyard of my father's home – me, my father Abdurrahmān and my mother's brother Ahmad, may Allāh be well pleased with them, and a few other army officers, all good friends of my father. A man of means, he had invited them to a feast in his home, for no particular reason – just to share a few 'raisins of life' together, as he used to call such moments of leisure and laughter among friends. We were enjoying the most succulent dishes of lamb and fowl, and many—too many—pitchers of cool wine; it all tasted wonderful on a calm and balmy evening after a hot and strenuous day. The conversation had taken us from lamb and the best ways to cook it, to cloves, pepper and other condiments, to tiger hunting, elephants and horses, life in the army, and Emperor Jahāngīr's successful campaigns in Mewār. I said little, listening to the elder men's conversation and busying myself with drinking, something to which I was at that time not at all accustomed.

Late in the night, when all the guests had left, and my father rose to retire to his bedchamber, I heard myself saying: 'Father, there is something that I have been wanting to ask you for a long time.' My speech sounded more slurred than I had hoped, and I instantly regretted my impertinence.

My father's face registered surprise. 'This must be very important, that you want to bring it up at this late hour,' he said softly, 'but go ahead.'

It was too late to go back now. 'I have been meaning to ask you,' I said, trying to sound as articulate as possible, 'you are a wealthy and powerful man, Father; the emperor has promoted you several times, he entrusts you with tasks of high import. . . .'

'And?' There was irritation in his voice.

'And yet, people say—to be honest, everybody says—that my revered grandfather Abū-l Fazl, may Allāh be well pleased with him, was assassinated on orders of that same Emperor Jahāngīr!'

'That is, alas, correct.'

'But why?'

'Jahāngīr—Shāhzāda Salīm at the time—was estranged from his father. I should rather say, he was in open rebellion against him, for he was holding his own court in Allāhābād, against his father's wishes. Why he had your grandfather killed, I do not know for sure. For some reason, he suspected him of setting Emperor Akbar against him, of trying to persuade the emperor to appoint Shāhzāda Khusrau as his successor.'

'And was that true?'

'No, that I do not believe. It is true that your grandfather did not think much of Salīm, but I am convinced he never tried to harm him. But he was extremely close to Emperor Akbar and he had his ear, and that is why Salīm resented and feared him.'

'But when he became emperor, did he leave our family alone?'

'He did. . . . To be honest, I was very afraid when he became emperor. I thought he would have me and my entire family assassinated or at least banned, if only to prevent us from taking revenge, or to get his hands on your grandfather's considerable wealth! But for some reason, he chose not to; he left us in peace. He also forgave Khusrau and his supporters, as he had promised he would.'

'And have you never . . . ?' I did not dare to finish my sentence.

'I know what you are going to ask. Have I never considered avenging my father? Yes, I have, and more than once! In fact, when people told me in what a terrible way my poor father had met his end, I could think of little else than revenge. But what could I do? Salīm was closely guarded all the time; I could not even come anywhere near him. Besides, had I not my family to think about? You were only twelve at the time!

'Still, the thought of revenge never left me, and I promised myself that one day, I would kill Salīm. Three and a half years later, when Emperor Akbar had passed away and Salīm—Jahāngīr—had succeeded him to the throne, I suddenly saw my opportunity. He was inspecting his troops outside the Āgrā fort, early in the morning, and contrary to his usual routine, he was casually walking among the ranks, all alone. . . . He also passed by me, very slowly; he stopped briefly and looked at me, then turned his back and continued his way. I only had to draw my dagger and plunge it in his back. Of course, I would be killed myself as well, probably after unspeakable torture, but at least the honour of our family would be avenged. Then again, I did not mind dying myself, but what about my family? I was still hesitating, when Jahāngīr suddenly turned around, and looked me in the eye. Instantly I knew with absolute certainty, that he sensed what I was thinking.

'Shaykh Abdurrahmān,' he said, in a soft, surprisingly friendly tone of voice, 'we would like to have a word with you, in private. Kindly present yourself at the Diwān-i-Khās, one hour from now.'

When I arrived at the hall, the guards let me pass without a word; they clearly had received their instructions. Surprisingly, they did not ask me to hand over my sword and dagger as they always do. I went into the hall and found Emperor Jahāngīr sitting cross-legged on a cushioned platform. In front of him lay his sword, and a bit further, a beautifully bound copy of the Holy Qur'ān on a small, jewel-encrusted bookstand. I bowed, touching the floor with my right hand, and he signalled me to approach the platform.

'You and I need to talk, Shaykh Abdurrahmān,' Jahāngīr said slowly, a tired smile on his face, as I was approaching the platform.

'You know, Shaykh Abdurrahmān,' he proceeded, 'that I have just succeeded my revered father, may Allāh receive him in His mercy, to the throne of Hindustān, and much is expected from me. It is my god-given task to perpetuate and augment what my revered father, and may I add, also your father, have worked for all their lives. Shaykh Abdurrahmān, I want to know, with absolute certainty that I can rely on you, just like my revered father has been able to rely on yours.'

Before I could answer, Jahāngīr proceeded, 'I know, Shaykh Abdurrahmān, you probably dislike me – no, you probably hate me. You feel that I have wronged your father. Well, I confess. Although I did not think so at the time, I must admit, with the wisdom of hindsight, that I probably have wronged him. You know, my father and I were estranged at the time, and I was convinced, mistakenly no doubt, that your father was bent on my ruin. I also was convinced that, the shameless flatterer that he was, he had nothing but his own private interests at heart.

'I confess: Maybe, probably, I have judged him too harshly. Despite the fact that I distrusted him and resented the influence he had on my father, I have to admit that he was a clever, hardworking and highly competent man, and that he served Hindustān well. One thing is for sure – what has happened cannot be undone. And, tell me, Shaykh Abdurrahmān: If your father could talk to you now, what do you think his advice to you would be? Would he advise you to try and take your vengeance, bring ruin to yourself and your family, and go to your grave as the traitor who endangered the empire, or would he tell you to go on living honourably in the service of the empire that he has helped my father to build?

'I am ready to forget the past, if you are ready too, Shaykh Abdurrahmān, but I want your answer, and I want it now. As a man of honour, put your right hand on the Holy Qur'ān and pledge your loyalty to me and the empire; if you cannot, go in peace and take your family and your belongings to another country: I will not try to stop you, and I will even provide you with a strong escort, so that you may travel safely. Or,' his voice flattened out until it was barely a whisper 'if you must, reach for your dagger or your sword or both, and fight me.'

He caressed the jade, horse-shaped hilt of his own dagger, and casually took out a golden coin from his belt. 'I do believe I am stronger than you,' he said, casually bending the coin in two between his thumb and forefinger, 'but who knows? Perhaps you are quicker or more agile than I am . . .'

The emperor took the Holy Qur'ān from the bookstand and held it out towards me, with both hands. If I was to draw my sword, he would be at a disadvantage. I looked at the Qur'ān, at the hilt of my sword, only a palm's breath away from my hand. Then, I bowed my head, laid my right hand on the Holy Book, and in a calm, surprisingly firm voice, swore to Emperor Jahāngīr that I would serve him and Hindustān with my life.

There was kindness, and I think honest gratitude in Jahāngīr's eyes, as he nodded and said: 'Thank you, Shaykh Abdurrahmān. I knew you are a true son of your father, may Allāh be pleased with him. Go in peace; may god protect you and your loved ones.'

My father stared at the candles, many of which had already died out. He helped himself to another beaker of wine, and poured me one as well.

'I have often thought back to that morning, my son. Time and again, I have searched my soul and challenged myself, but each time, I have come to the conclusion that I have made the right choice, and that my father, had he been in my stead, would have done the same. I know what he would have said to me: "My son, there are things in life that are more important than our own wants and needs. You may hate Shāhzāda Salīm for what he did, but it is your duty, before god, to honour and obey Jahāngīr pādshāh. To betray him, is to betray everything I have worked for all my life.'"

He took a sip of his wine; then a second, larger draught.

'I know,' he continued, as if he guessed what I was thinking, 'I know, Jahāngīr does not have the genius and stamina of Akbar. I know, some speak of him as a fickle-minded tyrant, a pleasure-seeking weakling, slave of leisure, wine, women, and opium. Well, although there is much truth in it, that reproach is not entirely fair. On the whole, he is a noble man who sincerely tries to rule with justice, and treat all his subjects equally, irrespective of religion, rank or birth. Such is his respect for justice that he has a long silver chain with a bell suspended from his balcony; whosoever of his subjects rings the bell and thus appeals to the emperor's justice, can be ensured that Jahāngīr pādshāh will personally hear his case.

'It is true that at times, he can be subject to fits of rage and can be extremely cruel, but following the example of his father, he has issued instructions that when he condemns someone to capital punishment, the order is not to be executed before sundown.

'He is deservedly popular with the common people for the peace and prosperity he has brought to the land. There is no hunger in Hindustān, no unjust taxation, people live in safety, and commerce flourishes.

'He is respectful to his mother and the members of his family. Although he did rebel against his father, I believe he did so under the influence of evil people. In any case, now that he is in possession of the throne and his father is dead and no longer a rival to him, he has really changed. He cherishes his father's memory, and holds him in great reverence. Whenever he resides in Āgrā, he often visits his father's mausoleum in Sikandra. He always dismounts at the gate, and walks on foot to the tomb; each time, at the entrance, he gets down on both knees, and rubs his forehead on the marble doorstep.'

Annexure j

Akbar's first letter to the Jesuits of Goa[324]:

In the name of God,
>Letter of Jalāl-ud-dīn Muhammad Akbar,
>King placed in the Seat of God.
>To the Chief Priests of the Order of Saint Paul:

Be it known to them that I am a great friend of theirs.

I have sent thither Abdullāh my ambassador, and the translator Domenico Perez, in order to request you to send back to me two of your learned men, who should bring books of the Law, and above all the Gospels, because I truly and earnestly desire to understand their perfection; and with great urgency, I again demand that they should come with my ambassador aforesaid, and bring their books. For, from their coming I shall obtain the utmost consolation; they will be dear to me, and I shall receive them with every possible honour.

As soon as I shall have become well instructed in the Law, and shall have comprehended its perfection, they will be able, if willing, to return at their pleasure, and I shall send them back with great honours, and appropriate rewards. Let them not fear me in the least, for I receive them under my pledge of good faith and assure them concerning myself.

(. . .)

---

324. Smith, pp. 120-21

Annexure JJ

Letter of Pope Gregory XIII to Akbar – Rome, 18 February 1582 [325]

Gregorius Episcopa
Servant of the Servants of God
to Akbar
Illustrious King of Mogor

May the merciful god, Who deigned to inspire you to listen to the teaching of the evangelical doctrine, transfer you as soon as possible from darkness to light. This we expect from the interest which, as it reached our ears, you have shown in the Christian religion. First of all, you summoned to your court our dear sons, priests of the Society of Jesus and ministers of the true faith. You received them graciously and heard them discussing on the kingdom of god. All these are clear indications of your zeal and useful steps to receive the truth, but in such an important matter no delay should be admitted, lest this movement of your spirit, which undoubtedly comes from god, be frustrated by tardiness in deliberation. Your Majesty should place, so to say, in one plate of the scales your kingdom, power, sons, the countless subjects, all riches and goods of this world; and in the other the dignity of your soul and the salvation promised by Christ to those who believe in Him. If you weigh it aright, you will find in comparison with the latter that those are worth nothing; an everlasting kingdom compared with one of short duration, perishable

---

325. *Letters from the Mughal Court*, pp. 119-120

and subject to many contingencies; transform your mortal power into undying bliss; prepare for yourself a new family and treasures in heaven. God will perhaps grant you that, if it be expedient for your salvation, you enjoy also this earthly kingdom. Life is short and human condition uncertain. See that you do not neglect your own salvation or appear to fail to the grace of god that calls you. Meanwhile, do not brush aside this thought, and continue listening as you did before, to the aforesaid priests (by the help of whose prayers and labours, both in the past and in the future, you will be greatly helped in a matter of such moment), whom I recommend to you. Your personal interest and concern for them shall not go unrewarded by Him, Who invites you to acknowledge the truth, the lord god almighty.

Given in Rome at Saint Peter's, in the year 1581 of the lord's incarnation, the 18th day of February, the 10th year of Our Pontificate.

Annexure III

Jahāngīr's account of the murder of Abū-l Fazl[326]:

Towards the end of my exalted father's reign, Shaykh Abū-l Fazl, one of the Shaykhzādas of Hindustān who was outstanding in his learning and wisdom, had ostensibly adorned himself with loyalty and sold it to my father for an exorbitant price.

    He was summoned [by my father] from the Deccan, and since he was suspicious of me, he was always making snide remarks. At that time, because of the corruption of mischief-makers, my exalted father's mind was quite turned against me, and it was certain that if Abū-l Fazl succeeded in reaching him, he would have created more discord and prevent me from rejoining my father. It was therefore absolutely necessary that he be prevented from reaching him. Since Bīr Singh Deo's territory lay in his path, and at that time Bīr Singh was in the circle of insurgents, I sent him a message that he should waylay the miscreant and dispatch him to nonexistence, in return for which he could expect great rewards from me. Success smiled on the endeavour, and as Abū-l Fazl was passing through Bīr Singh Deo's territory, Bīr Singh blocked his path, scattered his men in a skirmish, and killed him, sending his head to me at Allāhābād. Although this caused great distress to His Majesty Arsh-Ashyānī [Akbar], in the end it resulted in my being able to proceed to kiss the threshold of my exalted father's court without fear, and little by little the bad blood between us subsided.

---

326. *Jahāngīrnāmā*, pp. 32-33

Annexure IV

Jahāngīr's account of his drinking habits

I myself did not drink until the age of eighteen. After that, I started drinking wine, increasing it day by day until grape wine had no longer an effect on me, and I started drinking liquor. Over the next nine years, it increased to twenty phials of double-distilled spirits, fourteen during the day and the rest at night. Things became so bad that my hands shook and trembled so badly I could not drink myself, but had to have others help me. Finally I summoned Hakīm Humam, Hakīm Abū'l Fath's brother and one of my exalted father's confidants, and informed him of my condition. In perfect sincerity and compassion he said, with no beating around the bush: 'Highness, with the way you are drinking, in another six months—god forbid—your situation will be beyond remedy.' Since his words were spoken in benevolence, and life is precious, it made a great impression on me.

From that date, I began to decrease the amount I drank. Over a period of seven years, I got it down to six phials, the weight of a phial being seventeen and three-quarters mithcals. I have now been drinking like this for fifteen years without increase or decrease. [327]

---

327. *Jahāngīrnāmā*, p. 21.

Annexure V

Jahāngīr on his father:

My exalted father's good characteristics were too many to be described. If books were to be composed of his good qualities, without exaggeration and disregarding our father-son relationship, not even a small portion could be contained therein. Despite his rulership and such treasuries and treasures beyond enumeration, despite his war elephants and Arabian horses, never did he place his foot one iota above the level of humility before the divine court, and he considered himself the least of all creatures. Not for an instant was he unaware of god.

Followers of various religions had a place in the broad scope of his peerless empire – unlike other countries of the world, like Irān, where there is room for only Shiites, and Rum, Turān, and Hindustān, where there is room for only Sunnis. Just as all groups and the practitioners of all religions have a place within the spacious circle of god's mercy, in accordance with the saying that a shadow must follow its source, in my father's realm, which ended at the salty sea, there was room for practitioners of various sects and beliefs, both true and imperfect, and strife and altercation were not allowed. Sunnī and Shiite worshipped in one mosque, and Frank and Jew in one congregation. Utter peaceableness was his established way. He conversed with the good of every group, every religion, and every sect, and gave his attention to each in accordance with their station and ability to understand.

His nights were spent in wakefulness and he slept so little during the day that in a twenty-four-hour period he slept no more than a watch and a half, and he considered vigilance at night to be a renewal of life.

His courage and bravery were so great that he could ride uncontrollable, enraged elephants, and subdue into obedience elephants so murderous they wouldn't allow their mates near them. Usually, no matter how bad-tempered an elephant may be, it doesn't harm its mate or its keeper. Nonetheless, when an elephant so frenzied that it might have killed its keeper and wouldn't allow its mate near, or an elephant that had killed its mahout and gone berserk passed by a wall or tree, my father, relying on divine grace, would throw himself on the elephant's back, and as soon as he sat down, he would bring the elephant under control and calm it down. Such a scene has been witnessed more than once.[328]

---

328. *Jahāngīrnāmā*, p. 26, and pp. 184-85.

Historical Notes and Acknowledgements

While every attempt has been made to paint an historically accurate picture of Akbar's life and reign, *The Emperor's Writings* is, and remains, a novel: It is a romanced attempt, by a twenty-first century Western European, to read into the mind of a sixteenth century Indian monarch. To avoid any misunderstandings about what is actual fact and what is fiction, I have thought it appropriate to add a few comments below. Generally speaking, it can be stated that, with the notable exception of Akbar's writing skills and suicide, all the characters and events in the novel are authentic, whereas the dialogues, letters and personal memoirs are not.

Akbar's Persona

Abū'l Muzaffar Jalāl-ud-dīn Muhammad Akbar (1543-1605), pādshāh of Hindustān, was a truly remarkable human being. Conqueror of a vast empire, ranging from present-day Afghanistan to Bangladesh and from the Himalayas to the Deccan, aptly called Akbar-e-Āzam (Akbar the Great) by his own contemporaries, and still deservedly popular in present-day India, he was the true founder of the Mughal Empire and the greatest of the so-called Great Mughals. Not only was he among the most powerful and wealthiest sovereigns of his time, but without any doubt, also one of the most enlightened ones.

Educated as a pious Sunni Muslim, Akbar quickly revealed himself a highly unorthodox eclectic. It is well documented that throughout his life, he has been fascinated—not to say obsessed—by religion, increasingly skeptical of all fundamentalisms, and a firm proponent of universal tolerance and freedom of worship.

His practical, political views on religious diversity can be summarised in two simple lines:

- every human being is free to worship the divine in whatever way he or she pleases, provided he or she does not hurt other people in the process; and the
- duty of any sovereign is to put himself above all these differences, and to treat all his subjects justly and equally.

Akbar eagerly welcomed to his court learned representatives of all religions and factions known to him[329]: Sunni and Shiite Muslims, Hindus, Jains, Parsis, Jews, and even Jesuit priests from the Portuguese settlements in Goa. In a splendid, if vain, attempt to resolve all differences between those various creeds, he even attempted to establish a completely new, ecumenical cult, the Dīn-e-Illāhī, which means religion of the one god, that he hoped would peacefully unite people from all religions.

The Emperor's Writings has been written from Akbar's personal perspective and that of his most ardent supporters; it should therefore come as no surprise that the portrait painted of him in this book is biased, and arguably, altogether much too flattering. Did Akbar actually deserve his famous epithet of 'The Great'? In reality, if he has had many admirers, there have also been quite a few harsh critics, and over the years, many people have argued that his reign and persona have been grossly over-idealised in popular tradition. Admittedly, Akbar's critics do have a point: In today's terms, he was an unashamed, ruthless imperialist, who did not hesitate to act with merciless brutality whenever it suited him. Measured by the standards of his own time, however, he was exceptionally broad-minded, forgiving and tolerant. As stated above, he actively protected religious freedom in his dominions, forbidding only those practices which he considered to be unjust or inhuman (including, for instance, child marriage and the forcible burning of widows). In an age where 'cruel and unusual punishment' was the rule rather than the exception,

---

329. Buddhists were a notable exception.

he was altogether quite moderate; it is well documented that he even issued orders that the death penalty could never be executed, unless he had personally reconfirmed it three times. Unlike other absolutist rulers of his age (including Humāyūn and Jahāngīr), he never ordered a convict to be flayed alive.

From a personal point of view, he appears to have been an exceptionally captivating personality: imposing, majestic and daunting, yet at the same time, congenial, kind and charming. I imagine he must have been an excellent judge of character, and gifted with a manipulative, 'Godfather-like' personal style, that mixture of awe and personal charm which one tends to find in most great leaders, good or bad, from Caesar to Hitler.

Near the end of his authoritative biography *Akbar the Great*, the great historian Vincent A. Smith writes: '(Akbar's) ruling passion was ambition. His whole reign was dedicated to conquest. His aggressions, made without the slightest regard to moral considerations, were not determined in any instance by a desire to better the condition of the people in the kingdom attacked'. Smith's judgement is quite harsh, but not entirely unjustified: Akbar was an absolutist if there ever was one. Neighbouring states were attacked by him without provocation, and scores of people, whose only crime it had been that they had wanted to stay independent, were ruined, imprisoned, or killed.

However, despite the many reservations one may have vis-à-vis this brutal, unapologetic imperialism, it is impossible to deny that, in spite of his many faults and shortcomings, Akbar really was one of the most enlightened monarchs of his time, a king who sincerely desired the welfare of his subjects, and attempted to treat each and every one of them justly and equally. His character was a remarkable combination of mysticism, rationalism and melancholy, he genuinely and honestly aspired to know the Divine will and lead his life in submission to god. Whatever criticism one may want to express concerning his maladroit, impractical and vainglorious attempt at creating a new creed to unite all religions—Smith, for instance, states[330] quite pertinently that the *Divine Faith* was a monument of Akbar's folly, not of his wisdom—it cannot be denied that Dīn-e-Illāhī was also one of the very first conscious attempts

---

330. *Akbar the Great Mogul*, p. 160.

to create a 'secular' state, where the sovereign obligates himself to remain neutral and impartial, and to treat all his subjects equally. His tolerance in religious matters, which he pushed through in spite of stiff opposition and at great personal risk, was truly exceptional, and that alone merits him a place among the greatest rulers in history.

Whether we choose to like him or not, Akbar's story deserves to be remembered and reflected upon. To quote the phrase used by Father du Jarric in his account of the Jesuit missions, my chief regret is that *so rich a subject has not been dealt with by a worthier pen.*

Dyslexia?

It is a well documented historical fact that Akbar was, as Abraham Eraly phrased it, an illiterate savant. Other than signing his own name, he is not known to have written anything, and Jahāngīr in his memoirs confirms that his 'illustrious father' was indeed illiterate. This, however, did not prevent him from being a great lover of study and literature: Whenever he had a moment's leisure, he had books of all kinds read out to him, and in his conversations with learned men from all religions, he amazed everyone with the breadth of his knowledge and the quickness of his wit. People who did not know him could hardly believe that a man of such vast knowledge was unable to read.

It has been speculated that Akbar may have had some knowledge of reading and writing despite his dyslexia. Be that as it may, it is a historical fact that no one has ever witnessed him reading or writing anything.

Suicide?

Akbar died of dysentery, on Thursday, 27 October 1605, or 17 October of the Julian calendar (which was still in use by the British at that time). His illness had started three weeks before, the day after a fight between Salīm's famed prize elephant Girānbār and Ābrūp, the champion of his eldest grandson Khusrau. The open animosity between the supporters of both princes during, and after, the fight had greatly upset Akbar. The next morning, he was taken ill with the intestinal disease that would eventually kill him.

The illness showed a rather erratic course, with brief intervals of improvement, alternating with acute attacks. Despite the desperate efforts of his personal physician Hakīm Alī Gilanī, the symptoms gradually worsened. When his condition had become critical, the emperor sent for his son, and gestured him to put the imperial turban on his head and gird himself with Humāyūn's sword, thus confirming him as his legitimate successor.

There is no evidence that Akbar's death was due to anything other than natural causes. As usual under these circumstances, there have been widespread speculations (all of them unproven) that he had been the victim of poisoning, probably by Salīm's or Khusrau's supporters. It even has been suggested that his death was accidental, and that he mistakenly took poison which was, in fact, intended to kill someone else[331].

I have used the latter hypothesis (for which, it should be repeated, there is no historical evidence whatsoever) as the storyline of this book, hypothesising that Akbar killed himself, not by accident, but deliberately, in order to prevent civil war and ensure an orderly succession.

Bairām Khān

The importance of Akbar's faithful atālīq cannot be overestimated. Without Bairām Khān, the Mughal Empire would never have come into existence. Whatever Akbar's shortcomings, he was not dishonest, and he has always acknowledged the debt of gratitude he owed to his guardian. The story of their estrangement and reconciliation is not known in full detail, but did develop along the lines of the narrative in the book. Bairām Khān's second (and victorious) battle against Akbar's vanguard under Sultān Husayn Jalāir is only mentioned by a limited number of sources, but the story of their reconciliation, including the fact that Akbar took his own scarf to wipe off Bairām Khān's tears, is historical, as is the account of Akbar taking Bairām Khān's family under his care after his old friend had been assassinated.

Hamīda Bānū Bēgam

Akbar undoubtedly loved and greatly respected his mother, but it seems the two did not get along too well. It is well documented that Hamīda

---

331. Smith, pp. 234-35

Bānū resented her son's liberal attitude towards firanghīs and other infidels, and that she preferred to live on her own rather than taking up residence in the imperial zanāna.

Māham Anaga, Adham Khān

The pernicious influence of Akbar's foster mother Māham Anaga and her overly ambitious, unruly son Adham Khān is historically accurate, as is the account of their downfall.

Salīmā Sultānā Bēgam, 'Mākhfī'

Unlike other great Mughal emperors (including Jahāngīr and Shāh Jahān), it seems Akbar was not a very romantic man. While he did sleep with countless many women, particularly when he was still young, it seems he had no real 'love of his life'. It is, however, well documented that his cousin Salīmā Sultānā, whom he married after Bairām Khān's death, was clearly his favourite, in spite of the fact that she did not bear him any children. She was highly influential, probably much more than Akbar's mother was, and Akbar greatly valued her opinion. She appears to have been intelligent, exceptionally well-read, and an accomplished poetess, but to my knowledge, she has not left any published memoirs to posterity.

The story of her escape from Gujarāt after Bairām Khān's assassination is authentic, as is the fact that she personally travelled to Allāhābād and brought about the initial reconciliation between Salīm and his father. The detailed story of her betrothal to Akbar and their joint hunting trip are fictional.

Maryam uz-Zamānī, Jahāngīr's mother

Surprising though it may be, the name of Jahāngīr's mother (Akbar's first Rājpūt wife) appears not to be known with absolute certainty, apart from her title of honour (*Maryam uz-Zamānī*, 'Mary of the Age'), which she received when she gave birth to Salīm. In Abū-l Fazl's *Akbar Nāmā* (translated by H. Beveridge), she is identified as the eldest daughter of Rājā Bihārī Mal of Amber, but her maiden name is not mentioned. Popular tradition in India calls her by the name Jodhā Bai or Jodh Bai, which means 'Lady of Jodh(pur)'. However, the consensus among the vast majority of scholars is that Akbar never did marry any princess from the Jodhpur area, and that he certainly never had a wife called or nicknamed Jodhā Bai. Most historians correctly reserve the name Jodhā Bai for one of Jahāngīr's wives, namely Manmati, the daughter of the so-called 'Mota Rājā (fat Rājā)' Udai Singh of Jodhpur.

Ruby Lal (Lal 2005, 170) states she was called Harkha. Indeed, the current consensus among historians seems to be that Maryam uz-Zamānī's maiden name was Rājkumari Hira Kunwari, alias Harkha Bai: that is what Salman Rushdie calls her in his novel *The Enchantress of Florence*. I have, however, elected to avoid the controversy.

Mīr Abdul Latīf

The influence of Akbar's venerable old teacher cannot be overestimated. It is Mīr Abdul Latīf who imparted on his pupil the concept of *Sulh-i-Kul*, or Peace for All. The old man's memoirs quoted in the book are, of course, fictitious.

Shaykh Salīm Chishtī

Akbar's reverence for the old Shaykh who predicted the birth of his three sons has been recorded extensively. His decision to build his capital city near the old Shaykh's dwelling is historical, as is the fact that he abandoned the city fourteen years later.

Hakīm Alī Gilanī

It is a historical fact that Hakīm Alī Gilanī was Akbar's treating physician during his terminal illness. However, Hakīm Alī's close personal relationship with the emperor and Mīr Abdul Latīf remains a matter of speculation: He was without any doubt an important courtier, but probably not as close to Akbar as is intimated in this book.

Bīrbal, Todar Mal, Abū-l Fazl and the others

'Bīrbal-and-Akbar stories' are immensely popular in India. In reality, Bīrbal was probably much less influential and important than these stories suggest. Akbar did enjoy Bīrbal's company and appreciated his wit, but as administrators and army leaders, the roles played by Todar

Mal, Rājā Mān Singh, and Abdurrahīm Khān Khanān have been of much greater importance.

From a political point of view, Akbar has been deeply influenced by the views of his teacher Mīr Abdul Latīf, later reinforced by Abū-l Fazl and his father Shaykh Mubārak. The so-called *Infallibility Decree*[332] has been written by Mubārak, most probably assisted by Abū-l Fazl.

Contemporary sources describe Abū-l Fazl as an exceptionally erudite, highly intelligent man, with an almost prodigal capacity for hard work. His manner appears to have been perfectly courteous and amiable – his only obvious weakness (well known to his contemporaries) being an extraordinarily voracious appetite. A shameless flatterer and quick-witted freethinker, Abū-l Fazl had Akbar's ear and sympathy; no courtier has been more influential. Abū-l Fazl was the architect behind the infamous Dīn-e-Illāhī cult, as well as its main proponent. His enemies—of whom he had many among the ulamā—have claimed he was an atheist. This may or may not be true; he was at least firmly convinced of the fundamental equality of all faiths and denominations. His views are probably best summarised in the following verses he wrote towards the end of his life[333]:

O god, in every temple I see people that are seeking You,
and in every language I hear, people are praising You!
Polytheism and Islām feel after You,
each religion says, 'You are One, without equal!'

If it be a mosque,
people murmur the holy prayer,
and if it be a Christian church,
people ring the bell
out of love to You.

Sometimes I frequent the Christian cloister, and sometimes the mosque,
but it is You whom I search, from temple to temple.

---

332. The all-important formal declaration giving Akbar precedence over the ulamā (mentioned towards the end of the *29th Letter*).
333. Fragment of an inscription on a temple in Kashmīr, quoted in the introduction to the *Ā'īn-i-Akbarī* cited below, pp. liv-lv.

Bishotan, grandson of Abū-l Fazl

There is no evidence whatsoever (and it is, admittedly, highly unlikely as well) that a conversation like the one related in Epilogue 3 ever took place between Jahāngīr and Abū-l Fazl's orphaned son Abdurrahmān.

It is, however, historically correct that Jahāngīr, upon his accession, took no vindictive action whatsoever against Khusrau's supporters or anyone else who had opposed him. He was magnanimous enough to appoint Abū-l Fazl's son Abdurrahmān as a high-ranking officer in the cavalry. Also Bishotan, Abdurrahmān's son, was an eager officer in Jahāngīr's army.

Ibādat-Khāna, Dīn-e-Illāhī

The public debates on religion have actually taken place: between Muslims at first, and later between Muslims and representatives of other faiths. The discussions were probably much less erudite or systematic than is suggested in *The Emperor's Writings*, but it is certain that they have had tremendous influence on Akbar's thinking. His unorthodox eclecticism is to no small extent due to the contempt in which he came to hold all fundamentalism and bigotry. Critics of Akbar will never fail to point out that it was his all-consuming lust for power that was the real motive behind his religious tolerance and the ill-advised establishment of a cult of his own. This is only partially correct: It is true that Akbar did not want religion to interfere with his subjects' loyalty towards him; on the other hand, however, it cannot be denied that his attitude of tolerance also reflected his strong personal convictions on the matter.

Did Akbar renounce Islām?

Hundreds, if not thousands, of pages have been written about Akbar's religious beliefs and practices.

From a dogmatic point of view, Akbar's beliefs appear to have been the result of two competing tendencies in his mind. On the one hand, he had an inquisitive, fundamentally rationalist mind: According to him, beliefs were to be based solely on evidence and reason – had he been a European monarch, he would have been called a typical Renaissance man. On the other hand, he was also a melancholy mystic, with a deep and unfeigned reverence for the creator and an almost obsessive interest in religious truth.

Did he renounce Islām? As I have Hakīm Alī Gilanī state in *Epilogue 1*, the answer appears to be dependent on one's definition of Islām. If a Muslim is defined as a person who holds the profound belief that there is one god, lord of the universe, to Whom every human being should humbly submit, then Akbar was still a devout Muslim. However, when one considers the other central tenets of Islām, and in particular, the unique position held by the Holy Qur'ān and the Prophet Muhammad, Akbar was no longer a Muslim, or at best a highly unorthodox one, for in his mind, the Prophet Muhammad and the Holy Qur'ān occupied a much less prominent place than they do in orthodox Islām. It has frequently been pointed out that if Akbar was tolerant towards other religions, he was much less so towards Islām. More than one chronicler has claimed that he actually persecuted the religion of his ancestors, or at least was clearly prejudiced against it. While the evidence for that is less clear than some sources suggest, it is definitely true that Akbar was extremely critical of the Muslim clerics of his time – partly for religious, but mostly for political reasons. Akbar was an absolutist, with very little tolerance for any real power next to him. Both the so-called Infallibility Decree and the Dīn-e-Illāhī cult were deliberate attempts to neutralise the power of the Muslim jurists and strengthen his own position as pādshāh, Sultān and Khalīfah. However, it is equally important to emphasise that Akbar never formally renounced Islām, and never converted to any other religion, publicly or privately. He had an unfeigned and profound respect for Jesus of Nazareth, but clearly rejected the fundamental tenets of Christianity, i.e. the divinity of Christ and the concept of the holy trinity. It is equally clear that he never became a Hindū or a Jain or a Parsī, impressed and heavily influenced though he was by their philosophy, practices and symbols.

Akbar fundamentally was an eclectic, a rationalist as well as a mystic, who came to regard all religions as merely human attempts to honour and serve an ineffable, unattainable reality. In his own words: 'Each person, according to his personal condition, gives the Supreme Being a Name, but in reality, to name the Unknowable is vain.'

Historical Notes and Acknowledgements 595

Transcription and Spelling

Transcription of Perso-Arabic words into Roman alphabet is notoriously challenging. In the end, the writer inevitably needs to select one of many possibilities and variants between two extremes, i.e., on the one hand, a 'scientific' transcription – with a well-nigh illegible set of confusing apostrophes, accents and diacritical marks, utterly meaningless except to a few specialists; and on the other hand, an easily legible but hardly accurate westernised approximation (e.g., *Koran* instead of *Qur'ān*).

For a number of reasons, esthetic as well as practical, I have opted for a kind of middle ground, taking into account that the testimonials in the novel supposedly have been written in Persian, by native or at least habitual speakers of that language. Akbar himself, for instance, had had a bilingual education; and though he fluently spoke the Chagatai Turkish of his ancestors (he must have spoken it, occasionally at least, with other Turks like Bairām Khān, his aunt Gulbadan and his wives Ruqayya and Salīmā), he usually spoke Persian, the official lingua Franca at his court. His knowledge of Arabic (which he never spoke, except when reciting the Qur'ān) and of the local Hindustānī dialects must have been less than perfect, and it can readily be assumed that his pronunciation of other languages was strongly influenced by Persian.

The following principles have been applied:

- A clear distinction has been made between long and short vowels (an essential distinction in both Hindi and Persian), and also between the Arabic letters K and Q[334], (a distinction that educated Muslims will not fail to make). I have followed (in that order) the spelling used in Beveridge's translation of Abū-l Fazl's works, Irfan Habib's *Atlas of the Mughal Empire*, and R.C. Majumdar's *History of India*.
- Typically Arabic glottal stops have only been indicated occasionally, and no attempt has been made to distinguish between the letters Alif, Hamza and 'Ayn[335].
- The distinction between so-called retroflex and non-retroflex consonants (highly important in the pronunciation of Hindī and

---

334. ك and ق
335. ا, ء, and ع.

- most other languages on the subcontinent) has not been indicated either, as it does not occur in Persian[336].
- Generally speaking, an attempt has been made to remain as close as possible to both the original Perso-Arabic spelling and at the same time to the pronunciation, although this is not always possible without at least some kind of compromise. I have, for instance, opted not to use unaesthetic transliterations like *Mueen od Deen, Mooeen-oddeen*, etc., although they arguably are closer to the pronunciation in English; nor have I opted for *Muīn Al Dīn*, which would be the literal transcription of the actual Perso-Arabic letters, but *Muīn-ud-dīn*, which does respect the original spelling, while at the same time taking into account the different pronunciation of so-called 'Sun' and 'Moon' letters in Arabic. The distinction between 'Sun' and 'Moon' letters is also the reason why I have preferred to write, for instance, Abdurrahīm, Abdurrahmān, and Shams-ud-dīn.
- In all scientific transcriptions of Hindī, the long 'o' sound (somewhat like the 'o' in the French word '*corps*') is transcribed as 'au'. As this could be confusing for most Western readers, I have elected to write *Kalānor* instead of Kalānaur, *Chittor* instead of Chittaur, etc.

---

336. For example, the sounds त and ट have both been transcribed as **T**; and थ and ठ, as **TH**.

Bibliography

It will be clear that any historical novel with some pretence to authenticity cannot be written without extensive reference to, and indeed, borrowing from, various sources. In the bibliography below, I have added the references to the books I am most indebted to. May these references be an encouragement for interested readers to find out for themselves what scholarly history has to say about Akbar and his reign.

Historical Documents

Abū'l Fazl Allamī, *The Ā'īn-ī-Akbarī (Institutions of Akbar)*, Vol. I, translated from the Persian by H. Blochmann (1873), revised by D.C. Phillott (1927), Vols. II & II by H.S. Jarrett (1893-96), revised by Jadunath Sarkar (1949), *Bibliotheca Indica No 61*, reprinted Delhi, 1988.

Abū'l Fazl Allamī, *The Akbarnāmā*, trans. H. Beveridge, Delhi: Atlantic Publishers, 1989.

Ibn al-'Arabī, *El secreto de los Nombres de Dios*, Introducción, edición, traducción y notas de Pablo Beneito, Murcia: Regional de Murcia, 1996.

Ibn al-'Arabī, *El tratado de la unidad y otros textos sufíes*, Barcelona: Jose J. de Olaneta, 1987.

Bābur, Emperor of Hindustan, *The Baburnama: Memoirs of Babur, Prince and Emperor*; trans. and ed. Wheeler M. Thackston, New York: Oxford University Press, 1996.

Badauni (Mulla 'Abdul-Kadir Muluk Shah of Badaun), *Tarikh-i Badauni (Muntakhabu-t Tawarikh)*, in *The History of India: As Told By Its Own Historians, The Muhammadan Period, The Posthumous Papers of the Late Sir H.M. Elliot*, ed. Prof. John Dowson, Calcutta, 1875, 3rd reprint 1961.

Al Fārābī, *El camino de la felicidad (Kitāb al-tanbīh 'ala sabīl al-sa'āda)*, trans. Rafael Ramon Guerrero, Madrid, 2002.

Al-Ghazâlî, *Les dix règles du Soufisme (Al Qawâ 'id-l-'ashra)*, trans. Muhammad Diakho, Paris: Albouraq, 1999.

Al-Ghazâlî, *O Disciple*, translated by George H. Scherer, Beirut: Catholic Press, 1951.

Father Pierre du Jarric, S.J., *Akbar and the Jesuits: An Account of the Jesuit Missions to the Court of Akbar*, trans. C.H. Payne, New Delhi: Munshiram Manoharlal Publishers, 1999. First published by G. Routledge & Sons in 1926.

Father Fernão Guerreiro, S.J., *Jahangir and the Jesuits, With an Account of the Travels of Benedict Goes and the Mission to Pegu*, trans. C.H. Payne, New Delhi: Munshiram Manoharlal Publishers, 1997. First published by G. Routledge & Sons in 1930.

Jahāngīr, Emperor of Hindustan, *The Jahangirnama: Memoirs of Jahangir, Emperor of India*, trans. and ed. Wheeler M. Thackston, New York: Oxford University Press, 1999.

Letters from the Mughal Court, The First Jesuit Mission to Akbar (1580-1583), ed. John Correia-Afonso, Bombay: Gujarat Sahitya Prakash, Anand, 1980.

Muhammad Bāqir Najm-i-Sānī, *Advice on the Art of Governance (Mauizah-i-Jahāngīrī), an Indo-Islamic Mirror for Princes*, Persian Text with Introduction, Translation, and Notes by Sajida Sultana Alvi, New York: State University of New York Press, 1989.

Śiva Purāna, trans. and annotated by a Board of Scholars, ed. Professor J.L. Shastri, 4 vols., Delhi: Motilal Banarasidas, 1970.

R. Nath, *India as seen by Bābur (AD 1504-1530)*, Delhi: M.D. Publications, 1996.

Fakhr ad-Dīn ar-Rāzī, *Traité sur les Noms Divins, Lawāmi' al-baniyyāt fī al-asmāwa al-sifāt (Le Livre des Preuves Éclatantes sur les Noms et les Qualités*, 2 vols, trans. Maurice Gloton, Beirut: Editions Al-Bouraq, 2000.

Abū'l Walīd Ibn Rusd (Averroes), *El Libro de las Generalidades de la Medicina, [Kitāb al-Kulliyyāt fīl-tibb]*, trans. María de la Concepción Vázquez de Benito and Camilo Álvarez Morales, Madrid: Trotta, 2003.

Joseph A. Kechichian and R. Hrair Dekmijian, *The Just Prince: A Manual of Leadership, Including Sulwan al-Muta' Fi 'Udwan al-Atba' (Consolation for the Ruler During the Hostility of Subjects)*, by Muhammad ibn Zafar al-Siqilli, London: Saki, 2003.

Upanisads, trans. Patrick Olivelle, New York: Oxford University Press, 1996.

Religion & Philosophy

Khaled Abou El Fadl, *The Place of Tolerance in Islam, with Tariq Ali, Milton Viorst, John Esposito, and others*, ed. Joshua Cohen and Ian Lague, Boston: Boston Review, 2002.

Montserrat Abumalham, ed., *Textos fundamentales de la tradición musulmana*, Madrid: Trotta, 2005.
Peter Adamson and Richard C. Taylor, ed., *The Cambridge Companion to Arabic Philosophy*, London: Cambridge University Press2005.
Khwaja Jamil Ahmad, *Hundred Great Muslims*, Chicago: Kazi Publications, 1987.
Salahuddin Ahmed, *A Dictionary of Muslim Names*, New York: New York University Press, 1999.
Shabbir Akhtar, *The Possibility of a Philosophy of Islam, in History of Islamic Philosophy*, Vol 1 of Routledge Histories of World Philosophies, ed. Seyyed Hossein Nasr and Oliver Leaman, London: Routledge, 1996.
Self Building: An Islāmic Guide for Spiritual Migration towards God, writings of Āytullāh Ibrāhīm Amīnī, trans. Sayyid Hussein 'Alamdār, Qum: Ansarian Publications, 1997 (ISBN 964-438-000-2).
(Thomas Aquinas, *Summa Totius Theologiae*) Saint Thomas d'Aquin, *Somme théologique: La Trinité; traduction Française par H.F. Dondaine, O.P.*, 2 Vol., Paris-Tournai-Rome, 1942.
Ulfat Aziz-us-Samad, *A Comparative Study of Christianity & Islām*, New Delhi: Adam Publishers, 2007 (ISBN 81-7435-294-5).
Wahid Bakhsh Rabbani, *Islamic Sufism: The Science of Flight in God, with God, by God, and Union and Communion with God, also showing the tremendous Sufi influence on Christian and Hindu Mystics and Mysticism*, Lahore: Al-Faisal, 1984.
Hans Bakker & Martin Gosman (red.), *De Oriënt: Droom of Dreiging?, Het Oosten in Westers perspectief*, Kampen: Agora, 1988.
Bernhard Bartmann, *Katholieke Dogmatiek, vertaald uit het Duitsch (2de uitgave) door J. Lammertse Lz., met een voorwoord van Dr. A. Terstappen*, Roermond, 1935 (Dutch translation of *Grundriss der Dogmatik*, Freiburg im Breisgau, 1931).
Bâtonnier A. Benzakour, & Maître T. Bouab, *L'Islam et la liberté de culte*, Casablanca, 1992.
Thomas Bokenkotter, *Dynamic Catholicism: A Historical Catechism*, New York: Image Books, 1985.
D. Bont and C.F. Pauwels O.P., *De katholieke Kerk, Godsdienstleer en Apologie*, 3 vols, Brussels: Utrecht, 1946.
Jan Bor en Karel van der Leeuw, *25 eeuwen Oosterse filosofie: teksten, toelichtingen*, Amsterdam: Boom, 2003.
H. Brink O.P., *Theologisch Woordenboek*, Roermond: J.J. Romen, 1952.
Titus Burckhardt, *Introduction aux doctrines ésotériques de l'Islam*, Paris: Dervy, 1969.

Brian Carr and Indira Mahalingam. ed., *Companion Encyclopedia of Asian Philosophy*, London: Routledge, 1997.

P.N. Chopra, ed., *Religions and Communities of India*, New Delhi: Vision Books, 1982.

Henry Corbin, *Histoire de la philosophie islamique*, Paris: Gallimard, 1964.

Diané Collinson, Kathryn Plant and Robert Wilkinson, *Fifty Eastern Thinkers*, London: Cambridge University Press, 2000.

Edward Craig, ed., *Routledge Encyclopedia of Philosophy*, 10 Volumes, London: Routledge, 1998.

Ali Daddy, *Le Coran contre l'intégrisme*, Paris: Castells, 2000 (ISBN 2-912587-33-6).

Mawil Izzi Dien, *Islamic Law, From Historical Foundations to Contemporary Practice*, Edinburgh and Notre Dame: Edinburgh University Press, 2004.

E. van Donzel, *Islamic Desk Reference, Compiled from The Encyclopaedia of Islam*, Leiden: Brill Academic Publishers, 1994.

John Dowson, *A Classical Dictionary of Hindu Mythology & Religion: Geography, History, Literature*, New Delhi: Rupa & Co., 1982.

Eknath Easwaran, *Thousand Names of Vishnu, A Selection with Commentary*, Mumbai: Jaico, 1997.

Carl W. Ernst, *The Shambhala Guide to Sufism: An Essential Introduction to the Philosophy and Practice of the Mystical Tradition of Islam*, Boston: Shambhala, 1997.

John L. Esposito, *The Oxford Dictionary of Islam*, New York: Oxford University Press, 2003.

Michael Frassetto and David R. Blanks, *Western Views of Islam in Medieval and Early Modern Europe: Perception of Other*, New York: Palgrave Macmillan, 1999.

Shems Friedlander with al-Hajj Shaikh Muzaffereddin, *Ninety-nine Names of Allāh, The Beautiful Names*, San Francisco: HarperSanFrancisco, 1993.

Marc Gaborieau, *Un autre Islam: Inde, Pakistan, Bangladesh*, California: Icon Group International, 2007.

Maneka Gandhi, *The Penguin Book of Hindu Names*, New Delhi: Penguin, 1992.

Maneka Gandhi and Ozair Husain, *The Complete Book of Muslim and Parsi Names*, Delhi: Penguin, 2004.

Narayani Ganesh, ed., *The Best of Speaking Tree*, vols 1-4, New Delhi: Times Group Books, 2006.

Norman L. Geisler and Abdul Saleeb, *Answering Islam: The Crescent in Light of the Cross*,Michigan: Baker Books, 1993.

Cyril Glassé, *The Concise Encyclopaedia of Islam*, London: Harper & Row, 1989.
Paul J. Griffiths, ed., *Christianity through Non-Christian Eyes*, New York: Orbis Books, 1990.
Ludwig Hagemann, *Christentum contra Islam: Eine Geschichte gescheiterter Beziehungen*, Darmstadt: Primus, 1999.
Peter Heehs, *Indian Religions: The Spiritual Traditions of South Asia*, New Delhi: Permanent Black, 2002.
A.M. Heidt, *Catholica, Geïllustreerd encyclopedisch vademecum voor het katholieke leven*, The Hague: NV Pax Publishing, 1955.
A.G. Hogg, *The Christian Message to the Hindu: being the Duff Missonary Lectures for nineteen forty five on the challenge of the Gospel in India*, London: S.C.M. Press, 1947.
Richard Holloway, *Godless Morality: Keeping Religion out of Ethics*, Edinburgh: Cannongate, 1999.
Thomas Patrick Hughes, *Dictionary of Islam, Being a Cyclopaedia of the Doctrines, Rites, Ceremonies, and Customs, together with the Technical and Theological Terms of the Muslim Religion*, Chicago: kazi Publications, 1994. First published 1885 by Allan Publishing.
Enrique Gallud Jardiel, *Diccionario de Hinduismo*, Madrid: Alderaban, 1999.
Abd Al-Rahmān Ibn Al-Jawzī, *The Attributes of God*, trans. Abdullāh bin Hamīd 'Alī, Bristol: Amal Press, 2006.
V.P. Hemant Kanitkar and W. Owen Cole, *Teach Yourself Hinduism*, London: Teach Yourself, 2003.
Subodh Kapoor, *A Short Introduction to Vaisnavism*, New Delhi: Cosmo Publications, 2002.
Katechismus van de katholieke kerk, Vaticaanstad, Baarn, Brussel.
The Muslim Jesus: Sayings and Stories in Islamic Literature, ed. and trans. Tarif Khalidi, Massachusetts: Harvard University Press, 2001.
Hazrat Inayat Khān, *The Wisdom of Sufism: Sacred Readings from the Gathas*, Boston: Houghton Mifflin, 2000.
Gardens of the Righteous (Riyadh as-Salihin) of Imam Nawawi, trans. Muhammad Zafrulla Khān, London: Routledge, 1995 (ISBN 0-7007-0073-0).
Farida Khanam, *A Simple Guide to Sufism*, New Delhi: Goodword Books, 2006.
Al-Kindī, *Apología del cristianesimo*, trans. Laura Bottini, Milano: Bur Biblioteca University, 1996.
Anton Koch S.J., *Praedica Verbum, Homiletisch Handboek, Bronnen, thema's, schetsen en plannen, voorbeelden en gelijkenissen ten dienste van de geloofsverkondiging der christelijke heilsleer en heilsmysteries*, 15 delen,

Hasselt, 1956-1966 (vertaald uit het Duits, Freiburg im Breisgau – Würzburg, 1937).

Stella Kramrisch, *The Presence of Śiva*, Varanasi: Motilal Banarasidas, 1988.

James Kritzeck, ed., *Anthology of Islamic Literature: From the rise of Islam to modern times*, New York: Holt, Rinehart, and Winston, 1964.

Bharatan Kumarappa, *The Hindū Conception of the Deity as Culminating in Rāmānuja*, London: Luzac, 1934.

Henri Laoust, *Gli scismi nell'Islam, Un percorso nella pluralità del mondo musulmano*, Genova: ECIG Ed., 2002.

Oliver Leaman, *An Introduction to Classical Islamic Philosophy*, London: Cambridge University Press, 2002 0-521-79757-8).

Michiel Leezenburg, *Islamitische filosofie: Een geschiedenis*, Amsterdam: Bulaaq, 2001.

Donald S. Lopez, Jr., *Religions of Asia in Practice: An Anthology*, New Jersey: Princeton University Press, 2002 (ISBN 0-691-09061-0).

Pierre Lory, *La science des lettres en Islam*, Paris: Dervy, 2004.

Gabriele Mandel, *I novantanove Nomi di Dio nel Corano*, Milano: Edizoni San Paolo, 1995.

Axel Michaels, *Hinduism: Past and Present*, trans. Barbara Harshav, New Jersey: Princeton University Press, 2004.

Maulānā Muhammad 'Alī, *The Religion of Islām: A comprehensive discussion of the sources, principles and practices of Islām*, Lahore: Ahmadiyya Anjuman Isha'at Islam, 1936.

———, *A Manual of Hadith*, Lahore: Ahmadiyya Anjuman Isha'at Islam, 1944

——— *Introduction to the study of the Holy Qur'ān*, Lahore: Ahmadiyya Anjuman Isha'at Islam, 1936.

——— *The Living Thoughts of the Prophet Muhammad*, Lahore: Ahmadiyya Anjuman Isha'at Islam, 1947.

——— *Muhammad and Christ*, Lahore: Ahmadiyya Anjuman Isha'at Islam, 1921.

——— *The Muslim Prayer-Book*, Lahore: Ahmadiyya Anjuman Isha'at Islam, 1939.

Seyyed Hossein Nasr, *The Garden of Truth: The Vision and Promise of Sufism, Islam's Mystical Tradition*, New York: HarperOne, 2007.

Seyyed Hossein Nasr and Oliver Leaman, *History of Islamic Philosophy*, Routledge Histories of World Philosophies, vol. 1, London: Routledge, 2001pp. 1162-1172.

Seyyed Hossein Nasr, *Islam and the Plight of Modern Man*, Chicago: Kazi Publications, 2001.

Reynold A. Nicholson, *The Mystics of Islam*, London: G. Bell & Sons, 1914.

Constance E. Padwick, *Muslim Devotions: A Study of Prayer-Manuals in Common Use*, London: Oneworld Publications, 1996.
Pietro Parente, Antonio Piolanti, and Salvatore Garofalo, *Dictionary of Dogmatic Theology*, Milwaukee: Bruce Publishing, 1957.
The Parsis, Classic Collection (set of Martin Haug, *The Parsis, Essays on their Sacred Language, Writings and Religion*; John Wilson, *The Parsi Religion*; and Rustam Masani, *Zoroastrianism: The Religion of the Good Life*); New Delhi: Indigo Books, 2003.
Bansi Pandit, *The Hindu Mind: Fundamentals of Hindu religion and Philosophy for All Ages*, Delhi: New Age Books, 2001.
I.P. Petrushevsky, *Islam in Iran*, trans. Hubert Evans, London: Athlone, 1985.
Emilio Platti, *Wat gelooft een goede moslim?*, Amsterdam, 1996.
Utz Podzeit, *Duisternis uit het Oosten, Goeroes, sekten en valse hoop als voorlopers van de Antichrist*, trans. R.C. Vink, Vaassen: Medema, 1982.
Mgr. P. Potters, *Verklaring van den Katechismus der Nederlandsche Bisdommen*, 7 Vols., 's-Hertogenbosch, 1940.

Holy Qur'ān comments and translations:

The Holy Qur'ān, Transliteration in Roman script, by M.A. Haleem Eliasii, with original 'Arabic Text, English Translation by Abdullah Yūsuf Alī, Lahore, 1934; Eliasii Family Book Service, Charminar, Hyderabad-India, 2000.
The Holy Qur'ān, with English Translation and Commentary, by Maulānā Muhammad 'Alī, 1st, ed., 1917; 2002 edition Dublin, Ohio (ISBN 0-913321-01-X).
The Message of the Qur'ān, The Full Account of the Revealed Arabic Text Accompanied by Parallel Transliteration, trans. Muhammad Asad, Bristol: The Book Foundation, 1980.
Concordance of the Qur'ān, Extracted from the M.H. Shakir translation of The Qur'an, New York: Tahrike Tarsile Qur'an, 2005.
Ahmad ibn Naqib al-Misri, *Reliance of the Traveller: The Classic Manual of Islamic Sacred Law*, trans. Nuh Ha Mim Keller, Beltsville: Amana1997.
Sayyid Abūl A'lā Maudūdī, *Towards Understanding Qur'ān*, ed and trans. Zafar Ishaq Ansari, Delhi: The Islamic Foundation, 2006.
Mawlana Abul Kalam Azad, *The Opening Chapter of the Qur'ān (Sūrah al-Fātihah)*, ed. and trans. Syed Abdul Latif, Kuala Lumpur: Islamic Book Trust, 2001.
Farid Esack, *The Qur'an, A User's Guide*, London: Oneworld Publications, 2005.
Muhammad Taqi-ud-Dīn Al-Hilālī, and Muhammad Muhsin Khān, *Interpretation of the Meanings of the Noble Qur'ān in the English Language: A Summarized*

Version of At-Tabarī, Al-Qurtubī and Ibn Kathīr with Comments from Sahīh Al-Bukhārī, Ryadh: Darussalam Publishers, 1996.

An Interpretation of the Qur'an, English Translation of the Meanings, A Bilingual Edition, trans. Majid Fakhry, New York: New York University Press, 2002.

De Koran Arabisch-Nederlands; De Heilige Qor'aan, met Nederlandse vertaling, onder auspiciën van Hazrat Mirza Bashir-ud-Din Mahmud Ahmad, hoofd van de Ahmadiyya Beweging, Rahwah, Pakistan – Soest, Holland, 1953-1994 (ISBN 90-72540-52-2).

Sarvepalli Radhakrishnan and Charles A. Moore, *A Source Book in Indian Philosophy*, New Jersey: Princeton University Press, 1957.

Al Rāzī, *La conducta virtuosa del filósofo*, Madrid: Trotta, 2004.

John Renard, *Responses to 101 Questions on Hinduism*, New York: Paulist Press, 1999.

Abdullah Saeed, *Islamic Thought: An Introduction*, London: Routledge, 2006.

Omid Safi, ed., *Progressive Muslims on Justice, Gender and Pluralism*, London: Oneworld Publications, 2003.

Leo Schaya, *La doctrina sufí de la unidad*, Barcelona: José J. de Olañeta, 1985.

Stephan Schuhmacher and Gert Woerner, ed., *The Rider Encyclopaedia of Eastern Philosophy and Religion: Buddhism, Taoism, Zen, Hinduism*, London: Rider & Co., 1989.

Theodor Schneider E.A., *Manual de teología dogmática*, Barcelona: Herder, 1996.

Michael A. Sells, ed. and trans., *Early Islamic Mysticism: Sufi, Qur'an, Mi'Raj, Poetic and Theological Writings*, New York: Paulist Press, 1996.

Shāh Ismail Shaheed, *Taqwiyat ul-Imān (Strengthening of the Faith)*, Riyadh, 1995.

M. Saeed Shaikh, *A Dictionary of Muslim Philosophy*, New Delhi: Adam Publishers, 2006.

Arun Shourie, *The World of Fatwas, or, the Shariah in Action*, New Delhi: ASA Publications, 1995.

Janine Sourdel et Dominique Sourdel, *Dictionnaire historique de l'islam*, Paris: Presses universitaires de France 1996.

Mazheruddin Siddiqi, *Modern Reformist Thought in the Muslim World*, Islamabad: Islamic Research Institute, 1982.

Fauozi Skali, *Jésus dans la tradition soufie*, Paris: Albin Michel, 2004.

Mokhtar Stork, *A-Z Guide to the Ahadith: A Must-have Reference to Understanding the Traditions of the Noble Prophet Muhammad*, Singapore: Times Editions, 2004.

Mokhtar Stork, *A-Z Guide to the Qur'an: A Must-have Reference to Understanding the Contents of the Islamic Holy Book*, Singapore: Times Editions, 1998.

Wolf-Dieter Storl, *Shiva, The wild God of Power and Ecstasy*, Vermont: Inner Traditions International, 2004.
Satguru Sivaya Subramuniyaswami, *Dancing with Śiva, Hinduism's Contemporary Catechism*, Hawaii: Himalayan Academy Publications, 1997.
Yembal P.V. Thajamul Mohammad, *Religious Harmony: An Islamic Doctrine*, Pudukottai: Newlight Book Corner, 2000.
Mel Thompson, *Teach Yourself Eastern Philosophy*, London: McGraw Hill, 2003.
Āyatullāh Al-'Uzmā Hājj and Shaykh Lutfullāh Sāfī Gulpāygānī, *Discusions Concerning al-Mahdi (May Allāh hasten his return)*, trans. Sayyid Sulaymān 'Alī Hasan, Canada: Islamic Humanitarian Service & Fath al-Mubin Publications, 2000.
Rianne van der Smitte and Jan van der Hoeven, *Als het licht duisternis is . . ., een aangrijpend getuigenis en onthullende feiten over new-age en occultisme*, Hoornaar, 1989.
Viswanathan, ed., *Am I a Hindu?: The Hinduism Primer*, Columbia: South Asia Books, 1992.
Benjamin Walker, *Hindu World: An Encyclopedic Survey of Hinduism*, London: Allen & Unwin, 1968.
A.J. Wensinck and J.H. Kramers, *Handwörterbuch des Islam*, Leiden: Brill, 1941.
Tim Winter, ed., *The Cambridge Companion to Classical Islamic Theology*, London: Cambridge University Press, 2008.
Integral Yoga Institute, *Dictionary of Sanskrit Names*, London: Integral Yoga Publications, 1989.
R.C. Zaehner, *Hindi and Muslim Mysticism*, London: Oneworld Publications, 1995.
Imam A'li Ibnul-Husayn Zaynul-A'Abideen as-Sajjad, *The Psalms of Islam (As'-S'ah'eefatul-KaamilatusSajjaadeetah)*, trans. William C. Chittick, London: Muhammadi Trust of Great Britain and North Ireland, 1988.

Cultural, Political and Military History

Franco Adravanti, *Tamerlano, La stirpe del Gran Mogol*, Milan: Rusconi, 2003.
Muzaffar Alam and Sanjay Subrahmanyam, ed., *The Mughal State 1526-1750*, Oxford in India Readings, Themes in Indian History, New Delhi: Oxford University Press, 1998.
S. Alexandre, *Judeus, Cristãos-novos e a Inquisição*, Lisbon: Fedrave, 2002.
M. Athar Ali, *Mughal India: Studies in Polity, Ideas, Society, and Culture*, New York: Oxford University Press, 2006.
Mehdi Aminrazavi, *The Wine of Wisdom: The Life, Poetry and Philosophy of Omar Khayyam*, London: Oneworld Publications, 2005.

Catherine B. Asher, *Architecture of Mughal India*, The Cambridge History of India, New York: Cambridge University Press, 1992.

António Baião, *A Inquisição de Goa: Tentativa de Historia da sua Origem, Estabelecimento, Evolução e Extinção (Introdução á Correspondência dos Inquisidores da India 1569-1630)*, Vol. I, Academia das Ciências, Lisboa, 1945; and Vol. II, Coimbra, Imprensa da Universidade, 1930; (Vol. II was published before Vol. I).

S.R. Bakshi, and S.K. Sharma, ed., *Akbar the Great Moghul*, New Delhi: Deep & Deep, 2000.

S.R. Bakshi, and S.K. Sharma, ed., *Humayun: The Great Moghul*, New Delhi: Deep & Deep, 2000.

S.R. Bakshi, and S.K. Sharma, ed., *Jahangir: The Great Moghul*, New Delhi: Deep & Deep, 2000.

A.L. Basham, ed. *A Cultural History of India*, New York: Oxford University Press, 1984.

Valérie Berinstain, *Mughal India, Splendours of the Peacock Throne*, trans. Paul G. Bahn, London: Thames & Hudson, 1998.

Michele Bernardini, *Il mondo iranico e turco*, in *Storia del mondo islamico (VII-XVI secolo)*, vol.2, Italy: Einaudi, 2003.

Stephan Conermann, *Das Mogulreich, Geschichte und Kultur des muslimischen Indien*, Munich: Beck, 2006.

Frederick Charles Danvers, *The Portuguese in India, Being a History of the Rise and Decline of their Eastern Empire*, 2 vols., first published 1894, repr., London: Frank Cass, 1966.

Leo de Hartog, *Genghis Khan, Conqueror of the World*, London: Sterling, 1999.

S.M. Edwardes, and H.L.O. Garrett, *Mughal Rule in India*, New York: AMS Press, 1976.

Abraham Eraly, *The Mughal throne: The Saga of India's Great Emperors*, New Delhi: Phoenix, 2004.

Abraham Eraly, *The Mughal World: India's Tainted Paradise*, (originally published under the title *The Last Spring: The Lives and Times of the Great Mughals*, New Delhi: Viking, 1997), London: Orion, 2007.

Jorge Flores and Nuno Vassallo e Silva, ed., *Goa and the Great Mughal*, London: Scala, 2004.

www.fourmilab.ch The free Calendar Convertor (which can be found on this highly interesting website under the section *Astronomy and Space*) has been invaluable to me for the conversion of Muslim and Persian dates into Julian and Gregorian (Common Era) calendar dates and vice versa. I have also used it to check the position of Venus and the other planets at the time of Humāyūn's death.

Bamber Gascoigne, *A Brief History of the Great Moguls*, New York: Carrol and Graf, 2002.
R.C. Gaur, *Excavations at Fatehpur Sikri*, New Delhi: Aryan Books International, 2000.
Rumer Godden, *Gulbadan, Portrait of a Rose Princess at the Mughal Court*, London: Pan Macmillan, 1980.
Jos Gommans, *Mughal Warfare: Indian Frontiers and High Roads to Empire, 1500-1700*, New York: Routledge, 2002.
Olivinho J.F. Gomes, *The Religious Orders in Goa (XVIth-XVIIth Centuries)*, Chandor: Konkani Sorospot Prakashan, 2003.
Gul-Badan Begam, *Humāyūn Nāmā: The History of Humāyūn*, tr. Annette S. Beveridge, New Delhi: Oriental Books Reprint Corp., 1983.
Irfan Habib, *An Atlas of the Mughal Empire: Political and Economic Maps with Detailed Notes, Bibliography and Index*, New Delhi: Oxford University Press, 1986.
Irfan Habib, ed., *Akbar and his India*, New Delhi: Oxford University Press, 1997.
Gavin Hambly, "Asia Central", in *Historia Universal Siglo Veintiuno*, Vol. 16, Madrid (1972).
J.C. Harle, *The Art and Architecture of the Indian Subcontinent*, The Pelican History of Art series, London: Penguin, 1986.
Ibn Hasan, *The Central Structure of the Mughal Empire, and Its Practical Working up to the Year 1657*, Karachi: Oxford University Press, 1967. .
J.Hellings S.J., *De Geestelijke Oefeningen van de Heilige Ignatius van Loyola, Tekst, uitleg, overwegingen*, Voorhout (NL), 1953.
Dilip Hiro, *History of India, Rough Guide Chronicle*, London: Rough Guides, 2002.
H. Hosten S.J., 'List of Jesuit Missionaries in "Mogor" (1580-1803)', *Journal of the Asiatic Society of Bengal*, Vol. 6, no. 10 (1910): pp 527-541.
Takeo Kamiya, *The Guide to the Architecture of the Indian Subcontinent*, ed. Annabel Lopez and Bevinda Collaco. Trans. Geetha Parameswaran. Goa: Bardes, 2004.
John Keay, *India: A History*, London: HarperCollins, 2000.
A. Khoshkish, *Fársi Robáiyáte Omar Xayyám; Omar Khayyam, in English by Edward J. Fitzgerald, en Français par J.B. Nicolas ou C. Grolleau*, Los Angeles, 1997.
Ebba Koch, *Mughal Architecture: An Outline of its History and Development (1526-1858)*, Munich: Prestel, 1991.
Ruby Lal, *Domesticity and Power in the Early Mughal World*, London: Cambridge University Press, 2005 (ISBN 0-521-61534-8).

A.K.S. Lambton, *Persian Vocabulary*, London: Cambridge University Press, 1954.
Ira M. Lapidus, *A History of Islamic Societies*, New York: Cambridge University Press, 1988.
Stanley Wolpert, *India*, 3rd edition, Berkeley: University of California Press 2005.
Elias Lipiner, *Os baptizados em pé, Estudos acerca da origem e da luta dos Cristãos-Novos em Portugal*, Lisbon: Vega, 1998.
R.C. Majumdar (Ed.), *The Mughul Empire: The History and Culture of the Indian People*, Vol. 7, Bombay: Bharatiya Vidya Bhavan, 1974.
E.D. Maclagan, "Jesuit Missions to the Emperor Akbar." Journal of the Asiatic Society of Bengal, Vol. LXV, (1896): pp 38-113.
G.B. Malleson, *Akbar and the Rise of the Mughal Empire*, New Delhi: Rupa & Co., 2005.
Justin Marozzi, *Tamerlane, Sword of Islam, Conqueror of the World*, London: HarperCollins, 2004.
K.S. Mathew, Teotonio R. de Souza, and Pius Malekandathil, *The Portuguese and the Socio-cultural Changes in India, 1500-1800*, Tellichery: Meshar, 2001.
Antoni de Montserrat, and Josep Lluís Alay, *Embajador en la corte del Gran Mogol, Viajes de un Jesuita Catalán del siglo XVI por la India, Paquistán, Afganistán y el Himalaya*, Lleida, 2006, translated from Catalan (Barcelona, 2002).
Harbans Mukhia, *The Mughals of India*, Oxford: Blackwell, 2004.
R. Nath, *Private Life of the Mughals of India (1526-1803 AD)*, Jaipur: Historical Research Documentation Programme, 1994.
David Nicolle and Angus McBride, *Mughul India 1504-1761*, Oxford: Osprey Publishing, 1993.
Konstantin S. Nossov and Brian Delf, *Indian Castles 1206-1526: The Rise and Fall of the Delhi Sultanate*, Oxford: Osprey Publishing, 2006.
Ahsan Jan Qaisar, *Building Construction in Mughal India: The Evidence from Painting*, New York: Oxford University Press, 1989.
Muhammad Qamaruddin, *A Politico-Cultural Study of The Great Mughuls (1526-1707)*, New Delhi: Adam Publishers & Distributors, 2004.
Religion at Akbar's Court, www.columbia.edu/itc/mealac/pritchett/00islamlinks/ikram/part2_12.html
Francis Robinson, *The Mughal Emperors and the Islamic Dynasties of India, Iran and Central Asia, 1206-1925I*, London: Thames & Hudson, 2007.
Isaías Rosa Pereira, *A inquisição em Portugal, Séculos XVI-XVII-Período Filipino*, Lisban: Vega, 1993.

J.J. Saunders, *The History of the Mongol Conquests*, New York: Barnes & Nobles, 1971.
Annemarie Schimmel, *As Through a Veil: Mystical Poetry in Islam*, New York: Columbia University Press, 1982.
Annemarie Schimmel, *The Empire of the Great Mughals: History, Art and Culture*, with a Foreword by Francis Robinson, translated from German by Corinne AttwoodNew Delhi: Oxford University Press,2005.
Annemarie Schimmel, *Mystische Dimensionen des Islam, Die Geschichte des Sufismus*, München: Insel Verlag, 1992.
Annemarie Schimmel, *Islamic Names*, Edinburgh: Edinburgh University Press, 1989.
Robert Sigaléa, *La Médecine traditionnelle de l'Inde: Doctrines prévédique, védique, âyurvédique, yogique et tantrique; Les Empereurs Mogols, leurs maladies et leurs médecins*, Genève: Olizane, 1995.
Chob Singh Verma, *Mughal Romance*, New Delhi: Prakash Book Depot, 2004.
Som Prakash Verma, *Art and Material Culture in the Paintings of Akbar's Court*, New Delhi: Vikas Publishing House, 1978.
Vincent A. Smith, *Akbar the Great Mogul 1542-1605*, 3rd Indian ed. (Delhi: S. Chand, 1966); Second (Revised) Edition; Third Indian Reprint, 1966.
Vincent A. Smith, *The Oxford History of India*, Chennai: Oxford University Press, 2001. (First published 1919 by Clerendon Press).
G.H.R. Tillotson, *Architectural Guides for Travellers: Mughal India*, London: Viking, 1990.
S.A.I. Tirmizi, *Mughal Documents (1526-1627)*, New Delh: Manohar, 1989.
Roberto Tottoli, *Vita di Gesù secondo le tradizioni islamiche*, Italy: Sallerio Editore Palermo, 2000.
Carter Vaughn Findley, *The Turks in World History*, New York: Oxford University Press, 2005.
Joseph Velinkar, *India and the West: The First Encounters, A Historical Study of the Early Indo-Portuguese Cultural Encounters in Goa*, Mumbai: Heras Institute of Indian History and Culture, 1998.
Richard von Garbe, *Akbar, Emperor of India: A Picture of Life and Customs from the Sixteenth Century*, trans. Lydia G. Robinson, Montana: Kessinger Publishing, 2007.
Andrew Wheatcroft, *Infidels: A History of the Conflict between Christendom and Islam*, New York: Random House, 2005.
Zeenut Ziad (Ed.), *The Magnificent Mughals*, Karachi: Oxford University Press, 2002.

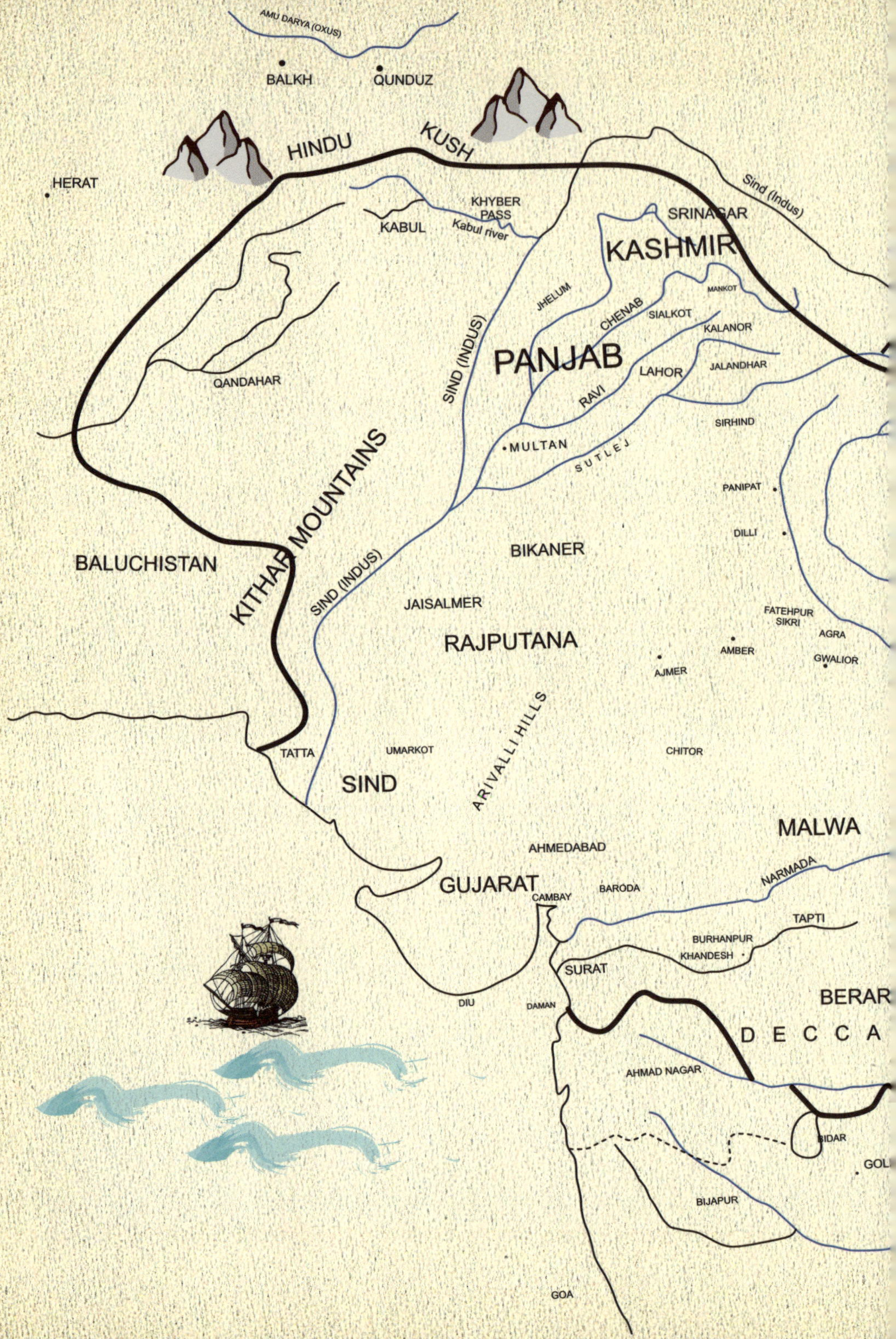

AMU DARYA (OXUS)
BALKH
QUNDUZ
HINDU
KUSH
HERAT
KHYBER PASS
KABUL
Kabul river
Sind (Indus)
SRINAGAR
KASHMIR
JHELUM
MANKOT
CHENAB
SIALKOT
KALANOR
PANJAB
LAHOR
JALANDHAR
RAVI
SIND (INDUS)
QANDAHAR
SIRHIND
MULTAN
SUTLEJ
PANIPAT
DILLI
KITHAR MOUNTAINS
BALUCHISTAN
BIKANER
SIND (INDUS)
JAISALMER
FATEHPUR SIKRI
AGRA
RAJPUTANA
AMBER
GWALIOR
AJMER
ARIVALLI HILLS
TATTA
UMARKOT
CHITOR
SIND
MALWA
AHMEDABAD
NARMADA
GUJARAT
CAMBAY
BARODA
TAPTI
BURHANPUR
KHANDESH
SURAT
BERAR
DIU
DAMAN
D E C C A
AHMAD NAGAR
BIDAR
BIJAPUR
GOA